MOON

COSTA RICA

NIKKI SOLANO

Contents

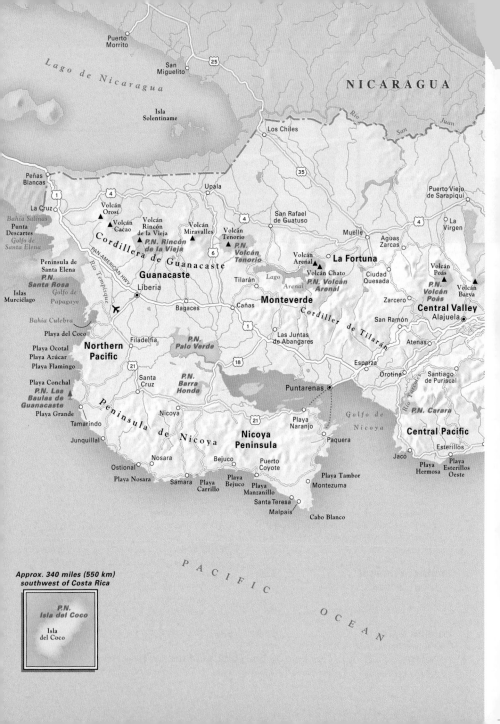

COSTA RICA

Caribbean Sea

Barra del Colorado

Tortuguero
P.N. Tortuguero

Caribbean Coast

Limón
Moín

P.N. Cahuita
Puerto Viejo de Talamanca
Manzanillo

Las Horquetas
Matina
Cahuita
Sixaola
Bribri

Guácimo
Siquirres
32

P.N. Braulio Carrillo
10
Guápiles

4
Volcán Turrialba
▲ P.N. Volcán Turrialba
Río Estrella

32
Volcán Irazú
▲ P.N. Volcán Irazú
Turrialba
Río Sixaola

Heredia
Highlands
Lago Cachí
Paraíso
Parque Internacional La Amistad
PANAMÁ

SAN JOSÉ
Cartago
P.N. Chirripó
Cerro Durika ▲

Orosi
Cordillera de
Cerro Chirripó ▲
Cerro Kamúk ▲

2
Cañón
Cerro de la Muerte ▲
Talamanca

San Ignacio de Acosta
P.N. Los Quetzales
Southern Inlands

Río Parrita
Río Naranjo

San Isidro de El General

Quepos
Savegre
Buenos Aires

Parrita
Manuel Antonio
P.N. Manuel Antonio
Playa Savegre
Dominical
Río General

Bahía de Coronado
P.N. Marino Ballena
Uvita
Palmar
2
San Vito

Ojochal

Sierpe
PAN-AMERICAN HWY

Bahía Drake
Península de Osa
Golfo Dulce
Golfito
Ciudad Neily

Osa Peninsula
Southern Pacific

Playa San Josecito
Puerto Jiménez
Playa Preciosa
Zancudo

Isla del Caño
P.N. Corcovado
Pavones

Carate
Cabo Matapalo
Península de Burica

Burica

Punta Burica

0   20 mi
0   20 km

© MOON.COM

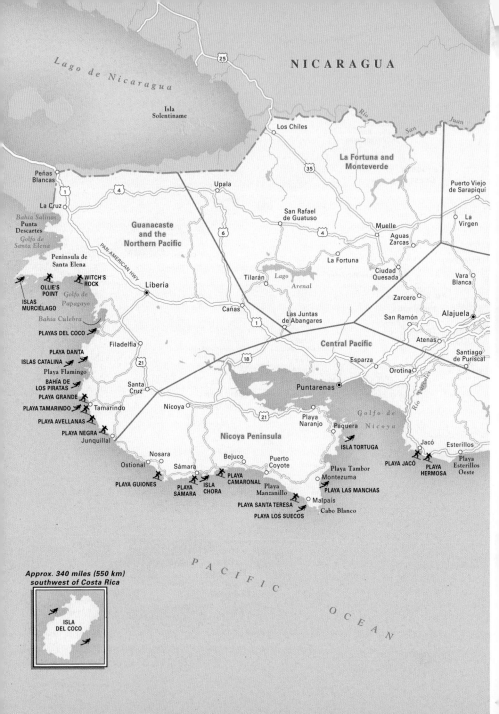

Lago de Nicaragua

Isla Solentiname

NICARAGUA

25

Los Chiles

Peñas Blancas

1

La Cruz

4

Upala

35

Río San Juan

La Fortuna and Monteverde

Puerto Viejo de Sarapiquí

Bahía Salinas
Punta Descartes

Golfo de Santa Elena

San Rafael de Guatuso

6

4

La Virgen

Península de Santa Elena

Muelle

Aguas Zarcas

Vara Blanca

Guanacaste and the Northern Pacific

Tilarán

Lago Arenal

La Fortuna

Ciudad Quesada

Zarcero

WITCH'S ROCK

OLLIE'S POINT

PAN-AMERICAN HWY

Liberia

San Ramón

Alajuela

ISLAS MURCIÉLAGO

Golfo de Papagayo

Cañas

1

Las Juntas de Abangares

Bahía Culebra

PLAYAS DEL COCO

Atenas

Central Pacific

Santiago de Puriscal

PLAYA DANTA

Filadelfia

18

Esparza

Orotina

ISLAS CATALINA

Playa Flamingo

21

Santa Cruz

BAHÍA DE LOS PIRATAS

Puntarenas

PLAYA GRANDE

PLAYA TAMARINDO

Tamarindo

Nicoya

Golfo de Nicoya

PLAYA AVELLANAS

21

Playa Naranjo

PLAYA NEGRA

Junquillal

Nicoya Peninsula

Paquera

Nosara

Bejuco

ISLA TORTUGA

Jacó

Esterillos

Ostional

Sámara

Puerto Coyote

Playa Tambor

PLAYA JACÓ

Playa Esterillos Oeste

PLAYA GUIONES

PLAYA SÁMARA

ISLA CHORA

PLAYA CAMARONAL

Playa Manzanillo

Montezuma

PLAYA LAS MANCHAS

PLAYA HERMOSA

PLAYA SANTA TERESA

Malpaís

PLAYA LOS SUECOS

Cabo Blanco

P A C I F I C

O C E A N

Approx. 340 miles (550 km) southwest of Costa Rica

ISLA DEL COCO

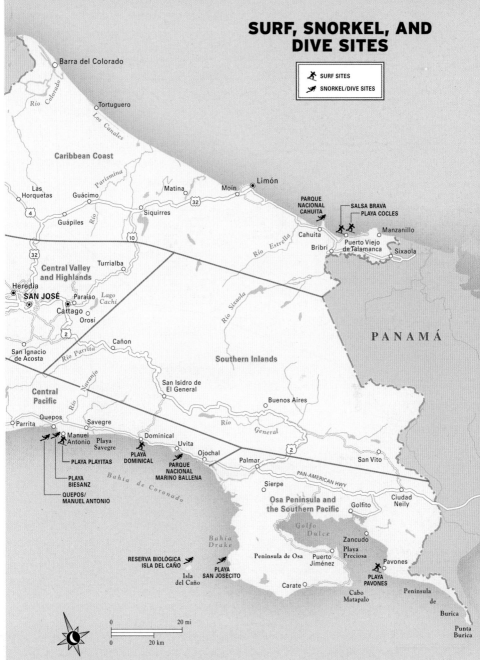

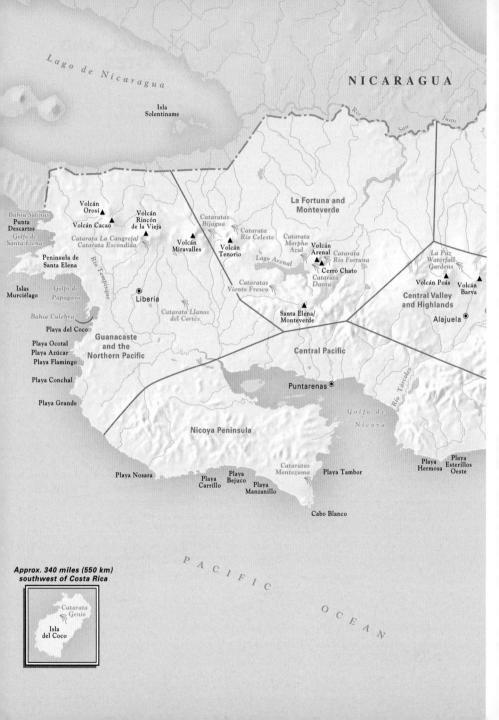

Lago de Nicaragua

NICARAGUA

Isla Solentiname

Río San Juan

La Fortuna and Monteverde

Volcán Orosí

Volcán Cacao

Volcán Rincón de la Vieja

Cataratas Bijagua

Catarata Río Celeste

Catarata Morpho Azul

Volcán Arenal

Catarata Río Fortuna

La Paz Waterfall Gardens

Catarata La Cangreja/ Catarata Escondida

Volcán Miravalles

Volcán Tenorio

Cerro Chato

Catarata Danta

Volcán Poás

Volcán Barva

Bahía Salinas

Punta Descartes

Golfo de Santa Elena

Península de Santa Elena

Lago Arenal

Central Valley and Highlands

Islas Murciélago

Golfo de Papagayo

Río Tempisque

Liberia

Cataratas Viento Fresco

Santa Elena/ Monteverde

Alajuela

Bahía Culebra

Playa del Coco

Catarata Llanos del Cortés

Playa Ocotal

Playa Azúcar

Playa Flamingo

Guanacaste and the Northern Pacific

Central Pacific

Playa Conchal

Puntarenas

Playa Grande

Río Tárcoles

Golfo de Nicoya

Nicoya Peninsula

Playa Hermosa

Playa Esterillos Oeste

Playa Nosara

Playa Carrillo

Playa Bejuco

Playa Manzanillo

Cataratas Montezuma

Playa Tambor

Cabo Blanco

PACIFIC OCEAN

Approx. 340 miles (550 km) southwest of Costa Rica

Catarata Genio

Isla del Coco

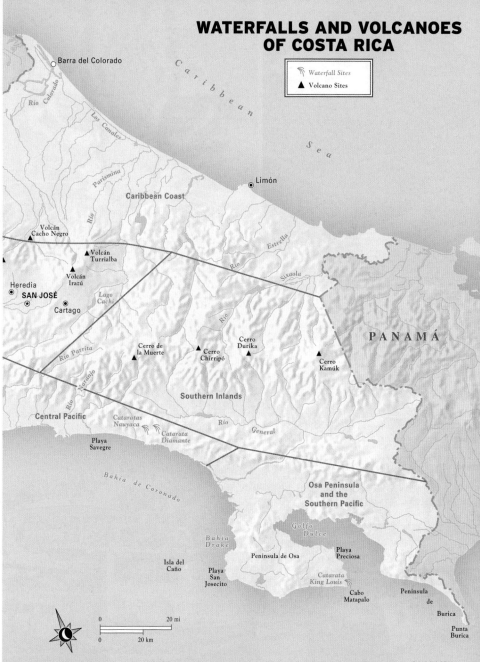

WATERFALLS AND VOLCANOES
OF COSTA RICA

⚡ *Waterfall Sites*
▲ Volcano Sites

Caribbean Sea

Barra del Colorado

Río Colorado

Los Canales

Parismina

Río

Limón

Caribbean Coast

Volcán
Cacho Negro

▲ Volcán
Turrialba

Río Estrella

Volcán Irazú

Río Sixaola

Heredia
SAN JOSÉ
Cartago

Lago Cachí

PANAMÁ

Río Parrita

Cerro de
la Muerte

▲ Cerro
Chirripó

Cerro
Durika

Río

▲ Cerro
Kamúk

Río Naranjo

Southern Inlands

Central Pacific

Cataratas
Nauyaca ⚡

Catarata
Diamante ⚡

Río General

Playa
Savegre

Bahía de Coronado

**Osa Peninsula
and the
Southern Pacific**

*Golfo
Dulce*

*Bahía
Drake*

Isla del
Caño

Playa
San
Josecito

Peninsula de Osa

Playa
Preciosa

Catarata
King Louis ⚡

Cabo
Matapalo

Peninsula
de
Burica

Punta
Burica

0 ____ 20 mi
0 ____ 20 km

© MOON.COM

DISCOVER

Costa Rica

One day early on in my career in Costa Rica, I was typing on a laptop while lounging in a hammock when a three-toed sloth appeared within a few feet of me. For nearly two hours, I watched the creature crawl around the rainforest canopy. From that day forward, I knew that Costa Rica is a place where magic is real—and within arm's reach.

Costa Rica will amaze you. Opportunities for immersion in nature, wildlife-spotting, and fantastic photography are everywhere, so seize them. Boat safaris wind through monkey-lined rivers, mangroves, and canals. Treetop excursions provide panoramic forest, volcano, lake, and ocean views. Exhibits and nature trails showcase reptiles, amphibians, insects, and plants. Parks, reserves, and refuges, spanning more than a quarter of the country's landmass, protect the immense biodiversity that makes Costa Rica unique.

Prefer to be thrilled? Imagine yourself zip-lining through the cloud forest, rafting over raging rapids, rappelling down waterfalls, exploring mysterious caves, or summiting Costa Rica's highest peak. Although diminutive in size, Costa Rica is vast in opportunities for rip-roaring adventure.

Clockwise from top left: Volcán Arenal; ocelot; *mamón chino* (rambutan); Spanish colonial-style building in Puntarenas; a frog nearly camouflaged in a pond; fishing boats on the central Pacific coast.

To relax or reenergize, pamper yourself in paradise with hot springs, mud baths, yoga, and wellness retreats. Several beaches on the Pacific and Caribbean coasts are known for their remoteness, tranquil sunrises, or rainbow-colored sunsets.

Costa Rica's laid-back *pura vida* attitude will change you. Costa Ricans are a friendly, inviting group who are proud of their country and welcome you to explore it.

Travel mindfully and you'll reap bountiful rewards from this tiny corner of the world where people greet one another with a smile. A truly magical experience is yours for the taking.

Clockwise from top left: vibrant colors and exquisite details on the wheel of a Costa Rican oxcart; typical beachside food stand; malachite butterfly; cacao pod cultivated in the Caribbean.

COPOS CON HELADO – CONOS – CEVICHE
CALDOSAS Y PIPA FRIA

CEVICHE #1000
CALDOSAS #1000
PIPA FRIA #500

10 TOP EXPERIENCES

1 **Encounter Wildlife:** Wildlife can be seen and heard everywhere in Costa Rica. Catch a glimpse of sloths snoozing in treetops, sea turtles laying their eggs on the beach, or toucans flying around cloud forests (page 479).

2 **Fly on a Zip Line:** Glide through the treetops to see Costa Rica from above. For the best thrills, zip among the clouds in **Monteverde** (page 180) or cruise alongside Volcán Arenal in **La Fortuna** (page 143).

>>>

3 **Ride the Waves at a Surf Town:** Costa Rica is a surf mecca. Dreamy beach destinations like bustling **Tamarindo** (page 253), quiet **Nosara** (page 274), remote **Santa Teresa** (page 311), and laid-back **Puerto Viejo de Talamanca** (page 435) offer stupendous waves and vibrant surf culture.

>>>

4 **Hike in Rainforests and Cloud Forests:** Explore the misty **Reserva Biológica Bosque Nuboso de Monteverde** (page 189) or the humid and remote **Parque Nacional Corcovado** (page 395). Stroll through **Parque Nacional Carara** (page 345) or take a thrilling trek in **Parque Nacional Chirripó** (page 472).

5 **Soak in Hot Springs:** Relax and rejuvenate at the volcanic mineral hot springs around Volcán Arenal near La Fortuna. Both luxury resorts and budget-friendly options are abundant (page 140).

6 **Beach-Hopping:** Boasting coastlines on both the Pacific Ocean and the Caribbean Sea, Costa Rica offers plenty of pristine beaches to choose from. Many are located close to each other, so you can sample them before you pick your favorite one (page 41).

7 **Take a Floating Safari:** Float through canals in **Tortuguero** (page 456), mangrove forests at **Isla Damas** (page 349), or down the **Río Peñas Blancas** (page 144), **Río Tenorio** (page 203), or **Río Sarapiquí** (page 421).

>>>

8 **Taste Coffee and Chocolate at their Source:** Tour a working coffee plantation or roastery in the Central Valley and Highlands (page 103) or a chocolate farm on the Caribbean coast (page 445).

<<<

9 **Go White-Water Rafting:** Home to the country's wildest white-water rapids, **Río Pacuare** is an unmissable attraction for adrenaline junkies— but beginners can join in the fun too (page 424).

>>>

10 **Swim Beneath a Waterfall:** Take a dip in a refreshing waterfall pool, like the one at the gentle and family-friendly **Catarata Llanos del Cortés** (page 206) or below the three cascades that form the **Cataratas Montezuma** (page 300). Swims at the peaceful **Cataratas Nauyaca** (page 367) are free from distractions.

Planning Your Trip

Where to Go

San José

Thanks to the proximity of Aeropuerto Internacional Juan Santamaría, many travelers experience San José briefly as a vacation start or end point. But there is much to see and do in the nation's capital city, a vibrant metropolis steeped in culture, character, and charm. Consider visiting the **Teatro Nacional de Costa Rica,** touring the **Museo del Oro Precolombino** or the **Museo del Jade,** and shopping among locals at **Mercado Central.** To top off a perfect day, enjoy a night on the town with dinner, drinks, music, or dance.

Central Valley and Highlands

In the Central Valley and on the slopes of its picturesque highlands, life operates at a slower pace than in San José. Cities and small rural communities share the land, which is home to a trio of popular volcanoes: **Volcán Poás, Volcán Irazú,** and **Volcán Turrialba.** Beloved tourist attractions like the **La Paz Waterfall Gardens,** the artisan town of **Sarchí,** and **coffee plantations** offer a nice balance of nature exploration and authentic cultural experiences.

La Fortuna and Monteverde

Welcome to the epicenter of adventure! **Volcán Arenal** is the backdrop to **adventure parks** in **La Fortuna** that feature **hiking trails, zip lines, hanging bridges,** and other thrills. The area's **hot springs** and **Catarata Río Fortuna,** a rushing waterfall, should not be missed.

In **Monteverde,** similar adventures take place in the **cloud forest.** Take your pick from early

cloud forest canopy

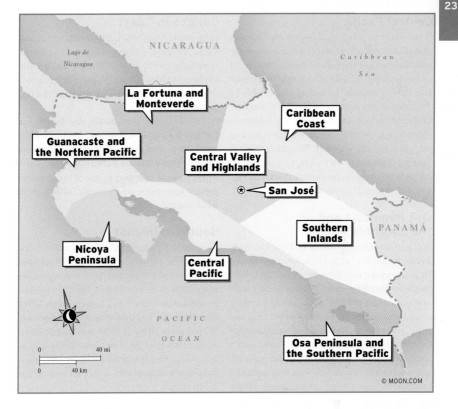

La Fortuna and Monteverde

Caribbean Coast

Guanacaste and the Northern Pacific

Central Valley and Highlands

San José

Southern Inlands

Nicoya Peninsula

Central Pacific

Osa Peninsula and the Southern Pacific

NICARAGUA

Lago de Nicaragua

Caribbean Sea

PANAMÁ

PACIFIC OCEAN

0   40 mi

0   40 km

© MOON.COM

morning **bird-watching** tours, **day hikes,** or **night tours** through the **Reserva Biológica Bosque Nuboso de Monteverde** and other local reserves.

Guanacaste and the Northern Pacific

Guanacaste is Costa Rica's driest province, but what it lacks in green landscape it makes up for in heart. Cowboy culture is the thing here: **Rodeos** and *fiestas cívicas* (civic festivals) are common and rustic ranches and resorts around **Volcán Rincón de la Vieja** feature **farm tours** and **horseback riding.**

Along the northern Pacific coast, **Bahía Murciélago** and **Islas Catalina** are two of the country's best **dive sites.** The **surfing** is notorious at **Ollie's Point** and **Witch's Rock.** Bird enthusiasts shouldn't miss the inland **Parque Nacional Palo Verde.**

Nicoya Peninsula

When people long for **sun, sand,** and **solitude,** they come to the Nicoya Peninsula. Travelers who make the trek are rewarded with **quiet towns,** beautiful and empty **beaches,** and little distraction. Fittingly, **yoga, surf,** and **health retreats** are draws here, luring those in search of **relaxation** and beach time.

The region also boasts the undeveloped paradise of **Isla Tortuga,** the exciting falls at **Cataratas Montezuma,** and the chance to watch **sea turtles nesting** at the **Refugio Nacional de Vida Silvestre Ostional.**

Central Pacific

If you want to combine **beach** time with adventure and **nature tours,** this is the region for you. Beaches line the central Pacific coast from end to end, yet the area is also **mountainous** and rich in wildlife, including **crocodiles** in **Tárcoles,** birds in **Parque Nacional Carara,** **sloths** in **Parque Nacional Manuel Antonio,** **monkeys** at the **Isla Damas mangroves,** and marine life in the waters of **Parque Nacional Marino Ballena.** From backpackers in friendly **hostels** to couples in romantic **resorts,** this region welcomes all travelers.

Osa Peninsula and the Southern Pacific

Much of the Osa Peninsula and the southern Pacific region has yet to be explored by visitors. In areas where development exists, establishments are **low-key,** environmentally conscious, and sometimes **off the grid.** While traveling to and through the region requires patience and time, **hikes** in the renowned **Parque Nacional Corcovado** and underwater exploration within the **Reserva Biológica Isla del Caño** make the trip worthwhile. Those who visit reap bountiful rewards, including immersion in nearly **virgin forest** and **wildlife-watching** opportunities of the highest caliber.

Caribbean Coast

With pretty **beaches, coral reefs,** and decent **surf,** the palm-backed southern Caribbean coast is loved for its **laid-back vibe.** It's also the home of **Afro-Costa Rican culture,** which delights visitors with delicious cuisine and reggae music.

To the north, the **canals** and beaches of **Parque Nacional Tortuguero** beckon wildlife watchers, as does the **rainforest** around the inland **Puerto Viejo de Sarapiquí.** This is also where you can take part in one of the country's greatest adventures, **white-water rafting** on the **Río Pacuare.**

Southern Inlands

Tourism in the southern inland region is scarce. Much of the region is made up of **indigenous reserves** and **protected land.** The region appeals most to fit and fearless **hikers** who wish to stand atop Costa Rica's highest point, **Cerro Chirripó,** in **Parque Nacional Chirripó.** A secondary draw is **bird-watching,** either at the **Refugio de Aves Los Cusingos** or around the **San Gerardo de Dota** area, where **resplendent quetzals** and other bird species are frequently seen.

When to Go

Costa Rica is a **year-round destination.** Experiences vary greatly between the **high season, mid-December through April** and the **low season, May through mid-December.** High season aligns with **summer** and is also known as the **dry season.** The low season aligns with the **green season,** colloquially referred to as the **wet season,** which is considered Costa Rica's **winter.**

The **shoulder season,** which spans the **end of June to mid-August,** sees a surge in visitors.

Some accommodations increase their rates during this period.

The Caribbean's weather patterns differ from those of the rest of the country. September and October, two of the wettest months in most areas of the country, are notoriously dry and sunny on the Caribbean coast, especially in the southern part of the region.

High Season

Generally, the high season runs from

If You're Looking For...

CANYONEERING
Visit La Fortuna or Manuel Antonio.

CAVING
Visit the Terciopelo cave in Parque Nacional Barra Honda on the Nicoya Peninsula. Or go cave camping near Dominical in the central Pacific region.

CULTURE
Visit San José for museums; Sarchí for artisan creations; the Caribbean coast for cuisine; or Guanacaste for *fiestas cívicas*. To learn more about some of Costa Rica's indigenous groups, visit San Rafael de Guatuso or Bribri village.

HOT SPRINGS
Visit La Fortuna.

MOUNTAIN BIKING
Visit Turrialba in the Central Highlands, La Fortuna, or bike parks near Las Catalinas and Bagaces in Guanacaste.

NIGHTLIFE
Visit San José; Playas del Coco or Tamarindo in Guanacaste; Jacó or Quepos in the central Pacific region; or Puerto Viejo de Talamanca on the Caribbean coast.

SCUBA DIVING
Visit Isla del Coco off the central Pacific coast; Bahía Murciélago or Islas Catalina off the northern Pacific coast; or Isla del Caño off the Osa Peninsula.

SEA TURTLE NESTING
Visit Parque Nacional Marino Las Baulas in Guanacaste, the Refugio Nacional de Vida Silvestre Ostional on the Nicoya Peninsula, or Parque Nacional Tortuguero in the Caribbean region.

SURFING
Don't miss the breaks at Witch's Rock, Ollie's Point, Playa Grande, Playa Tamarindo, and Playa Avellanas off the northern Pacific coast; Playa Guiones, Playa Camaronal,

rainforest trail in La Fortuna

and Playa Santa Teresa off the Nicoya Peninsula; Playa Hermosa and Playa Dominical off the central Pacific coast; or Salsa Brava off the Caribbean coast.

TREKKING
Summit Cerro Chirripó in the southern inland region, explore challenging trails in Parque Nacional Corcovado on the Osa Peninsula, or hike between La Fortuna and Monteverde.

TUBING
Visit La Fortuna or Bijagua.

WHITE-WATER RAFTING
Sign up for a tour on the Río Pacuare, accessible from the Caribbean region, San José, or La Fortuna.

YOGA AND WELLNESS RETREATS
Visit Nosara or Santa Teresa on the Nicoya Peninsula.

ZIP-LINING
Visit La Fortuna or Monteverde.

Explore the treetop canopy from a hanging bridge.

capuchin monkey

mid-December to the end of April. It begins no later than January 1 and ends no sooner than Easter. During the season, reservations for hotels, tours, and transportation can be tight, prices are high (notably for accommodations), and **crowds** are common at popular attractions.

The biggest draw is **favorable weather,** including sunny skies, warm temperatures of 75-85°F, and little rain; this translates to optimal driving conditions. The most expensive time to travel to Costa Rica is during brief **peak periods** around Christmas, New Year's, and Easter, when accommodation prices are hugely inflated.

Low Season
The low season runs from the **beginning of May** to mid-December. Sometimes, it can begin immediately after Easter and last until December 31. The low season offers **quiet trails, smaller tour groups,** and **cheaper prices.** Since most tour operators require a minimum of two people to run tours, solo travelers can find it a challenge to travel at this time of year. Some businesses close or undergo renovations between September and November.

Unfavorable weather, marked by heavy rain, whipping winds at high elevations, and occasional thunderstorms can cause landslides, traffic delays, flooding, road closures (typically only in back-road areas), and last-minute tour cancellations.

Before You Go

Passports and Visas
All visitors must have a **valid passport** to enter Costa Rica. **Proof of exit intent,** in the form of a ticket to travel to another country, is required to receive a passport entry stamp. Most stamps expire within 90 days of issuance.

Vaccinations
Costa Rica does not require North American travelers to provide proof of vaccination. Nationals of some countries (namely African and South American countries) are required to show proof of yellow fever vaccination. Recent travelers

to countries in those areas of the world may be asked to show the same.

Transportation

Near the center of Costa Rica and the capital city, the **Aeropuerto Internacional Juan Santamaría** (Juan Santamaría International Airport, SJO) is a great jumping-off point to destinations all around the country.

If you plan to explore Guanacaste or the northern Nicoya Peninsula, fly into the **Aeropuerto Internacional Daniel Oduber Quirós** (Daniel Oduber Quirós International Airport, LIR) in Costa Rica's northwest corner. If your itinerary takes you across the country, consider flying into one airport and out of the other to avoid backtracking.

Getting around is easy. The **public bus system** is well-coordinated and reliable, as are **tourist-geared shared shuttle services** and **private transfer services.** Some tour outfitters provide **post-tour onward transportation,** allowing you to travel between destinations while experiencing an adventure along the way.

Renting a car provides endless opportunities to explore, though a **4x4 vehicle** is required in many areas and recommended in most others.

Domestic flights, water taxis, and **ferries** connect several destinations and help save travel time.

Advance Reservations

Reserve tours, accommodations, and transportation services in advance. Last-minute requests and drop-ins are accepted in some cases, but most tour operators and attractions require prior notice. Secure reservations before you travel so you can take advantage of early-booking **discounts** and handle payment from home. Most businesses have **flexible cancellation policies.**

SIGHTS AND EXPERIENCES

It can be tempting to delay booking your tours until you have a better sense of what weather to expect. But doing so means that the tours you want may not have openings; delaying can also create a rush of last-minute arrangements. Most tours run **rain or shine.**

During the high season, when spaces fill up quickly, book early to get your preferred date, time slot, and guide. In many cases, advance reservations are **required.** This includes the trek to **Cerro Chirripó,** overnight stays in **Parque Nacional Corcovado,** visits to **Volcán Poás,** and activities run by small organizations or indigenous groups, as well as most bird-watching and night tours.

ACCOMMODATIONS

During the low season, most accommodations have rooms to spare, and advance reservations are not required. Availability tightens around the **shoulder season,** when you should book a **few months** prior to your travel dates.

During the mid-December through April high season, the best accommodations sell out well in advance, typically by **September.** Other options fill up soon after. Stays during **peak periods** are the most sought-after; some accommodations receive requests for rooms **up to a year** in advance.

TRANSPORTATION

Most transportation services, including shared shuttle services, private transfer services, organized tour transportation services, domestic flights, and water taxis, will not take passengers who don't have an advance reservation. Many can be booked up to the **day before departure** (year-round), availability permitting, but it's best to make reservations as soon as your itinerary is finalized.

During the high season, rental agencies either **sell out** of vehicles or have only non-4x4 vehicles or expensive high-end vehicles to loan. Agency lots are typically stocked with all vehicle types during the low season.

Most public bus companies do not accept reservations.

Choose Your Adventure

The six mini-itineraries here are a selective sampling of Costa Rica's most popular destinations and not-to-miss experiences. Combine them to form one comprehensive trip that merges adventure, nature, culture, and relaxation for an unforgettable, fast-paced, two-week travel experience. Or mix and match the itineraries to create the trip that best suits your interests.

You can drive yourself to many destinations in a rental vehicle, or rely on Costa Rica's extensive, tourist-oriented transportation system to get around. Private **transfer services,** shared **shuttle services,** and **outfitters** that offer transportation with **organized tours** provide several ways to travel between cities, beach towns, and mountainous inland areas, making it easy to connect the dots and maximize your time.

A Taste of the Caribbean

A quick visit to the Caribbean coast provides an opportunity to experience the Jamaican-inspired side of Costa Rica, as well as a mix of downtime at the beach and wild, white-water adventure.

Day 1
Fly into the **Aeropuerto Internacional Juan Santamaría** on the outskirts of **San José** as early in the day as possible. Take a bus, a shared shuttle service, or a private transfer service to the laid-back beach town of **Puerto Viejo de Talamanca** (a 4.5-hour drive from the airport) for two nights on the sultry southern Caribbean coast. Spend the evening exploring the small

beach in Puerto Viejo de Talamanca

community on foot, kicking back to reggae beats at the **Salsa Brava Rasta Bar** and sinking into the slow pace of the region.

Day 2

Rise early and take a taxi or bus to **Parque Nacional Cahuita** in nearby **Cahuita.** Arrive before 8am (when organized tour groups begin to enter the park) and spend a few hours on the easy **nature trail** that parallels the coast and the light sand that spans **Playa Blanca.** Upon exiting, grab lunch at **Soda Kawe** in Cahuita, then head back to Puerto Viejo de Talamanca.

Pop in at the café and bakeshop **Caribeans** at 2pm to catch their **chocolate tour;** drop-ins are welcome. Take in the sunset at **Playa Cocles** across the street and return to Puerto Viejo de Talamanca for a dinner full of traditional Caribbean foods at **Lidia's Place.**

Day 3

Ready yourself for a day of extreme adventure on **Río Pacuare,** Costa Rica's top river for white-water rafting (no previous experience is required). You'll get breakfast, lunch, 3-4 hours of paddling time, and an opportunity to experience Costa Rica's jungle up close during the adrenaline-packed session. Your tour will include transportation from your hotel in Puerto Viejo de Talamanca to the river (a 2-hour drive), and either return transport or onward service to a new destination once the tour is over.

With More Time

Consider taking a tour of the **Jaguar Rescue Center** outside of Puerto Viejo de Talamanca or a side trip to **Parque Nacional Tortuguero** in the northern Caribbean region.

Easy Excursions from Here

Visits to the Caribbean are best combined with **La Fortuna** and **Monteverde.** The **Pacuare River Rafting Tour** from Exploradores Outdoors includes transportation between Puerto Viejo de Talamanca and La Fortuna. It's the best option for travel between the two destinations.

River tubing is a less extreme but still adventurous alternative to white-water rafting.

forest in the Northern Inlands

the Catarata Río Celeste in Parque Nacional Volcán Tenorio

Adrenaline Rush in La Fortuna and Monteverde

You'll be amazed by how many experiences you can pack into only three days in La Fortuna and Monteverde, two of Costa Rica's top adventure and nature destinations.

Day 1

Begin your adventure in the northern inland region in action-packed **La Fortuna.** Maximize your time by participating in a full-day **Arenal Combo Tour,** which combines an early morning guided tour through **Místico Arenal Hanging Bridges Park,** a visit to the powerful **Catarata Río Fortuna,** an afternoon hike to **Volcán Arenal,** and an evening spent soaking in thermal pools at **The Springs Resort & Spa.** Conveniently, lunch, dinner, and transportation to each activity are provided with the tour.

Day 2

In the morning, pick up a 4x4 vehicle from a car rental agency in La Fortuna and hit the road to **Monteverde;** the drive takes 3-3.5 hours. Enjoy the scenic route around **Lago Arenal** and the gradual climb to the **cloud forest.**

Plan to eat lunch in **Santa Elena** (the "downtown" of the Monteverde region) at the **Orchid Coffee Shop,** then drive north of town to **Monteverde Sky Adventures Park.** Spend the afternoon soaring above the treetops during the **Sky Trek canopy tour** zip-line excursion and its complimentary **aerial tram ride.**

Day 3

Drive to the neighboring **Reserva Biológica Bosque Nuboso de Monteverde** early in the day to hike the lush, misty reserve's **nature** trails when birds and wildlife are most active. Give yourself a few hours to explore, then exit the reserve and visit the free **Hummingbird Gallery** to see charms of hummingbirds flying freely.

Grab lunch at the Costa Rica-themed **Sabor Tico #2** on your way back and spend the afternoon driving to your next destination. Plan to arrive before dark.

With More Time

Take a one-day tour from La Fortuna to the underground caves at **Cavernas Venado,** the **Refugio Nacional de Vida Silvestre Mixto Caño Negro** for bird-watching, or **Parque Nacional Volcán Tenorio** to see the bright-blue **Río Celeste.**

Easy Excursions from Here

Trips to the centrally located northern inland region are easy to combine with visits to most areas in the country, including destinations on the **Pacific** and **Caribbean coasts.**

Soak Up the Sun on the Pacific Coast

This laid-back, two-day trip connects the northern Pacific region with the Nicoya Peninsula and showcases the distinct vibes of each region.

Day 1

Soak up some rays on the Pacific coast in the vibrant and social community of **Tamarindo.**

Spend the day strolling and shopping along the town's beachside boulevard and sunbathing on **Playa Tamarindo.** If you **surf,** take advantage of the area's consistent waves; **surf lessons** are available if you want or need them.

Midafternoon, head up the hill to **Black Stallion Eco Park** for a **sunset horseback**

Playa Tamarindo

Family-Friendly Fun

Costa Rica is one big eco-adventure park, with scenic sights, thrilling experiences, and wildlife encounters that make learning fun. Various activities and attractions are suitable for children; consider incorporating the following kid-friendly experiences into your travel plans to make the trip memorable for the whole family.

GO ZIP-LINING

Many zip-lining tours allow kids to participate. A favorite is the Big AMA Canopy Tour at Arenal Mundo Aventura Ecological Park in La Fortuna, which wows kids with views of Volcán Arenal and two waterfalls.

VISIT A NATURE-BASED THEME PARK

Entertain everyone in the family with the attractions at Selvatura Park in Monteverde. These include hanging bridges, a snake and amphibian exhibit, butterfly and hummingbird gardens, and an insect museum.

TOUR OR VOLUNTEER AT A WILDLIFE RESCUE CENTER

Get up close and personal with rescued wildlife at Rescate Animal Zooave in Alajuela or while volunteering for a few hours at the Proyecto Asis Wildlife Refuge Center near La Fortuna.

A young traveler prepares to ride a zip line.

LEARN HOW CHOCOLATE IS MADE

The Rainforest Chocolate Tour in La Fortuna and the Costa Rica Chocolate Tour in Alajuela both include tasty samples and are free for kids five and younger.

SWIM AT AN ACCESSIBLE WATERFALL

Some of Costa Rica's waterfalls can be tough to access or too powerful for swimming. Great for children, the Catarata Llanos del Cortés near Liberia has a shallow wading area and a lifeguard on duty. It's only a five-minute walk from the parking lot and is free for kids six and younger.

TAKE A BEGINNER SURF LESSON

Lots of surf schools welcome children. Have the kiddies start in Sámara; the area has a calm bay with gentle waves perfect for beginners.

DINE AT A FUN RESTAURANT

Keep young ones smiling with meals at El Avión in Manuel Antonio—a restaurant that's set in a cargo plane—and the Tree House Restaurant & Café in Santa Elena. Are the kids jonesing to see some animals while they eat? At Restaurante Las Iguanas near La Fortuna, you can see hundreds of iguanas in the trees outside. Lola's on Playa Avellanas has a resident pig.

riding tour, followed by one of the park's legendary **buffet dinners.** Back in Tamarindo, experience a mix of the town's notorious **nightlife** while **barhopping** along the beach.

Day 2

Trade eventful Tamarindo for the low-key Nicoya Peninsula by making the two-hour drive to the unassuming beach town of **Sámara.** Sprawl out on the light sand of **Playa Sámara** and enjoy gentle swims in the area's calm bay.

Grab lunch and dinner whenever you please at **beachside restaurants** like the **Lo Que Hay Bar & Taquería,** but make sure you're at the crescent-shaped **Playa Carrillo** at sundown to witness a spectacular sunset.

With More Time

Schedule a surf trip to the breaks at **Witch's Rock** and **Ollie's Point,** scuba dive at **Islas Murciélago** or **Islas Catalina,** go bird-watching at **Parque Nacional Palo Verde,** or take in a sea turtle nesting tour.

Easy Excursions from Here

The northern Pacific and the Nicoya Peninsula are best reached directly from Costa Rica's international airports (especially Liberia's **Aeropuerto Internacional Daniel Oduber Quirós**), or following a visit to **La Fortuna** and **Monteverde.**

Central Pacific Road Trip

The central Pacific coast is great for road-tripping. With this three-day itinerary, you'll travel from one end of the region to the other, stopping to take in key experiences along the way.

Day 1

Take the day to travel to **Manuel Antonio** by rental car, making sure to stop along the way at the **Crocodile Bridge** in **Tárcoles** and in the beach town of **Jacó** to shop for an hour or two and take photos at its magnificent lookout spots. If you're there over lunchtime, eat at the **Green Room.**

Arrive in Manuel Antonio before 5pm so you can watch the sun go down over the ocean while enjoying a grilled dinner at **El Lagarto.**

Day 2

Rise early and drive to **Parque Nacional Manuel Antonio** on the south side of town. Plan to be at the park when it opens at 7am to avoid most of the crowds. Give yourself a few hours to traverse nature trails and swim at beaches in the park, especially **Playa Manuel Antonio.**

Take a relaxing **boat** or **kayak tour** through the mangroves at **Isla Damas** in the afternoon. (If the tide requires the mangrove tour to be run in the morning, reverse the order of the day's activities.) If lunch isn't included with your mangrove tour, grab a light meal before the excursion at **El Patio de Café Milagro.** For dinner, treat yourself to fine dining at **La Luna.**

Day 3

Spend this day exploring the coast south of **Quepos** along Highway 34. Detour north on Road 243 at **Dominical** to the **Cataratas Nauyaca,** where a challenging hike will reward you with a refreshing swim in a picturesque two-tier waterfall.

Return to Dominical and grab a quick bite

Parque Nacional Manuel Antonio

at **Café Mono Congo,** then continue south on Highway 34 to **Parque Nacional Marino Ballena.** Enter through the community of **Bahía** to access **Playa Uvita,** where (at low tide) you can walk one kilometer into the ocean along the **whale-tail sandbar.**

With More Time

Give yourself an extra day in Manuel Antonio to experience the **Santa Juana Lodge's** Rural Mountain Adventure Tour or enjoy a **sailing, snorkeling, and dolphin-watching tour** along the Pacific coastline.

Easy Excursions from Here

The central Pacific coast is easily reached from any region in the country except for the Caribbean. This mini-itinerary is a great way to bridge the gap between the **Nicoya Peninsula** and the **Osa Peninsula.**

Are you backpacking around Costa Rica on a tight budget? If so, stick to low-key experiences that cost little, allow for self-guided exploration, and provide an opportunity to make a friend or two along the way.

LOUNGE AROUND A WATERFALL

Head to the Cataratas Montezuma in Montezuma or the Catarata Río Fortuna in La Fortuna to spend a few hours relaxing at a beautiful waterfall amid a lush forest setting. No tour guide is required.

HIKE THROUGH A NATURE RESERVE OR NATIONAL PARK

At your own pace, hike through one of Costa Rica's many protected land areas, such as the Reserva Biológica Bosque Nuboso de Monteverde, which has 13 kilometers of interweaving trails.

DINE AT A SODA RESTAURANT

Save money by dining at inexpensive, informal sodas that serve traditional Costa Rican meals. Soda Víquez in La Fortuna is one of the country's best.

CURB THE MUNCHIES WITH CHEAP EATS

Between meals, turn to roadside stalls and beach vendors for snacks and beverages. Raw-fish ceviche, pork chicharrones, refreshing pipa fría, and sweet copos are must-haves.

SHOP AT A FARMERS MARKET

Visit a weekly farmers market like the ones in Jacó, Quepos, and Uvita on the central Pacific coast for unique handmade items that make great and inexpensive souvenirs.

SPEND A DAY BEACH-HOPPING

Extend your beach reach by walking, biking, taking a bus, or hailing a taxi between multiple sandy spots. The 13-kilometer stretch between Puerto Viejo de Talamanca and Manzanillo on the Caribbean coast has five beaches you can visit in one day.

a bar in beach town Jacó

STAY AT A SOCIAL HOSTEL

Looking to meet new people? The Room 2 Board Hostel in Jacó, the Selina in Manuel Antonio, and Playa 506 in Puerto Viejo de Talamanca have an energetic feel and host social events.

CHECK OUT BEACH TOWN BARS OR JOIN A PUB CRAWL

The coastal towns of Tamarindo and Jacó have tons of bars you can hop between. In San José, the Carpe Chepe Pub Crawl visits four bars and includes a shot of liquor at each.

RENT YOUR OWN EQUIPMENT

Shops and hotels in coastal communities rent surfboards, stand-up paddleboards, boogie boards, snorkeling equipment, kayaks, bikes, ATVs, and other items that aid in self-guided exploration of the country. Embrace your wanderlust!

Escape to the Osa Peninsula

This brief, two-day itinerary is an introduction to Costa Rica's most remote region. In most cases, meals are provided by small-scale, all-inclusive accommodations.

Day 1

Set off on your journey to Costa Rica's most remote region from the riverside village of **Sierpe.** Catch the 11:30am boat to **Bahía Drake,** which is a scenic and wild one-hour ride through the **Humedal Nacional Térraba-Sierpe** and the Pacific Ocean.

Spend the afternoon at your accommodation, relaxing and appreciating the stillness of the area. At 7:30pm, take a **night tour with the Bug Lady** to discover how the forest awakens after dark.

Day 2

To experience the best of Bahía Drake, take a one-day tour of either **Parque Nacional Corcovado** (if you're in search of nature and wildlife) or the **Reserva Biológica Isla del Caño** (if you want to explore Costa Rica's underwater world and marine species). Tours to each attraction depart by boat from most area accommodations.

In the evening, prepare for your departure from the area by catching a return boat to Sierpe the next day or a domestic flight from **Aeropuerto Bahía Drake** to San José or another destination.

With More Time

Give yourself an extra day in Bahía Drake to experience both Parque Nacional Corcovado and the Reserva Biológica Isla del Caño. Alternately, lengthen your visit to Parque Nacional Corcovado so you can spend one night (or more) at the **ranger station** within the park.

Easy Excursions from Here

Jaunts to the Osa Peninsula best follow time spent in the **central Pacific region** if you plan to travel via ground transportation. By air, the region can be reached from most destinations in Costa Rica that have a domestic airport.

A Day in San José

Have time to spare at the end (or start) of your trip? This daylong circuit allows you to explore Costa Rica's capital city on foot.

Morning

Begin as early as 8:30am at the corner of Avenida Central (a **pedestrian mall**) and Calle 7. Stroll one block west to the **Plaza de la Cultura,** which showcases the eye-catching **Teatro Nacional de Costa Rica** on its south side. Take an educational, 45-minute guided **theater tour,** then continue walking five blocks west to **Mercado Central,** where you'll find hordes of locals going about their daily routine. Shop for souvenirs and grab a snack at one of the many informal eateries that fill the congested indoor market.

Afternoon

Exit Mercado Central at Avenida 1 and walk two blocks east to Calle 2. Turn left and you'll see the striking golden **Edificio Central de Correos y Telégrafos** that consumes the block. On the building's north side is Avenida 3; head east on the avenue for four blocks to the parkland trio of **Parque Morazán,** the **Jardín**

Teatro Nacional de Costa Rica in San José

de Paz, and **Parque España.** If you wish to purchase indigenous art, don't miss the collection at **Galería Namu,** one block north of Parque Morazán on Avenida 7.

Continue one block east of Parque España to **Parque Nacional,** where you can enjoy a take-out picnic lunch in the park prepared by the **Maza Bistro** (on the east side of the park). After lunch, walk south from the park on Calle 15 for two blocks to Avenida Central, where the yellow fortress of **Museo Nacional de Costa Rica** lies ahead, and the tall, gray **Museo del Jade** can be seen to the right.

Spend a few hours perusing the pre-Columbian artifacts within the modern Museo del Jade, then walk three blocks west to return to the corner where you began the journey. **Hotel Presidente** marks the spot.

Evening

End the day with dinner and drinks at Hotel Presidente's eclectic rooftop restaurant and bar **Azotea Calle 7.** Alternately, to experience several of San José's nightlife establishments, sign up for a **beer tour** or **pub crawl** around the capital.

With More Time

With more time, consider touring additional **museums** in the city's center or straying outside of the capital (ground transportation required) to see attractions in the surrounding **Central Valley and Highlands.**

Easy Excursions from Here

San José is best explored the day before or after you pass through the **Aeropuerto Internacional Juan Santamaría.** If you wish to tour the city, do so on either your last or first day in Costa Rica.

Isn't It Romantic?

The Springs Resort & Spa

Costa Rica's abundant waterfalls, hot springs, beaches, and resorts provide no shortage of romantic settings, perfect if you're on your honeymoon, celebrating a wedding anniversary, or marking another milestone.

SPLURGE ON A ROOM AT A LUXURY RESORT

Surround yourself with Costa Rican luxury at the **Andaz Costa Rica Resort** in Papagayo, **Florblanca** in Santa Teresa, or **Lapa Ríos** in Matapalo.

SOAK IN SOME HOT SPRINGS

The myriad of dimly lit thermal pools and lagoons at **The Springs Resort & Spa** in La Fortuna are romantic and relaxing.

PLAY A ROUND OF GOLF

Book a tee time for two at the immaculate Ocean Course at **Peninsula Papagayo** or the **Garra de León Golf Course,** both in the northern Pacific region.

BOOK A SUNSET SAIL

Enjoy the sunset (and an open bar) while sailing peacefully along the Pacific coastline, especially the scenic stretch between **Quepos** and **Parque Nacional Manuel Antonio.**

TAKE A SCENIC DRIVE

Venture around the quiet countryside of the **Valle de Orosí** east of Cartago and picnic at one of the area's scenic viewpoints.

HIKE TO BEAUTIFUL WATERFALLS

Waterfall scenes are wildly enchanting. Tour a series of five tall cascades at the popular **La Paz Waterfall Gardens,** then treat yourself to a meal or an overnight stay at the on-site **Peace Lodge.** Alternately, escape crowds by delving into the jungle, where you can swim at the base of secluded cascades like the **Catarata King Louis.**

ZIP-LINE IN TANDEM

Try zip-lining alongside your partner with the side-by-side cables provided at **Diamante Eco Adventure Park** near Playas del Coco.

ENJOY DINNER AND DRINKS BY THE WATERFRONT

Spoil yourself with oceanside dining at the candlelit restaurant **Locanda** in Sámara, which has tables on the sand and occasional musical serenades.

Pura Vida Adventures

If you live for adventure, you'll love Costa Rica. It boasts seemingly infinite opportunities for rafting, canyoneering, zip-lining, tubing, caving, hiking, mountain biking, scuba diving, and surfing.

La Fortuna and Monteverde

La Fortuna and Monteverde provide the greatest selection of adventure activities. In La Fortuna, you can **rappel** down a rock face during the **Canyoning in the Lost Canyon Tour**, go **tubing** at the **Club Río Outdoor Center**, and **hike** up and over mountains of **lava rocks** at the **Arenal 1968** reserve. If you enjoy mountain biking, Arenal 1968 also has 16 kilometers of rugged **mountain biking** trails.

In Monteverde, try the wild **canopy tours** provided by **100% Aventura**, which has the longest superman cable in Latin America, or **Monteverde Extremo**, which has a subterranean superman cable that zips through a dark tunnel. Both experiences include a thrilling Tarzan swing.

For a rugged challenge, travel between La Fortuna and Monteverde via the **Big Forest Hike**.

Guanacaste and the Northern Pacific

The northern Pacific coast means open water. Go **scuba diving** with **bull sharks** at **Islas Murciélago** or **manta rays** at **Islas Catalina**.

Surf the legendary breaks at **Witch's Rock** and **Ollie's Point** within **Parque Nacional Santa Rosa** or visit **Playa Grande, Playa Tamarindo,** or **Playa Avellanas,** where you'll find good waves and surf.

On land, avid and experienced **mountain bikers** get their fill at the **bike trails** in **Las Catalinas** and at the **Río Perdido Activity Center** near Bagaces.

At Arenal 1968, you can hike over lava rocks.

Nicoya Peninsula

Although the Nicoya Peninsula is known for its calm, zen-like vibe, the heart-racing descents into the deep, dark **Terciopelo cave** at **Parque Nacional Barra Honda** are anything but relaxing.

The great **surf** off **Playa Guiones, Playa Camaronal,** and **Playa Santa Teresa** provide the coast's biggest thrills.

Central Pacific

A sensational overnight experience near Dominical, **cave camping** at **Catarata Diamante** includes the rush of sleeping next to a thundering **waterfall.**

The multiday **boat trip** on a liveaboard vessel to **Parque Nacional Isla de Coco** is arguably Costa Rica's most exotic adventure. The experience invites you to **scuba dive** with **hammerhead sharks** and set foot on uninhabited land.

Awesome adventures on or near the mainland include the jam-packed 10-in-1 combo tour from **Amigos del Río, white-water rafting** tours on **Río Savegre** and **Río Naranjo,** and **surfing** off **Playa Hermosa** and **Playa Dominical.**

Osa Peninsula and the Southern Pacific

Great **scuba diving** awaits at the **Reserva Biológica Isla del Caño,** a marine life haven off the coast of the Osa Peninsula at Bahía Drake.

One of the world's longest left **surf breaks** curls in front of **Pavones** and treats advanced-level surfers to legendary hollow runs.

Caribbean Coast

For **surfing** on the Caribbean coast, make your way to the crashing waves of the **Salsa Brava** surf break at **Puerto Viejo de Talamanca.**

The best place for **white-water rafting** in Costa Rica is **Río Pacuare.**

Southern Inlands

For a true challenge, **hike** to the peak of Costa Rica's highest mountain. Summit **Cerro Chirripó** on a multiday trek in **Parque Nacional Chirripó.**

Playa Avellanas

The Best Beaches for You

Parque Nacional Manuel Antonio

With coasts on the Pacific Ocean and the Caribbean Sea, Costa Rica offers no shortage of beaches.

GREAT FOR SINKING YOUR TOES INTO

Playa Flamingo and the west end of Playa Conchal in Guanacaste have sand soft enough to snuggle in.

BEST FOR SPOTTING WILDLIFE

Troops of monkeys play around the beach at Playa Manuel Antonio in Parque Nacional Manuel Antonio and Playa Blanca in Parque Nacional Cahuita. Other wildlife species make occasional appearances.

PERFECT FOR SWIMMING IN TIDE POOLS

At low tide, the rocky shores of Playa Los Suecos and Playa Pelada on the Nicoya Peninsula provide little pools that you'll love wading in.

MOST SPECTACULAR SUNSETS

Sunsets along both coasts are incredible, but the most jaw-dropping are seen from Playa Carrillo on the Nicoya Peninsula and Playa Hermosa in Guanacaste.

IDEAL FOR TAKING LONG WALKS

At low tide, visit the sun-soaked Playa Uvita in Parque Nacional Marino Ballena and walk the giant, whale tail-shaped sandbar that juts out into the ocean.

MOST IDYLLIC

The blissful cove at Playa Biesanz on the central Pacific coast is a great place to kick back, as is the remote-feeling Isla Tortuga, with its soothing turquoise waters off the Nicoya Peninsula.

OFF THE BEATEN PATH

Playa San Josecito on the Osa Peninsula, Playa Garza on the Nicoya Peninsula, and Playa Chiquita on the Caribbean coast are beautiful and quiet beaches less frequented than most.

Get Back to Nature

Costa Rica is filled with national parks, biological reserves, and other protected areas where waterfalls flow, birds fly, and all kinds of wildlife species can be spotted.

Central Valley and Highlands
The best nature experiences close to San José are tucked away in the Central Highlands. **Hike** around **waterfalls** and check out **wildlife** exhibits at **La Paz Waterfall Gardens** near Alajuela. Visit the crater of **Volcán Irazú** within **Parque Nacional Volcán Irazú** near Cartago.

La Fortuna and Monteverde
Escape to the lush **rainforest** and **cloud forest** that blanket La Fortuna and Monteverde. In this area, you can explore a series of **hanging bridges,** search for nocturnal species after dark during a **night tour, hike nature trails** through several **private reserves,** and admire the powerful **Catarata Río Fortuna.**

North of La Fortuna, there's great **bird-watching** at the **Refugio Nacional de Vida Silvestre Mixto Caño Negro.** The shockingly blue **Río Celeste,** within **Parque Nacional Volcán Tenorio,** showcases some of Mother Nature's best work.

Guanacaste and the Northern Pacific
In the interior of Guanacaste, you can **hike** past **steam vents** and around bubbling **mud pots** within **Parque Nacional Rincón de la Vieja** and go **bird-watching** at **Parque Nacional Palo Verde.**

By the coast, tour **wildlife exhibits** at **Diamante Eco Adventure Park.** Watch **leatherback sea turtles** crawl ashore on the sands of Playa Grande, within **Parque Nacional Marino Las Baulas.**

Some of Costa Rica's forests are home to trees with giant root systems.

Coffee, Cuisine, and Culture

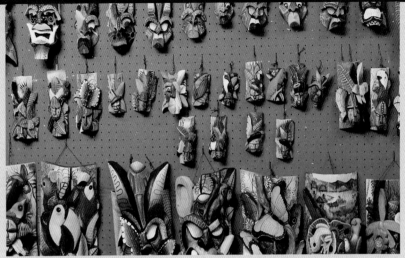

masks made by indigenous Boruca people

Costa Rican culture is an eclectic mix of history, lively celebrations, rich foods, artisan creations, and diverse groups of people. Immerse yourself in the beautiful blend to get the most out of your trip.

LEARN ABOUT GROWING COFFEE

The large **Doka Estate** near Alajuela uses old-fashioned machinery. The **Café Britt Coffee Roastery** in Heredia is entertaining for kids. **El Toledo Coffee**, near Atenas, is a small-scale, family-run operation that you can tour.

SAMPLE CARIBBEAN CUISINE

You can get high-quality, flavorful food at **Soda Kawe** in Cahuita and **Lidia's Place** in Puerto Viejo de Talamanca.

EXPLORE A MUSEUM

Step back in time and learn about Costa Rica's history through informative, interactive, and artifact-filled museum displays. The modern **Museo del Jade** and **Museo del Oro Precolombino** in San José are the best.

ATTEND A *FIESTA CÍVICA*

Don't miss the **Fiestas de Palmares,** Costa Rica's biggest party, in January. If you can't make the event, catch one of many lively and traditional civic festivals in Guanacaste.

CHECK OUT AN ARCHAEOLOGICAL SITE

The **Monumento Nacional Guayabo** in Turrialba is full of **petroglyphs,** tombs, and other interesting finds.

PERUSE ARTISAN SHOPS

Watch artists build and decorate **iconic oxcarts** at the *fábricas de carretas* (cart factories) in Sarchí or browse **art studios** in Monteverde.

VISIT AN INDIGENOUS RESERVE

At the **Reserva Indígena Maleku,** watch members of the indigenous group demonstrate the significance of dress, art, and medicinal plants.

WATCH A GAME OR PERFORMANCE

If you're into sports, catch the **national team** playing *fútbol* at the **Estadio Nacional de Costa Rica.** If you prefer the arts, take in a performance at the **Teatro Nacional de Costa Rica.** Both venues are in San José.

LIVE LIKE A LOCAL

Shop, dine, and **people-watch** like a Tico at the **Mercado Central** in San José.

hikers on a black sand beach in Parque Nacional Corcovado, on the Osa Peninsula

Nicoya Peninsula

The **Cataratas Montezuma** in the southern half of the Nicoya Peninsula provide an opportunity to swim in natural waterfall pools.

The northern half of the peninsula hosts Costa Rica's largest **sea turtle nesting** events, where thousands of **olive ridley sea turtles** come to lay their eggs in the sand at the **Refugio Nacional de Vida Silvestre Ostional.**

Central Pacific

Tour **Parque Nacional Carara** in search of **macaws** and other **tropical birds** just inland from the central Pacific coast. Farther south, the busy **Parque Nacional Manuel Antonio** houses numerous **wildlife** species, and **Isla Damas** invites its visitors to learn about **mangrove ecosystems.** Inland from Dominical, the **Cataratas Nauyaca** are must-see natural **cascades.**

Osa Peninsula and Southern Pacific

Hike through the remote **Parque Nacional Corcovado,** one of the most **biodiverse** places on the planet, for total immersion in nature. **Multiday treks** from Bahía Drake and Puerto Jiménez mean more opportunities to spot wildlife that few travelers ever get the chance to see.

Caribbean Coast

In the northern part of the region, the rainforest research center **Estación Biológica La Selva** and the peaceful canals of **Parque Nacional Tortuguero** offer glimpses of precious ecosystems. Parque Nacional Tortuguero is also home to a variety of **nesting sea turtles** and a handful of sea turtle conservation organizations where you can volunteer your time.

Southern Inlands

Birders and botanists shouldn't miss this region, namely the **bird-watching tours** around **San Gerardo de Dota,** the **Refugio de Aves Los Cusingos,** and the **Wilson Botanical Garden.**

San José

San José, Costa Rica's capital city, is a vibrant, bustling, and, yes, congested metropolis steeped in a blend of Costa Rican and expat cultures. Chepe, as the city is affectionately referred to by Josefinos (San José residents), is wildly diverse, at least when compared with the rest of the country. Within its relatively small center of roughly 15 square kilometers, the city provides a vast range of sights, experiences, and environments.

Casual markets and upscale shops sit side by side on the same avenue. Typical Costa Rican dishes are served next door to world-class international cuisine. Businesspeople, families, students, and street performers intermingle in plazas and parks. At its core, San José is a mosaic.

Highlights

Look for ★ to find recommended sights, activities, dining, and lodging.

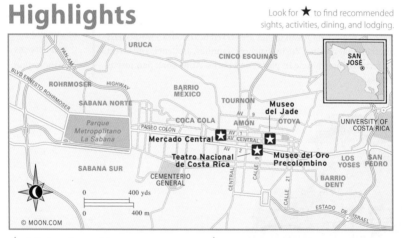

© MOON.COM

★ **Admire the architecture** and opulent decor of the **Teatro Nacional de Costa Rica** (page 51).

★ **View pre-Columbian gold artifacts** at the vast **Museo del Oro Precolombino** (page 53).

★ **Learn about Costa Rica's archaeological history** through the interactive displays at the **Museo del Jade** (page 54).

★ **Shop like a local** at the **Mercado Central** (page 63).

Once a coffee-trading outpost, San José has urbanized light-years beyond its agricultural roots. Still, it maintains much of its dashing old-world charm in striking colonial-style buildings around the city that now function as hotels, restaurants, and bars. The city's history is proudly preserved in statues, monuments, and museums.

Located in the middle of the country, the greater San José area serves as a popular hub where visitors begin and end their time in Costa Rica. Many overlook the capital as a potential destination in favor of spending more time in inland areas or along either coast. But there's enough here to pique the interest of most travelers.

PLANNING YOUR TIME

To really get to know San José, you would need weeks to explore the jam-packed city. Realistically, you'll probably only have **one day** (or two, at the most) to get the gist of it, so you'll want to fill the time with as many sights as you can. Plan your itinerary in advance so you can maximize your visits and minimize your walking time or taxi fare. If you're not up for coordinating your own route, several San José walking tours handle the mapping; all you need to do is show up and keep up.

Fortunately, the city's highlights can be experienced in a day. If you station yourself downtown, you can take in the architecture of the **Teatro Nacional de Costa Rica**, eye precious artifacts at the **Museo del Oro Precolombino**, see authentic urban life while shopping at the **Mercado Central**, and learn about jade and pre-Columbian history at the **Museo del Jade** all before nightfall, leaving your evening free to dine out, take in a show, attend a *fútbol* game, or have a few drinks at a bar. Your busy day will be long and tiring, but also revelatory and rewarding.

Weather and Transportation

San José, low in the Central Valley, has temperatures that average in the low 70s Fahrenheit. Sunshine is common but often interrupted by sporadic periods of rainfall, especially between May and November.

San José's paved, multilane highways offer well-marked exits. In the downtown core, streets narrow and traffic regularly backs up, but the roads are in decent condition and don't require a 4x4 vehicle. The biggest hazards to look out for are other drivers, many of whom speed and change lanes without signaling. Drive defensively and use a GPS to help you navigate. Occasional road closures can cause frustrating delays.

Traveling throughout San José is made quick and easy by the east-west passage of Highway 2. The highway begins in West San José and serves as the city's main thoroughfare. It sails through Central and East San José for six kilometers before turning south toward Cartago.

ORIENTATION

Greater San José is comprised of more than 100 barrios (neighborhoods); many are residential and pleasant, some are touristy, and others are very poor. It's hard to tell where one ends and the next begins. It's easier to navigate the city by breaking it into three main areas: **Central San José, East San José, and West San José.**

Most streets in San José follow a **grid pattern.** Generally, *avenidas* (avenues) run east-west and *calles* (streets) run north-south. Road numbers can help you get your bearings. Avenues north of Avenida Central have odd numbers and avenues south of Avenida Central have even numbers. Streets east of Calle Central have odd numbers and streets west of Calle Central have even numbers.

Most establishments in San José don't use numbered addresses. Instead, they're

---

Previous: Edificio Central de Correos y Telégrafos; Museo Nacional de Costa Rica; entrance to the Teatro Nacional de Costa Rica.

San José

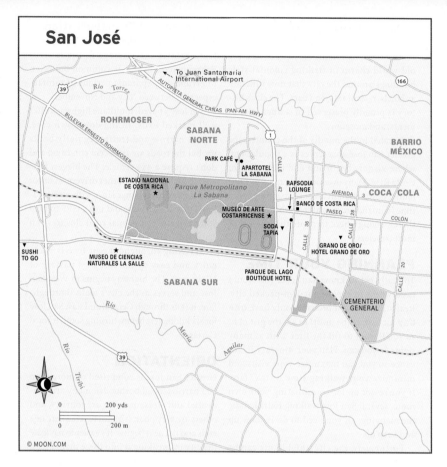

referenced by streets and avenues, common landmarks, or both. Familiarize yourself with basic directional words and phrases in Spanish. Most distances are in *metros* (meters); blocks in San José typically run 75-150 meters. You might see the address of the Museo del Jade referenced as any of the following: Avenida Central y Calle 13 (Central Avenue and 13th Street); Avenida Central, 30 *metros al este de la* Calle 13 (Central Avenue, 30 meters to the east of 13th Street); or Avenida Central, *en el lado oeste de la* Plaza de la Democracia (Central Avenue, on the west side of the Plaza de la Democracia).

Throughout West San José and upon entry into the central zone, Highway 2 is known as **Paseo Colón.** In the downtown core, Highway 2 is referred to as **Avenida 2.** In East San José, Highway 2 is sometimes cited as **Avenida del Libertador Juan Rafael Mora Porras.**

Highway 2 in Central San José is an eastbound one-way street. **Avenida 3** (three blocks north of Hwy. 2) is a westbound one-way street. In the center of the city, **Calle 1** (a southbound one-way street) and **Calle 3** (a northbound one-way street) form **Highway 32,** which connects the capital to the Caribbean coast.

Central San José

The city's core, in the middle of Central San

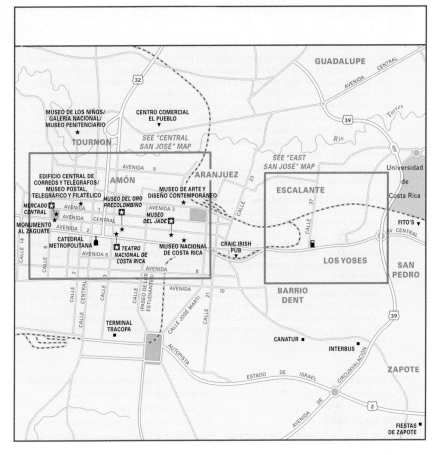

José, is a primarily flat, walkable stretch that's roughly 20 blocks wide and 6 blocks deep. **San José Centro** (San José Center), as the locals call it, or simply **downtown,** contains most of the city's attractions, parks, and pedestrian malls. Station yourself here if you wish to be in the middle of the action and within walking distance of most attractions.

The intersection of **Calle Central** and **Avenida Central** pinpoints the center of the city. In the downtown core, popular avenues are **Avenida 1, Avenida 2, Avenida 3,** and Avenida Central, which is closed to vehicles between Calle 9 and 14.

Northeast of downtown are some quaint neighborhoods including **Barrio Amón** and **Barrio Aranjuez,** home to some of the city's most eye-catching historical buildings.

Northwest of downtown is one of the city's roughest areas, and south of downtown offers little interest to foreigners. Both vicinities should be avoided.

East San José

The city's **University District** takes up much of East San José. Close to the campus of the Universidad de Costa Rica are **Barrio Los Yoses,** a quiet community with a handful of inexpensive lodging options, and **Barrio Escalante,** with a great selection of casual but high-end restaurants. If you're a night owl or looking to socialize, you'll love the

Reasons to Visit San José

Most Costa Rica travelers arrive into and depart from the country via the Aeropuerto Internacional Juan Santamaría (Juan Santamaría International Airport, SJO), in Alajuela, about 15 kilometers northwest of San José. If you're spending a night in the region either before or after your flight, you can stay on the outskirts of the capital or in the thick of the city.

It's possible to skip the country's center altogether. Alajuela and Ciudad Cariari in the Central Valley and Highlands provide plenty of accommodations in close proximity to the airport; Escazú and Santa Ana add unique and chic choices. If, however, you wish to immerse yourself in a metropolitan culture, you'll want to check out downtown San José. Plan a visit if the following attractions pique your interest:

- **Museums:** San José is Costa Rica's museum capital. The metropolis has exhibits galore, from gold and jade to art, history, and natural science.

- **People-watching:** People-watching opportunities abound in San José. Stroll around commercial districts where businesspeople hustle to and from work or take a seat in a plaza or park where Costa Rican families gather and kids play.

- **Varied cuisine:** Tired of rice and beans? The capital city's cosmopolitan culinary scene provides plenty of diverse meal options and settings for dining. Alternately, if there's a specific Costa Rican food you're tempted to try, there's bound to be a restaurant, market, or food stall that serves it.

- **Eclectic shops:** Traditional souvenirs can be purchased all over Costa Rica, but items that are difficult to come across elsewhere hide among San José's unique collection of stores and markets. To shop like a Tico, don't miss brand-name stores and markets in the city's concentrated center. To blend in with the masses, window-shop along San José's always-bustling pedestrian malls.

lively atmosphere that the east end of the city provides.

West San José

Closest to the upscale town of Escazú, West San José—much of which is referred to as **La Sabana**—has executive-style hotels, classy restaurants, and swanky clubs. It also has **Parque Metropolitano La Sabana,** the largest park in the city, and a softness that is missing from the downtown core. Business travelers and others looking to splurge stay here, if they're not in a ritzy hotel in the central zone.

SAFETY CONCERNS

There is a significant amount of crime in San José. This means visitors should have higher levels of alertness and preparedness than in other parts of Costa Rica. Plan where you want to go in the city, know how to safely get to and from each site, and stick to your itinerary. Aimless wandering can quickly lead you into dangerous neighborhoods.

Pickpocketing, petty theft, and vehicle break-ins are the most common crimes against tourists. Don't wear valuable jewelry, expose expensive cameras longer than necessary, or carry or display lots of cash around town. Keep your passport in your hotel, ideally in a safe. Only carry a copy of your passport with you around town. Park your rental vehicle only in secure lots.

Come nightfall, the potential for danger increases greatly. If you wish to experience San José after dark, go out with other people, stick to well-populated and well-lit areas (avoid parks and side streets), and always keep your wits about you. Do not visit an ATM at night; cash should be retrieved only during daylight hours.

If you're traveling on a shoestring, set aside funds in your budget for taxi transportation in San José. It can be tempting to walk everywhere in the city, especially to or from bus stations, but many are in dicey areas. It's best to take a cab from place to place instead of walking between destinations. Limit your walks around the city to popular and low-risk areas, and rely on paid transportation, such as official red taxis, buses, and drivers arranged through your hotel.

Sights

CENTRAL SAN JOSÉ

Catedral Metropolitana

Downtown San José's **Catedral Metropolitana** (Metropolitan Cathedral, Calle Central between Avenida 2 and Avenida 4, 6am-7:30pm Mon.-Sat., 6am-9pm Sun.) was reerected in 1871, decades after its initial construction and following an earthquake that battered the building. In the core of the city, this religious institution on the east side of Parque Central is the gathering place of local Roman Catholics. From the exterior, the stone-white, boxy cathedral resembles a courthouse, complete with a wide concrete staircase and eight tall columns at its entrance. The exterior is unembellished, but inside are ornate details like dark-wood pews, gold candelabras, decorative floor tiles, and stained-glass windows.

The music played on the 19th-century pipe organ is beautiful, unhurried, and contemplative. Mass takes place regularly, with four services throughout the day Monday through Saturday, and seven services on Sunday. On Saturdays, the 4pm service is conducted in English.

Plaza de la Cultura

The centrally located outdoor **Plaza de la Cultura** (Culture Plaza, Calle 5 at Avenida Central) is the perfect place to stop and rest during a stroll around San José. Following a multimillion-dollar renovation in 2016, the plaza—formerly no more than a concrete slab—is now a vibrant square where floor tiles act as water fountains; the space doubles as a children's **splashpad** (10am-6pm daily). At night (6pm-10pm daily), colorful lights and music accompany spurts of water and make for a synchronized, whimsical display in the city's center. The Gran Hotel Costa Rica towers over the plaza from the west, the Teatro Nacional de Costa Rica abuts its south side, and the subterranean Museo del Oro Precolombino hides underneath. Eateries and shops surround the plaza. Foot traffic passes through in all directions, making this an ideal spot for people-watching.

★ Teatro Nacional de Costa Rica

San José's distinguished **Teatro Nacional de Costa Rica** (National Theater of Costa Rica, Calle 5, adjacent to the Plaza de la Cultura, tel. 506/2010-1129, www.teatronacional.go.cr, 9am-5pm daily or later on performance nights) is easily identifiable. It's the large, lavish neoclassical building on the south side of the Plaza de la Cultura. In a country where coffee plantations and small houses dominate the landscape, this elegant, opulent theater in the heart of downtown San José is one of the few overt displays of luxury. The theater, inaugurated in 1897, hosts the country's top drama, music, and dance performances.

Statues adorn the exterior, the entrance, and the lobby of the theater, the last of which is a white marble masterpiece clad in gold trim and velvet ropes. The second-floor foyer is equally stunning, with its tall columns, hand-painted ceiling, and luxuriant curtains. Marble staircases connect floors via soft curves, and murals decorate most of the ceilings. The most famous work of art in the place, *El Alegoría del Café y el Banano (The Allegory of the Coffee and the Banana),* was also on the back of one of the old five-colón bills. Inside the shimmery,

Central San José

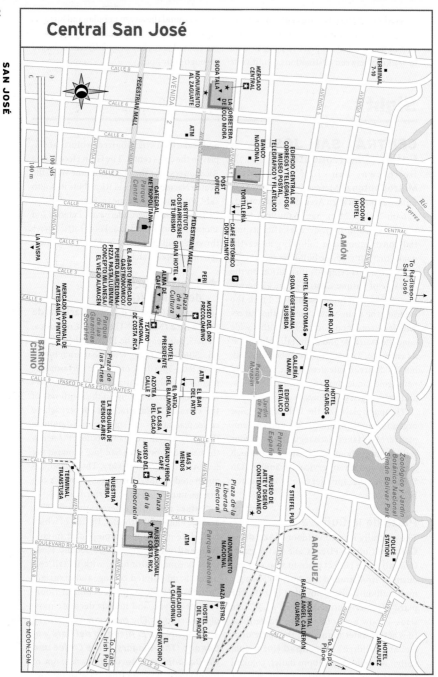

gold-accented auditorium are three levels of balconies arranged in a horseshoe shape around floor-level seating. Paintings of angels and cherubs fill the room's circular ceiling, warmly lit by a magnificent chandelier.

You can visit the theater for free to admire the beautiful lobby, visit the gift shop, and grab something to eat or drink at the on-site **Alma de Café** (9am-7pm Mon.-Sat., 9am-6pm Sun.), which serves delicious soups, salads, sandwiches, and other light fare. If you don't have tickets for a performance, you can see the theater beyond the lobby on a **guided tour** (hourly 9am-4pm daily, 45 minutes, $10 pp). The tour explores the building from top to bottom and discusses its history, artworks, and famous past performers.

Museo de los Niños

Located near one of San José's dodgiest neighborhoods and set, strangely, in a restored penitentiary, the interactive **Museo de los Niños** (Children's Museum, Calle 4 at Avenida 9, tel. 506/2258-4929, www.museocr.org, 8am-4:30pm Tues.-Fri., 9:30am-5pm Sat.-Sun., $4 adults, $3.50 children 0-15) has over 40 exhibit rooms that teach kids about everything from earthquakes and energy to dinosaurs and space technology. Signage is in Spanish. Regardless, there's plenty of hands-on learning and fun to be had. The place is packed on September 9 each year, when Costa Ricans celebrate the Día del Niño (Day of the Child).

Also at this location are the **Galería Nacional** (National Gallery, free), which displays Costa Rican and international drawings, paintings, photography, and other art forms, and the **Museo Penitenciario** (Penitentiary Museum, $4 adults, $3.50 children 0-15), where you can learn about the penitentiary's history and view prison relics. Both attractions operate on the same schedule as the children's museum.

Edificio Central de Correos y Telégrafos

Stroll past the **Edificio Central de Correos y Telégrafos** (Central Post Office and Telegraph Building, Calle 2 at Avenida 3, tel. 506/2223-6918, 8am-5pm Mon.-Fri.) and you may mistake the ornate structure for a palace. Constructed in 1917, the butter-yellow building proudly displays Costa Rica's coat of arms above its entrance. Today it's a fully functional post office that also serves as the country's postal headquarters.

Venture inside to see displays in the **Museo Postal, Telegráfico y Filatélico** (Postal, Telegraphic and Philatelic Museum, www.museocostarica.go.cr, $1.50 pp) of a variety of unique pieces, like antique phones in working condition and both domestic and international stamps (including Costa Rica's first). Bring a pen when you visit; the entrance fee buys you a postcard that can be sent anywhere in the world. Send it from the post office or keep it as a souvenir.

★ Museo del Oro Precolombino

Enter the subterranean **Museo del Oro Precolombino** (Pre-Columbian Gold Museum, Calle 5 at Avenida Central, under the Plaza de la Cultura, tel. 506/2243-4202, www.museosdelbancocentral.org, 9:15am-5pm daily, $13 pp), which dives three levels underground, and you'll feel like you've jumped back in history to pre-Columbian times. Reopened in 2019 following a vast renovation, the sleek-looking museum has nine exhibits that explore the behaviors and values of indigenous Costa Ricans, including their migration routes, farming and hunting techniques, trading practices, spiritual beliefs, and gender roles.

Exhibits contain gold, stone, and ceramic pieces; dioramas; interactive displays; sculptures; and informative placards with descriptions in both Spanish and English. The museum's standout feature is its large collection of antique gold relics; among the items on display are arm and ankle bands, headpieces, necklaces, and figures that represent fauna, humans, and spiritual beings.

The museum also showcases a 300-piece numismatic collection that details the history of Costa Rica's currency. Coins, banknotes, and private currencies used from the 18th century to present times can be examined at close range, and you can read about the Casa de la Moneda, Costa Rica's mint.

★ Museo del Jade

The well-organized, modern **Museo del Jade** (Jade Museum, Avenida Central at Calle 13, tel. 506/2521-6610, www.museodeljadeins.com, 10am-5pm daily, $15 pp) is rich in history. Along with its collections of pre-Columbian artifacts, it offers visually appealing displays documented in both Spanish and English, and interactive education centers with fun games and puzzles to aid young learners. An efficient five-floor design (elevators are available) minimizes time spent walking between exhibits. Each floor focuses on different aspects of pre-Columbian history. The discovery, use, and preservation of jade is covered, as are the routines and rituals of pre-Columbian peoples. Most displays are life-size, crafted with incredible detail, and supplemented with in-depth descriptions. While the *Night* exhibit (which covers the underworld, war, and burial ceremonies) is the favorite of many museumgoers, I prefer the colorful *Day* exhibit for its exploration of flora and fauna.

Don't miss the room full of glass display cases that contain thousands of Costa Rica's most important archaeological finds, including stone, ceramic, and jade pieces, many of which continue to be studied. You don't need to be a history buff to enjoy the place. The museum is entertaining and informative enough to hold your attention and make the visit worthwhile.

If you're feeling parched or peckish, the on-site, cafeteria-style **Grano Verde Café** (10am-5pm daily, $3-12) is a great little spot that serves 11 kinds of coffee and green smoothies, plus healthy sandwiches and salads, pizzas, lasagnas, and scrumptious desserts.

Museo Nacional de Costa Rica

The **Museo Nacional de Costa Rica** (National Museum of Costa Rica, between Avenida Central and Avenida 2, just east of Calle 13, tel. 506/2211-5700, www.museocostarica.go.cr, 8:30am-4:30pm Tues.-Sat., 9am-4:30pm Sun., $9 pp 12 years and older) is Costa Rica's most eclectic compilation of artifacts from all corners of the country. The displays span pre-Columbian times through the colonial era to modern-day Costa Rica, showcasing everything from indigenous tools and carvings to precious metals and stones, as well as topographic maps, old cars, and *carretas* (oxcarts). You can fit in a quick overview of the country at this museum in only a few hours, thanks to placards in Spanish and English—perfect if the rest of your trip focuses on Costa Rica's recreational attractions.

The yellow, castle-like museum, which served as a fortress until 1948, upon the end of the civil war, is on the east side of the concrete Plaza de la Democracia. Included in your visit is a walk through the museum's enclosed **butterfly garden.**

Museo de Arte y Diseño Contemporáneo

What once oozed booze as Costa Rica's national liquor factory now houses San José's most progressive museum. The **Museo de Arte y Diseño Contemporáneo** (Museum of Art and Contemporary Design, MADC, Avenida 3 at Calle 15, tel. 506/2257-9370, www.madc.cr, 9:30am-5pm Tues.-Sat., $3 pp, min. age 5) has five small rooms that can be toured rather quickly. Exhibitions rotate regularly; most focus on culture, gender, language, or other social issues. Also here is a video library and documentation center where museum archives can be accessed. Prior reservations are required to access the archives, most of which are in Spanish. Museum entry is free on the first Tuesday of every month.

1: Catedral Metropolitana 2: part of the *Day* exhibit in the Museo del Jade

Monumento al Zaguate

A heartwarming tribute you'll appreciate if you love animals are the six comical and colorful iron dog sculptures that adorn Avenida Central on the south side of Mercado Central. Known as the **Monumento al Zaguate** (Monument to the Mutt), the collection pays homage to the stray dogs that roam aimlessly around San José and throughout the country. Costa Rican artist Francisco Munguía crafted the pieces in honor of the 23 *zaguates* (mutts) he welcomed into his home.

EAST SAN JOSÉ

Universidad de Costa Rica

Much of the northeast side of San José is consumed by the main campus of the **Universidad de Costa Rica** (University of Costa Rica, UCR, in the block northeast of Hwy. 2 and Hwy. 39, tel. 506/2511-4000, www.ucr.ac.cr). Costa Rica's oldest and highest-ranking public university educates more than 40,000 students annually. Of all places on campus, strangely, the Escuela de Música (Music School) houses an impressive display of thousands of pinned insects in the **Museo de Insectos** (Insect Museum, tel. 506/2511-5318, 8am-noon and 1pm-4:45pm Mon.-Fri., $2.50 adults, $1 children 0-11). More fittingly, the Escuela de Biología (Biology School) has a *mariposario* (butterfly garden, www.mariposario.biologia.ucr.ac.cr). Although this small butterfly garden with roughly 20 live species in its collection is largely a research center utilized by students, it's open to the public for **self-guided visits** (8am-noon Mon.-Fri., $2 pp). The guided **Chepe Hidden Nature Tour** (8am and 1:30pm daily, 2.5 hours, $35 pp) run by **ChepeCletas** (tel. 506/2222-7548, www.chepecletas.com) tours the butterfly garden as well as the university's on-site nature reserves in search of birds and wildlife hidden within the concrete jungle.

WEST SAN JOSÉ

Estadio Nacional de Costa Rica

The **Estadio Nacional de Costa Rica** (National Stadium of Costa Rica, Road 104, west side of Parque Metropolitano La Sabana, tel. 506/2549-0985, www.estadionacionalcr.com) is arguably Costa Rica's most modern sports and event center. The all-white arena holds more than 35,000 seats and features a giant retractable roof. This spiky structure will catch your eye throughout West San José. Several events, from concerts to fashion shows, are hosted at the venue, but it is best known for being the home stadium of the **Selección Nacional,** Costa Rica's national *fútbol* team. Here, Costa Rica's best *fútbol* players represent their country in international sport competitions. Thousands of other Ticos—young and old—fill the stands to cheer them on during sold-out games.

Museo de Arte Costarricense

Housed in a defunct terminal of Costa Rica's first international airport, the Aeropuerto Internacional La Sabana (La Sabana International Airport), is the **Museo de Arte Costarricense** (Museum of Costa Rican Art, Hwy. 1 at Hwy. 2, on the east side of Parque Metropolitano La Sabana, tel. 506/4060-2300, www.mac.go.cr, 9am-4pm Tues.-Sun., free). The small attraction displays a rotating collection of Costa Rican and international pieces both inside and in the sculpture garden out back. Enter the museum just south of the west end of Paseo Colón, where the road meets the Parque Metropolitano La Sabana.

Take time to visit the **Salón Dorado** on the second floor. All four walls of the bronze-colored room feature nearly floor-to-ceiling stucco carvings that present a 360-degree visual interpretation of Costa Rica's history. The details are immaculate.

Museo de Ciencias Naturales La Salle

A hit with Costa Rican children, the **Museo de Ciencias Naturales La Salle** (La Salle Museum of Natural Sciences, just south of Road 167, southwest corner of Parque

East San José

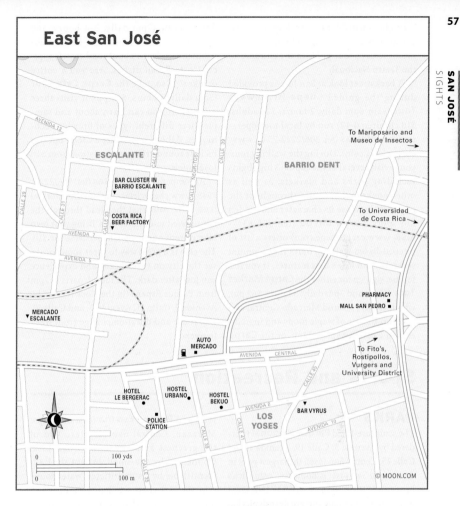

Metropolitano La Sabana, tel. 506/2232-1306, www.museolasalle.ed.cr, 8am-4pm Mon.-Sat., 9am-5pm Sun., $2.50 adults, $2 children 2-12, cash only) satisfies curious young minds with fossils and shells, rocks and minerals, pinned insects and butter-flies, the bones of dinosaurs and marine life, and lots of taxidermy. Depending on who you talk to, the canisters of formalde-hyde that contain odd creatures—including two-headed, mutated species—are either creative or creepy.

WALKING AND SIGHTSEEING TOURS

Looking to jam a ton of sights, stories, and knowledge into a few short hours in San José? The city is full of fun narrated walk-ing tours. My favorite is the **San José Free Walking Tour** (tel. 506/8721-9443, http://sanjosewalking.com, 9am daily, 3 hours, donations accepted). This all-encompassing walking tour covers the downtown core and includes talk of art, history, politics, and ev-eryday life in the capital. Best of all, the tour is run by spirited locals who love their city. Advance reservations aren't required; just meet the day's tour guide at the entrance to the Teatro Nacional.

A backstreet look at San José is provided during the guided **Chepe Hideaways Tour** (8am-6pm daily, 2 hours, $20 adults, $10 children 0-12) run by local tour operator **ChepeCletas** (tel. 506/2222-7548, www.chepecletas.com). During the walking tour, you'll visit several of the capital's highlights including parks and markets, as well as other nooks and crannies throughout the city that showcase its character and hidden hot spots. **Carpe Chepe** (tel. 506/8347-6198, www.carpechepe.com) offers a list of interest-based walking tours that pinpoint several of San José's best features. If you're a foodie, sign up for either the **Carpe Market Tour** (10am and 3pm daily, 3 hours, $62 pp), which centers around Mercado Central and explores the use of staple foods and ingredients in Costa Rican cooking, or the **Carpe**

Sabor Tour (7pm daily, 3-4 hours, $60 pp), which visits a handful of local establishments to learn about (and taste!) typical Costa Rican dishes. Are you a coffee drinker? If so, take the **Carpe Café Tour** (3pm daily, 3 hours, $60 pp); it visits three cafés where you can learn about and sample three different types of brewing techniques. All of Carpe Chepe's tour options include round-trip transportation from San José hotels.

Accompany **ChepeCletas** (tel. 506/2222-7548, www.chepecletas.com) on the informal **free bike tour** that they lead through the city on Wednesday evenings. Bring your own bike or rent one from ChepeCletas for $10. The ride is a great way to meet some locals, see the city on two wheels, and experience San José after dark. The tour departs at 7pm from Parque España (in the block formed by Avenida 7, Calle 11, Avenida 3, and Calle 9). The route and duration change from week to week.

Sports and Recreation

PARKS

The sculpture-filled **Parque Nacional** (bordered by Avenida 3, Calle 19, Avenida 1, and Calle 15, Central San José), the largest park in downtown San José, is home to Costa Rica's bronze **Monumento Nacional** (National Monument), perhaps the greatest depiction of national pride in the capital. It represents Costa Rica's regained identity following the defeat of American William Walker during the War of 1856. Choose this park if you're looking to picnic outdoors. The cute, vine-enclosed **Maza Bistro** (east side of the park at Hostel Casa Del Parque, tel. 506/2248-4824, 9am-6pm Tues.-Sun., $9-13) can prepare basket-packed meals for your enjoyment in the park.

Neighbors **Parque Morazán** (Avenida 3 between Calle 5 and Calle 9, Central San

José) and **Parque España** (east of Parque Morazán, Central San José) are two of the greenest areas in Central San José. Connected by the small **Jardín de Paz,** identifiable by its multitiered water fountain, the parks have manicured gardens and host the occasional artist as well as groups of street performers who use the gazebo in Parque Morazán as a place to practice their skills. The most noteworthy structure is the **Edificio Metálico** (north side of the Jardín de Paz), home to an elementary school. The striking blush-pink building resembles an all-metal Buckingham Palace.

On the west side of the city is the beloved **Parque Metropolitano La Sabana** (bordered by Road 104, Hwy. 1, and Hwy. 27, West San José), a rectangular 178-acre space comprising sport facilities, forest, and an

Fútbol Fever

Fútbol is an institution in Costa Rica. Children play it every day, teenagers dream of becoming professional players, and older folks rarely miss televised games. Eyes stay fixed on the national league's team standings from week to week. During international competitions, most notably the FIFA World Cup, there's hardly a dry eye in the country when the Selección Nacional, Costa Rica's national team (also known as La Sele), steps onto the field.

Fútbol fever spikes in San José, where the competitive blood of many residents runs purple, the official color of the city's home team of Saprissa (www.deportivosaprissa.com). It's arguably the most beloved team in the country. A great rivalry exists between the club and those of two neighbor cities, Alajuela's La Liga and Heredia's Los Florences. San José's fans are the wildest. They paint their faces, wave flags, jump, fist-pump, shout, and sing songs about the team to show their support. When the game's announcer calls *"goooooooooooooooool,"* chaos ensues, and the quintessential *fútbol* chant of *"ole, ole, ole, ole"* (followed by "Ticos, Ticos") bellows throughout the stadium.

Experience *fútbol* fever for yourself by watching a game in a stadium or at a bar, by striking up a conversation about teams with Ticos, or by simply looking for people wearing *fútbol* jerseys everywhere you go. Sport unifies people in Costa Rica—citizens, expats, and visitors alike. Join in if you get the chance.

artificial lagoon. The park feels out of place in the bustling capital, but it's well enjoyed by locals. The main entrance is on the east side, at the west end of Paseo Colón and just north of the Museo de Arte Costarricense. A tall statue of ex-president Leon Cortés marks the spot. Just beyond is a forest full of rainbow eucalyptus trees.

SPECTATOR SPORTS
Fútbol

Fútbol (soccer, to Americans and Canadians) is the most popular sport in Costa Rica. San José is home to two of the country's most visited stadiums. The **Estadio Nacional de Costa Rica** (National Stadium of Costa Rica, Road 104, west side of Parque

locals playing *fútbol* in front of the Estadio Nacional de Costa Rica

Metropolitano La Sabana, tel. 506/2549-0985, www.estadionacionalcr.com) hosts the Costa Rican national *fútbol* team, the **Selección Nacional.** When La Sele, as they're known, play in San José, there's no bigger event in the city. Don red, white, and blue and ready yourself for wild fandom. Purchase tickets in advance; some games sell out.

The **Estadio Ricardo Saprissa Aymá** (Ricardo Saprissa Aymá Stadium, Hwy. 32, 3.5 km north of Avenida 3, tel. 506/2240-0190) is where San José's city team, **Saprissa** (www.deportivosaprissa.com), plays games within the Liga Nacional de Fútbol (National Fútbol League). They're the most popular regional team in the country, and they regularly rank at the top of the league.

Entertainment and Events

NIGHTLIFE

San José's bar scene offers different strokes for different folks. You're guaranteed to find a place that fits your style, and several more that will introduce you to new sights, tastes, vibes, music, and dance moves. There are some sketchy dive bars that are unsafe to visit. To avoid these, stick to venues recommended in this guide.

If you prefer to barhop leisurely, the community of **Barrio Escalante** (a six-square-block area northeast of Avenida 3 and Calle 23), which draws a mature crowd, and the lively, student-filled **University District** (bordered by Hwy. 2, Calle 57, and Calle 61/Calle de la Amargura)—both in East San José—provide decent clusters of bars. In the north of the city, a group of about 20 bars forms the Centro Comercial El Pueblo (Calle 9, just north of Road 108), but this area can be dangerous. Don't go unless you're part of a group, ideally with a local who knows the place.

The *Tico Times* (www.ticotimes.net), an online English-language newspaper geared toward expats, posts evening events in their Arts & Culture and Dining & Nightlife sections. Spanish-language resources for events happening around the city (and the country) include local newspaper *La Nación* (www.nacion.com), the leading news station **Teletica** (www.teletica.com, channel 7 countrywide), and the **Sistema de Información Cultural Costa Rica** (http://si.cultura.cr).

Their websites are enabled to work with Google Translate, which can provide basic translations.

Local tour operator **Carpe Chepe** (tel. 506/8347-6198, www.carpechepe.com) offers **guided night tours** if you'd feel more comfortable hitting the town with a local or if you're simply looking to meet new people. The **Carpe Craft Beer Tour** (7:30pm Mon.-Sat., 3-4 hours, $79 pp, min. age 18) visits four bars and teaches you about pairing food and beer. The tour includes samples of four different kinds of beer and a souvenir glass. The **Carpe Chepe Pub Crawl** (7pm Fri.-Sat., 5.5 hours, $55 pp, min. age 18) visits four unique bars and includes a shot at each establishment. Round-trip transportation to and from your hotel is included in the cost of either tour, so consider your designated driver hired.

Pubs and Bars

For a low-key evening spent socializing with your travel mates and sipping artisan brews, pull up a stool at one of San José's awesome pubs. The two-story home that holds the **Stiefel Pub** (Avenida 7, 75 m east of Parque España, Central San José, tel. 506/8850-2119, 11:30am-2pm and 6pm-2am Mon.-Fri., 6pm-2am Sat.) is one of the city's best, with its lineup of more than 20 craft beers (bottled and on tap), tasting flights, knowledgeable staff, and funky walls and tabletops plastered with beer labels.

The **Craic Irish Pub** (corner of Hwy. 2 and Calle 25A, Central San José, tel. 506/2221-9320, 6pm-2am Mon.-Sat.) captures the essence of a true Irish bar. It caters to local workers fresh off a shift, boasts an atmosphere of camaraderie, and proudly overuses shamrocks for its decor. It's also the best place in the city to order a stout, with several varieties of this ale to choose from.

Just about every kind of beer imaginable can be had at the laid-back **Costa Rica Beer Factory** (Calle 33 at Avenida 7, East San José, tel. 506/6015-1745, noon-midnight Mon.-Wed., noon-1am Thurs.-Sat., noon-11pm Sun.). It isn't a pub per se but rather a casual, open-air spot where you can quench your thirst with international imports, Costa Rican domestic beers, and local microbrews.

For drinks outdoors, don't miss the beer garden at **Mercadito La California** (Calle 21, between Avenida Central and Avenida 1, Central San José, 6pm-3:30am Thurs.-Sat., 4pm-1:30am Sun.). Locals gather in the courtyard (which is tucked away from the street) under twinkling lights to enjoy the secluded hot spot's assortment of beers and cocktails.

Clubs

For *discos* (clubs) and dancing, take your pick between the fun and always full **Rapsodia Lounge** (tel. 506/2248-1720, 4pm-6am Fri.-Sat.), which blasts Latin and American top hits, or the Moroccan-themed **Club Vertigo** (tel. 506/2257-8424, www.vertigocr.com, 10pm-6am Fri.-Sun.), which plays house, hip-hop, and reggae. Both are upscale, offer bottle service, host guest DJs, and are on Paseo Colón (just east of Parque Metropolitano La Sabana, West San José); the clubs are about a block away from each other.

At **Bar Vyrus** (Avenida 8 at Calle 45, East San José, tel. 506/2280-5890, 4pm-midnight Wed.-Thurs., 4pm-2am Fri., 6pm-2am Sat.), students let loose to groovy tunes from the 1970s, classic rock songs straight out of the 1980s, and other retro hits.

Castro's (corner of Avenida 13 and Calle 22, West San José, tel. 506/2256-8789, 1pm-4am daily), with a tropical atmosphere, is the go-to spot for Latin dancing. It draws a mature crowd, but beginners are welcome. Cab, don't walk, to or from this place; it's in one of the city's roughest neighborhoods.

La Avispa (Calle 1, halfway between Avenida 8 and Avenida 10, Central San José, tel. 506/2223-5343, www.laavispa.com, 8pm-6am Thurs.-Sat., 5pm-6am Sun., entrance permitted until 3am) is the city's top gay and lesbian bar. The large club has been around since the late 1970s, offers dance floors that pump to a mix of electronic and Latin music, and has a quieter upstairs area that mimics a sports bar. Guest DJs and performers put on wildly entertaining shows.

Live Music

Live jazz, blues, and R&B music is best heard at the **Jazz Café** (Hwy. 2, 200 m east of the University District, East San José, tel. 506/2253-8933, 5pm-midnight Mon.-Thurs., noon-midnight Fri.-Sun.), which has a classy but relaxed atmosphere.

In the heart of the downtown core, the rustic but upscale **El Bar del Patio** (Avenida Central, halfway between Calle 7 and Calle 9, Central San José, tel. 506/2222-5022, www.balmoral.co.cr, 4pm-10pm Mon.-Thurs., 4pm-11pm Fri.-Sat.) provides live music during most weekday dinner hours.

THE ARTS

El Observatorio (Calle 23, halfway between Avenida Central and Avenida 1, tel. 506/2223-0725, www.elobservatorio.tv, 6am-2am Mon.-Sat.) hosts all kinds of live music events in an art-filled venue with a distinguished vibe.

San José is home to several small community theaters. However, top performances that catch the attention of most visitors are held at the **Teatro Nacional de Costa Rica** (National Theater of Costa Rica, Calle 5, adjacent to the Plaza de la Cultura, tel. 506/2010-1129, www.teatronacional.go.cr, 9am-5pm daily). The theater's website displays updated events, including plays, cultural presentations, and performances by Costa Rica's Latin Grammy-winning **Orquesta Sinfónica Nacional** (National Symphony Orchestra, www.cnm.go.cr).

FESTIVALS AND EVENTS

September 15, Costa Rica's **Día de la Independencia** (Independence Day), is celebrated enthusiastically in San José with music and dance performances, parades, and fireworks. Expect closures of Paseo Colón and Avenida 2, as torchbearers (who carry a flame through Central America in honor of the holiday) take the route to Cartago. Banks and government offices close for the day, but other businesses and nearly all tourism operations function as per normal.

December brings a string of festive events to the city beginning with the **lighting of the Museo de los Niños** (Children's Museum, Calle 4 at Avenida 9,), which showcases the museum aglow with thousands of Christmas lights. The event typically occurs within the first few days of the month and takes place shortly after sundown (6pm). Mid-month, you can catch the evening light parade **Festival de la Luz** (Festival of Light); it usually departs from the east side of the Parque Metropolitano La Sabana around 6pm. The parade travels east down Paseo Colón and Avenida 2 before ending near the Museo Nacional de Costa Rica. Christmas and New Year's mean it's time for the annual **Fiestas de Zapote,** San José's contribution to the country's *fiestas cívicas* (civic festivals). The lively event has fair rides, games, and food, but it also showcases traditions central to Costa Rica's rural roots, like *topes* (equestrian parades).

young Ticas in traditional dress on Costa Rica's Día de la Independencia

Shopping

Interesting stores and markets dot Costa Rica's capital city, but most—including those listed in this guide—are in **Central San José.** It's quite the cultural experience to see where locals shop and which products differ from those you see at home.

A word to the wise: Don't barter. As a rule, Costa Ricans don't lower prices significantly unless you make bulk purchases, and they tend to frown upon people who assume they're entitled to a bargain.

MARKETS

Offering a large selection of typical souvenirs including hats, shirts, keychains, bags, and more is the indoor **Mercado Nacional de Artesanía y Pintura** (National Market of Crafts and Paintings, south side of Parque de las Garantías Sociales, 8am-7pm daily). The stalls of this bustling market sell similar products, and vendors compete for your cash. You'll feel a bit like a pinball as you make your way through, bouncing back and forth between tables, sellers, and offers, but the adventure's a hoot.

Northeast of downtown is the city's best farmers market, **Feria Verde** (Green Market, east side of the *fútbol* field, 1 block north of Hotel Aranjuez and Kap's Place, 7am-12:30pm Sat.). This market may just be the happiest place in San José, where friendly residents turn out in droves to shop and mingle with their neighbors. Vendors will introduce you to their homemade, usually organic products, such as foods, drinks, plants, bath products, and crafts.

★ Mercado Central

The labyrinth of indoor vendors and narrow walkways that form the **Mercado Central** (Central Market, bordered by Avenida 1, Calle 6, Avenida Central, and Calle 8, 6:30am-6pm Mon.-Sat.) is one of my favorite places in San José. It's convoluted, stuffy, and noisy—but awesome nonetheless. The food and craft market, a mainstay of San José's economy since 1880, sells essentials like coffee beans, fresh meat and fish, and sugary treats. There are buckets full of tropical flowers, bolts of textiles, dry sprigs of medicinal plants, and thousands of other odds and ends. The market houses a slew of souvenir stalls that sell wood items, pottery, jewelry, and trinkets; it also has several informal eateries.

PEDESTRIAN MALLS

Window-shopping in the downtown core couldn't be easier, thanks to the city's handful of pedestrian malls. Closed to vehicular traffic, these boulevards are lined with clothing and department stores and filled with traveling passersby. Sculptures and other art pieces, as well as occasional street performers, enliven the streets. The primary thoroughfare is **Avenida Central** (between Calle 9 and Calle 14). **Avenida 4** (between Calle 9 and Calle 14) is an alternative that provides additional shopping opportunities, but it shouldn't replace a walk down Avenida Central.

GALLERIES

Galería Namu (Avenida 7 between Calle 5 and Calle 7, tel. 506/2256-3412, www.galerianamu.com, 9am-6:30pm Mon.-Sat., 1pm-5pm Sun. Jan.-Apr., 9am-6:30pm Mon.-Sat. May-Dec.) is the country's go-to shop for tribal art. The fair trade gallery is chock-full of pieces crafted by members of each of Costa Rica's indigenous tribes as well as tribal groups from other countries. Best of all, the owners of the family-run gallery know the background and significance of each piece they sell.

Food

San José's food scene is diverse, combining traditional Costa Rican foods and international cuisines. No matter what you're craving, you can find it in the city, from *chifrijo*—San José's specialty dish, which combines rice, beans, and fried pork rinds, among other fixings—to signature culinary choices from countries around the world.

In the same neighborhood, you can find top-notch restaurants helmed by esteemed and innovative chefs, and family-owned food stalls that stick to beloved recipes. Decor, atmosphere, prices, and service vary across San José's eclectic mix of dining establishments. Try a few different types of places to get a taste of both ancestral San José and its cosmopolitan contemporary culinary scene.

Most San José hotels and many hostels include breakfast in their rates, so it's unlikely you'll need to find a place to eat first thing in the morning.

CENTRAL SAN JOSÉ
Costa Rican
The most authentic dining experience you can have in San José is to eat at one of the many ★ *sodas* (traditional Costa Rican family restaurants) crammed inside **Mercado Central** (Central Market, bordered by Avenida 1, Calle 6, Avenida Central, and Calle 8, 6:30am-6pm Mon.-Sat.). All boast a similar diner-style design, give off a laid-back vibe, and offer relatively quick service. A plateful of Costa Rican cuisine goes for $5.50-13.50 at most. Don't concern yourself with seeking out the best: Just grab a chair, stool, or bench at one and give the place a go. If you must have a starting point, the well-liked **Soda Tala** (tel. 506/2222-8054, 6:30am-6pm Mon.-Sat.) has been around for decades.

Nuestra Tierra (corner of Avenida 2 and Calle 15, tel. 506/2258-6500, 6am-midnight daily, $8-23.50) is decked out with plenty of Costa Rican character. Animal statues and coffee-basket lanterns decorate the restaurant, and there are bunches of plantains and bird nests hanging from the ceiling. All kinds of typical foods can be ordered here, including the San José specialty dish *chifrijo*. Most plates are served tropical-style, on a banana leaf.

Steeped in history and full of civil war memorabilia, the small, vintage-style **Café Histórico Don Juanito** (corner of Avenida 1 and Calle Central, tel. 506/2221-4598, 7am-8pm daily, $5.50-7.50) has breakfast plates and sandwiches named after prominent war figures, plus display cases full of baked goods. Order a *café* (coffee) *con leche* (with milk), *con azúcar* (with sugar), or *negro* (black), and enjoy it while reading the list of 4,000 names on the café's wall of heroes.

Next to the Café Histórico Don Juanito, the woodsy, chalet-like ★ **La Tortillería** (tel. 506/2221-0880, www.tortilleriaycafe.com, 6am-8pm daily, $4-9) maintains one of the country's precious culinary traditions: tortilla making. Melt-in-your-mouth tortillas are served both individually ($2.50 each) and as a base to Costa Rican meals that include rice, beans, meats, and vegetables. Delectably rich and cheesy are the *tortillas rellenas* (stuffed tortillas) filled with *queso maduro* (aged cheese). The restaurant also has a small corner store where sweets like *cajetas* (sugary, chewy dessert bars) are sold.

For a helping of ice cream, head to **La Sorbetera de Lolo Mora** (Mercado Central, tel. 506/2256-5000, 9:30am-5:30pm Mon.-Sat., $2-5) inside Mercado Central. The multigenerational establishment, in business since 1901, imbues cloves, cinnamon, and nutmeg in its 100 percent homemade blend. The ice cream here has the consistency of a thick milkshake and is served in a glass. The most popular order is *vainilla* (vanilla).

1: banana leaves used to prepare tamales 2: Parque Morazán 3: souvenirs at the Mercado Nacional de Artesanía y Pintura 4: Plaza de la Cultura

At La Casa del Cacao (Calle 11 at Avenida Central, tel. 506/2221-9287, 10am-6pm Mon.-Thurs., 10am-7pm Fri.-Sat., $2-6), you can treat yourself to crepes, hot chocolate drinks, and molded chocolate desserts—some of which take the shape of cell phones, shoes, or tools. Each is prepared with chocolate produced at the eatery's chocolate factory, which is upstairs. Sign up for an on-site chocolate workshop (1 hour, $15 pp) to learn about cacao processing and make your own chocolate.

International

For an intimate dinner out on the town, choose La Esquina de Buenos Aires (corner of Calle 11 and Avenida 4, tel. 506/2223-1909, www.laesquinadebuenosaires.net, 11:30am-3pm and 6pm-10:30pm Mon.-Thurs., 11:30am-11pm Fri., 12:30pm-11pm Sat., noon-10pm Sun., $10-31). This classy little Argentinean place has a sophisticated vibe, South American music, and fabulous pairings of food and beverages thanks to the restaurant's extensive drinks menu. Most sought-after are the meat dishes, especially the *lomito* (beef tenderloin).

For *bocas* (Costa Rica's take on Spanish tapas) and light conversation, I like the rooftop ★ Azotea Calle 7 (Hotel Presidente, tel. 506/2010-0000, www.hotel-presidente.com, 4pm-11pm Sun.-Wed., 4pm-midnight Thurs.-Sat., $5-26), a place that feels like two restaurants in one. Grab a cast-iron seat in the outdoor garden and you'll be surrounded by greenery and mountain views. Indoors, the restaurant is a chic lounge that fuses historical decor with industrial elements like exposed brick walls. Tasty dinners and drinks go down effortlessly in both comfortable settings.

Large and open, the fern-filled El Patio del Balmoral (Avenida Central, halfway between Calle 7 and Calle 9, tel. 506/2222-5022, www.balmoral.co.cr, 6am-10pm Mon.-Thurs., 6am-11pm Fri.-Sat., 6am-9pm Sun., $6.50-35) has plenty of natural light. You can get almost everything to eat here, including sandwiches, soups, salads, hamburgers, pastas, and meat and seafood dishes. Tables by the street are great for people-watching as they offer a front-row view of the city's principal pedestrian boulevard.

El Abasto Mercado Gastronómico (south side of Teatro Nacional de Costa Rica, tel. 506/2101-8199, 7am-10pm Mon.-Wed., 7am-11pm Thurs.-Fri., 11am-11pm Sat., 11am-9pm Sun.) is a food hall with five individual eateries: Puerto Barcelona (Spanish, $15-30), Pizza Pasta (Italian, $13-19), Lubnan (Lebanese, $13-17.50), Concepto Milanesa (Argentinean, $14-25) and El Viejo Almacén (café and dessert bar, $4-6). Hand-painted murals on the walls and floors give the place an artistic feel, and varied furniture and decor create diverse settings across the five eateries. The space leans toward high-end cuisine and service, attracting a mature clientele.

Vegetarian and Vegan

Fresh and filling servings are provided by the Vietnamese-inspired Café Rojo (Avenida 7, 20 m east of Calle 3, tel. 506/2221-2425, noon-7pm Sun.-Thurs., noon-8pm Fri.-Sat., $5.50-9), a quirky, inviting spot just north of downtown that constructs healthy meals prepared with love. Pick your base (a noodle bowl, a sandwich, a rice plate, or a salad) and add your veggies (or meats, for non-vegans and -vegetarians). Eating a meal loaded with proteins and good fats, you'll feel righteous—and less guilty when you top off your visit with a slice of the café's famous carrot cake.

If you like Asian cuisine, especially if it's inexpensive and flavorful, you'll love Soda Vegetariana Susbida (Calle 5 at Avenida 7, tel. 506/2256-2400, 11:30am-4pm daily, $3-7), which fuses their dishes with vegetarian ingredients. Meal and snack options include soups with dumplings and noodles, chop suey and fried rice with vegetables, and vegetarian sushi. You could easily walk past this place, merely a hole-in-the-wall with barely enough room for a handful of two-seat tables, without knowing the value that lies inside.

Franchises for Foodies

San José boasts a repertoire of diverse restaurants like no other place in the country. Unique, independent restaurants are all around, as are several staple franchises that locals frequent when hunger strikes. Keep your eyes open for the below eateries; they've already won over many Ticos, and they may impress you, too.

- **Spoon** (www.spooncr.com): This restaurant will satisfy your taste buds and fill your stomach with its delicious platters of Costa Rican and international dishes. It offers one of the best menus I've come across, full of rich meals, healthy options, and a long list of drinks and desserts. It also identifies which dishes include common allergens and ingredients associated with digestive system upsets, making it ideal for cautious eaters.

- **Rostipollos** (www.rostipolloscostarica.com): The Costa Rican/Nicaraguan equivalent of Swiss Chalet, this eat-in restaurant never disappoints with its *pollo asado* (roasted chicken) cooked rotisserie-style. Other meal options include chicken fajitas, chicken salads, chicken wings, and arroz con pollo (rice with chicken).

- **Sushi to Go** (www.sushicr.com): At the premier sushi spot in the country, small establishments typically provide a handful of tables, a sophisticated vibe, and an array of Asian-inspired dishes. There are also some vegetarian options and a children's menu.

- **Musmanni** (www.musmanni.com): My favorite of the chains, this delectable-smelling bakery always has fresh baked goods on hand, including artisan breads, muffins, cakes, and *costillas* (turnover-style pastries, often filled with apple, pineapple, guava, or other fruits). Treats here are best ordered *para llevar* (to go).

- **POPS** (www.pops.co.cr): A scoop of one of the 32 flavors of ice cream at POPS is fabulous on a hot day. Look past the common flavors to rare ones inspired by Costa Rican food and drink, like *leche condensada con higos* (condensed milk with figs), *rompope* (an eggnog-like drink), or *dulce de leche* (caramel).

San José is rife with international food and drink chains. If you fancy a taste of the familiar, you'll find Papa John's, Popeyes, Kentucky Fried Chicken, Pizza Hut, Taco Bell, Burger King, McDonald's, Subway, Quiznos, Starbucks, and other recognizable franchises in the region.

EAST SAN JOSÉ

In East San José, an amazing cluster of high-quality but family-friendly dining establishments hides in the gastronomy market known as ★ **Mercado Escalante** (Calle 29 at Avenida 3, 4pm-11pm Thurs., 9am-midnight Fri.-Sat., 9am-9pm Sun., prices vary by establishment). Stroll around the open-air market and you'll find nine separate food booths offering everything from exquisite raw seafood to traditional tacos to scrumptious French toast.

My favorite restaurant in the University District is ★ **Fito's** (Calle 57, 175 m north of Hwy. 2, 11am-2am Mon.-Sat., $4.50-14), which is both adored by students and a historical site. Originally built in the late 1880s and restored in 2008 following a fire, the Costa Rican restaurant offers a young, hip, inviting atmosphere. It's a lively place great for visiting with friends. Portions are large and full of meat or fish, rice, and chunky vegetables. Group platters are available. *Noches parrilleras* (barbecue nights, every Wed., Fri., and Sat.) serve roasted chicken, potatoes, and corn on the cob.

For vegan burgers, visit the fast-food café **Vurgers** (Calle 71, 275 m north of Hwy. 2, tel. 506/4701-2950, www.vurgers.com, noon-8:30pm Mon.-Sat., $5.50-9). You can pick your preferred patty (soy, mushroom, or chickpea with quinoa) and add extra toppings if you wish. Also offered are quinoa salads, nachos, quesadillas, sandwiches, and even desserts—all vegan, nutritious, and delicious.

WEST SAN JOSÉ

On the north side of Parque Metropolitano La Sabana, the ★ **Park Café** (Calle 48, 150 m north of Road 104, tel. 506/2290-6324, www.parkcafecostarica.blogspot.com, 9am-5pm Mon.-Tues., 9am-5pm and 7pm-9pm Wed.-Sat. Nov.-Aug., $9-20) is an example of gastronomic excellence with its impeccable ingredient pairings, fanciful food presentations, and attentive service. It's a traditional tapas restaurant by day, but come nightfall, visitors are treated to the chef's tasting menu ($120 pp). Best of all are the intimate dining spaces: a peaceful, garden-adorned courtyard and a living-room setting with exotic antiques.

Worldly in its architecture and design, the Victorian-period restaurant **Grano de Oro** (corner of Calle 30 and Avenida 4, tel. 506/2255-3322, www.hotelgranodeoro.com, 7am-10pm daily, $15.50-39) is in the hotel of the same name. Offering classic and sophisticated indoor and outdoor seating areas, the fine dining restaurant serves top-notch French and Mediterranean fare like *pato con higo carmelizado* (duck with caramelized fig) and *cerdo en salsa tamarindo* (pork in tamarind sauce). If you're a wine connoisseur, you'll be pleased to know the hotel has one of the city's best wine cellars.

Soda Tapia (Hwy. 1, 125 m south of Paseo Colón, tel. 506/2222-6734, 6am-2am Mon.-Wed., 6am-midnight Thurs., 24 hours Fri.-Sat., 6am-midnight Sun., $2-7) is a decent place in the west end of the city if you want fast food on the cheap. The informal diner is busy and noisy, but if you're trying to save a buck, you'll love the $2 hamburgers, $6 *casados*, and $2-3 fruit *batidos* (smoothies).

Accommodations

San José poses several safety concerns after dark. It pays to choose a secure accommodation, so consider splurging on at least a midrange lodging. Gated entrances, security staff and cameras, guarded parking lots, and functional room locks—ideally with dead bolts and swinging door guards—should be on your checklist. It's acceptable to ask to see an available room before making a last-minute reservation. Security information is not generally available online, so contact the hotel to clarify any safety concerns before making advance reservations.

CENTRAL SAN JOSÉ
Under $50

The best hostel near the center of the city is the 1950s Spanish revival home ★ **Hostel Casa Del Parque** (Calle 19, east side of Parque Nacional, tel. 506/2233-3437, www.hostelcasadelparque.com, dorm $14 s, private $49 s/d), with two large dorms; one has 6 single cots, and the other has 12. This isn't your average party spot: You'll love this accommodation if you appreciate charming accents like decorative wood floors and pretty indoor gardens. Cozy up with a book in the homey living room.

Clean and fresh, the three-story, 43-room **Cocoon Hotel** (Avenida 9 at Calle Central, tel. 506/2256-6463, www.cocoonhotel.cr, dorm $21 s, private $60 s/d) has crisp, white, minimalist decor and pops of vibrant Granny Smith apple green. Small-scale dorms (women-only options are available) have three twin beds and private bathrooms. Private rooms include a television, one or two double beds, a fan or air-conditioning, and breakfast. The hotel's delightful butterfly motif is displayed in prints of the species on the walls and in chairs that resemble leaves.

$50-100

The 25-room **Hotel Santo Tomas** (Avenida 7 between Calle 3 and Calle 5, tel. 506/2255-0448, www.hotelsantotomas.com, $60 s/d), a block north of Parque Morazán, is one of several historical buildings that fill the vicinity's Barrio Amón. Hallways and stairways have decorative tile floors, rooms come with antique dressers and mirrors, and beds are adorned with carved wooden headboards. Wrought iron elements like railings are everywhere you look. The hotel has a pool and a Jacuzzi, a gym, and an open-air restaurant that overlooks the courtyard, where a hot breakfast is served. Stay here and you'll feel like you've traveled a few centuries back in time.

Kap's Place (Calle 19 at Avenida 11, tel. 506/2221-1169, www.kapsplace.com, $50 s, $60 d) is a tropical, colorful, flora-filled collection of interconnecting rooms and common areas in San José's Aranjuez district. I love the vibe here, which is lively, laid-back, and reminiscent of the coasts—far from the country's urban center. The 23 eclectic rooms (no two are alike) have double or twin beds, tile floors, shelves, and a hodgepodge of decorative linens, wallpapers, and hand-painted designs. Several common spaces and a game room are great for socialization; some are arranged like living rooms, and others are occupied by hammocks.

Down the street from Kap's Place is ★ **Hotel Aranjuez** (Calle 19 at Avenida 11, tel. 506/2256-1825, www.hotelaranjuez.com, $52 s, $62 d), a five-building collection of 35 rooms built in the 1930s that display vintage flair in the form of clapboard walls, French doors and windows, and tranquil courtyards. Rooms (which sleep 1-4 people) are comfortable and relaxing spaces lit dimly and decorated in soothing earth tones. Foodies, you'll love the hotel's substantial gourmet breakfast buffet; it's worth the cost of the room. The in-house baker in particular is phenomenal.

Dream of staying in the home of past presidents? **Hotel Don Carlos** (Calle 9, 25 m south of Avenida 9, tel. 506/2221-6707, www.doncarloshotel.com, $75 s, $80 d) offers the opportunity in its 32-room, three-story building. Viewed as classy by some and gaudy by others, the hotel has a unique charm that is best appreciated during a stroll through the Victorian-style courtyard or while eyeing the many old paintings that adorn the walls. Each room is decorated differently but has the same old-world feel. One or two beds, a television, and a desk furnish each.

$100-150

My go-to accommodation in downtown San José is the high-rise ★ **Hotel Presidente** (Avenida Central at Calle 7, tel. 506/2010-0000, www.hotel-presidente.com, $147 s/d). You can't beat its location on a pedestrian boulevard within walking distance of most attractions in the city, but its interior equally warrants a stay. The 100 sleek, contemporary, climate-controlled rooms done in ebony and ivory tones have full closets, mini-fridges, flat-screen televisions, and one king or two double beds that are plush enough to sink into. Best of all, the hotel has a fabulous rooftop restaurant and bar. If you come across a seven-story building covered in a mural of bright colors, geometric shapes, and the peeking eyes of an elusive cat, you've found the hotel.

$150-250

Although it's a typical American chain hotel, I like the three-story **Radisson San José** (Avenida 21, 125 m east of Calle Central, tel. 506/2010-6000, www.radisson.com, $179 s/d), which has interconnected buildings that enclose a private outdoor courtyard and a lagoon-like pool area. Rooms (210 in total) are furnished with desks, vanities, blackout panels, and beds draped with luxuriant duvets. While the hotel's concrete exterior is cold and off-putting, the lobby is warm and inviting, and the café-style breakfast hall couldn't be cuter. A bountiful breakfast buffet is included in the cost of your stay.

In the center of the city, you'll find the perfect blend of luxury, modernity, and historical preservation in the ★ **Gran Hotel** (Avenida Central, on the west side of the Plaza de la Cultura, tel. 506/2103-9000, www.curiocollection.com, $219 s/d). It's worth the splurge at this high-end, 79-room, five-story hotel, the country's first private hotel. Built in 1930, it closed in 2016 for a complete overhaul and opened in mid-2018 as a relic reborn. Upscale offerings include pillow-top mattresses in spotless and streamlined rooms, a fabulous on-site restaurant and piano bar, valet parking ($30 per night), and a top-floor panorama accessible via a glass elevator: Don't miss the view at night when the city sparkles with twinkling lights.

EAST SAN JOSÉ

Lively and great for backpackers looking to socialize, **Hostel Urbano** (Calle 39 between Avenida 2 and Avenida 8, tel. 506/2253-4130, www.hostelurbano.com, dorm $12 s, private $32 s/d) is near the University District's concentrated bar scene. This spot has eight private rooms, 6- and 8-bed mixed dorms, and 6- and 10-bed women's dorms. The dorms are stuffed with oak bunk beds, each of which has its own locker. There are also cool extras like a billiard table and a comfortable, well-furnished television lounge. The outdoor space is sparse; a small terrace and a few hammocks provide seating. A pancake breakfast is included in the price.

A stone's throw east of Hostel Urbano is **Hostel Bekuo** (Avenida 8 between Calle 39 and Calle 41, tel. 506/2234-1091, www.hostelbekuo.com, dorm $13 s, private $38 s/d), a vibrant hostel with bright colors, wall murals, and an energetic atmosphere. The four dorms have basic bunk beds topped with plaid blankets. The five private rooms each have one queen bed, usually with a single bunk above it. A few common areas and friendly staff encourage guest socialization. No guests under the age of 15—regardless of whether they are accompanied by an adult—are permitted.

Arguably outdated in decor but charming nonetheless is **Hotel Le Bergerac** (Calle 35, 75 m south of Hwy. 2, tel. 506/2234-7850, www.bergerachotel.com, $50 s, $60 d). The French-style inn has 25 rooms with one or two beds, neoclassical furniture, glistening hardwood floors, and big windows that let in a lot of light. Some rooms have doors that open to private terraces or balconies. Stay here if you're on a budget and fancy a vintage accommodation with plenty of charm.

WEST SAN JOSÉ

My favorite accommodation in the west end is the quaint, two-story motel ★ **Apartotel La Sabana** (Calle 48, 150 m north of Road 104, tel. 506/2220-2422, www.apartotellasabana.com, room $89 s/d, apartment $130 s/d). You'll forget you're in the downtown core at this relaxing oasis, which wraps around a leafy, mosaic-adorned courtyard with a swimming pool. Standard rooms (with one queen or two single beds) and a variety of suite-style apartments are offered. Each features striking dark-wood furniture, large wardrobes, and comfortable beds; apartments also have kitchens and dining areas. Extras—like kind and helpful service, decorative flora, chaise longues around the pool, a complimentary airport transfer service, and a comprehensive breakfast buffet—add unbeatable value.

The five-floor **Parque Del Lago Boutique Hotel** (Calle 40 between Paseo Colón and Avenida 2, tel. 506/2547-2000, www.parquedellago.com, $136 s/d) resembles a small-scale international chain hotel. The executive-style hotel, which catches the eye of business travelers, has 39 rooms outfitted with king or queen beds, desks, luggage stands, coffee makers, and flat-screen televisions. Bathrooms provide walk-in showers, modern furnishings, and robes. Street noise can be a problem because of the location on the block behind one of the city's busiest intersections.

Hotel Grano de Oro (on the corner of Calle 30 and Avenida 4, tel. 506/2255-3322, www.hotelgranodeoro.com, $232 s/d) is a century-old Costa Rican home full of history and heart. It displays exquisite architecture, provides modern facilities and amenities, and

---

1: traditional tortillas, like the ones served at La Tortillería in Central San José **2:** Hotel Presidente **3:** one of San José's multi-lane highways **4:** a vehicle from the shared shuttle service Interbus

oozes sophistication. The 34 classy rooms in the upscale boutique hotel, which shows off a self-described tropical Victorian style, are immaculately kept and feature luxurious touches like high-quality linens and fine, decades-old furniture. The rooftop terrace with a double Jacuzzi is a great outdoor getaway within the confines of the mansion.

Information and Services

MEDICAL AND EMERGENCY SERVICES

San José has several hospitals. Widely regarded as two of the country's best are the private Hospital Clínica Bíblica (Avenida 14 between Calle Central and Calle 1, tel. 506/2522-1000, 24 hours daily) and Hospital Metropolitano (Calle 14 at Avenida 8, tel. 506/2521-9595, 24 hours daily). Additional hospitals include Hospital Rafael Ángel Calderón Guardia (1 block north of Parque Nacional, tel. 506/2212-1000, 24 hours daily) and Hospital San Juan de Dios (east end of Paseo Colón, tel. 506/2547-8000, 24 hours daily) in Central San José and Hospital México (Hwy. 1, 2.5 km northwest of Hwy. 2, tel. 506/2242-6700, 24 hours daily) in West San José.

There's a pharmacy on almost every street in downtown San José. Most are open from at least 8am to 7pm daily. Additional pharmacies can be found in Mall San Pedro (in the east end of the city) and along Paseo Colón (in the west end of the city).

Police stations (24 hours daily) are spread out around the city. You'll find them in Central San José northeast of downtown (Calle 15, 500 m north of Parque Nacional, tel. 506/2222-4171) and northwest of downtown (Calle 20, 200 m north of Hwy. 2, tel. 506/2257-3067), in East San José (Calle 37, 100 m south of Avenida Central, tel. 506/2225-6750), and in West San José (Calle 72, 2 blocks southeast of Hospital México, tel. 506/2296-7332).

VISITOR INFORMATION

The government-run Instituto Costarricense de Turismo (Costa Rican Institute of Tourism, ICT, tel. 506/2222-1090, www.ict.go.cr, 8am-5pm Mon.-Fri.) is the official source of everything tourism-related in the country. At their office in downtown San José (Avenida Central between Calle 1 and Calle 3), you can get your questions answered, pick up free maps and brochures, or, if need be, issue a complaint against a private tourism company. Esencial Costa Rica (www.visitcostarica.com) is the institute's online presence; the website offers a wealth of information for first-time visitors.

Canatur (tel. 506/2234-6222, www.canatur.org, 8am-5pm Mon.-Fri.) is the leading private tourism organization in Costa Rica. Their office in East San José (Road 204, 1 km southeast of Hwy. 2) provides primarily administrative services, but their booth at the Aeropuerto Internacional Juan Santamaría (Juan Santamaría International Airport) in Alajuela provides tourism-related information and resources.

Most other establishments in San José and elsewhere in the country that offer tourism-related information and sell tourist services are private businesses.

BANKS AND ATMS

If you need a bank or an ATM, there are plenty to choose from in the city. The Banco Nacional (tel. 506/2212-2000, 8:30am-7pm Mon.-Fri.) on Calle 4 between Avenida 1 and Avenida 3 is a cinch to spot because it's the tallest building in the downtown corridor. Banks that are convenient to access in other areas include West San José's Banco de Costa Rica (Paseo Colón, 100 m east of Parque Metropolitano La Sabana, tel. 506/2211-1111, 9am-4pm Mon.-Fri.) and East

San José's Banco Nacional (corner of Hwy. 2 and Calle 57, tel. 506/2212-2000, 8:30am-3:30pm Mon.-Fri.).

MAIL AND SHIPPING SERVICES

Costa Rica's central post office is the Edificio Central de Correos y Telégrafos (Central Post Office and Telegraph Building, Calle 2 at Avenida 3, tel. 506/2223-6918, 8am-5pm Mon.-Fri.). A second post office (Calle 38, 75 m north of Paseo Colón, tel. 506/2223-9766, 7:30am-5pm Mon.-Fri., 7:30am-noon Sat.) is in West San José, as are offices for FedEx (Paseo Colón, 250 m east of the Parque Metropolitano La Sabana, 8:30am-5pm Mon.-Fri.) and DHL (Paseo Colón, 550 m east of the Parque Metropolitano La Sabana, 8am-5:30pm Mon.-Fri.).

SUPERMARKETS

Supermarkets are all around San José. The easiest to get to are Peri (Calle 3, near the Plaza de la Cultura, 6:30am-8:30pm Mon.-Thurs., 6:30am-9pm Fri.-Sat., 9am-6pm Sun.) and Más x Menos (Avenida Central, 150 m west of the Museo Nacional de Costa Rica, 6:30am-10pm Mon.-Sat., 8am-10pm Sun.) in Central San José, Auto Mercado (beside the gas station on the corner of Avenida Central and Calle 37, 7am-9pm Mon.-Sat., 8am-8pm Sun.) in East San José, and AM PM (Paseo Colón, 300 m east of Parque Metropolitano La Sabana, tel. 506/2105-2400, 6am-midnight daily) in West San José.

GAS STATIONS

Gas stations dot the San José region. The easiest to access are on Highway 2 on your way into or out of the city. Coming from the west, there's a station on the corner of Paseo Colón and Calle 24 (800 m east of Parque Metropolitano La Sabana in West San José). Coming from the east, there's a station on the corner of Highway 2 and Calle 37 (600 m west of Hwy. 39 in East San José).

Transportation

GETTING THERE

San José is the most central transportation hub in Costa Rica. Transfer services depart from the city throughout the day, every day, for destinations around the country. Nearly everywhere your wanderlust takes you in Costa Rica, you can get there via San José.

Air

Alajuela's Aeropuerto Internacional Juan Santamaría (Juan Santamaría International Airport, SJO) is sometimes referred to as the San José airport, given its proximity to the capital. Most travelers headed for San José fly into the Aeropuerto Internacional Juan Santamaría and arrange ground transportation into the city. (For more information on the airport, see the *Central Valley and Highlands* chapter.)

Car and Taxi

Driving to San José is easy. Highway 1, Highway 2, Highway 27, and Highway 32 provide direct access to the area from multiple directions.

San José is a 20-kilometer, 30-minute drive southeast from downtown Alajuela via Highway 1. From downtown Liberia, it's a 220-kilometer, 3.5-hour drive southeast on Highway 1.

Bus
CENTRAL VALLEY AND HIGHLANDS

Public buses travel daily to San José from Alajuela (multiple times 4:20am-11pm daily, 35 minutes, $1), Atenas (multiple times 4:30am-8:30pm daily, 1-1.5 hours, $2), San Ramón (multiple times 5:50am-10pm daily, 2 hours, $2.50), **Zarcero** (5am, 5:30am, 12:15pm, and 2:45pm daily, 1.5-2 hours, $3), **Sarchí** (multiple times 5am-10pm daily, 1.5 hours, $2), **Grecia** (multiple times 4:30am-8:30pm daily, 1-1.5 hours, $2), **Heredia** (multiple times 5am-11pm daily, 30 minutes, $1), **Santa Ana** (multiple times 5am-10:30pm daily, 40 minutes, $1), **Escazú** (multiple times 5am-11pm daily, 30 minutes, $1), **Cartago** (multiple times 5am-11pm daily, 45 minutes, $1), and **Turrialba** (multiple times 5am-9pm daily, 2-2.5 hours, $1.50-2).

LA FORTUNA AND MONTEVERDE

Public buses travel daily to San José from **Ciudad Quesada** (multiple times 5am-6pm daily, 2.5 hours, $3.50), **La Fortuna** (9am, 12:30pm, and 2:30pm daily, 4 hours, $4), **Tilarán** (5am, 7am, 9:30am, 2pm, and 5pm Mon.-Sat., 7am, 9:30am, 2pm, and 5pm Sun., 4 hours, $7), **Guatuso** (8am, 11:30am, and 3pm daily, 4 hours, $5), and **Monteverde/Santa Elena** (6:30am and 2:30pm daily, 4 hours, $5).

GUANACASTE

Public buses travel daily to San José from **Liberia** (multiple times 4am-8pm daily, 4.5 hours, $7.50), **Cañas** (multiple times 4am-1:30pm daily, 3.5 hours, $5.50), **Playa Hermosa** (5am daily, 6 hours, $9), **Playas del Coco** (4am, 8am, and 2pm daily, 5.5 hours, $9), **Brasilito** (2:45am, 8:30am, and 3pm daily, 5.5-6 hours, $9), **Playa Flamingo** (2:45am, 8:30am, and 3pm daily, 6 hours, $10), and **Tamarindo** (5:30am, 7:30am, and 2pm daily, 5.5 hours, $9).

NICOYA PENINSULA

Public buses travel daily to San José from **Nosara** (12:30pm daily, 5.5 hours, $8.50), **Sámara** (4am and 8:30am daily, 5 hours, $8), **Nicoya** (multiple times 5am-5pm daily, 5 hours, $7), **Montezuma** (6am and 2pm daily, 5.5 hours, $13, includes ferry ticket), **Tambor** (6am and 2pm daily, 5 hours, $13, includes ferry ticket), and **Santa Teresa/Carmen** (2pm daily, 6 hours, $13, includes ferry ticket).

CENTRAL PACIFIC

Public buses travel daily to San José from **Puntarenas** (multiple times 5:30am-7pm daily, 3 hours, $4.50-5), **Jacó** (multiple times 5am-5pm daily, 2 hours, $4-4.50), **Tárcoles** (multiple times 6am-7:30pm daily, 2 hours, $4-4.50), **Herradura** (multiple times 6am-7:30pm daily, 2 hours, $4-4.50), **Quepos** (multiple times 5am-4:45pm daily, 3.5 hours, $8-8.50), **Dominical** (5:30am and 1:30pm daily, 5 hours, $8), and **Uvita** (5am and 1pm daily, 5.5 hours, $9.50).

OSA PENINSULA AND THE SOUTHERN PACIFIC

Public buses travel daily to San José from **Palmar** (multiple times 5am-6:30pm daily, 5.5-6 hours, $11), **Sierpe** (7:30am daily, 6 hours, $10.50), **Puerto Jiménez** (5am and 11am daily, 8 hours, $12.50), **Golfito** (5am and 1:30pm daily, 7 hours, $13), and **Ciudad Neily** (multiple times 4am-3:30pm daily, 8 hours, $13).

CARIBBEAN COAST

Public buses travel daily to San José from **Puerto Viejo de Sarapiquí** (multiple times 5am-5:30pm daily, 1.5 hours, $2-2.50), **Limón** (multiple times 5am-7pm daily, 3 hours, $5.50-6), **Cahuita** (7:15am, 8:15am, 9:45am, 11:45am, and 4:45pm daily, 4 hours, $8.50), **Puerto Viejo de Talamanca** (7am, 8am, 9:30am, 11:30am, and 4:30pm daily, 4.5 hours, $10), and **Manzanillo** (7am daily, 5-5.5 hours, $11).

SOUTHERN INLANDS

Public buses travel daily to San José from **San Isidro de El General** (multiple times 5am-7:30pm daily, 3 hours, $6) and **San Vito** (5am, 7:30am, 10am, and 3pm daily, 7 hours, $12-12.50).

BUS STATIONS

Several of San José's bus stations are in rough areas. Always remain vigilant and keep an eye on your belongings. If you must stow luggage in overhead racks or compartments under the bus, keep your identification, money, and any valuables with you at your seat. Take a taxi rather than walk to and from any bus station, especially at night.

The bus terminals that foreigners use most often are:

- **Terminal 7-10** (Avenida 7 between Calle 8 and Calle 10, www.terminal7-10.com): Provides transport to the La Fortuna and Monteverde region, some destinations in the Central Pacific, most of the Nicoya Peninsula, and Guanacaste as far north as Tamarindo.

- **Terminal del Atlántico Norte** (sometimes referred to as Terminal MEPE, corner of Avenida 9 and Calle 12, www.mepecr. com): Provides transport to Caribbean destinations southeast of Limón and to Puerto Jiménez on the Osa Peninsula.

- **Terminal Tracopa** (Calle 5 between Avenida 18 and Road 215, www.tracopacr. com): Provides transport to the southern zone, including the Osa Peninsula and Southern Pacific, the Southern Inlands, and some destinations in the Central Pacific.

Additional terminals service other areas of the country, including the **Gran Terminal del Caribe** (Calle Central, just east of the Museo de los Niños, www.grupocaribenos. net), which provides transport to Caribbean destinations Limón and Puerto Viejo de Sarapiquí; **Terminal Coca-Cola** (Avenida 1 between Calle 16 and Calle 18), which provides transport to many areas in the Central Valley and Highlands; **Terminal Empresarios Unidos** (Calle 16 and Avenida 12), which provides transport to Puntarenas and San Ramón; **Terminal Transtusa** (Calle 13 at Avenida 6, www.transtusacr.com), which provides transport to Turrialba; and **Terminal Tralapa** (Avenida 5 between Calle 20 and Calle 22) and **Terminal Pulmitan** (Calle 24, 100 m north of Avenida 5), both of which provide transport to destinations in Guanacaste.

Connections between Alajuela's Aeropuerto Internacional Juan Santamaría and San José take place at **Terminal Tuasa** (corner of Avenida 2 and Calle 12).

Organized Tour

Several adventure and nature tours, such as ones offered by **Exploradores Outdoors** (Avenida 11A, 75 m west of Calle 15, Barrio Amón, tel. 506/2222-6262, www. exploradoresoutdoors.com, 8am-9pm daily) and **Desafio Adventure Company** (tel. 506/2479-0020, www.desafiocostarica.com) include **post-tour onward transportation** to San José from a variety of destinations. White-water rafting tours, safari float tours, canyoning tours, zip-lining tours, and boat tours can be arranged to offer a pickup from your hotel in La Fortuna, Manuel Antonio, Puerto Viejo de Talamanca, Cahuita, Tortuguero, or Puerto Viejo de Sarapiquí, then a drop-off at your hotel in San José.

Private Transfer Service

Private transfer service vehicles travel from all corners of the country to San José. Prices vary significantly by route and service provider. Prices average around $175 from La Fortuna, $200 from Monteverde, $225 from Tamarindo or Manuel Antonio, $250 from Sámara, and $275 from Puerto Viejo de Talamanca. Vehicles vary in size, but most accommodate up to 8 people plus luggage. Some fit 28 passengers to accommodate larger groups.

- From La Fortuna and Monteverde: **Desafio Adventure Company** (tel. 506/2479-0020, www.desafiocostarica.com)

- From points in Guanacaste: **Ecotrans Costa Rica** (tel. 506/2654-5151, www. ecotranscostarica.com)

- From the Caribbean region: **Caribe Shuttle** (tel. 506/2750-0626, www. caribeshuttle.com) or **Exploradores Outdoors** (tel. 506/2222-6262, www. exploradoresoutdoors.com)

Shared Shuttle Service

Two of the country's most well-known and respected shared shuttle service providers are based in San José. Both **Interbus** (Road 204 at Hwy. 39, tel. 506/4100-0888, www. interbusonline.com, 7am-6pm daily) and **Grayline Costa Rica** (corner of Avenida 31 and Calle 56, tel. 506/2220-2126, www. graylinecostarica.com, 7am-5pm Mon.-Fri., 7am-noon Sat.) provide daily shared shuttle services to San José from La Fortuna, Monteverde, Rincón de la Vieja, Papagayo, Playas del Coco, Brasilito, Playa Flamingo, Tamarindo, Sámara, Tambor, Montezuma, Santa Teresa, Puntarenas, Jacó, Manuel Antonio, Puerto Viejo de Talamanca, and Cahuita. Grayline also travels to San José from Dominical, Uvita, and Sierpe. One-way services cost $44-98 per person. Most shuttles fit eight people with luggage and offer drop-offs at San José hotels.

Interbus offers a shared shuttle service ($19 adults, $9.50 children) from the **Aeropuerto Internacional Juan Santamaría** to your San José hotel, or vice versa. The service is available to anyone with a flight arrival or departure. Buses depart every two hours daily from the airport (6am-4pm) and from San José (7am-9pm). Reservations must be placed at least 72 hours in advance through Interbus's website.

GETTING AROUND

San José's downtown is easy to walk around. Most streets have sidewalks. In congested areas, you'll walk shoulder to shoulder with Ticos. Pedestrian-only streets in the downtown corridor, most notably **Avenida Central** (between Calle 9 and Calle 14) and **Avenida 4** (between Calle 9 and Calle 14) provide significant roaming space, freedom from noisy vehicles, and air that is less polluted. Be careful stepping off curbsides onto streets; San José drivers aren't always cautious and courteous, nor do they always acknowledge a pedestrian's right of way.

Bus

To get around San José by bus, take one of two bus lines that loop outward from the city's center. The **western loop** travels around Parque Metropolitano La Sabana and the downtown core. Get off at Parque Central if you wish to explore downtown. The **eastern loop** connects Mall San Pedro at the corner of Highway 2 and Highway 39 to the downtown core. Get off at the corner of Avenida Central and Calle 9, one block east of Hotel Presidente, if you wish to explore downtown. On both routes, buses run regularly (usually every 8-10 minutes, 5am-11pm daily) and charge $0.50 (280 colones) per person. Payment should be made in colones.

Car and Taxi

Driving through the city, primarily around the downtown core, is a pain. One-way roads, pedestrian-only boulevards, bumper-to-bumper traffic, and carefree motorcycles (which zip between car lanes; check your blind spot regularly) make the feat stressful. These obstacles can also turn the six-kilometer drive between West San José and East San José into a seemingly never-ending journey. If you must drive, park your vehicle—ideally in a secure lot—for the duration of your stay once you get to the city, and walk, take a taxi, or use the public bus system to get to wherever you need to go.

To help combat traffic and air pollution in the downtown core, the government bans vehicles with particular license plate numbers from driving through the city on certain weekdays between 6am and 7pm. While rental cars aren't exempt, most agencies obtain permissions that allow their customers to skirt the rule. If in doubt, have your rental agency confirm whether you're required to abide by the law.

Parking lots are scattered around town. If you don't have access to a secure lot provided by an accommodation, stick to the handful of parking lots clustered around, and just east of

Calle 1 on Avenida 1. They're closest to sights and attractions near the city's center.

Most hotels and restaurants will call you a cab if you need one. Alternately, you can hail one yourself almost anywhere in town; you'll find many by the Teatro Nacional and between Parque Central and the Catedral Metropolitana. Be sure that the driver turns on the vehicle's *maría* (meter) and that the fare displayed is the current base rate. Rates start around 670 colones (US$1.11) for the first kilometer, 630 colones (US$1.05) per kilometer thereafter, and an additional 8,850 colones (US$6.40) per hour of wait time. It is common (and legal) for rides after 10pm to include a 20 percent surcharge.

The smartphone application **Taxi Shake** (www.taxishake.com) offers an on-demand ride-hailing service. Taxi Shake is operated by the Autoridad Reguladora de los Servicios Públicos (Public Services Regulatory Authority, ARESEP, www.aresep.go.cr) and uses the country's official **red taxis** for transport. Simply download the Taxi Shake app and create an account (both are free) and you can arrange a pickup service with an available driver in the area. See ARESEP's website for the most updated taxi fare base rates.

Central Valley and Highlands

Outside of Costa Rica's capital city, the land rises in all directions, a 360-degree wall of mountains and volcanoes. The interior basin, known as the Central Valley, and the slopes of the Central Highlands beyond contain more than two-thirds of the country's population, counting San José's residents. Spread out across cities like Alajuela and Cartago; charming small towns like Zarcero, Sarchí, and Grecia; and the affluent area of Escazú are Ticos who preserve Costa Rica's heritage through cultural events, religious ceremonies, and traditional cuisines. Most will tell you that this region—smack-dab in the middle of the country with a rugged exterior and a heart of gold—is authentic Costa Rica.

Highlights

Look for ★ to find recommended sights, activities, dining, and lodging.

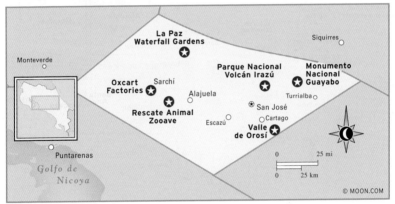

La Paz Waterfall Gardens

Siquirres

Monteverde

Oxcart Factories — Sarchí

Parque Nacional Volcán Irazú

Monumento Nacional Guayabo

Alajuela

Turrialba

Rescate Animal Zooave

San José

Escazú — Cartago

Valle de Orosí

Puntarenas

Golfo de Nicoya

0   25 mi
0   25 km

© MOON.COM

★ **Explore Rescate Animal Zooave** to see some of the 7,500 animals that the wildlife center rescues every year (page 83).

★ **Watch artisans** build the traditional carts that are a symbol of Costa Rican history at **oxcart factories** (page 95).

★ **Admire beautiful waterfalls** and diverse wildlife at **La Paz Waterfall Gardens** (page 100).

★ **See how coffee beans are harvested,** dried, and made into the beloved brew on a **coffee tour** (page 103).

★ **Take a road trip** through the picturesque hills and pastoral scenes around the **Valle de Orosí** (page 116).

★ **Peer over the edge of a deep crater** at **Parque Nacional Volcán Irazú,** home to Costa Rica's tallest volcano (page 119).

★ **Examine petroglyphs** and explore the archaeological remains of an indigenous civilization at the **Monumento Nacional Guayabo** (page 120).

Previous: a country road weaving through coffee and sugarcane plantations; Cartago's Ruinas de Santiago Apóstol; view of the Central Valley from Hotel Buena Vista.

Central Valley and Highlands

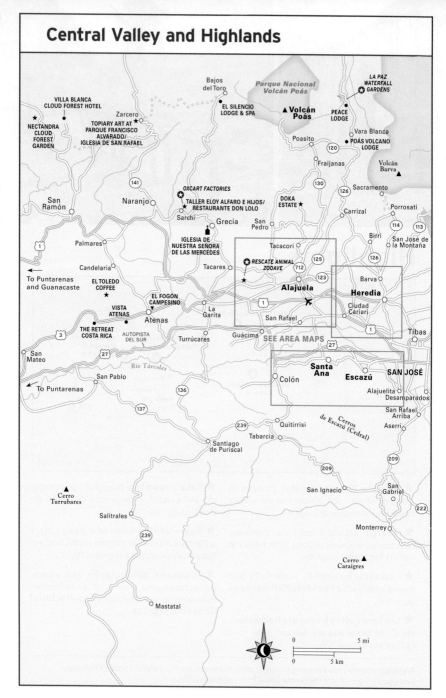

LA PAZ
WATERFALL
GARDENS

VILLA BLANCA
CLOUD FOREST HOTEL

Bajos
del Toro

Parque Nacional
Volcán Poás

PEACE
LODGE

EL SILENCIO
LODGE & SPA

▲ Volcán
Poás

NECTANDRA
CLOUD
FOREST
GARDEN

Zarcero

TOPIARY ART AT
PARQUE FRANCISCO
ALVARADO/
IGLESIA DE SAN RAFAEL

Poasito

Vara Blanca

POÁS VOLCANO
LODGE

120

Fraijanas

Volcán
Barva ▲

141

OXCART FACTORIES

DOKA
ESTATE ★

130

126

Sacramento

San
Ramón

Naranjo

TALLER ELOY ALFARO E HIJOS/
RESTAURANTE DON LOLO

Carrizal

Porrosati

Sarchí

Grecia

San
Pedro

Birrí

114

113

San José de
la Montaña

IGLESIA DE
NUESTRA SEÑORA
DE LAS MERCEDES

Tacacori

125

126

Palmares

712

Tacares

RESCATE ANIMAL
ZOOAVE

123

Barva

Candelaria

EL TOLEDO
COFFEE ★

Alajuela

Heredia

To Puntarenas
and Guanacaste

EL FOGÓN
CAMPESINO

Ciudad
Cariari

VISTA
ATENAS

La
Garita

1

1

THE RETREAT
COSTA RICA

Atenas

San Rafael

Tibas

AUTOPISTA
DEL SUR

Turrúcares

Guácima

SEE AREA MAPS

27

San
Mateo

27

Río Tárcoles

Santa
Ana

Escazú

SAN JOSÉ

San Pablo

Colón

To Puntarenas

136

Alajuelita

Desamparados

137

San Rafael
Arriba

239

Quitirrisi

Cerros
de Escazú (Cedral)

Aserrí

Tabarcia

Santiago
de Puriscal

209

209

▲
Cerro
Turrubares

San Ignacio

San
Gabriel

222

Salitrales

Monterrey

239

Cerro ▲
Caraigres

Mastatal

0   5 mi

0   5 km

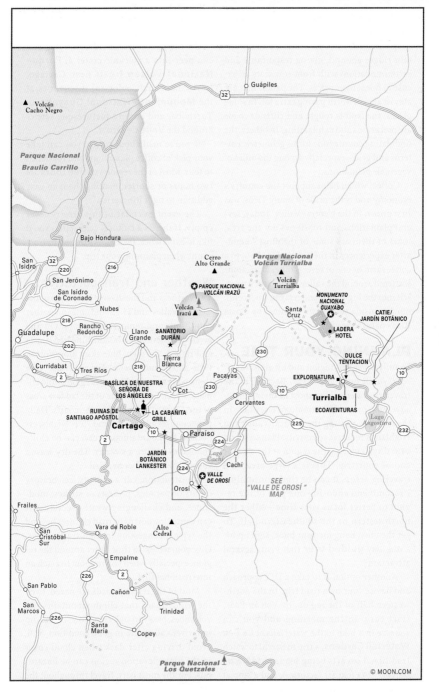

© MOON.COM

The region's uneven terrain is a thrilling landscape. Dramatic vistas of rolling hills, deep canyons, volcanic craters, and mountain ridges abound, giving restaurants and accommodations with front-row seats an excuse to boost their prices. The panoramas are almost always worth paying extra for. In some places, the land is rough, and cliffside roads are precarious and exhilarating. In others, the undulating countryside forms geometric patterns and grids, especially among the miles of vegetable plantations.

Coffee, which helps support the country's economy and is the pride of many Ticos, was first grown in the Central Valley. Today, several plantations and roasteries dot the area; tours of them are some of the most sought-after experiences in the region. Head out to a coffee farm or one of several other attractions scattered around the valley. Or just tuck yourself into the highlands and relax in a peaceful, mountainside setting surrounded by Costa Rica's natural beauty.

PLANNING YOUR TIME

To fully cover this region and hit all its must-sees, you'll need **5-6 days.** Because many travelers prefer to allot most of their time to adventure or beach destinations elsewhere in the country, visiting the Central Valley and Highlands requires selectivity. Plan to spend **one day** exploring the region at the start or end of your trip. This is a large area, and traveling across it can be time-consuming. I recommend choosing one part of the region to better focus your time—either the northwestern or the southeastern half. To get the most bang for your buck, sign up for a one-day **guided tour** that visits several attractions.

Another option is to take a DIY approach and devise your own road trip. In the northwestern half of the region, by Volcán Poás, start early in the morning and you can squeeze in a hike to the waterfalls at **La Paz Waterfall Gardens,** a trip to Sarchí to watch traditional oxcarts being made at *fábricas de carretas* (oxcart factories), and a stop at

the wildlife rescue center **Rescate Animal Zooave** near Alajuela.

On the southeastern side, in a day you can peer into a volcanic crater at **Parque Nacional Volcán Irazú** near Cartago, learn about archaeological discoveries at the **Monumento Nacional Guayabo** in Turrialba, and admire picturesque scenes around the **Valle de Orosí.**

If you're mad about coffee, you can take your pick of coffee plantations and roasteries to tour. Most of the region's **coffee tours** are two hours or shorter, making them an easy addition to tight itineraries.

The event calendar of this area is never empty. If there's a cultural celebration you'd like to experience, take its scheduling into account when planning your trip.

Weather and Transportation

The vastness and the diverse elevations of the Central Valley and Highlands mean weather conditions and temperatures vary. On any given day, there could be sunshine in Alajuela and rain in Cartago, blue skies atop Volcán Poás and cloud cover at Volcán Irazú. One thing you can count on is the region's mild climate, which makes it one of the coldest areas of the country compared to the coasts. Daily temperatures average around 70°F. Nights, especially in mountainous areas, can be chilly enough to require a sweater. The dry season runs from December to April.

Construction, car accidents, celebratory events or parades, protests or strikes, mudslides, and challenging weather conditions can cause slowdowns or road closures beyond the typical congestion in high-traffic areas. Give yourself extra time to get around the region, especially when you're about to catch an international flight.

Most of the region's roads are paved. Even the windy roads that climb mountains and volcanoes, pass through cloud forests, and dip into river valleys are in good condition. Still, avoid driving after dark when cloud cover in the high-elevation region can be hazardous. For the most part, travel throughout the

Central Valley and Highlands does not require a 4x4 vehicle.

ORIENTATION

The oval Central Valley engulfs the cities of Alajuela, Heredia, and Cartago, as well as the capital city. Clockwise around the valley are the Central Highlands: the vicinities of Alajuela to the west and northwest, Poás to the northwest, Heredia to the north and northeast, Cartago and Turrialba to the east and southeast, and Escazú to the west and southwest. Each highland region is elevated above the valley and stretches into mountainous territory. Near the region's center is the **Aeropuerto Internacional Juan Santamaría,** Costa Rica's main airport.

The region is the primary jumping-off point to destinations throughout the country, including the Caribbean coast, the Central Pacific coast, Guanacaste, and the Nicoya Peninsula. The fast-paced **Carretera Interamericana** (Inter-American Highway), also known as the **Pan-American Highway** or Highway 1, Highway 27, Highway 3, Highway 39, and Highway 2 expedite east-west travel into and out of the valley. Most north-south routes are country roads.

Alajuela and Vicinity

More than 1.3 million tourists each year visit the Alajuela vicinity, home to the Aeropuerto Internacional Juan Santamaría. The airport, dubbed erroneously by many travelers the San José airport, lies on the southern edge of the city of Alajuela in the district of Río Segundo, an approximate 20-minute drive northwest of San José. Receiving three times as many travelers as the international airport in Liberia, this is Costa Rica's busiest entry point.

Beyond the airport, the congested Highway 1 and Highway 3 provide routes toward all corners of Costa Rica. But with time to spend in the area, you'll discover plenty of quiet and picturesque towns worth exploring. From the coffee farms of Atenas and the cloud forest at San Ramón to the triad of culturally rich villages at Zarcero, Sarchí, and Grecia, the Alajuela area is much more than a concrete landing strip.

ALAJUELA

Alajuela is the country's fourth-largest city in terms of population. The city's grid of streets is regularly clogged with traffic, making passage through the area a frustrating chore. The airport is four kilometers south of the city center.

Downtown Alajuela is the area contained within Highway 3, Calle 3, Avenida 9, Calle 12, and Avenida 10. It is a nexus of history, religion, and modern-day life in Costa Rica. Stroll around the city and you'll find an eclectic mix of sculptures of local dignitaries, ornate churches, and students in parks.

Sights
★ RESCATE ANIMAL ZOOAVE
One of Costa Rica's most well-known and well-respected wildlife rescue centers is **Rescate Animal Zooave** (Hwy. 3, 10 km west of Aeropuerto Internacional Juan Santamaría, tel. 506/2433-8989, www. rescateanimalzooave.org, 9am-5pm daily, $20 pp). You can walk around at your leisure and see wildlife up close at this outdoor center with large, fenced enclosures spread out around a jungle-clad property. The low-key wildlife rescue center functions as a reproduction center, education center, research center, and animal hospital. Each division is partly funded by the entrance fee, meaning visits here help protect and care for wildlife. The operation's primary purpose is to rehabilitate birds and other animals and release them into the wild (or house them when health or social conditions mean they can't return to the wild), not to entertain wide-eyed visitors. For this

You've Got to Pay the Toll

Several highways in the Central Valley and Highlands require on-the-spot cash payment at *peajes* (tollbooths). As you approach one, look for the lane marked *Via Manual*. The booth in this lane is staffed and equipped with change. Payment is preferred in colones, but small denominations of American dollars (not coins) are accepted. If you accidentally enter the lane marked *Voluntario*, you must pay with 100-colón coins and change is not given. When approaching a tollbooth, mind the street vendors, who will try to sell you everything from snacks and drinks to stuffed animals, flowers, and phone chargers.

Below are the locations of the region's tollbooths.

HIGHWAY 1

· Between San José and Alajuela (75 colones or US$0.15)

· Between Alajuela and San Ramón (150 colones or US$0.25)

HIGHWAY 2

· Between San José and Cartago (75 colones or US$0.15)

HIGHWAY 32

· Between San José and the Parque Nacional Braulio Carrillo (250 colones or US$0.50)

HIGHWAY 27

· At Escazú (370 colones or US$0.65)

· At San Rafael (560 colones or US$1)

· At Atenas (740 colones or US$1.25)

· At Pozón (560 colones or US$1)

When Highway 27 is driven end to end, all four tolls must be paid. Additional tolls may apply if you take Highway 27 off-ramps at the following locations:

· Ciudad Colón (180 colones or US$0.30)

· La Guácima (420 colones or US$0.70)

· Siquiares (440 colones or US$0.75)

· Atenas (370 colones or US$0.65)

· Pozón (180 colones or US$0.30)

reason, you won't find the place as developed or as tourist-centered as several other attractions in the country. Informational signage is sparse, and there are no tours here; the staff mostly work behind the scenes, caring for the animals.

Each year, the center rescues about 7,500 animals. The revolving roster of inhabitants includes over 125 species of birds, mammals, and reptiles. A wheelchair-accessible concrete trail system throughout the center is easy to traverse but does have some inclines and declines. Colorful scarlet macaws, comical capuchin monkeys, and a toucan named Grecia—the country's first toucan to receive a prosthetic beak—reside on the premises, among scores of other wildlife. Iguanas and peacocks wander the trails freely. Try to

Alajuela and Vicinity

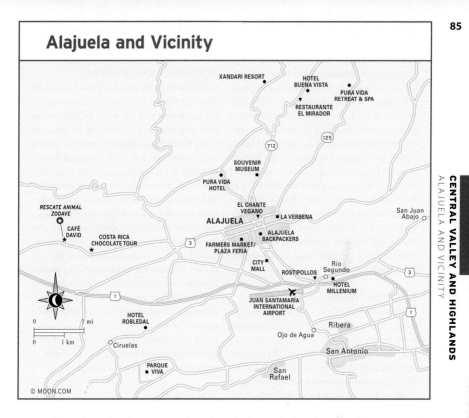

avoid disturbing the ubiquitous spiderwebs that hide among the flora growing throughout the facility.

On hot days, prepare yourself for stagnant, humid conditions. The center's tall trees, bamboo plants, and leafy canopy restrict airflow and keep the place moist. Give yourself at least one hour (ideally 2-3) to visit the series of enclosures. With additional time, you can grab a drink or food at the on-site restaurant, **Café David** (11am-6pm daily, $7-21).

Chocolate Tours

One of my favorite chocolate tours in the country is Alajuela's **Costa Rica Chocolate Tour** (Hwy. 3, 9 km west of Aeropuerto Internacional Juan Santamaría, tel. 506/2433-2730, www.choco-tour.com, 9am, 11am, 1pm, and 3pm daily, 90 minutes, $25 adults, $10 children 6-12). A passionate

chef-turned-chocolatier and his team of knowledgeable tour guides run this informative tour out of a large, open-air, roadside stall beside a grove of cacao trees. During your visit, you'll take a light walking tour around the property to stations that showcase cacao at its various stages. You'll discover how the delicacy we consume today is far from raw cacao nibs and how modern-day processing differs from traditional cacao processing by indigenous groups. Taste testing of cacao from bean to bar (plus an opportunity to make your own chocolate treat) is included. Various chocolate treats are available for purchase, including bars produced by other cacao growers around the country.

Recreation

To blend in with locals, don black-and-red garb and head to the outdoor,

18,000-person-capacity **Estadio Alejandro Morera Soto** (Alejandro Morera Soto Stadium) on nights when the **Liga Deportiva Alajuelense** (Alajuela Sport League, www.lda.cr), referred to by most as **La Liga,** is scheduled to play a home game. The *fútbol* club is the beloved team of Alajuelenses (Alajuela residents) and is one of the country's best competitors in the national Liga de Fútbol de Primera División (First Division Football League). La Liga plays in two annual seasons that run roughly from February to June and July to December. Buy tickets ($5-34 pp) and see the most up-to-date schedule on the team's website. Most games are tame events, but matches against San José's home team, Saprissa, can draw large, loud, competitive crowds.

Entertainment and Events

Parque Viva (Road 124, 10 km west of the Aeropuerto Internacional Juan Santamaría, www.parqueviva.com) is one of Costa Rica's largest outdoor concert venues. The modern, open-air, and wheelchair-accessible structure has a giant stage, covered stadium seating for 7,000 people, and space for an additional 9,000 attendees on a sloped lawn at the back of the venue. The amphitheater regularly hosts music acts from all over the world, plus a handful of festivals.

FESTIVALS AND EVENTS

Each year on **April 11,** a day known as **Día de Juan Santamaría,** Costa Ricans recognize the anniversary of the death of Alajuelense Juan Santamaría, a 24-year-old drummer in Costa Rica's now-abolished army, who played an instrumental role in the **Second Battle of Rivas** in 1856 in Nicaragua. Alajuela's festivities include parades, food stalls, costumes, and fireworks. Fittingly, drummers and other musicians fill the streets with music and dancing. My favorites are the spirited children who come to watch the parade; some grasp homecrafted decorative torches and wave them in the air to salute the fallen hero. The parade typically takes place midday and travels north on Road 712 and east on Avenida 5 to Calle 7. Driving through downtown Alajuela is best avoided on this day if you don't plan to take in the festivities. Confirm locations and start times with a local hotel or tour operator, as event details are subject to change.

Shopping

One of the country's largest **farmers markets** is held in Alajuela's **Plaza Feria**

Try a sample of cacao nibs during the Costa Rica Chocolate Tour.

(Avenida 4 just west of Calle 12, 1pm-9:30pm Fri., 5am-2:30pm Sat.). You can shop rain or shine at the roofed 7,600-square-meter warehouse for just about every fruit and vegetable grown in the country. Don't leave without trying slices of sweet, delicious mango; the area's many fruit trees are responsible for Alajuela's nickname, La Ciudad de los Mangos (The City of Mangos). La Verbena (in the park at Avenida 5 and Calle 15, 7:30am-1pm Sun.), a second market in Alajuela, sells fresh bread, sauces and spreads, jewelry, natural products like oils and soaps, and tons of other artisanal creations. La Verbena features mainly organic and environmentally friendly products.

Souvenir shopping is best accomplished at the Souvenir Museum (Road 712, 2 km north of downtown Alajuela, tel. 506/2441-5639, www.souvenirmuseumcr.com, 10am-6pm Mon.-Sat.). The small store has a contemporary art-gallery feel and sells creations of artists from all walks of Costa Rican life. Works by artists from various indigenous groups are widely represented. You can learn about the shop's collection, including where pieces came from, by asking a staff member to give you a tour (10am-3pm Mon.-Sat., 20 minutes, $6 pp).

The modern City Mall (Calle Francisco Orlich, 750 m northwest of the Aeropuerto Internacional Juan Santamaría, tel. 506/4200-5100, www.citymall.net, 10am-9pm Mon.-Sat., 10am-8pm Sun.) is full of Costa Rican, American, and European stores. This is a good place to wander if you have time to kill before heading to the airport.

Food

My go-to restaurant in downtown Alajuela is ★ El Chante Vegano (Avenida 5, 25 m west of the post office, tel. 506/2440-3528, www.elchantevegano.com, noon-8pm Tues.-Sat., noon-4pm Sun., $6-9.50). There's no question the casual, colorful eatery is a hole-in-the-wall, but its all-vegan menu surprises most diners and easily competes with some of the country's best health food restaurants. Even meat eaters like the place. Dishes include hamburgers, pastas, nachos, sandwiches, pizza, and Asian fare.

On the outskirts of town, ★ Restaurante El Mirador (Road 712, 5.5 km north of downtown Alajuela, tel. 506/2441-9347, www.restelmiradorcr.com, noon-10:30pm Mon.-Thurs., noon-11:30pm Fri.-Sat., noon-9:30pm Sun., $9-21) serves up a classy experience in addition to delicious food. The atmosphere here is sophisticated, though the space itself is casual, and the skilled chefs prepare high-quality seafood and beef cuts. This mountainside establishment has a spectacular view of the city. On top of all that, the service is superb. Reservations for dinner, when the place oozes with romance, are strongly recommended.

If you need fast food before or after a flight, head across the street from the airport to Rostipollos (tel. 506/2443-8739, www.rostipolloscostarica.com, 11am-10pm Sun.-Thurs., 11am-11pm Fri.-Sat., $7-9), a popular Costa Rican/Nicaraguan franchise that specializes in roasted chicken dishes.

Accommodations
UNDER $50
If money is tight, stay at the low-key Alajuela Backpackers (corner of Calle 4 and Avenida 4, tel. 506/2441-7149, www.alajuelabackpackers.com, dorm $14 pp, private $55 s/d). This four-story high-rise hostel is dark, bare, and lacking in overall service, but its location is ideal if you want to base yourself in downtown Alajuela. Some rooms offer city views, and guests like the open-air restaurant and bar. Overnight stays include an airport shuttle service. Most of the dorm rooms (which sleep 4, 6, or 10 people) are small, stuffed with bunk beds, and equipped with blackout curtains.

$50-100
My preferred budget lodging near the airport is Hotel Millenium (Hwy. 3, 1.5 km east of Aeropuerto Internacional Juan Santamaría, tel. 506/2430-5050, www.hotelmilleniumcr.com, $61 s, $67 d). Through the street-facing

entrance of the motel-style accommodation is a row of 12 private rooms, each equipped with one or two beds, a television, and air-conditioning. A small bar and a restaurant that serves a complimentary breakfast are on-site. You can watch airplanes fly overhead from the small seating area outside of your room. Apart from the planes, the place is quiet; it's also clean and safe. A taxi to the airport runs $6.

Run by a Costa Rican family, the 15-room ★ **Hotel Robledal** (Road 124, 6 km west of the Aeropuerto Internacional Juan Santamaría, tel. 506/2438-3937, www. hotelrobledal.com, $94 s/d) is quiet, cozy, and comfortable. You'll think you've joined their clan when you receive their warm service. Rooms sleep 1-4 people and have flat-screen televisions, safes, and garden or pool views. Best of all, the authentic hotel serves a healthy, hearty breakfast with a buffet bar and made-to-order plates. Set in a quiet suburb a 10-minute drive from Alajuela and the airport, the hotel feels private and remote, in part because of its secure gated entrance.

$100-150

Kind hospitality is provided by the cheerful, good-humored owners of the **Pura Vida Hotel** (Road 727, 2 km north of downtown Alajuela, tel. 506/2430-2630, www. puravidahotel.com, $149 s/d), who strive to help you enjoy your time at their garden-adorned property, a former coffee farm. Four freestanding casitas and two rooms off the main building are intimate spaces for quiet relaxation. Most have one or two beds, tiled bathrooms, and an outdoor seating area. The on-site restaurant, decorated with an array of wild orchids, is equally peaceful. The property's unobstructed vista of Volcán Poás is impossible to miss.

$150-250

When I wish to see the twinkle of city lights in the Central Valley, I book a stay at ★ **Hotel Buena Vista** (Road 712, 10 km north of Aeropuerto Internacional Juan Santamaría, tel. 506/2442-8595, www.hotelbuenavistacr. com, room $200 s/d, villa $313 s/d). Located a 25-minute drive up the mountain north of Alajuela, the Spanish colonial-style hotel has a beautiful view of the area, including a few volcanoes. It also has a nature trail, a pool, a restaurant, and 25 homey rooms (some sleep five people) with plush king and queen beds. In addition, five spacious villas feature upscale bathrooms, bedrooms, and living rooms. Each villa can accommodate six guests.

OVER $250

The 40-acre **Xandari Resort** (off Road 712, 10 km north of Aeropuerto Internacional Juan Santamaría, tel. 506/2443-2020, www. xandari.com, $295 s/d) is the area's most exotic accommodation. Twenty-four villas, clustered in buildings with 2-4 villas in each, have eclectic decor with bright walls and textiles, smooth tile floors, and natural wood ceilings. Each features a beautiful view of the valley from the hotel's position in the Central Highlands. Explore the property's forest trails to natural waterfalls, sink in the sunset-facing pool come sundown, practice yoga, or enjoy a natural body treatment in a hot-tub-equipped spa hut. Xandari aims to pamper you.

The luxurious **Pura Vida Retreat & Spa** (Road 125, 11 km north of Aeropuerto Internacional Juan Santamaría, tel. 506/2483-0033, www.puravidaspa.com, $295-535 s/d, all-inclusive) provides eight different types of accommodations, ranging from hybrid tent bungalows to ultramodern suites, spread out across a mountainside. The eight-acre property has four yoga halls, a fitness tower, and a wellness center that provides ayurvedic treatments, Watsu water massages, meditation sessions, bioenergetic healing practices, and traditional spa services. Three daily meals are included with each overnight stay. Wellness and yoga packages that cover room, board, yoga classes, and spa credits draw in multiday visitors.

Information and Services

Alajuela is one of the largest cities in Costa

Rica. It is home to Hospital San Rafael (Calle Francisco Orlich, 1 km northwest of Aeropuerto Internacional Juan Santamaría, tel. 506/2436-1001, 24 hours daily), a post office (Avenida 5 at Calle 2, tel. 506/2443-2653, 8am-5pm Mon.-Fri., 8am-noon Sat.), a police station (Road 712 at Avenida 7, tel. 506/2430-1085, 24 hours daily), and many supermarkets.

At least 10 pharmacies dot the downtown core, including three of the well-known and well-stocked franchise Fischel. Most are open 9am-9pm daily, but the location at Highway 3 and Avenida 6 has extended hours (7am-midnight Mon.-Sat., 9am-9pm Sun.).

Banks and ATMs also fill the city. The easiest to access are on Avenida Central between Calle 2 and Calle 4.

If you would prefer to avoid downtown Alajuela, a post office, pharmacy, bank, ATM, and supermarket can be found inside City Mall (Calle Francisco Orlich, 750 m northwest of Aeropuerto Internacional Juan Santamaría, tel. 506/4200-5100, www.citymall.net, 10am-9pm Mon.-Sat., 10am-8pm Sun.).

Transportation

Costa Rica's busiest airport is Aeropuerto Internacional Juan Santamaría (Juan Santamaría International Airport, SJO), four kilometers south of downtown Alajuela in the district of Río Segundo. The transportation hub services a long list of international airlines. Domestic flights operated by SANSA Airlines (tel. 506/2290-4100, www.flysansa.com) fly to Alajuela daily from Liberia, La Fortuna, Tamarindo, Nosara, Tambor, Quepos/Manuel Antonio, Palmar, Bahía Drake, Puerto Jiménez, Golfito, Limón, Tortuguero, and San Isidro de El General.

Alajuela is a 20-kilometer, 30-minute drive northwest from downtown San José via Highway 1. From downtown Liberia, it's a 200-kilometer, three-hour drive southeast on Highway 1.

Nearly every road in the city's center is a one-way street. Not all streets have signs that indicate *una via* (one-way) or *no hay paso* (no entrance). Watch for—and follow—the general flow of traffic.

Public buses travel daily to Alajuela from San José (multiple times 4:15am-11pm daily, 35 minutes, $1), Liberia (multiple times 4am-8pm daily, 4 hours, $7), Puntarenas (multiple times 4am-9pm daily, 2 hours, $4.50), and La Fortuna (9:10am, 12:45pm, 2:45pm, and 4:10pm daily, 3.5 hours, $4-4.50).

Several adventure and nature tours, such as those from Desafio Adventure Company (tel. 506/2479-0020, www.desafiocostarica.com), include post-tour onward transportation to Alajuela. White-water rafting tours, safari float tours, Tortuguero canal tours, canyoneering tours, zip-lining tours, and boat tours can be arranged to include a pickup from your hotel in La Fortuna, Puerto Viejo de Talamanca, Cahuita, Puerto Viejo de Sarapiquí, or Manuel Antonio, then a drop-off at your hotel in Alajuela.

ATENAS

About 20 kilometers west of Alajuela, the neighborly community of Atenas is along Highway 3, once the oxcart trail used to transport coffee beans from the Central Valley to the port town of Puntarenas. Blessed with a temperate climate, the slow-paced town has a friendly vibe and is surrounded by coffee, cattle, and *caña de azúcar* (sugarcane) farms. Quaint accommodations including bed-and-breakfasts and vacation home rentals will wow you with vast valley and highland views. There's little to do in the town center, but the low-key locale works well as a home base for day trips to nearby attractions.

Coffee Tours

The hardworking family behind El Toledo Coffee (Calle Pocitos, 7 km northwest of downtown Atenas, tel. 506/8711-1221, www.eltoledocoffee.weebly.com, 8am-5pm daily) declares, "We have nothing but the coffee we produce." Here's your chance to tour a small-scale organic *finca* (farm) and learn about coffee directly from three generations of a family

whose livelihood depends on its production. During the on-site **coffee tour** (10am and 2pm daily, other times upon special request, 2 hours, $20 pp 10 years and older), you'll walk through dense natural forest on a barely flattened trail to see where coffee plants grow on hillsides. Various stations around the plantation demonstrate different stages of bean processing, including drying and roasting. The production of coffee at this farm, unlike some other coffee plantations, is largely carried out by hand to create a healthier and more sustainable product. Capping off the informative experience is a cup of El Toledo's organic brew.

Food and Accommodations

Off the tourist radar is ★ **El Fogón Campesino** (Hwy. 3, 200 m northeast of downtown Atenas, tel. 506/4701-3238, 11am-9pm Tues.-Thurs., 8am-9pm Fri.-Sat., 8am-6pm Sun., $4.50-11). I love the little house-turned-restaurant, which cooks up the area's best Costa Rican cuisine with its outdoor woodburning *fogón* (stove). Try *chorreadas* (sweet corn pancakes) for breakfast, *olla de carne* (beef stew) for lunch or dinner, or any other *comida típica* (typical food) at the low-key, low-price, authentic establishment.

Vista Atenas (700 m south of Hwy. 3, 3 km west of downtown Atenas, tel. 506/2446-4272, www.vistaatenasbnb.com, $75 s/d) is a welcoming little bed-and-breakfast tucked away in the hills of Atenas. This modest, well-priced accommodation has six rooms and two cabins, each with a splash of color and furnishings that make the place feel like home, including mini-fridges, coffee makers, and desks. The view of the valley from the pool and outdoor terraces is unbeatable.

Luxury near Atenas is provided by **The Retreat Costa Rica** (800 m south of Hwy. 3, 7 km west of downtown Atenas, tel. 506/8947-0707, www.theretreatcostarica.com, $269 s/d), a small-scale wellness resort with eight double-occupancy rooms and three freestanding casitas that each sleep five guests. Pastel-hued rooms with whitewashed beds, light wood floors, and large windows that draw in tons of light give the accommodation a soothing, beachy feel. The resort's pool, Jacuzzi, steam room, and yoga studio encourage complete relaxation. A health-conscious breakfast is included with your stay; all-inclusive meal plans are offered.

Information and Services

The closest hospital is Alajuela's **Hospital San Rafael** (Calle Francisco Orlich, 1 km northwest of Aeropuerto Internacional Juan Santamaría, Alajuela, tel. 506/2436-1001, 24 hours daily). Atenas has several **clinics,** including **Clínica Atenas** (Calle 6 at Avenida 6, tel. 506/2446-5522, 7am-10pm Mon.-Thurs., 7am-9pm Fri., 7am-6pm Sat.-Sun.), and **pharmacies,** including **Farmacia Sucre** (Calle Central at Avenida Central, tel. 506/2446-1235, 8am-8pm Mon.-Sat.).

Atenas also has a **post office** (Avenida 2 between Calle Central and Calle 2, tel. 506/2455-0065, 8am-5pm Mon.-Fri.), a **police station** (Avenida 2 between Calle 6 and Calle 10, tel. 506/2446-5063, 24 hours daily), and **supermarkets.**

There are a few **banks** in Atenas. **Banco de Costa Rica** (Calle Central at Avenida 2, tel. 506/2446-7300, 9am-4pm Mon.-Fri.) has an **ATM** (5am-midnight daily).

Transportation

Atenas is a 40-kilometer, 40-minute drive west on Highway 27 or Highways 1 and 3 from downtown **San José.** From downtown **Liberia,** Atenas is a 180-kilometer, 2.5-hour drive southeast on Highway 1 and Highway 27. From **Alajuela,** Atenas is a 25-kilometer, 30-minute drive west on Highway 1 and Highway 3.

Access to Atenas is provided by the northeast-southwest run of Highway 3, which runs past the north end of town. Watch for one-way streets and avenues in Atenas proper.

Public **buses** travel daily to Atenas from

1: capuchin monkeys at Rescate Animal Zooave **2:** the charming Hotel Robledal **3:** La Paz Waterfall Gardens **4:** topiary art in front of the Iglesia de San Rafael in Zarcero

San José (multiple times 5:40am-10pm Mon.-Fri., 6am-10pm Sat., 6:30am-10pm Sun., 1-1.5 hours, $2) and **Alajuela** (multiple times 5:50am-10:30pm Mon.-Fri., 7am-10:30pm Sat., 7:45am-10:30pm Sun., 1 hour, $1.50).

SAN RAMÓN

On the west side of the Central Highlands is the colonial city of San Ramón. Recognized nationally for its knack of producing presidents and poets, the city is best known to foreigners as the most frequented gateway to La Fortuna and the northern inland area. While there is little to see in the city, the curvy but paved Road 702 north of San Ramón provides an eyeful as it zips through pretty pastures and forest-flanked mountain crevices amid cloud forest. If possible, avoid the drive after sundown, when darkness coupled with thick cloud cover can cause very poor visibility.

Nectandra Cloud Forest Garden

Not long after setting out on the dense forest trails that wind through the serene **Nectandra Cloud Forest Garden** (Road 702, 15 km north of Hwy. 1, tel. 506/8535-5382, www.nectandra.com, 8am-3pm daily, by guided tour only), you'll know you've stumbled upon one of the country's best-kept secrets. The 320-acre premontane cloud forest preserve is a haven for horticulturists and a beautiful sight for any nature lover. A rare collection of trees, plants, and flowers can be admired in their natural environment, thanks to the landowners' sustainability efforts.

The grounds are open to the public via guided tours with advance reservation. At this less-visited site, you and your tour guide are bound to have the quiet, damp, and moss- and lichen-filled forest all to yourselves. During the **garden tour** (7am-3pm daily, 2-3 hours, $54 pp), you'll learn about Nectandra's work in nature conservation, traverse trails past gentle waterfalls and streams, and likely encounter area inhabitants including butterflies, insects, reptiles, and birds, especially charms (groups) of hummingbirds. Most stunning,

however, is the display of botanicals, especially the orchids and bromeliads.

Festivals and Events

Costa Rica's biggest *fiesta civica* (civic festival) is the **Fiestas de Palmares,** hosted by the sleepy town of Palmares, six kilometers southeast of San Ramón. During the Fiesta de Palmares, you'll be able to enjoy carnival rides and games, food tents and bars, live acts and disco dancing, and traditional cultural events like bull-riding competitions, bullfights, and *topes* (equestrian parades). The two-week celebration in mid-January draws a Woodstock-like mass of music lovers and partygoers for its spectacular fireworks shows and concerts by world-renowned artists. Sate your hunger with churros, *algodones* (cotton candy), *chicharrones con yuca* (fried pork rinds with yuca), chop suey, and *arroz cantonés* (Cantonese rice). Wash it all down with a can of Costa Rican beer brewed by Imperial, the primary sponsor of the event. The fair is as safe as an outdoor gathering of hundreds of thousands of people can be, and it is applauded for its safety measures and heavy police presence.

Food and Accommodations

On the main road that connects San Ramón to the northern inland area is **Mi Rancho** (Road 702, 8 km north of Hwy. 1, tel. 506/2445-1551, 11am-11pm Mon.-Fri., 7am-midnight Sat.-Sun., $6.50-18.50). The rustic roadside restaurant is the Tico equivalent of a steak house and provides a great rest stop where you can grab a big meal (including beef tenderloin) or *chicharrones* to snack on. Don't miss the small *mirador* (lookout) across the street that captures views of hills full of cattle farms in multiple shades of green.

Just west of the southern entrance to San Ramón is **Restaurante El Jardín** (Hwy. 1, 4 km west of Road 156, tel. 506/2445-8397, www.eljardin.co.cr, 5:30am-9pm daily, $10-12). This diner has a long buffet bar stocked with more than 20 typical Costa Rican food preparations. Select whichever ones catch your eye to create your own custom plate.

The specific dishes can change, but rice, beans, meats in sauce, and mixed vegetables are staples. The informal, cafeteria-style place also has a large souvenir shop with well-priced items. There's a photo-worthy arrangement of plants and flowers behind the restaurant.

The ★ **Villa Blanca Cloud Forest Hotel** (7 km north of Road 702, 13 km north of Hwy. 1, tel. 506/2461-0300, www.villablanca-costarica.com, $166 s/d) is San Ramón's one and only upscale accommodation, with 35 individual hilltop casitas designed like chalets. Wood furnishings, rocking chairs, and fireplaces help create warm, inviting room environments on chilly days when the outside air is crisp and breezy. The main hacienda has a restaurant and a bar with forest views on clear days. Beause the hotel is set amid the cloud forest, it is often engulfed in a haze of white. If you dream of a remote accommodation that hides among the clouds, Villa Blanca provides a lofty escape.

Affordable lodging is supplied by **Casa Amanecer** (1 km northeast of Road 703, 4 km north of Hwy. 1, tel. 506/2445-2100, www.casa-amanecer-cr.com, $90 s/d), a quaint bed-and-breakfast just north of downtown San Ramón. It has five small, simple rooms with surprisingly modern bathrooms outfitted with vessel sinks and glassed-in stone showers. Each room opens to a shared veranda with a great view of the area's lush surroundings. Gracious hosts and a fresh, bountiful breakfast boost the B&B from being a place to lay your head to an enjoyable and rewarding experience.

The vegan-friendly hotel **Lands in Love** (Road 702, 34 km north of Hwy. 1, tel. 506/2447-9331, www.landsinlove.com, $117 s/d) is in the mountains north of San Ramón. Hidden in a forest regularly drenched in cloud mist are 33 modest rooms with floral prints and hand-painted art; two restaurants with separate vegetarian and vegan menus; and an adventure center that operates its own zip-line tour. The decor is decades old, but that is easy to overlook when you consider the owners' love for animals and their on-site dog and cat rescue center, funded in part by your overnight stay.

Information and Services

San Ramón's **hospital, Hospital Carlos Luis Valverde Vega** (corner of Avenida 11 and Road 703, tel. 506/2456-9700, 24 hours daily) has a **bank** (tel. 506/2211-1111, 11am-6pm Tues.-Fri., 8:30am-3:30pm Sat.) and a 24-hour **ATM** on-site. Additional banks and ATMs are scattered throughout the city, as are plenty of **supermarkets.**

San Ramón also has a **post office** (corner of Avenida 2 and Calle 4, tel. 506/2445-7606, 8am-5pm Mon.-Fri.) and a **police station** (Avenida 0 between Calle 0 and Calle 1, tel. 506/2445-5127, 24 hours daily). There are many **pharmacies** on Road 703/Calle 0; hours vary, but most are open at least 8am-6pm daily.

The large **supermarket Maxi Palí** (Road 703, just north of the hospital, tel. 506/2445-9606, 7:30am-10pm daily) at the north end of town is a great place to stock up on snacks and drinks before embarking on the mountainous drive to La Fortuna.

Transportation

San Ramón is a 60-kilometer, one-hour drive northwest of downtown **San José** via Highway 1. From **Alajuela,** San Ramón is a 45-kilometer, 45-minute drive northwest on Highway 1. From **La Fortuna,** it's a 70-kilometer drive south on Road 702 that takes one hour and 45 minutes. All roads in downtown San Ramón are one-way.

Public **buses** travel daily to San Ramón from **San José** (multiple times 4am-10:30pm daily, 2 hours, $2.50), **Alajuela** (multiple times 4:30am-11pm daily, 1.5 hours, $2.50), and **La Fortuna** (5:30am, 9am, 1pm, and 4pm daily, 3 hours, $4-4.50).

ZARCERO, SARCHÍ, AND GRECIA

The small towns of **Zarcero, Sarchí,** and **Grecia** are three reasons to explore the Central Highlands northwest of Alajuela.

Each has something different to offer. Zarcero, an agricultural town praised for its progressive organic farming practices, surprises visitors with displays of imaginative topiary art.

Sarchí, 20 kilometers southeast of Zarcero, is the artisan capital of Costa Rica. Thousands of brightly colored model oxcarts—including the world's largest oxcart, on display in the town's central park—adorn Sarchí and help boost the local economy.

In Grecia, seven kilometers southeast of Sarchí, a merlot-red church constructed entirely out of metal is a striking sight and a stark contrast to the softness of the understated town.

The towns, connected by Roads 141 and 118, make an easy day trip from San José or Alajuela; the best way to approach this trip is to drive out to Zarcero, the town farthest from Alajuela, and work your way back by visiting Sarchí, then Grecia. Another option is to visit Grecia, Sarchí, and then Zarcero as you leave the Central Valley bound for La Fortuna.

Accommodations in the Zarcero, Sarchí, and Grecia areas are limited. An overnight stay isn't required to experience all three towns in one day: You can return to Alajuela or continue on to La Fortuna and arrive before nightfall if you set out early in the morning. If you must spend the night, Grecia has quaint accommodation that's suitable for a pit stop.

Zarcero

The small and concentrated agricultural town of Zarcero is fresh-feeling, brisk, and sometimes smothered with clouds. Originally named Alfaro Ruiz (some people and maps still refer to the town by this name), Zarcero hides 50 kilometers northwest of Alajuela, high up in the Central Highlands, 1,736 meters above sea level. The town is set among a row of mountains that separates the region from the northern inland area. To locals, Zarcero is best known for its dairy products and vegetables, many of which are organic. Roadside stalls along Road 141, which leads north-south through town, sell several of the town's signature products, including *queso*

palmito (heart of palm cheese), a soft and pliable white cheese that is wound into balls and sold in plastic bags. Most interesting to visitors are the lovely topiary art that fills the town's central park, and the adjacent Iglesia de San Rafael.

TOPIARY ART

Zarcero's main attraction is its whimsical **topiary art.** Since the 1960s, local resident Evangelista Blanco Brenes has been sculpting cypress trees in the town's **Parque Francisco Alvarado** (Francisco Alvarado Park, Road 141 between Avenida Central and Avenida 2) into amusing figures, including dinosaurs, animals, and cheerful-looking humans, as well as abstract designs like spirals. Wander around the collection of more than 15 freestanding sculptures scattered around the one-block park, and take a stroll through the row of carved-shrub archways that runs east-west through the middle of the park.

IGLESIA DE SAN RAFAEL

On the east side of Zarcero's central park is the ornate, picturesque **Iglesia de San Rafael** (San Rafael Church). The exterior of this large church, which has two domed towers, is a cold-looking, smoke-gray color with white trim and a red roof. Inside, the church is more attractive and has a warm atmosphere. Notable features include cream-colored walls and swooping archways adorned with paintings of religious scenes, a blue-and-yellow geometric-patterned tile floor, and stained-glass side windows that let in beams of colorful light.

INFORMATION AND SERVICES

The closest hospital is San Ramón's **Hospital Carlos Luis Valverde Vega** (corner of Avenida 11 and Road 703, San Ramón, tel. 506/2456-9700, 24 hours daily), a 22-kilometer, 35-minute drive southwest of Zarcero. The town has a **clinic, Ebais Zarcero** (Calle 4 just west of Calle 2, tel. 506/2463-3201, 7am-5pm Mon.-Fri.), and **pharmacies,** including **Farmacia Central**

(Road 141, 35 m north of the central park, tel. 506/2463-2444, 8am-8pm Mon.-Sat., 8am-noon Sun.).

Zarcero has a **police station** (Road 141, 400 m north of the central park, tel. 506/2463-3231, 24 hours daily) and a **post office** (Avenida 1 between Calle Central and Calle 1, tel. 506/2463-3276, 8am-5pm Mon.-Fri.).

There are a couple of **banks. Banco Nacional** (50 m north of the central park, tel. 506/2212-2000, 8:30am-4pm Mon.-Fri.) has an **ATM** (5am-11pm daily). Zarcero also has a few **supermarkets.**

TRANSPORTATION

There are two ways to get to Zarcero from downtown **San José.** The most common and direct route follows Highway 1 northwest from San José to Road 141, which leads north to Zarcero. This route is a 70-kilometer drive that takes approximately one hour and 40 minutes. A more scenic trip passes through Grecia and Sarchí, following Highway 1 northwest from San José to Alajuela, along Highway 3 to Road 118, and connecting with Road 141, which provides direct access to Zarcero. This route is a 72-kilometer, two-hour drive. Both options arrive at Zarcero from the south.

The same two routes to Zarcero can also be taken from **Alajuela.** The direct route via Highway 1 and Road 141 is a 50-kilometer drive northwest from Alajuela that takes just over an hour. The scenic route, via Highway 1, Highway 3, Road 118, and Road 141, is a 52-kilometer, 1.5-hour drive northwest from Alajuela.

From downtown **Liberia,** Zarcero is a 180-kilometer, three-hour drive southeast via Highway 1, Road 703, and Road 141.

Public **buses** travel daily to Zarcero from **San José** (multiple times 5am-8:20pm Mon.-Sat., 9:15am-8:20pm Sun., 1.5-2 hours, $3).

Sarchí

Roughly 25 kilometers northwest of Alajuela is Sarchí, a quaint, small, and sprawling countryside town that serves as the artisan capital of Costa Rica. Despite being a quiet local town, Sarchí receives a consistent stream of foreign visitors who come to admire the fine craftsmanship and intricate paintwork of the destination's beloved oxcarts, which are on display and available to purchase at countless *fábricas de carretas* (cart factories) in town. You'll also find the most talented *artesanos* (artisans) with impeccable wood-shaping and hand-painting skills in Sarchí. Some of them helped create the world's largest oxcart—you can't miss it in the town's center. Even the street signs here are decorated with colorful oxcart wheels, a proud nod to Sarchí's contribution to Costa Rica's cultural scene.

The town is divided into **Sarchí Norte** and **Sarchí Sur,** both accessed along Road 118.

★ OXCART FACTORIES

Sarchí's *fábricas de carretas* (oxcart factories) are the country's go-to stores for handcrafted traditional oxcarts and other wood creations. Most of the oxcarts on display in restaurants, tour operator offices, and hotel lobbies around the country were constructed at the factories in Sarchí, which also sell smaller oxcarts in varying sizes that make great souvenirs.

Several factories are scattered around town, but particularly worthy of a visit is **Taller Eloy Alfaro e Hijos** (Eloy Alfaro and Sons Workshop, Calle 1, 200 m north of Road 118, North Sarchí, tel. 506/2454-4131, www.souvenirscostarica.com, 7am-5pm daily). This factory's two side-by-side, two-story buildings offer a nice balance of old and new. Built in 1923 and showing its age, the workshop is a large, multiroom, windowless wood building that you can walk around to observe all stages of oxcart craftsmanship, from construction to the hand painting of pieces. Most unique is Eloy Alfaro's exclusive, intricate process of binding and pinning 16 pie-shaped wood pieces together to form an oxcart's wheel. A giant waterwheel powers the entire operation.

Next to the workshop, a more modern but rustic building partly covered in murals houses the factory's large souvenir store and

The Iconic Oxcart

Oxcarts are a symbol of Costa Rica's labor culture.

No other object symbolizes Costa Rica's work culture quite like the oxcart—a sturdy, two-wheeled, rectangular wood cart, traditionally 1.5 meters long and 1 meter wide, with a 3-meter, front-facing shaft. It has long been part of the country's agricultural roots. Ticos used these oxen-driven carts years ago—and some still use them today—to haul products like coffee beans between towns. Today, the oxcart also demonstrates the creativity of artisans who craft decorative replica oxcarts. Many residents and business owners proudly display oxcarts in their homes and workplaces, but miniature versions in the form of keychains, napkin or postcard holders, and decorative conversation pieces for a shelf are easy to take home as souvenirs.

But the oxcarts aren't just souvenirs—they're artistic expressions, nods to Costa Rican heritage, and, in some cases, exhibitions of skills passed down through generations. What began as bare carts painted in one of three colors to protect the cart's wood from the rain have since been transformed into bold, multicolored oxcarts adorned with exquisite geometric and kaleidoscopic designs. If you're unable to make it to Sarchí to view the carts as they're being crafted and painted, you'll find displays elsewhere in Costa Rica, including in restaurants, offices of tourism-related businesses, and hotel lobbies, and in celebratory parades like Escazú's **Día de los Boyeros** (page 109).

a restaurant. In addition to oxcarts, the store has all kinds of wood pieces for sale, from tables, rocking chairs, and an endless list of kitchen items (think bowls, napkin holders, cutting boards, and so on) to rosaries and nativity scenes.

FOOD AND ACCOMMODATIONS
On the second floor of Taller Eloy Alfaro e Hijos is **Restaurante Don Lolo** (Calle 1, 200 m north of Road 118, North Sarchí, tel. 506/2454-1389, 11am-3pm daily, $5-16.50), a great place to enjoy a traditional Costa Rican lunch. You can build a custom plate from a buffet that rotates items like rice, beans, mixed vegetables, meat, soups, and salads. This large, informal, cafeteria-style restaurant is filled with tables and offers additional balcony seating. Some round tables are built like oxcart wheels and have geometric designs in natural woods.

Tucked away in the mountains 20

kilometers north of Sarchí (and 15 kilometers east of Zarcero) is the **El Silencio Lodge & Spa** (off Road 708, tel. 506/2476-0303, www.elsilenciolodge.com, $385 s/d). At this remote luxury hotel, one of the quietest places in the country, you'll be surrounded by birdsongs and the natural soundtrack of the cloud forest. Each of the 20 bungalow-style suites has resort-quality beds and linens, an in-room lounge area, floor-to-ceiling glass walls, an outdoor viewing deck with rocking chairs, elegant bathrooms, and a private outdoor Jacuzzi enclosed in bamboo. This hotel is a 50-minute drive from Sarchí. Choose El Silencio if you want to spend a night or two at a secluded site, ideally between a visit to Sarchí and time spent at a destination farther north, such as La Fortuna or Puerto Viejo de Sarapiquí.

INFORMATION AND SERVICES

Sarchí has a **post office** (Road 118, across from the *fútbol* field, tel. 506/2454-4533, 8am-5pm Mon.-Fri.), a **police station** (Calle 2, 1 km north of Road 141, tel. 506/2454-4021, 24 hours daily), a **pharmacy** called **Nuestra Señora Virgen de Loreto** (Road 118, northwest corner of the *fútbol* field, tel. 506/2454-1485, 7am-10pm Mon.-Sat., 7am-9pm Sun.), a **clinic** called **Ebais Sarchí Sur** (Calle Ratoncillal, 600 m northeast of Road 118, tel. 506/2454-2856, 24 hours daily), and a branch of **Banco de Costa Rica** (tel. 506/2211-1111, 9am-4pm Mon.-Fri.) with an **ATM** (5am-11pm daily). There are also a few **supermarkets.**

TRANSPORTATION

There are two ways to get to Sarchí from downtown **San José.** The most common and direct trip follows Highway 1 northwest from San José to Road 715 and Road 118, which leads northeast to Sarchí. This route is a 50-kilometer drive that takes approximately one hour and 15 minutes. A more scenic trip that passes through Grecia follows Highway 1 northwest from San José to Alajuela, then travels along Highway 3 to Road 118, which provides direct access to

Sarchí from the southeast. This route is 47 kilometers and takes roughly one hour and 20 minutes to drive.

Sarchí can also be reached from **Alajuela** via either of the same two routes. The direct route via Highway 1, Road 715, and Road 118 is a 30-kilometer, 45-minute drive northwest from Alajuela. The scenic route via Highway 1, Highway 3, and Road 118 is a 27-kilometer, 50-minute drive northwest from Alajuela.

From downtown **Liberia,** Sarchí is a 175-kilometer drive southeast on Highway 1, Road 141, and Road 118 that takes two hours and 45 minutes.

Public **buses** travel daily to Sarchí from **San José** (12:15pm and 5:30pm Mon.-Fri., noon Sat.-Sun., 1.5 hours, $2) and **Alajuela** (multiple times 6am-10:20pm daily, 1 hour, $1.50).

Grecia

The low-key but bustling town of Grecia sits atop a small plateau on the slopes of Volcán Poás, roughly 20 kilometers northwest of Alajuela. This concentrated, midsize town, which is larger than Zarcero and Sarchí, still feels more rural than urban. It is quiet, clean, and surrounded by sprawling fields. Laid-back living is practiced throughout Grecia's blended community, made up of local coffee, pineapple, and sugarcane farmers as well as a growing group of expat retirees. At the town's core is a two-block public park that has pretty palms, evergreens, and a decorative fountain. Grecia's primary attraction, the Iglesia de Nuestra Señora de las Mercedes, takes up the park's eastern block.

IGLESIA DE NUESTRA SEÑORA DE LAS MERCEDES

In the middle of town is the large, two-story, merlot-red **Iglesia de Nuestra Señora de las Mercedes** (Our Lady of Mercedes Church, Road 154 between Calle Central and Calle 1), Grecia's most attractive feature. Constructed entirely out of metal pieces imported from Belgium in the late 1890s, this long church is anchored by a tall steeple on each side of its entrance. White trim adorns several upper- and lower-floor windows. Inside, the church is stark white, has shiny but subtle gold embellishments, and is filled with striking redwood pews.

FOOD AND ACCOMMODATIONS

Arguably the best restaurant in Grecia, **La Casa de Miguel** (Road 118, between Calle 3 and Calle 5, tel. 506/2444-6767, 11am-9pm Tues.-Thurs., 11am-10pm Fri.-Sat., 11am-5pm Sun., $7.50-20.50) is two blocks east of Iglesia de Nuestra Señora de las Mercedes. This two-story restaurant has indoor tables and a few tables on a small veranda out back. It's a casual, affordable place, but high-quality menu options and good service help the restaurant feel sophisticated. Prepared fresh and nicely presented are seafood plates (locals love the ceviche), dishes made with local or imported meats, pastas, sandwiches, soups, salads, and a few desserts that feature Costa Rican fruits.

If you must spend a night in Zarcero, Sarchí, or Grecia, my preference is Grecia's **La Terraza Guest House** (Calle Salguero, 550 m north of Road 711, tel. 506/2494-0970, www.laterrazab-b.com, $79 s/d suite or cottage). This charming, two-story, two-building B&B sits up a hill north of Grecia and is a mere five-minute drive from the center of town. The main building has a dining area, one suite, and a veranda shared by all guests. Next door are two freestanding cottages and a building with three additional suites with terraces. Suites and cottages sleep 1-4 guests and are clean, cozy, comfortable spaces that feel like mini Costa Rican homes. I particularly love that the quiet property is gated and full of beautiful natural gardens you can wander

around. This place also has a warm, welcoming expat owner who specializes in helping retirees nail down the logistics of moving to Costa Rica.

INFORMATION AND SERVICES

Grecia's hospital, **Hospital San Francisco de Asís** (Road 154, 750 m west of Road 118, tel. 506/2437-9500, 24 hours daily), serves the Grecia and Sarchí areas. Grecia also has a few **pharmacies**, most of which are open 8am-8pm daily, on Avenida 2, east of the hospital.

The town has a **post office** (Avenida 1, just west of Road 118, tel. 506/2494-4501, 8am-5pm Mon.-Fri.) and a **police station** (Calle 6 at Avenida 10, tel. 506/2494-8750, 24 hours daily), as well as a few supermarkets.

Banco de Costa Rica (tel. 506/2211-1111, 9am-4pm Mon.-Fri.) is on Road 154 between Calle Central and Calle 1. There's an **ATM** (5am-11pm daily) on the same road just 200 meters west.

TRANSPORTATION

Grecia is a 20-kilometer, 40-minute drive northwest of **Alajuela** via Highway 3 and Road 118. From downtown **San José**, you can bypass Alajuela by taking Highway 1 northwest to Road 154, which leads north to Grecia. This route is a 45-kilometer, one-hour drive. From downtown **Liberia**, Grecia is a 185-kilometer, three-hour drive southeast on Highway 1, Road 141, and Road 118.

Road 118 enters and exits town, but driving through is a game of zigzags as the town's core is full of one-way streets.

Public **buses** travel daily to Grecia from **San José** (multiple times 5:40am-10:20pm daily, 1-1.5 hours, $2) and **Alajuela** (5am-10pm daily, 45 minutes, $1.50-2).

Volcán Poás

An imposing wall of mountains provides a dramatic backdrop in Alajuela. The northern slopes belong to Volcán Poás, which draws in travelers from all over Costa Rica to eye its crater within Parque Nacional Volcán Poás. Alajuela serves as the principal gateway to the park. However, the park can also be reached from San José, Heredia, and other cities and towns in the Central Valley.

Strict time limits enforced by the park keep trips to the volcano short, so it's best to also visit other sights in the Alajuela vicinity to make the most of your time in the area. Area attractions and businesses, capitalizing on the volcano's popularity, offer a convincing argument that your trip to this volcanic region should be a full day or more in order to include other highlights like waterfalls, wildlife encounters, coffee plantations, and breathtaking valley views from mountaintop accommodations. An overnight stay isn't necessary, though if you want one, quiet communities around Volcán Poás such as Poasito and Vara Blanca provide a lovely but limited selection of hotels. Alternately, you can visit the volcano during travel between Alajuela and destinations in the northern inland area, including La Fortuna.

PARQUE NACIONAL VOLCÁN POÁS

Before spring 2017, **Volcán Poás** had been Costa Rica's easiest volcano to access and explore. People are drawn to the park to see the Tiffany-blue pool in the volcano's crater, which is roughly 1,300 meters wide and a piping hot 122°F. Due to dangerous volcanic activity, **Parque Nacional Volcán Poás** (Poás Volcano National Park, Road 120, 9 km northwest of Road 146, tel. 506/2482-2165, www.sinac.go.cr, 7am-2pm daily, $15 adults, $5 children 2-12) was closed from April 2017 to August 2018. After reopening, the park quickly regained its position as one of the Alajuela area's top attractions.

But operations surrounding the 16,000-acre protected land area and its resident volcano have completely changed. The only way to visit now is by **guided tour.** Tours provide a maximum of 20 minutes of viewing

Volcán Poás

time at the principal crater. Tickets must be prepurchased through the website of Costa Rica's **Sistema Nacional de Áreas de Conservación** (National System of Conservation Areas, SINAC, www.sinac.go.cr). In addition, electronic tickets—which must be printed in advance and shown upon arrival at the park—are assigned for set days and time slots. Given the region's changeable weather and traffic conditions, it can be hard to nail down a specific day and time to visit. No refunds are given for missed reservations or if the crater is clouded over during your visit. Regardless, the opportunity to spot the volcano's blue pool amid dissipating clouds—sometimes just for a moment—is enough of a thrill to encourage many people to make the trip.

Varied wildlife, including birds, rabbits, armadillos, skunks, coyotes, and weasels, exists within the park but is scarce. The most interesting critter you may come across is arguably the rare, yellow-tinged Bangs's mountain squirrel, nicknamed the Poás squirrel.

At the park's entrance are a **visitors center,** bathrooms, and a parking lot ($3.50 per car).

Hiking

The park has a handful of trails, but since its reopening, only one is open to the public. The wheelchair-accessible **Sendero Principal** (Main Trail, 600 m one-way, 10 minutes, easy) is a paved path that connects the visitors center to the main crater. Park regulations require that you be accompanied by a tour guide on this walk. At the end of the trail, you'll come to a clearing edged by a guardrail and a small, one-story observation tower. On clear days, you can admire the crater at a distance from anywhere along the guardrail; unobstructed photos are best taken from the observation tower. When clouds roll in, typically late in the morning or in the afternoon, there is nothing to see but fog.

Getting There

From downtown Alajuela, it's a 30-kilometer, 50-minute drive north to reach the park. Take Road 712 due north for 18 kilometers until the community of Fraijanes. Here, Road 712 connects with Road 146 and continues north toward Poasito. Look for Road 120, which is well marked with signs for the park. Road 120 leads west for nine kilometers and ends at the park entrance.

From San José, the park is a 50-kilometer drive northwest on Highway 1, Highway 3, Road 712, Road 146, and Road 120 that takes roughly one hour and 20 minutes. These paved routes do not require a 4x4 vehicle.

Buses to the park depart once daily from San José (8:30am daily, 1.5 hours, $3) and Alajuela (9am daily, 1 hour, $2).

AROUND VOLCÁN POÁS

North of Alajuela, several paved but narrow roads ascend mountains past coffee plantations and cow pastures to the quiet communities of **Poasito** and **Vara Blanca.** The tiny agricultural towns southeast of Volcán Poás enjoy warm days, brisk nights, and beautiful views. They're also home to a small collection of hotels and attractions that suffered financial hardship following the closure of Parque Nacional Volcán Poás. The vicinity also endured one of the country's deadliest earthquakes in 2009 and has yet to recover fully from the disaster; it stands to benefit greatly from tourism.

Sights

★ LA PAZ WATERFALL GARDENS

One of Costa Rica's best nature- and wildlife-based theme parks is **La Paz Waterfall Gardens** (Road 126, 6 km north of Road 120, tel. 506/2482-2720, www.waterfallgardens.com, 8am-5pm daily, $44 adults, $28 children 3-12). This attraction on the eastern slopes of Volcán Poás has it all—a well-kept animal sanctuary that features one of the country's largest and most diverse displays of rescued Costa Rican wildlife, a lush property that hides five glorious waterfalls, and modern, secure facilities. You can spend several hours here, strolling around exhibits to see and hear some of the country's most beloved species (like sloths, hummingbirds, colorful tree frogs, toucans, and a magnificent jaguar) and hiking to powerful, photo-worthy waterfalls. An ideal stop if your time in the country is limited, the park makes it easy to check off several experiences on your list with a single visit.

This is one of Costa Rica's most organized tourist attractions, so it's a great choice for families with children. Visits run like clockwork, even as busloads of travelers arrive each day. If you're accustomed to traveling off the beaten path, you may feel like you're on a conveyor belt, being ushered from one sight to the next, but it's still worth going. You can take more time to explore what piques your interest and bypass anything that doesn't. Reception staff are welcoming, helpful, and happy to point you in the right direction to start your exploration.

In the park, paved paths lead to exhibits that showcase birds, butterflies, monkeys, snakes, frogs, and jungle cats within large aviaries and glass enclosures that allow species to be admired at close range. Also on view are an orchid display, a trout pond, and a small ranch where you can see a traditional oxcart strapped to oxen. A rougher trail departs from the exhibits and descends west into the forest toward the waterfalls: The Catarata Templo (Templo Waterfall) has upper-lever and lower-level lookouts. The Catarata Magia Blanca (Magia Blanca Waterfall) provides a photo opportunity behind the cascade. Catarata Encantada (Encantada Waterfall) and Catarata Escondida (Escondida Waterfall) are side by side. The site's namesake, Catarata La Paz (La Paz Waterfall), can only be seen from above. Come prepared for hilly trails and steep staircase descents into—and climbs out of—waterfall viewpoints.

Just north of Catarata La Paz is a gift shop and rest stop where shuttle buses depart regularly to return tired hikers to the reception area.

If you don't have a rental car (a 4x4 is not required), the attraction operates a midmorning **tour** (10:30am daily, 7 hours, $92 adults,

$82 children 3-12) that includes round-trip transportation from San José, the entrance fee, and lunch. Alternately, scores of other tour operators and agencies run day tours here, many of which combine the trip with stops at Parque Nacional Volcán Poás and/or the Doka Estate.

The park is often visited during travel between San José or Alajuela and La Fortuna. If you make the drive, the waterfall you'll approach on the south side of Road 126, 1.5 km north of the entrance, is Catarata La Paz.

COFFEE TOURS

The hacienda-style **Doka Estate** (3 km north of Sabanilla, 12 km north of Hwy. 1, tel. 506/2449-5152, www.dokaestate.com, 6:30am-5pm daily) is Costa Rica's oldest wet mill. It's a lovely place and a popular day trip from San José, sometimes to the point of becoming crowded. Doka Estate has been around since the 1940s and uses some machinery that's over 120 years old to produce a variety of coffee. The plantation's **coffee tour** (9am, 11am, 1:30pm, and 2:30pm Mon.-Fri., 9am, 11am, 1:30pm, 2:30pm, and 3:30pm Sat.-Sun., 1.5-2 hours, $22 adults, $10 children 6-12) is a journey through time. At stations around the plantation, you'll get to see demonstrations of traditional methods of coffee processing. After the light walking tour (suitable for children), wander around the estate and explore a butterfly garden, a hydroponic orchard, a bonsai garden, and a beautiful view, as well as a store stocked full of Doka's finest blends.

Food and Accommodations

Roadside stalls selling *fresas* (strawberries) are scattered along the slopes of Volcán Poás. You won't find any fresher fruit than here, which is largely why the strawberry drinks and desserts at **Freddo Fresas** (Road 146, 800 m south of Road 120, tel. 506/2482-2800, 7am-4pm daily, $4-8.50) are indescribably delicious. Stop at this cabin-style restaurant just southwest of Poasito for a quick refreshing beverage, meal, or snack on your way to or from the volcano or other nearby attractions.

One of the best nature lodges in Costa Rica is the rustic but luxurious ★ **Peace Lodge** (La Paz Waterfall Gardens, Road 126, 6 km north of Road 120, tel. 506/2482-2720, www.waterfallgardens.com, $495 s/d). On the grounds of the La Paz Waterfall Gardens, the 18-room resort features natural wood and stone finishes with luxurious touches and an aura of quiet elegance. You can soak in a Jacuzzi, snuggle by a fireplace, relax on a forest-facing balcony in a rocking chair or a hammock, or crawl under the covers of your soft canopy bed, all in the comfort of your private room. The courteous and helpful staff go out of their way to make guests happy.

The 11-room ★ **Poás Volcano Lodge** (off Road 120, 500 m west of Road 126, Vara Blanca, tel. 506/2482-2194, www.poasvolcanolodge.com, $100 s, $145 d) is intimate, homey, and chalet-like. I particularly love the architecture and design of this hotel. Each room is slightly different; some have wall-to-wall windows and tall, sloped ceilings that mimic the area's mountainous slope, and others have wood-paneled or stone walls softened by in-room lounge areas. Several fireplaces and a glassed-in sitting room that doubles as a library contribute to the property's cozy feel. Bird-watching opportunities and a game room provide on-site entertainment.

Don't be put off by the lackluster roadside front of the **Poás Lodge** (Road 120, 4 km west of Road 146, tel. 506/2482-1091, www.poaslodge.com, $85 s/d). Beyond the entrance, an expansive valley view is impressive both during the day and at night. When the valley is full of clouds, you'll realize how high you are in the mountains—and just four kilometers shy of an active volcano—at the small, five-room hotel. Rooms, outfitted simply with one king or queen bed, and the on-site restaurant capture the scene. The resident owners are friendly and hospitable.

Information and Services

The closest hospital is Alajuela's **Hospital San Rafael** (Calle Francisco Orlich, 1 km northwest of Aeropuerto Internacional Juan Santamaría, Alajuela, tel. 506/2436-1001, 24 hours daily).

Just west of Poasito, where Road 146 meets Road 120 at the turnoff for Parque Nacional Volcán Poás, are a **Super Poasito supermarket,** an **ATM** (5am-midnight daily), and a **tourist police office** (tel. 506/2586-4402, 24 hours daily) with officers available to assist foreign travelers.

South on Road 146 are the community's **clinic, Ebais Poasito** (tel. 506/2482-2121, 7am-4pm Mon.-Fri.), and a **pharmacy, Farmacia El Volcán** (tel. 506/2482-1150, 8am-6pm Mon.-Fri., 8am-noon Sat.).

Transportation

Poasito is a 20-kilometer, 40-minute drive north of **Alajuela** via Road 712 and Road 146. The 40-kilometer drive from downtown **San José** to Poasito via Highway 1, Road 712, and Road 146 takes one hour and 10 minutes. From downtown **Liberia,** Poasito is a 220-kilometer drive southeast via Highway 1, Road 712, and Road 146 that takes roughly three hours and 45 minutes.

Vara Blanca is six kilometers beyond Poasito to the east, an approximate 10-minute drive on Road 120.

★ Coffee Culture: Costa Rica's Golden Bean

Though vast amounts of gold belonging to indigenous populations earned Costa Rica (the Rich Coast) its name, the phrase is also fitting thanks to the country's ample supply of coffee beans, rich in flavor and aroma. Nicknamed the golden bean, coffee is a cultural touchstone in Costa Rica and a treasured contributor to the country's economy. Much of it comes from the highlands around the Central Valley, where an ideal combination of altitude, climate, and fertile soils creates fruitful crops that deliver fine arabica beans.

The region also offers some of the country's best coffee tours. Several coffee plantations, *beneficios* (processing plants), and roasteries are open to the public and have field stations that demonstrate various stages of coffee production. At most properties, you can examine coffee plants and their fruit; watch how beans are harvested, washed, and dried; smell beans being roasted using different techniques; and enjoy a fresh cup of a signature brew. My three favorite coffee tours in the region appeal to different interests, and each offers a unique approach to learning about coffee.

- The organic coffee tour at the small, family-run **El Toledo Coffee** (page 89) demonstrates sustainable coffee farming and hand-operated processing techniques.

- The coffee tour at the charming **Doka Estate** (page 101) shows off some cool, old-fashioned farming machinery and teaches visitors about traditional coffee production.

- The engaging and entertaining coffee tour at the **Café Britt Coffee Roastery** (page 104) will hold the interest of kids, teaching them about coffee varieties.

Heredia and Ciudad Cariari

Costa Rica's smallest province, Heredia, splits Alajuela from San José at Ciudad Cariari, swallows the eponymous city of Heredia (four kilometers northeast of Ciudad Cariari), and extends past several towns and villages farther north. As the province's capital city, Heredia provides numerous services to locals, but it lacks obvious appeal to visitors. The area's biggest draws are the sprawling dark-green fields of coffee farms that span the city's outskirts. A few are open for touring if you're interested in learning how coffee is made.

A mere 10 kilometers southeast of Costa Rica's busiest airport is Ciudad Cariari, a concentrated collection of businesses catering to airport travelers. Accommodations in the small district provide an alternative to overnight stays in San José's chaotic core.

HEREDIA

A distance of only 10 kilometers separates downtown Heredia from downtown San José, but the two cities feel worlds apart. Even though it's the country's third-largest metropolis in terms of population, Heredia has a delightful small-city atmosphere. It also has a vibrant student population, thanks to several education centers including the main campus of Costa Rica's Universidad Nacional (National University, UNA).

Look to the environs of the city and you'll find faint traces of tourism. To the north and northeast, businesses hide on mountainous slopes where quaint residential towns like **Barva, San Rafael,** and **San Isidro** illustrate colonial-style housing, ornate churches, and unfiltered Costa Rican life. Additional

Heredia and Ciudad Cariari

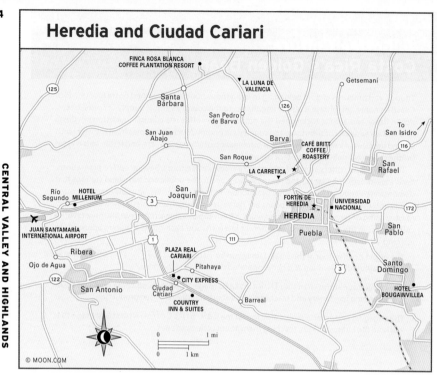

FINCA ROSA BLANCA
COFFEE PLANTATION RESORT •

125

Santa
Bárbara

LA LUNA DE
VALENCIA

Getsemaní

126

San Pedro
de Barva

To
San Isidro

San Juan
Abajo

Barva

116

CAFÉ BRITT
COFFEE
ROASTERY

San Roque

San
Rafael

LA CARRETICA ★

Río
Segundo

HOTEL
MILLENIUM

San
Joaquín

3

FORTÍN DE
HEREDIA ★

UNIVERSIDAD
NACIONAL

HEREDIA

172

JUAN SANTAMARÍA
INTERNATIONAL AIRPORT

1

111

Puebla

San
Pablo

Ribera

PLAZA REAL
CARIARI

Pitahaya

Santo
Domingo

Ojo de Agua

122

CITY EXPRESS

3

San Antonio

Ciudad
Cariari

COUNTRY
INN & SUITES

Barreal

HOTEL
BOUGAINVILLEA

0   1 mi
0   1 km

© MOON.COM

small towns, including **Santa Bárbara** (to the northwest) and **Santo Domingo** (to the southeast), contain Heredia's top hotels. Each town sits within a radius of 10 kilometers or less from downtown Heredia. Together, the city and its outskirts are considered the greater Heredia area, which is best explored with a rental car.

Sights

Towering over the city, as if to keep watch, are the 13-meter-tall ruins of the **Fortín de Heredia** (Heredia Fortress, Calle Central between Avenida Central and Avenida 1). The cylindrical tower's stone and brick exterior is worth a look if you're wandering around the city center, but inside access is prohibited. Built in 1876 as a guard tower within a Spanish fortress, the ruins are what remains of Spanish colonial construction in Heredia.

Coffee Tours

The **coffee tour** (9am, 11am, 1:15pm, and 3:15pm daily, 1.5 hours, $25 adults, $20 children 0-18) at the **Café Britt Coffee Roastery** (Avenida 17, 400 m southwest of Road 126, tel. 506/2277-1500, www.coffeetour.com, 8am-5pm daily) is a theatrical presentation, complete with costumes and enthusiastic actors, that explores the various stages of coffee production through visual aids and humor. During the experience, performed at Café Britt's aroma-filled roastery, you'll see a skit that explains why coffee is important to Costa Rica, learn how to correctly taste coffee, and have a chance to go outdoors to look at coffee seedlings in a nursery. As one of Costa Rica's largest coffee suppliers, Café Britt produces several types of coffee, including a variety of light roasts, dark roasts, and espressos. This tour does a great job of explaining how different coffee flavors are created. It's fun and engaging for children, and adults get to try samples of the different brews throughout the tour.

Entertainment and Events
FESTIVALS AND EVENTS
During the last week of March, the town of Barva, three kilometers north of Heredia, hosts a free, wild, artistic affair known as the **Feria de la Mascarada** (Masquerade Fair). During this time, *payasos* (clowns) and people donning oversize *máscaras* (masks) engage in theatrical performances during parades through Barva's streets. The masks, made of paper or fiberglass and typically resembling recognizable figures both real and imaginary, are central components of Costa Rican folklore. They're particularly important to Barva because several *mascareros* (mask makers) reside in town, and one of the country's first mask creators was from the area. The masks can also be seen in Barva during the last two weekends of August, when the town gathers to honor its patron saint, Bartholomew, and on October 31, the **Día Nacional de la Mascarada** (National Masquerade Day). Most festivities in Barva take place in or around the town's central park (Road 126 and Avenida Central). Confirm the schedule of events with a local hotel or tour operator. This part of town gets busy during the celebrations, so expect traffic conditions to be bad.

Food and Accommodations
Traditional and typical, the open-air restaurant **La Carretica** (Avenida 17 at Calle 22, tel. 506/2560-5750, 11:30am-8pm Mon., 7:30am-8pm Tues.-Sat., 7:30am-7pm Sun., $4.50-10.50) has wood tables and authentic ornaments inside and an oxcart out front. The laid-back spot has a seven-page menu full of Costa Rican favorites, including handmade tortillas, *sopa negra* (black-bean soup), and tropical juices made with *guanábana* (soursop) or *cas* (guava). If there's a Costa Rican food or drink you've been longing to try, there's a good chance La Carretica prepares it.

About seven kilometers north of Heredia is the Spanish restaurant ★ **La Lluna de Valencia** (750 m north of Road 128, 500 m east of Santa Bárbara, tel. 506/2269-6665, www.lallunadevalencia.com, 7pm-10pm Wed.-Fri., noon-10pm Sat., noon-5pm Sun., $10-31). The food, served by cordial and attentive staff, looks and tastes divine. There are eight kinds of paella, as well as beef and fish plates, salads, and a variety of tapas. Beverages include Spanish cocktails (like sangria) and wines. While you eat at one of the casual wood tables, you can enjoy the live music on Wednesday, Friday, and Saturday evenings and on Sunday afternoons.

The lovely **Hotel Bougainvillea** (Calle Santo Tomás, Santo Domingo de Heredia, tel. 506/2244-1414, www.hb.co.cr, $129 s/d) is a 10-minute drive southeast of downtown Heredia. The 81 rooms here are clean, carpeted, and furnished like executive-style suites. Tropical birds, butterflies, and colorful bougainvillea vines fill the property's 10-acre botanical gardens. The three-story hotel also has a restaurant, tennis courts, and a solar-heated pool.

If you're a coffee buff interested in staying at a working plantation, head for the ★ **Finca Rosa Blanca Coffee Plantation Resort** (750 m north of Road 128, 500 m east of Santa Bárbara, tel. 506/2269-9392, www.fincarosablanca.com, $330 s/d). Welcoming and service-minded, this ecofriendly, family-run hotel has spotless white adobe walls, handsome hardwood floors, and splashes of color provided by the owner's artwork and handicrafts. All 14 rooms differ greatly in architecture, decor, and furnishings, but each exudes calmness with a hint of romance. The property also has a gourmet restaurant and runs **coffee tours** (9am and 1pm daily, 2.5 hours, $40 pp 11 years and older) of its on-site plantation.

Information and Services
Heredia's hospital, **Hospital San Vicente de Paúl** (Avenida 16 between Calle 10 and Calle

14, tel. 506/2562-8100, 24 hours daily), is in the south end of the city.

One of the largest **banks** in the area is **Banco Nacional** (corner of Avenida 6 and Calle 6, tel. 506/2277-6900, 7:30am-4:30pm Mon.-Fri.). One block east are a 24-hour **pharmacy, Farmacia Sucre** (Avenida 6, 40 m east of Calle 6, tel. 506/2237-4673), and a well-stocked **Más x Menos supermarket** (Avenida 6, 40 m east of Calle 6). Three blocks farther is an **ATM** (Avenida 6 at Calle 1, 5am-midnight daily).

Heredia also has a **post office** (corner of Avenida Central and Calle 2, tel. 506/2237-2269, 8am-5pm Mon.-Fri., 8am-noon Sat.) and a **police station** (Road 126 between Avenida 5 and Avenida 7, tel. 506/2238-4314, 24 hours daily).

Transportation

Heredia is a 10-kilometer, 20-minute drive north from downtown **San José** via Highway 1 and Highway 3. From **Alajuela,** Heredia is a 13-kilometer, 20-minute drive east via Highway 3. From downtown **Liberia,** it's a 210-kilometer drive southeast via Highway 1 and Highway 3 that takes roughly 3.5 hours.

Highway 3 provides speedy entrance into the city from the west. On the city's east side, the highway turns sharply to the south and continues toward downtown San José. Look out for one-way streets, as Heredia has many.

Public **buses** travel daily to Heredia from **San José** (multiple times 5am-11pm daily, 30 minutes, $1) and **Alajuela** (multiple times 4am-10pm daily, 20 minutes, $1).

CIUDAD CARIARI

Sandwiched between Aeropuerto Internacional Juan Santamaría to the northwest and Costa Rica's capital city to the southeast is the developed district of Ciudad Cariari. Essentially an expansion of airport-area facilities rather than a sought-after destination in its own right, this community by the highway has a slew of hotels, restaurants, and shops most frequented by individuals going to or from the airport.

Shopping

Plaza Real Cariari (Hwy. 1, 6.5 km southeast of Aeropuerto Internacional Juan Santamaría, tel. 506/2293-3827, www.plazarealcariari.com, 10:30am-8pm Mon.-Sat., 11am-7pm Sun.), a large mall, has tons of international and Costa Rican stores for your shopping needs. There's a branch of the bookstore **Librería Internacional** (www.libreriainternacional.com), a Costa Rican chain with shelves of books about the country—including informative reads and photo-heavy coffee-table tomes—that typically sell for less than what you'll pay at shops inside the airport.

Food and Accommodations

Food options in Ciudad Cariari cluster around the **Plaza Real Cariari** (Hwy. 1, 6.5 km southeast of Aeropuerto Internacional Juan Santamaría, tel. 506/2293-3827, www.plazarealcariari.com, 10:30am-8pm Mon.-Sat., 11am-7pm Sun.). The mall has more than 20 dining options from fast food branches to American sit-down favorites like Applebee's. A lively **Hard Rock Café** (tel. 506/2239-2828, www.hardrock.com, noon-11pm Sun.-Wed., noon-2am Fri.-Sat., $11.50-28) is across the street.

Adjacent to the Plaza Real Cariari is the high-rise **City Express** (Hwy. 1, 6.5 km southeast of Aeropuerto Internacional Juan Santamaría, tel. 506/2209-2300, www.cityexpress.com, $86 s/d), a favorite among business travelers who love the hotel's stylish decor. All 134 fresh, minimalist rooms have one queen or two double beds, flat-screen televisions, funky plastic chairs, and light-wood wardrobes and desks. A small continental breakfast buffet is served in a cafeteria-style lounge.

One of my favorite international chain hotels in Ciudad Cariari is the superbly comfortable ★ **Country Inn & Suites** (Hwy. 1, 7 km southeast of Aeropuerto Internacional Juan Santamaría, tel. 506/2239-2272, www.countryinns.com, $98 s/d), built around a private courtyard with a pool, lounge chairs, and shaded huts. It's easy to forget that the relaxing space is just off the highway in the fast-paced Central Valley. The hotel is shockingly quiet and offers above-average rooms with high-quality mattresses and contemporary bathrooms. It's also one of the few non-Alajuela hotels with a complimentary airport shuttle. The staff is helpful, and the breakfast buffet choices are bountiful.

Information and Services

The closest hospital is Heredia's **Hospital San Vicente de Paúl** (Avenida 16 between Calle 10 and Calle 14, tel. 506/2562-8100, 24 hours daily), an eight-kilometer, 15-minute drive northeast of Ciudad Cariari.

Ciudad Cariari's services are primarily commercial. The plaza that is 200 meters northwest of the Country Inn & Suites has a **pharmacy, Farmacia Ciudad Cariari** (tel. 506/2293-7070, 9am-9pm Mon.-Sat., 9am-6pm Sun.), and an **ATM** (6am-10:30pm daily) inside the **Fresh Market supermarket.**

The **Plaza Real Cariari** (Hwy. 1, 6.5 km southeast of Aeropuerto Internacional Juan Santamaría, tel. 506/2293-3827, www.plazarealcariari.com, 10:30am-8pm Mon.-Sat., 11am-7pm Sun.) has additional ATMs, pharmacies, and **banks,** including **Banco Nacional** (tel. 506/2212-2000, 1pm-7pm Mon.-Sat.).

Transportation

Ciudad Cariari is a 10-kilometer, 15-minute drive northwest from downtown **San José** via Highway 1. From **Alajuela,** it's a 10-kilometer, 15-minute drive southeast via Highway 1. From downtown **Liberia,** it's a 205-kilometer, three-hour drive southeast via Highway 1.

Sailing past Ciudad Cariari to the northeast is Highway 1, which offers a turnoff to the district just beyond the overpass of Road 111.

To reach Ciudad Cariari by **bus,** hop on a *colectivo* (shared bus) that commutes between San José and Alajuela (from San José: multiple times 8:15am-11pm daily, 20 minutes, $1; from Alajuela: multiple times 4am-11pm daily, 15 minutes, $1). Be sure to ask the bus driver, *"¿Por favor, puede parar en Ciudad Cariari?"* ("Please, can you stop in Ciudad Cariari?"). The driver will drop you off alongside Highway 1 on the northeast side of the district.

Escazú and Santa Ana

Cosmopolitan Costa Rica shows itself in the affluent hills west of San José. Escazú, Santa Ana, and the outskirts of the two towns are largely occupied by Tico businesspeople, retirees, and wealthy expats. Here you'll find chic gourmet restaurants, high-end shops, and the country's best medical facilities, which serve international visitors who come to the country for medical tourism.

Pockets of historical Costa Rica peek through like rays of sun. Cute churches, decades-old businesses, and traditional celebrations exist, but they're largely overshadowed by the area's vast malls, high-rise hotels, country clubs, and residential compounds.

ESCAZÚ

Escazú shines in the Central Valley, its development and economic prosperity reflecting onto the rest of the country. It's home to millions of dollars' worth of modern shopping centers, hospitals, and mansions, especially within the community of **San Rafael de Escazú,** just off Highway 27. South of San Rafael, Escazú creeps up the hillside of the Central Highlands, where the downtown center (now considered **old Escazú**) and the community of **San Antonio de Escazú** embrace oxen-led carts over luxury cars.

Escazú and Santa Ana

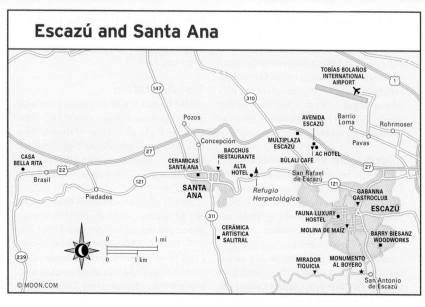

© MOON.COM

Entertainment and Events

NIGHTLIFE

A popular and sophisticated hangout spot in Escazú's San Rafael neighborhood is **Tintos & Blancos** (Multiplaza Escazú complex, tel. 506/2201-5935, www.tintosyblancos.com, noon-1am Sun.-Thurs., noon-2am Fri.-Sat.). This two-story, redbrick, Mediterranean-style tapas bar is the place to be if you enjoy drinking wine. It has more than 30 reds and whites that can be purchased by the glass, a cellar full of wines that can be purchased by the bottle, plus rosés, champagnes, ice wines, sangrias, and organic wines. Cocktails are also served. Reservations can be made through the bar's website and are recommended, especially for Friday and Saturday nights when there's live music.

If you're a beer drinker, you'll love the broad selection of brews at the **Costa Rica Beer Factory** (Avenida Escazú complex, tel. 506/2208–8757, noon-midnight Mon.-Wed., noon-1am Thurs.-Sat., noon-11pm Sun.). Escazú's location of this local chain has a cool look and vibe. The colorful establishment is essentially two spaces in one: An indoor area features strung lights, paper lanterns, a bar

made of bottle caps, and a wall displaying bottles of craft beer; an outdoor patio has several tables and booths arranged under pergolas. It's a chill place to grab a drink during the day and the vibe is fun and social after dark.

CULTURAL PERFORMANCES

Escazú has no shortage of lavish bars, but with a free evening in the area, I like to experience one of the cultural performances offered by two nearby mountainside restaurants. **Mirador Tiquicia** (Bebedero district, 5 km southwest of old Escazú, tel. 506/2289-7330, www.miradortiquicia.com), a quick 10-minute trek from town, hosts **Noche Tica** (7pm-9pm Thurs.-Fri.). **Ram Luna** (Road 209, 16 km southeast of old Escazú, tel. 506/2230-3022, www.restauranteramluna.com) presents **Tierra Tica** (7pm-10pm Wed.-Thurs.), a higher-quality show; it's also a more challenging 40-minute drive from Escazú. Both establishments host lively culture nights twice weekly with authentic music, folk dance presentations, and typical Costa Rican food. Thanks to their mountainous locations, both restaurants also offer spectacular views.

FESTIVALS AND EVENTS

On the weekend closest to March 14, the **Día de los Boyeros** (Day of the Oxcart Drivers) is celebrated with free parades through the community of San Antonio de Escazú. During this event, which pays homage to *boyeros* (oxcart drivers) and all of Costa Rica's agricultural laborers, you can see hundreds of oxen (some with decorative headpieces) pulling colorful, traditional oxcarts through the streets, usually with the herder's family in tow. The fun affair brings together *boyeros* from around Escazú and other nearby communities to celebrate the region's rural heritage. The procession typically begins in downtown Escazú and travels south to the community of San Antonio, gathering parade participants and spectators along the way; see the event's Facebook page for parade start times and other details. It's best to catch the procession near its end, usually the outdoor plaza just west of San Antonio's central church. If you miss the event, check out the remarkably detailed clay and concrete mural depicting *boyeros* and their oxcarts that is part of the community's **Monumento al Boyero** (Oxcart Driver Monument); it's in the same outdoor plaza.

Shopping

At the north end of Escazú, an area formed by Highway 27 (to the north), Road 105 (to the east), Road 121 (to the south), and Road 310 (to the west) contains the country's most concentrated collection of high-end shops. The two best shopping centers are neighbors **Avenida Escazú** (Hwy. 27, 3 km west of Hwy. 39, tel. 506/2208-8990, www.avenidaescazu.com, hours vary by store) and **Multiplaza Escazú** (Hwy. 27, 4 km west of Hwy. 39, tel. 506/2275-3900, www.multiplaza.com/escazu, 10am-9pm Mon.-Sat., 10am-8pm Sun.). Avenida Escazú, a commercial neighborhood comprising several contiguous buildings that are easy to hop between, has sleek-looking glass buildings, features outdoor sculptures, and offers valet parking. Contained in the swanky development are restaurants, a movie theater,

and a wide range of stores. You can buy everything from top-of-the-line home products, electronics, and sportswear to art and cigars here. Multiplaza Escazú is a modern, three-story shopping mall that's always bustling with shoppers. It looks like an ordinary mall on the outside, but inside it's full of international and national designer stores, including Calvin Klein, Carolina Herrera, Guess, Hugo Boss, Lacoste, Michael Kors, and Tommy Hilfiger, as well as popular jewelry stores and shoe stores. You'll also find a movie theater here, as well as over 40 places to eat.

Beautiful wood items buffed to perfection can be purchased at **Barry Biesanz Woodworks** (Calle 110, 1 km south of Road 177, tel. 506/2289-4337, www.biesanz.com, 8am-5pm Mon.-Fri., 9am-4pm Sat.), a private woodshop and gallery-like public showroom in a traditional Costa Rican home. Wood pieces crafted by the shop's namesake artist include boxes, bowls, cutting boards, chess sets, humidors, jewelry, and abstract art. They adorn the showroom, where Costa Rica's exotic woods shine in yellows, oranges, reds, purples, and browns. The shop is two kilometers southeast of Escazú proper. A well-marked, zigzagged route leads to its location in the suburbs.

Food and Accommodations

Expect to pay more for food and beverages in upscale Escazú than elsewhere in Costa Rica.

Swanky eateries abound in Escazú, but I'm partial to the ★ **Búlali Café** (Avenida Escazú complex, tel. 506/2519-9090, www.bulaliartesanal.com, 7:30am-8pm daily, $8.50-14.50). I like everything about the place, from its vintage style and outdoor terrace to its tasty specialties including artisanal bread, organic coffee, and combinations of fresh, healthy ingredients. Choose from soups, salads, sandwiches, cookies, cakes, teas, juices, and shakes. The café's prices are average for the area.

You can don a little black dress or a button-up shirt and live the champagne lifestyle among well-to-do Ticos, expats, and foreigners at the **Gabanna Gastroclub** (Road 105, 600 m south of Road 121, tel. 506/8622-4242, www.gabannagastroclub. com, noon-midnight Mon.-Sat., noon-9pm Sun., $10-28.50). The restaurant and tapas bar, which has a classy art-gallery look and an urban vibe, wins with delicious, unique entrées and appetizers, as well as skillfully prepared cocktails and desserts to die for—tequila truffles, anyone?

For a snack that provides the authentic flavor of Escazú, seek out **Molina de Maíz** (Road 105 between Avenida 34 and Avenida 36, tel. 506/2289-6618, 6am-5pm Mon.-Sat., $1) in the downtown corridor. From a take-out window, this unique little establishment serves freshly ground corn tortillas filled with cheese handmade by a local woman who has run the mini mill for more than 50 years.

Ritzy accommodations aren't just the norm in Escazú—they're part of the reason why travelers visit the city. Plenty of big-name brands (including InterContinental, Wyndham, and Sheraton) have resort-quality hotels in the upscale village. Taking the town by storm, however, is the seven-story, 122-room ★ **AC Hotel** (Avenida Escazú complex, tel. 506/2588-4500, www. marriott.com, $209 s/d), which opened in 2018. The Marriott-owned property is an ultra-sleek, pet-friendly property with in-door lounges decorated with futuristic-looking tables and chairs, and comfortable outdoor spaces with streamlined sofas. The calming rooms have neutral palettes, leather chairs and benches, a flat-screen television, soft linens, tile-walled bathrooms with glass showers, and one king or two queen beds as soft and fluffy as clouds. Best of all, the place is within walking distance of Escazú's quintessential shops.

If you're on a tight budget in this ritzy city, head to the **Fauna Luxury Hostel** (Avenida Manuel Zavaleta, between Calle 138 and Calle 140, tel. 506/2289-5020, www.faunahostel. com, dorm $13 pp, private $50 s/d). The inexpensive, uber-trendy accommodation has five- to eight-person pod-style dorms (each bed has its own privacy shade), a game room with table tennis and billiards, a bar, beanbag seating, a pool surrounded by gardens, and underground parking.

Information and Services

San Rafael de Escazú's **Hospital CIMA** (off Hwy. 27, just north of Avenida Escazú, tel. 506/2208-1000, 24 hours daily) is widely regarded as one of the country's best hospitals. There's also a **clinic, Ebais Escazú** (Avenida 30, 200 m east of the central park, tel. 506/2289-9497, 7am-4pm Mon.-Thurs., 7am-3pm Fri.), in town.

There are **banks** and **ATMs** all over, including a few in Escazú proper and others in shopping centers like **Multiplaza Escazú** (Hwy. 27, 4 km west of Hwy. 39, tel. 506/2275-3900, www.multiplaza.com/escazu, 10am-9pm Mon.-Sat., 10am-8pm Sun.). One of the easiest banks to access is **Banco de Costa Rica** (Road 105, just off Hwy. 27, tel. 506/2290-1129, 9am-4pm Mon.-Fri., ATM 5am-midnight daily). The same road, between Highway 27 and old Escazú, has a row of **pharmacies,** most of which are open 9am-9pm daily.

Escazú also has a **post office** (Avenida 28 at Calle 134, tel. 506/2288-0239, 8am-5pm Mon.-Fri., 8am-5pm Sat.) and a **police station** (off Road 105, just south of Road 121, tel. 506/2228-1274, 24 hours daily).

Transportation

Escazú is a 10-kilometer, 15-minute drive west from downtown **San José** via Highway 27 and Road 105. From **Alajuela,** it's a 20-kilometer, 30-minute drive south on Highway 1, Highway 39, Highway 27, and Road 105. From downtown **Liberia,** Escazú is a 210-kilometer, three-hour drive southeast via Highway 1, Highway 27, and Road 105.

Highway 27 whizzes past Escazú's commercial district, San Rafael de Escazú. The turnoff at Road 105 leads through old Escazú, which has a number of one-way streets, and San Antonio de Escazú.

Public **buses** travel daily to Escazú from

San José (multiple times 5am-10pm daily, 30 minutes, $1).

SANTA ANA

The valley town of Santa Ana is surrounded by a beautiful backdrop of steep hills topped by graceful wind turbines. Its sunny, low-key, and centuries-old downtown core prides itself on its ceramic handicrafts and a favorable climate.

The **Pozos** district exposes Santa Ana's alter ego: a rapidly growing commercial zone occupied by office buildings, condos, and modern hotels.

Refugio Herpetológico

The **Refugio Herpetológico** (Road 121, 2 km east of downtown Santa Ana, tel. 506/2282-4614, www.refugioherpetologico.com, 9am-4:30pm Tues.-Sun., by guided tour only), Santa Ana's small wildlife rescue center, has a big heart. The center's dedicated team is composed of a biologist, a veterinarian, and a few assistants. They rehabilitate (and release, when possible) snakes, turtles, monkeys, ocelots, caimans, tropical birds, and other wild inhabitants that have been rescued by the shelter. This unembellished attraction runs entirely on profits obtained from the **guided tour** (9am and 4:30pm Tues.-Sun., 45-60 minutes, $20 adults, $10 children 4-12), an easy walking tour on a wheelchair-accessible path around the refuge's enclosures. Visitors meet the animals, hear their backstories, and learn how the refuge is working to better the animals' lives.

Shopping

Pottery pieces and glazed creations can be purchased at Santa Ana's abundance of ceramic shops. **Ceramicas Santa Ana** (corner of Avenida Central and Calle 8, tel. 506/2282-6024, 7am-5pm Mon.-Fri., 7am-noon Sat.-Sun.) is operated by the Costa Rican family credited with first bringing pottery to Santa Ana in the 1960s. At **Cerámica Artística Salitral** (Road 311, 2 km south of downtown Santa Ana, tel. 506/2282-7536, 9am-4pm daily), you can witness clay being spun, shaped, and kilned at the on-site workshop. Typical pieces for sale include vases, pots, masks, piggy banks, and a slew of decorative trinkets.

Food and Accommodations

Fine-dining options dot the area. I like the intimate nook that is the **Bacchus Restaurante** (Calle 5 at Avenida 3, tel. 506/2282-5441, www.enjoyrestaurants.net, noon-3pm and 6pm-10pm Mon.-Fri., noon-10pm Sat., noon-8pm Sun., $12-26). Choose this place if you want artistic food presentations and a warm, inviting atmosphere ideal for a romantic night out. Substantial menus provide plenty of meal choices and wine varieties, but the Italian restaurant wins over most with its antipasti, pastas, and flatbreads. There are also several options for vegetarian and gluten-free diners.

Each of the five rooms at ★ **Casa Bella Rita** (off Hwy. 22, 2 km west of Hwy. 27, tel. 506/2249-3722, www.casabellarita.com, $119 s/d) provides a unique experience. One is a cozy, attic-like space, and another has an in-room tropical garden. Some have canyon views and all have comfortable memory foam mattresses to ensure a good night's sleep. The low-key B&B has long been a standout for its splendid service. Located on the outskirts of Santa Ana, the property is just shy of a 10-minute drive from the village's center.

The romantic **Alta Hotel** (Road 121, 2 km east of downtown Santa Ana, tel. 506/2282-8882, www.thealtahotel.com, $205 s/d) is softly lit with rustic chandeliers and pendant lights. The five-story Mediterranean-style building has a terra-cotta tile roof and arched wood doors and is decorated with antique furniture and historical Costa Rican photographs. Warm colors with bold textures add further interest. The hotel also has a 200-year-old guanacaste tree. The 23 clean, comfortable rooms, with one king or two queen beds and wide terraces, take in sweeping views of Santa Ana's hills.

Information and Services

Hospital Clínica Bíblica (off Hwy. 27, 400 m east of Road 147, tel. 506/2522-1000, 24 hours daily) opened in 2018 and is one of the country's top private hospitals. Santa Ana also has a branch of the private **Hospital Metropolitano** (Road 310, 900 m north of Hwy. 27, tel. 506/4035-1212, 24 hours daily), as well as a **clinic, Ebais Santa Ana** (Calle 2, 100 m south of Avenida Central, tel. 506/2282-5242, 7am-4pm Mon.-Thurs., 7am-3pm Fri.).

Santa Ana has a **post office** (Avenida 1, between Calle Central and Calle 2, tel. 506/2203-8364, 8am-5pm Mon.-Fri.), a **police station** (Road 121 at Road 147, tel. 506/2282-6347, 24 hours daily), and **banks,** one of which is **Banco de Costa Rica** (corner of Avenida 1 and Calle 2, tel. 506/2282-7273, 9am-4pm Mon.-Fri.).

There are a couple of **ATMs** (hours vary) and a **pharmacy, Fischel** (tel. 506/2282-2875, 9am-9pm daily), at the corner of Road 121 and Road 147.

Transportation

Santa Ana is a 15-kilometer, 30-minute drive west from downtown **San José** via Highway 27, Road 147, and Road 121. From **Alajuela,** it's a 15-kilometer, 20-minute drive south via Road 111 and Road 147. From downtown **Liberia,** Santa Ana is a 200-kilometer, three-hour drive southeast via Highway 1, Highway 27, Road 147, and Road 121.

The town is best accessed off Highway 27, which runs through the Pozos district. Downtown Santa Ana is two kilometers southeast of the turnoff for Pozos at Road 147. The old road to Santa Ana, Road 121, connects with Escazú five kilometers to the east.

Public **buses** travel daily to Santa Ana from **San José** (multiple times 5am-10pm daily, 40 minutes, $1).

Cartago and Vicinity

Costa Rica's capital city until 1823, the metropolis of Cartago is steeped in civic history and religious significance. As you enter Cartago from the west, you'll fly by high-rises and billboards along multilane highways, then journey past quiet plantations full of chayote along country roads that leave the city to the east. Though it's just 25 kilometers to the northwest, San José feels light-years away, especially along the scenic back roads around the villages of Orosí, Cachí, and Ujarrás. Cartago also serves as the gateway to Parque Nacional Volcán Irazú, whose namesake volcano can be seen to the north.

CARTAGO

Cartago is a great city to explore, ideally in a vehicle. Marvel at its Spanish colonial architecture, much of which has weathered several earthquakes. Of all the cities in the Central Valley, Cartago has the highest elevation. The chilly, sometimes misty city sits 1,435 meters above sea level and is nicknamed the Ciudad de las Brumas (City of the Fogs).

Sights

At the Byzantine-style **Basílica de Nuestra Señora de los Ángeles** (Our Lady of the Angels Basilica, corner of Avenida Central and Calle 15, 6am-7pm daily, free), statues of guardian angels on the facade preside over the gray, white, and gold architectural masterpiece. Within the sanctuary are tall wooden arches, decorative pillars, stained-glass windows, and an opulent altar that pays homage to La Negrita, the country's patron saint.

Several blocks west of the basilica, the Romanesque-style **Ruinas de Santiago Apóstol** (Santiago Apóstol Ruins, between Hwy. 10/Avenida 2 and Avenida Central, just west of Calle 1, 24 hours daily, free) will catch your eye. The decrepit church was abandoned, unfinished, in 1910. It currently serves as a public park. The roofless ruins fill the park with walls of gray stone and appear distressed and somber; you can wander through the tall archways. Cartago's occasionally foggy weather adds to the eerie aura of the place, as do legends that suggest the ruins may be haunted.

SANATORIO DURÁN

Sanatorio Durán (Road 219, 14 km north of downtown Cartago, tel. 506/2240-3016, 8am-4pm daily, $2 pp) is widely regarded as the country's most haunted site. In the early to mid-1900s, this was an institution housing tuberculosis patients and people diagnosed with mental illnesses. What remains of the abandoned sanatorium are rusty buildings with barred windows, boarded-over doors, and walls covered in graffiti and peeling paint. Eerie and empty, this place is a snapshot of a sad and painful time when Costa Ricans—many of them children—lived and died within the complex. On a visit here, you'll take an unguided walk around bare operating rooms, doctors' offices, patient dormitories, and the morgue. Most unsettling is the hallway lined with child-size handprints.

Individuals with an interest in paranormal activity come to catch a glimpse of the ghosts that are said to inhabit the sanatorium. Photos and videos taken here suggest there have been various encounters with spirits of both adults and children. Strange noises have also been reported. If you don't believe in the supernatural, this sanatorium may change your mind.

JARDÍN BOTÁNICO LANKESTER

One of the country's most impressive botanical gardens, the 27-acre **Jardín Botánico Lankester** (750 m southeast of Hwy. 10, 3 km southeast of downtown Cartago, tel. 506/2511-7939, www.jbl.ucr.ac.cr, 8:30am-4:30pm daily, $10 pp 6 years and older) is overseen by the Universidad de Costa Rica (University of Costa Rica). It's a marvelous showing of tropical plants, including bromeliads, heliconias, and palms, plus cacti and succulents. Most visitors are mesmerized by the extensive orchid collection, which contains roughly 1,000 varieties across native, exotic, and miniature species. Wander through various displays, such as a fern garden and a serene Japanese garden, at your own pace. Wheelchair-accessible trails make the garden easy to zip through, but you'll benefit from slow exploration.

Entertainment and Events
FESTIVALS AND EVENTS

A significant religious event for the Roman Catholic population is the **Romería de la Virgen de los Ángeles** (Pilgrimage of the Virgin of the Angels). Each year on August 1, over one million Costa Ricans walk more than 20 kilometers from San José to Cartago's **Basílica de Nuestra Señora de los Ángeles** (Our Lady of the Angels Basilica, corner of Avenida Central and Calle 15). Some crawl the last few meters on their hands and knees; others begin the walk days before from towns outside of the Central Valley. On August 2, known as the **Día de la Virgen de los Ángeles** (Day of the Virgin of the Angels), a mass (6pm) unites the townspeople and draws Costa Rican dignitaries. After mass, bishops lead prayers and a procession known as the **Santo Rosario de la Luz** (Holy Rosary of Light) through the plaza in front of the church.

Foreigners and nonreligious individuals are welcome to participate in all of the festivities. The volume of church visitors makes it difficult to attend the mass, but you can explore the church's interior before or after the ceremony; the church is open 24 hours on August 1 and 2. You can also join in with the crowd that congregates in the plaza to watch the evening procession.

Food and Accommodations

Conveniently located across the street from the basilica, ★ **La Cabañita Grill** (Avenida Central at Calle 15, tel. 506/7066-1337, 11am-9pm Mon.-Thurs., 8am-2am Fri.-Sat., 8am-8pm Sun., $5.50-17) is your best option for food or drinks in downtown Cartago. Cheesy thick-crust pizzas, stacked hamburgers, and

La Negrita

Every year on August 2, Cartago celebrates the **Día de la Virgen de los Ángeles** (Day of the Virgin of the Angels). The celebration marks the day in 1635 when a young girl came across a doll made of volcanic rock, graphite, and jade in the forest. She took it home to keep. The next day, the doll miraculously returned to the forest. When a priest attempted to keep the doll in a church tabernacle, it disappeared again, prompting belief that the figure represented the Virgin Mary with baby Jesus. The figure, called La Negrita, was later declared Costa Rica's patron saint. Today, the **Basílica de Nuestra Señora de los Ángeles** (Our Lady of the Angels Basilica) houses the doll in a shrine above the altar. It was supposedly built on the forested spot where La Negrita longed to reside.

typical Costa Rican dishes make up the comprehensive menu. The classy but casual spot, doubling as a bar come nightfall, also sells the Tico-preferred beverage *horchata,* a sweet and creamy blend of ground rice, condensed milk, and cinnamon.

On your way to or from Volcán Irazú, don't miss **Restaurante Linda Vista** (Road 219, 15 km north of Road 230, tel. 506/2530-8032, 8am-5:30pm daily, $6-15). Admittedly, the small roadside restaurant's food quality isn't as high as the prices, but it's neat seeing the thousands of business cards, notes, and dollar bills that cover the establishment's interior from floor to ceiling. If you go, be prepared to contribute something of your own. Food options include *casados* (traditional dishes of rice and beans, accompanied by a variety of side dishes).

Most people who visit Cartago don't stay overnight, unless they're visiting Volcán Irazú early the next morning. In that case,

1: an oversized mask that's typically seen in the Central Valley and Highlands **2:** the crater of Volcán Irazú **3:** Basílica de Nuestra Señora de los Ángeles in Cartago

book a night at **Grandpa's Hotel** (off Road 219, 200 m north of Road 230, tel. 506/2536-6666, www.grandpashotel.com, $76 s/d). This hotel is the preferred choice of local and international professional athletes, who come to train at high altitude. Each of the 11 basic rooms (some are built to look like log cabins) are clean and come with comfortable beds and in-room heaters to take the chill out of the brisk evening air.

Information and Services

Cartago has a hospital, **Hospital Maximiliano Peralta Jiménez** (Avenida 6 between Calle 2 and Calle 4, tel. 506/2550-1999, 24 hours daily), and a **police station** (Avenida 1 at Calle 11, tel. 506/2592-0648, 24 hours daily).

On the southwest corner of the Ruinas de Santiago Apóstol (between Hwy. 10/Avenida 2 and Avenida Central, just west of Calle 1) is a **pharmacy, Farmacia Central** (tel. 506/2551-0698, 7:30am-7:30pm Mon.-Sat., 7:30am-5:30pm Sun.). The city's **post office** (Hwy. 10 between Calle 5 and Calle 7, tel. 506/2553-2068, 8am-5pm Mon.-Fri.) is four blocks east. Two blocks west of the north side of the ruins is a **bank, Banco Nacional** (corner of Avenida Central and Calle 4, tel. 506/2212-2000, 8:30am-4pm Mon.-Fri.) with an **ATM** (5am-11pm daily). Additional banks, pharmacies, and **supermarkets** are spread out across the city.

Transportation

Cartago is a 25-kilometer, 40-minute drive southeast from downtown **San José** via Highway 2 and Highway 10. From **Alajuela,** it's a 45-kilometer, 70-minute drive southeast via Highway 1, Highway 39, Highway 2, and Highway 10. From downtown **Liberia,** Cartago is a 235-kilometer drive southeast via Highway 1, Highway 27, Highway 39, Highway 2, and Highway 10 that takes roughly three hours and 40 minutes.

Cartago is accessible from the west by Highway 2, which connects with Highway 10, the city's main thoroughfare. Highway 10 splits

Valle de Orosí

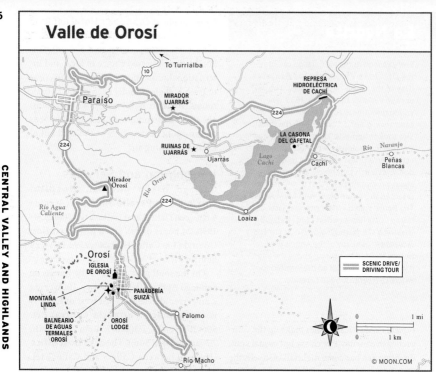

© MOON.COM

into two parallel streets as it crosses the city, Avenida Central (traffic flows to the east) and Avenida 2 (traffic flows to the west). Highway 10 exits Cartago's east side in the direction of Turrialba.

Public **buses** travel daily to Cartago from **San José** (multiple times 5:15am-midnight daily, 45 minutes, $1), **Orosí** (multiple times 4am-9pm Mon.-Fri., 5:20am-9pm Sat.-Sun., 45 minutes, $1-1.50), and **Turrialba** (multiple times 4:30am-9pm daily, 1-1.5 hours, $1.50).

★ VALLE DE OROSÍ

The **Valle de Orosí** (Orosí Valley) seems like it came straight from a postcard: Soft, rolling hills tumble toward quiet communities, winding country roads trace the mountainside, and fields of grasses sway in gentle breezes. This picturesque area of the Central Highlands is regarded as one of the country's prettiest destinations. Only after you see it for yourself and come to the same

conclusion will you know the beauty that Costa Rica hides among its arcadian back roads. Within the valley are the peaceful villages of **Orosí, Cachí,** and **Ujarrás.** Come prepared with an empty memory card for your camera, but know that photos pale in comparison to firsthand views of the dramatic countryside.

Give yourself **1-2 days** to road-trip around the valley and take in its various sights. Most fall along Road 224, which begins off Highway 10 at the town of **Paraíso** (7 km southeast of downtown Cartago) and loops around Lago Cachí (Cachí Lake) before returning to Highway 10. The 30-kilometer route takes 50 minutes to drive if you don't stop. A few accommodations cluster in Orosí, but others are spread out around the loop.

If ever there was a perfect place to picnic in Costa Rica, it's in the Valle de Orosí. Pack your own breakfast or lunch and enjoy a meal at one of many scenic spots along Road 224.

Otherwise, it's slim pickings for restaurants in the area.

Paraíso

Three kilometers south of Paraíso, the **Mirador de Orosí** (Orosí Lookout, Road 224, 8am-4:30pm daily) welcomes you with a spectacular view of the valley from above. At the spot, you can see the narrow **Río Orosí** flow gently alongside the distant town of Orosí, which sits at the base of lofty, verdant hills. This well-maintained lookout is up a flight of stairs, where a concrete path lined with a pretty, white fence leads to a grassy knoll. From the green space, you can picnic high above the valley and take pictures of pastures below.

Orosí

Five kilometers south of the *mirador,* you'll journey through the small town of Orosí, where the clouds sometimes feel close enough to touch. Here, the charming **Iglesia de Orosí** (Orosí Church, one block west of Road 224, opposite the *fútbol* field, 9am-5pm daily, free) brightens the community with white adobe walls and well-manicured gardens. Built in 1743, the small Roman Catholic church is one of the oldest churches in Costa Rica. Photographs without the use of flash are permitted.

HOT SPRINGS

With time to spend in Orosí, you can swim in the four hot spring pools at the **Balneario de Aguas Termales Orosí** (Orosí Hot Springs Spa, 200 m west of Road 224, south of the *fútbol* field, tel. 506/2533-2156, www.balnearioaguastermalesorosi.com, 7:30am-4pm Wed.-Mon., visitors pass $5 pp 2 years and older). Although foreigners are welcome, this spot is far more a hangout spot for locals than a tourist attraction. It's a perfectly fine place to take a rejuvenating soak in mineral-rich water, but don't expect a romantic setting or luxurious lagoons. The thermal water here is contained in rectangular swimming pools.

FOOD AND ACCOMMODATIONS

Your safest bet for food in Orosí proper is **Panadería Suiza** (Road 224, 100 m south of the bank, tel. 506/8706-6777, 6am-5pm Tues.-Sat., 6am-3pm Sun., $1-5). The tiny home-style bakery sells breads, cookies, cakes, muffins, and pastries, many of which taste especially delicious when slathered in marmalade. It's best visited for breakfast, when you can start your day with fresh coffee and a plateful of *gallo pinto* (a traditional blend of rice and beans).

The most attractive hotel in Orosí is the colorful, colonial-style ★ **Orosí Lodge** (next to the Balneario de Aguas Termales Orosí, tel. 506/2533-3578, www.orosilodge.com, $63 s/d). Rooms in the two-story hotel have custom bamboo furniture, beds with orthopedic mattresses, mini-fridges, coffee makers stocked with organic coffee straight from a farm up the street, and outdoor sitting areas in front of wild gardens. The upper-floor rooms face two of the region's volcanoes. The hotel's all-day breakfast ($8 pp) is worth the extra cost.

Orosí's dual hostel and hotel guesthouse, **Montaña Linda** (200 m west of Road 224, 200 m south of the *fútbol* field, tel. 506/2533-3640, www.montanalinda.com, dorm $9 pp, private $15 s, $22 d, guesthouse $30 s/d), has three dorms (with 2-4 bunk beds in each) and eight private rooms that cater to the budget-minded. Shared bathrooms, kitchens, living and dining rooms, and laundry facilities ($8 per load) make the quiet, humble abode feel like you've moved to the valley. One-on-one Spanish-language classes are taught on-site.

Cachí

Follow Road 224 for another 13 kilometers northeast to Cachí, where **Lago Cachí** (Cachí Lake) dominates the view. As seen from its eastern side, the lake is set amid a backdrop of mountains, some of which pop in shades of orange when the flowers on the *poro* trees bloom. As you drive through this section of the valley, be sure to pull over at the side of the road to snap a photo of the lake; you'll have several opportunities to do so. It's usually a green-blue hue, as smooth as glass, and adorned with clusters of aquatic plants. The pretty scene isn't one commonly seen elsewhere in the country. At the northeast end of the lake (2 km north of Cachí), you'll cross over Río Reventazón at the Represa Hidroeléctrica de Cachí (Cachí Hydroelectric Dam). Continued travel on Road 224 west of the dam showcases the lake's western side, where the views are less impressive but still beautiful.

FESTIVALS AND EVENTS

A half-hour drive northeast of Cachí via Road 225, the hamlet of Tucurrique hosts Costa Rica's annual **Feria de Pejibaye** (Peach Palm Fruit Fair). About the size of a plum, typically reddish-orange in color, and with a baked-potato-like texture when cooked, *pejibaye* (peach palm fruit) is a snack enjoyed by most Ticos, especially when cut in half and served with a dollop of mayonnaise. At the fair, you can try the fruit in various forms including soups, breads, desserts, preserves, and alcoholic beverages, all while you take in parades, fireworks, and music. The specific dates for the two-weekend fair vary from year to year but typically fall between the end of September and the beginning of November.

ACCOMMODATIONS

Elegant and romantic, **La Casona del Cafetal** (off Road 224, 550 m northwest of the *fútbol* field, tel. 506/2577-1414, www. lacasonadelcafetal.com, $130 s/d) is set amid a coffee plantation at the edge of Lago Cachí. Seven spacious, clean rooms have comfortable resort-quality beds, rich dark-wood furniture, high ceilings, warm lighting, and terraces. Concrete paths that skirt around the property's gardens connect rooms to the main building and the upscale on-site restaurant, which impresses most guests and caters to celiac travelers with a gluten-free menu.

Ujarrás

A few kilometers north of Cachí, Road 224 switchbacks and travels west to the village of Ujarrás. A quick turnoff from the road into the village takes you to the **Ruinas de Ujarrás** (Ujarrás Ruins), a crumbling, photoworthy limestone church fronted by a sign that details the history of this national monument. These ruins are believed to be the remains of Costa Rica's oldest church, erected in the late 1500s.

From the ruins, it's a three-kilometer drive northwest on Road 224 to the **Mirador**

Ticos celebrate the *pejibaye* (peach palm fruit) at an annual fair near Cachí.

Ujarrás (Ujarrás Lookout, Road 224, 8am-4:30pm daily). This spectacular observation deck, a few steps up from a roadside parking lot, overlooks the valley and captures views of Lago Cachí, the village of Ujarrás, and fields of coffee.

A short 1.5-kilometer sprint to Highway 10 concludes one of the most visually impressive in-country journeys you can make.

Information and Services

The closest hospital is Cartago's **Hospital Maximiliano Peralta Jiménez** (Avenida 6 between Calle 2 and Calle 4, tel. 506/2550-1999, 24 hours daily), an 18-kilometer, 30-minute drive northwest of Orosí.

In Orosí proper, a **pharmacy, Farmacia La Candelaria** (tel. 506/2533-1919, 11am-7pm Mon.-Sat.), **Banco Nacional** (Road 224, tel. 506/2212-2000, 8:30am-4pm Mon.-Fri.), an **ATM** (5am-11pm daily), and a few **supermarkets** line the main road that passes through town (Road 224).

Cachí has a **police station** (northeast corner of the *fútbol* field, tel. 506/2577-1022, 24 hours daily) and a couple of **supermarkets.**

Transportation

Orosí is a 40-kilometer, one-hour drive southeast from downtown **San José** via Highway 2, Highway 10, and Road 224. From **Alajuela,** it's a 65-kilometer, 1.5-hour drive southeast via Highway 1, Highway 39, Highway 2, Highway 10, and Road 224. From downtown **Liberia,** it's a 250-kilometer drive southeast via Highway 1, Highway 27, Highway 39, Highway 2, Highway 10, and Road 224 that takes a little over four hours.

Cachí is 12 kilometers (an approximate 20-minute drive) beyond Orosí to the northeast. Both destinations fall along the loop created by Road 224.

Public **buses** travel daily to Orosí from **Cartago** (multiple times 5:15am-9:30pm Mon.-Fri., 6:15am-9:30pm Sat.-Sun., 45 minutes, $1-1.50).

★ PARQUE NACIONAL VOLCÁN IRAZÚ

Costa Rica's tallest volcano, **Volcán Irazú** (Irazú Volcano) peaks at a whopping 3,432 meters above sea level and is the most visited attraction in the Cartago area. Not only are trips up the mountainside pleasant journeys that cut through picturesque villages and vast vegetable farms, but **Parque Nacional Volcán Irazú** (Irazú Volcano National Park, Road 219, 30 km north of downtown Cartago, tel. 506/2200-5025, www.sinac.go.cr, 8am-3:30pm daily, last entry 2:30pm, $15 adults, $5 children 2-12) also possesses a crater that's different from anything else you'll see in Costa Rica. Unlike the gradual basin that tops Volcán Poás, the crater at Volcán Irazú drops 300 steep meters from its rim into a pit. The dramatic display may quicken your heartbeat and have you grasping for the guardrail that lines the crater's edge.

The volcano's harsh environment doesn't support much wildlife. Volcano juncos (a kind of sparrow) and perhaps gray foxes are the most interesting finds.

From Road 219, a small booth marks the entrance to the park's **Crater Sector,** beyond which a 1.5-kilometer road ends at a public parking lot and a **visitors center** that has bathrooms and a small cafeteria. A second, less popular area of the park is the **Prusia Sector** (21 km southwest of the main ranger station off Road 219, tel. 506/2200-4422). You're welcome to explore either sector without a guide. Self-guided visits do not require advance reservations. It costs $2 to park in the Crater Sector's parking lot.

Within the Crater Sector, the 200-meter-long, wheelchair-accessible **Sendero Principal** (Main Trail) provides a direct path to the main crater from the parking lot. Here, you'll stand in a wide-open space grounded by dark volcanic sand and breathe in air laced with sulphuric and smoky scents. When the sky is clear—typically in the early morning, as clouds tend to roll in during the midmorning or afternoon—you can peer over the crater's edge into the seemingly bottomless pit, which once contained a bright-green lake. Remain mindful of the park's makeshift wooden guardrail and gaps in the rails large enough for young children to fit through. Don't just keep an eye on your little ones; keep them within arm's reach.

From the less-visited Prusia Sector, you can explore the park's coniferous forest via a 13-kilometer web of trails. Wildlife-spotting opportunities are limited.

The park averages 40-50°F, so wear pants and bring a sweatshirt or jacket. Sometimes it's sunny enough to warrant wearing sunscreen, and other times it's rainy. Come prepared for both scenarios.

Getting There

To get to the Crater Sector, take Road 219 for 30 kilometers (approximately 45 minutes) north out of Cartago. The paved route does not require a 4x4 vehicle and ends at the park's entrance.

The turnoff for the Prusia Sector, best accessed in a 4x4 vehicle, is off Road 219, 17 kilometers before the Crater Sector's entrance. From the turnoff, it's a four-kilometer drive north to the Prusia Sector entrance. From Cartago, it's a half-hour drive north to the Prusia Sector's entrance.

Buses to the park depart once daily from **San José** (8am daily, 2 hours, $4-4.50) and **Cartago** (8:45am daily, 1-1.5 hours, $4-4.50).

Turrialba

East of Cartago, Highway 10 and Road 230 climb steadily over mountainous terrain from the slopes of Volcán Irazú to those of Volcán Turrialba. Each route travels through several quiet communities that display authentic rural life in Costa Rica, where *campesinos* (farmers) raise families and have businesses that thrive from the fertile soils. Both roads hug the mountainside as they descend into a valley at the city of Turrialba, eventually meeting in its downtown core. They pass plantations of shiny-leafed plants, fields full of tall grasses, and cow-grazed pastures and farms that produce some of the country's best coffee beans, sugarcane, and cheese.

Despite the tourism boom that hit Costa Rica in the 1990s and has continued ever since, Turrialba feels impervious to change. On any given day, only a handful of foreigners can be seen roaming the downtown core, where Costa Ricans carry out daily routines and salute familiar faces with a smile. Occasionally, members of the indigenous Cabecar group visit Turrialba to purchase food and supplies that they'll later carry on their backs through thick forest to homes in the mountains southeast of town.

The closest most travelers, apart from off-the-beaten-path explorers, come to the city are the hamlets of Tres Equis and Santa Marta, halfway between Turrialba and the Caribbean town of Siquirres. The two communities provide access roads to Río Pacuare, where white-water rafters on organized day tours come from all over Costa Rica to raft raging rapids. (Most river put-ins are halfway between Turrialba and the town of Siquirres. See the *Caribbean Coast* chapter for more information.)

Sights

★ MONUMENTO NACIONAL GUAYABO

The archaeological findings at Costa Rica's protected national monument, the **Monumento Nacional Guayabo** (Guayabo National Monument, 4.5 km west of Road 415, 13.5 km north of downtown Turrialba, tel. 506/2559-1220, www.sinac.go.cr, 8am-3:30pm daily, $5 pp ages 2-65), are wildly intriguing. The one-of-a-kind, 50-acre excavation site is set within a 575-acre rainforest reserve and displays illustrative petroglyphs, deep well-like tombs, large mounds (on which homes were once built), cobblestone roads and steps, and an ingenious water filtration system. Each feature is a snapshot of indigenous life between 1000 BC and AD 1400, at a site that was occupied and then abandoned long before the Spanish colonization. Information placards around the monument explain much of what historians have confirmed about the site's inhabitants, including their hunting and farming techniques and their use of clan hierarchies topped by political chiefs and religious shamans. Only one-fifth of the archaeological site has been excavated so far.

Walks around the monument follow the one-kilometer **Sendero Los Montículos** (Los Montículos Trail), an easy hike (with short inclines, declines, and some stairs) to points of interest including a forest *mirador* where the grounds can be viewed from above. Additional observation points and the area's natural flora are showcased along the less popular 300-meter **Sendero Caragra** (Caragra Trail) and the one-kilometer **Sendero El Canto del Agua** (El Canto del Agua Trail).

It's easy to tour the historic site on your own, but guides can help explain the cultural significance of the many tools and objects you'll come across along the trek. Tour guides can be hired at the monument's entrance for $15 per person.

Guided tours ($65 pp) offered by Turrialba outfitter **Explornatura** (Hwy. 10, 75 km southwest of Calle 2, tel. 506/2556-0111, www.explornatura.com, 7am-7pm daily) include round-trip transportation between the monument and Turrialba hotels.

CATIE

Headquartered in Turrialba is the world-renowned **Centro Agronómico Tropical de Investigación y Enseñanza** (Tropical Agronomic Research and Education Center, Hwy. 10, 4 km southeast of downtown Turrialba, tel. 506/2558-2000, www.catie. ac.cr, 7am-4pm daily). Committed to the study of tropical agriculture, **CATIE,** as the center is known, is a large research site comprising farms, plantations, orchards, and greenhouses. Here, everything from cattle, coffee, and chocolate to plants, nuts, seeds, and acidic fruits is examined, and some rare species are well protected and bred to avoid extinction. The center also functions as a campus and offers graduate-level education to aspiring botanists and agronomists. Though CATIE isn't a tourist attraction per se, you're welcome to walk around some of the center's

view of the mounds at the Monumento Nacional Guayabo

field stations, the most popular of which is the on-site *jardín botánico* (botanical garden, 7am-4pm daily, $10 adults, $6 children 6-12), where more than 250 plant species fill a 111-acre space. If you want to see more of the center and learn about its research projects, staff run guided **day tours** ($26-55 adults) that include narrated walks around the property's botanical garden, coffee plantation, cacao plantation, seed bank, and sustainable dairy farm. Advance reservations are required.

Recreation
MOUNTAIN BIKING

The beloved sport of many active Turrialbeños (Turrialba residents) is mountain biking. If you journey to Turrialba, you're bound to come across several cyclists as they make their way up the hills and mountains that surround the town. Keep an eye out for them after dark, especially on narrow, winding, and shoulderless roads.

Ecoaventuras (Hwy. 10, 200 m west of the Maxi Palí supermarket, tel. 506/2556-7171, www.ecoaventuras.co.cr, 10am-8pm Mon.-Sat.), a small Turrialba tour operator with well-known adventure lovers as owners, runs the vicinity's most scenic mountain biking experience. Their **Mountain Bike Irazú-Turrialba Volcanoes Tour** (9am daily, 5 hours, $125 pp) follows a 50-kilometer, primarily downhill route from the height of Volcán Irazú to the valley of Turrialba. If you're most content exploring new places on a bike, you'll love this two-wheel tour of small-town Costa Rica.

Explornatura (Hwy. 10, 75 km southwest of Calle 2, tel. 506/2556-0111, www.explornatura.com, 7am-7pm daily) offers a flat, easy bike tour through the grounds of CATIE (Hwy. 10, 4 km southeast of downtown Turrialba, tel. 506/2558-2000, www.catie.ac.cr). Their **CATIE Mountain Bike Tour** (8:30am and 1pm daily, 2.5-3 hours, $60 pp, min. age 8) passes through the center's plantations and botanical gardens while a tour guide offers facts and findings about the fruits and flowers you see along the way.

Food and Accommodations

Clean, trendy-looking, and on the main drag (albeit at the north end of town) is the **Maracuyá Cafe** (Calle 2 between Avenida 10 and Avenida 12, tel. 506/2556-2021, 2pm-9:30pm Wed.-Mon., $5.50-7), a small, funky diner with menu options scribbled across chalkboard-style walls. You can get sandwiches, hamburgers, burritos, nachos, fish fingers, and pasta dishes here, plus desserts and drinks flavored with the house specialty: tart and seedy *maracuyá* (passion fruit).

★ **Dulce Tentación** (Calle 0, between Avenida 4 and Avenida 6, tel. 506/2556-0448, noon-9pm daily, $4-5.50) translates as Sweet Temptation and offers just that. It has crepes, cakes, and tons of chocolaty desserts that satisfy everyone with a sweet tooth, as well as fresh and savory salads, pitas, and wraps. Not hungry? Go for a beverage; the drink menu has inventive ice cream milkshakes like the fruit-based Colibri Morado and Mariposa Amarilla, and the caffeine-heavy Oreo Cookie Coffee. Seats on the terrace of the casual second-floor establishment are great for watching people as they enjoy the central park across the street.

The ★ **Ladera Hotel** (Road 230, 6 km north of downtown Turrialba, tel. 506/2556-9315, $72 s/d), formerly La Cascada B&B, feels like your own private mountainside residence. Five large, spotless rooms (two of which adjoin) occupy the homey building and face a covered open-air patio that overlooks the most beautiful panorama of Turrialba. In the daytime, clouds and birds glide through the dramatic valley below the hotel. After dark, the city lights flicker softly like a thousand distant candles. You won't find a more peaceful place for a better price in the area. Throw in warm hospitality from the Tico owner, and stays here are worth every penny.

Turrialba provides access to the famed Río Pacuare (see the *Caribbean Coast* chapter for more information), where white-water rafters come from all over Costa Rica to venture out in the raging rapids on organized

Volcano Photo Ops

an erupting Volcán Turrialba, as seen from the south

Legend suggests that **Volcán Turrialba** (Turrialba Volcano) took its name from Torre Alba, which supposedly means (but doesn't directly translate to) "White Tower." Recent years considered, the moniker fits. When the volcano awoke in 2010 with a startling eruption, giant plumes of smoke billowed out of the beast. Some eruptions were so large that drifting ash floated over San José, halting operations of Aeropuerto Internacional Juan Santamaría farther west in Alajuela. Residents (mainly farmers) who lived on the volcano's slopes were forced to relocate, leaving their homes and livelihoods behind.

Today, while the eruptions are believed to pose no significant threat to Turrialba, there is also no obvious sign that the volcano is tiring. Access to the volcano's namesake park, Parque Nacional Volcán Turrialba, is prohibited, but the volcano can be admired at a distance from several spots, including Turrialba's downtown core (along Highway 10), several accommodations on the town's outskirts, and the main highways that wind throughout the area. If you're lucky, you'll spot the volcano mid-eruption, when a flurry of smoke rises aggressively before dissipating. Below are three of the best volcano-viewing spots:

- In downtown Turrialba, make your way to Calle 2, anywhere between Avenida 2 and Avenida 14. Look up the street, to the northwest, and the volcano will be straight ahead.

- On Highway 10, roughly eight kilometers before you enter Turrialba from the west, around the suburb of Alto La Victoria, there are some clear sections of the highway where the volcano can be seen to the north.

- On Highway 10, as you approach Turrialba from the east, near the community of Jabillos, there are some clear sections of highway where the volcano can be seen to the northwest.

day tours. The garden-bedecked, two-story **Turrialtico Lodge** (Hwy. 10, 8 km east of downtown Turrialba, tel. 506/2538-1111, www.turrialtico.com, $75 s/d) is perched on a quiet mountaintop. The 15 rustic rooms have one or two double beds, private balconies or terraces, fans, and coffee makers. Brew a cup of local coffee and enjoy it from the hotel's reading nook or living room—or from the outdoor cliffside deck that showcases a breathtaking valley view. Situated along the access road to Río Pacuare put-in sites,

Turrialtico is the preferred accommodation of white-water rafters who tour the river out of Turrialba.

The priciest digs in the area are at the lakeside **Casa Turire** (off Road 255, 11 km southeast of downtown Turrialba, tel. 506/2531-1111, www.hotelcasaturire.com, $185 s/d), which, despite having an on-site playground, is enjoyed most by mature travelers. The three-story, colonial-style home has 16 rooms, a restaurant, a pool, a spa, and its own palm-lined entrance. The charming but rather outdated rooms come with one king or two queen beds flanked by wrought-iron headboards and footboard benches, linens in plaid and floral prints, in-room sofas and chairs, and balconies with views of Volcán Turrialba.

Information and Services

Turrialba has a **post office** (Calle 0, 200 m north of the central park, tel. 506/2556-7670, 8am-5pm Mon.-Fri.), a **police station** (Hwy. 10 at Avenida 9, tel. 506/2556-0030, 24 hours daily), and **Hospital William Allen Taylor** (Hwy. 10, across from the bus station, tel. 506/2558-1300, 24 hours daily).

Several **pharmacies,** most of which are open 8am-8pm daily, are along Highway 10/ Calle 2 in the city's core. There's a **Banco Nacional** (tel. 506/2556-1211, 8:30am-3:30pm Mon.-Fri.) with an **ATM** (5am-10pm daily) on Avenida 0 at the east end of town; a large **Megasuper supermarket** (8am-9pm Mon.-Sat.) is one block north on the corner of Avenida 2 and Calle 3.

Transportation

Turrialba is a 60-kilometer, 1.5-hour drive east from downtown **San José** via Highway 2, Road 219, Road 230, and Highway 10. From **Alajuela,** it's an 80-kilometer, two-hour drive east via Highway 1, Highway 39, Highway 2, Road 219, Road 230, and Highway 10. From downtown **Liberia,** it's a 270-kilometer drive southeast on Highway 1, Highway 27, Highway 39, Highway 2, Road 219, Road 230, and Highway 10 that takes slightly less than five hours.

Highway 10, the main road that enters the city from the west, loops around the downtown core and exits the area to the east, eventually turning north and climbing up a mountain before descending into Siquirres.

Public **buses** travel daily to Turrialba from **San José** (multiple times 5am-9pm daily, 2-2.5 hours, $1.50-2) and **Cartago** (multiple times 6am-10pm daily, 1-1.5 hours, $1.50).

La Fortuna and Monteverde

The northern inland area is undeniably touristy, but even adamant off-the-beaten-path travelers shouldn't miss it. Its anchors, La Fortuna and Monteverde, illustrate much of Costa Rica's appeal. Lush rainforest and cloud forest cover the majority of the region, keeping it green, gorgeous, and replete with wildlife year-round. Among the area's memorable features are deep valleys, rich agricultural plains, an idyllic lake sunken among rolling hills, and a conical stratovolcano that never fails to make jaws drop. Hundreds of guided excursions are available day and night, immersing travelers in rich biodiversity and providing many of the country's most thrilling adventures.

Highlights

Look for ★ to find recommended sights, activities, dining, and lodging.

© MOON.COM

★ **See rescued animals** up close at the **Proyecto Asis Wildlife Refuge Center** (page 132).

★ **Capture postcard-worthy snapshots** of **Catarata Río Fortuna** as it rushes into crystalline waters (page 135).

★ **Explore the rainforest** along a series of suspension bridges at the **Místico Arenal Hanging Bridges Park** (page 140).

★ **Soak in volcanic mineral pools** at **The Springs Resort & Spa** (page 141).

★ **Zip-line** around a volcano at **Arenal Sky Adventures Park** (page 159).

★ **Bird-watch** at the **Refugio Nacional de Vida Silvestre Mixto Caño Negro** (page 167).

★ **Admire** the brilliant blue hue of **Río Celeste** inside Parque Nacional Volcán Tenorio (page 171).

★ **Take a zip line** through a cloud forest at **Monteverde Sky Adventures Park** (page 175).

★ **Check out diverse wildlife** at the exhibits in **Selvatura Park** (page 175).

★ **Hike through the clouds** in the **Reserva Biológica Bosque Nuboso de Monteverde** (page 189).

But not all that shines in the region is glitzy and over the top. La Fortuna, Monteverde, and the host of other towns and communities that contribute to the area's allure provide sights and experiences that promote sustainability. A number of organic farms offer tours, volunteer opportunities, farm-to-table dining, and homestays. Tourism companies and tour guides demonstrate conscientious business and ecological practices. A vibrant art community thrives amid hordes of souvenir shops. Indigenous people welcome foreigners to learn about their heritage.

It's no wonder so many first-time Costa Rica travelers make it a priority to visit the northern inland area. Quite simply, it encompasses too many worthwhile experiences to skip. Perhaps more surprising and telling is that both La Fortuna and Monteverde remain favorites among return visitors—faithful lovers of the land who cannot seem to get their fill of adrenaline-inducing activities, nature expeditions, and community tourism.

PLANNING YOUR TIME

Travel to the northern inland area, especially for first-time visitors, is incomplete without a multiday stay in the La Fortuna or Monteverde region—or both. If you're up for ecoadventure, the plethora of experiences here will amaze and likely overwhelm you. Planning ahead is key and can significantly boost the quality and affordability of your trip. Secure reservations for accommodations, transportation, and activities a few weeks prior to your trip if you plan to travel between May and mid-December, or 3-6 months in advance if you will be in the country between the end of December and April. (Book even earlier if your visit coincides with Christmas, New Year's, or Easter.) Early bookings mean discounted prices, which can help offset the area's tourism-inflated costs.

La Fortuna is Costa Rica's epicenter of adventure. Aim for a minimum of **2-3 days** in the area but give yourself more if your vacation schedule and budget allow for it. Plan on being busy. Combination tours that group multiple activities into half- or full-day experiences can save you time and money. Relaxing soaks in the waters of the **Catarata Río Fortuna** and **The Springs Resort & Spa** (among other thermal-water attractions) are commonly paired with hikes around **Volcán Arenal** and nature exploration at the **Místico Arenal Hanging Bridges Park.** At the **Arenal Sky Adventures Park** and other one-stop-shop adventure centers, a number of experiences can be checked off your bucket list in one day.

If you're keen on exploring the cloud forest, you can hike through it at the **Reserva Biológica Bosque Nuboso de Monteverde** or one of many other nature reserves in the Monteverde vicinity. You can also play in the clouds at the **Monteverde Sky Adventures Park** and spy on the ecosystem's species up close at **Selvatura Park.** In **two days** you can hit the highlights, but with more time you can see the rural and cultural sides of Monteverde that locals know and love.

To escape the norm, spend **a night or two** at a less-visited destination, such as **El Castillo, Nuevo Arenal,** or **Bijagua.** Another option is to give yourself extra time in La Fortuna to experience the greater area via a day tour. During some tours, you can learn about efforts to protect the environment, preserve cultural heritage, and rehabilitate rescued animals, such as the work being done at the **Proyecto Asis Wildlife Refuge Center.** Tours to other sites, including the **Refugio Nacional de Vida Silvestre Mixto Caño Negro** and **Río Celeste** at the **Parque Nacional Volcán Tenorio,** will teach you why these prized jewels of the north are some of the country's best attractions.

Previous: Volcán Arenal; verdant forest in Monteverde; Reserva Biológica Bosque Nuboso de Santa Elena.

La Fortuna and Monteverde

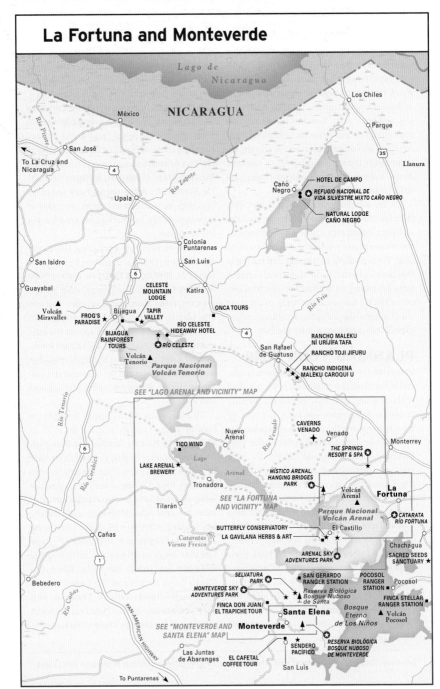

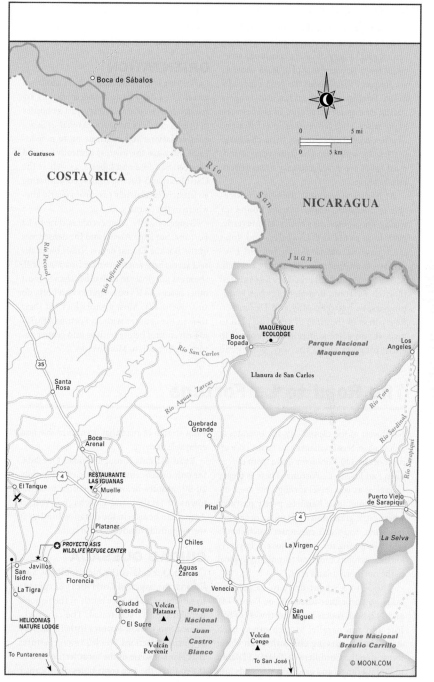

Weather and Transportation

The lowland areas in the region, which include La Fortuna, are consistently warm. Hot, sunny, and muggy days are common, especially from January to April. Rain showers are frequent throughout the year, especially in La Fortuna, but heavier and longer-lasting downpours are more likely between September and November. Fortunately, weather conditions present little challenge getting to and from the area year-round; most roads are paved and easy to maneuver, rain or shine.

At higher elevations, there is a noticeable temperature drop. If you're bound for windy and sometimes chilly Monteverde, pack long pants and a sweater, and don't fault your accommodation for not having air-conditioning—it's rarely needed. Although Monteverde receives less rainfall than La Fortuna, it sometimes has whipping winds between May and December. Regardless of the time of year you plan to visit, if you drive yourself, be prepared to encounter fog along the way, which can reduce visibility. Also make sure you rent a 4x4 vehicle; you'll need it to get to this mountainous destination.

ORIENTATION

La Fortuna is the hub of the country's tourism wheel. On a daily basis, flocks of visitors arrive from all over the country, just as hordes of others check out of their Arenal-area accommodations and continue on to new locales. Because the town is centrally located between San José and Liberia, as well as the Caribbean and Pacific coasts, coordinating a visit here is relatively easy from nearly anywhere in the country.

Geographically, Monteverde is close to La Fortuna, but Lago Arenal and the dense trees of the Bosque Eterno de los Niños block direct access between the two destinations. Still, the areas are closer to each other than to most other places, so if you intend to visit both, do so sequentially. Most visitors kick off their time in the country with La Fortuna's thrilling adventures before settling into gentler nature exploration in Monteverde.

The Road to La Fortuna

Northwest of the capital city, life operates at a slow pace. Small villages and farms take up most of the 140-kilometer drive from downtown San José to La Fortuna. There is plenty to gaze at as you travel through the area, including quiet little hamlets, pretty pastures where cattle graze, and fields full of ornamental plants. You won't encounter much that is worth stopping for, but the lovely, leisurely journey exhibits the rural tranquility typical of the northern inland area.

The 3- to 3.5-hour drive to La Fortuna takes you on either Road 702 or Roads 141 and 142; both routes begin northwest of San José and run parallel to each other. Each starts with a curving climb through cloud forest atop the Cordillera de Tilarán (Tilarán mountain range) and gradually descends into a flat stretch of road that is comfortable and enjoyable to drive.

Road 141 cuts through Ciudad Quesada, the only urban center in the vicinity. Roughly 20-30 minutes before La Fortuna, near the towns of Javillos and Chachagua, Volcán Arenal can be seen in the distance, hinting at the magnitude of adventure to come.

CIUDAD QUESADA

Ciudad Quesada is the metropolis of San Carlos, the largest of Costa Rica's 82 cantons by landmass and where much of the region's population is concentrated. The city, nicknamed San Carlos, features little in the way of tourist attractions. Nestled among pastures that blanket some of the most fertile land in the country, the area contributes significantly to the agricultural sector by way of cattle meat and dairy production.

The downtown core is bounded by Calle 1, Avenida 4, Calle 2, and Avenida 7.

Shopping

Special-interest shops in the area include *talabarterías* (saddleries) that produce and sell leather goods. The downtown core features two. **Talabartería La Moderna** (Avenida 3 between Calle 1 and Calle Central, tel. 506/2460-1761, 6am-7pm Mon.-Sat.) has been around since the 1950s and is a household name in town. **Talabartería La Ranita** (Calle Central just south of Avenida 4, tel. 506/2460-4980, 8am-6pm Mon.-Fri., 8am-4pm Sat.) is newer and caters to tourists; if you want a personalized souvenir from the region, artisans at the store can stamp the signature leather cowboy belts with your name or favorite catchphrase while you wait.

Food

For inexpensive food, check out the **Babaloo Coffee Restaurant** (Calle 2 between Avenida 6 and Avenida 10, tel. 506/4700-5578, 10am-6pm Mon.-Fri., 10am-4pm Sat., $3-8). The small diner serves staple Costa Rican dishes alongside Colombian specialties. A fancier establishment that offers a more comprehensive menu, albeit higher prices, is **Restaurante Coca Loca** (Calle 2 across from the central park, tel. 506/2460-3208, 11am-11pm daily, $8-20). This place has been cooking the perfect steak since 1992.

Information and Services

North of downtown, the **Hospital de San Carlos** (Road 141, 2 km north of the Catholic church, tel. 506/2401-1200, 24 hours daily) serves residents of Ciudad Quesada and its surrounding areas, including La Fortuna. A **pharmacy** is on-site. Other pharmacies, as well as **banks**, are around the central park in the middle of town.

The **police station** (Calle 1 just south of Avenida 3, tel. 506/2460-6079) is open 24 hours daily. The city has several **post offices**

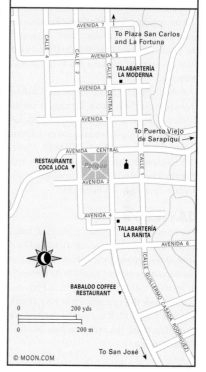

Ciudad Quesada

AVENIDA 7

To Plaza San Carlos and La Fortuna

CALLE 4 · CALLE 2 · CALLE CENTRAL · CALLE 1

AVENIDA 5

TALABARTERÍA LA MODERNA ■

AVENIDA 3

AVENIDA 1

To Puerto Viejo de Sarapiquí →

AVENIDA CENTRAL

RESTAURANTE COCA LOCA ▼

Parque

AVENIDA 2

AVENIDA 4

TALABARTERÍA LA RANITA ■

AVENIDA 6

CALLE GUILLERMO CASADA RODRIGUEZ

BABALOO COFFEE RESTAURANT ▼

0   200 yds

0   200 m

To San José ↘

© MOON.COM

(tel. 506/2460-3399, 8am-5pm Mon.-Sat.), the most central of which is on Avenida 4 just east of Calle Central. There are several **supermarkets** around town.

A number of **gas stations,** including two on Road 141 (at opposite ends of town), make filling up on your way into or out of the city a breeze.

Transportation

Ciudad Quesada is 95 kilometers northwest of downtown **San José** via Highway 1 and Road 141, about a two-hour drive.

Road 141, the main passageway that runs north-south through the city, splits into two streets in the downtown corridor: Calle 1 to the east and Calle 2 to the west. Both are one-way streets; traffic on Calle 1 flows north, and traffic on Calle 2 flows south. Official **taxis**

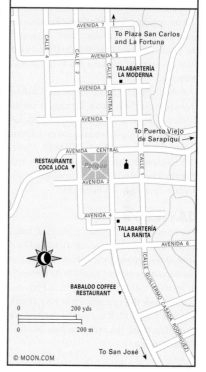

park on Avenida 1 between Calle Central and Calle 2 along the north side of the central park.

The regional **bus station** (Avenida 21 and Calle 4) is north of downtown. Taxis and the Ciudad Quesada city bus (both accessed from the station) can take you to the downtown core.

Public buses travel daily to Ciudad Quesada via **San José** (multiple times 4:30am-6:30pm daily, 2.5 hours, $3.50), **La Fortuna** (multiple times 4:25am-9:20pm daily, 1.5 hours, $2.50), **Tilarán** (7am, 12:15pm, and 3:30pm daily, 2 hours, $5), and **Puerto Viejo de Sarapiquí** (multiple times 4:40am-7pm daily, 2.5 hours, $3).

JAVILLOS

The hamlet of Javillos has a few local businesses and a *fútbol* (soccer) field huddled around the intersection of Road 141 (to the north and the east) and Road 738 (to the west). Its location makes it a gateway to La Fortuna.

Although the community is tiny (blink and you'll miss it), it has one of the region's best attractions: the Proyecto Asis Wildlife Refuge Center.

★ Proyecto Asis Wildlife Refuge Center

Most travelers sail through Javillos without looking back, but if you have an interest in wildlife—particularly rescued wildlife, animal rehabilitation efforts, and volunteer opportunities—don't miss the **Proyecto Asis Wildlife Refuge Center** (Road 738, 500 m west of Road 141, tel. 506/2475-9121, www. institutoasis.com, 8am-4pm Mon.-Sat., by guided tour only).

The center's **regular tour** (8:30am and 1pm Mon.-Sat., 2 hours, $33 general, $19 children 5-9) offers an introductory look at the project's efforts and the animals it has rescued. A guided stroll around the grounds from one wildlife enclosure to the next reveals many of the center's guests, including jungle cats, tropical birds, caimans, and monkeys. Your guide will discuss the eye-opening backstories

of the abuse, neglect, or illegal trafficking of different creatures, while explaining how the center helps to return as many animals as possible to the wild. The tour is suitable for kids, but some travelers may find the information to be heavy or boring.

If you're feeling philanthropic, I recommend helping out with food and toy preparation, enclosure cleaning, and other tasks via either the half-day **tour and volunteer experience** (8:30am and 1pm Mon.-Sat., 3.5 hours, $56 general, $33 children 5-9) or the **full-day activity** (8:30am Mon.-Fri., 7 hours, $88 general, $68 children 5-9). You may even get to feed some of the animals! Long-term volunteer stints that feature **homestays** with Costa Rican families are also available.

Every visit benefits the center. The government does not fund the project, and its success depends on private donations, tour proceeds, and volunteer program enrollment fees.

Food and Accommodations

Everything from typical Costa Rican dishes to fast food and kids' meals can be ordered at **El Gran Coloso Soda y Restaurante** (Road 141 across from El Colono, tel. 506/2475-5034, 11am-10pm Mon.-Sat., $3.50-8), an inexpensive restaurant to stop at if your stomach starts grumbling as you pass through the area.

The only well-known accommodation in the area is the **Tree Houses Hotel** (Road 141, 300 m north of the Santa Clara cemetery, tel. 506/2475-6507, www. treehouseshotelcostarica.com, $114 s/d), with its seven chalet-like rooms perched nine meters above the forest floor on metal structures. The rooms aren't luxurious, but they are novel and allow for a different way to appreciate the local flora and fauna. They are equipped with air-conditioning, a shower, and a refrigerator, so if you aim to live like Tarzan, you can swing it in comfort.

Transportation

Javillos is roughly halfway between Ciudad Quesada and La Fortuna (an approximate half-hour drive from both cities). The easiest way to reach Javillos is by car. From San José, the most popular route is via Highway 1 and Road 702, which passes through San Ramón; this drive is 110 kilometers and takes about 2.5 hours. Another option is to go via Highway 1 and Road 141, which passes through Ciudad Quesada. This route is also 110 kilometers but takes a little longer, up to three hours.

Buses travel regularly between Ciudad Quesada and La Fortuna. From **Ciudad Quesada** (45 minutes, $2.50), buses headed to La Fortuna depart multiple times each day from 4am to 10:10pm daily; they can stop in Javillos upon request. From **La Fortuna** (30-45 minutes, $2.50), buses headed to Ciudad Quesada leave multiple times each day from 4:25am to 9:20pm and can stop in Javillos upon request. On either route, ask the driver, *"¿Por favor, puede parar en Javillos?"* ("Please, can you stop in Javillos?") when you get on. Regardless of which city you depart from, make sure you board a bus labeled *"por El Tanque."* Not all buses labeled *"por Chachagua"* pass through Javillos. Schedule postings at bus stations, as well as signs displayed in the bus's front window, identify routes.

CHACHAGUA

A small community south of La Fortuna, Chachagua is slowly making an impression on tourism in the region. The town's appeal is its distance from La Fortuna's bustle. If you want to stay on the outskirts of La Fortuna but remain within driving distance of its activities, restaurants, and shops, consider one of Chachagua's remote accommodations.

Food and Accommodations

Restaurants in the Chachagua area are limited. Plan to eat at your hotel's on-site restaurant (the recommendations here each have one), or in La Fortuna if you're not opposed to making day trips into town.

The ★ **Heliconias Nature Lodge** (Road 702, 5.5 km south of downtown Chachagua, tel. 506/2468-0067, www. heliconiasnaturelodge.com, $125 s, $150 d)

is one of my favorite family-run hotels because it truly welcomes guests into the family. Taste age-old recipes honed by the owner's grandmother at the lodge's restaurant, drink Grandpa's secret honey moonshine, kick a soccer ball around or play in the pool with the owner's kids, and interact with siblings and aunts who operate the property's restaurant, farm, and salon. Hike nature trails, participate in an on-site coffee or chocolate tour, and soak in thermal-water pools, or just relax in one of the hotel's 18 beautiful bungalows (each sleeps 2-4 people). You'll feel right at home.

The most popular accommodation in the area is **Finca Luna Nueva Sustainable Rainforest Ecolodge** (2.3 km west of Road 702, from the paved road just north of the Peñas Blancas cemetery, tel. 506/2468-4006, www.fincalunanuevalodge.com, bungalows $152 s/d). Built in conjunction with a 200-acre biodynamic farm, the property offers wellness activities and workshops ranging from creative writing to yoga, meditation, and Reiki. The on-site **Sacred Seeds Sanctuary** also draws in visitors. Most who come stay in one of the ecolodge's seven bungalows; however, the property also has two rental homes (each sleeps 12 people) and an odd-looking "earthbag" house constructed with clay (sleeps 1-3 people).

The **Chachagua Rainforest EcoLodge** (2.5 km west of Road 702, from the gravel road 2 km south of downtown Chachagua, tel. 506/4000-2026, www. chachaguarainforesthotel.com, $149 s/d) has 28 individual bungalows with beautiful wood floors and vaulted ceilings, as well as a private front porch with a hammock. The hotel is also a working ranch, and its most impressive offerings are cowboy-led horseback-riding tours. For an added touch (and taste) of Costa Rican authenticity, some of the rides end with a lesson in traditional corn tortilla preparation.

Transportation

Chachagua is an approximate 45-minute drive from Ciudad Quesada. It's 20 minutes south

Sacred Seeds Sanctuary

The first time I was introduced to *gavilana* (jackass bitters), I was put off by its sharp, unpleasant taste. Then a tour guide told me that the plant deters parasites and pathogens, and that its leaves can supposedly be used to treat everything from traveler's diarrhea, infections, and the flu to lice infestations. The lesson was eye-opening and changed the way I see the country. I no longer search for the prettiest flowers or foliage in Costa Rica's forests; I am far more interested in uncovering the power rooted in each.

The *gavilana* leaf packs a powerful punch.

An international nonprofit called Sacred Seeds, an offshoot of the North American nonprofit conservation group known as United Plant Savers (www.unitedplantsavers.org), aids in the creation and maintenance of a number of medicinal gardens across the globe. The Sacred Seeds Sanctuary at Chachagua's Finca Luna Nueva Sustainable Rainforest Ecolodge (2.3 km west of Road 702, from the paved road just north of the Peñas Blancas cemetery, tel. 506/2468-4006, www.fincalunanuevalodge.com) is one of the project's founding gardens. It has roughly 300 medicinal plants in what workers refer to as the "botanical pharmacy." The sanctuary emphasizes two key ideas: that medicinal plants are a vital part of healthcare practiced around the world—not just in traditional medicine but as ingredients in modern-day prescriptions—and that these plants are essential to understanding unique cultural groups.

To see, smell, and even taste some of what the sanctuary has to offer, you can arrange a guided tour through Finca Luna Nueva. During your visit, you'll make your way through the garden's path. You'll learn how people benefit from using plant-based compounds, and how you can grow similar species in your own backyard.

If you visit, be brave and try the *gavilana*. Let its bitterness saturate your tongue; true healing power is right under your nose.

of La Fortuna by car. The easiest way to reach Chachagua is by car. From San José, the most popular route is via Highway 1 and Road 702, which passes through San Ramón; this route is 120 kilometers and takes 2.5 hours. Alternately, you can take Highway 1 and Road 141, which passes through Ciudad Quesada; this option is 125 kilometers and takes three hours.

Buses travel regularly between Ciudad Quesada and La Fortuna. From Ciudad Quesada (1-1.5 hours, $2.50), buses headed to La Fortuna depart multiple times each day from 4am to 10:10pm daily; they can stop in Chachagua upon request. From La Fortuna (30 minutes, $2.50), buses headed to Ciudad Quesada leave multiple times each day from 4:25am to 9:20pm and can stop in Chachagua upon request. On either route, ask the driver, *"¿Por favor, puede parar en Chachagua?"* ("Please, can you stop in Chachagua?") when you get on. Make sure you board a bus labeled *"por Chachagua."* Buses labeled *"por El Tanque"* do not pass through Chachagua. Schedule postings at bus stations, as well as signs displayed in the bus's front window, identify routes.

La Fortuna and Vicinity

The town of La Fortuna de San Carlos ("La Fortuna" for short) is geographically small but packed with restaurants, shops, and tourism offices. The area's biggest draw is adventure tourism, which is unrivaled elsewhere in the country.

Choose from a seemingly endless list of stand-alone day tours or visit one of several adventure parks that provide a variety of activities, from leisurely aerial tram rides to thrilling zip-line glides. Most of La Fortuna's experiences are family-friendly, but some outfitters enforce a minimum age requirement.

At the town's core is the **central park,** bordered to the west by the **central church.** From downtown La Fortuna, Road 142 (the main drag) departs west in the direction of Volcán Arenal. It skirts around the volcano and passes by countless hotels, hot spring properties, and other attractions before arriving at the Lago Arenal Dam. Most activity centers and accommodations that fall between La Fortuna's center and the dam are considered La Fortuna operations. The region at large is colloquially referred to as "Arenal."

SIGHTS
★ Catarata Río Fortuna

Imagine a rainforest scene so leafy and lush that it looks soft enough to snuggle in, a picture of vivid lime and emerald greens with a view that fills your gaze with gorgeous forest as far as your eyes can see. Now envision a stark white cascade slicing through the portrait and spilling into a river pool 70 meters below. Most people who visit the **Catarata Río Fortuna** (Río Fortuna Waterfall, Road 142, tel. 506/2479-9515, www.cataratalafortuna.com, 7am-5pm daily, last entry 4pm, $18 pp 8 years and older) have fun swimming in its waters and exploring its onsite **Orchid Garden,** but I love admiring the waterfall at a distance from the viewpoint just beyond the entrance.

You can catch an equally impressive view of the powerful waterfall from its base. The trail of 530 steps that leads down to the waterfall from the entrance is daunting (especially knowing that you'll have to return uphill), but worth every ounce of effort. Most visitors, including children, make the trek without a problem, and benches provide a break along the way. I don't recommend swimming in the waterfall's pool, as the current here is strong. It's better to wade in the calmer waters slightly downstream.

Although nearly every operator in town offers guided hikes to the waterfall for roughly $50 per person, the attraction is one you can easily navigate and explore on your own. Another option is to visit via a **guided horseback tour** (8am, 10:30am, and 1:30pm daily, 3 hours, $70 adults, $53 children 7-12, min. age 7) coordinated by the **Arenal Mundo Aventura Ecological Park** (Road 702, 1.5 km south of the central church, tel. 506/2479-9762, www.arenalmundoaventura.com); the tour departs from the adventure park.

If you would prefer to skip the trip down the steps and back up again, you can still see everything else that the site has to offer. A viewpoint, orchid garden, restaurant, and souvenir store are all located at the top of the property, a short and easy walk beyond the entrance.

Arenal Mundo Aventura Ecological Park

Nearly 1,400 acres of primary rainforest is protected by the **Arenal Mundo Aventura Ecological Park** (Road 702, 1.5 km south of the central church, tel. 506/2479-9762, www.arenalmundoaventura.com, 7am-5pm daily by tour only, cost varies by activity), where you can go zip-lining and rappelling or take a horseback ride to the nearby Catarata Río Fortuna. This is the first theme park in the

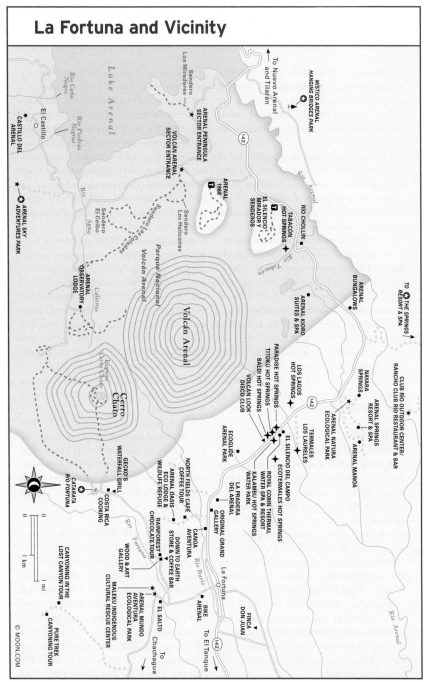

La Fortuna and Vicinity

© MOON.COM

country to receive the prestigious Sustainable Tourism Certification issued by the Instituto Costarricense de Turismo (Costa Rican Institute of Tourism). Through its adventure and nature tours, the park acts as an example of responsible ecotourism in La Fortuna. Each of its activities interacts harmoniously with the environment, and the park's business operations adhere to strict sustainability policies.

The park offers activities individually or as part of the **Full Day Combo** (8am and 10:30am daily, 5.5 hours, $129 adults, $90 children 7-12).

You can choose between two **zip-line tours:** the 12-cable **Big AMA Canopy Tour** (8am, 10:30am, and 1:30pm daily, 3.5 hours, $70 adults, $53 children 7-12) and the 7-cable **AMA Xtreme Canopy Tour** (8am, 10:30am, 1:30pm, and 3pm daily, 2.5 hours, $52 adults, $41 children 7-12).

The park also offers the chance to visit the nearby Catarata Río Fortuna via a **guided horseback tour** (8am, 10:30am, and 1:30pm daily, 3 hours, $70 adults, $53 children 7-12, min. age 7); the tour departs from the adventure park.

To try your hand at canyoneering, sign up for the **rappel tour** (8am, 10:30am, and 1:30pm daily, 3 hours, $75 adults, $56 children, min. age 12). There's just a single rappel descent, but it's the highest around at 80 meters. If you combine the tour with some of the park's other activities, the lone rappel run is far more affordable.

The park also offers **guided walking tours** of its private reserve (7am-5pm daily, 2.5 hours, $53 adults, $38 children 4-12).

MALEKU INDIGENOUS CULTURAL RESCUE CENTER

Inside the Arenal Mundo Aventura Ecological Park, the **Maleku Indigenous Cultural Rescue Center** invites visitors to learn about the culture of the indigenous Maleku people. The guided **Maleku Indian Village Tour** (7am-5pm daily, 2 hours, $36 adults, $20 children 4-12) offers a peek into Maleku life.

You'll witness ceremonial rituals performed in cultural dress, learn about the use of food and medicinal plants, and listen to Maleku people speak Jaíca (sometimes spelled Jaíka or Ihaíca)—their traditional language. My favorite part of the experience is when tribe members explain how birds and other wildlife symbolize virtues such as love, power, and fidelity. The symbols are common throughout Maleku artwork, most notably in fruit, seed, and wood carvings. You can purchase many of these works at the end of the tour; each piece reads as a story and is believed to impart the gifts it symbolizes onto its beholder.

If you don't have time to participate in the full village tour, you can catch a shorter version of it by booking one of the park's nature or adventure tours. A brief stop at the village and a quick cultural demonstration is included with each zip-lining, rappelling, horseback riding, and walking tour.

Arenal Natura Ecological Park

Since its creation in 2010, I have enjoyed watching the **Arenal Natura Ecological Park** (200 m east of Road 142 just beyond the Volcano Lodge & Springs, tel. 506/2479-1616, www.arenalnatura.com, 8am-5:30pm daily, last entry 4pm, tour costs vary) grow into the multifaceted attraction it has become, complete with a butterfly garden, a frog garden, a snake garden, a crocodile and caiman lagoon, a turtle pond, and nature trails sprinkled with heliconias and orchids. The park is a true labor of love.

To get the most bang for your buck, take the **premium exhibit tour** (every hour on the hour 8am-4pm, 2 hours, $36 adults, $22 children 5-12), which walks you through all of the park's attractions. The trained eye of your naturalist guide can find even the tiniest creatures hidden in the park's forest and terrariums. If you're fearful and squeamish around snakes, prepare to have a change of heart; the guides speak about serpents with such admiration and compassion that you'll gain a new respect for the slithering kind. It's also possible to see the exhibits on your own, without

La Fortuna

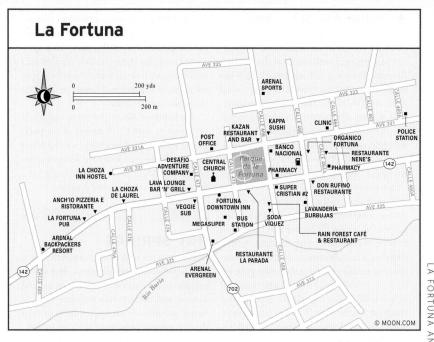

a guide, by paying the **unguided access fee** ($21 adults, $13 children).

If you're snap happy, sign up for the **photography tour** (6am-6pm, 3 hours, $119 adults, $66 children 5-12), a one-of-a-kind experience designed for both amateur and professional photographers. During this walking tour, guides help you get up close and personal with bird, insect, amphibian, and snake species commonly spotted around the park so you can photograph them. Camera and lighting equipment are not provided, so be sure to bring your own.

Club Río Outdoor Center

The upscale, mountainside Springs Resort & Spa shares part of its lower property with the **Club Río Outdoor Center** (4 km north of Road 142 just beyond the Arenal

Paraiso Resort, tel. 506/2401-3313, www.thespringscostarica.com, 9am-4:30pm daily by tour only), one of La Fortuna's newest adventure parks. You access Club Río by way of a complimentary and scenic 10-minute shuttle ride from the resort's main building to a reception area along the Río Arenal.

Although pricey, the center's **Multi-Adventure Package** ($119 adults, $99 children 3-12) offers incredible value. It includes two on-site adventure tours (choose from river tubing, river kayaking, horseback riding, rock climbing, and an early morning nature walk), lunch at the **Rancho Club Río Restaurant & Bar** (11am-4pm daily), and access to trails, hot springs, and the resort's upper property, including the Cascadas Calientes and Los Perdidos Hot Springs. To maximize your visit, save soaks in the hot springs at the upper property until after the outdoor center closes; those hot springs stay open until 10pm. If your itinerary is tight, you can fit all of Club Río's activities into a half-day visit; otherwise you can easily spend a full day at the resort.

1: an endangered spider monkey at Proyecto Asis Wildlife Refuge Center 2: white-water rafting on the Río Pacuare 3: rope swing at El Salto swimming hole in La Fortuna 4: Místico Arenal Hanging Bridges Park

★ **Místico Arenal Hanging Bridges Park**

Amid the tourist boom that sounds throughout La Fortuna, I seek respite at the **Místico Arenal Hanging Bridges Park** (2.5 km north of Road 142 just beyond the Lago Arenal Dam, tel. 506/2479-8282, www.misticopark. com, 6:30am-4:30pm daily, advance reservations required, general admission $26 adults, $16 children 11-18). It's one of the area's busiest attractions, yet it remains a peaceful place where you can hear a symphony of birdsongs, cicada buzzes, and monkey howls.

Visitors flock to the park to traverse its trail system comprising 16 bridges, 6 of which are suspended among the treetops and allow you to hover in midair over deep rainforest valleys. The park is home to insects, birds, and the occasional monkey or sloth; the best way to experience it is alongside a guide who is trained to spot wildlife. You can take the park's guided **Natural History Walk** (8am, 9am, 10am, noon, 1pm, and 2pm, 2.5 hours, $38 adults, $12 children 6-10). However, most tour operators in La Fortuna offer the same guided walk through the park, often coupling the experience with other area activities. Exploring without a guide is allowed, but all visits require advance reservations (via the park's website or by telephone, or through a third-party tour operator), as strict capacity limits are enforced. The park prohibits sandals and hiking shoes that expose sections of skin.

The park's **Sendero Principal** (Main Trail) is an oval circuit of over three kilometers, consisting of uphill and downhill sections. By completing the full loop, you'll cross all of the bridges, pass through a tunnel, and be able to access the **Catarata Morpho Azul**. The steep steps that lead down to the waterfall are easy to miss; look for them to your right after the Keel-Billed Toucan Bridge but before the Ant Hill Bridge. When hiked nonstop, the course takes roughly 90 minutes to complete.

The optional **Sendero de Observación de Aves** (Bird-Watching Trail) connects the north and south sides of park. Visitors hike it as a secondary trail in addition to the Sendero Principal, or as a shortcut that reduces the full circuit by 30 minutes and skips the toughest climb in the park. This aptly named trail cuts through a less-traveled area of the park with dense forest; I regularly spot members of the motmot family perched on trees that line the route.

The **Sendero Accesible** (Accessible Trail) explores the first 1,500 meters of the park; guests with limited mobility can check out this 30-minute mini loop that features seven bridges (including one suspension bridge) and only slight trail inclines and declines.

TOP EXPERIENCE

HOT SPRINGS

La Fortuna's hot springs offer one of the country's top experiences for visitors. Hot spring complexes are everywhere you look around Arenal, and competition between them is fierce. All provide an opportunity to reap the therapeutic benefits of soaking in thermal water. The properties vary in size, design, luxury, day-pass duration and price, child-friendliness, and pool variety.

Most complexes have a restaurant on-site and do not allow guests to enter with food or drinks purchased elsewhere. Many offer the option to include lunch or dinner in the cost of their visitors pass. The restaurants offer everything from full table service to a buffet. The food is typically Costa Rican and international cuisine. Tabacón Hot Springs and the Springs Resort and Los Perdidos Hot Springs provide the finest dining experiences. Many complexes also have on-site accommodations.

Baldi Hot Springs Hotel Resort and Spa

The **Baldi Hot Springs Hotel Resort and Spa** (Road 142, 4.5 km west of the central church, tel. 506/2479-2190, www. baldihotsprings.cr, 9am-10pm daily, visitors pass $36 adults, $18 children 6-10) is the most popular middle-of-the-road option. It is also one of the area's largest properties, with 25 thermal-water pools that rarely feel full. Despite the grandeur of the entrance, the grounds don't feel elegant, but the spa, swim-up bar, and steam room up the level of sophistication. If you have young children, don't miss the water activity park at the back of the property. There are two restaurants on-site. A buffet restaurant serves traditional Costa Rican food and an Italian restaurant provides à la carte options. Baldi also has a standard hotel on-site, offering basic rooms ($261 s/d) with balconies and terraces.

EcoTermales Fortuna

If you prefer nature over novelty, consider the **EcoTermales Fortuna** (Road 142, 4.5 km west of the central church, tel. 506/2479-8787, www.ecotermalesfortuna.cr, half-day sessions 10am-4pm or 5pm-10pm daily, visitors pass $40 adults, $26 children 5-11). Natural stone and tropical foliage border the property's five waterfall-fed hot springs and an additional non-thermal-water pool. Sip a cocktail poolside or while relaxing on a chaise lounge under swaying palms. Visit between May and November when access to this small, sought-after property is easier. Advance reservations are required due to the 150-person capacity for each session. Two on-site restaurants serve Costa Rican fare; one is a buffet.

Tabacón

Tabacón (Road 142, 11 km west of the central church, tel. 506/2479-2000, www.tabacon. com, half-day sessions 10am-2pm or 6pm-10pm daily, visitors pass $70 adults, $28 children 6-11) is renowned for the thermal-water river that flows throughout the property and the beautiful gardens that create a relaxing, romantic atmosphere. Step into the riverbed or one of five pools for a rejuvenating soak. Although newer luxury developments around Arenal give Tabacón a run for its money, this classic attraction remains a hit among couples and honeymooners. The visitors pass here includes lunch or dinner. Two open-air restaurants adjacent to gardens and the hot springs operate as buffets and provide à la carte options. Advance reservations are required. The on-site accommodations ($345 s/d) are liked for the classy rooms and fancy bathrooms.

★ The Springs Resort & Spa

I love the combination of luxury and lush surroundings at **The Springs Resort & Spa** (4 km north of Road 142 just beyond the Arenal Paraiso Resort, tel. 506/2401-3313, www. thespringscostarica.com, Cascadas Calientes 8am-10pm daily, Los Perdidos Hot Springs 10am-10pm daily, visitors pass $68 pp 4 years and older). The five-story open-air resort offers a panoramic view of Volcán Arenal from every level, multitiered hot springs with waterfalls and swim-up bars, and a waterslide that is as much fun for adults as it is for kids.

This is the largest hot springs attraction in the region. On the property, you'll find 12 pools, known as the **Cascadas Calientes**, near the resort's main building, and seven secluded lagoons, referred to as **Los Perdidos**, a brief walk away down a paved path. Visit during the day when you can admire the beauty of the resort's architecture and heliconia gardens or during the evening when the mood is idyllic and romantic. Advance reservations are required during peak periods (Christmas, New Year's, and Easter). At the four open-air restaurants in the resort's main building, enjoy Costa Rican and international food and drinks, along with fabulous service. Each one is sophisticated but comfortable, and overlooks the rainforest canopy. The on-site accommodations perfectly fuse rustic decor with luxury.

The resort's on-site adventure park, the **Club Río Outdoor Center** (4 km north of Road 142 just beyond the Arenal Paraiso Resort, tel. 506/2401-3313, www. thespringscostarica.com, 9am-4:30pm daily by tour only) has additional hot springs and a restaurant.

Paradise Hot Springs Thermal Water Resort

Built in 2011, one of the newest kids on the block is the **Paradise Hot Springs Thermal Water Resort** (Road 142, 5 km west of the central church, tel. 506/2479-1380, www. paradisehotspringscr.com, 11am-9pm daily, visitors pass $28 adults, $16 children 3-11). It is my go-to spot when I want to avoid crowds and overt lavishness while still pampering myself in a wallet-friendly way. Head to the thermal-water Jacuzzi first for a hydromassage, then gravitate toward the Palma Real pool with its permanent in-water lounge beds—perfect for a lazy snooze in the springs. The on-site restaurant, which serves mostly Costa Rican cuisine, provides a buffet and à la carte options. A separate *bocas* (Costa Rica's take on Spanish tapas) menu provides snacks inspired by American cuisine. The hotel ($190 s/d) here is standard, but it impresses with its rich, dark-wood furniture.

Los Lagos Hotel, Spa & Resort

The budget-friendly **Los Lagos Hotel, Spa & Resort** (Road 142, 5.5 km west of the central church, tel. 506/2479-1000, www. hotelloslagos.com, 9am-10pm daily, visitors pass $16 adults, $8 children 6-9) is gaining popularity, although much of its appeal has nothing to do with the thermal-water pools. The visitors pass here buys you access to the on-site butterfly garden, frog farm, and crocodile farm, so arrive prepared for nature exploration in addition to relaxation. This is one of the least expensive hot spring properties in La Fortuna; it also has some of the cheapest hotel rates ($166 s/d) of the hot springs complexes. An on-site restaurant offers Costa Rican food and a selection of dishes from international cuisines.

Titokú Hot Springs

The **Titokú Hot Springs** (Road 142, 4.5 km west of the central church, tel. 506/2479-7156, www.hotelarenalkioro.com, partial-day sessions 10am-1pm, 1pm-3pm, 3pm-5pm, or 5pm-8pm daily, visitors pass $32 adults, $16 children 4-11) is one of La Fortuna's hidden gems. This attraction is a free amenity enjoyed by guests of the nearby Arenal Kioro Suites & Spa, but few know that it's open to the public.

The hot springs are rarely full, which means you'll likely have some of the tiny property's eight sequential thermal-water pools to yourself. Advance reservations are required. There is no restaurant on-site, but visitors are welcome to dine at the restaurant at the Arenal Kioro Suites & Spa.

Termales Los Laureles

If you want to soak with locals, check out the **Termales Los Laureles** (Road 142, 5.5 km west of the central church, tel. 506/2479-1431, www.termalesloslaureles.com, 9am-9pm daily, visitors pass $12 adults, $5 children 3-10). On weekends, Arenal-area residents flock to its seven thermal-water pools, two cold-water pools, waterslides, and sport facilities for family get-togethers. The complex also houses 130 small, electricity-equipped open-air dining shelters, which are free for guests to use and perfect for large groups. There is no restaurant on-site. Outside food and drinks are permitted on the premises, so pack a picnic lunch or dinner to make the most of your visit.

Kalambu Hot Springs Water Park

In a league of its own is the **Kalambu Hot Springs Water Park** (Road 142, 4.5 km west of the central church, tel. 506/2479-0170, www.kalambu.com, 9am-8pm Mon.-Thurs., 9am-9pm Fri.-Sun., visitors pass $20 adults, $10 children 4-12). Play—not relaxation—is the attraction here. Multiple waterslides and an interactive water game zone overshadow the thermal-water pool. The four-story Mamut slide is the park's most unique feature and the region's only raft-run waterslide; try it in a tandem tube with a partner or as a group of up to four people in a raft. An on-site restaurant serves Costa Rican dishes, hamburgers, and pizzas.

RECREATION
Local Guides and Tours
Desafío Adventure Company (Calle 472 behind the central church, tel. 506/2479-0020,

www.desafiocostarica.com, 6am-10pm daily) is one of La Fortuna's most reputable adventure outfitters. When it comes to fun and exciting—but safe!—escapades with thoroughly trained guides, this operation cannot be beat. They are especially good at crafting tours that explore less well-trodden areas, in addition to ones that allow for participation in unique cultural experiences.

Desafio also offers a service called **Adventure Connections.** These tours depart from La Fortuna and provide onward transportation to a variety of destinations, rather than depositing you back in La Fortuna at the end of the day. Canyoning adventures ($133 pp) and white-water rafting trips on **Río Sarapiquí** and **Río Balsa** ($92-102 pp) allow for drop-offs in San José. White-water rafting and safari float excursions on **Río Tenorio** ($133-154 pp) are most often used to travel to Sámara and areas along the Guanacaste coast. Horseback riding tours and mountain biking tours ($88-92 pp) that explore scenic countryside trails around Lago Arenal are unique ways to get to Monteverde. A significant number of Desafio's tours are Adventure Connections; see the website for a complete list. Adventure Connections tour pricing varies according to activity type, route, and number of participants. In all cases, the company has factored the fee for the transportation service into the cost of the tour.

Canoa Aventura (Road 142, 1.5 km west of the central church, tel. 506/2479-8200, www.canoa-aventura.com, 6:30am-10pm daily) employs some of the most keen-eyed and knowledgeable naturalist guides with whom I've toured Costa Rica, many of them women. Within a male-dominated industry, the company is changing the norm. They are my go-to nature tour operator in La Fortuna, especially for safari float tours, boat tours, and canoe excursions, where they shine in wildlife-spotting and species identification.

In addition to running standalone tours, Desafio and Canoa offer **combination tours** that group multiple activities into half- or full-day experiences. Both operators run one of the area's most popular combination tours, known as the **Arenal Combo Tour** (sometimes called the **Arenal Highlights Tour**), which bundles visits to Místico Arenal Hanging Bridges Park, Catarata Río Fortuna, Volcán Arenal, and The Springs Resort & Spa (or another hot springs property).

Exploradores Outdoors (tel. 506/2222-6262, www.exploradoresoutdoors.com) is an adventure tour operator known for its long-standing river operations, spotless safety record, and humorous tour guides. They have offices in San José and Puerto Viejo de Talamanca, rather than La Fortuna, but they are still one of the most sought-after operators for their popular white-water rafting excursions on **Río Pacuare** ($99 pp). These trips are a **city-to-city transportation-inclusive tour,** meaning the price includes onward transportation to San José, Alajuela, Puerto Viejo de Talamanca, Cahuita, or Puerto Viejo de Sarapiquí; return transportation to La Fortuna is possible, too. The outfitter also runs rafting trips on **Río Reventazón** ($99 pp), multiday nature expeditions to the Tortuguero canals on the Caribbean coast ($154-224 pp), and combination white-water rafting and Tortuguero packages ($299-464 pp). Each includes transportation between La Fortuna and San José, Alajuela, Puerto Viejo de Talamanca, Cahuita, or Puerto Viejo de Sarapiquí.

TOP EXPERIENCE

Zip-Lining

Zip-line tours are very common in the Arenal region. When you sift through the mix, stick to the classics—tours offered by stand-alone ecoadventure parks, not add-on hotel features.

One of my favorite zip-line tours is the **Big AMA Canopy Tour** (8am, 10:30am, and 1:30pm daily, 3.5 hours, $70 adults, $53 children 7-12, min. age 7) provided by the **Arenal Mundo Aventura Ecological Park** (Road 702, 1.5 km south of the central church, tel. 506/2479-9762, www.arenalmundoaventura.com, 7am-5pm daily by guided tour only). The

12-cable experience traverses the forest and stuns with views of Volcán Arenal and the Catarata Piño Blanco. I love catching a bird's-eye view of the Catarata Río Fortuna and joshing with the witty tour guides. If your time is short, opt for the seven-cable **AMA Xtreme Canopy Tour** (8am, 10:30am, 1:30pm, and 3pm daily, 2.5 hours, $52 adults, $41 children 7-12, min. age 7). This condensed version of the Big AMA Canopy Tour still includes access to the volcano and waterfall viewpoints.

The 13-cable **canopy tour with Tarzan swing** (8am, 10:30am, and 1:30pm daily, 2 hours, $75 pp, min. age 2), run by the **Ecoglide Arenal Park** (Road 142, 3.5 km west of the central church, tel. 506/2479-7120, www.arenalecoglide.com, 7am-5pm daily), is a great choice for families with young children because it's one of the few in the area that welcome participation by young adventurers. If you want to try zip-lining in the dark, the tour can run at night (5:30pm daily, 2 hours, $100 pp, min. age 2).

White-Water Rafting

La Fortuna is a leading locale for white-water rafting tours. Trips down five different rivers scattered around the country leave from and return to La Fortuna daily. A number require a multi-hour drive from town.

Tours down the country's most notorious Class III and IV river, **Río Pacuare** (a two-hour drive from La Fortuna), are especially popular. **Exploradores Outdoors** (tel. 506/2222-6262, www.exploradoresoutdoors.com) runs the fantastic full-day **Pacuare River Rafting Tour** (5:30am daily, 12 hours, $99 pp, min. age 12), which includes breakfast, lunch, and a thrilling 30-kilometer ride over 38 rapids in the heart of the Costa Rican jungle.

As a Class II and III river, **Río Reventazón** (a two-hour drive from La Fortuna) is the smarter choice if you have young children or are in search of a tamer rafting experience. Exploradores Outdoors also runs the **Reventazón River Rafting Tour** (5:30am daily, 12 hours, $99 pp, min. age 6) that covers 10 kilometers of the river and maneuvers nine of its rapids.

Closer to La Fortuna are the Class III and IV **Río Sarapiquí** (a 90-minute drive from La Fortuna) and the Class II and III **Río Balsa** (a 40-minute drive from La Fortuna). The supreme rafting outfitter on these rivers is **Desafío Adventure Company** (Calle 472 behind the central church, tel. 506/2479-0020, www.desafiocostarica.com, 6am-10pm daily). Their **Sarapiquí River Extreme Rafting Tour** (8:30am daily, 8 hours, $95 pp, min. age 13) is the most common river trip booked from La Fortuna. Their **Balsa River Rafting Tour** (9am daily, 5 hours, $75 pp, min. age 10) is best done as part of a **combination tour** ($123-189 pp), where you select a second activity, such as canyoneering, mountain biking, zip-lining, horseback riding, or a hot springs visit, to create a full-day excursion.

Safari Float Tours

On the scenic **Río Peñas Blancas** (a 30-minute drive from La Fortuna), you can float down a slow-moving river where howler monkeys play in trees overhead and crocodiles sometimes sunbathe on its banks. The outfitter I go with most often is **Canoa Aventura** (Road 142, 1.5 km west of the central church, tel. 506/2479-8200, www.canoa-aventura.com, 6:30am-10pm daily). They offer **safari float tours** (7:30am and 2pm daily, 4 hours) where you travel by **kayak** ($59 pp, min. age 5), by **canoe** ($69 pp, min. age 5), or by **raft** ($59 adults, $30 children 3-11, min. age 3). Each option includes round-trip transportation between the river and La Fortuna hotels, and a knowledgeable tour guide who will steer your raft or float alongside your kayak or canoe while detailing flora and fauna encountered along the way. These laid-back float experiences are a refreshing contrast to the many high-octane activities in La Fortuna.

Canoeing, Kayaking, and Stand-Up Paddling

One of the best canoeing or kayaking experiences in this region is taking a **safari float** tour (7:30am and 2pm daily, 4 hours, $59 kayak, $69 canoe) on **Río Peñas Blancas** with **Canoa Aventura** (Road 142, 1.5 km west of the central church, tel. 506/2479-8200, www.canoa-aventura.com, 6:30am-10pm daily).

You can tour the large, sometimes choppy, open-water **Lago Arenal** by **kayak** (8am and 1pm daily, 2.5 hours, $65 pp, min. age 8) or by **stand-up paddleboard** (8am and 1:30pm daily, 2.5 hours, $65 pp, min. age 8). Both guided experiences, coordinated by **Desafío Adventure Company** (Calle 472 behind the central church, tel. 506/2479-0020, www.desafiocostarica.com, 6am-10pm daily), include round-trip transportation between La Fortuna hotels and the lake, as well as an opportunity to paddle around the lake and capture an unobstructed view of Volcán Arenal. If you're part of a group of 10 or more people, sign up for Desafío's **stand-up paddling Team Building Experience** (7:30am and 1:30pm daily, 5 hours, $103 pp, min. age 8). It uses games, races, and challenges on the lake to foster communication, leadership, and teamwork among participants.

Waterfall Jumping Tours

Are you intrepid and a bit wild? If so, sign up for waterfall jumping through **Desafío Adventure Company** (Calle 472 behind the central church, tel. 506/2479-0020, www.desafiocostarica.com, 6am-10pm daily); it's the latest craze to hit La Fortuna. During the **Gravity Falls Waterfall Jumping Tour** (6:30am daily, 6 hours, $125 pp, min. age 16), professional tour guides teach you how to safely launch yourself off a series of secluded waterfalls and cliffs into refreshing pools tucked away in the forest. If you really want to work up a sweat, challenge yourself to the **Extreme Gravity Falls Waterfall Jumping Tour** (6:30am daily, 10 hours, $189 pp, min. age 16). It throws mountain biking and white-water rafting into the mix to provide the ultimate jungle workout! Both experiences include a hearty homemade lunch.

Canyoneering

Some of the country's best canyon descents lurk in the crevices and gullies that surround La Fortuna. The **Canyoning Tour** (7am and noon daily, 4 hours, $101 pp, min. age 5) provided by **Pure Trek** (across from the Arenal Natura Ecological Park, tel. 506/2479-1313, www.puretrek.com, 7am-5pm daily) feels like a jungle obstacle course. There are four rappel descents (three of which parallel waterfalls), a brief rock ascent, and a rappel and zip-line cable combo coined the "Monkey Drop." It's loads of fun to complete, especially for kids. Tour guides prioritize safety throughout.

The **Canyoning in the Lost Canyon Tour** (7:30am, 10am, and 1pm daily, 4 hours, $99 pp, min. age 13) is for adults looking to be challenged. This activity is one of the best offered by canyoning pioneers **Desafío Adventure Company** (Calle 472 behind the central church, tel. 506/2479-0020, www.desafiocostarica.com, 6am-10pm daily). After being shuttled from your La Fortuna hotel to the canyon in a 4x4 nicknamed the Jungle Limo, you'll rappel down waterfalls, pause for a photo op in a canyon amid a river's rush, and throw caution to the wind during a secure and exhilarating freefall. The tour ends with a tough 15-minute uphill hike and a well-deserved buffet meal of home-style eats.

To merely sample canyoneering, try the **abseiling tour** (8am, 10:30am, and 1:30pm daily, 3 hours, $75 adults, $56 children, min. age 12) at the **Arenal Mundo Aventura Ecological Park** (Road 702, 1.5 km south of the central church, tel. 506/2479-9762, www.arenalmundoaventura.com). There is only one rappel descent, but it is the highest around at 80 meters. Your heart will race at the top of the line as you search for the forest floor below, but after completing the thrilling descent alongside the powerful Catarata Piño Blanco, you'll feel fearless. If you combine the tour with some of the park's other activities, the lone rappel run is far more affordable.

Bird-Watching

Nearly every tour operator in town offers

guided birding excursions. I like the **bird-watching tour** (5:30am daily, 2-4 hours, $53 adults, $38 children 4-12) at the **Arenal Mundo Aventura Ecological Park** (Road 702, 1.5 km south of the central church, tel. 506/2479-9762, www.arenalmundoaventura. com), as well as the **bird-watching tour** (6am daily, 3 hours, $50 adults, $33 children 5-12) provided by the **Arenal Natura Ecological Park** (200 m east of Road 142 just beyond the Volcano Lodge & Springs, tel. 506/2479-1616, www.arenalnatura.com). Since both parks tour their own private land, you're bound to see and hear more birds at each than if you opted to explore a public area or a more popular hiking trail in the region. Both of these tours begin before the parks open to the public, and advance reservations are required. Tour guides provide spotting equipment, but you're welcome to bring your own.

You can cross bird-watching and hiking hanging bridges off your to-do list with the specialized **Birding Guided Tour** (6am daily, 2.5 hours, $49 adults, $23 children 6-10) at the **Místico Arenal Hanging Bridges Park** (2.5 km north of Road 142 just beyond the Lago Arenal Dam, tel. 506/2479-8282, www.misticopark.com, 6:30am-4:30pm daily). Thanks to the early start, you'll see and hear the variety of songbirds that awaken the park, and you'll gain access to the property's trails and bridges before the majority of visitors. This tour requires advance reservations; book via the park's website or by telephone. The park supplies all equipment needed for bird observation free of charge.

Mountain Biking

One of the country's leading bike outfitters is based in La Fortuna. **Bike Arenal** (corner of Road 142 and Avenida 319, tel. 506/2479-9020, www.bikearenal.com, 8am-5pm Mon.-Sat.) wows with a number of well-thought-out half- and full-day **guided bike treks** ($45-110) that vary in difficulty, distance, and duration. Most cycle past parts of the region that remain untouched by tourism, including small villages, cattle farms, and vegetable plantations that you're unlikely to see during participation in other La Fortuna activities.

If you think you can handle it, give the guided **Madness Hill to Zarcero Road Cycling Tour** (8am daily, 7 hours, $110 pp) a whirl. The paved-highway ride is 88 kilometers long, has an elevation gain of 2,800 meters, and weaves through the mountains and clouds around San Ramón (the namesake Madness Hill). Prior biking experience is an asset but is not required. A safety vehicle is available at all times in case you cannot finish the climb. Bike Arenal also offers multiday bike tours that travel through various destinations around Costa Rica.

If you would rather bike on your own, head to the private reserve **Arenal 1968** (1.5 km south of Road 142, 500 m north of the Parque Nacional Volcán Arenal's main ranger station, tel. 506/2462-1212, www.arenal1968. com, 8am-6pm daily, $15 pp). The reserve has 16 kilometers of private forest and river trails for you to maneuver at your own pace. You can rent a bike through **Bike Arenal** (corner of Road 142 and Avenida 319, tel. 506/2479-9020, www.bikearenal.com, 8am-5pm Mon.-Sat.). The outfitter includes a helmet, gloves, spare kit bag, pump, and lock with each bike ($25-65 per day).

Night Tours

A variety of nocturnal specimens—including amphibians, reptiles, insects, and night-blooming flowers—enliven La Fortuna after dark. Try your luck at seeing them in the wild via the guided **Místico Night Walk** (6pm daily, 2.5 hours, $49 adults, $23 children, min. age 10). Held at the **Místico Arenal Hanging Bridges Park** (2.5 km north of Road 142 just beyond the Lago Arenal Dam, tel. 506/2479-8282, www.misticopark.com), the tour explores the same three-kilometer trail system and hanging bridges that day visitors see, albeit alongside a tour guide who will explain how the rainforest changes at night. Advance reservations are required.

For guaranteed sightings, head to the **Arenal Natura Ecological Park** (200 m east of Road 142 just beyond the Volcano Lodge & Springs, tel. 506/2479-1616, www. arenalnatura.com) and take their **night walk** (6pm daily, 2 hours, $45 adults, $26 children 5-12). The park's terrariums present a unique opportunity to spy on deadly frog and snake species—creatures awake and active after dark—secured behind glass enclosures. A knowledgeable tour guide identifies unique species and their behaviors as you stroll around the park from one enclosure to the next. Advance reservations are required.

If you have a specific interest in seeing frogs in the open forest, don't miss the guided **Frog Watching Night Walk** (5:45pm daily, 2 hours, $40 adults, $20 children 5-11) conducted at the **Arenal Oasis Eco Lodge & Wildlife Refuge** (2 km west of the central church, 1 km south on Calle 506, tel. 506/2479-9526, www.arenaloasis.com). The property has carefully crafted ponds and trails that over 28 frog species call home. Led by members of the Costa Rican family that owns the refuge, the evening nature walk progresses at a leisurely pace and is perfect for kids, especially those hoping to see the lime-green red-eyed tree frog, which is regularly spotted.

Swimming Holes

On hot and humid days, cool off where the locals do, at the swimming hole and rope swing known as **El Salto** (Road 702, 1.5 km south of the central church, under the east side of the bridge, free). Most congregate at the spot to sunbathe on boulders and take turns swinging into Río Fortuna. If you find the area too noisy, follow the trail behind the rope swing that descends into the forest; after five minutes, you'll arrive at a more private space near a shallow stretch of the river perfect for wading.

Another popular hangout is **Río Chollin** (Road 142, 11 km west of the central church, under the bridge, free), a swimming spot that taps into the same river system that feeds the elite **Tabacón Hot Springs** (tel. 506/2479-2000, www.tabacon.com). The budget-minded love this place, but it lacks the safety and cleanliness that La Fortuna's formal hot spring properties provide. If you must go and you're a backpacker, stay at **La Choza Inn Hostel** (Avenida 331, 300 m west of the post office, tel. 506/2479-9091, www.lachozainnhostel.com, dorm $8 pp, private $36 s/d); it shuttles hostel guests to the river for free.

ENTERTAINMENT AND EVENTS
Nightlife

The most notable and happening club in the area is the **Volcán Look Disco Club** (Road 142, 4.5 km west of the central church, tel. 506/8836-1166, 8pm-3am Wed.-Sat., cover $9 and up). It features theme nights, various types of music, and DJs from all over the country. From time to time it hosts special events (see their Facebook page for listings), especially on holidays.

To learn how to cook and dance like a Costa Rican, sign up for the **Cooking and Salsa Dance Lesson Combo** (5pm daily, 3.5 hours, $64 pp, min. age 6). First, you'll cook like a Costa Rican as you prepare a traditional dinner alongside a local chef. Then, after enjoying your culinary efforts, you'll learn how to dance merengue, cumbia, and salsa, step by step. Coordinated through **Desafio Adventure Company** (tel. 506/2479-0020, www.desafiocostarica. com), the lesson takes place at **Hunters and Gatherers** (Road 702 just north of El Salto, www.huntersandgathererscostarica.com), Desafio's private buffet restaurant. Lone dancers are welcome.

You can chill at a number of laid-back pubs. The small **La Fortuna Pub** (Road 142, 350 m west of the central church, tel. 506/2479-1511, noon-midnight Mon.-Wed., noon-1am Thurs.-Sun.) is my favorite, thanks to its extensive craft beer collection, live music, and plenty of board games including Jenga Giant. Don't forget to eternalize your visit by writing your moniker or a philosophical point to ponder on the wall beside hundreds of other "wuz here" declarations.

The open-air **Kazan Restaurant and Bar**

(on the corner of Calle 468 and Avenida 331, tel. 506/2479-7561, 11am-midnight daily) offers the best location for people-watching at the park across the street. Grab a beer or a cocktail and a table out front on the patio.

On the main drag, the **Lava Lounge Bar 'n' Grill** (Road 142, 25 m west of the central church, tel. 506/2479-7365, www. lavaloungecostarica.com, 7am-10pm daily) glows in the evening with lanterns and colorful lights. Its reggae-inspired vibe and picnic table seating make it the town's coolest hangout joint for enjoying tropical cocktails, wine, and artisanal beer.

SHOPPING

Souvenir shops, especially in La Fortuna's downtown core, are abundant. Shop around and compare costs. Many of the same items are for sale at a variety of stores, at different prices.

For unique wood pieces, I head to two galleries on the outskirts of town, where woodworkers craft on-site. The **Original Grand Gallery** (Road 142, 2 km west of the central church, tel. 506/2479-8037, http://original-grand-gallery.negocio.site, 8am-8pm daily) will catch your eye with its giant polished-wood sculptures at the entrance. Cutting boards, bowls, figurines, and other items fill tables inside, and you can see works in progress at the back of the shop. The **Wood & Art Gallery** (1.5 km south of the central church, 2 km west on Road 301, tel. 506/2479-7638, 9am-5pm daily) is smaller in size but offers rare pieces carved out of fallen wood and branch remnants. I have yet to find artwork like it anywhere else in Costa Rica.

If you forget to pack any gear (such as rain jackets, hiking shoes, and backpacks), visit the outdoor supplies store **Arenal Sports** (Calle 468, 150 m north of the central park, tel. 506/2479-9760, www.arenalsports.com, 8am-8pm daily).

FOOD
Food and Farm Tours
The **North Fields Café** (Calle 506, 700 m south of Super Cristian #4, tel. 506/2479-7195, www.northfieldscafe.com) will lure you into their small establishment with the rich aroma of roasted coffee beans. During a guided, interactive **coffee tour** (8am, 10am, noon, 2pm, and 4pm daily, 2 hours, $40 adults, $20 children 8-17), you'll take an easy walk around the café's property to see coffee plants, try your hand at picking and grinding coffee beans, and drink a cup of the café's finest brew. The tour covers various stages of coffee production, and taste-testing cacao and sugarcane are also part of the experience.

The best chocolate-centered activity in La Fortuna is the **Rainforest Chocolate Tour** (Road 301, 1 km west of Road 702, tel. 506/2479-0090, http://rainforestchocolatetour.com, 8am, 10am, 1pm, and 3pm daily, 1.5 hours, $26 adults, $18 children 6-14). This educational class, taught at a cacao farm, covers the historical and modern-day processing of cacao in Costa Rica. Knowledgeable, passionate tour guides make for a fun experience. Pick up a bar (or 10) at the on-site shop to take home. I recommend the organic 100 percent cacao bar. It is bitter, but as you'll learn during the tour, it's the best for you.

Costa Rica Cooking (Road 301, 300 m east of Catarata Río Fortuna, tel. 506/2479-1569, www.costaricacooking.com) brings the outside in. Their guided **Farm to Table Tour** (8am and 1pm daily, 2 hours, $75 pp) invites you to explore an organic and sustainable farm, and treats you to a lunch full of homemade goodies. To try your hand at food preparation or to watch an internationally trained chef work his magic in front of you, register for a **cooking class** (2pm daily, 3.5 hours, $125 pp). All-you-can-drink cocktails and a three-course meal are included.

Costa Rican
Restaurante La Parada (Road 142, across from the central park, tel. 506/2479-9119, www.restaurantelaparada.com, 10am-

---

1: Soda Víquez 2: souvenir store in downtown La Fortuna 3: Arenal Springs Resort & Spa

midnight daily, $4-9) is an informal, well-priced diner that is easily accessible on La Fortuna's main street. It serves a mix of traditional Costa Rican dishes alongside American favorites like pizza and hamburgers, and has a display case of baked goods near the cashier. Stock up on *pan dulce* (sweet bread) and other delights as you pass through or roam around town.

To sample a variety of Costa Rican foods, don't miss the small and homey ★ **Soda Víquez** (Calle 468, 60 m south of the central park, tel. 506/2479-8772, 7am-10pm daily, $5-11). The restaurant is a favorite among locals for its flavorful food and fair prices. In addition to ordering entrées from the menu, you can visit the small buffet at the back of the restaurant. The buffet features side dishes like *ensalada rusa* (Russian salad; a combination of beets, potatoes, eggs, and mayonnaise), *yuca frita* (fried yuca or cassava; similar in taste and appearance to thick french fries), and other preparations you may never have tried before. If a number of these catch your eye, skip the menu and ask the waitstaff for a custom plate comprised entirely of side dishes.

For a more elegant dining experience than what is typical in La Fortuna, plan a dinner out on the town at ★ **Restaurante Nene's** (50 m north of the pharmacy on Road 142, tel. 506/2479-9192, www.nenescr.com, 10am-11pm daily, $9-20). The small establishment provides soft lighting, quiet music, and attentive service yet maintains a rustic charm with its wood decor. A broad selection of seafood and meat preparations is offered (filet mignon is hard to come by elsewhere), as are impressive flambéed dishes, but the diverse lineup of red and white wines is the standout here.

If you want a place that includes cultural representations with its cuisine, look no further than **La Choza de Laurel** (Road 142, 250 m west of the central church, tel. 506/2479-7063, http://lachozadelaurel.com, 11am-10pm daily, $12-21). The restaurant is touristy, but for good reason—waitstaff don traditional red, white, and blue dress; iconic oxcarts adorn the property; and you can hear the tropical sound of marimba instruments. Go for lunch or dinner and choose from plenty of salads, seafood platters, and barbecued meats. You're in for a treat if you order a cup of coffee; it will be prepared at your table using an old-fashioned filter. Visit for the experience more than for the food.

International

There is pub grub galore at **Gecko's Waterfall Grill** (200 m before Catarata Río Fortuna, tel. 506/2479-1569, 11am-4:30pm daily, $6-10), including wraps, quesadillas, and tacos. If you're parched or exhausted after hiking the nearby Catarata Río Fortuna, stop by to hydrate yourself with an energizing fruit drink.

For thin-crust and wood-fired pizza, nowhere beats **Anch'io Pizzeria e Ristorante** (Road 142, 350 m west of the central church, tel. 506/2479-7024, noon-10:45pm Wed.-Mon., $9-19). The small, open-air Italian restaurant soothes with soft lighting and a pleasant ambience ideal for a date night, not to mention the decadent desserts including tiramisu.

The best American steakhouse in town is the **Don Rufino Restaurante** (corner of Road 142 and Calle 466, tel. 506/2479-9997, http://donrufino.com, 11:30am-9:45pm daily, $10-42). It is a bit pretentious but deserves its accolades. Choose from above-average meat, seafood, pasta, and sandwich offerings that pay attention to detail. The pottery serving pieces created specifically for the restaurant by artisans in Santa Ana are a nice touch.

Kappa Sushi (Calle 468, 50 m north of the central park, tel. 506/2479-1639, noon-10pm daily, $5-12) is a hole-in-the-wall that produces sushi of the highest caliber. It has only a handful of tables and borders on a fast-food joint (consider taking your food to go), but the menu's extensive vegetarian and vegan offerings are impressive. Best of all is the imaginative presentation: Colorful arrangements of rolls and decorative seeds and sauces fill the sushi boats from bow to stern.

Vegetarian and Vegan

★ **Orgánico Fortuna** (Calle 466, immediately south of Banco San José, tel. 506/2572-2115, 9am-8pm Mon.-Sat., $5-18) is an organic market and restaurant in one. Its style is hippieish, its food is healthy, and the variety of vegetarian, vegan, and gluten-free options (all easily identifiable on the menu) will make you happy. Salads, sandwiches, breads, and smoothies are abundant, as are signs and slogans that preach peace and love. If you have a craving for health food, satisfy it in the eatery's small but cozy space.

For good-for-you eats, try **Veggie Sub** (corner of Road 142 and Road 702, tel. 506/2479-8080, www.veggiesubcr.com, 7am-9:30pm daily, $5-12). Meals are 100 percent vegetarian, with a handful of vegan dishes too. There is plenty to eat besides sub sandwiches: Three different kinds of vegetarian burgers, a list of appetizers, and ample creative breakfast choices will bring you back time and time again.

Cafés and Bakeries

When I want a rich cup of coffee, I head to either the **Rain Forest Café & Restaurant** (Calle 468, 50 m south of the central park, tel. 506/2479-7239, 7:30am-10pm daily) or the **Down to Earth Store & Coffee Bar** (Road 301, 1 km west of Road 702, tel. 506/2479-8568, www.godowntoearth.org, 8am-5:30pm daily). At the Rain Forest Café, treat yourself to a pastry or a piece of cake and wash it down with coffee prepared by skillful baristas. At Down to Earth, you can cool off with an iced coffee, learn about bean varieties, and purchase bagged coffee as a souvenir.

ACCOMMODATIONS

There are over 100 hotels and hostels to choose from in the La Fortuna region, and countless other apartment and vacation home rentals. Many come with an above-average price tag but still manage to sell out months in advance for travel during the high season, from mid-December through April.

The least expensive accommodations, which include hostels, economy hotels, and some standard hotels, are in downtown La Fortuna. Higher-quality hotels and resorts are scattered outside of town, typically west of La Fortuna, close to Volcán Arenal.

Many of the hot springs attractions in the vicinity of La Fortuna also have on-site accommodations. (For more information on these attractions, see the *Hot Springs* section on page 140.)

Downtown La Fortuna
UNDER $50

The **Arenal Backpackers Resort** (Road 142, 500 m west of the central church, tel. 506/2479-7000, www.arenalbackpackers.com, dorm $15 pp, private $110 s/d) is the go-to hostel in the area, probably because it is priced like a budget property but barely resembles one. The hostel attracts a youthful, energetic crowd with its pool, wet bar, lounge chairs, hammocks, and fun games to pass the time, including a slip and slide. It has four dorm rooms that sleep up to eight people, six private rooms (for 1-4 people), and nine camping huts with beds (for 1-3 people, $50).

$50-100

On the main drag across from the central church is the **Fortuna Downtown Inn** (Road 142, tel. 506/4000-2027, www.fortunadowntowninn.com, $81 s/d). I have seen the property change its owners, name, and design a handful of times, but its current setup is the best so far. For a standard hotel, the rooms are more modern than most in the category, likely the result of its repeated renovations. Ask for a room that faces the street and you'll have a perfect view of the central park from your balcony.

Beyond Downtown La Fortuna
$50-100

The best-value hotel in the region is ★ **La Pradera Del Arenal** (Road 142, 2.4 km west of the central church, tel. 506/2479-9597, www.lapraderadelarenal.com, room $85 s/d, bungalow $105 s/d). Opt for one of the 25 quaint and quiet rooms or try one of the eight bungalows; both sleep 1-4 people. Both the rooms and the bungalows offer standard amenities, a volcano view, and a hearty breakfast for a fair price. Well-manicured shrubs and flowers decorate the clean property, which has a pool, a hot tub, and a game room. High-quality stays around Arenal aren't usually this cheap.

$100-150

The **Arenal Bungalows** (Road 142, 9.3 km west of the central church, tel. 506/2479-1629, www.arenalbungalows.com, $112 s, $126 d) offer one of the best views of Volcán Arenal. The property's location allows for views of both the green east side and the gray west side of the volcano, and big windows in each of the 12 bungalows help you enjoy the unobstructed vistas. There is not much to the property beyond the rooms and a communal kitchen near the reception, but that makes it the perfect choice if you want a place that is free of noise and distractions. This is one of the few La Fortuna hotels that will permit six people to stay in a room, which is ideal for budget-conscious groups.

$150-250

If you're looking for an accommodation with a natural feel that doesn't compromise on quality, choose **El Silencio del Campo** (Road 142, 5 km west of the central church, tel. 506/2479-2201, www.hotelsilenciodelcampo. com, $226 s/d). The property has 23 individual wood villas that are finely furnished, with modern bathrooms and chandeliers that bring a touch of class to the otherwise rustic setting. During your stay you can relax on your villa's front porch or in the hotel's hot springs, while appreciating the peacefulness of the hotel and its numerous gardens showcasing heliconias, bromelias, and other colorful native flora.

OVER $250

I'm partial to the ★ **Arenal Springs Resort & Spa** (7 km west of the central church, 1 km east off Road 142 after the Volcano Lodge & Springs, tel. 506/2479-1212, www.

hotelarenalspring.com, $257 s/d) with its aura of sophistication and friendly, accommodating staff. People love this 90-room resort, especially for its adjoining rooms (perfect for families) and two upscale restaurants. The resort's best features include a yoga deck, vegetable garden, spa, and swim-up sushi bar, as well as hot springs and bird-watching gardens (pick up a free bird booklet at reception). There are even rooms designed for asthma and seasonal allergy sufferers.

Arenal Manoa (7 km west of the central church, 1 km east off Road 142 after the Volcano Lodge & Springs, tel. 506/2479-1111, www.arenalmanoa.com, $260 s, $280 d) is a superior-quality hotel that has 102 junior suites with modern furnishings, spacious bathrooms, and terraces with a volcano view. Built on a cattle farm established in the 1960s, the hotel maintains its rural roots by fusing overnight stays with farm visits. Guests are treated to the hotel's dairy farm tour, where you'll see pigs, chickens, and sheep. You can even try milking a cow if you're up for the challenge.

Long to stay at a lavish hotel in La Fortuna? Look no further than the five-story, 54-room **Royal Corin Thermal Water Spa & Resort** (Road 142, 4.8 km west of the central church, tel. 506/2479-2201, www.royalcorin.com, $310 s/d). Luxurious marble and tile work in the reception, contemporary room design, top-of-the-line room amenities, and red leather furniture in the fifth-floor **Lava Bar** all contribute to the resort's chicness. Hot spring pools, multiple Jacuzzis, and a sauna aim to pamper you, but you'll be truly spoiled by the view of Volcán Arenal from your room's balcony and the restful night's sleep you'll have on a most comfortable bed.

The Springs Resort & Spa (8 km west of the central church, 4 km north off Road 142 after the Arenal Paraiso Resort, tel. 506/2401-3313, www.thespringscostarica. com, low season $490 s/d, high season $615 s/d) is an immaculate multitiered structure on the side of a mountain that overlooks the Arenal valley. The region's most luxurious

Hot Springs Hotels

Arenal Springs Resort & Spa

Several of La Fortuna's most popular hot springs attractions have on-site accommodations, so you can stay the night after relaxing in their pools.

· **Baldi Hot Springs Hotel Resort and Spa** (page 140)

· **Tabacón** (page 141)

· **The Springs Resort & Spa** (page 141)

· **Paradise Hot Springs Thermal Water Resort** (page 141)

· **Los Lagos Hotel, Spa & Resort** (page 142)

In addition to its publicly accessible hot springs, La Fortuna is also home to resorts and hotels with hot springs that are open only to overnight guests.

· **Arenal Springs Resort & Spa** (page 152)

· **Royal Corin Thermal Water Spa & Resort** (page 152)

· **El Silencio del Campo** (page 152)

· **Nayara Springs** (page 153)

accommodation provides guests with complete privacy from its remote location 20 minutes from town. The property has 75 rooms and villas; the smallest is perfect for couples, and the largest can accommodate up to 14 people. You can rent the property's most magnificent villa for a whopping $5,000 per night, but even its least expensive room stuns with an extravagant marble bathroom and a private terrace with a volcano view.

★ **Nayara Springs** (7 km west of the central church, 1 km east off Road 142 after the Volcano Lodge & Springs, tel. 506/2479-1600, www.nayarasprings.com, low season $488 s/d, high season $885 s/d) is La Fortuna's sole adults-only accommodation. It comprises 35 individual luxury villas (each sleeps 1-3 people) with exquisite furnishings including a canopy bed, a patio with a daybed, and a private pool. The hotel has seven restaurants, so you need not stray far for food. Drink coffee at **Mi Cafecito,** experience a wine-pairing dinner at the **Nostalgia Wine & Tapas Bar,** and don't miss the boldly decorated **Amor Loco** for fine dining.

INFORMATION AND SERVICES

La Fortuna does not have a hospital, but two clinics, **Centro Medico Sanar La Fortuna** (corner of Avenida 331 and Calle 464, tel. 506/2479-9420, 8am-midnight Mon.-Sat., 8am-10pm Sun.) and **Sucursal Fortuna de San Carlos** (corner of Avenida 333 and Calle 466, tel. 506/2479-9055, 7am-4pm Mon.-Fri.), can attend to medical issues. Centro Medico Sanar La Fortuna tends to be less busy. A few **pharmacies** are scattered throughout the downtown core along the main drag; most are open 9am-9pm daily.

The city has a **police station** (corner of Avenida 331 and Calle 460A, tel. 506/2479-9689, 24 hours daily) and a **post office** (Avenida 331 across from the central church, tel. 506/2479-8070, 8am-5:30pm Mon.-Sat., 8am-noon Sun.).

The most well-stocked grocery stores are **Super Cristian #2** (corner of Road 142 and Calle 468) and **Megasuper** (100 Centro Comercial Adifort), beside the regional bus station.

There are a number of banks in town. The easiest to spot is **Banco Nacional** (on the corner of Avenida 331 and Calle 468, tel. 506/2212-2000, www.bncr.fi.cr, 8:30am-3:45pm Mon.-Fri.). It has an **ATM** (5am-11pm daily).

There's a **gas station** on the corner of Road 142 and Calle 466.

Many hotels in the area offer laundry services to guests. Otherwise, you can have your clothes washed at **Lavandería Burbujas** (Calle 466, 75 m south of Road 142, 8am-8pm Mon.-Sat., 8am-6pm Sun.).

TRANSPORTATION
Getting There

If you're heading to La Fortuna by way of San José, the Central Valley and Highlands, or the Caribbean, you will enter town from either the east or the south. If you arrive via Guanacaste, access is from the west.

AIR

The **Aeropuerto Arenal** (FON) is eight kilometers east of downtown La Fortuna, roughly a 10-minute drive. **SANSA Airlines** (tel. 506/2290-4100, www.flysansa.com) offers direct flights to La Fortuna from San José, Liberia, and Tortuguero daily. The flight time from San José is approximately one hour.

There's no taxi stand at the airport. Call the taxi dispatch line **Central de Taxis La Fortuna** (tel. 506/2479-9605, 6am-10pm daily) to request a taxi to pick you up from the airport to take you wherever you need to go. Expect to pay $15 to downtown La Fortuna, more to reach hotels on the outskirts of town.

BOAT

If you plan to visit La Fortuna from the Monteverde vicinity, boat crossings over **Lago Arenal** save ground transportation time. The entire trip—which consists of ground transportation from Santa Elena (Monteverde) to the lake, a boat ride across the lake, and ground transportation on to La Fortuna—is known as the **van-boat-van service** (formerly called the jeep-boat-jeep service, sometimes referred to as the taxi-boat-taxi service, $30-45 pp) and takes approximately 3.5 hours to complete. A number of companies provide the service, typically twice daily, once in the morning and again in the afternoon. Those with the best reputations include **Aventuras Arenal** (Road 702, 750 m south of Road 142, tel. 506/2479-9133, www.aventurasarenal.com, 7am-8pm daily) and **Desafio Adventure Company** (Calle 472 behind the central church, tel. 506/2479-0020, www.desafiocostarica.com, 6am-10pm daily).

CAR

Most people visit La Fortuna directly from San José. The most popular version of this drive is 130 kilometers and takes three hours via Highway 1 and Road 702, which passes through San Ramón. Another option is 140 kilometers and takes 3.5 hours via Highway 1 and Road 141, which goes through Ciudad Quesada.

Getting to La Fortuna from **Liberia** requires a 135-kilometer, 2.5-hour drive via Highway 1 and Road 142. From **Monteverde,** it's a 115-kilometer, 3.5-hour drive via Roads 606, 145, and 142.

The roads that lead to La Fortuna are generally paved, well maintained, and safely maneuvered by the average driver. Travel to La Fortuna from the west (along Road 142 between Tilarán and the Lago Arenal Dam) is curvy in many places but primarily flat. South of La Fortuna is rather mountainous, especially Road 702 between San Ramón and Bajo Rodríguez, and Road 141 between Ciudad Quesada and Santa Clara. Each of these routes is easily passable with slow and cautious driving; aim to make the trip early in the day when fog cover is less of an issue. Access to La Fortuna from the east (via Highway 4 from Puerto Viejo de Sarapiquí) offers the fewest twists.

BUS

La Fortuna's regional **bus station** is on the corner of Calle 470 and Avenida 325.

Public buses travel to La Fortuna daily. You can catch one from **San José** (5am, 6:15am, 8:40am, and 11:50am daily, 4 hours, $4), **Ciudad Quesada** (multiple times 4am-10:10pm daily, 1.5 hours, $2.50), **San Ramón** (5 times daily, 2.5 hours, $4), and **Tilarán** (7am, 12:15pm, and 3:30pm daily, 2 hours, $5).

PRIVATE TRANSFER SERVICE

Most La Fortuna tour operators (and nearly all transportation service providers in the country) can get you to La Fortuna from any destination by way of a private transfer service. My votes go to **Desafío Adventure Company** (Calle 472 behind the central church, tel. 506/2479-0020, www. desafiocostarica.com, 6am-10pm daily) and **Ride Costa Rica** (2.5 km southwest of Los Ángeles, 10 km east of La Fortuna on Road 141, tel. 506/2469-2525, www.ridecr.com, 7am-8pm Mon.-Sat.) for their free onboard Wi-Fi. Prices average around $175 from San José or Liberia, and $200 from Monteverde. Vehicles vary in size. Most accommodate up to eight people plus luggage. Larger vehicles, which are great for groups, can transport up to 28 occupants.

SHARED SHUTTLE SERVICE

Interbus (tel. 506/4100-0888, www. interbusonline.com), **Ride Costa Rica** (tel. 506/2469-2525, www.ridecr.com), and **Grayline Costa Rica** (tel. 506/2220-2126, www.graylinecostarica.com) can shuttle you to La Fortuna from many popular tourist towns. Morning and afternoon departures are available from most destinations daily. One-way services to La Fortuna cost $44-90 per person. Most of these eight-person shuttles offer drop-offs at La Fortuna hotels.

ORGANIZED TOUR

A number of adventure and nature tour operators, such as **Desafío Adventure Company** (tel. 506/2479-0020, www. desafiocostarica.com) and **Exploradores Outdoors** (tel. 506/2222-6262, www. exploradoresoutdoors.com), offer post-tour **onward transportation** to La Fortuna from various cities around the country. Tours can be arranged to include pickups at hotels in San José, Monteverde, Puerto Viejo de Talamanca, Cahuita, Tortuguero, Puerto Viejo de Sarapiquí, Manuel Antonio, Sámara, and a variety of Guanacaste beach towns, and drop-offs at hotels in La Fortuna.

Getting Around
CAR AND TAXI

Driving around downtown La Fortuna is generally easy. In the middle of town, Road 142 becomes a one-way street (traffic flows west) between Road 702 and Calle 464. Parking is available but limited; there are usually free spaces along the north side of the central church across the street from the post office.

Official **taxis** line up along Calle 468 between Road 142 and Avenida 331 on the east side of the central park; unlicensed drivers station themselves along the park's south side.

BICYCLE AND SCOOTER

Bike Arenal (on the corner of Road 142 and Avenida 319, tel. 506/2479-9020, www.bikearenal.com, 8am-5pm Mon.-Sat.) offers daylong bike rentals for $25. High-quality road bikes will run you closer to $65 per day. All bike rentals include a helmet, gloves, spare kit, pump, and lock. If you want a bike for a shorter period, **Montaña de Fuego** (Road 142, 8.5 km west of the central church, tel. 506/2479-1220, www.montanadefuego.com) rents bikes by the hour ($8) or in four-hour periods ($15).

Arenal Sports (Calle 468, 150 m north of the central park, tel. 506/2479-9760, www.arenalsports.com, 8am-8pm daily) rents two-rider scooters ($12 per hour, $30 for 8 hours, $38 for 12 hours, and $45 for 24 hours) complete with a helmet, a reflective strap, and insurance.

SHARED SHUTTLE SERVICE

La Choza Inn Hostel (Avenida 331, 300 m west of the post office, tel. 506/2479-9091, www.lachozainnhostel.com) operates the **Arenal Shuttle Pass** ($15 pp), which includes unlimited transportation on a preset pickup and drop-off schedule between their property in downtown La Fortuna and a number of noteworthy sights around town. With the pass, you can visit El Salto, the Catarata Río Fortuna, Río Chollin, Lago Arenal, and the Parque Nacional Volcán Arenal as many times as you like over the course of your stay in La Fortuna. You'll receive a paper copy of the service provider's schedule upon purchase of the pass.

PARQUE NACIONAL VOLCÁN ARENAL

Much of the land that fills the space between La Fortuna and the Lago Arenal Dam is protected, either by the government or by private parties. **Parque Nacional Volcán Arenal** (Arenal Volcano National Park, main ranger station 2 km south of Road 142, tel. 506/2200-4192, www.sinac.go.cr, 8am-4pm daily, last entry 2:30pm, $15 adults, $5 children 2-12), home to the conical and picturesque **Volcán Arenal** and its dormant neighbor **Cerro Chato,** occupies the bulk of it.

The park's main **ranger station** marks its most popular entrance and provides access to the **Volcán Arenal Sector.** Nearly every tour operator in La Fortuna runs daily guided tours on the trails within this sector, typically once in the early morning and again in the early afternoon. Coupling a volcano tour with a visit to one of La Fortuna's famed hot springs is common.

A second, less popular area of the park is the **Arenal Peninsula Sector** (2 km northwest of the main ranger station, 8am-4pm daily, last entry 2:30pm). A bumpy road (4x4 recommended but not required) connects the peninsula sector's entrance to the main ranger station. You're welcome to explore either area without a guide. Self-guided visits do not require advance reservations.

Volcán Arenal

Visits to La Fortuna are incomplete without a lesson in the sad history that haunts Volcán Arenal. After the volcano was dormant for hundreds of years, an abrupt and devastating eruption in 1968 killed 87 people and left many others displaced. Following this catastrophic event that pummeled the volcano's west side with piping hot boulders and swallowed three communities whole, the volcano remained active for over 40 years. Frequent smoke clouds and lava-laced fireworks displays astonished survivors and residents of La Fortuna, who had escaped the eruption's wrath. In 2010, the volcano grew quiet, and today only the occasional gas emission can be seen.

Today, tours of the park focus on the area's history, flora, and fauna. Hiking trails around the volcano's base provide an up-close look at lava field striations on the ashy west side and opportunities to climb over the giant lava rocks that shot out of the belly of the beast. Ascents of the volcano, including hikes to the crater, are not permitted.

Hiking

Three trails are accessible beyond the main ranger station. The flat **Sendero Las Coladas** (Las Coladas Trail, 2 km one-way, 30 minutes, easy) is the park's principal route. It follows a straight line from the entrance to the back of the park, where you can see and stand atop lava rocks at a lookout point reachable by a brief but steep climb. Note that the lookout point is a deviation from the principal trail and may be skipped if preferred.

From Las Coladas, you can take the **Sendero El Ceibo** (El Ceibo Trail, 2 km one-way, 30 minutes, easy) for an extra two kilometers and 30 minutes but no additional difficulty. This trail forms a half-circle that connects at two points along Las Coladas. Its main draw is the tall, 400-year-old ceiba tree encountered along the way and its jungle gym of giant roots.

Just past the ranger station at the entrance to the park, the **Sendero Las Heliconias** (Las Heliconias Trail, 1-km loop, 20 minutes, easy) is a short circuit that can be toured on its own if your mobility is limited, or as a third walk if you want to leave no trail unseen.

Within the Arenal Peninsula Secor, the **Sendero Los Miradores** (Los Miradores Trail, 1.2 km one-way, 20 minutes, easy) is the most accessible. It's paved from start to finish. Of the park's various nature trails across its two sectors, this is the best trail for bird-watching. It also offers a view of Volcán Arenal from an observation platform and a view of Lago Arenal from the peninsula's tip.

Getting There

The drive from downtown La Fortuna to the entrance to the Volcán Arenal Sector is 17 kilometers and takes 20-25 minutes. Take the gravel side road known as "the road to El Castillo" off Road 142 (15 km west of La Fortuna center) to the main ranger station. A 4x4 vehicle is not required. The turnoff is well marked with signs for the park, as well as signs to the Arenal Observatory Lodge, Rancho Margot, and Sky Adventures. There's a large parking lot at the entrance.

You can hire a **taxi** ($25 one-way) to take you to the park; staff at the ranger station

lava rocks at the Parque Nacional Volcán Arenal

Hiking Around Volcán Arenal

In addition to the trails within Parque Nacional Volcán Arenal, other trails worthy of a visit weave around the volcano's base. Tour them with a guide or on your own. Note that if you have reserved an Arenal Volcano Tour through any operator or agency in the country, a walk inside the park is not guaranteed unless confirmed. Here are some of the trails you might find yourself on:

ARENAL 1968

At the private reserve Arenal 1968 (road to El Castillo, tel. 506/2462-1212, www.arenal1968. com, 8am-6pm daily, last entry 3-4pm, $15 pp 12 years and older), you'll find the most breathtaking and unobstructed volcano views. The reserve, also called Sendero 1968 (1968 Trail) offers two overlapping loops, the Sendero Bosque 1968 (Forest 1968 Trail, 5-km loop, 2.5 hours, moderate-difficult) and the Sendero Colada 1968 (Lava Flow 1968 Trail, 4-km loop, 1.5-2 hours, moderate).

Getting There: The drive from downtown La Fortuna to Arenal 1968 is 16 kilometers and takes 20-25 minutes. After about 15 kilometers on Road 142, turn south onto the gravel side road known as the road to El Castillo. A 4x4 vehicle is not required. The turnoff is well marked with signs for Parque Nacional Volcán Arenal, the Arenal Observatory Lodge, Rancho Margot, and Sky Adventures. If you reach the main ranger station for Parque Nacional Volcán Arenal, you've gone roughly 1 kilometer too far.

EL SILENCIO MIRADOR Y SENDEROS

Six trails snake throughout the private reserve known as El Silencio Mirador y Senderos (Road 142, 1.5 km west of Tabacón, tel. 506/2479-9900, www.miradorelsilencio.com, 7am-6:30pm daily, $7 pp 7 years and older). The Sendero Los Sainos (Los Sainos Trail, 1.5 km one-way, 30-45 minutes, moderate) is aptly named: The first peccary I saw in Costa Rica was along this route. Most trails lead through forested areas to the Mirador Volcán Arenal (Volcán Arenal Lookout). This lookout spot can be accessed on foot or by car.

Getting There: The drive from downtown La Fortuna to El Silencio Mirador y Senderos is 13 kilometers and takes 15-20 minutes. The entrance to the reserve is on the south side of Road 142, roughly 2 kilometers after Tabacón. A 4x4 vehicle is not required.

can call a taxi to the park when you're ready to leave. Another option is to purchase the Arenal Shuttle Pass ($15 pp) provided by La Choza Inn Hostel (Avenida 331, 300 m west of the post office, tel. 506/2479-9091, www. lachozainnhostel.com). The main ranger station is one of the shuttle's pickup and drop-off points.

To get to the Arenal Peninsula Sector from downtown La Fortuna, drive to the Volcán Arenal Sector and turn right on the unnamed road 50 meters beyond the main ranger station. Continue on this road for two kilometers to reach the entrance. Alternately, to access the sector from the west via destinations around Lago Arenal, take the unnamed road to your right immediately after you cross the bridge at the Lago Arenal Dam. Continue on this road for two kilometers to reach the entrance.

Lago Arenal and Vicinity

West of La Fortuna, a handful of small towns—El Castillo, Nuevo Arenal, and Tilarán—are scattered around the 85-square-kilometer Lago Arenal, which is nearly 30 kilometers long from west to east. In all three towns, you'll find privacy, peace, and a respite from tourist traps. Many expats live here, including retirees who have settled in the region. Gentle breezes off the lake, distant mountain and volcano views, and an aura of calm make this area a good place to escape the frenetic adventure destinations nearby.

EL CASTILLO

A dozen kilometers south of the Lago Arenal Dam is the small, quiet community of El Castillo. Although its attractions, accommodations, and restaurants are often advertised as being part of La Fortuna, El Castillo is an approximate half-hour commute from the city.

★ Arenal Sky Adventures Park

The most popular tourist attraction in the area, the **Arenal Sky Adventures Park** (off Road 142, 7 km south on the road to El Castillo, tel. 506/2479-4100, www.skyadventures.travel, 7am-9pm daily, price varies by tour) draws in visitors from downtown La Fortuna and beyond. It is one of the region's largest and most modern theme parks, offering a plethora of recreational activities. Large numbers of people visit the park each day, yet tours run like clockwork and the staff are friendly.

The guided **Sky Tram aerial tram ride** (multiple times 8am-3pm daily, 1 hour, $48 adults, $33 children 0-12), **Sky Trek canopy tour** (multiple times 8am-3pm daily, 2.5 hours, $84 adults, $58 children 5-12, min. age 5), and **Sky Walk hanging bridges tour** (multiple times 7am-2pm daily, 3 hours,

$41 adults, $28 children 0-12)—known as the classics—are the most popular park offerings. If you opt for the three-activity **combo tour** (multiple times 7am-11:30am daily, 5.5 hours, $104 adults, $72 children 5-12, min. age 5), you'll glide amid the rainforest on a tram ride, zip back and forth above it during your canopy tour, and explore it from within while traversing five hanging bridges, all in a day's work.

My favorite feature is the **Sky Limit Adrenaline Challenge** (9am and 12:30pm, 3 hours, $84 pp, min. age 15). This fun obstacle course incorporates zip lines, a rappel, a Tarzan swing, a superman cable, a ladder bridge, high ropes, and other hurdles. Give it a go solo to test your own abilities, or else challenge your travel mates for some friendly competition.

Additional guided adventures offered by the park include off-site **river tubing, mountain biking,** lake **kayaking,** and **fly boarding.** For these tours, Sky Adventures provides complimentary transportation.

The same Costa Rican family that oversees the Monteverde Sky Adventures Park in the Monteverde vicinity owns and operates this attraction. If you drive to the park, you'll find ample free parking out front. Alternately, Sky Adventures can provide round-trip transportation ($17 pp) between the park and La Fortuna hotels.

Shopping

If you know what microbes, aquaponics, and tinctures are, you'll marvel at what's in the works at **La Gavilana Herbs & Art** (500 m south of the Butterfly Conservatory, tel. 506/8533-7902, www.gavilana.com, 8am-5pm Mon.-Fri., 9am-2pm Sat.). If you don't, the shop's owners will happily chat with you about fermentation and food forests. Everything the store sells is crafted on-site, from snacks and drinks rich in nutrients, enzymes, and

Lago Arenal and Vicinity

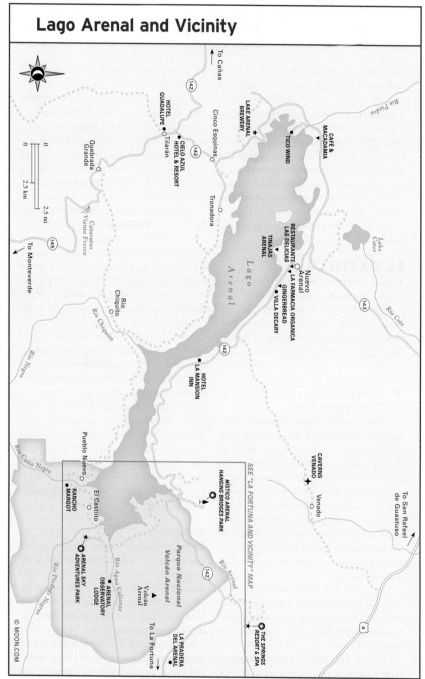

To Cañas

142

Cinco Esquinas

LAKE ARENAL BREWERY

HOTEL GUADALUPE

CIELO AZUL HOTEL & RESORT

Tilarán

Quebrada Grande

142

Tronadora

Cataratas Viento Fresco

145

To Monteverde

Río Chiquito

Río Chiquito

Río Negro

Río Caño Negro

Pueblo Nuevo

El Castillo

RANCHO MARGOT

ARENAL SKY ADVENTURES PARK

Río Piedras Negras

Río Agua Caliente

ARENAL OBSERVATORY LODGE

Parque Nacional Volcán Arenal

Volcán Arenal

MÍSTICO ARENAL HANGING BRIDGES PARK

Río Arenal

142

To La Fortuna

LA PRADERA DEL ARENAL

SEE "LA FORTUNA AND VICINITY" MAP

THE SPRINGS RESORT & SPA

4

To San Rafael de Guastuso

Venado

CAVERNS VENADO

143

Río Cote

Lake Cote

Río Piedra

Lago Arenal

TICO WIND

CAFÉ & MACADAMIA

RESTAURANTE LAS DELICIAS

TINAJAS ARENAL

Nuevo Arenal

LA FARMACIA ORGANICA

GINGERBREAD

VILLA DECARY

HOTEL LA MANSION INN

© MOON.COM

0   2.5 mi
0   2.5 km

biotic content, to the area's famous El Millón Original Salsa Picante hot sauce, to the artwork that hangs on the walls.

Food

El Castillo has only a few restaurants, but nearly all of them offer fantastic food. One of my favorites is the modest **La Ventanita Café** (300 m south of the El Castillo school, tel. 506/2479-1735, 10:30am-9pm daily, $3-6), which serves wraps, nachos, quesadillas, and burritos to patrons relaxing on its covered patio. Another is **Soda La Mesa de Mamá** (across from the El Castillo school, tel. 506/2479-1954, www.lamesademama. com, 7am-9pm daily, $5-11). I don't dare go anywhere else if I want the best homemade *casado* (a traditional dish that marries rice and beans on a plate, accompanied by a variety of side dishes) for lunch or for dinner, or a tasty serving of *gallo pinto* (a traditional rice and bean blend) for breakfast.

Accommodations

Stays at the ★ **Arenal Observatory Lodge** (off Road 142, 8.5 km south on the road to El Castillo, tel. 506/2290-7011, www. arenalobservatorylodge.com, $106 s/d) are an unmatchable experience. The property has 48 spacious and clean rooms, all without televisions so you can hear the natural soundtrack of the nearby national park. Two fully equipped and furnished two-story villas (sleep 8 and 10 people, $450-650) are a one-kilometer walk from the hotel's main building. The quiet, remote lodge offers unobstructed views of Volcán Arenal as well as a volcano museum with a live seismometer. Coatimundis and oropendolas inhabit the property, which has observation decks and nature trails of varying difficulties. Don't miss the Catarata Danta (Danta Waterfall), reached via the moderate hike along the Sendero Catarata (Catarata Trail). Nonguests can visit the property with a day pass (5am-11pm daily, $10).

In the heart of El Castillo is **Castillo del Arenal** (400 m south of the El Castillo school, tel. 506/2479-1146, www. hotelcastillodelarenal.com, $45 s/d), a run-of-the-mill standard hotel with simple accommodations for a decent price. Down the road is the equally budget-friendly **Essence Arenal** (800 m south of the El Castillo school, tel. 506/2479-1131, www.essencearenal.com, $48 s/d), which you would never guess provides an organic farm, a vegetarian restaurant with **Demo Cuisine** (hands-on meal preparation alongside a chef), a yoga studio, a *temazcal* (sweat lodge), and mud-wrap spa treatments.

If you want to go off the grid, escape to ★ **Rancho Margot** (4.5 km southwest of the El Castillo school, tel. 506/8302-7318, www.ranchomargot.com, private room $110-190, bungalow $159-249 d). The sustainable ranch, adorned with living roofs and furniture made from fallen wood, recycles everything imaginable: Who knew cooking oil could be reused as detergent and soap? As a guest, you'll swim in a pool built around a tree trunk, practice yoga twice a day, fish for *guapote* (rainbow bass), and hand milk a cow. For privacy and comfort, choose one of the property's 19 bungalows (sleeps up to 5 people); each has its own hammock and terrace. The bunkhouse provides 20 private rooms (for 1-2 people) with bunk beds and communal bathrooms.

Transportation

From **La Fortuna,** El Castillo is a 25-kilometer, 40-minute drive west on Road 142 and south on the gravel road known as "the road to El Castillo."

A **local bus** ($2.50) travels between La Fortuna and El Castillo once daily in each direction. The bus leaves El Castillo around 6:45am, stops in La Fortuna, then continues to Ciudad Quesada. From Ciudad Quesada, the bus leaves at 3:30pm, stops in La Fortuna, then continues to El Castillo.

Local resident Arturo operates an inexpensive **shuttle service** (tel. 506/8887-9141) that commutes between La Fortuna and El Castillo three times daily (departs El Castillo 8am, noon, and 4pm; departs La Fortuna 9am, 1:30pm, and 6:30pm). It leaves from La Fortuna in front of Super Cristian #1 (Road 702, 125 m south of Road 142) and travels to most El Castillo hotels. The cost varies by drop-off location, but the most expensive ride (La Fortuna to Rancho Margot) is only $10 per person.

The fit and fearless can reach El Castillo from Monteverde via the **Big Forest Hike** (8am daily, 8 hours, $159 pp, min. age 12), a combined horseback ride and challenging hike through the dense forest that separates the two areas. The folks at **La Gavilana Herbs & Art** (500 m south of the Butterfly Conservatory, tel. 506/8533-7902, www.gavilana.com, 8am-5pm Mon.-Fri., 9am-2pm Sat.) organize the feat, promoting the experience as a means of crossing the **Continental Divide** without using fossil fuels. Your luggage can be transported between towns for $10 per bag.

It's beneficial to have a rental car if you're staying in El Castillo. The community is a $30 taxi ride from La Fortuna center, and most La Fortuna tour operators charge transportation fees for pickups and drop-offs at El Castillo accommodations. You can avoid paying these if you drive yourself to and from La Fortuna where most tours start and end.

NUEVO ARENAL

From the Lago Arenal Dam, Road 142 zigzags west for 30 kilometers to the town of Nuevo Arenal. Aside from the views, you won't encounter much along the way, with the exception of groups of coatimundis that barricade the street from time to time. Keep your eyes out for them when driving, especially as you make your way around sharp corners.

Most travelers pass Nuevo Arenal on their way from one city to the next. Few stop and stay awhile, but those who do are treated to a slice of tranquil lake life. The community promotes stillness and solitude over organized tours.

Sights
SCENIC VIEWS OF LAGO ARENAL
The road to Nuevo Arenal offers panoramic views of **Lago Arenal**—a scene set with lush, rolling hills and sparkling waters. On clear days, if you time it right (around 5pm-6pm), you can witness the lake aglow in shades of pink, orange, and yellow as the sun sets.

For your safety and that of other drivers, do not pull over to the side of the curvy road to take in a view of the lake. Instead, head to **Tinajas Arenal** (off Road 142, 1.5 km southwest of Nuevo Arenal, tel. 506/2694-4667, 9am-8pm daily, $6-15), a small restaurant in the Nuevo Arenal vicinity that offers whimsical dishes, bioorganic meal options, and the best view of Lago Arenal at water level. If you would rather enjoy the *vista* (view) from higher up, check out **Café & Macadamia** (Road 142, 10 km west of Nuevo Arenal, tel. 506/2448-0030, www.cafe-macadamia.com, 8am-5pm daily, $4-12). The establishment draws in crowds with its mouthwatering baked goods and fruit smoothies, but you can enjoy the delicacies all the more from a cliffside table that overlooks the lake from above.

Food and Accommodations
Nuevo Arenal is loaded with expats, many of whom own restaurants. International cuisines with mainly American, Italian, German, and Swiss influences overshadow Costa Rican cooking in the region, although locals cherish my go-to *soda* (traditional Costa Rican family restaurant), **Restaurante Las Delicias** (Road 142, 20 m south of the gym, tel. 506/8320-7102, 7am-9:30pm daily, $6-15).

The laid-back **Gingerbread** (Road 142, 1.5 km east of Nuevo Arenal, tel. 506/2694-0039, www.gingerbreadarenal.com, 5pm-9pm Tues.-Sat., bar open until 11pm, $15-30, cash only), an avant-garde restaurant admired for its Mediterranean, French, and American fusion fare and its focus on fine dining, is a great option here. If you're not sure what to order, ask chef Eyal Ben-Menachem to surprise you with a series of creative, custom plates.

La Farmacia Orgánica (Road 142, 200 m

south of the gym, tel. 506/2694-4033, 10am-6pm Mon.-Sat.) is worth popping into. The business is not your average pharmacy; rather, it's a health food store where you can buy fresh and organic fruits and vegetables, salads, vegan ice cream, healthy chocolate, and other yummy snacks to munch on as you journey around the lake.

My favorite accommodation in the area is the quaint bed-and-breakfast **Villa Decary** (Road 142, 1.5 km east of Nuevo Arenal, tel. 506/2694-4330, www.villadecary.com, room $109 s/d, casita $164 s/d). This country hotel provides standard facilities and amenities but excels at putting guests' experience first. From fruit strewn about the seven-acre property to increase bird-watching opportunities, to friendly chats with the owners over hearty homemade breakfasts, there's no doubt you'll feel appreciated and looked after during a stay here. Choose one of five basic, white-walled rooms with colorful textiles in the hotel's main building, or one of three freestanding casitas equipped with a kitchen. Each option has a comfortable outdoor seating area.

Halfway between the Lago Arenal Dam and Nuevo Arenal, the **Hotel La Mansion Inn** (Road 142, 12 km east of Nuevo Arenal, tel. 506/2692-8018, www.lamansionarenal.com, $184 s/d) isn't luxurious, but it is the area's most elite accommodation, offering a leg up on its competitors with an infinity pool, Jacuzzi, and 14 multiroom villas. The villas vary in size and feature ornate, wrought-iron king- or queen-size beds, showy tilework, and hand-painted murals of tropical scenes. Each comes with a television, refrigerator, and air-conditioning. Guests can participate in the **Selva Leona Primary Rainforest Tour** (7:15am daily, 8 hours, $150 pp, min. age 5), a combined horseback riding and hiking experience exclusive to the hotel. The guides who lead this tour speak limited English.

Information and Services

For a small community, Nuevo Arenal offers a surprising number of services. The town's core houses a **clinic, Surcursal Nuevo**

Arenal (Nuevo Arenal center, tel. 506/2694-4650, 7am-3pm Mon.-Thurs., 7am-2pm Fri.) and a **pharmacy, Farmacia Santa Fe** (75 m west of Road 142, tel. 506/2694-4474, 8am-8pm Mon.-Sat.), as well as **supermarkets, banks,** and a **police station** (Nuevo Arenal center, tel. 506/4001-6911, 24 hours daily).

Transportation

From **La Fortuna,** it's a 45-kilometer, one-hour drive to Nuevo Arenal west on Road 142. Road 142 runs through town, which is identifiable by the corner **gas station.**

You can also get to Nuevo Arenal via **public bus** from either **La Fortuna** (8am, 1:30pm, and 5:30pm daily, 2 hours, $5) or **Tilarán** (4:45am, 5:45am, 10am, 2:45pm, and 4:45pm Mon.-Sat., 10am and 4:45pm Sun., 1 hour, $2).

TILARÁN

Tilarán is a peaceful town unbothered by passersby making their way to or coming from Liberia, La Fortuna, or Monteverde. Set atop the Cordillera de Tilarán (Tilarán mountain range), this highland town is a refreshingly cool place to visit, both in temperature and ambience. If I ever decide to move to the inlands of the Guanacaste province, the slow pace of life in Tilarán and the friendly disposition of its inhabitants would push it to the top of my list.

Sights

LAKE ARENAL BREWERY

If you're both a beer lover and a conservationist, you'll appreciate the 100 percent solar-powered **Lake Arenal Brewery** (off Road 142, 8 km north of Tilarán, tel. 506/2695-5050, http://lakearenalhotel.wixsite.com/lakearenalbrewery, 7am-9pm daily). Ingeniously, spent grain (used in the beer-making process) is fed to local cows to increase their milk and cheese production; the brewery also runs off methane gas from cow manure. At the **LAB Pub Taproom,** the on-site restaurant and bar, you can admire a gorgeous view of Lago Arenal and purchase

a beer ($3-6) made with spring-fed water or a sample flight of what's on tap ($2). Try seven different brews ranging from pale ales to stouts; some are infused with the flavors of Costa Rican mangoes, pineapples, and chilies. It's entertaining to learn about the operation and partake in a beer tasting, but be aware that the waitstaff can be unattentive and sometimes rude.

CATARATAS VIENTO FRESCO

If you have an hour or two to spare in Tilarán—ideally on your way to or from Monteverde—head to the **Cataratas Viento Fresco** (Viento Fresco Waterfalls, Road 145, 11 km southeast of Tilarán, tel. 506/2695-3434, www.vientofresco.net, 8:30am-5pm daily, last entry 3pm, $15 adults, $10 children 6-12), five waterfalls that you can explore courtesy of the farm that's located here. The cascades range in height from 15 to 90 meters and can be reached via a short trail that descends sharply into the forest; an uphill climb is required to get out. Most people spend about one hour hiking in and back out.

With more time, you can play in the caves on either side of the **Catarata Escondida,** wade in the small, shallow pool at the base of the **Catarata Arco Iris,** and treat yourself to a natural hydromassage provided by the **Catarata Tobogán.** Regardless of when you visit, you'll almost surely have the place to yourself.

Recreation

Impossible to miss around Tilarán (most notably north of town around the community of Tejona), stark white wind turbines populate the area's rolling hills and pastoral scenes. Favorable wind conditions between Nuevo Arenal and Tilarán not only satisfy the Instituto Costarricense de Electricidad (the Costa Rican Institute of Electricity), they

delight windsurfers and kitesurfers who flock to **Lago Arenal** for gusts that produce chops and swells up to 1.5 meters tall.

Tico Wind (Road 142, 14 km north of Tilarán, tel. 506/8383-2694, www.ticowind. com) has the most comprehensive offering of windsurfing and kitesurfing lessons, ranging from hour-long classes to multi-hour courses ($50-590) and equipment rentals (including board, helmet, harness, and wetsuit rentals; cost varies by type). They operate from December to April when the wind is best.

To maximize your surf opportunities, give yourself ample time in the area; I have waited for hours for lake conditions to be just right before getting on the water. Some travelers wait for days. Participation in either sport is entirely weather-dependent, and requires as much patience as it does skill.

Accommodations

Most travelers skip overnight stays in Tilarán, but if you need a place to lay your head, go with either the 12-room **Cielo Azul Hotel & Resort** (Road 142, 500 m north of Tilarán, tel. 506/2695-4000, www.hotelcieloazulresort. com, $50 s, $75 d) on the outskirts of town, or the 36-room **Hotel Guadalupe** (corner of Calle 1 and Avenida 4, tel. 506/2695-5943, www.hotelguadalupe.co.cr, $38 s, $58 d) in the downtown core. Both offer basic, clean, and safe rooms at fair prices.

Information and Services

Tilarán provides all the standard services of a midsize Costa Rican town. There's a **clinic, Clínica Tilarán** (corner of Avenida 2 and Calle 6, tel. 506/2695-5093, 24 hours daily) and a nearby **pharmacy, Farmacia Tilarán** (Avenida 2 between Calle Central and Calle 2, tel. 506/2695-6255, 7am-7pm Mon.-Fri.).

The town also has a **post office** (Avenida 1 between Calle 1 and Calle 3, tel. 506/2695-6230, 8am-5pm Mon.-Fri.), a **police station** (corner of Avenida Central and Calle 4, tel. 506/2695-5001, 24 hours daily), **supermarkets,** and **banks.**

1: scenic view of Lago Arenal from Café & Macadamia, west of Nuevo Arenal **2:** the Sky Tram at Arenal Sky Adventures Park **3:** sunset on Lago Arenal

Transportation

From **La Fortuna,** Tilarán is a 75-kilometer, two-hour drive west and south on Road 142. From **Santa Elena,** it's a 35-kilometer, 1.5-hour drive northwest on Road 606 and Road 145.

Road 142 passes right through town. Note that as you enter Tilarán from the north, a turn is required to stay on Road 142; the clearly marked turn occurs near the **gas station.** If you miss it, Road 142 becomes Calle 1 and continues south through town until it ends at Avenida 6.

It's possible to get to Tilarán by public **bus.** The regional **bus station** is on Avenida Central just west of the central park. Service is available from **San José** (7:30am, 12:45pm, 3:45pm, and 6:30pm daily, 4 hours, $7), **Ciudad Quesada** (6:30am, 11:30am, and 3:55pm daily, 3 hours, $5), **Cañas** (multiple times 6am-9pm Mon.-Sat., 7am-7pm Sun., 30 minutes, $1), **La Fortuna** (8am, 1:30pm, and 5:30pm daily, 2 hours, $5), **Nuevo Arenal** (5:45am, 7:20am, 12:30pm, 4pm, and 5:45pm, 2 hours, $1.50), and **Monteverde** (5am, 7am, noon, and 4pm Mon.-Sat., 7am and 4pm Sun., 1.5-2 hours, $2.50).

Northern Inlands

Some of the region's most picturesque scenes hide in the inland area north of La Fortuna. Swampy marshes and river tributaries twine around the tiny village of Caño Negro. Kilometers of dry rice fields span open plains near the town of San Rafael de Guatuso. Vast mountains tower over the community of Bijagua.

Rural community tourism is on the rise in the vicinity. Two of the region's most sought-after attractions—the Refugio Nacional de Vida Silvestre Mixto Caño Negro and Río Celeste within the Parque Nacional Volcán Tenorio—are additional draws.

MUELLE

Approximately 25 kilometers east of La Fortuna is the small community of Muelle de San Carlos (known as just "Muelle"). Marked by the intersection of Highway 4 (east-west) and Highway 35 (north-south), Muelle is significant not as a tourist destination but as a crossroads. To the east, the highway leads to Puerto Viejo de Sarapiquí—a gateway to the Caribbean. To the south is a route to San José. To the northwest, the highway travels through the Northern Inlands, passing by San Rafael de Guatuso, which itself is a gateway to Parque Nacional Volcán Tenorio. To the north is the Refugio Nacional de Vida Silvestre Mixto

Caño Negro and Los Chiles, just shy of the border with Nicaragua.

There are a couple of unique restaurants and lodgings close to Muelle if you need a break on your way elsewhere.

Food and Accommodations

Less than a five-minute drive north of the intersection, **Restaurante Las Iguanas** (Hwy. 35, 1.5 km north of Muelle, tel. 506/2462-1102, 7am-8pm daily, $6-9) sells typical Costa Rican rice and meat dishes, with ice cream for dessert. What the restaurant does best, however, doesn't come from its menu—it is home to hundreds of iguanas that bask in the sun on trees beside the property. Nowhere else in the country can you see such a high number of iguanas both on demand and in the wild. The sight is particularly memorable for kids.

Northeast of Muelle is the ★ **Maquenque EcoLodge** (Boca Tapada, 50 km northeast of the intersection at Muelle, tel. 506/2479-8200, www.maquenqueecolodge.com, $110 s, $138 d), where you're likely to see great green macaws flying around the banks of Río San Carlos. Choose from 15 cozy wood bungalows (sleep 1-4 people), most of which have views of the property's lagoon. Stays at this remote spot include breakfast only; lunch and dinner can be purchased at the on-site buffet restaurant, which serves typical Costa Rican fare. During your stay, you can plant a tree, canoe for free, and visit a local school.

Transportation

From **La Fortuna,** Muelle is a 25-kilometer, 20-minute drive east on Road 142 and Highway 4. From **Guatuso,** it's a 55-kilometer, one-hour drive southeast on Highway 4 to reach Muelle.

★ REFUGIO NACIONAL DE VIDA SILVESTRE MIXTO CAÑO NEGRO

Ornithologists and avid birders shouldn't miss the **Refugio Nacional de Vida Silvestre Mixto Caño Negro** (Caño Negro Wildlife Refuge, tel. 506/2471-1309, www.sinac.go.cr, 8am-4pm daily, $5 pp), a 25,000-acre protected area approximately 60 kilometers north of Muelle, sandwiched between Highway 4 and Highway 35. The grassy and marshy swamps here provide some of the country's best bird-watching opportunities, especially from December to April, when North American waterfowl migrate to the refuge to escape the chilly north. Home to a slew of other wildlife, including monkeys, iguanas, and lizards, the refuge's most obvious

inhabitants are the hundreds of caimans that lurk in its waters and nap on its shores. Contained within the refuge, the small community of Caño Negro is the departure point for the refuge's boat tours.

Exploring the Refuge

You can explore this area one of two ways. The most popular option is to tour **Río Frío,** the river that borders the refuge. Guided excursions advertised throughout the country as **Caño Negro tours** are almost always of this kind, unless specified otherwise. Most depart from La Fortuna, although tours to the river can be arranged from elsewhere in the northern inland area, San José, or Guanacaste.

You can also explore the refuge from within by visiting the small community of **Caño Negro.** These **boat tours** (2-2.5 hours, captains can be hired at the community's dock) include stops at an 18-meter-tall observation deck that overlooks the wetlands and an area of the refuge that has wheelchair-accessible pathways. The tours cost around $65 (1-5 people) and include the services of a Spanish-speaking captain. Expect to pay roughly $20 extra to be accompanied by an English-speaking tour guide. Currently, construction is underway to create a visitors

a caiman in the Refugio Nacional de Vida Silvestre Mixto Caño Negro

center, **El Sitio,** in the southwest end of Caño Negro.

If you're visiting the community of Caño Negro, you may want to hole up at one of the few accommodations in the area for a night or two and participate in activities arranged by your hotel, such as **kayaking** and **fishing**—most famously, tarpon fishing between August and March. My two favorite places to stay are the fairly priced **Hotel de Campo** (Caño Negro, tel. 506/2471-1012, www.hoteldecampo.com, $95 s/d) and the superior-quality **Natural Lodge Caño Negro** (Caño Negro, tel. 506/2471-1426, www.canonegrolodge.com, $130 s/d).

BOAT TOURS ON RÍO FRÍO

Tour operator **Canoa Aventura** (tel. 506/2479-8200, www.canoa-aventura.com) runs three similar, slow-moving **Río Frío float tours** (7:30am, 7.5 hours) from La Fortuna daily, on which you can spot birds and other wildlife around the peaceful refuge. The **Unique Caño Negro tour** ($65 adults, $46 children 4-11) traverses the river in a covered pontoon boat that can protect you from the sun or rain. Alternately, you can float down the river in a motorized raft during the **Caño Negro Eco Safari** ($89 pp, min. age 3). For a rare opportunity to go canoeing in Costa Rica, treat yourself to the **Caño Negro canoe tour** ($108 pp, min. age 5)—it's Canoa Aventura's specialty!

BIRD-WATCHING

Bird-watching during boat tours is the foremost activity around the refuge. The list of bird species that call the refuge home is far too long to detail, but sightings of cormorants, herons, egrets, ibises, and Costa Rica's tallest bird, the **jabiru stork,** are definite draws. The brilliant pink **roseate spoonbills,** which I have been fortunate enough to spy in great numbers at the refuge, always dazzle me.

Transportation

To reach the community of Caño Negro from **La Fortuna,** it's a 110-kilometer, two-hour drive north on Road 142, Highway 4, Highway 35, and Route 138. You'll pass through the town of Muelle on this drive. A 4x4 vehicle is required on the incredibly bumpy Route 138.

There is no direct bus service to Caño Negro from La Fortuna.

SAN RAFAEL DE GUATUSO

West of Muelle, Highway 4 angles north and cuts through the region. It divides mountains on the left from plains on the right and passes through the small farming community of San Rafael de Guatuso (simply "Guatuso" to locals). Home to the highest concentration of the indigenous Maleku people, Guatuso is also the eastern gateway to Parque Nacional Volcán Tenorio.

Sights
RESERVA INDÍGENA MALEKU

Guatuso is home to **Margarita, Tonjibe,** and **El Sol,** the three primary *palenques* (communities) that make up the village **Reserva Indígena Maleku** (Maleku Indigenous Reserve).

An assortment of Maleku cultural centers cluster around Highway 4, a few kilometers southeast of Guatuso. At the **Rancho Toji Jifuru** (Palenque Tonjibe, 4 km south of Hwy. 4 at Margarita, 4 km southeast of Guatuso, tel. 506/6060-8874, www.malekuindianscostarica.com, 7am-4pm daily by guided tour only, 3-4 hours, $65 pp), you can learn about the history of the Malekus and the importance of their medicinal gardens on a guided walk through the tribe's reforestation project. **Rancho Maleku Ní Uríjifa Tafa** (Hwy. 4, 3 km southeast of Guatuso, tel. 506/8559-1767, 9am-5pm daily by guided tour only, 3 hours, $35 pp) is run by female tribe member Hiqui, who specializes in cultural *charlas* (talks) about the importance of dress, plants, and art to the Malekus. At the **Rancho Indígena Maleku Caroqui U** (Hwy. 4, 4.5 km southeast of Guatuso, tel. 506/8637-6229, 8am-6pm daily by guided tour only, 2.5-3 hours, $65 pp), male tribe member Jaquíma leads nature tours around the indigenous village. All three locales offer demonstrations of traditional ceremonies (advance reservations are required by telephone or through Facebook) and sell original Maleku artwork.

If you're interested in spending a night at the reserve, **Galería Namu** (Avenida 7 between Calle 5 and Calle 7, San José, tel. 506/2256-3412, www.galerianamu.com, 9am-6:30pm Mon.-Sat., 1pm-5pm Sun. Jan.-Apr., 9am-6:30pm Mon.-Sat. May-Dec.), an indigenous art gallery that works with the Maleku community, can arrange the experience. Their overnight **Eco-Ethno Maleku Village Tour** (10am daily, $125 pp) is an opportunity to visit, dine, and stay with a Maleku family who will show you around their forest, workshops, and cemetery.

CAVERNAS VENADO
The area's deepest and darkest secrets are hidden among the **Cavernas Venado** (off Hwy. 4 at Jicarito, 3 km west of Venado, tel. 506/2478-8008, www.cavernasdelvenadocr.com, 8am-3pm daily by tour only), a series of traversable caves that are about three kilometers west of the community of Venado, southwest of Highway 4. Provided you are not claustrophobic or opposed to getting dirty and wet, you'll love exploring the murky underground chambers. Be prepared to climb, crouch, duck, crawl, and squeeze your way through the hollows as you search for insects, arachnids, and bats in the crevices of stalactites overhead and stalagmites below.

The owners offer a **cave tour** (hourly 8am-2pm daily, 1.5 hours, $28 adults, $25 children 5-10, min. age 5), but it's also possible to visit with a La Fortuna tour operator. Most operators run jaunts to the attraction daily, typically once in the morning and again in the afternoon. Round-trip transportation is included in the tour cost.

From La Fortuna, the 40-kilometer route via Road 142 and Highway 4 takes roughly 45 minutes to an hour. Getting there doesn't require a 4x4, but it does require patience, as the last three kilometers are bumpy. Watch for signs for the caverns that indicate the turnoff from Highway 4.

Information and Services
Guatuso does not have a hospital, but it has a **clinic, Sucursal Guatuso** (Road 143, 1.5 km south of Hwy. 4, tel. 506/2464-0161, 7am-4pm Mon.-Fri.). It also has several **pharmacies,** one of which is **Farmacia Guatuso** (Road 143 between Avenida 4 and Avenida 6, tel. 506/2464-0017, 7am-8:30pm Mon.-Fri., 7am-noon Sun.). There are also **banks, supermarkets,** and a **police station** (Hwy. 4 at Calle 1, tel. 506/2464-0257, 24 hours daily) in town.

Banco Nacional has an **ATM** (corner of Road 143 and Avenida 12, 5am-10pm daily). There is one **gas station** (Road 143, 400 m south of the central park) in Guatuso.

Transportation
Highway 4 passes through Guatuso. From **Muelle,** Guatuso is a 55-kilometer, one-hour drive northwest on Highway 4. From **La Fortuna,** it's a 45-kilometer, 50-minute drive east on Road 142 and northwest on Highway 4.

Guatuso's regional **bus station** is on Calle 2 on the east side of town, 50 meters south of Highway 4. Buses to Guatuso run from **San José** (5am, 8:40am, and 11:50am daily, 4 hours, $5) and **La Fortuna** (multiple times 5am-11pm daily, 1-1.5 hours, $5).

PARQUE NACIONAL VOLCÁN TENORIO
The not-to-be-missed attraction in the Northern Inlands is **Parque Nacional Volcán Tenorio** (Tenorio Volcano National Park, tel. 506/2206-5369, www.sinac.go.cr, 8am-4pm daily, last entry 2pm, $12 adults, $5 children 2-12). Covering more than 30,000 acres, the park spans much of the land northwest of Lago Arenal, between the towns of Guatuso (to the east) and Bijagua (to the west). From a distance, the lush, dense, forest-filled and stream-strewn park resembles a mountain. It conceals **Volcán Tenorio** (Tenorio

Volcano), whose crater is inaccessible to the public. Thanks to **Río Celeste,** the jaw-dropping, bright blue river that weaves its way throughout the park, the hiking hot spot is on most travelers' to-do lists.

The main entrance is via **El Pilón ranger station** (9.5 km east of Bijagua, 23 km west of Guatuso) on the north side of the park. A lesser-known entrance exists on the west side of the park via the private **Las Heliconias Lodge and Rainforest** (off Hwy. 6, 300 m southeast of Bijagua, tel. 506/2466-8483, www.heliconiascr.com). The lodge has its own hanging bridges trail, from which you can access the park's Sendero Lago Danta (Lago Danta Trail).

Operators all over the country offer guided tours to the park. Tours typically start and end in La Fortuna or at destinations in Guanacaste. The park's main trail can be hiked independently, however.

★ Río Celeste

Río Celeste's striking blue color is the foremost draw of the park. Entering the park through El Pilón ranger station, you can witness the river change from a clear, colorless stream to a cloudy azure waterway. Most vibrant in color during the high season (when rainfall that can diminish the potency of the river's hue is minimal), Río Celeste is a natural phenomenon you must see for yourself. Note that swimming in the river anywhere inside the park is not allowed.

Río Celeste's most noteworthy features include the striking **Catarata Río Celeste** (Río Celeste Waterfall); a mountain *mirador* (lookout); the calm blue pool known as **Laguna Azul** (Blue Lagoon); piping-hot riverside gas vents that create the Jacuzzi-like **Borbollones** ("gushing waters" or "bubbling waters"); and **Los Teñideros** (The Dyers)—the area where the color of the river's water transforms from a crystal-clear silver to

an opaque, celestial blue. Hiking the park's Sendero Principal (Main Trail) takes you to all these.

Catarata Río Celeste

The park amazes visitors with the picturesque, 30-meter-tall **Catarata Río Celeste** (Río Celeste Waterfall), which spills out of the rainforest and into an aquamarine pool. You can get relatively close via a steep, 250-step staircase that branches off from the Sendero Principal (Main Trail) and leads down to the waterfall's base. Swimming is not allowed. You'll approach the staircase to the waterfall on your left, roughly halfway (1.5 km) into the hike.

Hiking

Just beyond El Pilón ranger station you'll find the **Sendero Principal** (Main Trail, 3 km one-way, 1.5-2 hours, moderate, last entry 2pm). This moderately difficult trail heads southwest through the park, parallel to Río Celeste, the park's main attraction. As you hike, you'll encounter the river's best features: Catarata Río Celeste (Río Celeste Waterfall); a mountain-top lookout; Laguna Azul (Blue Lagoon); the Jacuzzi-like Borbollones ("gushing waters" or "bubbling waters"); and Los Teñideros (The Dyers)—the area where the water goes from clear silver to opaque blue. The trail comprises mud, tree branches, and rocks, all of which are trickier to traverse when wet. Keep this in mind if you plan to visit during the low season, when rainfall is most common, and dress accordingly; rubber boots can be rented near the park's entrance ($4). You can hike the trail without a guide, but it's also a popular outing offered by tour operators across the country.

To hike the park's challenging **Sendero Lago Danta** (Lago Danta Trail, 2.5 km one-way, 2 hours, difficult, guide required, last entry 1pm), you need preapproval by **Las Heliconias Lodge and Rainforest** (off Hwy. 6, 300 m southeast of Bijagua, tel. 506/2466-8483, www.heliconiascr.com), as

1: an elegant casita at the Río Celeste Hideaway Hotel 2: a bridge over Río Celeste in Parque Nacional Volcán Tenorio 3: a carving made by a member of the Maleku indigenous group

the trail is accessible only through this private property. Because the trail is rough and rarely trekked, hiking it requires a guide. Tour guides are best booked through the lodge; expect to pay $65 for 1-2 people and $25 per additional person. This trail does not offer views of Río Celeste.

Las Heliconias also has its own **hanging bridges trail** (2.5-km loop, 1.5 hours, moderate, 7am-5:30pm daily, last entry 4pm, $12 adults, $8 children 6-11), open to the public for self-guided hikes. You can hire tour guides through the lodge for about $45 for 1-2 people and $15 per additional person. From the hanging bridges loop trail, the Sendero Lago Danta branches off to the southeast and begins a steep climb up to Lago Danta.

Getting There

The park can be reached from Bijagua or Guatuso via the unnamed road that connects the two.

From Guatuso, it's a 23-kilometer, 35-minute drive to the park. From Highway 4, at the north end of Guatuso, the unnamed road will be on your left (south), just beyond the bridge over Río Frío. Look for the sign for the Río Celeste Hideaway Hotel.

From Bijagua, it's a 9.5-kilometer, 15-minute drive to the park. From Highway 6, at the northeast end of Bijagua, the unnamed road will be on your right (east) as you exit town. Look for the sign for Parque Nacional Volcán Tenorio.

To reach the park from La Fortuna, take the route through Guatuso. Guatuso is a 45-kilometer, 50-minute drive east on Road 142 and northwest on Highway 4 from La Fortuna.

There's no direct bus service to the park. Instead, you can take the **La Fortuna to Río Celeste Shuttle** (departs La Fortuna 7:30am daily, departs park 1pm-2pm daily, 1.5-2 hours, $50 pp round-trip) provided by tour outfitter **Arenal Evergreen** (tel. 506/2479-8712, www.arenalevergreen.com). Advance reservations are required.

BIJAGUA

Smack dab in the middle of Volcán Tenorio and Volcán Miravalles is the town of Bijagua, the western gateway to Parque Nacional Volcán Tenorio (Tenorio Volcano National Park). Although the famed Río Celeste may draw you to the Northern Inlands, Bijagua's handful of other attractions will give you a reason to stay.

Sights
CATARATAS BIJAGUA

After you've visited Parque Nacional Volcán Tenorio, head west of town to reward yourself with the **Cataratas Bijagua** (Bijagua Waterfalls, 7am-5:30pm daily, last entry 2:30pm, $6 adults, $3 children 0-5), a series of small, swimmable waterfalls and one powerful, 40-meter cascade. You can reach the waterfalls via a difficult three-hour, out-and-back hike (2.5 km each way) through rainforest. **Cataratas Bijagua Lodge** (off Hwy. 6, 2 km west of Bijagua, tel. 506/8937-4687, www.cataratasbijagua.com), on whose property the trail begins, grants access to the trail. Although it's not required, hiring a guide for this hike provides an extra pair of eyes for spotting snakes and other creatures camouflaged along the trail. Tour guides are best booked through the lodge and charge approximately $32 per person. If you're a lodge guest, the entrance fee is included in the cost of your stay, but the guide fee still applies.

FROG'S PARADISE

The perfect way to cap off a day of hiking and swimming around the Cataratas Bijagua is with an evening of leisurely exploration at **Frog's Paradise** (off Hwy. 6, 500 m west of Bijagua, tel. 506/8634-7402, by guided tour only). At this reforested farmland, you can join Spanish-speaking Tío (Uncle) Miguel on his **night tour** (5:30pm daily, 2 hours, $15 adults, $7.50 children 3-12) as he welcomes you to see where frogs, reptiles, and insects roam free. Tío Miguel's son provides basic

English translations. If you would rather have a guide who is fluent in English, hire one through **Bijagua Rainforest Tours** (tel. 506/8515-4463, www.bijaguarainforesttours.com) for $30 per person.

TAPIR VALLEY

At the private reserve **Tapir Valley** (off Hwy. 6, 4.5 km east of Bijagua, tel. 506/8312-1248, www.tapirvalley.org, by guided tour only), across the road from Parque Nacional Volcán Tenorio, you might catch a glimpse of the endangered Baird's tapir. Take a **guided walking tour** (6am and 3pm daily, 2 hours, $48 adults, $24 children 0-10) through the reserve's rainforest and wetlands. Tours can be arranged through the reserve directly or the Casitas Tenorio B&B (tel. 506/8312-1248, www.casitastenorio.com), the owners of which also oversee the reserve. Self-guided exploration is not permitted.

FARM TOURS

For a comprehensive farm visit, head to the **Finca Verde Lodge** (off Hwy. 6, 1.5 km south of Bijagua, tel. 506/2466-8069, www.fincaverdelodge.com), also known as Finca Gavilan. The lodge's **farm tour** (8am, 10am, noon, 2pm, and 4pm daily, 2 hours, $14 pp) provides a bit of everything, including nature exploration, discussion of organic farming, and a visit to a butterfly garden.

Recreation

LOCAL GUIDES AND TOURS

Bijagua Rainforest Tours (tel. 506/8515-4463, www.bijaguarainforesttours.com) is your best bet for organized tours around Bijagua. Tour guide and owner Marlon Calderón Brenes is fluent in English and French, and runs all kinds of nature tours in the area, including day hikes, specialized bird-watching tours, and night tours, as well as horseback riding and mountain biking excursions. Allow Marlon's keen spotting skills—and his adorable tagalong son—to enhance your exploration of the region.

TUBING

Tubing on **Río Celeste** within Parque Nacional Volcán Tenorio is not permitted. However, you can go tubing on the river's lower section, which flows outside the park's boundary. The area's leading tubing tour operator is **Onca Tours** (off Hwy. 4, 2.5 km south of Katira, tel. 506/8399-2757, 7am-7pm daily), but they can be difficult to track down. It's best to book their **Río Celeste Tubing Tour** (9am and 1pm daily, 2 hours, $50 adults, $25 children 4-10, min. age 4) through a third party, such as your lodging in this region.

Food and Accommodations

For a hands-on farmstay, book a casita at **Casitas Tenorio B&B** (off Hwy. 6, 2.5 km southeast of Bijagua, tel. 506/8312-1248, www.casitastenorio.com, $100-140 s/d). As an advocate of rural community tourism in Bijagua, the accommodation welcomes guests to milk cows and make cheese, among other farm activities. The six casitas here, which sleep 1-5 people, are rustic, freestanding structures with bedrooms, bathrooms, and a kitchen.

The ★ **Río Celeste Hideaway Hotel** (1.5 km east of El Pilón ranger station, tel. 506/2206-4000, www.riocelestehideaway.com, low season $200 s/d, high season $300 s/d) is the closest lodging to the entrance of Parque Nacional Volcán Tenorio. It brings elegance to the region with its swim-up bar and 26 exquisite casitas—freestanding mini-homes that have a canopy bed, private garden, and an outdoor stone shower. You can even stroll along a section of Río Celeste that flows through the property. When I want to feel spoiled, a stay here does the trick. This is a romantic spot that's great for couples and honeymooners.

Second only to the Río Celeste Hideaway Hotel in proximity to the park, the **Catarata Río Celeste Hotel** (2 km east of El Pilón ranger station, tel. 506/2200-0176, www.cataratarioceleste.com, $49 s, $75 d) is your best option if you want a small accommodation that is less expensive than most others in the region but has clean and spacious rooms.

If you're traveling on a shoestring, you can save money by staying at the **Río Celeste Backpackers** (Hwy. 6, 200 m south of Banco Nacional, tel. 506/2466-8600, www. bijaguabackpackers.jimdo.com, dorm $18 pp, private $41 s/d), a small, one-story, hacienda-style accommodation. It has one dorm room, equipped with bunk beds for eight people. There are also two lovely, comfortable private rooms (with a shared bathroom) for 1-2 people. If you don't have a rental car, the hostel—which feels more like a B&B—is a 10-minute walk (along a highway without sidewalks) from downtown Bijagua and a 15-minute drive or taxi ride from Parque Nacional Volcán Tenorio.

Deserving of attention, the ★ **Celeste Mountain Lodge** (1.5 km east of El Pilón ranger station, tel. 506/2278-6628, www. celestemountainlodge.com, $110 s, $150 d, with all-inclusive meals $165 s, $210 d) is a two-story, 18-room hotel with showstopping contemporary design; open-air communal areas bring the outdoors in to make you feel like you're right in the forest. Volcán Tenorio and Volcán Miravalles surround the pretty, well-manicured property. Although rooms are on the small side, all have floor-to-ceiling windows that maximize the views. Breakfast, lunch, and dinner can be included in your stay.

Transportation

Bijagua is easy to access by car, as it falls along Highway 6. From **Guatuso,** Bijagua is a 33-kilometer, 50-minute drive on the unnamed road that connects the two towns. From the north end of Guatuso on Highway 4, get on the unnamed road by turning south just past the bridge over Río Frío.

To get to Bijagua from **Cañas,** it's a 40-kilometer, 35-minute drive north on Highway 6. This flat drive is particularly scenic as it passes pretty cattle pastures and showcases the vast Volcán Tenorio to the east and Volcán Miravalles to the west.

There are two options to reach Bijagua from **La Fortuna.** The shortest (80 km) and fastest (1.75 hours) route is through Guatuso. From La Fortuna, take Road 142 east, then Highway 4 north to Guatuso and turn left (south) onto the unnamed road that ends in Bijagua. An alternate route (135 km, 2.5 hours) leads west out of La Fortuna on Road 142 to Cañas, where Highway 1 connects with Highway 6 and leads north to Bijagua. This route provides a lovely drive around Lago Arenal.

There is no place to get fuel in the vicinity; the closest **gas station** is on Highway 6, 23 kilometers north of Bijagua.

To reach Bijagua by bus from **Cañas,** hop on one that passes through town on the way to Upala (multiple times 4:30am-5:30pm daily, 1-1.5 hours, $3). To ensure that your bus will stop in Bijagua, ask the driver *"¿Por favor, puede parar en Bijagua?"* ("Please, can you stop in Bijagua?") when you board. There's no direct bus service to Bijagua from Guatuso.

Monteverde and Santa Elena

With an elevation just shy of 1,500 meters, the Monteverde region is one of the best places in Costa Rica to experience a cloud forest ecosystem. Puffy clouds waft through the air, sometimes dense enough to swathe your surroundings in a blanket of white—but only for a moment. As quickly as the haze creeps up on you, it carries on down the road.

Steady low-cloud cover keeps the area cool and refreshing, and the land moist. Myriad tree, lichen, flower, fern, and moss species flourish in the climate and create a rich environment for wildlife. The diversity of vegetation around Monteverde—the "Green Mountain"—draws botanists, ornithologists, biologists, and naturalists from all over the globe, as well as casual visitors who flock to the region to gaze at its pretty forests.

The town of Santa Elena, the center of the region, has a cluster of restaurants, shops, and accommodations nestled within walking distance of one another. Although Santa Elena and Monteverde are considered one area, they are technically separate. The community of Monteverde is 2.5 kilometers southeast of Santa Elena town, not far from the entrance of the Reserva Biológica Bosque Nuboso de Monteverde. The small community of **Cerro Plano** divides the two.

SIGHTS

★ Monteverde Sky Adventures Park

If your time in the area is limited, head straight to the **Monteverde Sky Adventures Park** (off Road 619, 3.5 km north of Santa Elena, tel. 506/2479-4100, www.skyadventures. travel, 7am-9pm daily, prices vary by activity). The multifaceted operation is one of Monteverde's best one-stop-shop adventure centers and receives hundreds of visitors daily. The famed theme park (a sister company of Arenal Sky Adventures Park on the outskirts of La Fortuna) offers a number of quintessential Monteverde experiences, including a guided tram ride, zip-line course, and hanging bridges tour. If you want to maximize your experience in Monteverde and minimize precious travel time, no place in the area combines nature exploration with adventure excursions better than this park.

During the **Sky Tram aerial tram ride** (multiple times 8am-3pm daily, 1 hour, $48 adults, $33 children 0-12), you'll glide above the treetops up to the Continental Divide, where Monteverde's lush landscape can be seen for miles.

You'll make eerie but thrilling zips across cables that speed through the clouds during the **Sky Trek canopy tour** (multiple times 8am-3pm daily, 2 hours, $84 adults, $58 children 5-12, min. age 5), and throw caution—and your body—to the wind during an adrenaline-inducing bungee jump called the

"Vertigo Drop" (free with zip-lining tour). This is the only zip-line tour in the area that allows participants to brake with metal handlebars, as opposed to gripping the cables by hand using a thick leather glove. Included with the tour is a complimentary jaunt in an aerial tram; the gondola ride takes you to the top of the forest where the zip-line tour begins.

While walking through the forest during the **Sky Walk hanging bridges tour** (multiple times 8am-2pm daily, 2 hours, guided tour $41 adults, $28 children 6-12, self-guided tour $27 adults, $19 children 6-12), you'll see and hear a variety of plant and animal species that contribute to the region's famed biodiversity. On this tour, you'll cross a 236-meter hanging bridge, the longest in the area. The three-activity, five-hour **combo tour** ($104 adults, $72 children 5-12) runs multiple times between 8am and 1pm daily and allows you to maximize your time at the park.

The park's modern, two-story facility has a comfortable lounge, lockers for storing your belongings, and ample free parking. Sky Adventures can provide round-trip transportation ($10 pp) between the park and Santa Elena and Monteverde hotels.

★ Selvatura Park

If admiring some of Costa Rica's most cherished creatures is your thing, don't miss **Selvatura Park** (off Road 619, 2 km north of Santa Elena, tel. 506/4001-7899, www. selvatura.com, 7am-4pm daily by tour only, prices vary by activity), where you'll have the chance to check out hummingbirds, snakes, butterflies, and other species that contribute to the area's biodiversity. The park, which also offers zip-lining and hanging bridges tours, has three live animal exhibits and one insect museum (each one a short walk from the rest) that are only accessible by guided tour.

The guided exhibit tours occur every 15 minutes (8:30am-2:30pm daily). The most immersive exhibits are those with creatures that fly: At the **Hummingbird Garden** (30-40 minutes, $5 pp), a small outdoor patio

Monteverde and Santa Elena

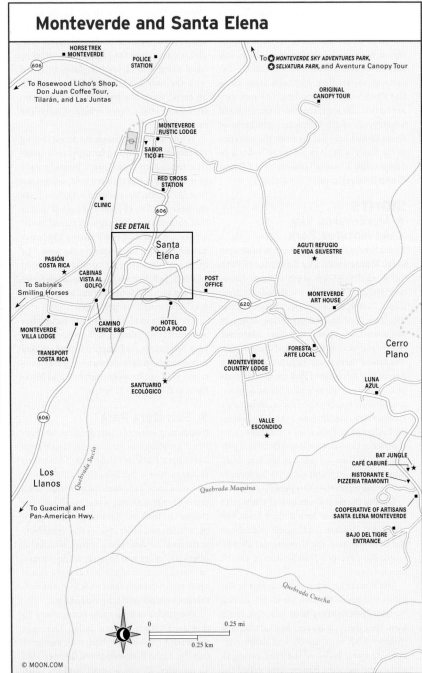

HORSE TREK MONTEVERDE

POLICE STATION

To ⭐ MONTEVERDE SKY ADVENTURES PARK, ⭐ SELVATURA PARK, and Aventura Canopy Tour

606

To Rosewood Licho's Shop, Don Juan Coffee Tour, Tilarán, and Las Juntas

ORIGINAL CANOPY TOUR

MONTEVERDE RUSTIC LODGE

SABOR TICO #1

RED CROSS STATION

CLINIC

606

SEE DETAIL

Santa Elena

AGUTI REFUGIO DE VIDA SILVESTRE

PASIÓN COSTA RICA

CABINAS VISTA AL GOLFO

POST OFFICE

To Sabine's Smiling Horses

620

MONTEVERDE ART HOUSE

MONTEVERDE VILLA LODGE

CAMINO VERDE B&B

HOTEL POCO A POCO

TRANSPORT COSTA RICA

FORESTA ARTE LOCAL

Cerro Plano

SANTUARIO ECOLÓGICO

MONTEVERDE COUNTRY LODGE

LUNA AZUL

VALLE ESCONDIDO

606

BAT JUNGLE

CAFÉ CABURÉ

RISTORANTE E PIZZERIA TRAMONTI

Los Llanos

Quebrada Sucia

Quebrada Maquina

COOPERATIVE OF ARTISANS SANTA ELENA MONTEVERDE

To Guacimal and Pan-American Hwy.

BAJO DEL TIGRE ENTRANCE

Quebrada Cuecha

0   0.25 mi

0   0.25 km

© MOON.COM

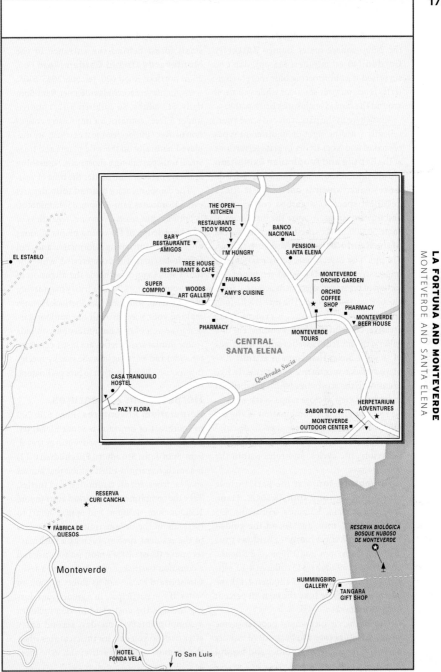

THE OPEN KITCHEN

RESTAURANTE TICO Y RICO

BANCO NACIONAL

BAR Y RESTAURANTE AMIGOS

I'M HUNGRY

PENSION SANTA ELENA

EL ESTABLO

TREE HOUSE RESTAURANT & CAFÉ

FAUNAGLASS

MONTEVERDE ORCHID GARDEN

SUPER COMPRO

WOODS ART GALLERY

AMY'S CUISINE

ORCHID COFFEE SHOP

PHARMACY

MONTEVERDE BEER HOUSE

PHARMACY

CENTRAL SANTA ELENA

MONTEVERDE TOURS

Quebrada Sucia

CASA TRANQUILO HOSTEL

PAZ Y FLORA

HERPETARIUM ADVENTURES

SABOR TICO #2

MONTEVERDE OUTDOOR CENTER

RESERVA CURI CANCHA

FÁBRICA DE QUESOS

RESERVA BIOLÓGICA BOSQUE NUBOSO DE MONTEVERDE

Monteverde

HUMMINGBIRD GALLERY

TANGARA GIFT SHOP

HOTEL FONDA VELA

To San Luis

equipped with benches and tables, expect several hummingbirds to whiz past your nose as they visit several freestanding feeders. Inside the 2,500-square-meter, domed **Butterfly Garden** (40-60 minutes, $15 pp), don't be surprised if a shimmering blue morpho butterfly lands on your shoulder while you stroll around the humid enclosure's brick paths.

Elsewhere in the park, you can scare yourself silly with the sight of 30 different types of snakes and frogs living in glass terrariums at the **Reptile and Amphibian Exhibition** (40-60 minutes, $15 pp), including a fer de lance snake, which is one of Costa Rica's deadliest species, large boa constrictors, and tiny tree frogs. Admire the intricacies of some 50,000 insect specimens at the **Jewels of the Rainforest Insect Museum** (1 hour, $15 pp). The insect museum is particularly impressive as it boasts a world-renowned collection of preserved specimens acquired from Costa Rica and beyond. The owner's lifelong commitment to the project is evident in the creative, colorful displays. Reminiscent of a gallery, the museum's walls feature hundreds of shadow boxes that contain artfully displayed insect specimens. I particularly like examining the scorpions, which are difficult to find and view at close range in the wild.

You can visit any combination of the exhibits. Tour guides narrate at each, discussing topics such as species identification, behaviors, life cycles, and roles within the ecosystem.

Adventure tours at the park include a zip-lining **canopy tour** (8:30am, 11am, 1pm, and 2:30pm, 2.5 hours, $50 adults, $35 children 4-12, min. age 4) and the guided **Treetop Walkways hanging bridges tour** (8:30am, 11am, 1pm, and 2:30pm, 2-2.5 hours, guided tour $50 adults, $35 children 4-12, self-guided tour $35 adults, $25 children 4-12); the latter is a moderate hike through 90 percent virgin forest.

One of the vicinity's most popular theme parks, Selvatura caters to busloads of visitors daily and has modern facilities and helpful employees.

Monteverde Orchid Garden

Rumor has it that Monteverde has the highest diversity of orchids in the world. The small forest behind the entrance to the **Monteverde Orchid Garden** (Road 606, 25 m north of Road 620, tel. 506/2645-5308, www.monteverdeorchidgarden.net, 9am-5pm daily, $12 adults, $6 children 5-12, children under 5 free) contains an impressive collection of over 400 species, most of which are displayed naturally on the wild plants and trees you'll walk past along a short path. Something is always in bloom, no matter the time of year.

The complimentary **guided tour** (departs every 15 minutes 9am-4:15pm, 35-45 minutes) is optional but wows everyone, regardless of any knowledge of flowering plants. Guides offer enough intriguing information and cool facts to fascinate the uninterested, while the tour's short run time holds the attention of even young visitors. With a trusty magnifying glass in hand, you'll feel like Sherlock Holmes making your way through the outdoor garden in search of tiny but miraculous orchids (some miniature varieties are just 1 centimeter wide) and learning how the sneaky species ingeniously disguises itself to lure pollinators.

Herpetarium Adventures

Herpetarium Adventures (Road 620, 200 m southeast of downtown Santa Elena, tel. 506/2645-6002, www.skyadventures.travel, 9am-8pm daily, $16 adults, $10 children 0-12) is a small, terrarium-filled exhibit that houses snakes, frogs, toads, tarantulas, and turtles. Take the complimentary **guided tour** (noon, 1:30pm, 3pm, 4:30pm, and 6pm, 1 hour) to learn about the unique traits and behaviors of the resident species, such as a bushmaster snake (Costa Rica's most poisonous) and a common basilisk, better known as a Jesus Christ lizard because of its ability to walk on water. If you participate in a guided tour during the day, the cost of admission includes a complimentary same-day, second entry after dark so you can see the creatures when they're most vocal and active; aim to be there at 6:30-7pm.

Bat Jungle

Monteverde's **Bat Jungle** (Road 620, 2 km southeast of Santa Elena, tel. 506/2645-9999, www.batjungle.com, 9am-6pm daily, $7) is the only bat-centered museum in Costa Rica. Though it's possible to tour the small premises on your own, the Bat Jungle's tour guides share ample information about the mammals—and are anxious to debunk myths about them—so opt for the **guided tour** (hourly 9am-5pm daily, 45 minutes, $15 adults, $12 children 6-18). Either way, you'll receive access to the habitat where bats fly freely behind a glass wall. Schedule your visit in advance and you can coordinate it with feeding time.

Hummingbird Gallery

Totally free and worth a visit is the **Hummingbird Gallery** (Road 620, 25 m south of the Reserva Biológica Bosque Nuboso de Monteverde, tel. 506/2645-5030, 9am-5pm daily, free). The gallery's biggest draw is the charms of hummingbirds that fly freely around the property and hover in midair as they drink from feeders. On occasion, olingos and coatimundis visit the spot too. Spend as much time as you like admiring and photographing the creatures, but remain quiet and avoid using the flash on your camera. Visits do not require a guide or an advance reservation.

The gallery's gift shop sells artwork and photographs by indigenous artists. If you don't buy anything at the shop, you can express your gratitude for the attraction and help further hummingbird research by leaving a tip. Avoid visiting in the late morning when tour groups departing from the nearby nature reserve make their way toward the gallery.

San Luis

One of the scariest drives I have made in Costa Rica was down the steep, narrow, cliffside path known as **La Trocha a San Luis.** Although I do not recommend driving the route yourself (taxis are far more skilled at handling the bumpy terrain and hairpin turns), the trip is worth taking for the stunning scenes of pristine mountain terrain—always green and gorgeous. The road descends into a valley speckled with immaculate farmland cherished by inhabitants of **San Luis** (4 km south of Monteverde), a community of roughly 350 people.

A number of farms around Monteverde offer farm tours. In San Luis, at least eight farms have opened their properties for touring. At these farms, you can watch sugarcane and coffee demonstrations, hike forested trails, learn about conservation efforts, and take a dip in a swimming hole.

To learn more about the farms or to pre-arrange a visit, contact the **Asociación de Desarrollo Integral de San Luis** (San Luis Development Association, San Luis community center, tel. 506/2645-7485, www.sanluis.or.cr). You can also visit San Luis by reserving a spot on the town's own **El Cafetal Coffee Tour** (250 m north of the community center, tel. 506/2645-7329, www.elcafetaltour.com, 8am, 10am, and 2pm daily, 2 hours, $35 adults, $15 children 6-12), an informative and laid-back tour that details coffee production from bean to beverage. Run by a local family, the tour also invites participants to have a cup of their finest brew and homemade baked goods. Transportation between Monteverde and San Luis is included, sparing you the daunting drive on La Trocha a San Luis.

RECREATION

This region is known for its many outdoor adventures. Stand-alone outfitters offer zip-lining and tree-climbing tours, as well as horseback rides and farm visits.

Two popular adventure parks in the area also offer the chance to experience multiple activities at one place. At **Selvatura Park** (off Road 619, 2 km north of Santa Elena, tel. 506/4001-7899, www.selvatura.com, 7am-4pm daily by tour only, prices vary by activity), you can go zip-lining and tour hanging bridges. The park is home to a butterfly garden, a hummingbird garden, a reptile and amphibian exhibit, and an insect museum, too. At **Monteverde Sky Adventures Park** (off Road 619, 3.5 km north of Santa Elena, tel. 506/2479-4100, www.skyadventures.travel, 7am-9pm daily, prices vary by activity), you can go zip-lining, tour hanging bridges, ride an aerial tram, and try tree climbing. Both parks are adjacent to the Reserva Biológica Bosque Nuboso de Santa Elena.

Local Guides and Tours

MONTEVERDE TOURS

Monteverde Tours (Road 620, 25 km east of Road 606, tel. 506/2645-5874, www.monteverdetours.com, 7:30am-6pm Mon.-Fri., 10am-6pm Sat.-Sun.) is a divison of La Fortuna's **Desafio Adventure Company** (tel. 506/2479-0020, www.desafiocostarica.com). Upholding the same high standards for safety and customer service that Desafio Adventure Company is known for, Monteverde Tours focuses on helping visitors experience highlights of the Monteverde vicinity.

Through Desafio Adventure Company, Monteverde Tours provides a helpful service known as **Adventure Connections.** These tours provide onward transportation to various destinations once your tour is over, saving you the hassle of arranging transportation. There are several Adventure Connections in the Monteverde area; see the Monteverde Tours website for a complete list. You can do a **white-water rafting** or **safari float excursion** on Río Tenorio, then travel to Sámara or areas along the Guanacaste coast ($129-153 pp). Another option is to go on a **horseback riding** or **mountain biking tour** around Lago Arenal, then travel to La Fortuna ($88-92 pp). The **crocodile boat tour** breaks up travel to the central Pacific coast and can provide drop-offs around Manuel Antonio ($164 pp). Adventure Connections tour pricing varies according to activity type, route, and number of participants. In all cases, the fee for the transportation service is already factored into the tour cost.

PASIÓN COSTA RICA

For a selection of less-common experiences, check out the tour offerings of **Pasión Costa Rica** (150 m north of the Santa Elena cemetery, tel. 506/8304-7161, www.pasioncostarica.com, 8am-4pm daily). Co-owner and certified naturalist guide Marcos Méndez Sibaja is a fantastic resource for unique explorations of Monteverde's smaller nature reserves and its most popular cloud forest attractions. His company's name (which means "Passion Costa Rica") speaks to his enthusiasm for guiding. As he's a one-man show, book early, especially if you'll be traveling during the high season. Half-day tours start at $57 per person (min. 2 people); full-day tours start from $66.50 per person (min. 2 people).

NASUA TOURS

Nasua Tours (tel. 506/8313-6679, www.nasuatours.com) is a small outfitter operating from Santa Elena. Owner Oscar Castillo Mejia is not only a trained tour guide but also an enthusiastic person who is a joy to explore Monteverde with. He specializes in day tours, night tours, and bird-watching expeditions. It's best to book in advance, especially for tours during the high season. Half-day tours run $25 per person; full-day tours are $220 per group.

Zip-Lining

Canopy tours speckle the Monteverde region. In order to be competitive, each outfitter offers something different from the next.

Monteverde Sky Adventures Park (off Road 619, 3.5 km north of Santa Elena, tel. 506/2479-4100, www.skyadventures.travel, 7am-9pm daily) offers the favorite **Sky Trek canopy tour** (8am-3pm daily, 2 hours, $84 adults, $58 children 5-12, min. age 5). It's the only option in the area where you brake with metal handlebars instead of your gloved hand.

Leading the way in excitement and thrills are **100% Aventura** (Road 619, 3.5 km north of Santa Elena, tel. 506/2645-6388, www.

aventuracanopytour.com, 7am-4pm daily) and **Monteverde Extremo** (off Road 606, 5.5 km north of Santa Elena, tel. 506/2645-6058, www.monteverdeextremo.com, 8am-5pm daily). If you want to experience a **superman cable,** a forward-facing zip line that allows you to fly through the air like Superman— no cape required—100% Aventura's **canopy tour** (8am, 11am, 1pm, and 3pm, 2 hours, $50 adults, $40 children 5-12, min. age 5) has the longest one in Latin America at more than 1,500 meters. To experience a superman cable in the dark, Monteverde Extremo's **canopy tour** (8am, 11am, and 2pm, 2.5 hours, $50 adults, $40 children 3-12, min. age 3) provides a **subterranean superman cable** that whizzes through a fabricated tunnel. Both outfitters' tours include a Tarzan swing and a rappel for added fun.

If you want to give zip-lining a try but don't consider yourself an adrenaline junkie, head to either the **Original Canopy Tour** (off Road 620, 1.5 km north of Santa Elena, tel. 506/2645-5243, www.canopytour.com, 7:30am-5pm daily) or **Selvatura Park** (off Road 619, 2 km north of Santa Elena, tel. 506/4001-7899, www.selvatura.com, 7am-4pm daily by tour only, $50 adults, $35 children). Both locations offer slightly mellower zip-lining experiences. OCT's **canopy tour** (7:30am, 10:30am, and 2:30pm, 2-2.5 hours, $45 adults, $35 children 5-12, min. age 5) has been running since the mid-1990s and pioneered the practice of zip-lining in Costa Rica. The operation's owner has been embattled in court for years as part of a lengthy saga over zip-lining rights; if the court rules that he holds the patent for the activity, this could mean an end to all non-partnered zip-lining tours in the country.

Horseback Riding

Horse Trek Monteverde (Road 606, 1.5 km north of Santa Elena, tel. 506/8359-3485, www.horsetrekmonteverde.com) provides the region's most extensive repertoire of horseback tours. Half-day ($49-65 pp), full-day ($85-120 pp), and multiday excursions

($399-1,595 pp) that range in difficulty are available. Choose from mountain and farm rides at sunset, combined hiking and horseback tours to a waterfall, rides along the Continental Divide, and more. You can also create your own custom tour.

Sabine's Smiling Horses (off Road 606, 2 km west of Santa Elena, tel. 506/8385-2424, www.horseback-riding-tour.com, 6am-9pm daily, $45-105 pp) is a small operation but one that has contributed to the Santa Elena and Monteverde horseback riding scene for years. The company's twilight rides ($60 pp) on evenings with a full moon are unique.

Tree-Climbing Tours

Finca Modelo Ecológica (off Road 606, 4.5 km northwest of Santa Elena, La Cruz, tel. 506/2645-5581, www.treetopclimbingmonteverde.com, 8am-4pm daily) is home to a 40-meter hollow ficus tree that can be climbed from the outside or the inside—but avoid the latter if you suffer from claustrophobia. The farm's **Tree Top Climbing Tour** (7:30am, 10:30am, and 1:30pm, 3 hours, $45 pp, min. age 12) allows you to choose your preferred route up the tree, as well as the method used to get back down— either rappelling or climbing in reverse.

At the **Arboreal Tree Climbing Park** (at the Monteverde Sky Adventures Park, off Road 619, 3.5 km north of Santa Elena, tel. 506/2479-4100, www.skyadventures. travel, 7am-9pm daily), take the park's **tree-climbing tour** (1.5 hours, $42 adults, $29 children 5-12, min. age 5) to experience a climbing course that will have you shimmying and safely free-falling down from a number of trees.

ENTERTAINMENT AND EVENTS
Nightlife

Head to the **Monteverde Beer House** (Road 620, 100 m east of downtown Santa Elena, tel. 506/2645-7675, 10am-10pm daily) for craft ales. It has two-for-one cocktails during happy hour (5pm-7pm daily), samples of beer on

tap, live music and theme nights on occasion, and a full restaurant. If nothing on the menu catches your eye, sister property **The Open Kitchen** (Road 606, 25 m north of downtown Santa Elena, tel. 506/2645-5775, 11am-9pm daily, $6-12) will deliver food from their menu to the beer house for free.

After dark, quiet Santa Elena comes to life at **Bar y Restaurante Amigos** (Road 606, 25 m west of the central church, tel. 506/2645-5071, www.baramigos.com, 11:30am-2am daily). Every ingredient needed for a fun night out is here, including a dance floor, a DJ, food, drinks, televisions, and pool tables. Visit before sundown and you can admire the view of one of Monteverde's many valleys from the back of the property. If you're in the area on a Sunday, you can stop by an authentic Costa Rican disco. Covered with colorful artwork, the spot is impossible to miss downtown.

SHOPPING
Art Studios and Galleries
The Monteverde vicinity is jam-packed with beautiful art. A number of artists own studios or shops that are open to the public, and you can easily spend a half day hopping from one gallery to the next (this is best done with a rental car).

In the heart of Santa Elena, the **Woods Art Gallery** (Road 606, 40 m south of the central church, tel. 506/2645-6668, 8:30am-9pm Mon.-Sat., 9am-9pm Sun.) stocks all kinds of Costa Rican souvenirs. It is one of the town's biggest souvenir stores—certainly the most commercial—and conveniently located on the main drag.

A small shop worth peeking your head into is **Faunaglass** (Road 606, 15 m south of the central church, tel. 506/2645-7598, www.faunaglass.com, 11am-8pm Mon.-Sat., 11:30am-6pm Sun.). Also known as the Glass Art Studio, the store features glass-blown replicas of Costa Rican animals, including

hummingbirds, turtles, sloths, and a variety of frogs. Time flies as you watch artist Angel Castellanos Gomez shape his creations before your eyes.

The **Foresta Arte Local** (Road 620, 1 km southeast of Santa Elena, tel. 506/2645-6081, 10am-6pm daily) displays jewelry, clothing, and items made with batik (hand-dyed) fabrics.

At the **Monteverde Art House** (100 m north of Road 620, 200 m north of Foresta Arte Local, tel. 506/2645-5275, www.monteverdearthouse.com, 9am-6pm daily), you can purchase the paintings of local artists, as well as wood carvings and masks.

Luna Azul (Road 620 at Pensión Santa Elena, tel. 506/2645-6638, www.shopmonteverde.com, 10am-7pm daily) has a great selection of handcrafted jewelry and clothing designed by Costa Ricans.

The **Cooperative of Artisans Santa Elena Monteverde** (CASEM, Road 620, 2 km southeast of Santa Elena, tel. 506/2645-5190, www.casemcoop.blogspot.com, 9am-5pm daily) sells an assortment of crafts, including dolls and stuffed animals, bags and wallets, bookmarks, bracelets, hair ties, and more. CASEM is a nonprofit organization; purchases help support impoverished local families and the cooperative's artists (mainly women).

For unique handmade wooden pieces, head to the hidden gem **Rosewood Licho's Shop** (Road 606, 2.5 km northwest of Santa Elena, tel. 506/2645-6456, www.rosewoodmtv.weebly.com, 8am-6pm daily). Friendly craftsman Jose Luis Arguedas Jimenez (known as "Licho") is almost always on the premises and can show you around the workshop where he produces bowls and plates out of fallen rosewood. He also offers free informal walks around his farm's gardens; impromptu visits are permitted.

FOOD
Food and Farm Tours
For a coffee education direct from the farm, I favor the operation at **Finca Don Juan**

1: cacao pods at Finca Don Juan **2:** a traditional tamale, like the kind served at Sabor Tico **3:** a snake at Selvatura Park **4:** the rustic Monteverde Country Lodge

(Road 606, 2.5 km northwest of Santa Elena, tel. 506/2645-7100, www.donjuancr.com/monteverde, 8am-5pm daily), where the charming Don Juan makes an effort to greet customers and is a pleasure to chat with. His jam-packed **Coffee, Chocolate, and Sugarcane Tour** (8am, 10am, 1pm, and 3pm daily, 2 hours, $35 adults, $15 children 6-15) provides great value by explaining the processing of three tasty products. During the tour you'll visit stations around the farm to see coffee plant seedlings; the working coffee plantation; the coffee pulping, drying, and shelling processes; and the bean roasting house. You'll also visit a station that explains how cacao is produced, as well as a station that demonstrates how sugarcane is made. Samples of chocolate and sugarcane are provided during the tour, and you can try a complimentary cup of coffee upon tour completion. Lined with accessible trails, the farm offers an experience for the whole family.

The **El Trapiche Tour** (Road 606, 3 km northwest of Santa Elena, tel. 506/2645-7650, www.eltrapichetour.com, 10am and 3pm Mon.-Sat. and 3pm Sun., 2 hours, $33 adults, $12 children 6-12) focuses on the production of sugarcane, though it also includes chocolate and coffee components. During your visit, you can ride around in an oxcart, see how three different types of sugarcane mills operate, and make your own sugarcane candy. Advance reservations are recommended.

Santa Elena
COSTA RICAN

Sodas are traditional Costa Rican family restaurants. When looking for a *soda* in Santa Elena, I usually end up at **Restaurante Tico y Rico** (Road 606, 35 m north of the central church, tel. 506/2645-5204, 10am-10pm daily, $5-10). Their menu is full of staple Costa Rican dishes from *casados* (traditional dishes of rice and beans on a plate, accompanied by a variety of side dishes), to desserts, and they make mean *patacones* (smashed and fried green plantains).

INTERNATIONAL

The ★ **Tree House Restaurant & Café** (Road 606, 15 m south of the central church, tel. 506/2645-5751, www.treehouse.cr, 11am-10pm daily, $12-28) is something you won't see every day—a dining establishment with an ancient ficus tree in the center. Head to the top floor where you can watch passersby on the main street while dining on American, Mexican, or Peruvian fare. The first floor sometimes has live music. Note that the restaurant's dishes are more expensive than others in town; what you're really paying for is the feeling of dining in a treehouse.

Santa Elena has a few restaurants called **I'm Hungry** (Road 606 across from the central church, tel. 506/2645-6878, $4-7) that snuggle close to each other on the main drag. Expect inexpensive eats but unimpressive service from these places. All are informal, hole-in-the-wall restaurants, but the largest one, with the longest menu, is an American fast-food joint (11am-10pm daily). Oddly, it serves fantastic French crepes. For complete indulgence, order the *crepa éxtasis,* which is loaded with bananas, caramel, and Baileys Irish Cream. Just steps up the street are two neighboring I'm Hungry restaurants (11am-11pm daily); one serves Chinese food, and the other is a pizzeria.

VEGETARIAN AND VEGAN

Three establishments around Santa Elena's core can prepare a variety of non-meat (and in some cases, non-dairy) meal options, although none is specifically vegetarian or vegan. At the ★ **Orchid Coffee Shop** (Road 620, 25 m east of Road 606, tel. 506/2645-6850, www.orchidcoffeecr.com, 7am-8pm, $9-14), choose from plenty of breakfast selections (omelets, waffles, and crepes) and lunch options (soups, salads, and sandwiches). The restaurant is one of my favorites in Monteverde because of its laid-back vibe, homey ambience, friendly service, and delicious fresh food and drinks, including rich coffee and flavorful smoothies. **Amy's Cuisine** (Road 606, 20 m south of the central church, tel. 506/2645-7272, www.amyscr.com, 11am-10pm, $8-24) offers extensive lunch and dinner entrée choices, including pasta, quesadilla, fajita, rice, and wrap options. **Paz y Flora** (Road 606, 250 m southwest of downtown Santa Elena, beside Casa Tranquilo Hostel, tel. 506/6336-6956, noon-8pm, $7-10), a restaurant with vibrant colors and design, can turn any dish on its menu into a vegetarian or vegan one if it isn't already meatless or dairy-free to begin with.

Monteverde

COSTA RICAN

First-time visitors to Monteverde shouldn't miss either ★ **Sabor Tico #1** (Road 606, 750 m north of downtown Santa Elena, tel. 506/2645-5827, www.restaurantesabortico.com, 7am-9pm daily, $5-12) or ★ **Sabor Tico #2** (Road 620, 250 m southeast of downtown Santa Elena, tel. 506/2645-5827, www.restaurantesabortico.com, 7am-10pm daily, $5-12). Both restaurants showcase Costa Rican cuisine in establishments with plenty of Tico pride, where traditional oxcart art and red, white, and blue banners are displayed. The smaller, original restaurant, #1, is likely to be the less busy of the two. Although #2 is larger and usually louder, the second-floor restaurant is perfectly positioned to take in the sunset and a delightful breeze. Both restaurants share the same menu, which features mini corn tamales ($2) traditionally prepared and served wrapped in a banana leaf.

If you only need a snack, stop by the **Fábrica de Quesos** (Road 620, 3 km southeast of Santa Elena, tel. 506/2645-6889, 9am-5pm Mon.-Sat., 10am-4pm Sun.). Although the cheese factory no longer has tours, you can still buy dairy products from its shop. The ice cream, raved about more than the cheese, comes in a variety of unique flavors (including macadamia nut and Monteverde coffee) and can also be enjoyed as a milkshake.

To try one of Costa Rica's most guilty culinary pleasures—*chicharrones* (fried pork rinds)—venture out to **Chicharronera Monteverde** (Road 619, 3 km north of Road 606, tel. 506/8986-5917, noon-9pm Wed.-Sun.,

$5-7). You may be the only non-Costa Rican at the place, but you'll be welcome anyway, especially if you end up loving the delicacy that locals go nuts for. Other dishes (mainly pork-based selections) are served, but they're not the main reason to go. Visit during the day to take in the restaurant's fabulous mountaintop view of layers of forested hills, or on a Saturday night for karaoke.

INTERNATIONAL

★ **Ristorante e Pizzeria Tramonti** (Road 620, 2 km southeast of Santa Elena, tel. 506/2645-6120, www.tramonticr.com, 11:30am-9:45pm daily, $5-16) has fantastic Italian food. I'm a sucker for their wood-fired pizzas. Twinkling lights and elegantly set tables keep the rustic restaurant classy, creating the perfect setting for a romantic or relaxing night out. As good as the entrées are, don't fill up on them; save room for tiramisu, panna cotta, or an ice cream off the dessert menu.

Café Caburé (Road 620, 2 km southeast of Santa Elena, tel. 506/2645-5020, www.cabure.net, 9am-9pm daily, $4-15) will get your mouth watering if you're a chocolate fan. The homemade goodies in the café's chocolate shop are most delectable; choose from truffles, turtles, and chocolate-covered coffee beans, all made with Costa Rican cocoa beans. If you're hungry for a full meal, the café covers breakfast, lunch, and dinner with a menu that spans Argentinean, Chinese, and Mexican creations.

ACCOMMODATIONS

If you want to save a buck (or bucketloads) on accommodations, Santa Elena has plenty of shared room options. At least 10 hostels (pensions and B&Bs with dormitory rooms included) are spread throughout the downtown core.

My favorite Monteverde-area accommodations are outside of Santa Elena. On the outskirts of town are woodsy rooms, cabins, lodges, and villas, most of which offer tranquil properties where you can appreciate the sights and sounds of the mountain's biodiversity.

Santa Elena

UNDER $50

The most popular of Santa Elena's several budget accommodations, **Pensión Santa Elena** (Road 606, 25 m south of Banco Nacional, tel. 506/2645-5051, www.pensionsantaelena. com, dorm $11.50 pp, private $32 s/d) is the best option if you're looking to socialize, especially with free-spirited individuals. It wins with friendly, welcoming, and helpful staff—plus, it has terrific tacos. The motel-style, two-story pension has one dorm for six people and 32 private rooms for 1-4 guests. Each room is slightly different, but most feature natural wood decor, pops of color, and warm bedding that you'll appreciate on chilly nights.

Down the road from Santa Elena's center but still within walking distance is the **Casa Tranquilo Hostel** (Road 606, 250 m southwest of downtown Santa Elena, tel. 506/2645-6782, www.casatranquilobackpackers.com, dorm $11 pp, private $25 s/d). Visits to the property, formerly a Costa Rican house, feel like homestays. There are three dormitories (each sleeps 1-4 people) and eight private rooms (each sleeps 1-5 people); some have hand-painted artwork across concrete walls, which match the building's colorful exterior, while others are constructed entirely of wood. The hostel runs its own **canyoneering tour** (7:20am daily, 5 hours, $60 pp, min. age 18), but if you would rather just relax at the hostel, you can chill in a hammock, strum the communal guitar, or pet the resident Labrador.

For inexpensive but clean rooms, I lean toward **Cabinas Vista al Golfo** (off Road 606, 350 m southwest of downtown Santa Elena, tel. 506/2645-6321, www.cabinasvistaalgolfo. com, dorm $14 pp, private $37 s/d), with 16 vibrant, private rooms (for 1-4 people each) with windows that let in lots of light. A modern dorm is equipped with bunk beds that sleep 19 guests, and each bed comes with a locker. Although the hotel resembles a one-story lodge from the street, the back actually spans two floors and is built into the mountainside. For the price, it's hard to beat the property's valley view, which you can enjoy from the communal area; some rooms have balconies.

$50-100

An accommodation you cannot go wrong with is the ★ **Camino Verde B&B** (off Road 606, 350 m southwest of downtown Santa Elena, tel. 506/2645-5641, www.hotelcaminoverde. com, $75 s/d). The budget-friendly two-story home has 19 simple but quiet rooms; all are private, but a few have shared bathrooms. Request a private bathroom upon booking if that is your preference. What sells me on the hotel is the super service provided by friendly staff who are eager to please. Regardless of whether it is sunny, cloudy, or rainy, plan to spend the majority of your time at the B&B relaxing on the covered deck; it's the best spot in the place.

When in Santa Elena, the place I stay at most often is the ★ **Monteverde Villa Lodge** (off Road 606, 750 m southwest of downtown Santa Elena, tel. 506/2645-7283, www.monteverdevillalodge.com, $75 s, $78 d). I love the four spacious cabins in particular (for 1-5 people); the four rooms (for 1-4 people) in the main building of the small, family-run hotel are also worthy of a stay. All are immaculately kept and have natural mixed-wood decor; some have murals of rainforest scenes. The best feature of all is the hearty breakfast, sometimes accompanied by fresh jam made from fruit collected around the premises. If you would like to join the chef in the kitchen and take part in meal preparation, you're welcome to do so; inform the owners of your interest the day before. Sister property the **Monteverde Rustic Lodge** (off Road 606, 750 m north of downtown Santa Elena, tel. 506/2645-6256, www.monteverderusticlodge.com, $75 s/d) is equally comfortable and hospitable—and fittingly named. The owners, who are skilled at both woodworking and storytelling, built nearly every rustic furnishing in the small two-floor, 14-room hotel. If you want to know about Monteverde's history, strike up a conversation with one of them during your stay; they'll be happy to share their heritage with you. The hotel's clean, quaint, and cozy rooms sleep 1-5 people.

Monteverde

$50-100

With its inviting wood terraces and peaked roof, the 60-room **Monteverde Country Lodge** (off Road 620, 1.5 km southeast of Santa Elena, tel. 506/2645-7600, www. monteverdecountrylodge.com, $96 s/d) reminds me of a Swiss lodge or a ski chalet. The two-story lodge has pretty gardens, patios, and trickling water fountains, giving the eco-conscious hotel a soothing atmosphere for relaxation. The property is incredibly quiet; not only is it removed from the stir of Santa Elena, but it is also two side streets away from one of the region's most traveled roads, so you won't be bothered by a steady sound of cars whizzing by. All rooms sleep 1-5 people.

$150-250

The modern ★ **Hotel Poco a Poco** (off Road 620, 500 m south of Santa Elena, tel. 506/2645-6000, www.hotelpocoapoco.com, $165 s/d) brings a touch of elegance to the vicinity yet remains unpretentious. It has indoor fine dining, casual patio dining, and a spa, and each of the hotel's 34 rooms (for 1-4 people) features hypoallergenic bedding, blackout curtains, bathrobes, and contemporary bathroom finishes. Roofs and sunshades provide cover throughout the property, so when it rains, you can walk around, swim in the pool, or soak in the Jacuzzi without being bothered by a drop.

What I love best about **Hotel Fonda Vela** (Road 620, 3.5 km southeast of Santa Elena, tel. 506/2645-5125, www.fondavela. com, $170 s, $192 d) are facilities that are rare finds in the Monteverde region, including a swimming pool and Jacuzzis, a restaurant where you can dine by a fireplace, and a mini sports bar equipped with a pool table. It is also a hop, skip, and jump away from the area's most famous nature reserve, and

shares many of the same bird-watching opportunities. The two-story hotel has 24 oversize rooms (each with one king or two queen beds) that showcase gorgeous hardwood handicrafts and forest views.

The only resort-like property in the vicinity is ★ **El Establo** (off Road 620, 1.5 km southeast of Santa Elena, tel. 506/2645-5110, www. elestablo.com, $225 s/d), a large mountainside hotel with over 150 rooms (each sleeps 1-4 people), two restaurants, two pools, sports fields and courts, and a spa. It even runs its own zip-line tour and night tour, and has a trail system that invites self-guided hikes and mountain bike rides. The best of the rooms' features are beds with orthopedic mattresses and balconies or terraces that boast a beautiful view of the Nicoya Gulf. Some spacious suites have two floors.

INFORMATION AND SERVICES

The Monteverde region does not have a hospital, but there is a **clinic, Sucursal Monteverde** (200 m southwest of the *fútbol* field, tel. 506/2645-5076, 7am-4pm Mon.-Thurs., 7am-3pm Fri.), just outside of the downtown core. **Farmacia Vitosi** (Road 606 beside Beso Espresso, tel. 506/2645-5004, 8am-8pm daily) and other **pharmacies** can be found in the heart of Santa Elena.

A **police station** (250 m north of Road 606, 1 km north of Santa Elena center, tel. 506/2645-7074, 24 hours daily) and a **post office** (Road 620, 400 m southeast of Santa Elena center, tel. 506/2645-5042, 8am-5pm Mon.-Fri.) are on the outskirts of town.

The grocery store **Super Compro** (Road 606, 100 m west of Santa Elena center, tel. 506/7209-2612, 7am-9pm daily) is within walking distance of most establishments in downtown Santa Elena.

Money can be obtained from **Banco Nacional** (Road 606, the northeastern side of Santa Elena's downtown triangle, tel. 506/2645-5610, www.bncr.fi.cr, 8:30am-3:45pm Mon.-Fri.) or the **ATM** just up from the Super Compro.

TRANSPORTATION
Boat

If you plan to visit the Monteverde vicinity from La Fortuna, one of the best ways to reach Santa Elena is by a boat crossing over **Lago Arenal.** The **van-boat-van** service (formerly called the jeep-boat-jeep service, sometimes referred to as the taxi-boat-taxi service, $30-45 pp) combines ground transportation from La Fortuna to the lake, a boat ride across the lake, and further ground transportation on to Santa Elena. The entire route takes approximately 3.5 hours to complete and typically operates twice daily—once in the morning and once in the afternoon. The two best service providers are **Aventuras Arenal** (Road 702, 750 m south of Road 142, La Fortuna, tel. 506/2479-9133, www.aventurasarenal.com, 7am-8pm daily) and **Desafío Adventure Company** (Calle 472 behind the central church, La Fortuna, tel. 506/2479-0020, www.desafiocostarica.com, 6am-10pm daily).

Car and Taxi

The roads around Santa Elena are a mixed bag—some are freshly paved, and others are gravel and dirt paths that require driving at slow speeds. Prepare yourself for mountainous driving, including sharp turns, steep cliffs, and bumpy stretches. A 4x4 vehicle is recommended regardless of when you plan to visit, but is required during the low season when rainfall contributes to a messy drive. You're bound to encounter cloud cover as the drive increases in elevation, so avoid driving at night as darkness only worsens the hazard. However, the views of the rich landscape more than make up for the rough drive.

From **San José** to Santa Elena, the 150-kilometer drive on Highway 1 and Road 606 takes about three hours.

From **La Fortuna,** the 115-kilometer drive around Lago Arenal on Roads 142, 145, and 606 takes about 3.5 hours.

From **Liberia,** the 110-kilometer drive on Highway 1, Road 145, and Road 606 takes around two hours.

The smoothest route into town is via the southeast. Road 606 between Highway 1 and the community of Guacimal (20 kilometers south of Santa Elena) is entirely paved. Other routes to Santa Elena, via the southwest and the northwest, also offer paved sections but require longer drives on poorer roads.

There are **gas stations** on Highway 1 before the turnoff for Las Juntas de Abangares (coming from Liberia), at the main intersection in Tilarán (coming from La Fortuna), and on the outskirts of Santa Elena as you enter town.

Driving around the center of Santa Elena is much easier; the roads are hilly but smooth. Note that Road 606—the main drag—takes the shape of a triangle, and all three sides are one-way streets where traffic flows counterclockwise. Parking spaces line the westernmost side of the triangle, which is also where **taxis** (up to $12) can be hailed; they can take you wherever you need to go.

Bus

The regional **bus station** is on Road 620, 250 meters southeast of Santa Elena's center. Public buses travel to Santa Elena daily. You can catch one from **San José** (6:30am and 2:30pm daily, 4 hours, $5), **Tilarán** (3:50am, 9:30am, 12:30pm, and 4:30pm Mon.-Sat., 4am and 12:30pm Sun., 1.5-2 hours, $2.50), and **Puntarenas** (8am, 1pm, 1:30pm, and 2:15pm daily, 3 hours, $3). If you plan to travel to Santa Elena via Sardinal (Guacimal) or Las Juntas de Abangares, buses from Puntarenas pass through one or the other.

Private Transfer Service

Vehicles for private transfer service vary in size. Most accommodate up to eight people plus luggage. Prices are determined by route, departure time, and number of passengers (depending on the service provider, the cost may be for 1-8 people, or 1-5 people with an extra fee imposed for additional passengers). Prices average around $235 from San José, $195 from Liberia, and $200 from La Fortuna. Some operators offer vehicles that fit 28 passengers, perfect for larger groups.

Monteverde Tours (Road 620, 25 km east of Road 606, tel. 506/2645-5874, www. monteverdetours.com, 7:30am-6pm Mon.-Fri., 10am-6pm Sat.-Sun.) is the satellite office of La Fortuna-based Desafio Adventure Company (tel. 506/2479-0020, www. desafiocostarica.com). The operator can provide transportation to the region from all over Costa Rica.

Operating directly from Monteverde is Transport Costa Rica (Road 606, 500 m southwest of Santa Elena center, tel. 506/2645-6315, www.transportcostarica.com, 6am-8pm daily). They can get you to Santa Elena from virtually any destination countrywide.

Shared Shuttle Service

Well-known service providers Interbus (tel. 506/4100-0888, www.interbusonline.com) and Grayline Costa Rica (tel. 506/2220-2126, www.graylinecostarica.com) can shuttle you to the Monteverde region from the country's most frequented areas, including La Fortuna, Manuel Antonio, San José, and many others. Daily morning and afternoon departures are available from most cities. Depending on the route, one-way services to Santa Elena range $55-90 per person. Most shuttles fit eight people with luggage and offer drop-offs at Monteverde-area hotels.

Organized Tour

A number of adventure and nature tours include post-tour onward transportation to the Monteverde vicinity from a variety of cities. White-water rafting tours, safari float tours, horseback riding tours, mountain biking tours, and boat tours can be arranged to offer pickups at hotels in La Fortuna, Manuel Antonio, Sámara, and several Guanacaste beach towns; you are dropped off afterward at hotels around Monteverde. Desafio Adventure Company (tel. 506/2479-0020, www.desafiocostarica.com), which operates the local Monteverde Tours (Road 620, 25 km east of Road 606, tel. 506/2645-5874, www.monteverdetours.com, 7:30am-6pm Mon.-Fri., 10am-6pm Sat.-Sun.), provides

this service under the name Adventure Connections.

If you plan to travel to Monteverde following a stint in La Fortuna, and if you're up for a challenging hike and horseback riding combo experience, the Big Forest Hike (8am daily, 8 hours, $159 pp, min. age 12) is worth looking into. Offered by La Gavilana Herbs & Art (500 m south of the Butterfly Conservatory in El Castillo, tel. 506/8533-7902, www.gavilana. com, 8am-5pm Mon.-Fri. and 9am-2pm Sat.), the tour starts in El Castillo (a $30 taxi ride from La Fortuna center) and ends at the Mirador San Gerardo Lodge (a $20 taxi ride to Santa Elena center).

TOP EXPERIENCE

★ RESERVA BIOLÓGICA BOSQUE NUBOSO DE MONTEVERDE

From Santa Elena, Road 620 weaves southeast for several kilometers (passing through Cerro Plano and Monteverde along the way) and ends at the entrance of the Reserva Biológica Bosque Nuboso de Monteverde (Monteverde Cloud Forest Biological Reserve, Road 620, 5.5 km southeast of Santa Elena, tel. 506/2645-5122, www. reservamonteverde.com, 7am-4pm daily, last entry 2pm, $22 adults, $10 children 6-12), the region's most-visited cloud forest reserve. The nearly 26,000-acre space is lush and jungle-like, with giant tree trunks, intertwining roots and branches, moist and sometimes musky air, and regular wafts of fog.

The protected land area is a beacon of biodiversity in Costa Rica. More than 100 species of reptiles, 60 species of amphibians, and 6 species of jungle cats (among other mammals, including monkeys, bats, peccaries, and tapirs) inhabit the reserve, along with an immeasurable number of insects and birds. Nonstop visitor flow during operating hours makes wildlife-watching a challenge, but certainly not impossible. Easier to see is evidence of the reserve's extraordinary collection of over 3,000 species of plants and trees. Low montane rainforest encompasses the majority, where it is estimated that up to 10 percent of the flora is endemic to the area.

Guided tours come in the form of the early morning **bird-watching tour** (6am, 4.5 hours, $65 pp), the daytime **natural history walk** (11:30am and 1:30pm, 2.5 hours, $39 pp), and the **night tour** (6pm, 2 hours, $20 pp). You can arrange tour guides directly through the reserve—which is managed by the Centro Científico Tropical (Tropical Science Center)—or through tour operators in town. Advance reservations for tours are required; they can be made via telephone or the reserve's website. The park's trails can also be explored without a guide. Advance reservations for unguided visits are recommended (but not required), especially if you plan to visit during the morning, when the reserve is the busiest. Since entry is restricted to 250 people at a time, without a reservation you may end up waiting at the entrance indefinitely.

Hiking

The reserve boasts an impressive 13-kilometer trail system beyond the main **visitors center.** If you are a beginner hiker or are restricted to a tight timeline, choose one or two of the principal trails where the majority of visitors trek. With a free day and a generous amount of energy, you can explore the mystical cloud forest extensively by covering every one of the park's paths.

The **Sendero Bosque Nuboso** (Bosque Nuboso Trail, 2 km one-way, 45 minutes, moderate) and the **Sendero Camino** (Camino Trail, 2 km one-way, 30-45 minutes, easy-moderate) are the most frequented trails. Both start at the reserve's entrance and run parallel to each other, following a jagged line that ascends to the east and ends near **La Ventana** (The Window)—a lookout point over the Continental Divide. The Sendero Bosque Nuboso is named "cloud forest" for a reason; the narrow path cuts through dense forest where the air is moist and usually cluttered with clouds. It is the prettiest trail in the

park, and perfectly resembles the scene you probably envision when you think of a cloud forest. In contrast, the Sendero Camino offers less rugged terrain, a wider track, and an easier hike, but at the cost of a less scenic experience.

Varying in distance, duration, and difficulty are eight other routes that complete the reserve's trail system, referenced by some as "the triangle." Most notably, the **Sendero Wilford Guindon** (Wilford Guindon Trail, 1.7 km one-way, 30 minutes, moderate) provides access to the reserve's one and only **hanging bridge** (not to be confused with the Monteverde region's famed hanging bridges, located off-site); the **Sendero El Río** (El Río Trail, 1.5 km one-way, 20-30 minutes, easy-moderate) leads to a small but tranquil waterfall.

Continental Divide

One of Monteverde's claims to fame is the passage of the Continental Divide, the ridge that separates water flow to the Atlantic from water flow to the Pacific, through the region. The divide offers a beautiful and seemingly endless view, although gusty trade winds keep it clouded over most of the time. Within the reserve, you can find the divide at the end of the **Sendero Bosque Nuboso** (Bosque Nuboso Trail) and the **Sendero Camino** (Camino Trail). A sign at **La Ventana** marks the spot.

Bird-Watching

The reserve is a fantastic locale for bird-watching, especially from December to April, when over 20 percent of the protected land area's migratory species come to visit. Rife with fruit and insects, the reserve pleases the **resplendent quetzal,** a brightly colored and sometimes long-tailed trogon (a type of tropical bird) that can be seen in the vicinity. More likely to be heard, however, is the **three-wattled bellbird.** Their tinny "bonk" is easily recognizable; it sounds throughout the reserve like a rusty swing.

Getting There

To drive to the reserve, exit Santa Elena to the east and take Road 620 as far as you can, roughly 5.5 kilometers. From downtown Santa Elena, the drive is 12 minutes. A 4x4 vehicle is recommended but not required. Parking is available at the trailhead.

You can hire an official taxi to take you to the reserve, or take the public bus that travels between downtown Santa Elena and the reserve (6:15am, 7:30am, and 1:15pm daily, departures to Santa Elena at 11am, 2pm, and 4pm daily, 20 minutes, $1.25). By taxi, a one-way trip from downtown Santa Elena costs approximately $10. If you're staying at an accommodation along Road 620, you can catch the bus as it travels between town and the reserve.

TOP EXPERIENCE

RESERVA BIOLÓGICA BOSQUE NUBOSO DE SANTA ELENA

Cloud forest immersion awaits at the **Reserva Biológica Bosque Nuboso de Santa Elena** (Santa Elena Cloud Forest Biological Reserve, off Road 619, 3.5 km northeast of Santa Elena, tel. 506/2645-5390, www.reservasantaelena. org, 7am-4pm daily, last entry 2:30pm, $16 adults, $7 children 8-12). This 766-acre reserve is significantly smaller, slightly higher in elevation, and noticeably less busy than the Monteverde cloud forest reserve. The lush and jungle-like scenery and wildlife-spotting opportunities at both reserves are similar.

Through the **visitors center,** you can obtain a tour guide who will lead you on a **natural history walk** (7:30am, 9:15am, 11:30am, and 1pm daily, 2.5 hours, $33 adults, $20 children 8-12) through the property's secondary and premontane wet forest. All guided bookings require at least two days' notice; reserve by telephone or through the reserve's website. Self-guided exploration is encouraged, and walk-ins are welcome. The price of the tour includes admission.

Hiking

The **Sendero Encantado** (Encantado Trail, 3.5-km loop, 2-3 hours, moderate) and the **Sendero del Bajo** (Del Bajo Trail, 2.5-km loop, 1.5 hours, moderate) both present opportunities to appreciate the forest's tall trees and lush surroundings without working too hard. The **Sendero Caño Negro** (Caño Negro Trail, 5 km one-way, 3-4 hours, moderate-difficult) is a semicircular trail accessed from Sendero del Bajo or Sendero Encantado. It provides the roughest, most adventurous trek of the reserve's five trails.

On clear days, you can see Volcán Arenal from the observation deck along the leisurely **Sendero Youth Challenge** (Youth Challenge Trail, 1.5-km loop, 45 minutes, easy-moderate). The short **Sendero Mundo Jóven** (Mundo Jóven Trail, 500-m loop, 10 minutes, easy) is entirely paved and wheelchair-accessible.

Getting There

To drive to the reserve, exit Santa Elena to the north on Roads 606 and 619 and continue until Road 619 forks. Stay right on the unnamed road for 3.5 kilometers, following the signs to the reserve or to Selvatura Park. From downtown Santa Elena, the drive is 15 minutes. A 4x4 vehicle is recommended but not required. There's a small parking lot at the trailhead.

Francisco Torres operates a **shuttle service** (tel. 506/8725-4335, 6:30am, 8:30am, 10:30am, and 12:30pm daily, departures back to Santa Elena at 9am, 11am, 1pm, and 4pm daily, 30 minutes, $3) to the reserve from downtown Santa Elena or accommodations along the way. Advance reservations are required and can be placed through area hotels. The shuttle departs from downtown Santa Elena at the Cámara de Turismo de Monteverde (Monteverde Chamber of Tourism, Road 606, 50 m south of the central church). You can also hire an official **taxi** to take you to the reserve. A one-way trip from downtown Santa Elena costs approximately $12.

Hiking Around Monteverde

The Reserva Biológica Bosque Nuboso de Monteverde, the Reserva Biológica Bosque Nuboso de Santa Elena, and the Bosque Eterno de los Niños are three of the largest and most-visited nature reserves in the Monteverde vicinity. With extra time in the area, or if you enjoy hiking or bird-watching along unfrequented forest trails, consider exploring a less popular reserve. Most permit self-guided exploration but also offer guided tours. Advance reservations for guided tours are recommended. Here are some quiet, worthwhile options:

RESERVA CURI-CANCHA

As many as seven intertwined trails provide relatively easy hikes through Reserva Curi-Cancha (300 m northeast of Road 620, 3 km southeast of Santa Elena, tel. 506/2645-6915, www. reservacuricancha.com, 7am-4:30pm daily, last entry 3pm, $15 adults, $7 children 7-20). Half of the 200-acre reserve is primary forest, and the other half is a mix of secondary forest and pastureland. It's a great spot for bird-watching on your own. The reserve also runs guided bird-watching tours, as well as guided day hikes and night tours.

Getting There: The drive from downtown Santa Elena to Reserva Curi-Cancha is three kilometers and takes seven minutes. Exit Santa Elena to the east on Road 620 and turn left on the unnamed road at the large Fábrica de Quesos (cheese factory). The reserve is roughly 250 meters northeast of the cheese factory.

SANTUARIO ECOLÓGICO

The family-owned reserve Santuario Ecológico (850 m southwest of Road 620, 1.2 km south-east of Santa Elena, tel. 506/2645-5869, www.santuarioecologico.com, 7am-5pm daily, last entry 3:30pm, $15 adults, $7 children 0-11) has trails that meander past plantations, a hollow ficus tree, and a waterfall. Reserve staff offer guided day hikes, night tours, tours of a coffee plantation, and traditional cooking classes.

Getting There: The drive from downtown Santa Elena to Santuario Ecológico is two kilometers and takes five minutes. Exit Santa Elena to the east on Road 620 and turn right on the unnamed road at the school. The reserve is at the end of the road, roughly 850 meters beyond the turn.

VALLE ESCONDIDO

With valley and waterfall viewpoints, and a stunning look at the Golfo de Nicoya, the small, 40-acre Valle Escondido (750 m southwest of Road 620, 1.2 km southeast of Santa Elena, tel.

BOSQUE ETERNO DE LOS NIÑOS

What began as a fundraising effort led by children is now the largest private reserve in Costa Rica—the Bosque Eterno de los Niños (Children's Eternal Rainforest, www. acmcr.org, adults $13, children 6-12 $8, children under 6 free). The massive reserve spans over 55,000 acres of land between Monteverde and La Fortuna.

The majority of visitors who tour the reserve do so a stone's throw from Santa Elena at Bajo del Tigre (off Road 620, 2.5 km southeast of Santa Elena, tel. 506/2645-5305, 8am-5pm daily), a subset of the full reserve. An information center marks the entrance.

The reserve can also be accessed via the ranger stations at San Gerardo (tel. 506/2200-0313, by appointment only), Pocosol (tel. 506/2468-8282, by appointment only), and Finca Stellar (tel. 506/8726-1675, 8am-4pm Mon.-Fri.). San Gerardo is on the west side of the reserve, not far from Santa Elena and Monteverde. The entrances to both Pocosol and Finca Stellar are on the east side of the reserve in the San Carlos region and are unreachable via Monteverde. Visits to any of the three stations require advance reservations.

506/2645-5156, www.escondidopreserve.com, 6am-4:30pm daily, last entry 3pm, $15 adults, $10 children 5-17) is my favorite reserve in the area for scenic views. Reserve staff run bird-watching tours, day hikes, and night tours.

Getting There: The drive from downtown Santa Elena to Valle Escondido is two kilometers and takes five minutes. Exit Santa Elena to the east on Road 620 and turn right on the unnamed road at the school. After 350 meters, turn left on the unnamed road signed for the Night Walk Hidden Valley Trail. The reserve is at the end of the road, roughly 400 meters beyond the turn.

AGUTI REFUGIO DE VIDA SILVESTRE

The nature trails at the Aguti Refugio de Vida Silvestre (400 m north of Road 620, 700 m southeast of Santa Elena, tel. 506/4000-3385, www.agutimonteverde.com, 7am-4:30pm daily, last entry 3:30pm, $15 pp, cash only), which was established in 2017, are currently being developed and improved. Some paths are already paved, making this reserve a good option for travelers with impaired mobility or families with young children.

Getting There: The drive from downtown Santa Elena to the Aguti Refugio de Vida Silvestre is slightly more than one kilometer and takes three minutes. Exit Santa Elena to the east on Road 620 and turn left on the unnamed road at the Banco de Costa Rica. The reserve is roughly 400 meters north of the bank.

SENDERO PACÍFICO

Construction is underway to create a trail system throughout the bellbird corridor that connects Monteverde to the Golfo de Nicoya. The Sendero Pacífico (Pacífico Trail, www.senderopacifico.net) is a work in progress; the only paths currently open to the public are those that connect the communities of San Luis and Guacimal. Treks along the off-the-beaten-path trails require a tour guide; you can arrange this through the Asociación de Desarrollo Integral de San Luis (San Luis Development Association, San Luis community center, tel. 506/2645-7485, www.sanluis.or.cr).

Getting There: Current access to the Sendero Pacífico is permitted through the community of San Luis. The drive from downtown Santa Elena to San Luis is eight kilometers and takes 20 minutes. Exit Santa Elena to the east on Road 620 and turn right on La Trocha a San Luis just beyond Hotel Fonda Vela. San Luis is roughly four kilometers south of the turn. A 4x4 vehicle is required.

Hiking

Bajo del Tigre has a wonderful collection of short, easy trails that nicely balance the challenging hikes at other reserves in the Monteverde area. You can hike with a guide during the day tour (8am-4pm daily with advance reservation, 2 hours, $32 adults, $24.50 children 6-12) or on your own.

Bajo del Tigre's night tour (5:30pm daily, 2 hours, $23 adults, $18.50 children 6-12) is my favorite of the kind in the area, offering the chance to trek through the forest in complete darkness. The hike starts out with a striking view of the valley, made even more beautiful by a gorgeous sunset (weather permitting). It continues into the forest, where a different world emerges after dark. With a little luck, you'll see spiders, bats, and sleeping birds. All of the tour's proceeds go toward conserving the reserve.

If you are an avid hiker and want to go where most others don't, plan a day trip, an overnight outing, or a multiday visit to the ranger station at San Gerardo. Access is granted through the Reserva Biológica Bosque Nuboso de Santa Elena, where a forested trail (3.5 km one-way, 1.5 hours, moderate-difficult) awaits. The hike descends into the forest toward the station and climbs out of it once you leave. The station itself has a web of six trails, most of them moderate in difficulty, so you'll get your fill of remote exploration and exercise with the visit.

Getting There

To reach Bajo del Tigre by car, exit Santa Elena to the east on Road 620 and continue for 2.5 kilometers until you see the welcome sign on your right. From downtown Santa Elena, the drive is five minutes. There's a small parking lot at the trailhead.

You can hire an official **taxi** to take you to the reserve. A one-way trip from downtown Santa Elena costs approximately $4.

It's possible to take the **public bus** (6:15am, 7:30am, and 1:15pm daily, departures back to Santa Elena at 11am, 2pm, and 4pm daily, 20 minutes, $1.25) that travels between Santa Elena town and the Reserva Biológica Bosque Nuboso de Monteverde. Tell the driver *"Bajo del Tigre, por favor"* upon boarding. The bus will stop a quick two-minute walk from the reserve entrance.

To reach San Gerardo ranger station, head to the Reserva Biológica Bosque Nuboso de Santa Elena; you access the ranger station from within the reserve. Exit Santa Elena town to the north on Roads 606 and 619 and continue until Road 619 forks. Stay right on the unnamed road for 3.5 kilometers, following the signs to the reserve or to the Selvatura Park. A 4x4 vehicle is recommended but not required. There's a small parking lot at the trailhead.

Guanacaste and the Northern Pacific

In Guanacaste, Costa Rica's hottest and driest region, you'll find a reprieve from the heat under the shade of its eponymous trees, also known as elephant-ear trees. For much of the year, this deciduous giant—the country's national tree—is full and emerald green. In contrast, during the drought season from January to April, it's bare and brown. This transformation is echoed throughout the region, which is predominantly tropical dry forest. Comprising plants, trees, and vines, the threatened tropical dry forest struggles to survive when rainfall is sparse. It loses some of its fauna to wetter areas, and it is most susceptible to forest fires. During this period, under the lustrous rays of a beating sun, Guanacaste glows in golden hues.

Highlights

Look for ★ to find recommended sights, activities, dining, and lodging.

★ **Swim at the base of a waterfall** at **Catarata Llanos del Cortés** (page 206).

★ **Go boating** and bird-watching at **Parque Nacional Palo Verde** (page 208).

★ **Visit a rustic ranch resort** around Volcán Rincón de la Vieja (page 219).

★ **Dive with bull sharks** in **Bahía Murciélago** (page 223).

★ **Surf the breaks** at **Witch's Rock and Ollie's Point** (page 226).

★ **Zip-line** in tandem at **Diamante Eco Adventure Park** (page 229).

★ **Try diving with manta rays** at **Islas Catalina** (page 246).

★ **Sunbathe** on white sand at **Playa Conchal** (page 250).

★ **Experience ranch life** and barbecue fiestas at **Black Stallion Eco Park** (page 253).

★ **Watch sea turtles nesting** at **Parque Nacional Marino Las Baulas** (page 266).

A microcosm of Costa Rica, Guanacaste has friendly people, delicious food, wild adventure, diverse landscapes, and a relaxed *pura vida* attitude. Nicknamed the Gold Coast, Guanacaste is most adored for its coastal communities and pristine beaches. No matter what you're looking for—lively beach towns with waterfront bars, quiet villages that have spectacular sunset views, all-inclusive resorts mere steps from the beach, or your own remote oasis—Guanacaste has it. It's family-friendly, idyllic enough for honeymooners, and thrilling for water sport enthusiasts, so it's no surprise that Guanacaste attracts just about every type of traveler.

This region is also steeped in rich tradition, and locals revel in it. Guanacaste hosts some of the best parties, parades, rodeos, and other cultural events that celebrate its people's vivacity and their national and provincial heritage.

PLANNING YOUR TIME

A popular option—especially among resort goers—is to use Guanacaste as a base from which to take **day trips,** including **boat tours** around **Parque Nacional Palo Verde** to view rare migratory birds, **nighttime tours** to see leatherback turtles nest on the beach at **Parque Nacional Marino Las Baulas,** and trips to the **Catarata Llanos del Cortés,** where you can swim at the gentle cascade's base. You can also visit theme parks like **Diamante Eco Adventure Park** or **Black Stallion Eco Park** and go tandem zip-lining or take part in a barbecue fiesta at a cowboy saloon, respectively.

If you're splitting your time in Costa Rica across two or more regions, Guanacaste makes a great last destination. Seemingly **endless coastline** provides plenty of peaceful beaches to relax at during your last few days in paradise: Don't miss the white sand at **Playa Conchal.** Desire a grand finale? Dive with bull sharks in **Bahía Murciélago**

and manta rays at **Islas Catalina,** or ride the notorious surf at **Witch's Rock** and **Ollie's Point.** You'll need a full day for any one of these four extreme adventures.

If you're not looking for more beach time, explore Guanacaste's **inland region.** A fabulous collection of accommodations and adventure parks is scattered about the slopes of **Volcán Rincón de la Vieja.** Opposite the large, modern properties that line the coast, the mountain's low-key **rustic ranch resorts** are worth a day trip or an overnight stay. They'll wow you with authenticity and traditional Tico hospitality.

Weather and Transportation

Guanacaste is hot! The region has an average temperature over 80°F, receives very little rainfall (with next to none from January through March), and boasts the highest percentage of sunshine across Costa Rica. Although areas at higher elevations east of Liberia provide cooler temperatures, plan for scorching sun along the coast. Take water, a hat, and sunscreen wherever you go. If you plan to be active, prepare yourself for dry air and infrequent shade. Rain showers between May and November provide some relief. The wettest months are June, September, and October.

A few paved highways make it easy to travel throughout most of Guanacaste. Side roads can be comprised of asphalt, flattened gravel, or dirt. Most routes between Liberia and the popular beach destinations do not require a 4x4 vehicle, but it's smart to have one if you plan to explore back roads (including the infamous Monkey Trail) or venture out into mountainous areas. During wet periods, rain can make poorly maintained roads impassable.

ORIENTATION

Guanacaste takes up the northwestern corner of the country. From the border at Nicaragua,

---

Previous: stand-up paddle surfers; fishing boats off Playa Potrero; a boardwalk at Parque Nacional Palo Verde.

Guanacaste and the Northern Pacific

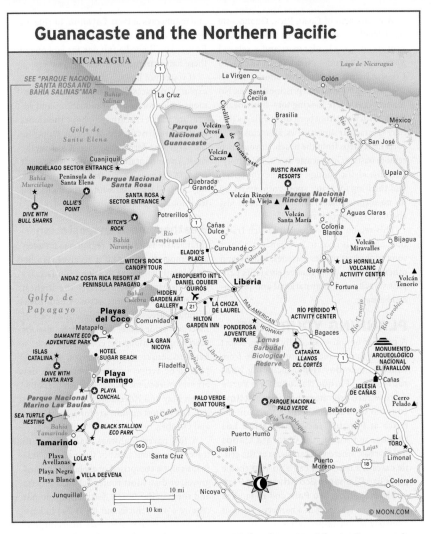

it stretches as far south as the Nicoya Peninsula and the central Pacific coast, and as far east as the northern inland area. The **Carretera Interamericana** (Inter-American Highway), also known as the **Pan-American Highway** or Highway 1, draws a vertical line through the region and passes by agricultural towns. Many of Guanacaste's most visited adventure parks and protected land areas are accessible via side roads that branch off from the highway in all directions.

Within the region, Liberia, Guanacaste's largest city, and its airport, the **Aeropuerto Internacional Daniel Oduber Quirós,** are centrally located. If you travel to Guanacaste from other areas in the country, you'll likely pass through Liberia on your way to the region's mountainous inlands or the coast.

The region's coast is split into a northern and southern half, as a result of access roads that cluster around two separate areas of Highway 21. The northern half of Guanacaste's coast reaches from Papagayo down to Playas del Coco. **Playas del Coco** is that section's hub. The southern half of the coast stretch from Las Catalinas to Playa Junquillal; its hub is **Tamarindo.**

Highway 21, one of the region's main thoroughfares, originates at Highway 1 in Liberia. From there, it moves west toward the Pacific coast. Several roads branch off from Highway 21 and provide access to most of the region's coastal communities and beaches. **Road 253** leads north to Papagayo. **Road 254** leads west to Bahía Panamá; here, **Road 159** travels south to Playa Hermosa. **Road 151** leads west to Playas del Coco and connects with Road 159 and Playa Hermosa to the north. **Road 155** leads south to Tamarindo. You'll travel these roads often if you plan to beach hop or make frequent day trips between towns.

The Road to Liberia

Highway 1 divides mountainous terrain to the north from the Golfo de Nicoya (Nicoya Gulf) to the south. The highway connects San José to Liberia, offering a leisurely 3.5-hour drive between the two metropolises. Relatively straight, flat, and well maintained, the route is a pleasant one, though you'll share it with big-rig trucks carrying loads of coffee, pineapples, and bananas.

As you approach the southern part of Guanacaste and the community of Limonal, you'll experience a shift in climate, scenery, and pace. Mountains distance themselves from the road and leave dusty plains in their place. The temperature rises, the humidity drops, and the surrounding greenery fades to brown due to seasonal drought from January to April. Roadside merchants slump in their chairs, tucked away in shaded areas to escape the scorching sun, sometimes under the broad, dense cover of a guanacaste tree, one of the country's national treasures. Welcome to the dry forest.

LIMONAL

The small hamlet of Limonal offers little in the way of attractions, but it is a great place to stop if you need a break from driving. A small

seed pod of Costa Rica's national tree, the guanacaste

Rodeos and *Sabaneros*

Rodeos are plentiful in Costa Rica. They top the lineups of nearly all *fiestas cívicas* (civic festivals) countrywide, but Guanacaste is king of the ring, with the most traditional and rustic versions.

Across the province, bucolic arenas with wood *graderías* (bleachers) remain impervious to modernization. Inside, *vaqueros* (cowboys) or *sabaneros* (the Guanacaste-specific term for a cowboy) saddle up horses for competitions in *lazos de lujo* (roping) and timed obstacle-course runs. They also ready bulls for *montas de toro* (bull riding) and no-kill *corridas de toro* (bullfights).

Sometimes cows are let loose in the *plaza de toros* (bullring), where fearless Ticos play *fútbol* (soccer) while simultaneously trying to dodge the beasts. Kids join in by getting their faces painted or by mounting a horse and participating in a *tope infantil* (kids' equestrian parade). Traditional adult-led *topes* are one of my favorite cultural events. They demonstrate dressage—horse obedience and movement precision. I love watching horses eloquently lift their legs and hop to commands or musical beats. The horses dance during parades with as much spirit as their joyful riders.

The festivities provide a unique peek into the recreational life of locals. They also are an opportunity to hear catchy mariachi-inspired *rancheros* (ranch music), try authentic dishes, and listen to *retahílas*—quickly recited poems that Costa Ricans use to playfully provoke others, much like the prodding of a bull. The entire affair is, as locals say, *puro Tico* (purely Costa Rican).

If you want to experience one of Guanacaste's best rodeos, the inland town of Santa Cruz (1 hour south of Liberia, 45 minutes east of Tamarindo, or 1 hour north of Sámara) hosts a weeklong party around mid-January each year. A true local event, the rodeo is largely advertised through word of mouth and takes place at the Plaza de los Mangos (Calle 1, 500 m south of Hwy. 21) in the town's center.

collection of restaurants around the corner of Highway 1 and Highway 18 invites you to pull over and grab a bite or a drink before continuing on your way. If you're headed for the Nicoya Peninsula, note that Limonal marks the turnoff to the Paseo del Tempisque (Tempisque Walk) or Highway 18, which leads to the peninsula and connects with other highways that carry on toward the coast.

El Toro

Limonal is as impossible to miss as its giant bull statue, known as El Toro (The Bull, in front of the BBQ Tres Hermanas restaurant, on the corner of Hwy. 1 and Hwy. 18). Cowboy country begins just beyond the hefty beast. Yes, the multistory statue is gimmicky, but the big guy (who restaurant staff call Aladdino) makes a great photo subject.

Food and Accommodations

If Limonal's bull statue makes you pull off the highway to get a better look, BBQ Tres Hermanas (corner of Hwy. 1 and Hwy. 18,

tel. 506/2662-8584, www.bbqtreshermanas. com, 7am-9pm daily, $7-22) has already earned your visit. Mosey on in to the alfresco steak house and prepare for big eats. The restaurant is all about meat; it serves steaks, pork chops, ribs, roasted chicken, and hamburgers, among a list of other Costa Rican dishes. If you only need a snack, skewers of freshly prepared potato chips called Papas Twisters are easy to take on the road. Several tour operators and private transfer services stop at this restaurant with travel groups, so there's regularly a mix of local and foreign diners.

Across the highway from BBQ Tres Hermanas, the bare-bones Restaurante Mi Finca (corner of Hwy. 1 and Hwy. 18, tel. 506/2662-8686, 6am-9pm daily, $8-23) is smaller and less polished than the busy steak house across the street, but it's equally popular with tourists thanks to a flock of uncaged scarlet macaws out back. Service is typically quick, especially if you order what almost everyone else does—*casado* (a traditional dish of rice and beans, accompanied by a variety of side dishes). The restaurant also operates a small, on-site bakery where you can stock up on fresh-baked snacks, including muffins and cookies.

Transportation

From **San José,** Limonal is a 140-kilometer, 2.5-hour drive northwest on Highway 1. From **Liberia,** Limonal is a 70-kilometer, one-hour drive southeast on Highway 1.

CAÑAS

Roughly 20 kilometers northwest of Limonal, Cañas is a midsize, rural-feeling, authentic Costa Rican town that's home to some of the region's cowboys and a handful of off-the-beaten-path experiences. The first thing you'll notice when you enter town or drive by it on Highway 1 is the **Plaza de Toros Chorotega** (Chorotega Bullring), the area's trusty and rusty bullring. It hosts the city's *fiestas cívicas* around March each year and enlivens the quiet town with bull riding, bullfighting, and concerts.

A few outfitters in Cañas operate whitewater rafting tours and safari float tours on Río Tenorio and Río Corobici. Though tours to either river can be arranged to provide transportation from destinations elsewhere in Guanacaste, as well as from La Fortuna, Monteverde, and beach towns on the Nicoya Peninsula, Cañas serves as the meeting point for these boating trips.

In Cañas center, Road 142, the main passageway that runs east-west through the city, splits into two streets in the downtown corridor: Avenida 1 to the north and Avenida Central to the south. Both are one-way streets; traffic on Avenida 1 flows west and traffic on Avenida Central flows east.

Sights

IGLESIA DE CAÑAS

The eye-catching **Iglesia de Cañas** (Cañas Church, Avenida Central and Calle 1) in the center of Cañas is a midsize Catholic church with a noteworthy exterior covered in multicolor broken-tile mosaics. Thousands of tile pieces (many in geometric shapes) create the work of art, which displays abstract backgrounds and a few figures and symbols, including San José, the church's patron saint, and a star believed to represent wisdom. Established in 1966, the church underwent an exterior restoration in 2009 to replace fading mosaics. Today, the sight is particularly beautiful under Guanacaste's shining sun, when the reflective tiles sparkle and add pizazz to the simple town.

CERRO PELADO

For one of the best panoramic views in Costa Rica (and certainly the best in Guanacaste), hike to the top of the dormant volcano known as **Cerro Pelado** (Bare Hill, 10 km east on Road 926, 3.5 km south of Cañas, free). The attraction is one of the province's least frequented, but it is well-known among locals and a must-do for any avid hiker. Guided tours are not provided. Due to the remote location, only hikers experienced in off-the-beaten-path treks should attempt this hike, ideally with another person.

Most of the hike is an uphill climb. An unpaved **trail** (4 km one-way, 1.5-2 hours, moderate-difficult) leads through forest, then across open pastures Windy conditions atop the mountain help cool the hot temperatures but can also throw you off-balance at a moment's notice. Be cautious of your footing as you climb up and over rocks to the summit, especially around Punto Cerro Pelado (Bare Hill Point), a peak with incredibly steep sides.

From the top, the view is incredible. You can see mountains in the distance that appear like waves in the sea, and Guanacaste's savanna-like landscape fills the lowlands in between. To optimize your experience, head out as early as 5am to catch the sunrise and to avoid being on the mountaintop when the sun's rays are the strongest.

The drive to the trailhead begins 3.5 kilometers south of Cañas. Take Road 926 off Highway 1 at the small village of Jabilla, drive for roughly 30 minutes until you see the sign marked "Cerro Pelado," and enter through the wood gate. A 4x4 vehicle is not required, and you can park your car by the roadside once inside the gate. Keep a few dollars on hand to give to Wilbert Barrantes, the owner of the land beyond the gate. He permits free entry but charges roughly $5 to keep an eye on parked cars.

MONUMENTO ARQUEOLÓGICO NACIONAL EL FARALLÓN

Some 15 kilometers north of Cañas, you can glimpse petroglyphs at the **Monumento Arqueológico Nacional El Farallón** (Farallón National Archaeological Monument, 9 km north of Sandillal, tel. 506/2200-0073, 8am-noon Tues.-Sun., advance reservations required by phone, $7). The monument, a rock wall, preserves petroglyphs inscribed by the indigenous Corobici people. Hundreds of petroglyphs depict animals, humans, ceremonies, and clan hierarchies. A member of the Costa Rican family that owns the property provides guided visits to the monument; however, English is not spoken. If you do not understand Spanish, book your own English-speaking tour guide; you can hire freelance guides through most Guanacaste tour operators and agencies.

The monument is north of the community of Cedros, beyond the Finca Las Lomas farm, down a rugged path. To reach the farm, take Highway 1 northwest from Cañas for three kilometers and turn right on the unnamed road that leads to the community of Sandillal. From here, unnamed country roads zigzag toward the monument. The unsigned route is best navigated with a GPS or a mobile device with Wi-Fi and access to a map.

Recreation

LOCAL GUIDES AND TOURS

The **Tenorio Adventure Company** (Hwy. 1 at Río Corobici, 5 km northwest of Cañas, tel. 506/2668-8203, www. tenorioadventurecompany.com, 8am-10pm daily) is a partner of La Fortuna's **Desafio Adventure Company** (www. desafiocostarica.com). The company is one

of two outfitters in the Cañas area that handle the majority of Guanacaste's river operations, including **white-water rafting excursions** on the **Río Tenorio** as well as **safari float tours** on a slower-moving stretch of the same river.

The Tenorio Adventure Company also runs **hiking tours** (9 hours, $149 pp) to **Río Celeste** at Parque Nacional Volcán Tenorio. Round-trip transportation from Cañas is included, but the tour can be arranged to depart from La Fortuna and finish at one of Guanacaste's many beach destinations (or vice versa) at no extra cost.

RCR Rafting (Hwy. 1 at Río Corobici, 5 km northwest of Cañas, tel. 506/2669-6161, www. raftingguanacaste.com, 8am-5pm daily) is a division of San José's **Ríos Tropicales** franchise. They provide **white-water rafting tours** on Río Tenorio and **safari float tours** on **Río Corobicí.** The outfitter caters to foreigners who book day tours through Guanacaste-based tour operators and agencies. Their river trips generally depart from and return to the same destination, typically one of the many coastal communities that fall between Papagayo and Tamarindo.

Each tour operator services different areas if you need to coordinate tour transportation from outside Cañas. RCR can provide transportation from Tamarindo, Playas del Coco, and Liberia with a minimum of four people. The Tenorio Adventure Company can pick you up in beach towns along the coast between Papagayo and Tamarindo, as well as destinations in other regions, including La Fortuna, Monteverde, and Sámara, with a minimum of two people.

WHITE-WATER RAFTING

Río Tenorio offers the best white water in Guanacaste and thrills rafters with a 3.5-meter drop over **Cascabel Falls.** The Tenorio Adventure Company's **Tenorio River Rafting Tour** (9am daily, 7 hours, $98 adults, $88 children 8-10, min. age 8) competes with RCR's **Tenorio River Rafting Tour** (9am daily, 4.5 hours, $105 pp, min.

age 12) for adrenaline-hungry thrill seekers. The essence of the two river trips is similar, but each tour operator services different areas if you need to coordinate tour transportation from outside Cañas.

SAFARI FLOAT TOURS

RCR Rafting's **Corobici River Floating Tour** (8am-3pm daily, 2.5 hours, $65 adults, $55 children 3-12) and the Tenorio Adventure Company's **Tenorio River Safari Float Tour** (9am daily, 3 hours, $57 adults, $51 children 6-10, min. age 6) are, like the white-water trips, similarly matched. Both leisurely river trips pass through dry forested areas and provide the same wildlife-spotting opportunities. There's a good chance you'll see a variety of birds, including tall herons and tiny kingfishers, plus iguanas, otters, and crocodiles.

SWIMMING HOLES

Roughly 10 minutes north of Cañas is one of my favorite swimming holes in the country, **La Poza de los Paredones** (The Pool of the Walls, 5.5 km north of Cañas center, Cedros de Cañas, free). Locals congregate at this small canyon filled with water. The miniature gorge is deepest under a nearby 12-meter bridge, so you'll likely see people jumping off the bridge into the refreshing pool below. If you would rather not jump, you can swim downstream; the water has hardly any current and is easy to wade into. There are no bathrooms or restaurants on-site. The friendly and social locals who frequent the spot are happy to share it with the occasional foreigner.

Food and Accommodations

Make time to stop at the **Restaurante Rincón Corobici** (Hwy. 1, 5 km northwest of Cañas, tel. 506/2669-6161, www. raftingguanacaste.com, 8am-5pm daily, $12-32), a pretty, open-air structure on the banks of Rió Corobici. If you dine in for breakfast or lunch, ask for a table near the river's edge. The sound of water will serenade you as it skips along the riverbed. Menu choices include typical Costa Rican breakfasts, meat and fish plates, and international foods like pasta and hamburgers.

Supported by natural wood posts and joists, the wall-less **Cocobolo Restaurant** (Hwy. 1, 4.5 km northwest of Cañas, tel. 506/2669-6191, 7:30am-7pm daily, $6-15) is a small, rustic restaurant with a casual atmosphere and only a handful of tables. But it has just about everything you can eat, from soups and sushi to cheesecake and *casado*. Special requests to customize dishes according to gluten-free, vegetarian, and vegan diets are accepted.

At **Hacienda La Pacifica** (Hwy. 1, 4.5 km northwest of Cañas, tel. 506/2669-9393, www. pacificacr.com, $72 s, $87 d), a herd of white-tailed deer (Costa Rica's national animal) meanders freely about the property, which is shared with cattle and covered with rice fields and tilapia ponds. Once owned by a former Costa Rican president, the hacienda provides subtle elegance. Its 19 spacious rooms feature vaulted ceilings with rustic wood beams. Although the quality of the furnishings is standard, the hotel is the nicest in the area. It is also easy to spot from the highway; look for the row of international flags.

Information and Services

Cañas is the largest city between Puntarenas (to the southeast) and Liberia (to the northwest). **Hospital de Cañas** (Road 142, 1.5 km north of Cañas, tel. 506/2668-4300, 24 hours daily) is the city's hospital. Several **pharmacies,** including **Farmacia Sucre** (Calle Central, 35 m north of Avenida 1, tel. 506/2668-7127, 8am-8pm Mon.-Sat., 9am-5pm Sun.), are scattered throughout the downtown core along or just off Avenida 1 and Avenida Central.

The city has a **post office** (near the corner of Hwy. 1 and Avenida 3, tel. 506/2671-1119, 8am-5pm Mon.-Sat.), a **police station** (Hwy. 1, 650 m north of Road 142, tel. 506/2669-0057, 24 hours daily), and many **supermarkets.**

The downtown core also houses several **banks,** including a branch of **Banco de Costa Rica** (Avenida Central, 100 m east of

Hwy. 1, tel. 506/2669-9090, 9am-4pm Mon.-Fri.) with an **ATM** (5am-midnight daily).

If you need fuel, grab it at the **gas station** on the corner of Highway 1 and Avenida Central (Road 142). It is conveniently located at the turnoff to the route that leads northeast to Tilarán.

Transportation

Cañas is 160 kilometers, a drive of 2.5-3 hours, northwest of downtown **San José** via Highway 1. From downtown **Liberia,** it's 50 kilometers, an approximate 40-minute drive, southeast via Highway 1.

The **regional bus station** is on Avenida 11 between Calle 1 and Calle Central. **Public buses** travel daily to Cañas from **San José** (multiple times 9:30am-5pm daily, 3.5 hours, $5.50), **Puntarenas** (multiple times 5am-5pm daily, 2 hours, $3-3.50), **Tilarán** (multiple times 5am-8pm daily, 30 minutes, $1), and **Liberia** (multiple times 5:30am-9:30pm daily, 1 hour, $2.50-3).

The **Tenorio Adventure Company** (Hwy. 1 at Río Corobici, 5 km northwest of Cañas, tel. 506/2668-8203, www.tenorioadventurecompany.com, 8am-10pm daily) runs several tours that may be used as **Adventure Connections.** The tour operator offers a pickup in one city, a river or hiking tour, and onward transportation to a new destination. Hiking, white-water rafting, and safari float tours ($125-149 pp, depending on tour type and start/end destinations) can be used to travel to or from any combination of the following areas: La Fortuna, Monteverde, Sámara, Liberia, and several areas along the Guanacaste coast, including Papagayo, Playa Hermosa, Playas del Coco, Potrero, Playa Flamingo, Brasilito, and Tamarindo.

If you need a **taxi,** you can find one on Calle Central between Avenida 11 and Avenida 13 near the regional bus station.

BAGACES

As it cuts through Guanacaste, Highway 1 barrels by Bagaces, roughly halfway between Cañas and Liberia. The sleepy agricultural town contributes little in the way of tourism but serves as a gateway to two of the province's biggest draws: the majestic Volcán Miravalles and the Parque Nacional Palo Verde.

In Bagaces center, Road 164—the main route that passes through town and continues north to Volcán Miravalles—splits into two streets in the downtown corridor: Calle Central to the east and Calle 2 to the west. Both are one-way streets; traffic on Calle Central flows south and traffic on Calle 2 flows north.

Volcán Miravalles

Volcán Miravalles (Miravalles Volcano) sits at 2,208 meters in the Cordillera de Guanacaste (Guanacaste mountain range), positioned on the boundary that separates the Guanacaste and Alajuela provinces. Its east side is green and reminiscent of the lively, lush landscape that runs rampant in the Northern Inlands. From the east at Bijagua, you can access hikes around the volcano's foothills that traverse forest trails and pass remote waterfalls. From the west, the volcano appears coarse, patchy, and partly brown.

The volcano is part of the Zona Protectora Miravalles (Miravalles Protective Zone). The protected land area does not have a ranger station, a visitors center, or well-marked and maintained trails. There are, however, fun things to do in the vicinity that invite volcano experiences of a whole different kind, like taking a dip in a pool of volcanic clay, biking around the volcano's slopes, and soaking in volcano-fed, themal-water hot springs.

Las Hornillas Volcanic Activity Center

My favorite way to experience Volcán Miravalles is by soaking in the clay at the **Las Hornillas Volcanic Activity Center** (25 km north of Bagaces, tel. 506/2100-1233, www.hornillas.com, 8am-5pm daily, $25 adults,

1: Río Corobicí, a pretty setting for safari float tours **2:** Iglesia La Agonía in Liberia **3:** the giant El Toro statue in Limonal **4:** the gentle cascade of Catarata Llanos del Cortés

$20 children 4-10). During a self-guided visit to Las Hornillas, you'll dunk yourself into a *baño de lodo* (mud bath) filled with mineral-rich clay from the volcano. There are two mud baths (one large and one small), as well as showers for rinsing off the clay after it has dried on your body. Changing rooms are provided, but towels are not, so be sure to bring your own. You can also sit in a sauna, relax in three thermal-water pools, and tour a raised path that winds through a live crater amid its bubbly spurts and smoking fumaroles.

In addition, the center boasts two rather impressive waterfalls, one with a deep-enough pool you can jump into from a platform at its side. You can experience both via the center's guided **waterfall tour** (9am, 11am, 1pm, and 3pm daily, 2 hours, $30 adults, $25 children 4-10), comprising a combined tractor ride, forest hike, and bridge crossing. I particularly love the view of the dry forest captured from the bridge, a kaleidoscopic scene of green or gold forest (depending on when you visit), red soil, and yellow-tinged riverbanks from sulphur-laced rivers.

Río Perdido Activity Center

The **Río Perdido Activity Center** (25 km north of Bagaces, tel. 506/2673-3600, www.rioperdido.com, 8am-6pm daily, day pass $30-40, adventure package $110-120) is the area's most glamorous construction. In a peaceful, remote location in the foothills of Volcán Miravalles, the adventure center features a multitiered design, a high-end restaurant with nearly 360-degree views of endless dry forest, modern pools, and elegant furnishings throughout. This is the place to be if you want to combine adventure with relaxation around Bagaces. Here you'll find an on-site thermal river, natural river pools, hot springs, and nature trails. You can go on a guided white-water tubing or canyoneering tour, or ride in the center's mountain bike park. A luxury hotel on-site has 20 ultramodern bungalows ($320 s/d).

To squeeze every drop of goodness out of your visit, reserve the **Total Adventure Package** ($120 adults, $110 children 3-12). It offers access to the property's river, pools, hot springs, and trails, as well as guided adventure tours: a rough white-water tubing run and a canyon adventure that is a mash-up of zip lines, bridges, via ferratas, and swings.

If you would rather skip the adrenaline, choose the activity center's **day pass** ($40 adults, $30 children 3-12), which allows access to the rivers and pools but skips the adventure tours.

All guests can take part in any of the activity center's on-site and unguided activities, including soaking in a medicinal spring, walking 1 kilometer to a waterfall, hiking 3.5 kilometers to a lookout point to see Volcán Miravalles in the distance, and tackling a difficult 5-kilometer trek along Sendero Las Tumbas (Las Tumbas Trail).

Biking enthusiasts will love the on-site **mountain bike park** (enter between 5am-3:30pm daily, visitors pass $12). Trails vary by distance and terrain, but all cater to experienced riders. If you don't feel comfortable heading out onto the trails on your own, a guide from the activity center can accompany you ($25 per hour). Bring your own bike or rent one through the center ($60 per day). Purchasing the Total Adventure Package or the day pass provides complimentary access to the bike park. Advance reservations are required if you want to enter the bike park before 8am.

★ Catarata Llanos del Cortés

It's amazing that the **Catarata Llanos del Cortés** (Llanos del Cortés Waterfall, tel. 506/8777-3014, $7 adults, $4 children 7-12) isn't more sought after. The beautiful waterfall is only a half-hour drive from Liberia, and you don't need to complete a difficult hike or have a 4x4 vehicle to reach it.

A five-minute walk down a set of concrete stairs is all that's required to access the waterfall. You can picnic and relax on the flat, sandy clearing in front of the cascade (it has sunny and shady spots), or else swim in the large pool at its base. The waterfall isn't one compact stream but rather a wide and gentle 25-meter cascade that spans much of the rock face it tumbles over. Its power is dispersed across the wall, making for an enjoyable swim in relatively calm water. Swimming here is suitable for kids; there are plenty of shallow spaces for wading, the pool deepens gradually, and a lifeguard is on duty. Resist the urge to climb behind the spray or hike above the waterfall to its edge. Although locals regularly frequent both spaces, slippery rocks make the areas unsafe.

Bathrooms and a free parking lot (a security guard here keeps watch over visitor vehicles) are just beyond the entrance, where the stairs to the waterfall's base are found. The waterfall is best accessed from the northwest. From Liberia, take Highway 1 southeast for approximately 20 kilometers and turn right onto the unnamed dirt road near the pedestrian walkway that crosses over the highway. From the turnoff, it's an approximate two-kilometer, 10-minute drive to the entrance. Make another right-hand turn onto a road signed for the waterfall. If arriving from the southeast via Bagaces, a median prohibits left-hand turns onto the unnamed dirt road from the highway. There is a break in the median just north of the pedestrian walkway where you can turn around and backtrack toward the dirt road.

Food and Accommodations

Since 1984, **Soda La Fuente** (Calle Central, 750 m north of Hwy. 1, tel. 506/2671-1620, www.sodalafuente.wordpress.com, 6:30am-10pm daily, $4-7) has been cooking up the best Costa Rican food in Bagaces. Try not to be put off by its unfinished walls or roof; the restaurant excels at cooking, not decorating. Its flavorful *casados* are tasty, but save room for a traditional treat, like an ice cream and Coca-Cola float, called a *vaca negra* (black cow).

Many attractions around Bagaces provide on-site accommodations, but if you need to spend a night in the heart of town, stay at **Cabinas Tamarindo** (Avenida 7, 200 m east of Avenida 3, tel. 506/2671-2695, $26 s, $35 d). The motel's six rooms sleep 1-3 people each and don't provide much more than a bed, but the property is clean, the owners are friendly, and the price is right if you're looking for a place to lay your head.

Information and Services

The closest **hospital** is the **Hospital de Cañas** (Road 142, 1.5 km north of Cañas, tel. 506/2668-4300, 24 hours daily) in Cañas, a 20-kilometer, 15-minute drive southeast of Bagaces. Alternately, the **Hospital Enrique Baltodano Briceño** (Calle 3 between Avenida Central and Avenida 2, tel. 506/2690-5500, 24 hours daily) in Liberia is a 25-kilometer, 20-minute drive northwest of Bagaces. On the south side of Highway 1 opposite the entrance to Bagaces is the town's **clinic, Sucursal Bagaces** (Road 922 at Hwy. 1, tel. 506/2671-1429, 8am-5pm Mon.-Fri.). The **pharmacy,** known as **Farmacia Zavaqui** (Avenida Central, between Avenida 3 and Calle 2, tel. 506/2671-1511, 8am-8pm Mon.-Sat., 9am-2pm Sun.), is easy to find in the center of Bagaces.

Although Bagaces is small, it has a **police station** (Calle 2, 85 m north of Hwy. 1, tel. 506/2671-1173, 24 hours daily), a **post office** (Calle 2, 50 m north of Hwy. 1, tel. 506/2671-1119, 7am-4pm Mon.-Fri.) and **supermarkets.** There are a few **banks** in town, including **Banco Nacional** (Calle 2, 500 m north of Hwy. 1, tel. 506/2212-2000, 8:30am-3:30pm Mon.-Fri.), which has an **ATM** (5am-10pm daily).

You can fill up on fuel at the **gas station** just off Highway 1 between Calle 1 and Calle Central.

Transportation

To get to Bagaces from downtown **San José,** it's a 185-kilometer, three-hour drive northwest on Highway 1. From downtown **Liberia,** it's a 25-kilometer, 20-minute drive southeast on Highway 1 to Bagaces.

It's possible to reach Bagaces by bus. **Public buses** commute between Liberia and Cañas. From **Liberia** (multiple times 5:30am-9:30pm daily, $1.50), it's a half-hour ride southeast to Bagaces. From **Cañas** (multiple times 4:30am-8:30pm daily, $1.50), it's a half-hour ride northwest to Bagaces.

If you need a **taxi** in town, you can find one parked on Avenida Central one block west of the central park.

★ PARQUE NACIONAL PALO VERDE

Smack dab in the middle of the country's driest province, **Parque Nacional Palo Verde** (Palo Verde National Park, 21 km south of Bagaces, tel. 506/2680-6596, 8am-4pm daily, $12) is a protected land area of over 45,000 acres. It's one of the best places in the country to spot waterfowl and other creatures that wander through waterlogged marshes, mangroves, and swamps.

Spillover from river flooding during part of the year transforms the area's tropical dry forest into wetlands. Resident bird species turn out in abundance between May and December as the dry forest blooms. From January to April (as the water recedes), the park welcomes flocks of annual migratory birds, as well as avid birders who are anxious to spot the avian visitors. Other notable animals in the park include crocodiles, peccaries, monkeys, and bats.

The entrance to the park (where the admission fee is paid) is marked by a small, signed booth. The largest development within the park is the **biological station** overseen by the **Organization for Tropical Studies** (OTS, 7 km southwest of the park entrance, tel. 506/2661-4717, www.tropicalstudies.org). You can tour the park with one of the organization's representatives as part of a **regular guided walk** (8am-3pm daily, 2 hours, $30 adults, $20 children 5-12) or else seize the rare opportunity to explore the protected land after dark during the **Nocturnal Wildlife Walk** (7pm daily, 2 hours, $48 adults, $30 children

5-12). Both experiences require advance reservations made by telephone or through the OTS website.

Most visitors experience the park on a trip down the Río Tempisque in a pontoon boat. Arranged through OTS, boat tours depart from the park's dock, 3.5 kilometers west of the biological station.

Hiking

You can explore the many trails beyond the Organization for Tropical Studies biological station on your own. The most notable include the easy **Sendero Mapache** (Mapache Trail, 700 m one-way, 20-30 minutes, easy), which passes through three types of forest (limestone, deciduous lowland, and evergreen), and the more challenging **Sendero Roca** (Roca Trail, 500 m one-way, 30 minutes, moderate) and **Sendero Pizote** (Pizote Trail, 800 m one-way, 20 minutes, easy-moderate), which both reward adventurous hikers with views of the Nicoya Gulf as well as the park's plains, wetlands, river, and lagoon.

Boat Tours

Boat captains pilot the non-narrated **boat tours** (7:30am, 10:30am, and 1:30pm daily, 2 hours, $57 adults, $35 children 5-12) offered by OTS on Río Tempisque. Hiring a tour guide is strongly recommended to help you correctly identify and understand the importance of the park's sights, including its 15 different habitats and the many kinds of wildlife.

Luckily, nearly every Guanacaste and Nicoya Peninsula tour operator and agency runs guided tours of Río Tempisque. Each tour provides a similar experience: A knowledgeable tour guide discusses the flora and fauna encountered during a quiet and gentle float down a slow-moving river. Tours depart from popular coastal communities daily. Round-trip transportation is almost always included; tour prices vary by departure location but average $85-120 per person.

If you have a rental vehicle, you can save money by driving yourself to Río Tempisque and joining a local tour. La Fortuna outfitter **Aventuras Arenal** (tel. 506/2479-9133, www.aventurasarenal.com) runs guided boat tours (9:45am daily, 2.5 hours, $89 adults, $44.50 children 6-11) from the communities of Bebedero (in the north) and Puerto Humo (in the south). **Palo Verde Boat Tours** (Ortega center, tel. 506/2651-8001, www.paloverdeboattours.com) runs a guided boat tour (8am, 10:30am, and 11am daily, 1.5 hours, $50 adults, $45 children 3-9) by way of the community of Ortega. If you choose to see the river with Palo Verde Boat Tours, allot extra time before or after your tour experience to visit the hacienda at **El Viejo Wetlands** (4 km north of Ortega, tel. 506/2296-0966, www.elviejowetlands.com, 9am-5pm daily, free). A 10-minute drive up the road from the tour operator's office, the worn yet well-preserved house pays homage to the country's heritage as far back as the 1800s.

Bird-Watching

Bird-watching is the park's foremost draw, so much so that it hosts the annual **Festival de Aves** (Bird Festival, tel. 506/8871-3401) around March of each year.

Anhingas, storks, cormorants, ibises, spoonbills, and herons are only a few of the species of great interest, and many can be spotted at the park's 5.5-acre **Isla Pájaros** (Pájaros Island). Not all boat tours visit the island, so check with your chosen outfitter about whether it's included on your preferred trip. The volume of birds that frequent the island (*pájaro* means "bird") makes it one of the best areas in the park for bird-watching. Though you cannot walk on the island, boats can get you close enough to it to see several bird species in close range.

Getting There

The only official and direct route to Palo Verde is from the north, via the unpaved but drivable Road 922. It covers about 23 kilometers between Bagaces and the entrance to the park. A 4x4 vehicle is recommended but not required.

Unofficial park access is possible from the south by way of the community of Puerto Humo. With this more complicated option, you'll need to hire a boat at the dock in Puerto Humo to cross Río Tempisque, then walk approximately two kilometers inland to end up at the OTS biological station.

A host of Guanacaste and Nicoya Peninsula tour operators will happily shuttle you to and from the park as part of an organized day tour. The excursion is one of the most popular guided tour offerings in the western half of the country. Tour prices vary by departure location but average $85-120 per person.

Liberia

The city of Liberia is both the capital of Guanacaste and a symbol of Costa Rica's *sabanero* (cowboy) soul. Cattle ranching remains the livelihood of many residents. Evidence of the city's age and resilience is everywhere, from the small, plain, stark white **Iglesia La Agonía** (La Agonía Church, Avenida 1, 1.5 km east of Hwy. 1), erected in the mid-1800s, to numerous illustrations of colonial-era architecture and design (including corner houses with double sun doors, adobe construction, and whitewashed buildings) that landed it the nickname La Ciudad Blanca (The White City).

Home to the Aeropuerto Internacional Daniel Oduber Quirós, Liberia marks the start and end of many travelers' journeys to Costa Rica. Others briefly pass through the city as they travel between the northern inland area and Guanacaste's famous beaches. Although Liberia is rarely visited as a destination in itself, it's a good place to shop for authentic souvenirs, wander through informal museums, people-watch, and see for yourself

Liberia

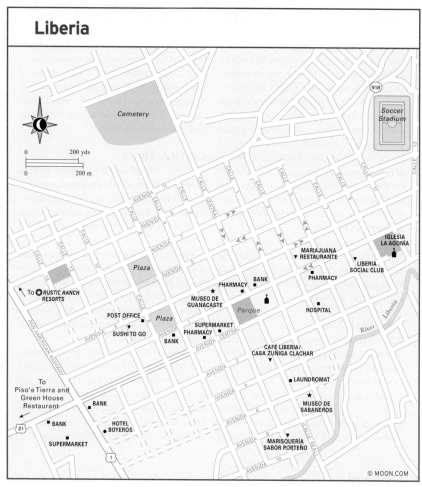

what typical city life is like for Guanacastecos (residents of Guanacaste).

SIGHTS

You'll find this small metropolis easy to explore on foot.

Museo de Sabaneros

The small **Museo de Sabaneros** (Cowboy Museum, corner of Avenida 6 and Calle 1, tel. 506/2665-7114, 9am-5pm Mon.-Sat., 1pm-4pm Sun., free), in Liberia's Casa de la Cultura (Culture House), has a lofty goal: It

aims to preserve artifacts and celebrate civic values central to the region's cowboy culture. Historical photographs, saddles, and lassos capture the feeling of days gone by, as well as pay homage to a culture that continues to thrive in the area.

Museo de Guanacaste

If you are interested in Costa Rica's military, or rather its lack thereof, you can visit what used to be the country's military barracks and armory at the **Museo de Guanacaste** (Guanacaste Museum, Avenida 1 between

Celebrating the Annexation of Guanacaste

July 25 marks the **Anexión de Guanacaste** (Annexation of Guanacaste), the day that a large percentage of Guanacaste was first declared Costa Rican territory. In many town centers all around the province—including Liberia, Playas del Coco, and Tamarindo—you can catch parades and fireworks displays and hear the tropical trills of Costa Rica's national instrument: the xylophone-inspired marimba. Plenty of rodeos, cattle shows, and dances take place, and you may also spot children marching around in cultural dress or in costumes that depict traditional characters. Taste the local culture by purchasing food from pop-up stalls or restaurants that prepare special menus for the day.

Although the date is only casually celebrated outside of Guanacaste, many businesses across the country (including government offices and banks) close for the day.

Calle 2 and Calle 4, tel. 506/2665-2996, 8am-4pm Mon.-Fri., free). There are few furnishings inside (the museum is a work in progress), but you're welcome to walk through the historical fortress to see what remains of its sleeping quarters, offices, prison cells, and other rooms.

Ponderosa Adventure Park

The closest theme park to Liberia is **Ponderosa Adventure Park** (off Hwy. 1, 9.5 km southeast of Liberia, tel. 506/2288-1000, www.ponderosaadventurepark.com, 8am-5pm daily). With its proximity to the airport, the park will happily fill some time if you have a few spare hours after your flight arrives or before it departs. Guided activity offerings include kayaking Río El Salto, visiting a waterfall, gliding across zip-line cables, and participating in an **African Safari,** during which you'll be driven through large animal enclosures to see giraffes, zebras, and other exotic animals up close. Each of the four activities ($35 adults, $20 per child) is suitable for kids over the age of five and takes no more than an hour to complete. A combination package ($75 adults, $68 children) allows you to experience all of the park's attractions.

ENTERTAINMENT AND EVENTS
Nightlife

Even though its cheeky-sounding name may cause you to do a double take, one of my favorite places to grab drinks is **Mariajuana Restaurante** (Calle 3, between Avenida 1 and Avenida 3, tel. 506/2665-7217, 11:30am-11pm Mon.-Sat., 1pm-10pm Sun.). I love the casual tree-stump seating and extensive drink menu. Grab a mojito, piña colada, or fruit daiquiri if you're the cocktail type, or try the province's own Guanaca beer, a honey blonde ale. There's live music on Friday and Saturday nights. A cover ($6-8) is sometimes charged when big-name performers play here.

The upscale **Liberia Social Club** (Calle 7, between Avenida 1 and Avenida Central, tel. 506/2665-4050, noon-midnight Mon.-Sat., 4pm-10pm Sun.) has an ample selection of wines, but it also makes good margaritas and sangrias. Opened in 2017, this lounge and restaurant hasn't garnered much attention yet, but it's worth checking out. Take your drink out on the small, outdoor patio.

SHOPPING

The best souvenir shopping in Liberia is on the outskirts of town.

La Gran Nicoya (Hwy. 21, 19 km west of Hwy. 1, tel. 506/2667-0062, www.lagrannicoya.com, 8am-6pm daily) has been the area's go-to store since 1997. It is a decent size, offers ample parking, and is easy to access just off the highway. A large selection of all kinds of souvenirs is available, including indigenous artwork, hand-carved wood products, clothing, jewelry, and bags of Tío Leo Coffee. You can learn about the bean from Tío

(Uncle) Leo himself, who runs on-site **coffee tours** (9am and 1pm Mon.-Sat. with advance reservation, 2.5-3 hours, $15 adults, $10 children 10-18). Worth snapping photos of are the traditional clay and stone *fogón* (oven) and the antique, wood marimba instrument stationed at the entrance to the shop.

If you're looking for the perfect conversation piece to take home, you'll likely find it at the **Hidden Garden Art Gallery** (Hwy. 21, 17 km west of Hwy. 1, tel. 506/2667-0592, www.hiddengardenart.com, 10am-4pm Tues.-Sat.). The shop is one of the best galleries in the country featuring original Costa Rican artwork. It showcases hundreds of paintings and sculptures, conveniently organized by genre in a 15-room facility. If you're not in the market for new art but still want to admire the incredible talent on display, the gallery is free to tour.

FOOD
Costa Rican
Your Liberia experience will be incomplete without having a slab of beef. Get one at **Piso'e Tierra** (Hwy. 21, 2 km west of Hwy. 1, tel. 506/4700-8746, www.d5liberia.wixsite.com/pisoetierra, 7am-9pm daily, $6-18), where the only fancy thing in the place is its steak cuts. The restaurant isn't your typical upscale steak house—informal tables and bar seating fill the small establishment, which is no more than an outdoor patio with a concrete floor and a tin roof. Its meat, however, rivals some of the country's best. You'll find both locals and foreigners at the spot, jointly appreciative of the fair portions and prices.

La Choza de Laurel (Hwy. 21, 9 km west of Hwy. 1, tel. 506/2668-1018, http://lachozadelaurel.com, 11am-8pm Wed.-Mon., $12-21), nearly across the street from the airport, brings Costa Rican culture to the forefront of its cuisine. If you have kids, they'll get a kick out of standing behind photo cutouts of figures wearing traditional garb. My favorite dish is the Volcano Rice, which includes an edible "lava flow." There's a sister location in downtown La Fortuna.

The finest seafood in Liberia is served at the down-to-earth **Marisquería Sabor Porteño** (Calle 2 between Avenida 8 and Avenida 10, tel. 506/2665-7337, www.saborporteno.com, 11:30am-3pm and 6pm-9:30pm Wed.-Sun., $8-28). Fish, shrimp, and other seafood specialties delight, but the most exotic thing on the menu is the *pulpo* (octopus). If you're not sure what to order, the restaurant's television displays a video of its offerings to help you decide. Groups of locals gather at the restaurant, known for its casual, social, and family-friendly vibe.

International
The light and airy **Green House Restaurant** (Hwy. 21, 2 km west of Hwy. 1, tel. 506/2665-5037, 11am-10pm Mon.-Sat., $10-40) is well-known. It has above-average prices but also top-notch service. The ultramodern restaurant, which features floor-to-ceiling walls of glass, a shiny tile floor, and sleek furniture, serves tasty sandwiches, hamburgers, wraps, and chicken wings. The ambience here is a step up from Liberia's usual casual scene. Choose this spot for a date night or a special outing.

If you need something quick to munch on, head to **Sushi To Go** (Calle 10, between Avenida 1 and Avenida 3, tel. 506/2666-0674, www.sushicr.com, 11:30am-3pm and 5pm-10pm Mon.-Fri., noon-10pm Sat., noon-9pm Sun., $5.50-14). When this well-loved San José franchise set up shop in Liberia, it brought over 50 sushi selections to Guanacaste, and other delights as well, including miso soup, chicken teriyaki bowls, and green salad with diced tuna. Try the Tico Roll, which features *pejibaye* (peach palm fruit).

Vegetarian and Vegan
Café Liberia (Calle Central, between Avenida 2 and Avenida 4, tel. 506/2665-1660, www.sdevenelle4.wixsite.com/cafe-liberia, 3pm-9pm Mon., 9am-9pm Tues.-Sat., $6-14) provides the city's best vegan and vegetarian meal selection, even though its menu overall is rather limited. Choose from ceviche, salads,

or a vegetarian sandwich while dining inside one of the city's oldest and most exquisite homes. The neoclassical-style Casa Zuñiga Clachar is an architectural and cultural artifact that's furnished to replicate the building's original era. Even if you're not hungry for a meal, drop by the café for a coffee and a look at the antique furniture and art.

ACCOMMODATIONS

Not surprisingly, Liberia's highest-quality accommodation is also its most expensive. The five-story **Hilton Garden Inn** (Hwy. 21, 10 km west of Hwy. 1, tel. 506/2690-8888, www.hiltongardeninn3.hilton.com, $117 s/d) surpasses competitors with its comfortable beds, gym, pool, and buffet breakfast, but what it really sells is convenience, with a complimentary shuttle service to and from the airport across the street. The hotel is part of Solarium, a massive, in-progress commercial center that will eventually house restaurants and shops.

The quaint, fairly priced **Hotel Boyeros** (Calle 12 between Avenida 2 and Avenida 4, tel. 506/2666-0722, www.hotelboyeros. com, $68 s, $78 d) offers good value. It has 70 standard-quality rooms and a pool, is just off the highway, includes a complimentary breakfast in its rates, and allows children under eight to stay for free. It is one of the few hotels in the area with a pool.

INFORMATION AND SERVICES

The city's hospital is **Hospital Enrique Baltodano Briceño** (Calle 3 between Avenida Central and Avenida 2, tel. 506/2690-5500, 24 hours daily). **Pharmacies** are scattered throughout the downtown core; many are on Avenida Central. The easiest pharmacy to access is **Farmacia Sucre** (Centro Comercial Santa Rosa, corner of Hwy. 1 and Hwy. 21, tel. 506/2665-7065, 8am-10pm daily). The **police station** (Hwy. 1, 1 km north of Hwy. 21, tel. 506/2665-0609, 24 hours daily) is just north of the city.

The city has several **supermarkets** and **banks** in the downtown core. The plaza on the corner of Highway 1 and Highway 21 houses a **Banco de Costa Rica** (Centro Comercial Santa Rosa, tel. 506/2211-1111, 8am-10pm daily) with an **ATM** (5am-midnight daily).

You can wash your clothes at **Lavandería Calle Real** (Calle Central between Avenida 4 and Avenida 6, tel. 506/2665-4010, 8am-7pm Mon.-Fri., 8am-6pm Sat.). Send mail from the **post office** (tel. 506/2666-1649, 8am-5pm Mon.-Fri., 8am-noon Sat.) on the corner of Avenida 3 and Calle 8.

There are a few **gas stations** in Liberia's center, as well as along Highway 1 both north and south of the city. The easiest one to access is on the corner of Highway 1 and Highway 21.

TRANSPORTATION
Getting There
AIR

The **Aeropuerto Internacional Daniel Oduber Quirós** (LIR) is a 10-kilometer, 10-minute drive west of Liberia's main intersection, where Highway 1 and Highway 21 meet. **SANSA Airlines** (tel. 506/2290-4100, www.flysansa.com) offers direct flights to Liberia daily from San José, La Fortuna, Nosara, and Tambor. The flight time from San José is about 50 minutes.

CAR AND TAXI

From downtown **San José,** Liberia is a 210-kilometer, 3.5-hour drive northwest on Highway 1. The roads that feed into the city are paved and easy to drive.

BUS

Public buses travel to Liberia daily from a multitude of destinations, most notably **San José** (multiple times 6am-8pm daily, 4.5 hours, $7.50), **Puntarenas** (multiple times 5am-5pm daily, 3 hours, $5-5.50), **Cañas** (multiple times 4:30am-8:30pm daily, 1 hour, $2.50-3), **Peñas Blancas** (multiple times 5am-6:30pm daily, 2 hours, $3), **Playa Panamá** (multiple times 6am-7pm daily, 1 hour, $1-1.50), **Playa Hermosa** (multiple times 6am-7pm daily, 1 hour, $1-1.50),

Playas del Coco (multiple times 5am-8pm daily, 1 hour, $1.50), Playa Flamingo (5:10am, 10:30am, 12:30pm, and 3:40pm daily, 2.5 hours, $2.50), and Tamarindo (multiple times 3:30am-6:30pm daily, 2.5 hours, $2.50). Depending on where your trip began, you'll be dropped off at one of two regional bus stations, either on Avenida 5 between Calle 10 and Calle 12, or two blocks north on the corner of Avenida 7 and Calle 12.

PRIVATE TRANSFER SERVICE

If you need to get to Liberia from anywhere east of the city, Desafio Adventure Company (tel. 506/2479-0020, www.desafiocostarica.com) provides private transfer services that depart from most popular destinations, including La Fortuna, Monteverde, Manuel Antonio, and San José, among others. They offer complimentary Wi-Fi in their vehicles.

If you plan to travel to Liberia from the west (namely from one of Guanacaste's coastal destinations), turn to the friendly folks at Ecotrans Costa Rica (tel. 506/2654-5151, www.ecotranscostarica.com). They're always on time, they offer a large fleet of reliable vehicles, and they're one of Guanacaste's most well-known transportation providers. Their vehicles also have complimentary Wi-Fi.

Private transfer service vehicles vary in size. Most accommodate up to eight people plus luggage. Prices range $50-100 from origin points throughout Guanacaste.

SHARED SHUTTLE SERVICE

Interbus (tel. 506/4100-0888, www.interbusonline.com) and Grayline Costa Rica (tel. 506/2220-2126, www.graylinecostarica.com) can shuttle you to Liberia from popular tourist towns around the country. One-way services cost $54-93 per person. Morning and afternoon departures are available from most destinations.

Ecotrans Costa Rica ($20-30 pp, depending on route) can shuttle you to Liberia from Playa Hermosa, Playas del Coco, Potrero, Playa Flamingo, Brasilito, and Tamarindo. Most shuttles fit eight people with luggage. All shuttles offer drop-offs at Aeropuerto Internacional Daniel Oduber Quirós; some, time permitting, can provide drop-offs at Liberia hotels.

ORGANIZED TOUR

A few tour operators include post-tour onward transportation between coastal destinations in Guanacaste and destinations in the northern inland area including La Fortuna and Monteverde. Although most of the tours speed through Liberia on their way to other areas, operators can provide drop-offs directly in Liberia upon special request.

White-water rafting tours, safari float tours, and hiking tours to Río Celeste at Parque Nacional Volcán Tenorio can be arranged with Tenorio Adventure Company (tel. 506/2668-8203, www.tenorioadventurecompany.com) to include a pickup from your hotel in La Fortuna, Monteverde, Sámara, Papagayo, Playa Hermosa, Playas del Coco, Potrero, Playa Flamingo, Brasilito, or Tamarindo, then a drop-off at your hotel in Liberia.

Getting Around
CAR AND TAXI

The many one-way streets in downtown Liberia make driving here a nuisance. In general, every other calle (street) and avenida (avenue) flows in the same direction. Keep your eyes open for road signs that note una vía (one-way) or una vía adelante (one-way up ahead).

1: Río Negro Hot Springs, near Hacienda Guachipelín 2: fumarole at Parque Nacional Rincón de la Vieja 3: a gazebo at a park in Liberia

Rincón de la Vieja

The country's northwest corner is comprised almost entirely of undeveloped land protected by the government as part of the Área de Conservación Guanacaste (Guanacaste Conservation Area). The mass of nearly 400,000 acres reaches as far west as the Pacific Ocean and increases in elevation as it moves inland, eventually hopping over the Continental Divide and sliding down toward the Caribbean Sea. In order to best protect the ecosystems and wildlife within the conservation area (including threatened dry forest and near-threatened jaguars), tourist services are minimal in this part of Guanacaste, which is commonly referred to as Rincón de la Vieja. Named after Parque Nacional Rincón de la Vieja, the area's national park and primary draw, this quiet, forest-filled, wilderness destination is worth retreating to and offers a nice balance to beach days spent lounging by the coast.

Isolated lodgings and adventure parks dot the territory around the national park. Choose one to visit for an entire day and stay overnight if accommodations are provided onsite. Few services are available in Rincón de la Vieja outside of these establishments, so plan to dine and participate in tours at whichever one you select. Most adventure parks offer horseback riding, zip-lining, and visits to hot springs with mud pools, and nearly all provide a full-day combination tour designed to maximize your time in the region.

PARQUE NACIONAL RINCÓN DE LA VIEJA

The Guanacaste region's most-visited inland destination is the **Parque Nacional Rincón de la Vieja** (Rincón de la Vieja National Park, tel. 506/2666-5051, www.sinac.go.cr, hours vary by sector, $15 adults, $5 children 6-12). Although the forested park has over 300 species of birds and other kinds of wildlife, its main attractions are bubbling mud pots, billowing steam vents, natural hot springs, and refreshing waterfalls. A variety of well-traveled hiking trails and manageable road access add to the park's appeal.

The 40,000-acre park has two sectors: the **Pailas Sector** (25.5 km northeast of Liberia, 7:30am-5pm Tues.-Sun.), on the park's southwestern side, and the **Santa María Sector** (23 km northeast of Liberia, 7:30am-5pm daily), on the park's southeastern side. **Ranger stations** mark the entrance to each. You're welcome to explore either sector without a guide. If you would prefer one, most adventure parks in the vicinity run guided tours to the park daily, as do most tour operators and agencies that operate elsewhere in Guanacaste.

Volcán Rincón de la Vieja

The mammoth 15-kilometer-wide **Volcán Rincón de la Vieja** (Rincón de la Vieja Volcano) dominates the large park. Just shy of 2,000 meters tall, the dormant Santa María crater is the park's highest peak. At least eight other craters (including the Von Seebach crater and the Rincón crater) and Lago Los Jilgueros (Jilgueros Lake) hide in the volcano's girth. Over 30 rivers flow on its slopes, which are a mosaic of premontane wet forest, dry forest, and cloud forest.

Hiking

The most popular trail in the park is the Pailas Sector's 3.5-kilometer **Sendero Las Pailas** (Las Pailas Trail, 3.5-km loop, 1.5 hours, easy-moderate). It is also the easiest trail to trek, as it is primarily flat; the first section is even wheelchair accessible. As you complete the loop, you'll encounter piping-hot steam vents and their sulphuric stench, a spurting mini volcano known as **Volcancito** (Little Volcano), bubbling mud pots, and small, boiling hot springs (swimming is not permitted in these). All serve as obvious reminders that

Rincón de la Vieja

although visits to the park are considered safe, the attraction is home to an active volcano. For your own safety, stick to the park's trails, obey signage, and stay behind trail guardrails.

Also within the Pailas Sector, the out-and-back **Sendero Catarata La Cangreja** (La Cangreja Waterfall Trail, 5 km one-way, 2.5 hours, moderate) leads to the blue-tinged Catarata La Cangreja (La Cangreja Waterfall). Two kilometers into this trail from its starting point just beyond the Las Pailas entrance, an **unnamed side trail** (2 km one-way, 1 hour, moderate) shoots off to the right and leads to the **Catarata Escondida** (Escondida Waterfall). Unless you have much of the day open to spend in the park, choose to visit only one of the waterfalls. You'll need to hike on an incline, withstand the region's beating heat, and make your way over and under several obstacles (like small rivers and giant tree branches) regardless of which route you choose. In either case, you'll earn the same reward: views of a beautiful clear waterfall. (Swimming in the waterfalls' pools is prohibited.)

Additional trails, including trails beyond the Santa María Sector, lead to the volcano's craters. Due to increases in volcanic activity, the crater trails are closed indefinitely.

Getting There

From downtown Liberia, it's a 25-kilometer, 45-minute drive to the Pailas Sector. Take Highway 1 north for 5.5 kilometers and turn right at the sign for the park and the community of Curubande. Continue traveling east for

20 kilometers. The route passes through private property at Hacienda Guachipelín; expect to pay $1.50-2 for passage through the private property. The road ends at the ranger station. A 4x4 vehicle is not required.

To get to the Santa María Sector from downtown Liberia, it's a 25-kilometer, one-hour drive. Take Road 198 (Avenida 1 in Liberia center) 20 kilometers east. Turn left at the sign for the park and drive to the community of Colonia Blanca. After one kilometer, turn left again, and continue driving for two kilometers until you reach the ranger station. Although a 4x4 vehicle is not required, having one is recommended.

You can reserve a seat on the **shared shuttle service** provided by **Offitours Adventures** (tel. 506/8899-8149, www.offitours.com, $20 pp). It travels daily between Liberia and the Pailas Sector ranger station (1 hour). The round-trip service departs from Liberia at 9am and leaves the park between 4 pm and 5pm. Have the driver confirm the exact return pick-up time. There is no shuttle service to the Santa María Sector.

HACIENDA GUACHIPELÍN

Rincón de la Vieja's most popular and authentic rustic ranch is **Hacienda Guachipelín** (21.5 km northeast of Liberia, tel. 506/2690-2900, www.guachipelin.com, activity costs vary; rooms $92 s, $112 d). Spread out over 3,400 acres of farmland, the sustainable ranch offers 64 clean, cozy rooms for overnight guests, a spa, a vegetable garden, a greenhouse, and a restaurant that serves food grown or raised on-site. Hacienda Guachipelín is one of the most organized and comprehensive adventure parks in the region, serving hundreds of day visitors and overnight guests daily.

Located on the road that leads to the Pailas Sector of Parque Nacional Rincón de la Vieja, Hacienda Guachipelín is the accommodation and adventure center closest to the park. If you want to experience a slew of ranch activities and hike through the park, opt to stay at this property, giving yourself a minimum of two days to explore the area.

Choose from a list of activities to fill your day at the ranch: zip-lining, waterfall rappelling, mountain biking, river tubing, horseback riding, or exploring butterfly, snake, frog, and lizard exhibits. Or opt for a combination package with either the **One-Day Adventure Pass** ($93 adults, $83 children 4-12) or the **One-Day Nature Pass** ($60 adults, $40 children 4-12). Designed for active explorers, the Adventure Pass offers zip-lining, river tubing, horseback riding, and a visit to the hot springs. The Nature Pass includes easy walking tours around the property's butterfly garden, herpetarium, and frog exhibit, as well as visits to a waterfall and the hot springs. Lunch is included with either pass. The cost of the activities is not included with an overnight stay.

As a working ranch, the hacienda specializes in cowboy-led activities. Its nine different horseback riding tours range from easy two-hour waterfall rides to full-day **"cowboy for a day" experiences** ($27-60 adults, $22-50 children 4-10) that will have you riding around the ranch, saddling horses, herding cattle, and completing other chores in the corrals. You can even travel between Hacienda Guachipelín and the national park on **horseback** ($40 adults, $30 children 4-10).

The folks at Hacienda Guachipelín also oversee operation of the off-site **Río Negro Hot Springs** (2.5 km southeast of Hacienda Guachipelín, 10am-6pm daily, visitors pass $20 adults, $15 children 4-11, free for hotel guests), which features 10 small, thermal-water pools hidden in remote forest at the edge of Río Negro. There's also a mud bath where you can paint yourself from head to toe with volcanic clay.

BUENA VISTA DEL RINCÓN

Buena Vista del Rincón (29.5 km northeast of Liberia, tel. 506/2690-1414, www.buenavistadelrincon.com, activity costs vary; rooms $78 s, $90 d) is a full-service ranch,

★ Rustic Ranches and Resorts

Spread out on country back roads and carved into the widespread slopes of Volcán Rincón de la Vieja are several remote properties that showcase the rural side of Guanacaste. These arcadian ranches and resorts, most of which are on the southwest side of the volcano, feature rustic charm and warm service, as well as a chance to take horseback rides through the dry forest, hike around Volcán Rincón de la Vieja, and experience Costa Rica's peaceful backcountry. Some ranch properties also offer their guests the opportunity to participate in traditional farm activities. Each property offers its own take on the pastoral experience. Tour offerings and prices vary by location.

Also in the area are adventure parks, which resemble miniature theme parks. These parks are in quiet, rural settings and make great day trips from Liberia or beach towns along the coast.

one of the rustic rooms at Hacienda Guachipelín

PLANNING YOUR TIME

Rincón de la Vieja's ranches and resorts welcome both day visitors and overnight guests. While it's possible to spend just a day at one of these properties and experience the highlights, it's best to give yourself at least two days in the area. Spend one day participating in the property's on-site activities and the second day hiking through Parque Nacional Volcán Rincón de la Vieja.

To help maximize your time, most ranches and resorts offer a one-day tour option that combines multiple on-site activities and lunch. Advance reservations are usually required. These tours typically begin around 8am and end before sundown. If you plan to drive yourself to the property from elsewhere in the region, plan for an early morning departure and a late-evening return. If you do not have a rental vehicle, some properties can pick you up from destinations around Guanacaste at an extra cost. Most tours are family-friendly, but some activities have minimum age limits. Have the property confirm their policies in advance.

RANCHES

- Hacienda Guachipelín (page 218)
- Buena Vista del Rincón (page 218)

RESORTS

- Borinquen Mountain Resort (page 220)
- Blue River Resort (page 220)

ADVENTURE PARKS

- Vandará Hot Springs & Adventure (page 221)
- Vida Aventura Nature Park (page 221)

hotel, and activity center. You can go zip-lining or horseback riding, tour hanging bridges, and ride down a 425-meter waterslide through the rainforest. The property also features a cattle farm, a freshwater pool, five thermal-water pools, a mud bath, a peaceful lake (in which swimming is not permitted), a small spa, an organic garden, and three restaurants. Though the accommodations at this ranch are set up like a motel, the 76 rustic wood rooms are more reminiscent of log cabins.

The ranch's most popular offering is the **Day Experience** ($85 adults, $65 children 5-10), a guided tour that combines zip-lining, horseback riding, hanging bridges, and a waterslide run with visits to a waterfall and the on-site hot springs. Both day visitors and overnight guests can purchase this combination tour. Also available are several **cultural tours** (costs vary by activity) that showcase Guanacaste cooking techniques, artisan craft construction, cow milking, and cheese making.

Don't miss the property's spectacular, unobstructed view of Guanacaste's dry forest, the Pacific Ocean, and a distant Nicaragua. The scene is particularly beautiful from the property's *mirador* (lookout) at sunset.

Buena Vista del Rincón can be visited as a day trip, though a stay of two or more days is ideal in order to explore all its offerings.

BORINQUEN MOUNTAIN RESORT

The highest-quality accommodation in the Rincón de la Vieja area is the **Borinquen Mountain Resort** (30.5 km northeast of Liberia, tel. 506/2690-1900, www.borinquenresort.com, day pass cost varies; rooms $167 s/d). This resort is also an adventure center that offers zip-lining, horseback riding, hiking, and ATV tours. You can spoil yourself with visits to the resort's thermal-water pools, steam room, and mud bath, as well as the spa, which has an extensive list of massages and rejuvenating treatments. The hotel rooms are romantic and softly lit, and are outfitted with comfortable beds; rooms

also come with a private deck or balcony. The four well-designed restaurants and bars cover casual to fine dining, with a swim-up bar and a tiki-style snack hut thrown in for good measure.

The resort's **day pass,** referred to by most tour agencies as the Borinquen Adventure or something similar, allows day visitors to access all the available activities. The pass includes a horseback ride, a 12-cable zip-line tour, and access to the property's pools, steam room, and mud bath, as well as lunch. Pass prices vary by tour agency but average $135-180 per person, including round-trip transportation from most coastal destinations in Guanacaste. For overnight guests, each activity is available for purchase on a stand-alone basis. The day pass is not sold at the resort; buy one in advance from a tour agency.

Choose this quiet mountain resort for a relaxing stay, fun adventure, or a combination of the two. Plan to stay for two days or more to fully enjoy the resort's offerings.

BLUE RIVER RESORT

The **Blue River Resort** (54 km northeast of Liberia, tel. 506/2206-5000, www.blueriverresort.com, activity costs vary; rooms $157 s/d) offers a mind-boggling number of activities and amenities. At the resort you'll find pools and hot springs, botanical gardens, a mud bath, a sauna, a spa, and a butterfly garden. Most impressive, however, is the long list of guided activities available at the on-site adventure center: a nine-cable zip-line route, hiking tours to a few waterfalls, guided horseback rides around the volcano's foothills, white-water rafting, and tubing. For overnight guests, the resort has 25 spacious and simple wooden, cabin-style rooms.

The on-site adventures are priced individually, so you can pick and choose your experiences. Day visitors must purchase a **day pass** ($20 adults, $15 children 4-12), which buys access to the hot springs, mud bath, and butterfly and botanical gardens. Tours ($65-120 pp) can be added to the day pass at an extra cost. You can also choose from one of the resort's many **day tours** ($105-180 pp) that include round-trip transportation from most coastal towns in Guanacaste.

Although you can visit the resort as a day trip, it's a 90-minute drive from Liberia, so it's worth staying at least one night here. The resort is on the north side of Parque Nacional Rincón de la Vieja and is also close to two beautiful, bright-blue rivers, Río Azul and Río Pénjamo.

Blue River also operates the nearby **Dinosaur Park** (4 km southeast of the Blue River Resort, tel. 506/6067-1081, 8am-5pm daily, $45 adults, $35 children 0-11), a touristy attraction that features mechanical dinosaurs built to scale.

VANDARÁ HOT SPRINGS & ADVENTURE

Vandará Hot Springs & Adventure (23.5 km northeast of Liberia, tel. 506/4001-5344, www.vandara.travel, 8am-3pm daily, activity costs vary) is an adventure park that warrants a road trip from anywhere in Guanacaste. Far more than just hot springs, the well-developed property has a wet bar, Jacuzzi, restaurant, spa, mud bath, 400-meter waterslide, and *trapiche* (sugarcane mill). Guided activities include zip-lining, horseback riding, and an informative farm tour. The **full-day ticket** ($67 adults, $57 children 4-12, children under

4 free) provides access to everything the park has to offer, as well as lunch. Spa services are an extra fee.

If you're staying in Liberia, Vandará is a great day-trip destination; it's only a half-hour drive north of the city.

VIDA AVENTURA NATURE PARK

The only adventure park on the southeastern side of Parque Nacional Rincón de la Vieja, near the Santa María Sector, is **Vida Aventura Nature Park** (26 km northeast of Liberia on Road 918, tel. 506/2668-0148, www. vidaaventurapark.com, 9am-4pm daily). Of the many adventure parks scattered throughout the region, this one is the least commercial, the least visited, and, not surprisingly, the quietest. It has thermal-water pools, a mud bath, horses to ride on forest trails, a zipline tour, and a restaurant that serves traditional Costa Rican food. The park's **One-Day Adventure Pass** ($85 adults, $42.50 children 10 and under) includes access to every experience the park has to offer, as well as a tasty lunch at the restaurant.

This is an easy day trip from Liberia, as the park is only about a 45-minute drive from the city. If you want to stay overnight, check out the vacation home rental ($90-500), which can accommodate up to 10 people.

Parque Nacional Santa Rosa and Bahía Salinas

Guanacaste's northwestern coast is dominated by the forested Parque Nacional Santa Rosa. The national park is on the Santa Elena Peninsula, which juts out some 25 kilometers into the Pacific Ocean. The protected waters on the south side of the peninsula are rich in marine life and blessed with world-class surf breaks. Scores of advanced scuba divers are drawn to Bahía Murciélago to swim with sharks. Experienced surfers come to ride the

waves at renowned surf sites Witch's Rock and Ollie's Point.

North of the park, Bahía Salinas is a picturesque and peaceful crescent bay that's not well-known to tourists. The biggest draw in this corner of the country is kitesurfing. Several operators offer lessons around the bay, which has ideal conditions for the sport.

Highway 1 bisects this region, running north from Liberia all the way to the

Nicaraguan border. Routes that lead to the national park and Bahía Salinas depart from Highway 1 to the west. They include Road 913, Road 914, and Road 935.

PARQUE NACIONAL SANTA ROSA

Although **Parque Nacional Santa Rosa** (Santa Rosa National Park, Road 913, tel. 506/2666-5051, www.sinac.go.cr, 8am-3:30pm daily, last entry 2:30pm, $15 adults, $5 children 6-12) isn't one of the country's top national parks, it has a few unique points of interest. If you're drawn to history, you'll love the on-site museum, where you can learn about historic events that took place here. If you're a surfer or scuba diver, you simply cannot miss the renowned surf and dive sites a few kilometers offshore. If you're a die-hard off-roader, the bumpy and rugged routes that wind throughout the park and offer what locals call "Tico massages" will put a smile on your face. Additionally, this is one of Costa Rica's few national parks with a paved and wheelchair-accessible trail.

The park marks the spot where invaders, under the command of American William Walker, were confronted and defeated by Costa Rica's militia in 1856. Long after the triumph of the Batalla de Santa Rosa (Battle of Santa Rosa) and a couple of other nearby conflicts, the area was designated as Costa Rica's first national park.

There are three sectors in the park. The park's largest and most popular area is the **Santa Rosa Sector.** A ranger station marks its entrance, beyond which you'll encounter nearly everything the park has to offer. The remote, less-visited **Murciélago Sector** (Road 937) provides little apart from a few desolate beaches. The entrance to Murciélago is unattended (meaning help will not be close by if you need it), and the roads to reach its beaches are long, treacherous, and unfrequented. Self-guided exploration of both sectors is allowed and does not require advance reservations. Sandwiched between the Santa Rosa Sector and the Murciélago Sector is the **Santa Elena Sector,** which is closed to the public.

Museo Histórico Casona de Santa Rosa

The park's greatest attraction and the gem of the Santa Rosa Sector is the **Museo Histórico Casona de Santa Rosa** (Santa Rosa Casona Historical Museum, 8am-11:30am and 1pm-3:30pm daily, free with park admission),

Museo Histórico Casona at the Parque Nacional Santa Rosa

referred to by most locals as **La Casona.** Though the museum is small, it displays well-preserved wartime relics, including saddlery and traditional clothing. The modern-day building that houses the museum is a replica of the original, which burned to the ground in the early 2000s.

Out back, plaques list the names of the Costa Rican troops who fought in the Batalla de Santa Rosa, forming the **Monumento a los Héroes** (Monument to the Heroes). Don't miss the viewpoint just beyond the monument; it has a distant vista of the volcano-speckled Cordillera de Guanacaste.

Hiking

The best area for exploring the park's tropical dry forest is the Santa Rosa Sector. The Murciélago Sector is difficult to access, and its beaches aren't especially noteworthy.

The short, paved, and wheelchair-accessible **Sendero Indio Desnudo** (Indio Desnudo Trail, 750 m one-way, 10 minutes, easy) is the Santa Rosa Sector's only fully developed path. It departs from the sector's entrance just beyond the parking lot and offers little to see apart from the peeling bark of the trail's namesake naked Indian tree, birds, and the occasional anteater.

The remainder of the Santa Rosa Sector is in poor condition, requires a durable 4x4 vehicle to access, and is best avoided between May and November, when heavy rainfall can cause the area's rocky, rutted roads to become impassable. If you're up for a challenge, you can drive through the park to the **Sendero Los Patos** (Los Patos Trail) or the **Sendero Valle Naranjo** (Valle Naranjo Trail) and hike to either path's viewpoint, or else continue in your vehicle toward the coast (past three other trails), where you'll find a stretch of sand at **Playa Naranjo.**

★ Diving with Bull Sharks

Dives in the **Bahía Murciélago** (Bat Bay), specifically around the **Islas Murciélago** (Bat Islands) are some of the country's best. The experience is well worth the trip from any corner of Guanacaste if you are an advanced diver who is not put off by strong and rough dive conditions. Collectively, the dive sites at Islas Murciélago are referred to as "The Bats."

You're likely to see sea turtles, rays, and many varieties of fish in the dive site's clear waters, where humpback whales have been known to make an appearance. But none of those sightings top the rush of sharing the open water with stocky **bull sharks.** These sharks can be spotted in the area, especially between May and November, when the water is calmest and visibility is optimal.

Nearly all dive operators that run trips to the bay from towns along Guanacaste's coast are familiar with the best dive spots. If in doubt, request a trip to **Black Rock,** a spot rampant with rays. The **Summer Salt Dive Center** (Calle La Chorrera, 25 m north of Road 151, Playas del Coco, tel. 506/2670-0308, www.costaricadivecenter.com, 7am-6pm daily) and **Rich Coast Diving** (Road 151, 400 m south of the beach at Playas del Coco, tel. 506/2670-0176, www.richcoastdiving.com, 7am-6pm daily) operate dive excursions to the bay from Playas del Coco. With Summer Salt, **Islas Murciélago dives** (6am daily, 8 hours, $190-220 pp for 2-3 tanks) include equipment rental. With Rich Coast Diving, less expensive **Islas Murciélago dives** (6am daily, 8 hours, $165-195 pp for 2-3 tanks) require separate equipment rental fees ($25 pp).

Though bull sharks have a reputation for being aggressive, you'd never know it from watching the species gracefully glide through the water. There have been very few attacks on humans by any species of shark in Costa Rica, but it's important to take every safety precaution and only go out with a reputable dive operator. Summer Salt Dive Center and Rich Coast Diving have plenty of experience with safe shark encounters here—they know where sharks are commonly spotted, they maintain a safe distance, and they never provoke the animals.

Parque Nacional Santa Rosa and Bahía Salinas

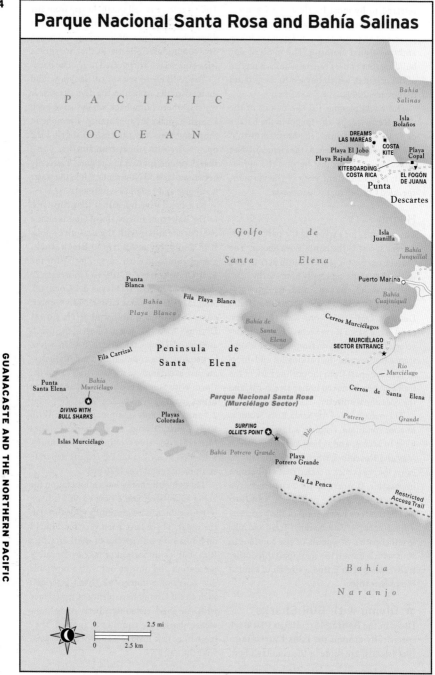

PACIFIC

OCEAN

Bahía Salinas

Isla Bolaños

DREAMS LAS MAREAS
COSTA KITE
Playa El Jobo
Playa Rajada
Playa Copal
KITEBOARDING COSTA RICA
EL FOGÓN DE JUANA
Punta

Descartes

Golfo de

Isla Juanilla

Santa Elena

Bahía Junquillal

Punta Blanca

Puerto Marina

Fila Playa Blanca

Bahía Playa Blanca

Bahía de Santa Elena

Cerros Murciélagos

Bahía Cuajiniquil

MURCIÉLAGO SECTOR ENTRANCE

Fila Carrizal

Peninsula de
Santa Elena

Río Murciélago

Punta Santa Elena

Bahía Murciélago

Cerros de Santa Elena

DIVING WITH BULL SHARKS

Playas Coloradas

Parque Nacional Santa Rosa
(Murciélago Sector)

Potrero Grande

SURFING OLLIE'S POINT

Río

Islas Murciélago

Bahía Potrero Grande

Playa Potrero Grande

Fila La Penca

Restricted Access Trail

Bahía

Naranjo

0   2.5 mi

0   2.5 km

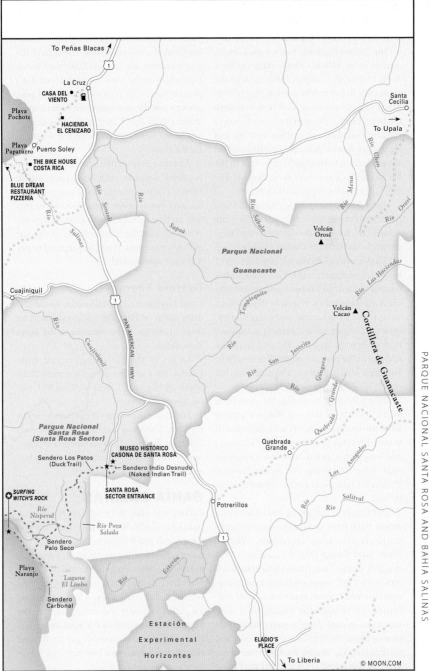

To Peñas Blacas
La Cruz
CASA DEL VIENTO
Santa Cecilia
Playa Pochote
HACIENDA EL CENIZARO
To Upala
Playa Papaturro
Puerto Soley
THE BIKE HOUSE COSTA RICA
BLUE DREAM RESTAURANT PIZZERÍA
Río Sapoá
Río Sábalo
Río Mena
Río Orosí
Río Chon
Volcán Orosí
Parque Nacional
Guanacaste
Río Las Haciendas
Cuajiniquil
Río Cuajiniquil
PAN-AMERICAN HWY
Río Tempisquito
Volcán Cacao
Cordillera de Guanacaste
Río San Josecito
Río Gongora
Río Grande
Quebrada Grande
Parque Nacional Santa Rosa
(Santa Rosa Sector)
MUSEO HISTÓRICO CASONA DE SANTA ROSA
Sendero Los Patos (Duck Trail)
Sendero Indio Desnudo (Naked Indian Trail)
SANTA ROSA SECTOR ENTRANCE
Quebrada Grande
Río Los Ahogados
Río Salitral
SURFING WITCH'S ROCK
Río Nisperal
Río Poza Salada
Potrerillos
Sendero Palo Seco
Playa Naranjo
Laguna El Limbo
Río Esterón
Río
Sendero Carbonal
Estación
Experimental
Horizontes
ELADIO'S PLACE
To Liberia

© MOON.COM

★ Surfing at Witch's Rock and Ollie's Point

Two of the country's top surf spots are found off the Parque Nacional Santa Rosa's southwestern coast. **Witch's Rock,** known as Roca Bruja in Spanish, is impossible to miss; it's the giant rock (inhabited by a witch, legend suggests) just off the coast at **Playa Naranjo** (Naranjo Beach). The surf is stellar, thanks to the area's sandbar, and it offers both left and right wave breaks. Advanced surfers around the globe flock to this world-class spot in the North Pacific Ocean every day of the year. The surf is not safe for beginner surfers.

If you don't want to drive yourself to Playa Naranjo through the rough roads of the Santa Rosa Sector, hitch a ride with surfer and local guide Eladio Castro of **Eladio's Place** (Hwy. 1, 13 km north of Liberia, tel. 506/2691-0303, www.eladiosplacecr.com). This fun and humorous guide, who has been surfing since the 1980s, runs guided excursions to Witch's Rock in his trusty Land Cruiser and offers surf lessons to advanced surfers wanting to improve their skills at the famed locale, with an option to camp in the park overnight. Prices vary by excursion, lesson duration, and inclusions, but cost $150-350 for two people.

Ollie's Point is located up the coast from Witch's Rock, in front of **Playa Potrero Grande** (Potrero Grande Beach). Experienced surfers love this spot for its razor-cut walls and long rights, not to mention its appearance in the 1994 movie *The Endless Summer II*. Access to the sweet swell is permitted only by boat.

Surf trips to Witch's Rock and Ollie's Point depart daily from several Guanacaste beach towns, most notably Tamarindo. **Witch's Rock Surf Camp** (Playa Tamarindo, 350 m north of the Tamarindo Diria resort, tel. 506/2653-1262, www.witchsrocksurfcamp.com) is a well-known, experienced, and professional tour operator, backed by a team that loves to surf. They're particularly passionate about the breaks at Ollie's Point and their namesake, Witch's Rock. On one of the **Witch's Rock and Ollie's Point surf trips**

(departs 5:30am, 12 hours, $100 pp, 4-person min.), you can experience the thrill of both, when surf conditions permit. Trip scheduling depends on ocean conditions; have the tour operator confirm available surf dates. Equipment rental is not included. If you don't plan to travel with your own board and gear, you can rent the equipment you need through Witch's Rock Surf Camp or at a surf shop in one of the beach towns along the northern Pacific coast.

Advance reservations for surf trips are required. Because both breaks are within Parque Nacional Santa Rosa, you must pay the park entrance fee, even if you never step foot on land. Confirm with your chosen operator whether the fee is included in the cost of their excursions. If not, be prepared to pay it in cash upon arrival.

Getting There

From Liberia, it's a 45-kilometer, 40-minute drive north on Highway 1 and southwest on Road 913 to get to the entrance to the Santa Rosa Sector.

To get to the Murciélago Sector from Liberia, it's a 60-kilometer, 70-minute drive north on Highway 1, west on Road 914, and southwest on Road 937.

Travel to either sector of the park by bus is difficult. A one-way taxi ride from downtown Liberia to the Santa Rosa Sector costs approximately $40. Park staff can assist in calling you a cab for the ride back to Liberia.

BAHÍA SALINAS

Unless you plan to cross into Nicaragua, Bahía Salinas (Salinas Bay) is likely the farthest north you'll travel in Costa Rica. If you haven't heard of the destination, you're not alone. The bay, which lies north of Parque Nacional Santa Rosa, remained off the tourist radar until 2014, when a massive, all-inclusive resort was constructed in the region. The area offers a few adventure tours that cater primarily to resort guests. Beyond this, Bahía Salinas is a low-key area where locals go to kitesurf.

Development in the area is centered in **La Cruz,** a small, non-touristy town five kilometers due east of the bay. La Cruz serves as the gateway to Bahía Salinas. Road 935 provides access to the bay, branching off from Highway 1 in the center of La Cruz.

Beaches
PLAYA EL JOBO
Though the brown sand of the public **Playa El Jobo** is hardly noteworthy, the calmness of its small crescent bay, **Bahía Jobo,** is spectacular. The bay's gentle water is good for swimming. Stretches of mountainous land that jut out into the ocean frame the clear waters. The sight is particularly pretty between June and November, when the hills are lush and green. This is where you'll find the area's all-inclusive resort, Dreams Las Mareas. Off Road 935, Playa El Jobo is a five-kilometer, 10-minute drive west of Bahía Salinas.

PLAYA RAJADA
My favorite beach in the area is **Playa Rajada.** It is accessible by car, has space for parking, and offers shallow water that's great for wading. Located south of Playa El Jobo, the beach offers calm conditions, unlike those up the coast, which are some of the country's windiest places. The beach's best features are light-brown sand that's pretty and soft, a picturesque islet just offshore, and plenty of trees that provide cooling shade.

To reach this secret spot that is frequented by locals but off the tourist radar, follow Road 935 west of Bahía Salinas for 2.5 kilometers to the small village of El Jobo. Turn right on the unnamed road in the village's center (just past the *fútbol* field) and continue driving for three kilometers. The road ends at the beach.

Recreation
KITESURFING
The best kitesurfing in Costa Rica is in Bahía Salinas, specifically on **Playa Copal.** The bay provides strong winds, wind conditions that are favorable year-round, and a crescent coastline that protects the bay from big waves.

The windiest days are between November and May. The wind is so strong during January, February, and March that you'll need to wear a wetsuit to keep warm as you surf. Playa Copal is on the south side of the bay, just north of Road 935.

The region's three most reputable kitesurfing operators are **Blue Dream** (Road 935, 1.5 km east of Copal, tel. 506/2676-1042, www.bluedreamhotel.com, 8am-10pm daily), **Costa Kite** (3 km north of El Jobo, tel. 506/8907-9889, www.costakite.com, 7am-8pm daily), and **Kiteboarding Costa Rica** (Playa Copal, tel. 506/8370-4894, www.kiteboardingcostarica.com). These operators run kiteboarding schools around the bay where you can take a lesson. All have instructors certified by the International Kiteboarding Organization. Lessons run three hours ($90-135 pp) to nine hours ($230-405 pp). Experienced boarders can rent equipment through any of these three operators. Equipment offerings vary by operator, but most supply a kite, board, helmet, harness, and wetsuit (if needed). Renting equipment will cost you $50-65 per day.

MOUNTAIN BIKING
If you're looking to bike around the northwest corner of the country, **The Bike House Costa Rica** (Road 935, 8 km southwest of La Cruz, tel. 506/8704-7486, www.thebikehousecostarica.com) runs a few excursions, from half-day jaunts (from $65 pp) and single-track treks (from $99 pp) to bike camps (from $155 pp) and weeklong bike tours.

HORSEBACK RIDING
The dude ranch **Hacienda El Cenizaro** (Road 935, 3.5 km southwest of La Cruz, tel. 506/8630-5050, www.haciendaelcenizaro.com, 8am-5pm daily) has a **horseback riding tour** (8:30am, 11:30am, and 1:30pm daily, 2 hours, $50 pp, min. age 6) that provides a beautiful view of Bahía Salinas from above. You'll also learn how to make corn tortillas and other tasty treats at the hacienda's rustic old house during the excursion.

Food and Accommodations

My favorite restaurant in the area is **El Fogón de Juana** (Road 935, 750 m south of Playa Copal, tel. 506/8956-0372, 9am-9pm daily, $6-12). The small, open-air establishment is most reminiscent of a *soda* (traditional Costa Rican family restaurant), serving homemade Costa Rican dishes alongside lasagnas and pizzas. Most dishes are cooked in Juana's wood-fired oven. The best options are the seafood plates with catches from the bay.

The **Blue Dream Restaurant and Pizzeria** (Road 935, 1.5 km east of Copal, tel. 506/2676-1042, www.bluedreamhotel.com, 7am-9am, noon-2pm, and 6:30pm-9:30pm daily, $6-11) is the best place to eat if you want to hang out with your mates or meet new travelers. The Costa Rican, Mediterranean, and Italian restaurant serves five unique plates per day and rotates the selections throughout the week. In the evening, the terrace turns into a chill bar where music plays and videos of kite-surfing escapades are screened.

The sprawling **Dreams Las Mareas** (3 km north of El Jobo, tel. 506/2690-2400, www.dreamsresorts.com, $460 s/d, all-inclusive) sits just west of the bay. The smartly designed all-inclusive resort features 447 rooms, eight restaurants, and seven bars. Its lagoon-like pools, lined by palm trees and chaise longues, snake throughout the property from the main building to the beach. The resort is remote, so it's a good option if you don't plan on making many day trips off the property. Its sister property, Secrets Papagayo, is an all-inclusive resort down the coast at Bahía Culebra.

An economical accommodation in the area is **Casa del Viento** (Road 935, 700 m west of Hwy. 1 at La Cruz, tel. 506/2679-8060, http://casa-del-viento-cr.book.direct, dorm $13, private $29 s, $44 d). It offers basic private rooms and dormitory beds, includes breakfast in its rates, and has a pool. Casa del Viento has eliminated single-use plastic throughout their operation. You won't find a plastic dish, utensil, straw, or bag at the property.

Information and Services

The closest hospital is **Hospital Enrique Baltodano Briceño** (Calle 3 between Avenida Central and Avenida 2, Liberia, tel. 506/2690-5500, 24 hours daily) in Liberia, a 60-kilometer, one-hour drive southeast of La Cruz.

There is a **supermarket** on Road 935 just east of Playa Copal. Nearby La Cruz has additional services, including a **clinic** known as **Sucursal La Cruz** (corner of Hwy. 1 and Road 935, tel. 506/2679-9116, 24 hours daily); the town's principal **pharmacy, Farmacia La Cruz** (Calle Central, 100 m north of Road 935, tel. 506/2679-8048, 6am-10pm daily); and a **post office** (Road 935, 500 m west of Hwy. 1, tel. 506/2679-9329, 8am-noon and 1pm-5pm Mon.-Fri.).

There are a few **banks** in town, including a branch of **Banco de Costa Rica** (Road 935, 550 m west of Hwy. 1, tel. 506/2679-8161, 9am-4pm Mon.-Fri.) with an **ATM** (5am-midnight daily).

The closest **gas station** is on the corner of Highway 1 and Road 935 in La Cruz.

Transportation

La Cruz is a 270-kilometer, 4.5-hour drive northwest from downtown **San José** via Highway 27 and Highway 1. From downtown **Liberia,** it's a 60-kilometer, 50-minute drive northwest via Highway 1.

To reach Bahía Salinas by **car** from La Cruz, take Road 935 southwest for 14 kilometers. A more complicated route departs Highway 1 earlier, at Road 914, passing through the community of Cuajiniquil and heading north until Road 914 ends at Road 935. The bay is another five-kilometer drive west. This route is a 280-kilometer, 4.5-hour drive from downtown San José and a 70-kilometer, one-hour drive from downtown Liberia.

Playas del Coco and Vicinity

One of Guanacaste's most visited destinations is the area surrounding Playas del Coco, a beach town about 35 kilometers west of Liberia. The area's southernmost town has a lot to offer, including shops, accommodations, adventure tour operators, restaurants, and bars. Playas del Coco is popular with budget travelers because it's possible to get by in town without much money or a rental vehicle. The name Playas del Coco translates to "the Coconut Beaches," but you're more likely to hear it referred to in English as "Coco Beach."

The area's northernmost section contains Papagayo, Bahía Culebra, and Bahía Panamá, which draw in families and couples to their numerous luxurious resorts. Farther south, you'll find travelers of all ages in low-key Playa Hermosa.

PLAYAS DEL COCO

Playas del Coco is home to one of Guanacaste's most prominent social scenes. (The other is in Tamarindo, a surf town in the southern half of the region.) The beach town serves as the area's hub for adventure and nature tours, restaurants, bars, and shops. It's also the commercial center for the stretch of coast that spans the communities of Playa Ocotal, Playa Hermosa, Playa Panamá, and Papagayo.

Locals and the area's large expat community coexist harmoniously here, and everyone strolls around informally in their beach attire. Road 151, the main drag, passes through town and ends at the beach. A plethora of open-air establishments fill both sides of the narrow, tree-lined, and walkable street. You'll find souvenir stores draped in hammocks and sarongs, and sports bars stocked with *guaro* (sugarcane liquor). Despite the concentration of businesses, the vibe is surprisingly laid-back and cool.

Sights
PASEO PEATONAL AMOR DE TEMPORADA

One of my favorite things to do in Playas del Coco is people-watch. There is usually plenty of action around the waterfront: beach volleyball matches, vendors selling *copos* (snow cone-inspired desserts topped with syrup and condensed milk) from carts, boats coming and going from the shore. The best way to take it all in is by strolling along the **Paseo Peatonal Amor de Temporada,** a concrete, four-block **boardwalk** that runs parallel to the beach.

Don't miss the statue of Costa Rican crooner Héctor Zúñiga Rovira along the way. The boardwalk's name, which literally means "seasonal love," was taken from the title of his popular 1930s guitar ballad about unrequited love first encountered at Playas del Coco.

★ DIAMANTE ECO ADVENTURE PARK

The only theme park in the area is the **Diamante Eco Adventure Park** (off the unnamed road to the Riu resorts, tel. 506/2105-5200, www.diamanteecoadventurepark.com, 8:30am-4:30pm daily, tour prices vary), just a 30-minute drive southwest of Playas del Coco. Stretching from a hilltop down to the beach, the park has a lot of impressive features, including well-organized and fun tours, friendly staff, and clean facilities. You can take a guided horseback ride along forest trails to the coast, or drive an ATV around the mountainous property. Other options are strolls through the botanical gardens or around the animal sanctuary (complete with a butterfly conservatory) with its rescued sloths, snakes, birds, crocodiles, frogs, and jungle cats.

Don't leave without taking the park's **zip-line tour.** Purchase the **Aerial Pass** (multiple times 9am-3pm daily, 1.5 hours, $78

Playas del Coco and Vicinity

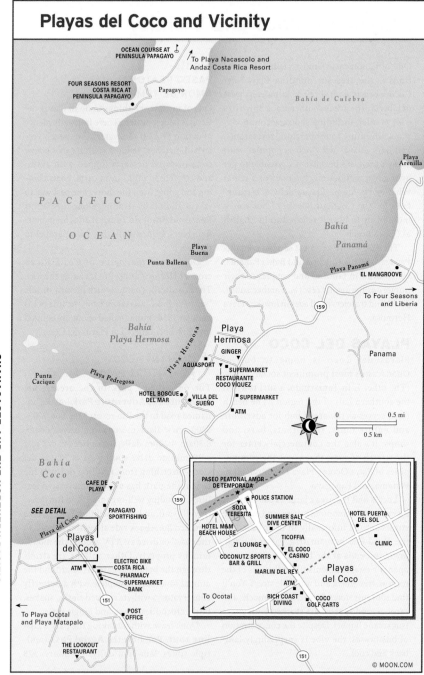

OCEAN COURSE AT
PENINSULA PAPAGAYO

To Playa Nacascolo and
Andaz Costa Rica Resort

FOUR SEASONS RESORT
COSTA RICA AT
PENINSULA PAPAGAYO

Papagayo

Bahía de Culebra

*Playa
Arenilla*

P A C I F I C

O C E A N

*Bahía
Panamá*

*Playa
Buena*

Punta Ballena

Playa Panamá
EL MANGROOVE

159

To Four Seasons
and Liberia

Playa
Hermosa

Panama

GINGER

*Bahía
Playa Hermosa*

AQUASPORT

SUPERMARKET

RESTAURANTE
COCO VIQUEZ

Punta
Cacique

Playa Pedregosa

HOTEL BOSQUE
DEL MAR

VILLA DEL
SUEÑO

SUPERMARKET

ATM

0   0.5 mi

0   0.5 km

*Bahía
Coco*

CAFE DE
PLAYA

PASEO PEATONAL AMOR
DE TEMPORADA

POLICE STATION

SODA
TERESITA

SUMMER SALT
DIVE CENTER

HOTEL PUERTA
DEL SOL

159

SEE DETAIL

PAPAGAYO
SPORTFISHING

HOTEL M&M
BEACH HOUSE

TICOFFIA

CLINIC

ZI LOUNGE

EL COCO
CASINO

Playas
del Coco

Playas
del Coco

COCONUTZ SPORTS
BAR & GRILL

MARLIN DEL REY

ATM

ELECTRIC BIKE
COSTA RICA

ATM

PHARMACY
SUPERMARKET
BANK

To Ocotal

RICH COAST
DIVING

COCO
GOLF CARTS

151

POST
OFFICE

To Playa Ocotal
and Playa Matapalo

THE LOOKOUT
RESTAURANT

151

© MOON.COM

adults, $63 children 5-10) to do the canopy tour, my favorite in all of Guanacaste, thanks to the tandem superman cable that allows you to soar toward the ocean with a friend at your side. The experience is rewarding year-round but particularly breathtaking between July and December when the landscape is vibrantly green. To do the zip-line tour together with other activities, choose the **Adventure Pass** (8:30am-11:30am daily, 5 hours, $118 adults, $95 children 5-10). The pass also includes a traditional Costa Rican lunch and use of kayaks, snorkel gear, and paddleboards at Playa Matapalo.

Advance reservations are recommended, but it's possible to sign up for activities on the spot, availability permitting.

Beaches
PLAYA DEL COCO

The town of Playas del Coco encompasses the long, brown-sand **Playa del Coco** (Coconut Beach or Coco Beach) that curves around **Bahía Coco** (Coconut Bay or Coco Bay). From town, you can walk along the beach one kilometer in either direction in search of the perfect unoccupied sunbathing spot. Finding one can be a challenge from mid-December to early February, throughout Easter week, during the first two weeks of July, and on weekends, as the coastal destination is a favorite among vacationing Ticos.

PLAYA OCOTAL

Four kilometers west of Playas del Coco, and separated from the town by a large headland, **Playa Ocotal** is a small, gray-sand beach that is sometimes beautified by shallow tide pools and other times spoiled by stones and debris. It's worth retreating to if Playa del Coco's noise or crowds aren't to your liking. The beach is a 10-minute drive from Playas del Coco on an unnamed but frequently traveled road. The road departs from Playas del Coco's main drag on the north side of the office for Rich Coast Diving. If you're more adventurous, you can walk or bike the route.

PLAYA MATAPALO

Playa Matapalo fronts the Riu brand's two all-inclusive resorts in the area. Non-resort guests are welcome to visit the public beach, which is notoriously clean. Stick to the westernmost side of the beach opposite the resorts if you want to sunbathe away from crowds of hotel guests. Thanks to light-gray sand, a view of Parque Nacional Santa Rosa over the horizon, and a backdrop of hills covered with dry forest, the scene at Playa Matapalo is much prettier than at other beaches immediately north along the coast.

Playa Matapalo is a 30-minute drive from Playas del Coco via the communities of Sardinal and Artola. To get here, follow the signs to the Riu hotels.

Recreation
FISHING

My preferred Guanacaste sportfishing operator is **Papagayo Sportfishing** (tel. 506/8331-2731, www.papagayosportfishing.com). The owner, Genaro Mendez, has been fishing from Guanacaste since he was a kid, and he knows the coast inside and out. The company serves nearly the entire coast, from as far north as Papagayo all the way down to Tamarindo, offering just about every kind of sportfishing experience. Options include inshore and offshore (deep-sea) tours, and half-day and full-day excursions. Trips run on one of the company's 15-boat fleet, ranging from small motorboats to large yachts. Tour rates are $375-3,500 for groups of 1-9 people. They offer complimentary pickups by boat at most beaches around Playas del Coco. An additional pickup fee may apply for transportation provided from other areas.

SNORKELING AND DIVING

Playas del Coco is a base for scuba excursions to several great Guanacaste dive sites. The most notable trips are up the coast to the marine-life haven of **Bahía Murciélago,** which hides the famed **Islas Murciélago** and batches of bull sharks, as well as trips down the coast to **Islas Catalina.** Both of

Sportfishing on the Northern Pacific Coast

Prices for sportfishing excursions vary considerably and depend on a variety of factors such as trip duration, boat type and size, group size, location (inshore or offshore), and optional inclusions. On average, charters will set you back $375 for a half-day, inshore trip (for up to three people) or over $3,500 for a full-day, offshore trip on a yacht (for up to nine people). Expect gear and tackle to be included, although you're welcome to bring your own.

Sportfishing excursions operated from a boat require the purchase of a fishing license. You can purchase a fishing license online ahead of time from the Instituto Costarricense de Pesca y Acuicultura (Costa Rican Institute of Fisheries and Aquaculture, www.incopesca.go.cr). Instructions in English are provided on the institute's website, and credit cards are accepted. License validity periods span 1-8 days ($15 pp), 30 days ($25 pp), or one year ($50 pp).

If your heart is set on baiting a specific species of fish along the northern Pacific coast, familiarize yourself with the area's fishing seasons before you confirm your travel dates:

- **sailfish:** year-round; best May-August

- **roosterfish:** year-round; best May-October

- **dorado:** June-September

- **snapper:** June-October

- **wahoo:** August-September

- **tuna:** year-round; best August-October

- **marlin:** August-March

these trips are for advanced divers. If you're a beginner, there are plenty of less challenging dive spots just off the coast of Playas del Coco including **Tortuga,** a dive site with two small shipwrecks, tons of fish, eels, seahorses, and whitetip sharks.

In town, at least five independent dive operations have solid reputations. My personal favorites are the **Summer Salt Dive Center** (Calle La Chorrera, 25 m north of Road 151, tel. 506/2670-0308, www.costaricadivecenter. com, 7am-6pm daily) and **Rich Coast Diving** (Road 151, 400 m south of the beach at Playas del Coco, tel. 506/2670-0176, www. richcoastdiving.com, 7am-6pm daily). Both are accredited PADI organizations that not only abide by strict safety regulations during open-water excursions but are also licensed to provide instruction for both discovery

and advanced courses as well as specialty certifications.

Summer Salt runs a number of trips daily, including local **daytime dives** (8am daily, 4 hours, $105-135 pp for 2-3 tanks), local **night dives** (5pm daily, 2 hours, $95 pp), **Islas Catalina dives** (7am daily, 6.5 hours, $135-165 pp for 2-3 tanks), and **Islas Murciélago dives** (6am daily, 8 hours, $190-220 pp for 2-3 tanks). The operator's prices are some of the most expensive in town, but rates include equipment rentals.

Rich Coast Diving has been a staple in Playas del Coco since 1993. They are my go-to dive operator for Guanacaste's most challenging descents at **Islas Murciélago** (6am daily, 8 hours, $165-195 pp for 2-3 tanks). They also offer local **daytime dives** (8am daily, duration varies, $85-115 pp for 2-3 tanks) and dives at **Islas Catalina** (6am daily, 7 hours, $135-165 pp for 2-3 tanks). Budget an extra $25 per person for equipment rentals.

1: zip lines at Diamante Eco Adventure Park
2: Playa del Coco

SAILING

Sailing and catamaran tours are a great way to spoil yourself with a hint of luxury in Playas del Coco. Most tours provide relaxing glides along the coast, during which your only job is to sit back, relax, and watch dolphins frolic in the waves. Tours typically include a stop at a snorkeling spot; participation is optional. To add romance to your journey, opt for an afternoon sail and end with a spectacular sunset (weather permitting).

My preferred sailing outfitter in Guanacaste is **Marlin del Rey** (Road 151, 300 m south of the beach at Playas del Coco, tel. 506/2670-1035, www.marlindelrey.com, 9am-6pm daily). They are headquartered in Tamarindo but have a satellite office in Playas del Coco and boats moored nearby. Choose between the **Morning Sailing Tour** (8am daily, 4 hours, $75 adults, $50 children 6-11) and the **Afternoon Sailing Tour** (1:30pm daily, 4 hours, $85 adults, $60 children 6-11).

Entertainment and Events

NIGHTLIFE

The place to be seen on Playas del Coco's main drag is **Zi Lounge** (Road 151, 200 m south of the beach, tel. 506/2670-1978, www.zilounge. com, 11am-2:30am daily), a popular bar and restaurant with live bands or DJs nightly and a seemingly endless happy hour (11am-7pm daily). On holidays like Halloween and New Year's Eve, the bar hosts over-the-top celebrations.

If you're a sports fan, you can catch Costa Rican *fútbol* matches, NFL games, and other American favorites on the screens at **Coconutz Sports Bar & Grill** (Road 151, 250 m south of the beach, tel. 506/2670-1982, www.coconutzbar.com, 9am-11pm or later daily). The place is usually filled with expats eating pub grub (pizzas, wraps, and seven different burger selections) and downing pints of beer. If you have one too many, you may end up across the street playing poker, blackjack, roulette, or the slots at **El Coco Casino** (Road 151, 250 m south of the beach,

tel. 506/2670-0555, www.elcococasino. com, casino 10am-2am daily, poker 2pm-5am daily).

For an evening unlike any other in Playas del Coco, head up the mountain on the outskirts of town to **The Lookout Restaurant** (Hotel Chantel, 3 km south of the beach, tel. 506/8696-7253, www.thelookoutcoco.com, 4pm-10pm Tues.-Sun.). The rooftop establishment is the area's only oyster bar, and it's wonderfully unpretentious. Grab a drink at the low-key but high-quality hangout and enjoy a killer panoramic view of Bahía Coco that you can't get anywhere else.

FESTIVALS AND EVENTS

Lively Playas del Coco rarely misses a party, so it's no surprise that key dates in Costa Rica's history are celebrated with vigor. On July 25, the **Anexión de Guanacaste** (Annexation of Guanacaste) is typically marked with a parade down the Paseo Peatonal Amor de Temporada. On the Saturday closest to July 16, all eyes are on the water as a procession of boats carries a statue of the Virgin to the bay in honor of the **Fiesta de la Virgen del Mar** (Virgin of the Sea Festival). Both events brighten the region with colorful decorations, music, dance, and fireworks.

Food

International cuisine dominates Playas del Coco's restaurant scene due to the town's hefty expat population and a consistent flow of foreign visitors. Most of the town's bars and grills offer every type of American pub food, and a variety of other establishments, from small gelato shops to cute bistros, serve French, Mexican, Italian, and Asian-inspired cuisines.

COSTA RICAN

★ **Ticoffia** (Road 151, 250 m south of the beach, tel. 506/6392-4270, www.ticoffia.com, 7am-6pm Mon.-Sat., 7am-3pm Sun., $5-15) is a great little spot to start your day. The specialty coffee shop serves light to dark roast coffee from the country's famed Tarrazú

Liquor Lingo

Cacique is Costa Rica's best-selling brand of *guaro* (sugarcane liquor).

Playas del Coco is known in part for the bucketloads of booze available in its bars. You'll be sure to see bottles of Cacique, a brand of **guaro** (sugarcane liquor). Residents can't get enough: They sip it slowly, throw it back quickly, and drink it as part of the spicy **Chiliguaro**—a shot or cocktail that blends the distilled spirit with lime, hot sauce, and salt. On its own, *guaro* has a taste that resembles a sweetened version of an inexpensive vodka. If you're not accustomed to its sharpness, consuming it in a cocktail infused with other flavors can help hide its bite.

Fitting in at any beach town's *disco* (nightclub) or bar (sometimes called a cantina) is easy if there is **Costa Rican rum** (try Ron Centenario) in your glass or if you're cradling a **cerveza** (beer). Don't be surprised if you hear locals ordering beer as **birra** (BEER-a), a slang term. You may also observe customers asking for an **águila** (eagle). What they really want is an Imperial, the country's best-selling lager, which features an eagle on its logo.

region, as well as cold drinks with a Tico twist, like the Horchata Cacao Frappe-Tico and the sugarcane-infused Caribbean Lemonade. Grab a chair out front and watch people stroll by on the main drag.

The long-standing Costa Rican diner **Soda Teresita** (Road 151 at the beach, tel. 506/2670-0665, 10am-10pm daily, $6-22) looks and feels like a fast-food restaurant, with menu boards above the cashier and a busy kitchen in the back. It is painted hot pink throughout and has a few tables inside, with a handful more under a covered patio outside. Spectacular *casados* are served here, among other traditional dishes.

INTERNATIONAL

Find international food of the highest caliber at ★ **Café de Playa** (Calle La Chorrera, 1 km northeast of Road 151, tel. 506/2670-1621, www.cafedeplaya.com, 11am-9pm daily, $9-40), a classy fine-dining establishment. Its menu is heavy on the "surf" and light on the "turf," which is typical for a fishing town. The oceanside restaurant's ambience is unbeatable. A table on the beach is the best place to enjoy the view.

If you're not opposed to making a trip 10 minutes outside town, **Father Rooster Bar & Grill** (on the beach at Playa Ocotal, tel. 506/2670-1246, www.fatherrooster.

com, 11:30am-9:30pm daily, $7-25) is worth a visit. Housed in a rustic but colorful hacienda built in 1917, the restaurant is a culinary melting pot. It serves meals you won't find elsewhere in the vicinity, including Middle Eastern kebabs, Mexican chalupas, and European gazpacho. Check the restaurant's website to coordinate your visit with special events such as sushi nights and live music performances.

If you make a day trip to Playa Matapalo, you must stop by **Monkey's Bar/Restaurant** (west end of Playa Matapalo, tel. 506/8650-7078, 10am-7pm daily, $10-30). This roadside, open-air restaurant is built off the side of a beach house on the main road that backs Playa Matapalo. It has several tables spread out on the sand under an extended roof, and the casual vibe invites swimmers and sunbathers to kick back under some shade. If you're hungry, there is seafood, and if you're thirsty, there are Margaronas—fishbowl-sized margaritas served with inverted bottles of Corona beer. Be sure to bring an extra dollar when you visit; you'll be asked to sign the bill and post it on the wall or ceiling alongside hundreds of others.

Accommodations

In and around Playas del Coco, there are economy and standard accommodations, high-end resorts—and not much else in between. Look to the small community of Playa Hermosa, 15 minutes north, for the quaint, fairly priced accommodations that Playas del Coco lacks.

UNDER $50

Right on the beach, the **Hotel M&M Beach House** (on the beach at Playas del Coco, 100 m southwest of Road 151, tel. 506/2670-1212, www.hotelmym.com, $27 s, $42 d) is the best of the low-cost options. Rooms are simple and without frills (there is no air conditioning), but the trade-off is convenience. You'll be steps away from the water, as well as from shops, restaurants, and bars clustered nearby.

$50-100

My favorite place to stay in town is the charming, well-kept ★ **Hotel Puerta del Sol** (250 m south of the beach at Playas del Coco, 300 m east of Road 151, tel. 506/2670-0195, www.lapuertadelsolhotel.com, $90 s, $110 d). The property boasts clean rooms, a cute bar, a pool with lounge chairs, and ample parking. It's a few blocks off the main drag and within walking distance of the beach. Breakfast is included in its fair rates.

OVER $250

Among the all-inclusive resorts in the area are the **Hotel Riu Guanacaste** (on the beach at Playa Matapalo, tel. 506/2681-2300, www.riu.com, $410 s/d, all-inclusive) and the **Hotel Riu Palace Costa Rica** (on the beach at Playa Matapalo, tel. 506/2681-2300, www.riu.com, $515 s/d, all-inclusive). The side-by-side, family-friendly properties take up the eastern half of Playa Matapalo. I prefer the pools at the Riu Guanacaste; their clover shape allows you to find a space of your own to swim in. But once you step inside, the Riu Palace wins with its funky bars and ultramodern rooms. It has a fresh and stylish feel, and wows with eye-pleasing architecture that resembles the Taj Mahal.

Information and Services

The hospital that serves most of the northern Pacific coast's communities is **Hospital Enrique Baltodano Briceño** (Calle 3 between Avenida Central and Avenida 2, Liberia, tel. 506/2690-5500, 24 hours daily) in Liberia, a 35-kilometer, 40-minute drive east of Playas del Coco. Additional **clinics,** like **Ebais Coco** (50 m south of Hotel Puerta del Sol, tel. 506/2670-0987, 7am-4pm Mon.-Fri.) are scattered throughout the downtown core.

The large Pacífico plaza on the east side of Road 151 contains a **Fischel pharmacy** (tel. 506/2670-2208, 9am-7pm daily). One of the town's best-stocked **supermarkets** is the **Auto Mercado** in the same plaza. Also in the plaza is **BAC San José** (tel. 506/2670-2226, 9am-6pm Mon.-Fri., 9am-1pm Sat.), a **bank** with an **ATM** (24 hours daily). Several other banks and ATMs line Playas del Coco's main drag. The most popular is **Banco Nacional** (550 m southeast of Playa del Coco, tel. 506/2670-0644, 9am-3:30pm Mon.-Fri.), with its own **ATM** (5am-10pm daily).

Playas del Coco also has a **post office** (Road 151, 1.5 km south of Playa del Coco, tel. 506/2670-0418, 8am-5pm Mon.-Fri.), a **police station** (Playa del Coco, tel. 506/2670-0258, 24 hours daily), and a **gas station,** which is on the unnamed road behind Banco Nacional, 350 meters southwest of the bank.

Transportation
GETTING THERE

Playas del Coco is easily accessible from Liberia by **car.** From **Liberia,** Playas del Coco is a short 35-kilometer, 40-minute drive west on Highway 21 and Road 151. From **Aeropuerto Internacional Daniel Oduber Quirós** (Daniel Oduber Quirós International Airport), it's an even quicker 25-kilometer, 30-minute drive on the same route. From downtown **San José,** Playas del Coco is a 245-kilometer, four-hour drive northwest on Highway 1, Highway 21, and Road 151.

Local buses regularly serve Playas del Coco. They depart from **Liberia** (multiple times 3:15am-6:10pm daily, 2.5 hours, $2.50) and **San José** (7am, 11:30am, and 4pm daily, 5.5 hours, $9). The bus can drop you off at Playas del Coco's **bus stop** (Road 151, 250 m south of the Pacífico plaza).

Ecotrans Costa Rica (tel. 506/2654-5151, www.ecotranscostarica.com) is your best bet for **private transfer services** to Playas del Coco from nearly anywhere in the country. Prices are $60-115 for pickups in Guanacaste and $180-300 for pickups elsewhere in the country. Their vehicles vary in size; most accommodate up to eight people plus luggage. Additional vehicles that fit 28 passengers can handle larger groups.

Shared shuttle services to Playas del Coco are available out of San José, Rincón de la Vieja, La Fortuna, Monteverde, Manuel Antonio, Dominical, Puntarenas, and Uvita with **Interbus** (tel. 506/4100-0888, www.interbusonline.com) and **Grayline Costa Rica** (tel. 506/2220-2126, www.graylinecostarica.com). One-way services cost $54-93 per person. Most shuttles fit eight people with luggage and offer drop-offs at Playas del Coco hotels.

A few tour operators, such as **Tenorio Adventure Company** (tel. 506/2668-8203, www.tenorioadventurecompany.com), include **post-tour onward transportation** to Playas del Coco. White-water rafting tours, safari float tours, and hiking tours to Río Celeste at Parque Nacional Volcán Tenorio can be arranged to include a pickup from your hotel in La Fortuna, Monteverde, Sámara, or a variety of Guanacaste beach towns, then a drop-off at your hotel in Playas del Coco.

GETTING AROUND

You can minimize travel time between beaches with the speedy **Coco Water Taxi** (on the beach at Playas del Coco, tel. 506/8830-9626, www.cocowatertaxi.com, 8am-5pm daily Nov.-Apr., noon-4pm Wed. and 10am-4pm Thurs.-Sun. May-mid-Sept., $15-30 pp, cash only). Use the water taxi to travel between Playas del Coco and Papagayo, Bahía Culebra, Bahía Panamá, Playa Hermosa, Playa Ocotal, and Playa Matapalo. Be aware that you'll need to walk knee-deep into the ocean to get on and off the boat.

Downtown Playas del Coco is flat, paved, and easy to drive and walk around. Although the downtown strip is somewhat narrow, there is parking on both sides of the road, as well as along the beach.

Electric Bike Costa Rica (Road 151, 600 m south of the beach, tel. 506/8593-5077, www.electricbikecostarica.com, 8am-6:30pm Mon.-Sat.) rents electric road ($20 for 1 hour), mountain ($20 for 1 hour), and even tandem bikes ($35 for 1 hour).

Coco Golf Carts (Road 151, 400 m south of the beach, tel. 506/8354-8669, www.cocogolfcarts.com, 8am-6pm Mon.-Sat.,

10am-5pm Sun.) has street-legal golf carts ($45 for 1 day, $280 for 1 week) and regular bike rentals ($10 per day).

PAPAGAYO, BAHÍA CULEBRA, AND BAHÍA PANAMÁ

Directly west of Liberia, the mainland narrows into a small peninsula referred to as Papagayo. The term is taken from the Golfo de Papagayo (Papagayo Gulf), the body of water that separates the peninsula's west side from the Pacific Ocean. To its east, the peninsula forms half of a horseshoe bay known as Bahía Culebra (Culebra Bay). On its south side, Bahía Culebra connects to the small cove of Bahía Panamá (Panamá Bay).

Around Papagayo is a cluster of the country's most visited resorts, many of which are all-inclusive properties. At least five recognizable brands have large-scale properties in the region. Little development exists beyond the resorts, except for the 184-slip Marina Papagayo on the north side of Bahía Culebra. Nearly all visitors to Papagayo stay at one of the resorts.

Beaches
PLAYA NACASCOLO

Experience a slice of Papagayo's peninsula with a visit to **Playa Nacascolo.** At this public beach on the east side of the peninsula, which only exists at low tide, you can stroll along the boardwalk and possibly even spot one of the resident capuchin monkeys. Here, shimmery, golden sand meets aquamarine water that gradually sinks into the dark-blue Bahía Culebra. You can dine at and rent equipment for water sports from the on-site **Beach House** (10am-5pm daily).

The beach is easy to access. It's possible to drive along the peninsula to the public parking lot (follow the signs to the Four Seasons resort), park your vehicle, and hop on one of many **public shuttles** (multiple times 8am-5pm daily, free) that commute between the lot and the beach. The shuttle will leave you at a **ranger station,** where there are bathrooms.

Lot parking, use of the shuttle service, and access to the beach are all free.

PLAYA PANAMÁ

There's no town surrounding **Playa Panamá,** the main beach of Bahía Panamá; it lies to the south of Bahía Culebra. This public beach draws in locals and tourists looking for an escape from the more popular beach communities nearby. Head here to swim in calm waters or to sunbathe in solitude. The beach isn't especially beautiful, with its gray-brown, somewhat drab sand. But it's easily accessible by car via Road 159 (from either Playas del Coco or Playa Hermosa to the south, or from Papagayo to the north) or Road 254 (from Liberia to the east). West of Road 159, you can park along the side of Road 254, which provides direct access to the signed beach.

Recreation
GOLFING

One of the country's most distinctive golf courses sits atop the hills of Papagayo and stretches across 220 acres of the peninsula. Ingeniously designed by professional golfer Arnold Palmer, the public **Ocean Course at Peninsula Papagayo** (Four Seasons Resort Costa Rica at Peninsula Papagayo, tel. 506/2696-0000, www.fourseasons.com, tee times 7am-4pm daily, pro shop 6am-8pm daily, greens fees $240 adults, $100 children 12-18) is an 18-hole, par-72 course with championship-level golfing alongside stunning bay and ocean views. The course is part of the Four Seasons Resort Costa Rica at Peninsula Papagayo. Advance reservations are required. Clubs and carts are available to rent.

ZIP-LINING

The one and only zip-lining tour operator in the area is **Witch's Rock Canopy Tour** (Road 253, 5 km northeast of Marina Papagayo, tel. 506/2696-7101, www.witchsrockcanopy.com, 8am-3pm Mon.-Fri.). Their **canopy tour** (9am, noon, and 3pm daily, 1.5 hours, $75 pp, min. age 3) zips around the area northeast of Bahía Culebra, high above Guanacaste's dry forest. During the tour, you'll travel past a waterfall, overlook the water from a distance, hike between platforms, and glide along 11 zip-line cables that span lengths up to 450 meters. Round-trip transportation from hotels in the Papagayo region is free, while transport from other cities along the northern Pacific coast, such as Liberia and Playas del Coco, is available for an additional fee.

Food and Accommodations

Dining options in the Papagayo area are limited. Most restaurants are on private resort properties that serve hotel guests only. Plan to eat at your resort's on-site restaurants, or pack a picnic lunch or dinner if you visit Papagayo as a day trip from another destination.

The **Four Seasons Resort Costa Rica at Peninsula Papagayo** (at the tip of the Papagayo peninsula via Road 253, tel. 506/2696-0000, www.fourseasons.com, $1,175 s/d) is one of Papagayo's most talked-about properties. It appeals to a variety of travelers, including couples and honeymooners, groups of friends, and families with children. Foodies love the resort's five restaurants and bars, occasional rum and chocolate tastings, and the option to select dinner from the catch of the day (Tues., Thurs., and Sun. at the Bahía restaurant). There is nonstop entertainment for kids and teens, and children up to the age of 17 stay for free. The cozy rooms feel like home—but with modern marble bathrooms.

One of my preferred Papagayo resorts is the ★ **Andaz Costa Rica Resort at Peninsula Papagayo** (Papagayo peninsula, 800 m west of the marina, tel. 506/2690-1234, www.papagayo.andaz.hyatt.com, $845 s/d), which is not all-inclusive. The resort's design, by distinguished Costa Rican architect Ronald Zurcher, makes bold use of shapes and textures that allow it to feel like a rainforest haven. It features three restaurants, access to three beaches, Zen-inspired room decor, and countless lounge and rest spots scattered around the property.

For an all-inclusive stay near Bahía Culebra, choose **Secrets Papagayo** (Road 159, 1.5 km north of Playa Panamá, tel. 506/2697-4400, www.secretsresorts.cr, $549 s/d, all-inclusive). In addition to meals and beverages provided by seven restaurants and five bars, the resort includes a ton of extras in its rates, such as rum- and wine-tasting, karaoke, water aerobics, and cooking classes. The adults-only resort has 202 Bali-inspired rooms and is the sister property of the all-inclusive resort Dreams Las Mareas, situated up the coast at Bahía Salinas.

Part of Marriott's Autograph Collection, ★ **El Mangroove** (Road 254, 200 m west of Road 159, tel. 506/2105-7575, www.elmangroove.net, $479 s/d) is one of my favorite resorts in the region. This small-scale resort is boho-chic. Individual cabanas adorned with lamps and pillows line the pool, pod chairs hang from terraces and patios, and rooms fuse a palette of whites with signature art pieces. The two on-site restaurants both serve exquisite cuisine. Best of all, the resort's location in front of Playa Panamá means it is a quick drive or taxi ride away from notable beach towns just down the coast. Optional all-inclusive packages may be added to your nightly stay; package add-ons start at $100 per person, per night.

Transportation

The peninsula is easily reached by **car.** Papagayo is about 240-255 kilometers northwest of downtown **San José** via Highway 1, Highway 21, and Road 253, a drive of about 4-4.5 hours. It's 30-45 kilometers west of downtown **Liberia** via Highway 21 and Road 253, a drive that takes about 30-50 minutes. Driving times and distance will vary based on your ultimate destination; Bahía Panamá is the closest point from either San José or Liberia.

Ecotrans Costa Rica (tel. 506/2654-5151, www.ecotranscostarica.com) is your best bet for **private transfer services** to Papagayo and its bays from multiple cities countrywide. Prices are $60-115 for pickups in Guanacaste and $180-300 for pickups elsewhere in the country. Their vehicles vary in size; most accommodate up to eight people plus luggage. Additional vehicles that fit 28 passengers can handle larger groups.

Shared shuttle services frequent the peninsula daily. **Interbus** (tel. 506/4100-0888, www.interbusonline.com) offers departures from San José, La Fortuna, Monteverde, and Rincón de la Vieja. **Grayline Costa Rica** (tel. 506/2220-2126, www.graylinecostarica.com) leaves from San José, La Fortuna, Monteverde, Manuel Antonio, Dominical, Puntarenas, and Uvita. One-way services to Papagayo cost $54-93 per person. Most shuttles fit eight people with luggage and offer drop-offs at Papagayo and bay-area hotels.

PLAYA HERMOSA

Playa Hermosa (not to be confused with the community of the same name on the central Pacific coast, just south of Jacó) is one of my favorite Guanacaste destinations. This beachside community is quiet and small, yet it is big enough to offer options for food, lodging, and activities to its handful of visitors. Although the area has little in the way of facilities and services, everything you might need during your stay can be obtained in Playas del Coco, one of the hubs of the northern Pacific coast, a mere 15-minute drive south from Playa Hermosa.

Two parallel, unnamed roads to the north and south enclose the town. Most development falls along the northernmost road; it runs east-west for 500 meters and connects the area's main thoroughfare, Road 159, to the town's namesake beach, Playa Hermosa. The community's southernmost road also branches off Road 159 to the west and ends at the same beach after 850 meters. The area's best accommodations are along this route.

Beaches

Whoever named the community's principal beach **Playa Hermosa,** "Beautiful Beach," must have witnessed one of its gorgeous sunsets due west of the beach. The sun sets perfectly between a headland that shapes Bahía

Hermosa and a small islet that floats off the coast. Sailboats, fishing boats, and small rowboats rock from side to side as gentle waves crash into the shore. The best view is from the south end of the beach. At the spot, you can stretch out on soft, gray-brown sand and take in the spectacle with minimal distraction. Locals and visitors alike enjoy walking and running along the bare beach. The bay is ideal for swimming.

Near the north end of the beach, the restaurant and equipment rental shop **Aquasport** (on the beach, near the end of the northern road, tel. 506/2672-0151, 11am-9pm daily) offers **kayak rentals** ($30 per hour).

Food and Accommodations

My go-to restaurant in town is ★ **Restaurante Coco Víquez** (on the northern road, halfway between Road 159 and the beach, tel. 506/2672-0029, 7am-10pm daily, $7-12). This casual, family-friendly spot serves delicious Costa Rican food at fair prices in line with a typical *soda*. The buffet bar is the best; stroll on in for breakfast, lunch, or dinner, peek at the day's delights, create a custom plate with whichever dishes look the tastiest (or try the restaurant's plate of the day), and enjoy a truly Tico meal! Grab a table at the front of the restaurant, which has a wall of sliding windows that open to views of the community's busiest street.

For fine dining and international cuisine, no establishment in the area beats **Ginger** (Road 159 at the northern road, tel. 506/2672-0041, www.gingercostarica.com, 5pm-11pm daily, $7-14). The swanky second-floor tapas bar features Asian-inspired dishes and an extensive wine list. Try the signature ahi tuna, then have the pavlova for dessert. If you're a vegetarian or need gluten-free choices, you'll find plenty of options clearly identified on the menu.

To dine near the water, head to the beachfront **Aquasport** (on the beach, near the end of the northern road, tel. 506/2672-0151, 11am-9pm daily, $6-17). The diner (and water sports shop) serves crowd-pleasing appetizers such as buffalo wings and chicken fingers alongside burgers, pizza, and seafood dishes. Fish entrées, including ceviche, fish tacos, and whole red snapper, are prepared fresh. Note that the establishment is casual; you can wander up to the spot in your bathing suit directly from the water.

Hotel Bosque del Mar (on the beach, at the end of the southern road, tel. 506/2672-0046, www.bosquedelmar.com, $210 s/d) is a much-loved accommodation in the area, primarily for its beachfront location and superior-quality rooms. If you're celebrating a milestone or are planning a romantic getaway, opt for one of the hotel's oceanfront suites. Each has a view of the Pacific Ocean and a Jacuzzi on a private, open-air terrace.

My preferred accommodation in the area is the two-story, 45-room, hacienda-style ★ **Villa del Sueño** (on the beach via the southern entrance to Playa Hermosa, tel. 506/2672-0026, www.villadelsueno.com, $110 s/d). The inviting rooms, decorated in warm, earthy tones, are outfitted with one queen or two single beds, air conditioning, a television, and a safe. The property is clean, quaint, quiet, and a four-minute walk from the beach. It also serves fantastic food on-site; the French-infused menu features crepes, almond-crusted brie cheese, and tarte Tatin.

Information and Services

The **hospital** that serves most of the northern Pacific coast's communities is **Hospital Enrique Baltodano Briceño** (Calle 3 between Avenida Central and Avenida 2, Liberia, tel. 506/2690-5500, 24 hours daily) in Liberia, a 32-kilometer, 35-minute drive east of Playa Hermosa.

Playa Hermosa has a couple of **supermarkets,** most notably **Supermercado Luperón** on Road 159. The supermarket has a small **pharmacy** (tel. 506/2672-0303, 8am-9pm Mon.-Sat., 8am-8pm Sun.).

Off Road 159 is the town's only **ATM** (250 m south of Supermercado Luperón, 24 hours daily).

Transportation
GETTING THERE
Playa Hermosa is a 240-kilometer, four-hour drive northwest from downtown **San José** via Highway 1, Highway 21, Road 254, and Road 159. It's a 35-kilometer, 35-minute drive west of downtown **Liberia** via Highway 21, Road 254, and Road 159.

Playa Hermosa can be accessed by **bus** from **Liberia** (multiple times 4:40am-5:30pm daily, 1 hour, $1-1.50) or **San José** (5am and 3:30pm daily, 6 hours, $9). The bus can drop you off at Playa Hermosa's **bus stop** (Road 159, in front of Supermercado Luperón).

Ecotrans Costa Rica (tel. 506/2654-5151, www.ecotranscostarica.com) is your best bet for **private transfer services** to Playa Hermosa from nearly any spot in the country. Prices are $60-115 for pickups in Guanacaste and $180-300 for pickups elsewhere in the country. Their vehicles vary in size; most accommodate up to eight people plus luggage. Additional vehicles that fit 28 passengers can handle larger groups.

Shared shuttle services frequent the beach town daily. **Interbus** (tel. 506/4100-0888, www.interbusonline.com) offers departures from San José, La Fortuna, Monteverde, and Rincón de la Vieja. **Grayline Costa Rica** (tel. 506/2220-2126, www.graylinecostarica.com) leaves from San José, La Fortuna, Monteverde, Manuel Antonio, Dominical, Puntarenas, and Uvita. One-way services to Playa Hermosa cost $54-93 per person. Most shuttles fit eight people with luggage and offer drop-offs at Playa Hermosa hotels.

GETTING AROUND
Road 159 connects Playa Panamá to Playas del Coco and passes through Playa Hermosa along the way.

It's a good idea to have a **rental car** so you can travel between the community's north and south ends as often as you need. A car will also come in handy if you wish to make day trips to nearby beaches and towns.

Playa Flamingo and Vicinity

The beachside town of Playa Flamingo and the surrounding coastal villages of Potrero, Surfside, Las Catalinas, and Brasilito are about 50 kilometers southwest of Liberia. These quiet beach communities line two neighboring bays, Bahía Potrero and Bahía Brasilito. Jutting out on a small, rocky peninsula between the two bays is Playa Flamingo, the area's most central town.

This is where to come to stretch out on soft, light-colored sand. Some of the country's most magnificent beaches sweep the coastline here, and the gentle waves and clear waters create ideal conditions for swimming. Beach-hopping to this centrally located area is easy from Playas del Coco to the north and Tamarindo to the south. The stunning Playa Conchal alone is worth the road trip.

The dive sites at Islas Catalina off the coast of Las Catalinas are some of the best in Costa Rica for spotting marine life.

Road 180 is the area's main thoroughfare. From Brasilito in the south, it travels north to Playa Flamingo, where it connects with Road 911. Road 911 then leads northeast through Surfside and into Potrero. At Potrero, a side road branches off Road 911 to the northwest and continues to Las Catalinas.

PLAYA FLAMINGO

The bustling little town of Playa Flamingo sits between Potrero and Brasilito. Its east side, overlooking Bahía Potrero, is monopolized by **Marina Flamingo,** a sleepy marina that is undergoing development. The west side of town faces Bahía Brasilito and is home to Playa Flamingo's biggest attraction, its namesake beach. The town's best accommodation, the Margaritaville Beach Resort, is on the west side too.

Playa Flamingo isn't your average Costa Rican beach town. It is the preferred coastal community of many wealthy Ticos and expats who reside or vacation in the luxury homes

that sit atop the peninsula's highlands. The obvious but not overwhelming development in town caters to this demographic. The few establishments that exist include a mini-mall, above-average restaurants, and a resort. Choose this destination if you want to surround yourself with American and other international influences.

Road 180, Playa Flamingo's primary access road and main drag, connects the two bays by cutting across the narrow peninsula. On the same road, midway across the peninsula, the commercial center known as La Plaza marks the town's center.

Beaches

Stunning **Playa Flamingo,** the town's name-sake beach, is the area's biggest draw. Filled with silky, postcard-worthy, nearly white sand, this deep beach has a wide-open view of Bahía Brasilito, which sparkles in emerald, teal, and steel-blue hues. Over one kilometer long, the beach provides more than enough room for stretching out away from others, and its proximity to a variety of restaurants means that food and drinks are never far away. If you're not staying in Playa Flamingo, this beach is a great day-trip destination that is worth the drive from farther-flung locales. To access the beach, follow Road 180 west through the town of Playa Flamingo. You'll find the beach 250 meters beyond La Plaza.

Recreation

Although several tours offer pickups from Playa Flamingo, few take place here. Most local operators will shuttle you to Tamarindo for an assortment of water sports.

If you would rather not stray from Playa Flamingo, try my favorite local activity: **stand-up paddling** around Bahía Potrero. **Point Break Surf Camp** (tel. 506/8866-4148, www.pointbreaksurf.com) offers a leisurely **stand-up paddling tour** (7am, noon, and

Playa Flamingo and Vicinity

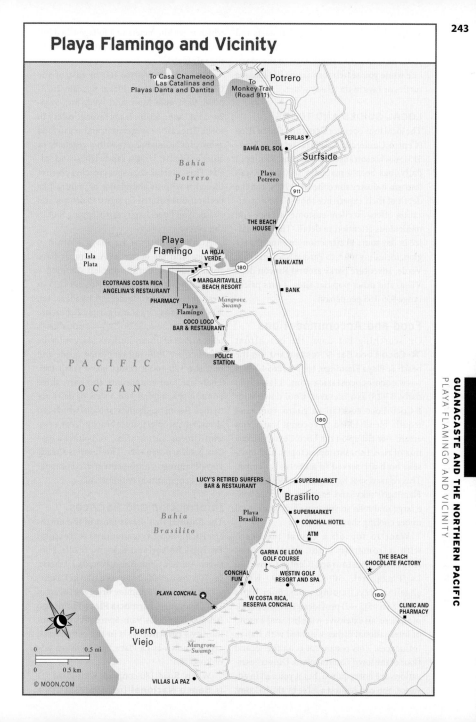

To Casa Chameleon
Las Catalinas and
Playas Danta and Dantita

To
Monkey Trail
(Road 911)

Potrero

PERLAS ▼

BAHÍA DEL SOL ●

Surfside

*Bahía
Potrero*

Playa
Potrero

911

THE BEACH
HOUSE ▼

Playa
Flamingo

LA HOJA
VERDE
▼

Isla
Plata

BANK/ATM

180

ECOTRANS COSTA RICA
ANGELINA'S RESTAURANT

● MARGARITAVILLE
BEACH RESORT

■ BANK

PHARMACY

*Mangrove
Swamp*

Playa
Flamingo

COCO LOCO
BAR & RESTAURANT

P A C I F I C

POLICE
STATION

O C E A N

180

LUCY'S RETIRED SURFERS
BAR & RESTAURANT

■ SUPERMARKET

Brasilito

Bahía

Playa
Brasilito

■ SUPERMARKET

Brasilito

● CONCHAL HOTEL

■ ATM

GARRA DE LEÓN
GOLF COURSE

THE BEACH
CHOCOLATE FACTORY
★

CONCHAL
FUN

● WESTIN GOLF
RESORT AND SPA

PLAYA CONCHAL ✪

180

★

W COSTA RICA,
RESERVA CONCHAL

CLINIC AND
PHARMACY
■

Puerto
Viejo

*Mangrove
Swamp*

0   0.5 mi

0   0.5 km

VILLAS LA PAZ ●

© MOON.COM

3:30pm daily, 2 hours, $75 pp) that starts and ends at Marina Flamingo. During the tour, you'll be treated to a scenic view of the coastline while you search for marine life like sea turtles or rays in the glassy water.

LOCAL GUIDES AND TOURS

The local tour operator **Ecotrans Costa Rica** (Centro Comercial La Plaza, tel. 506/2654-5151, www.ecotranscostarica.com, 8am-6pm daily) has been a mainstay in Costa Rica's tourism industry since the late 1990s, and the depth of their experience shows. The organization offers excellent customer service and meticulous attention to detail. They specialize in day tours to attractions around the region, including tours to Parque Nacional Palo Verde, adventure parks around Rincón de la Vieja, and other popular sites. Tours prices range $35-155 per person.

Food and Accommodations

On scorching hot days, the beachfront ★ **Coco Loco Bar & Restaurant** (on the beach at Playa Flamingo, tel. 506/2654-6242, www.cocolococostarica.com, 11am-9pm daily, $7-28) is a lifesaver. Cool down with a Coco Loco cocktail—a *guaro*, rum, and tequila blend added to coconut water and cream—or fill up on the Loco Coco entrée, a mix of rice, fish, shrimp, octopus, and mussels; both are served in an actual coconut. This relaxed spot has wooden tables on Playa Flamingo's silky sand, each one equipped with a large umbrella so you can enjoy your meal under cooling shade.

Want to top off a day at the beach with a romantic night on the town? **Angelina's Restaurant** (Centro Comercial La Plaza, tel. 506/2654-4839, www.angelinasplayaflamingo.com, 5pm-10pm Tues.-Sun., $15-42) provides a fine-dining atmosphere, an extensive wine list, and a menu of international dishes weighted with Italian influences. This restaurant is on the second floor of the town's central plaza. Dinner reservations are not required, but if you call in advance, you can request a table by the balcony, which is within meters of a foliage-filled hill and creates the feeling that you're dining in the rainforest.

★ **La Hoja Verde** (60 m east of the Centro Comercial La Plaza, tel. 506/2573-0096, 9am-4pm Mon. and Wed.-Fri., 9am-2pm Sat.-Sun., $5-10) is my favorite eatery in town. The café has vegetarian and vegan food galore, including burgers with a vegetable or chickpea patty, wraps, sandwiches, and salads. This colorful, cozy spot preaches positive thoughts with its abundance of mantra-like declarations painted on signs, tabletops, and chairs. You'll feel happy just stepping foot in this place.

Accommodations in Playa Flamingo are few and far between. A number have come and gone, but the one left standing—the **Margaritaville Beach Resort** (225 m west of the Centro Comercial La Plaza, tel. 506/2654-4444, www.margaritavillebeachresortcostarica.com, $229-239)—is no fallback option. Part of Jimmy Buffett's Margaritaville resorts since 2018 and renovated inside and out, the 120-room resort has a fresh feel. There are four restaurants and bars, three pools, a spa, a gym, and a slew of daily activities. Rooms and suites (some of which can sleep eight people) feature beachy decor, crisp white linens, sitting areas, and either a garden, pool, or ocean view. This resort is already Playa Flamingo's most popular accommodation. Its competition is almost nil.

Information and Services

The hospital that serves most of the northern Pacific coast's communities is **Hospital Enrique Baltodano Briceño** (Calle 3 between Avenida Central and Avenida 2, Liberia, tel. 506/2690-5500, 24 hours daily) in Liberia, a 75-kilometer, 75-minute drive northeast of Playa Flamingo. **Farmacia Plaza Flamingo** (tel. 506/2654-5524, 9am-6pm daily), the community's **pharmacy,** is in the commercial center known as La Plaza, on the north side of Road 180.

Where Road 180 connects with Road 911 is **Banco Nacional** (tel. 506/2212-2000,

8:30am-3:30pm daily), which has an **ATM** (5am-10pm daily). Playa Flamingo has a **police station** (1.5 km south of the Centro Comercial La Plaza, tel. 506/2654-5086, 24 hours daily) on the road that runs parallel to the beach.

The closest **gas station** is 12 kilometers south of Playa Flamingo, on Road 155 in the village of Huacas.

Transportation

From **Liberia,** Playa Flamingo is a 75-kilometer, 75-minute drive southwest on Highway 21, Road 155, and Road 180. From downtown **San José,** it's a 285-kilometer, 4.5-hour drive northwest on Highways 1, 18, and 21, Road 155, and Road 180.

From **Potrero,** Playa Flamingo is a five-kilometer, 10-minute drive south on Roads 911 and 180. From **Brasilito,** it's a five-kilometer, 10-minute drive north on Road 180.

Public **buses** serve Playa Flamingo daily from **Liberia** (4:30am, 6am, 8am, 11am, and 6pm daily, 2.5 hours, $2.50) and **San José** (8am, 10:30am, and 3pm daily, 6 hours, $10). The bus can drop you off at Playa Flamingo's **bus stop** (Road 180, 200 m south of La Plaza). **Ecotrans Costa Rica** (tel. 506/2654-5151, www.ecotranscostarica.com) is your best bet for **private transfer services** to Playa Flamingo from nearly any spot in the country. Prices are $80-140 for pickups in Guanacaste and $190-320 for pickups elsewhere in the country. Vehicles vary in size; most accommodate up to eight people plus luggage. Additional vehicles that fit 28 passengers can handle larger groups.

Interbus (tel. 506/4100-0888, www.interbusonline.com) offers daily **shared shuttle services** to Playa Flamingo from San José, La Fortuna, Monteverde, and Rincón de la Vieja. **Grayline Costa Rica** (tel. 506/2220-2126, www.graylinecostarica.com), another option for shared shuttle services, travels to Playa Flamingo from San José, La Fortuna, Monteverde, Manuel Antonio, Dominical, Puntarenas, and Uvita. One-way services cost $54-93 per person.

POTRERO, SURFSIDE, AND LAS CATALINAS

The quiet communities of Potrero, Surfside, and Las Catalinas occupy the coastline of Bahía Potrero. Largely unpopulated and off the tourist radar, this area has a mix of upper-end hotels and laid-back restaurants. The liveliest villages, Potrero and Surfside, offer a similar vibe to that of other small, self-sufficient beach towns in Guanacaste. Catering primarily to vacation home renters, Las Catalinas is a unique, isolated, and car-free community that meshes well with a long-term stay.

Surfside sits just north of where Roads 180 and 911 meet in Playa Flamingo. This is where you'll find Playa Potrero. Another few kilometers north, where Road 911 turns east, is the town of Potrero. Las Catalinas, the farthest north, is accessible only by taking the unnamed road that locals call "the road to Las Catalinas."

The area's infamous **Monkey Trail** (Road 911) provides a route into and out of the region via the inland hamlet of Sardinal. Make sure you have a 4x4 vehicle if you plan to tackle the route. Be prepared to maneuver a narrow, pressed-gravel and dirt road that kicks up dust when dry and can be muddy and slippery when wet. The trail is hilly, with plenty of inclines, declines, and curves that require you to drive slowly and cautiously, but it's passable. During extremely wet periods, you may need to ford a river along the way.

Skip the headache of the Monkey Trail altogether by taking Road 180 from the south. From Brasilito, Road 180 is an easy drive as far north as Playa Flamingo, where it connects with a much tamer stretch of Road 911 that delivers a pleasant drive into Potrero.

Beaches
PLAYA POTRERO

The main beach, **Playa Potrero,** lines the central stretch of Bahía Potrero and connects Potrero to Surfside. Dark sand keeps this area of the coast empty most of the time, as many of the region's visitors congregate at prettier light-sand beaches farther south. The view of the water from Playa Potrero is an attractive sight, as several fishing boats bob in the bay's gentle waves. You can see the rocky island formations of Islas Catalina in the distance. Swimming just off the beach in Bahía Potrero is a lovely experience once you're out from the shore, where black volcanic sediment gets kicked up.

PLAYA DANTA AND PLAYA DANTITA

Up the coast from Potrero, **Playa Danta** is tucked at the northern end of Bahía Potrero. This beach fronts the community of Las Catalinas. It has dark sand and draws few visitors apart from area residents, but its gentle waters are sought after for swimming, snorkeling, boogie boarding, kayaking, and stand-up paddling. It also has boccie ball, beach volleyball courts, and a parking lot.

If you would prefer a beach with prettier sand, visit **Playa Dantita.** This gorgeous little beach with light gray sand is an isolated oasis just north of Playa Danta. You can access the remote spot at low tide by climbing over the jagged outcrop that splits the beaches near the water. At high tide, hike up and over the forested hill that divides the beaches. An unnamed hillside **trail** (1 km one-way, 30 minutes, moderate) connects the two beaches and provides beautiful views of the bay among forest clearings. The trail to Playa Dantita is signed at the north end of Playa Danta.

Recreation
★ DIVING WITH MANTA RAYS

Ten kilometers off the coast of Las Catalinas, the **Islas Catalina** archipelago is a renowned dive site (for advanced divers only) where schools of fish reside among whitetip sharks, sea turtles, and nine species of rays. The showstoppers are giant **manta rays**—some as wide as six meters—that regularly occupy the area, especially from November to May when the water is cold and choppy. Although their size can be intimidating, witnessing the gentle giants floating within meters of you is a humbling experience not to be missed.

Numerous dive operators run tours to Islas Catalina. The majority are based out of Playas del Coco and Tamarindo, which are around the same distance from the archipelago (20 kilometers as the crow flies, roughly a 45-minute boat ride). The most common dive sites around the islands and islets are **La Pared, La Punta, La Viuda,** and **Los Sombreros.** Each provides an opportunity to spot rays. Collectively, the dive sites at Islas Catalina are referred to as "The Cats."

From Playas del Coco, the **Summer Salt Dive Center** (Calle La Chorrera, 25 m north of Road 151, tel. 506/2670-0308, www. costaricadivecenter.com, 7am-6pm daily) and **Rich Coast Diving** (Road 151, 400 m south of the beach at Playas del Coco, tel. 506/2670-0176, www.richcoastdiving.com, 7am-6pm daily) operate dive excursions to Islas Catalina. With Summer Salt, **Islas Catalina dives** (7am daily, 6.5 hours, $135-165 pp for 2-3 tanks) include equipment rental. With Rich Coast Diving, **Islas Catalina dives** (6am daily, 7 hours, $135-165 pp for 2-3 tanks) require separate equipment rental fees ($25 pp).

From Tamarindo, **Agua Rica** (corner of Calle Cardinal and Calle Tigris, tel. 506/2653-0094, www.aguarica.net, 7:30am-7pm daily) operates **Islas Catalina dives** (8:30am daily, 4 hours, $90 pp for 2 tanks). Equipment is not included; expect to pay $20 per person for diving gear.

MOUNTAIN BIKING

Las Catalinas is home to a whopping 30 kilometers of single-track mountain bike trails. Sign up with outfitter **Pura Vida Ride** (Playa Danta, tel. 506/2654-6137, www.puravidaride. com, 7am-5pm daily) to bike either the 10-kilometer **Short Loop** (7am-3:30pm, 1-1.5 hours, $100 per person) or the 25-kilometer **Long Loop** (7am-2pm, 2.5-3 hours, $150 per person). The cost includes instruction and the use of a bike and helmet—but note that this is not a guided tour. The principal trailhead is located at the north end of the community of Las Catalinas near Pura Vida Ride's office. The operator can provide a map.

STAND-UP PADDLING

Pura Vida Ride (Playa Danta, tel. 506/2654-6137, www.puravidaride.com, 7am-5pm daily) is the area's go-to provider for **water sport equipment rentals,** including paddleboards ($30 for 1 hour), kayaks (single $30 for 1 hour, double $45 for 1 hour), snorkeling gear ($15 for 1 day, $65 for 1 week), and boogie boards ($15 for 1 day). Specializing in stand-up paddling, the outfitter offers lessons (7am-4pm, 1.5 hours, $90 pp) and guided tours (7am-4pm, 3 hours, $120 pp).

Food and Accommodations

One of my favorite restaurants in the area is **Perlas** (corner of Road 911 and Avenida 3, Surfside, tel. 506/2654-4500, www.perlas. pub, 6am-midnight Mon.-Sat., food served until 10pm, $7-20). It serves sandwiches, salads, pastas, burgers (including the bunless Plantain Burger), surf and turf dishes, and plenty of options for vegetarian and gluten-free travelers. Come on a Friday night when you can buy a ticket ($2) for the restaurant's weekly lottery. Forty percent of the jackpot is donated to Abriendo Mentes, a Potrero-based organization that works with youth development, adult education, and women's empowerment projects. If you win the lottery, you take home 30 percent of the week's jackpot; the remaining 30 percent is added to the pot for the following week.

For lunch or dinner, head to the waterfront for a casual meal at ★ **The Beach House** (Playa Potrero, tel. 506/2654-6203, 11am-10pm daily, $6-30). The extensive menu of this colorful, family-friendly diner mixes American cuisine with locally caught seafood. They can also grill or fry any fish you catch for $6 (including accompanying side dishes). Vegans, don't miss the vegetarian ceviche, which swaps raw fish for chickpeas.

The best hotel in Surfside is the 35-room **Bahía del Sol** (Playa Potrero, tel. 506/2654-5339, www.bahiadelsolhotel.com, $256 s/d). Staying at this boutique accommodation comes with a high price tag. The expense will get you a clean and comfortable room, yoga classes, breakfast at the hotel's impressive, open-air **Nasu Restaurant** (tel. 506/2654-4671, 6:30am-10pm daily), and access to the on-site **Palapa Lounge** (5:30pm-9pm daily), which overlooks Islas Catalina. The property is steps away from the water and within walking distance of everything in town.

Offering great value, ★ **Hotel Sugar Beach** (Playa Pan de Azúcar, tel. 506/2654-4242, www.sugar-beach.com, $174 s/d), sits three kilometers north of Potrero, just south of Las Catalinas. This quiet, beachfront hotel, tucked among forested hills to the north and east, is the perfect choice if you're looking for a remote but affordable accommodation to escape to outside of town. The hotel's 27 spacious, contemporary, and superior-quality rooms are spread out across several one- and two-story buildings. Most have one king or two queen beds, streamlined tile bathrooms, and access to a patio or balcony. I particularly like the hotel's open-air restaurant, which overlooks the ocean and has a down-to-earth vibe. Playa Pan de Azúcar, a bare, light-sand beach that fronts the hotel, is great for sunbathing. Though the beach is public, limited access outside the confines of the hotel means guests regularly have the stretch of sand to themselves.

A unique, romantic, and extravagant place to escape to along Guanacaste's coast, the exquisite **Casa Chameleon Las Catalinas** (Las Catalinas, tel. 506/2103-1200, www. casachameleonhotels.com, $695 s/d) has 21 Bali-inspired villas perched atop the area's hill. Each villa captures a spectacular view of either the forest, Bahía Potrero, or the Pacific Ocean, perfect for admiring while you soak in your private saltwater plunge pool. Valet parking, shuttle services to and from Playa Danta, and breakfast are merely a few of the complimentary services provided by this adults-only resort.

Information and Services

The hospital that serves most of the northern Pacific coast's coastal communities is **Hospital Enrique Baltodano Briceño** (Calle 3 between Avenida Central and Avenida 2, Liberia, tel. 506/2690-5500, 24 hours daily) in Liberia, an 80-kilometer, 80-minute drive northeast of Potrero.

Both Potrero and Surfside have small **supermarkets.** There are **ATMs** in Potrero; the easiest to find is the ATM (5am-midnight daily) for **Banco de Costa Rica** (Road 911, 350 m after the road bends sharply to the east). The closest **gas station** is 15 kilometers south of Potrero on Road 155, in the village of Huacas.

Transportation

From **Liberia,** it's an 80-kilometer, 80-minute drive southwest to Potrero via Highway 21, Road 155, Road 180, and Road 911. This route loops south and comes up through Playa Flamingo, so you'll pass through Surfside two kilometers before reaching Potrero. To continue to Las Catalinas, you'll stay straight as Road 911 becomes "the road to Las Catalinas" (as known to locals); drive for another five kilometers (10 minutes).

To get to Potrero on the Monkey Trail (Road 911) from Liberia, you'll need a 4x4 vehicle. This route is shorter, only 50 kilometers, but takes roughly the same time (75 minutes) and requires advanced driving skills.

To reach Potrero, Surfside, or Las Catalinas from downtown **San José,** it's a 210-kilometer, 3.5-hour drive to get to Liberia. From there, you'll jump on Highway 21, then Road 155 and Road 180, which turns into "the road to Las Catalinas." The complete drive from San José to Las Catalinas is 290 kilometers and takes nearly five hours.

From **Playa Flamingo,** Potrero is a five-kilometer, 10-minute drive northeast on Roads 180 and 911. From **Brasilito,** it's an eight-kilometer (10-minute) drive northeast on Roads 180 and 911 to reach Potrero.

Public **buses** serve Potrero daily from

Playa Flamingo (multiple times 4:45am-8:30pm, 10 minutes, $1). The bus passes through Surfside approximately 5 minutes before reaching Potrero, and continues on to Las Catalinas, arriving roughly 10 minutes after departing from Potrero.

Ecotrans Costa Rica (tel. 506/2654-5151, www.ecotranscostarica.com) is your best bet for **private transfer services** to Potrero, Surfside, and Las Catalinas from nearly any spot in the country. Prices range $80-140 for pickups in Guanacaste and $190-320 for pickups elsewhere in the country. Their vehicles vary in size; most accommodate up to eight people plus luggage. Additional vehicles that fit 28 passengers can handle larger groups.

Interbus (tel. 506/4100-0888, www.interbusonline.com) offers daily **shared shuttle services** to Potrero, Surfside, and Las Catalinas from San José, La Fortuna, Monteverde, and Rincón de la Vieja. Another shared shuttle service, **Grayline Costa Rica** (tel. 506/2220-2126, www.graylinecostarica.com) travels to Potrero from San José, La Fortuna, Monteverde, Manuel Antonio, Dominical, Puntarenas, and Uvita. One-way services cost $54-93 per person.

BRASILITO

Unassuming Brasilito feels rather out of place in the region, with luxury homes and all-inclusive resorts both north and south of it. This unspoiled and down-to-earth beach town, just south of Playa Flamingo on Bahía Brasilito, is a favorite among young locals. Brasilito's main attraction is **Playa Conchal,** a beach made of soft shell fragments and white sand.

A five-kilometer, 10-minute drive south from Brasilito leads to Huacas, an inland, crossroads community sitting at the intersection of Road 180 and Road 155. This location means Brasilito is as accessible as Guanacaste's more frequented beach towns.

1: the Islas Catalina, off the coast of Las Catalinas **2:** the beachfront Coco Loco Bar & Restaurant in Playa Flamingo **3:** The Beach House in Potrero **4:** the pristine Playa Conchal

The Beach Chocolate Factory

The small chocolate shop known as **The Beach Chocolate Factory** (off Road 180 at The Village, #127, 2 km south of the beach at Playa Brasilito, tel. 506/4701-0536, www.beachchocolatefactory.com, 9am-5pm Mon.-Sat.) runs fun, interactive cacao-processing workshops in a casual and peaceful setting. On the lawn outside the shop, owner and chocolatier Henrik Bodholdt teaches a weekly **chocolate workshop** (9:30am Fri., 1.5 hours, $30 pp), where he discusses the history of cacao and demonstrates chocolate processing step by step. Be prepared to get your hands dirty—with delicious chocolate, that is—as you construct your own treat during the informal yet informative experience. Don't forget to visit the shop before you go; it has individual chocolates, chocolate bars named after Costa Rican destinations, and even chocolate-based beauty products for sale.

Beaches

★ PLAYA CONCHAL

Without a doubt, Brasilito's primary draw is **Playa Conchal.** Comprised of millions of tiny shell fragments and dusty, white sand, this is one of Costa Rica's most unique beaches. The stunning landscape sweeps the coastline just south of town, separated from Playa Brasilito by Punto Conchal, a red rock formation.

Shell fragments (and the occasional complete shell) fill the east end of the beach. Polished like sea glass, the shells are soft enough to walk on barefoot, and you'll love digging your feet into them for a natural foot massage. Long walks here can be a challenge, as you have to work harder than usual to pull your feet out of the sand each time you step. The view from this part of the beach is particularly pretty, as craggy headlands frame the coast to the north and south. Swimming is decent here around the shore of Bahía Brasilito, but beware of a rocky seabed immediately south of Punto Conchal. Nearest to Brasilito and a few high-end resorts, this eastern section of Playa Conchal is the most frequented.

The west end of the beach, separated from Punto Conchal by one kilometer, is wildly different. It has fine sand (arguably the lightest in the country), hardly any shells, and fewer visitors than the opposite end of the beach. A swim here, among aquamarine waters that glide into Playa Conchal in rows, is paradisiacal. Choose this section of Playa Conchal if you want to isolate yourself from other beachgoers.

Vegetation backs the entirety of the beach, but it is sparse in areas and offers no opportunities for shade in others. Come prepared to stretch out on a largely exposed beach.

As striking as the beach's shells may be, removing them from the beach is strictly prohibited. Also forbidden is driving anywhere on the beach between Brasilito and Playa Conchal.

To reach the east end of Playa Conchal from town, you can walk along Playa Brasilito and make a small, easy 100-meter climb up and over Punto Conchal. To reach the west end of Playa Conchal, you can drive or take a taxi to Playa Conchal's alternate access point at Playa Puerto Viejo.

PLAYA BRASILITO

You'll find most locals in Brasilito sprawled out on the light-brown sand of **Playa Brasilito.** This long beach stretches the length of the town and beyond. Although most foreigners spend their days at neighboring Playa Conchal, you can have an equally enjoyable time playing in the waves off Brasilito's shore or cooling off with a drink at the beachfront **La Casita Del Pescado** (Playa Brasilito, tel. 506/2654-6203, 11am-9pm daily).

Recreation

Conchal Fun (Playa Conchal, tel. 506/8557-2776, www.conchalfun.com, 6am-6pm daily, prices vary by tour) is a company of local tour guides who offer different experiences based on their individual specialties. Tour options include horseback rides, ATV tours, Jet Ski tours, and fishing excursions (including sportfishing, spearfishing, and fly-fishing).

Every guide is prompt, courteous, and professional. Conchal Fun provides the few tours that operate directly out of Brasilito and Playa Conchal; other operators run tours out of Tamarindo.

Food and Accommodations

Most of the food offerings in Brasilito are inexpensive *sodas* sandwiched between Road 180 and the beach. They're fine for a quick meal or a cold drink, but don't expect formal settings or service.

★ **Lucy's Retired Surfers Bar & Restaurant** (Playa Brasilito, tel. 506/4702-0826, www.lucysretiredsurfers.com, 10am-9pm Mon.-Fri., 9am-9pm Sat.-Sun., $7-18) is a vivacious sports bar and family-friendly restaurant that's a real hoot. Their American pub grub menu is amusing (start with the Rock-a-Mole guacamole and tortilla chips, then try the Juicy Lucy hamburger), but the cocktail and mocktail presentations are downright hilarious. Drinks come with little plastic whales, mermaids, and scorpions swimming in them. My favorite is the blue Ataque de Tiburón (Shark Attack), a vodka, rum, and tequila cocktail with a toy shark biting the side of the glass and drops of "blood" (grenadine) inside. The experience is fun for all ages. As their motto says, there's "no attitude on this latitude."

The best hotel in town is the bright, colorful ★ **Conchal Hotel** (Road 180, 400 m south of Playa Brasilito, tel. 506/2654-9125, www.conchalcr.com, $115 s/d). It has 16 clean and cozy guest rooms centered around the small property's flora-framed pool. A tropical buffet breakfast (included in the rate) is served on the second floor at the hotel's open-air **Papaya Restaurant** (6:30am-10am Wed., 6:30am-8:30pm Thurs.-Tues.). The restaurant has the healthiest food in the area and offers ample vegetarian and vegan options. Service at the hotel and the restaurant is above average. Stay here and the owners will make sure you know they appreciate your visit.

Southwest of Brasilito, on the west side of Playa Conchal, is one of my favorite accommodations in Costa Rica. Clustered within a private complex, ★ **Villas La Paz** (750 m south of Playa Puerto Viejo, just west of Playa Conchal, tel. 506/8307-9423, www.conchalcostarica.com, $80-250) has six tropical villas, each one unique in design, decor, and size (the largest sleeps 12 people). These villas are constructed to mimic mini houses; large villas resemble full-size homes and small villas feel like apartments. The complex is just a short walk south of Playa Conchal, and 4.5 kilometers north of the hamlet of Matapalo, the closest place to grab the groceries you need to prepare your own meals in your villa's fully equipped kitchen. I often spot monkeys, iguanas, and a variety of birds around the peaceful grounds, which have plenty of open-air gathering spaces, oversize rooms, and a communal pool. The Costa Rican family that owns the place goes above and beyond to make your stay memorable.

On the beach at Playa Conchal, the **W Costa Rica, Reserva Conchal** (Playa Conchal, tel. 506/2654-3000, www.reservaconchal.com, $377 s/d) is contained within a 2,300-acre private reserve. This family-friendly property has 151 lavish, fully furnished condos that attract travelers who prefer vacation homes over hotels. All of the condos share access to the facilities and amenities supplied by the reserve's **Beach Club,** which has a pool, restaurant, rooftop deck, gym, and spa. If you want to feel like you're living in luxury in Costa Rica, Reserva Conchal provides the experience. If you prefer to stay at a traditional all-inclusive resort, the **Westin Golf Resort and Spa** (off Road 180, 1 km south of the beach at Playa Brasilito, tel. 506/2654-3500, www.westinplayaconchal.com, $625 s/d, all-inclusive) shares the same property as Reserva Conchal.

Information and Services

The hospital that serves most of the northern Pacific coast's communities is **Hospital Enrique Baltodano Briceño** (Calle 3 between Avenida Central and Avenida 2, Liberia, tel. 506/2690-5500, 24 hours daily)

Golfing in Brasilito

The **Garra de León Golf Course** (tee times 6:30am-4pm daily, pro shop 6am-5pm daily, greens fees $150 adults, $20 children 0-13) is one of the top two courses in the country; it attracts golfers from around the world. The 18-hole, par-71 course, which is close to Playa Conchal, surrounds the W's Reserva Conchal resort and the Westin Golf Resort and Spa. Designed by renowned golf architect Robert Trent Jones II, the course is famous for the wide and hilly fairways that provide Pacific Ocean and mountain views.

Because the course is open only to guests of the W Costa Rica, Reserva Conchal (except by special request, and only when there's availability), your best chance to golf here is to book a stay at the resort. Advance reservations for tee times are required. Clubs and carts are available to rent.

in Liberia, a 70-kilometer, 70-minute drive northeast of Brasilito. The **Centro Médico Metropolitano** (Road 180, 2 km south of Brasilito center, tel. 506/4000-3822, 9am-5pm Mon.-Sat.) is the town's **clinic**. It has a **pharmacy** (9am-5pm Mon.-Sat.) on-site.

In town, you'll find **supermarkets** and an **ATM** (on Road 180, 800 m south of Playa Brasilito, 5am-midnight daily). The closest **gas station** is six kilometers south of Brasilito on Road 155 in the village of Huacas.

Transportation

To get to Brasilito from downtown **San José**, it's a 270-kilometer, 4.5-hour drive west on Highways 1, 18, and 21 and Roads 155 and 180. To get there from **Liberia**, it's a 70-kilometer, 70-minute drive southwest on Highway 21, Road 155, and Road 180.

From **Playa Flamingo,** Brasilito is a five-kilometer, 10-minute drive south on Road 180. From **Potrero,** it's an eight-kilometer, 15-minute drive southwest on Roads 911 and 180 to Brasilito.

Public **buses** serve Brasilito daily from **Liberia** (4:30am, 6am, 8am, 11am, and 6pm daily, 2-2.5 hours, $2) and **San José** (8am, 10:30am, and 3pm daily, 5.5-6 hours, $9). The bus can drop you off at Brasilito's **bus**

stop (Road 180, 150 m south of Lucy's Retired Surfers Bar & Restaurant).

Ecotrans Costa Rica (tel. 506/2654-5151, www.ecotranscostarica.com) is your best bet for **private transfer services** to Brasilito from nearly any spot in the country. Prices are $80-140 for pickups in Guanacaste and $190-320 for pickups elsewhere in the country. Their vehicles vary in size; most accommodate up to eight people plus luggage. Additional vehicles that fit 28 passengers can handle larger groups.

Interbus (tel. 506/4100-0888, www.interbusonline.com) offers daily **shared shuttle services** to Brasilito from San José, La Fortuna, Monteverde, and Rincón de la Vieja. Another shared shuttle service, **Grayline Costa Rica** (tel. 506/2220-2126, www.graylinecostarica.com) travels to Brasilito from San José, La Fortuna, Monteverde, Manuel Antonio, Dominical, Puntarenas, and Uvita. One-way services cost $54-93 per person.

The small operation **Avellanas Express** (tel. 506/2653-1400, $10 pp) can shuttle you to Brasilito from Tamarindo via their **blue line service** (Mon.-Sat.), which departs from the Neptuno Surf Shop in Tamarindo. As a surf-based shuttle service, they're happy to transport your board for free.

Tamarindo and Vicinity

Roughly 75 kilometers southwest of Liberia are the coastal destinations of Tamarindo and Playa Grande. Divided by the estuary of Río Matapalo and parkland belonging to Parque Nacional Marino Las Baulas, the two towns edge Bahía Tamarindo, one of the westernmost bays in the Guanacaste province. Though a mere four kilometers separates Tamarindo from Playa Grande to the north, the beach towns feel much farther apart, thanks to the estuary that divides them. The towns are connected via boat crossings and roads that skirt inland.

In the southwest corner of the northern Pacific coast, beginning nine kilometers down the coast from Tamarindo, are Playa Avellanas, Playa Negra, and Playa Junquillal, three tiny beach communities that attract off-the-beaten-path travelers.

You cannot find two neighboring destinations that are more different from each other than Tamarindo and Playa Grande. Tamarindo, the most popular tourist town in Guanacaste, is superbly energetic. It can feel a bit overwhelming during the high season, when the main drag is crowded and businesses vie for tourists' attention. Playa Grande is calm year-round. During a period of five months, the area awaits the arrival of leatherback turtles on the beach within the national park. Fewer travelers visit when there are no turtles to see, so the seven-month off-season is even quieter. For adventure and nightlife, choose Tamarindo. For nature and wildlife, go with Playa Grande.

One of Guanacaste's best-kept secrets is the 15-kilometer span of coastline from Playa Avellanas to Playa Junquillal—few foreigners even know it exists. The stretch is too far-flung for some people, but it impresses others with nearly virgin beaches. Visit if you want to center yourself in an isolated beach community with little development, where you can relax with little distraction.

TAMARINDO

Tamarindo is Guanacaste's most developed coastal destination—a tight-knit beach community bursting at the seams with accommodations, restaurants, bars, tour offices, and shops. The town officially begins at the south end of the estuary that separates it from Playa Grande. Playa Tamarindo, the area's main beach, begins at the estuary and stretches one kilometer south, spanning the entire town. Most businesses line the beachside Calle Central, the town's main drag, or are within walking distance. The town is known for its vibrant surf culture.

Tamarindo is more commercialized than other remote beach towns. However, the area's development means you can get by without a rental car, you have access to dining options of varied cuisines and prices, and numerous recreational options are at your fingertips. If you want space and solitude more than convenience and choice, though, Tamarindo may not be for you.

The downtown core is comprised of Calle Central, a north-south street that runs parallel to Playa Tamarindo, and Avenida Central, an offshoot of the main drag that runs east-west and perpendicular to the same beach. In the heart of town, Tamarindo Diria is the town's largest resort complex and a commonly cited point of reference on Calle Central.

★ Black Stallion Eco Park

Visits to Tamarindo are all about having fun in the sun. But what I love most about this place is that it pays homage to the region's *sabanero* roots. Just up the hill from town is the fantastic **Black Stallion Eco Park** (7.5 km east of Tamarindo, off Road 152/155, tel. 506/8869-9765, www.blackstallionhills. com, 8:30am-10pm Mon.-Sat.), a ranch where you can explore cowboy culture and take adventure tours all in one spot. Most authentic (and my favorite) are the ranch's

Tamarindo

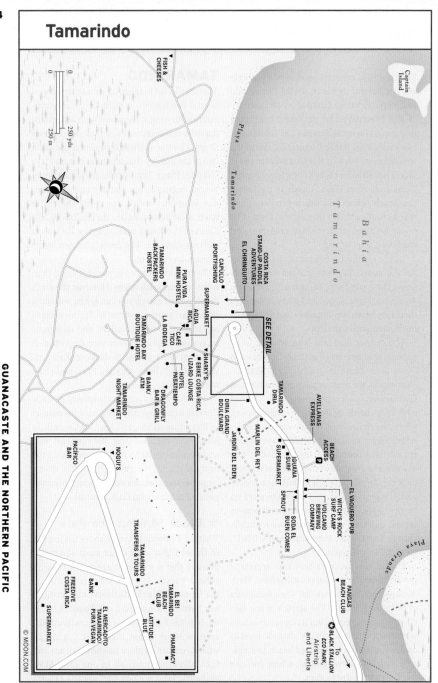

0 250 yds
0 250 m

Captain Island

Playa Tamarindo

Bahia Tamarindo

FISH & CHEESES

TAMARINDO BACKPACKERS HOSTEL

PURA VIDA MINI HOSTEL

CAPULLO SPORTFISHING

COSTA RICA STAND-UP PADDLE ADVENTURES

EL CHIRINGUITO

SUPERMARKET

AGUA RICA

LA BODEGA

CAFÉ TICO

TAMARINDO BAY BOUTIQUE HOTEL

SHARKY'S

LIZARD LOUNGE

EBIKE COSTA RICA

HOTEL PASATIEMPO

DRAGONFLY BAR & GRILL

BANK/ ATM

TAMARINDO NIGHT MARKET

SEE DETAIL

DIRIA GRAND BOULEVARD

TAMARINDO DIRIA

AVELLANAS EXPRESS

JARDIN DEL EDEN

MARLIN DEL REY

SUPERMARKET

IGUANA SURF

SPROUT

SODA EL BUEN COMER

VOLCANO BREWING COMPANY

WITCH'S ROCK SURF CAMP

EL VAQUERO PUB

BEACH ACCESS

Playa Grande

PANGAS BEACH CLUB

BLACK STALLION ECO PARK, Airstrip and Liberia

To

Detail

PACIFICO BAR

NOGUI'S

TAMARINDO TRANSFERS & TOURS

BANK

FREEDIVE COSTA RICA

SUPERMARKET

EL MERCADITO TAMARINDO/ PURA VEGAN

EL BEI TAMARINDO BEACH CLUB

LATITUDE BLUE

PHARMACY

Robert August's Endless Summer

If you're a diehard surfer, chances are you've seen *The Endless Summer*, the 1966 documentary starring American surfers Mike Hynson and Robert August as they travel across the world to chase waves. More than 50 years later, this cult surfing movie, directed and narrated by Bruce Brown, remains a classic.

In the 1990s, Brown began working on a sequel to the film, *The Endless Summer II*. This time, the filmmaker followed surfers Pat O'Connell and Robert Weaver as they retraced Hynson and August's path from the first movie. The sport had expanded, though, and more ground was covered. August, who relocated to Tamarindo after filming the first movie and became a regular rider of the area's waves, invited O'Connell and Weaver to Costa Rica to experience big thrills. August makes an appearance in the sequel, helping the two navigate breaks off Costa Rica's northern Pacific coast. The notorious surf at **Witch's Rock, Ollie's Point, Playa Tamarindo,** and **Playa Negra** made it into the film.

Today, August splits his time between Tamarindo and California. When he's in Costa Rica, he can usually be found at the small studio at **Witch's Rock Surf Camp** (Playa Tamarindo, tel. 506/2653-1262, www.witchsrocksurfcamp.com), where he makes custom surfboards by hand. He has also been known to teach surfing seminars and chat with camp guests.

barbecue fiestas, hosted in a rustic, all-wood saloon.

The guided adventures offered here include **zip-lining, ATV tours,** and a **rope course** called the **Monkey Walk.** The best option is the **Sunset Horseback Riding Tour** (3:30pm Mon.-Sat., 2.5 hours, $55 adults, $35 children 4-15, min. age 4), a horseback ride through the park's private, 1,500-acre property. The tour ends with a panoramic view of the Tamarindo highlands as the sun goes down. The tour wraps up in time to catch the legendary **buffet dinner** (6:30pm Mon.-Sat., $45 adults, $25 children 4-15, children under 4 free), a feast of ribs, sausages, chicken, rice, and potatoes hearty enough to feed a hundred cowboys. Drinks, both alcoholic and nonalcoholic, are included.

Beaches

The light-brown sand of the town's principal beach, **Playa Tamarindo,** is almost always speckled with sunbathers, pedestrians, and surfers, but this bustle is part of the beach's appeal. People looking to socialize congregate here, making Playa Tamarindo the place to be in town. The beach parallels much of Calle Central, ending at the estuary as its northern boundary. If you want space to yourself,

you can find it along the kilometer of beach that extends southwest past the end of Calle Central, toward the small village of **Playa Langosta.**

You can swim off Playa Tamarindo, but be aware that this popular surf destination has consistently choppy waters. Lifeguards keep watch 9am-6pm daily.

Recreation
SURFING

Surfing is the heart of Tamarindo. Umpteen surf schools and camps are located here—not to mention instructors offering impromptu lessons. Sizing up the options can feel like an endless chore. There are simply too many greats to note.

My top two recommendations are **Witch's Rock Surf Camp** (Playa Tamarindo, 350 m north of the Tamarindo Diria, tel. 506/2653-1262, www.witchsrocksurfcamp.com) and **Iguana Surf** (Playa Tamarindo, 100 m north of the Tamarindo Diria, tel. 506/2653-0091, www.iguanasurf.net, 8am-6pm daily). Both are mainstays in the region, backed by teams of good people.

Since 2001, Witch's Rock Surf Camp has been Tamarindo's premier full-service surf education provider. They have every aspect of the experience covered, from high-quality instruction to hotel accommodations and a restaurant on the beach where you can fuel up when you're not on the water. They provide weeklong **surf programs** that target beginner ($973-2,030 pp), intermediate ($1,078-2,135 pp), and advanced ($1,078-2,135 pp) surfers. The program packages include accommodations, breakfast, lessons, seminars, board rentals, and more. They even design custom family surf vacations.

If you're just interested in taking a class or two, Iguana Surf runs three different types of **surf lessons** (9am, 11am, 1pm, and 3pm daily, 1.5 hours): group ($45 pp, 4 students per instructor), semiprivate ($65 pp, 2-3 students per instructor), and private ($80 pp, 1 student per instructor). Each lesson includes a board and rash guard rental for the duration of the class. If you wish to keep renting the board until the end of the day (or for additional days), as a lesson graduate you'll pay half the standard rental rate.

If you just need a board, most surf schools and shops in town offer **surfboard rentals.** Iguana Surf keeps a variety of boards in stock, including shortboards, longboards, and funboard hybrids ($10 for 2 hours; $120 for 1 week). The optional board insurance is $5 per day. They also have stand-up paddleboards ($25 for 2 hours; $220 for 1 week) and boogie boards ($5 for 2 hours; $60 for 1 week).

SAILING

Sailing along the Pacific coast is one of my favorite activities. **Marlin del Rey** (Plaza Esmeralda, tel. 506/2653-1212, www.marlindelrey.com, 8am-6pm daily) provides an unforgettable sailing experience. The operator's **Morning Sailing Tour** (8am daily, 4 hours, $75 adults, $50 children 6-11) and **Afternoon Sailing Tour** (1:30pm daily, 4 hours, $85 adults, $60 children 6-11) both are opportunities to relax on a catamaran, search for dolphins and other marine life, and snorkel near the Bahía de los Piratas. A delicious homemade meal and drinks (both alcoholic and nonalcoholic) are included

with either tour. On the afternoon tour, you'll also be treated to a gorgeous sunset (weather permitting).

SNORKELING AND DIVING

The most well-known dive operator in Tamarindo is **Agua Rica** (corner of Calle Cardinal and Calle Tigris, tel. 506/2653-0094, www.aguarica.net, 7:30am-7pm daily). They specialize in **local day dives** (8:30am daily, 4 hours, $85 pp for 2 tanks, $20 equipment rental) around the Parque Nacional Marino Las Baulas. They can also arrange dive trips to the **Islas Catalina** archipelago, a 45-minute boat ride from Tamarindo. If you're not licensed to dive, opt instead for Agua Rica's **Snorkeling Tour** (8:30am daily, 3 hours, $55 pp), which also visits the waters within Parque Nacional Marino Las Baulas.

If you have ever tried free diving (also known as apnea diving), you know there is no other experience quite like it. Essentially, you're diving without the "scuba," so this exhilarating activity invites you into the underwater world in the least restrictive way possible. The sport is starting to catch on in Costa Rica, and Tamarindo operator **Freedive Costa Rica** (Plaza Conchal, off Calle Central, tel. 506/8353-1290, www.freedivecostarica.com, 9:30am-5pm Mon.-Sat.) is leading the movement. You can join in by taking a free-diving discovery course ($125 pp) or a PADI-certified free-diving course ($295 pp). If you like to fish, you can combine your free-diving discovery course with one in spearfishing ($260 pp for 2 discovery courses).

STAND-UP PADDLING

Adding to the plethora of water sports in Tamarindo is **Costa Rica Stand-Up Paddle Adventures** (50 m south of Nogui's, tel. 506/8780-1774, www.costaricasupadventures.com, 10am-6pm Mon.-Sat., 11am-4pm Sun.). You'll often see their boards lined up along

---

1: the saloon at Black Stallion Eco Park **2:** an estuary tour boat in Parque Nacional Marino Las Baulas **3:** El Vaquero Pub in Tamarindo **4:** view of the beach from Tamarindo Diria

the sand or out on flat water as beginners participate in **stand-up paddleboarding lessons** (2 hours, $85 pp). The company's most unique offering is lessons in **stand-up paddle surfing** (2-3 hours, $95 pp), the ingenious mashup of stand-up paddling and surfing; it's a lot harder than it looks! All lesson times are dependent on wind conditions, which can usually be predicted up to one week in advance. Advance reservations are required; the tour operator can confirm lesson start times a day or two before the lesson date.

FISHING

Capullo Sportfishing (tel. 506/8569-3516, www.capullo.com, 7am-5pm Sun.-Fri.) operates directly from Tamarindo. They'll save you from having to travel far, since their charter boats depart from Playa Tamarindo. Their operation is small, with just two boats to choose from, but they offer both inshore and offshore fishing trips. The smaller boat can take three people; excursions start at $475 for a half day. The larger boat can hold 6-7 people; excursions start at $900 for a half day. If Capullo doesn't have openings, consider hiring **Papagayo Sportfishing** (tel. 506/8331-2731, www.papagayosportfishing.com). They're based out of Playas del Coco up the coast, but they can pick you up in Tamarindo at an extra cost.

Entertainment and Events
NIGHTLIFE

There's a lot to do in Tamarindo after dark. Most of the action takes place on the beach, where you can kick back with a cocktail and listen to the waves roll in, or enjoy more lively entertainment. Stroll along the waterfront and you'll find happy hours and live music at **El Chiringuito** (Playa Tamarindo, near Calle Cruz, tel. 506/2438-9569, 7am-10pm daily), the **Pacífico Bar** (south end of Calle Central, tel. 506/2653-4406, 8pm-2:30am Mon.-Sat.), **El Be! Tamarindo Beach Club** (Playa Tamarindo, near Calle del Parque, tel. 506/2653-2637, 10am-10pm Tues.-Fri. and Sun., 10am-2:30am Sat.), and **Latitude**

Blue (Playa Tamarindo, 50 m south of the Tamarindo Diria, tel. 506/2653-2222, www.latblue.com, 11am-11pm daily). All four establishments are within walking distance of one another, making for easy barhopping along the shore.

The most upscale club in town is the **Lizard Lounge** (south end of Calle Central, tel. 506/2653-4406, 8pm-2:30am Mon.-Sat.), where DJs spin reggae, reggaeton, and hip-hop jams well into the morning. Across the street is **Sharky's** (Avenida Central, 150 m south of Calle Central, tel. 506/2653-4705, www.sharkysbars.com, 11:30am-12:30am daily), Tamarindo's best sports bar and one of my favorite hangout joints. On theme nights, they serve discounted cocktails (Margarita Mondays, Frozen Mojito Fridays, Sangria Saturdays, and so on). The evening will fly by while you're watching televised games, singing karaoke, and competing at beer pong.

For artisan beer brewed locally, head to **El Vaquero Pub** (Witch's Rock Surf Camp, Playa Tamarindo, tel. 506/2653-1262, 7am-10pm daily). It has pale and dark ales crafted by the town's own Volcano Brewing Company. **El Mercadito Tamarindo** (Calle del Parque, no phone, 11am-11pm daily) resembles a food court more than a bar, but it's a neat place to be on nights with live music (see their Facebook page for specific events). The **Tamarindo Night Market** (Plaza Palmas, corner of Avenida Central and Calle Cerritos, 6pm-9pm Thurs.) is a weekly pop-up market on Thursday evenings that showcases souvenirs made by local vendors and also hosts talented street acts that are always fun to watch.

FESTIVALS AND EVENTS

Tamarindo pulses to hard-hitting techno beats and house music during the first week of January each year when the **Ocaso Underground Music Festival** (www.ocaso-festival.com) takes over the beach town. The multiday party, which is spread out around beachfront bars, hilltop properties, and other venues in town, is one of Costa Rica's best EDM festivals. Go to dance, lose yourself in flashing lights, and listen to live music spun by top DJs from Costa Rica and around the world.

Shopping

From the northern entrance into town to the *rotonda* (roundabout) at the main drag's southernmost end, countless surf shops sell everything from surfboards and rash guards to general beach accessories, with a handful of souvenirs thrown in.

Most of the other shops around town are boutiques selling beachwear, jewelry, and wellness products. A number of these are scattered across Tamarindo's numerous plazas. For the most concentrated collection, stop by the **Diria Grand Boulevard** (Calle Central just south of the Tamarindo Diria, tel. 506/2653-4786, 10am-9pm daily).

A unique shop worth visiting is **Lydia Beech Art Boutique** (50 m south of Nogui's, tel. 506/8614-8529, 10:30am-5pm Mon.-Sat., 10:30am-3:30pm Sun.) on Playa Tamarindo. This small, beachfront shop is full of colorful pieces, including painted clothing, art prints, and handmade jewelry. Resident artist Lydia Beech specializes in pet portraits; if you supply her with a photo of your pet, you can go home with a beautiful painting, which makes a one-of-a-kind souvenir.

Food
COSTA RICAN

Foreigner-owned restaurants that serve international cuisines are becoming the norm in Tamarindo, with its high expat population. The town has only a handful of *sodas,* the worthiest being **Soda El Buen Comer** (Calle Central, across from Witch's Rock Surf Camp, tel. 506/2653-4691, 6am-10pm daily, $5-9). If you're craving local food, it serves classics like *casados,* as well as typical rice, seafood, meat, and pasta dishes. This tiny, informal, hole-in-the-wall is one of the few budget dining options in town.

A visit to the region isn't complete without a meal or drink at ★ **Nogui's** (south end of Calle Central, tel. 506/2653-0029, www. noguistamarindo.com, 6am-10pm Thurs.-Tues., $7-26), a Tamarindo institution. The restaurant is, as locals say, *"más Tico que el gallo pinto"* ("more Costa Rican than a spotted rooster"). It's most sought after for its seafood selections, especially the locally caught mahi-mahi and tuna. Locals also flock to this spot for less traditional treats like milkshakes and cream pies. The bright yellow, two-story,

Nogui's, one of Tamarindo's best restaurants

open-air establishment is hard to miss. Inside, it has café-style tables on the first floor and casual seating that creates a lounge setting on the second floor.

Finding Costa Rican coffee in Tamarindo is never a problem; cafés are all around. My favorite, **Café Tico** (Calle Tigris, tel. 506/8861-7732, 7am-3pm Mon.-Sat., 8am-1pm Sun., $4-8), has lattes, espresso, cappuccinos, iced coffee, and decaffeinated brews, as well as yummy baked goods and a full lunch menu.

INTERNATIONAL

Most restaurants that serve international cuisine offer selections of vegetarian and sometimes vegan dishes. **La Bodega** (Avenida Central at Hotel Nahua, tel. 506/2395-6184, www.labodegatamarindo.com, 7am-3pm Mon.-Sat., 7am-noon Sun., $5.50-10) is one such spot. A surprising number of its preparations do not include meat, like the breakfast specials, quiches, sandwiches, and salads.

On the main drag, you can't miss **Sprout** (Calle Central, across from Witch's Rock Surf Camp, tel. 506/4702-5960, www.sprouttamarindo.com, 7am-9pm daily, $8-13), a wonderful little health joint that has wraps, tacos, and sandwiches. The place doubles as a bar and has a well-loved happy hour (3pm-6pm daily) that will get you free beer with the purchase of an appetizer. Most patrons choose the crispy calamari.

Two of the finer places in town are the **Pangas Beach Club** (Calle Central, 750 m north of Tamarindo Diria, tel. 506/2653-0024, www.pangasbeachclubcr.com, 10am-10pm daily, $10-40) and the **Dragonfly Bar & Grill** (Calle Corona behind Hotel Pasatiempo, tel. 506/2653-1506, www.dragonflybarandgrill.com, 5:30pm-10pm daily, $7-20). I prefer Pangas for lunch, when I can take in the restaurant's view of nearby Parque Nacional Marino Las Baulas while dining on prime beef cooked tableside. My husband cannot seem to get enough of their smoked salmon lasagna. Dragonfly provides a more intimate setting, ideal for a romantic dinner. It serves elegant entrées like sesame-seared yellowfin tuna and filet mignon.

In the village of Playa Langosta, just southwest of Tamarindo, the superb **Fish & Cheeses** (Calle Cardinal, Playa Langosta, tel. 506/2653-1668, www.fishandcheeses.com, 11am-10pm Mon.-Fri., $10.50-28) is its own little Italy. At this restaurant, you'll find traditional carpaccios and tartares, bruschettas, and, naturally, dishes that feature fish and cheese. For a lighter meal, select a sandwich from a list of over 30 choices, each one prepared with fresh Tuscan bread.

VEGETARIAN AND VEGAN

The go-to place for vegans in town is the Thai-inspired **Pura Vegan** (El Mercadito Tamarindo, tel. 506/8488-7633, www.puravegancr.com, 11am-11pm daily, $5.50-10). It has pad Thai and curries, burritos and tacos, and decadent desserts you can wash down with kombucha.

Accommodations

UNDER $50

If you're in the market for an inexpensive night's stay, narrow your search to either the **Pura Vida Mini Hostel** (Calle Este, tel. 506/7020-4507, www.hostelminitamarindo.com, dorm $18, private $59 s/d) or its neighbor, the **Tamarindo Backpackers Hostel** (Calle Este, tel. 506/2653-1720, www.tamarindobackpackershostel.com, dorm $15, private $50 s/d). Pura Vida has hammocks, beanbag chairs, and a game room; Tamarindo Backpackers has a pool. Both properties have dorm rooms equipped with air conditioning, which runs 9pm-9am nightly.

$50-100

★ **Hotel Pasatiempo** (Avenida Central, 400 m south of the beach at Playa Tamarindo, tel. 506/2653-0096, www.hotelpasatiempo.com, $89 s/d) is Tamarindo's best-value standard accommodation. The hotel is tucked away enough from the main drag to feel private, yet it's within walking distance of nearly everything, including the beach. The 22 rooms are clean, and the beds are comfy, but the property's secluded location among the trees is the reason to visit. Don't be surprised if you see howler monkeys snooping around while you relax by the pool or in the on-site restaurant **Monkey La-La.**

$100-150

Tamarindo has plenty of high-priced and resort-quality places to stay, but the **Tamarindo Bay Boutique Hotel** (Calle Cruz, on the beach at Playa Tamarindo, tel. 506/2653-2692, www.tamarindobayhotel. com, $145 s/d) keeps luxury affordable. The adults-only accommodation's contemporary style and spectacular service are its standout features, but you'll also love the freebies that are included with your stay, such as use of bikes, boogie boards, and snorkel gear, and a made-to-order gourmet breakfast.

$150-250

Taking up much of the town's center is the 242-room resort complex ★ **Tamarindo Diria** (Playa Tamarindo, tel. 506/2653-0032, www.tamarindodiria.com, $212 s/d). This sprawling resort provides everything you might want—10 restaurants and bars, five pools, attentive and warm customer service, a central location in the heart of Tamarindo, and a big breakfast buffet that won't leave you hungry. Essentially three hotels in one, Tamarindo Diria consists of the Sunset Oceanview building (on the west side of Calle Central) with beachfront rooms and the Family Poolside and Tropicana Village buildings with additional rooms tucked back from Playa Tamarindo (on the east side of Calle Central). All rooms impress guests with beds as soft as clouds, flat-screen televisions, air conditioning, and spotless bathrooms. Though Tropicana Village is an adults-only section that provides a more intimate stay, the remainder of the complex is family-friendly.

Sister to Tamarindo Diria, the lovely adults-only ★ **Jardín del Eden** (100 m east of Playa Tamarindo, tel. 506/2653-0137, www.jardindeleden.com, $243 s/d) is its own little paradise with pretty gardens, a tranquil pool, and plenty of thatched-roofed cabanas equipped with queen-size daybeds perfect for lounging. Each of the hotel's 46 rooms has a king-size bed, soft lighting, tropical decor, and a romantic feel. Although the property isn't on the beach, a direct path from the hotel leads to Playa Tamarindo via a private waterfront garden shared with Tamarindo Diria.

Information and Services

The hospital that serves most of the northern Pacific coast's communities is **Hospital Enrique Baltodano Briceño** (Calle 3 between Avenida Central and Avenida 2, Liberia, tel. 506/2690-5500, 24 hours daily) in Liberia, a 75-kilometer, 75-minute drive northeast of Tamarindo. **Ebais Villareal** (4 km east of Tamarindo center, tel. 506/2653-0736, 7am-4pm Mon.-Fri.), the closest **clinic** to Tamarindo, is 15 minutes east of Tamarindo in the small village of Villareal.

Villareal also has a **post office** (3 km east of Tamarindo center, tel. 506/2653-0676, 8am-5:30pm Mon.-Fri.) and a **police station** (3 km east of Tamarindo center, tel. 506/2244-6173, 24 hours daily).

Downtown Tamarindo has a handful of **pharmacies,** including **Farmacia Pacífico** (Calle Central across from the Diria Grand Boulevard, tel. 506/2653-0711, 9am-8pm daily), as well as **supermarkets, banks,** and **ATMs,** along Calle Central and Avenida Central. The biggest bank in town, which provides an ATM, is **Banco Nacional** (Avenida Central, 350 m south of Calle Central, tel. 506/2653-1724, 8:30am-3:30pm Mon.-Fri.).

The closest **gas station** is seven kilometers northeast of Tamarindo, on Road 155, and two kilometers north of the village of Villareal.

Transportation

Tamarindo's roads are flat, paved, and lined with **parking** spaces. Although Tamarindo has a few **taxis,** the most common way to explore town is on foot. If the heat has you beat, seek out **eBike Costa Rica** (Centro Comercial

Plaza Tamarindo, tel. 506/8458-7963, www.ebikecostarica.com, 10am-6pm daily, rentals $15 for 2 hours; $200 for 1 week). Rent one of their funky electric bikes, easy riders, or street surfers to help you get around.

AIR

The fastest way to get to Tamarindo is by catching a domestic flight to **Aeropuerto Tamarindo** (TNO). **SANSA Airlines** (tel. 506/2290-4100, www.flysansa.com) flies to Tamarindo daily from Liberia (25 minutes) and San José (45 minutes).

CAR

The drive to Tamarindo from other parts of Guanacaste is easy, thanks to favorable road conditions and significant signage. To get to Tamarindo from **Liberia**, it's a 75-kilometer, 75-minute drive southwest on Highway 21, Road 155, and a signed side road that leads into town from the community of Huacas.

From **San José**, it's a 290-kilometer, 4.5-hour drive to Tamarindo, heading west on Highways 1, 18, and 21, Roads 160, 152, and the signed side road in Huacas.

From **Playa Flamingo**, it's a 25-kilometer, 30-minute drive to Tamarindo, heading south on Roads 180, 155, and the side road that departs from Huacas.

BOAT

Small boats commute between Tamarindo and Playa Grande multiple times daily. They do not operate according to set schedules or accept advance reservations. You can hire one of these boats at either of two docks in Playa Grande (Hotel Bula Bula or the southernmost end of Playa Grande). The boat will take you to the dock in Tamarindo (northernmost end of town, near the Pangas Beach Club). Expect to pay $2-6 per person for a brief ride that lasts 5-15 minutes, depending on where you depart from. Some boat captains speak English and others do not. To hire a captain, ask: *"¿Por favor, me puede llevar a Tamarindo?"* ("Please, can you take me to Tamarindo?"). To confirm the cost of the service, also ask:

"¿Cuánto cobra por el viaje?" ("How much do you charge for the trip?").

BUS

You can reach Tamarindo by **bus** from **Liberia** (multiple times 3:15am-6:10pm daily, 2.5 hours, $2.50) or **San José** (7am, 11:30am, and 4pm daily, 5.5 hours, $9). The bus can drop you off at the bus stop in Tamarindo (Calle Central, 150 m north of Tamarindo Diria).

PRIVATE OR SHARED TRANSFER SERVICE

Many **private transfer services** travel to and from Tamarindo daily. My top two recommendations are **Ecotrans Costa Rica** (tel. 506/2654-5151, www.ecotranscostarica.com) and **Tamarindo Transfers & Tours** (Centro Comercial Galerías del Mar, Tamarindo, tel. 506/2653-4444, www.tamarindoshuttle.com). With Ecotrans Costa Rica, prices range $80-140 for pickups in Guanacaste and $190-320 for pickups elsewhere in the country. With Tamarindo Transfers & Tours, prices range $75-120 for pickups in Guanacaste and $220-380 for pickups elsewhere in the country. Vehicles from both service providers vary in size; most accommodate up to eight people plus luggage. Additional vehicles that fit 28 passengers can handle larger groups.

Both Ecotrans Costa Rica and Tamarindo Transfers & Tours also provide **shared shuttle services** to Tamarindo, as do **Interbus** (tel. 506/4100-0888, www.interbusonline.com) and **Grayline Costa Rica** (tel. 506/2220-2126, www.graylinecostarica.com). Together, the four companies cover routes to Tamarindo from Liberia, San José, Rincón de la Vieja, La Fortuna, Monteverde, Nosara, Sámara, Malpaís, Montezuma, Manuel Antonio, Dominical, Puntarenas, and Uvita. One-way services cost $54-93 per person. Most shuttles fit eight people with luggage and offer drop-offs at Tamarindo hotels.

The small, Tamarindo-based operation **Avellanas Express** (Neptuno Surf Shop &

Deli, tel. 506/2653-1400, $10 pp) can shuttle you to Tamarindo from Brasilito on their **blue line service** (departs from Hotel Brasilito, Mon.-Sat.). They also offer service to Tamarindo from Playa Avellanas on their **green line service** (departs from Lola's, Tues.-Sun.). As a surf-based shuttle service, they're happy to transport your board for free.

ORGANIZED TOUR

A few tour operators, such as **Tenorio Adventure Company** (Hwy. 1 at Río Corobici, 5 km northwest of Cañas, tel. 506/2668-8203, www.tenorio adventurecompany.com, 8am-10pm daily), include **post-tour onward transportation** to Tamarindo. White-water rafting tours, safari float tours, and hiking tours to Río Celeste at Parque Nacional Volcán Tenorio can be arranged to include a pickup from your hotel in La Fortuna, Monteverde, Sámara, or a variety of Guanacaste beach towns, then a drop-off at your hotel in Tamarindo.

PLAYA GRANDE

Opposite Tamarindo to the south, the low-key beach town of Playa Grande sits three kilometers north of the area's estuary. Playa Grande has two distinct ends. Access to the north end, considered the community's center, is provided by Road 933. It enters the area from the east, passes through the sparse community, and ends at the town's namesake beach. The south end of Playa Grande occupies a land spit created by the estuary. It contains a residential community known as Palm Beach Estates, with a few noteworthy establishments and estuary docks. An unnamed dirt road connects the two areas, which are approximately two kilometers from each other.

Quiet Playa Grande is no ordinary coastal community. It is part of **Parque Nacional Marino Las Baulas,** one of the world's top nesting sites of leatherback sea turtles. Although most people who visit come to see turtles, the area also has great surfing and a handful of eclectic accommodations and restaurants. Steps from where Road 933

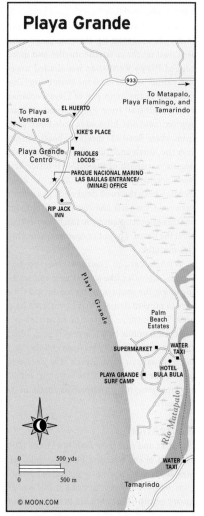

Playa Grande

meets the beach is the park's **Ministry of Environment and Energy** (MINAE) office, the best point of reference in Playa Grande.

There aren't many beachfront establishments in this community. Most businesses are set back at least 100 meters from the sand to protect turtle nesting grounds.

Beaches

Playa Grande, the town's namesake beach, is one of Costa Rica's biggest and barest beaches.

It offers plenty of light-brown sand to stretch out on, but hardly any shade. Swim at your own risk, as strong rip currents plague the area. Just up the coast, the smaller and more rugged **Playa Ventanas** has shaded areas and calmer waters ideal for swimming. You can walk to the south end of Playa Ventanas via a beach trail from Playa Grande; it's an approximate one-kilometer, half-hour walk from where Road 933 meets the beach. To access the north end, take the back road that begins just south of the MINAE office and leads northwest out of town. After one kilometer, where the road dead ends at another back road, turn left and continue driving for another kilometer until you reach the parking lot at the beach. The entire route takes roughly five minutes.

Within Parque Nacional Marino Las Baulas, activities like sunbathing and walking along the shore must be conducted with care to prevent damage to the protected land area. To minimize disruption to turtle nesting cycles, public beach access is prohibited from 6pm to 6am daily between October and late February or early March. The only way to visit the beach after dark is by participating in a government-approved turtle nesting tour.

Recreation

Outfitter and surf shop **Frijoles Locos** (500 m north of the beach at Playa Grande, tel. 506/2652-9235, www.playagrandesurfshop. com, 9am-6pm daily) offers a ton of **water sport equipment rentals** to amp up your enjoyment of the area. You can rent surfboards ($15 for 2 hours; $150 for 1 week), stand-up paddleboards ($30 for 1 day; $150 for 1 week), boogie boards ($5 for 4 hours; $35 for 1 week), and snorkeling equipment ($5 for 4 hours; $50 for 1 week), as well as handy extras like beach chairs (from $5 for 4 hours), coolers (from $5 for 1 day), and sun tents (from $10 for 1 day). They even have certified lifeguards for hire ($50 for 2 hours) to keep an eye on you or your little ones while you're swimming offshore.

SURFING

Although Tamarindo (a half-hour drive from Playa Grande) is known as the surfing mecca in Guanacaste, Playa Grande, with its year-round waves, comes in a close second.

Frijoles Locos (500 m north of the beach at Playa Grande, tel. 506/2652-9235, www. playagrandesurfshop.com, 9am-6pm daily), in the center of Playa Grande, is a reputable surf school, surf shop, tour concierge, and spa. They run two different types of **surf lessons** (on the hour 9am-4pm daily, 1.5 hours): group ($30 pp, 4 students per instructor, min. age 12) and private ($120 for 1-4 people). The private lessons are ideal for couples, small families, and children under the age of 12. Operating since 2008, this outfitter knows not only how to maneuver the area's swells but also how to avoid its difficult current to keep surfers safe.

The best surf camp in the area is the **Playa Grande Surf Camp** (3 km south of Playa Grande center, in Palm Beach Estates, tel. 506/2653-1074, www.playagrandesurfcamp. com). They offer weeklong **surf programs** that target beginner ($599 pp) and advanced ($999 pp) surfers. These packages include accommodations (dorm room with beginner package, private room with advanced package), breakfast or lunch, surf lessons, board rentals, and more. Perfectly suited for relaxed Playa Grande, the surf camp is a small but well-organized operation that prioritizes student experience through tailored instruction.

Food and Accommodations

When you're hungry, head to ★ **El Huerto** (Road 933, Playa Grande center, tel. 506/2653-1259, www.elhuertodeplayagrande.com, 10am-10pm daily, $9-26). Mixing casual dining with a sophisticated ambience, this restaurant features hanging lanterns, tropical plants, and beautifully crafted tables made from giant tree trunks. Its menu covers all the bases—salads, seafood, meat, pizza, and decadent desserts—but locals swear the linguine is the best around.

The most popular hangout spot in town is **Kike's Place** (Road 933, Playa Grande center, tel. 506/2653-0834, 7:30am-midnight daily, $5-20), which most closely resembles a *soda* (traditional Costa Rican family restaurant) but is larger and livelier. It serves Costa Rican food and plenty of booze, which never fails to draw in waterlogged beachgoers. Other draws are occasional live music, karaoke, a pool table, a dartboard, and televised sports games. Despite the young crowd, the restaurant is family-friendly and a good option for any budget-minded traveler.

The hotel with the funkiest vibe in town is the ★ **Rip Jack Inn** (100 m south of the MINAE office, tel. 506/2653-1636, www.ripjackinn.com, $105 s/d). I love this two-story boutique hotel's eight ornate rooms with touches like vintage-style wardrobes and mirrors. An on-site yoga shala, where the hotel runs yoga classes and retreats, adds to this place's uniqueness. The Rip Jack is named after the owners' beloved past dogs—Ripley and Jack—so it comes as no surprise that pets are welcome at the hotel (with prior approval).

At the southern end of Playa Grande, **Hotel Bula Bula** (3 km south of Playa Grande center, in Palm Beach Estates, tel. 506/2653-0975, www.hotelbulabula.com, $129 s/d) has lackluster rooms but spoils guests with a delicious made-to-order breakfast (included in the rate) direct from the hotel's restaurant, **The Great Waltini** (8am-9pm daily). There are menu options you won't find at most hotel breakfasts, like eggs Benedict, French toast, and custom-made omelets. Situated on the bank of the estuary, the hotel is a quick boat ride away from Tamarindo. Stay here if you plan to travel regularly between Tamarindo and Playa Grande.

Information and Services

The hospital that serves most of the northern Pacific coast's communities is **Hospital Enrique Baltodano Briceño** (Calle 3 between Avenida Central and Avenida 2, Liberia, tel. 506/2690-5500, 24 hours daily) in Liberia, a 75-kilometer, 75-minute drive northeast of Playa Grande.

The town's **supermarket,** known as the **Palm Beach Market** (tel. 506/2215-5321, 8am-8pm daily), is in Palm Beach Estates.

The closest **gas station** is 10 kilometers northeast of Playa Grande, on Road 155 in the village of Huacas.

Transportation

This area is best accessed by car. To get to Playa Grande from downtown **San José,** it's a 275-kilometer, 4.5-hour drive west via Highways 1, 18, and 21 and Roads 160 and 152/155. From **Liberia,** it's a 75-kilometer, 75-minute drive southwest on Highway 21, Road 155, and Road 933.

Playa Grande is a 20-kilometer, half-hour drive southwest from **Playa Flamingo** via Roads 180 and 933, through the town of Huacas and the hamlet of Matapalo.

From **Tamarindo,** the 20-kilometer, half-hour drive to Playa Grande loops around national park land on Roads 155, 180, and 933. This route also passes through Huacas and Matapalo. You can also reach Playa Grande from Tamarindo by taking a **boat** across the estuary. Small boats commute between Tamarindo and Playa Grande multiple times daily. They do not operate according to set schedules or accept advance reservations. You can hire one of these boats at the dock in Tamarindo (at the northernmost end of town, near the Pangas Beach Club). It will take you to one of two docks in Playa Grande (Hotel Bula Bula or the southernmost end of Playa Grande); specify your preference to the boat captain. Expect to pay $2-6 per person for the 5- to 15-minute ride. Some boat captains speak English and others do not. To hire a captain, ask: *"¿Por favor, me puede llevar a Playa Grande?"* ("Please, can you take me to Playa Grande?"). To confirm the cost of the service, also ask: *"¿Cuánto cobra por el viaje?"* ("How much do you charge for the trip?").

The outfitter and gear shop **Frijoles Locos** (500 m north of the beach at Playa Grande, tel. 506/2652-9235, www.playagrandesurfshop. com, 9am-6pm daily) can help you get around town. Their **Fetch Me, Frijoles service**

(9am-5:30pm daily with advance reservation) covers transportation between Playa Grande, the area's southernmost end (known as the Palm Beach Estates), and the estuary dock at Hotel Bula Bula. The service costs $5 per person, but the fee is returned to you as a credit that you can use in their shop. The vehicles are easily recognizable, multicolored Jeeps. Frijoles Locos also has beach cruiser **bike rentals** (from $5 for 4 hours) for local use.

PARQUE NACIONAL MARINO LAS BAULAS

Playa Grande's main attraction is **Parque Nacional Marino Las Baulas** (Las Baulas National Marine Park, 150 m northeast of the beach at Playa Grande, tel. 506/2653-0470, www.sinac.go.cr, 9am-4pm Mon.-Fri., free), the best spot along the northern Pacific coast to witness sea turtle nesting. This marine park engulfs over 54,000 acres, some 1,000 of which are land, including the stretch at Playa Grande. The well-regulated, accessible park exists to protect the hundreds of large, prehistoric-looking leatherback sea turtles that find their way to this park between October and March each year to nest. A small museum marks the park's official entrance.

★ Sea Turtle Nesting

Turtle nesting is known as *arribadas* (arrivals) in Costa Rica. Although the term refers to the act of adult sea turtles coming ashore to lay their eggs, which occurs from October to March (December and January produce the most turtle sightings), it's sometimes used informally—and incorrectly—by tour operators, agencies, and guides to address all kinds of turtle behavior, including egg hatching.

Observing these turtles during an *arribada* is one of the rarest, most breathtaking experiences in Costa Rica. You can watch as mother leatherback sea turtles that weigh a whopping 250-700 kilograms shimmy up the beach. Catch a glimpse of them burying upward of 100 eggs deep in the sand. If you visit during the middle or the end of the nesting season, you may also witness eggs hatch,

releasing baby sea turtles that scurry toward the ocean. Leatherback eggs typically hatch 60-65 days after nesting takes place.

To minimize harm to the endangered leatherbacks, Costa Rica's **Ministerio de Ambiente y Energía** (Ministry of Environment and Energy, MINAE, www.minae.go.cr) oversees activity within the park and regulates access during turtle nesting season (October to March). MINAE approves the only legal **turtle nesting tours** (start times and duration vary, $26 pp). Beware of lone individuals claiming to be tour guides and book your tour directly through MINAE. It's best to book at the **MINAE office** (150 m northeast of the beach at Playa Grande, tel. 506/2653-0470, 9am-4pm Mon.-Fri.) after you arrive in Playa Grande. Bring your passport when you visit the office, as you'll need it to register for the tour.

Estuary Tours

The estuary at **Río Matapalo** separates Playa Grande (to the north) from Tamarindo (to the south), weaving through the park and showcasing one of the country's most unique ecosystems, notable for its maze of tangled mangrove tree roots. The estuary can be toured by *panga* (a small boat that typically seats up to eight people), kayak, or canoe. Taking a peaceful float through the waterway provides an opportunity to spot monkeys, crocodiles, iguanas, and plenty of birds.

You can arrange tours rather informally at the dock beyond Playa Grande's Hotel Bula Bula, or else have your Playa Grande accommodation arrange one for you in advance. Prices are negotiable, but expect to pay at least $25 per person for a 2- to 2.5-hour tour. Tours also depart from the Tamarindo side of the estuary, but you'll pay $40-70 for the same experience.

Getting There

To get to the park's main entrance from the north or east, you'll take Road 933 through the town of Huacas and the hamlet of Matapalo; it leads right into Playa Grande and passes the

MINAE office a mere 150 meters before the road ends at the beach.

To get there from Tamarindo, you'll take a boat across the estuary. Small boats commute between Tamarindo and Playa Grande multiple times daily. They do not operate according to set schedules or accept advance reservations. You can hire one of these boats at the dock in Tamarindo (at the northernmost end of town, near the Pangas Beach Club). It will take you to one of two docks in Playa Grande (Hotel Bula Bula or the southernmost end of Playa Grande); specify your preference to the boat captain. Expect to pay $2-6 per person for the 5- to 15-minute ride. Choose to travel to the dock at Hotel Bula Bula if you want to get to the park's main entrance or if you want to participate in an estuary tour. Some boat captains speak English and others do not. To hire a captain, ask: *"¿Por favor, me puede llevar a Playa Grande?"* ("Please, can you take me to Playa Grande?"). To confirm the cost of the service, also ask: *"¿Cuánto cobra por el viaje?"* ("How much do you charge for the trip?").

PLAYA AVELLANAS TO PLAYA JUNQUILLAL

South of Tamarindo, beyond the 4,500-acre resort, ranch, and organic farm Hacienda Pinilla, are **Playa Avellanas, Playa Negra,** and **Playa Junquillal,** three beaches spread out over 15 kilometers of coastline that have managed to escape development and attention from tourists. Only a few businesses operate out of this area; most cater to surfers and the occasional sunbather who rolls in looking for peace and quiet. The majority of businesses are around the small village of **Pargos,** one kilometer inland from Playa Negra, and others are in the community of **Paraíso,** three kilometers inland from Playa Junquillal.

Farthest north and least developed, Playa Avellanas makes a great day-trip destination from Tamarindo. Both Playa Negra and Playa Junquillal provide a scattering of accommodations and restaurants, making either area a suitable option if you want a remote place by the coast to hole up in for a few days.

Beaches
PLAYA AVELLANAS

Of the few Guanacaste beaches that remain off the radar, **Playa Avellanas** is my favorite, with pretty, golden sand that shimmers in the sunset. Tropical palm trees tower overhead, providing shade. The beach also fronts the fabulous restaurant **Lola's** (Playa Avellenas, tel. 506/2652-9097, 11am-5pm Tues.-Sun.,

surfers at Playa Avellanas

$10-18), which has everything you might need during your visit. You can easily pass an entire day listening to waves roll in and watching surfers paddle out to ride them. It's pure paradise.

PLAYA NEGRA

Just 10 minutes south of Playa Avellanas, **Playa Negra** has a mellow surf-community vibe fueled by noteworthy breaks that were first widely acknowledged in the surf documentary *The Endless Summer II*. The beach isn't black, as its name suggests, but it has rocky outcroppings that darken the stretch. The best place to swim is south of the reef break, away from where the surfers congregate in the water.

PLAYA JUNQUILLAL

The nearly deserted **Playa Junquillal** is the southernmost of the three beaches, 15 minutes from Playa Negra and 25 minutes from Playa Avellanas. This gray-sand, brush-backed beach is also one of the area's longest. Take a lengthy, peaceful stroll along the waterfront—you'll see a cute little turtle hatchery along the way. Resist the urge to swim; strong currents plague the area. A much calmer swimming spot exists just up the coast at the pristine **Playa Blanca.** A small, raised escarpment divides the beaches, but it isn't safe to climb and cross on foot. Drive between the two beaches instead.

Recreation
SURFING

Avid surfers ride the waves around Playa Avellanas. Several breaks are nearby, but **La Purruja, El Parqueo, El Palo,** and **El Estero** are where most beginner-to-intermediate surfers congregate. The pros walk to the north end of Playa Avellanas (across the river mouth), where beautiful barrels await at the **Little Hawaii** break.

A fantastic small-scale operation, the **Avellanas Surf School** (Lola's, at Playa Avellanas, tel. 506/7105-8809, www.avellanas-surf-school.com, 8am-6pm daily) is driven by

passion for the sport and is particularly patient with young or novice surfers. They run three different types of **surf lessons** (times depend on the tide, 1.5 hours): group ($50 pp, 3 students per instructor), semi-private ($60 pp, 2 students per instructor), and private ($70 pp, 1 student per instructor). The school also has **water sport equipment rentals,** including surfboards ($10 for 1 hour; $105 for 1 week) and boogie boards ($5 for 1 hour; $75 for 1 week).

Food and Accommodations

Established in 1998, the laid-back ★ **Lola's** (Playa Avellenas, tel. 506/2652-9097, 11am-5pm Tues.-Sun., $10-18) has long served cold drinks and good eats to anyone who stumbled upon Playa Avellanas. It's now a modern, open-air structure that reminds me of a giant pergola. Lola's supplies beachgoers with shaded seating under umbrellas, hammocks for lounging, and bathrooms. Food options include burgers, salads, pizza, and tacos. Be sure to get a snap with the resident pig, Lolita, who saunters freely about the beach.

The best option for food near Playa Negra is **Café Playa Negra** (Pargos center, 900 m east of Playa Negra, tel. 506/2652-9351, www.cafeplayanegra.com, 7am-9pm daily, $6-14). Its huge menu features tasty breakfast creations, classics like sandwiches and salads, a selection of Peruvian entrées, and a bunch of seafood plates.

The **JW Marriott Guanacaste Resort & Spa** (Hacienda Pinilla, tel. 506/2681-2000, www.marriott.com, $429 s/d) is the area's most developed accommodation, though it's not all-inclusive. The three-story property has 316 rooms, seven restaurants and bars, a spa, a gym, and a free-flowing infinity pool that overlooks Playa Mansita, a beach just north of Playa Avellanas. The property is shared with the **Hacienda Pinilla Golf Course** (tel. 506/2681-4500, 18 holes, par 72, greens fee $150 adults, $35 children 14-18).

A handful of midrange accommodations are clustered around Playa Negra. The small, six-room ★ **Villa Deevena** (300 m east of Café Playa Negra, Pargos, tel. 506/2653-2328, www.villadeevena.com, $110 s/d) is a great choice. Extras like rainforest shower-heads, a saltwater lap pool, and patios with Adirondack chairs add comfort and a touch of elegance to the place. The on-site restaurant offers fine dining in a casual setting.

For a beachfront stay, **Hotel Playa Negra** (Playa Negra, tel. 506/2652-9134, www. playanegra.com, $100 s, $110 d) has 17 circu-lar, tiki hut-inspired bungalows that are steps away from the water. Each one features win-dows all around, a palm-thatched roof, and a small front porch. A pool, restaurant, surf shop, and yoga shala are on-site.

Information and Services

The hospital that serves most of the north-ern Pacific coast's communities is **Hospital Enrique Baltodano Briceño** (Calle 3 be-tween Avenida Central and Avenida 2, Liberia, tel. 506/2690-5500, 24 hours daily) in Liberia, an 85- to 90-kilometer, 1.5-hour drive northeast of Playa Avellanas, Playa Negra, and Playa Junquillal.

Each beach area has at least one small **supermarket.** You'll find **Mini Super Jose Pablo** (100 m south of the church in Pinilla, 6am-8pm daily) in Playa Avellanas, **Mini Super Los Pargos** (main street in Pargos, 7am-7pm Fri.-Wed.) in Playa Negra, and **Super Junquillal** (Road 928, halfway be-tween Paraíso and Playa Junquillal, 8am-8pm daily) in Playa Junquillal.

Make sure you fill up on gas before head-ing out to any of the beaches. The closest **gas station** to Playa Avellanas is 15 kilometers northeast of the beach, 2 kilometers north of the village of Villareal on Road 155. The closest gas station to Playa Negra and Playa Junquillal is 35 kilometers northeast of the beaches, on Highway 21 in Santa Cruz.

Transportation

Playa Avellanas, Playa Negra, and Playa Junquillal are each roughly 250-260 kilome-ters from downtown **San José,** an approx-imate 4.5-hour drive west on Highways 1, 18, and 21 and Road 160. The three beaches are about 85-90 kilometers from downtown **Liberia,** an approximate 1.5-hour drive southwest on Highway 21 and Road 160.

To reach Playa Negra and Playa Junquillal from inland locales, take Road 160 south-west to Road 928. The road leads into Playa Junquillal; follow the signs to Playa Negra.

Playa Avellanas is trickier to reach from in-land locales; it's best to have a GPS. Three ki-lometers south of Villareal, take the unnamed road west off Road 152 and follow the signs to Hacienda Pinilla. After two kilometers, the road forks at a bridge; stay left and follow the signs to Playa Avellanas. The route passes through the small community of Pinilla along the way. A 4x4 vehicle is recommended since many roads in the area are dirt.

The small, Tamarindo-based operation **Avellanas Express** (tel. 506/2653-1400, $10 pp) can shuttle you to Playa Avellanas from Tamarindo on their **green line service** (Tues.-Sun., departs from the Neptuno Surf Shop). They can also shuttle you between Playa Negra and Playa Avellanas (in ei-ther direction). As a surf-based shuttle ser-vice, they're happy to transport your board for free.

Nicoya Peninsula

It's 5:30pm and the sun is setting over western

Costa Rica. Surfers line up in the Pacific Ocean, eager to ride the day's last waves. Sunbathers relax on sand that glows in colorful hues under an iridescent sky. Yogis stretch out in peaceful shalas and welcome nightfall with a gentle namaste. This is the Nicoya Peninsula, a corner of the country where water, land, and spirit come together.

An assortment of travelers gathers in the beach towns that outline the peninsula. First-time and lifelong surfers, soul searchers, health nuts, socialites, artists, and bohemians are drawn to the region for different reasons, but they share a common interest in its slow-paced, tranquil way of life. Regardless of which coastal destination you choose, it will rid you of stress the moment you roll into town.

Highlights

Look for ★ to find recommended sights, activities, dining, and lodging.

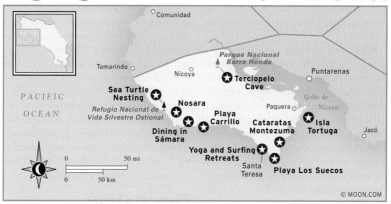

© MOON.COM

★ **Relax** in the tight-knit community of **Nosara**, a quiet, stress-free beach town (page 274).

★ **View sea turtles nesting** at the **Refugio Nacional de Vida Silvestre Ostional** (page 282).

★ **Dine right on the beach** in **Sámara** (page 290).

★ Watch the sun set over a crescent coast at **Playa Carrillo** (page 293).

★ **Descend into the Terciopelo cave** at **Parque Nacional Barra Honda** (page 299).

★ **Soak in waterfall pools** at the **Cataratas Montezuma** (page 300).

★ **Take a day trip to Isla Tortuga**, a postcard-worthy paradise (page 310).

★ **Swim, snorkel, and spy on bats** at **Playa Los Suecos** (page 313).

★ Get your zen on at **surfing and yoga retreats** in **Santa Teresa** (page 313).

The region's calm and positive vibe materializes in many forms. Resorts here are typically small-scale boutique hotels. Health food restaurants and shops are the norm, not anomalies. Organized tours are less popular than surf lessons, yoga classes, retreats, and other opportunities to better yourself or your skills. If you don't have a checklist of things to do or see while in Costa Rica, the Nicoya Peninsula is the place for you.

PLANNING YOUR TIME

The Nicoya Peninsula offers opportunities to relax. Visits to the peninsula are less about seeing and doing as much as possible and more about taking time to nourish yourself. To enjoy one or more of the peninsula's beautiful beaches, stay for at least **several days**—more, if possible. Whether you plan to practice yoga, surf, socialize, or seek solitude, the more time you have to let the Nicoya Peninsula work its rejuvenating magic on you, the better.

You'll need **one day** to visit key destinations like **Isla Tortuga** or the **Parque Nacional Barra Honda.** Most of the region's other highlights don't adhere to specific timelines. Spend as much or as little time as you want getting to know the community of **Nosara,** enjoying meals and beverages on the beach in **Sámara,** relaxing at **Playa Carrillo** (but plan to be there at sunset), hiking around the **Cataratas Montezuma,** or swimming at **Playa Los Suecos** (aim for low tide to climb around Punta Murciélago).

Independent **surfing** and **yoga** practice are possible from sunup to sundown. If you need more structure, though, you'll need to plan ahead and be patient: Surf lessons can depend on the tide, and yoga classes run according to set schedules. Organized **surf and yoga retreats** are multiday or sometimes multiweek programs.

To witness **sea turtles nesting** in the **Refugio Nacional de Vida Silvestre Ostional,** give yourself **several days** in the northern region of the Nicoya Peninsula. Be flexible, as turtle activity can be difficult to predict.

Closures of restaurants, bars, and shops in the peninsula's beach towns are common late in the low season, especially between September and November. Accommodations and tour operators tend to remain open throughout the year.

Weather and Transportation

The Nicoya Peninsula is loved in part for its favorable climate. Between December and July, the region is hot—temperatures average over 80°F—famously sunny, and dry. Rainfall is most significant between September and October, which is also when road conditions in the region are at their worst.

Despising the peninsula's roads is as easy as loving its pristine beaches. Some thoroughfares are paved highways and a pleasure to drive, but others will test your patience and driving abilities. Having a 4x4 vehicle is a must in areas where dirt roads, steep inclines or declines, and river crossings are common. Ongoing roadwork aims to maintain or improve the most popular routes in the region (namely sections of Highway 21 and the main coastal road), but in remote areas, especially the stretch between Carrillo and Santa Teresa, the roads are the worst of the bunch.

ORIENTATION

The broad, mountainous Nicoya Peninsula juts off Costa Rica's western side and curves south around the mainland. Thought of as its own region, the peninsula is part of Guanacaste province (in the northwest) and part of Puntarenas province (in the southeast). The provincial divide loosely follows the north-south run of **Road 162,** splitting the peninsula into two distinct halves: the

Previous: souvenirs for sale by the beach in Sámara; bridge from the mainland to the Nicoya Peninsula; Playa Guiones in Nosara.

Nicoya Peninsula

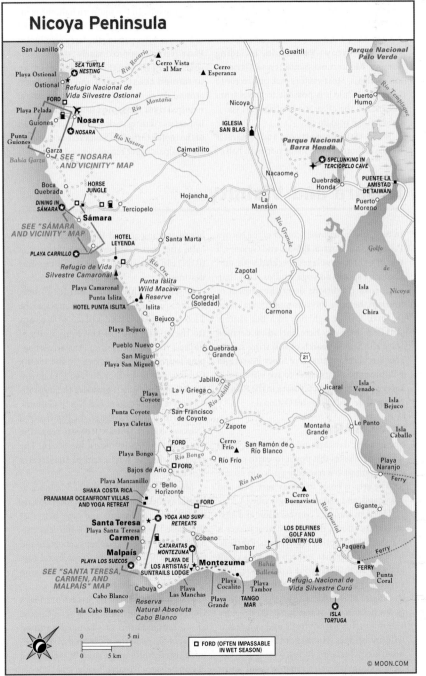

San Juanillo

SEA TURTLE NESTING

Río Rosario

Cerro Vista al Mar

Cerro Esperanza

Guaitil

Parque Nacional Palo Verde

Río Tempisque

Playa Ostional

Ostional

Refugio Nacional de Vida Silvestre Ostional

Río Montaña

Nicoya

Puerto Humo

FORD

Playa Pelada

Guiones

Nosara

NOSARA

Río Nosara

IGLESIA SAN BLAS

Parque Nacional Barra Honda

Punta Guiones

Garza

Bahía Garza

SEE "NOSARA AND VICINITY" MAP

Caimatilito

SPELUNKING IN TERCIOPELO CAVE

PUENTE LA AMISTAD DE TAIWÁN

Boca Quebrada

HORSE JUNGLE

Terciopelo

Nacaome

Quebrada Honda

Puerto Moreno

DINING IN SÁMARA

Sámara

La Mansión

SEE "SÁMARA AND VICINITY" MAP

HOTEL LEYENDA

Santa Marta

Río Ora

Río Grande

Golfo de Nicoya

PLAYA CARRILLO

Refugio de Vida Silvestre Camaronal

Zapotal

Isla Chira

Playa Camaronal

Punta Islita

HOTEL PUNTA ISLITA

Punta Islita Wild Macaw Reserve

Islita

Congrejal (Soledad)

Carmona

Playa Bejuco

Bejuco

Pueblo Nuevo

San Miguel

Playa San Miguel

Quebrada Grande

21

Jabillo

La y Griega

Río Jabillo

Jicaral

Isla Venado

Isla Bejuco

Playa Coyote

San Francisco de Coyote

Punta Coyote

Playa Caletas

Zapote

Montaña Grande

Le Panto

Isla Caballo

FORD

Cerro Frío

San Ramón de Río Blanco

Playa Bongo

Río Bongo

FORD

Río Frío

Playa Naranjo

Bajos de Ario

Ferry

Playa Manzanillo

Bello Horizonte

Río Ario

SHAKA COSTA RICA

PRANAMAR OCEANFRONT VILLAS AND YOGA RETREAT

FORD

Cerro Buenavista

Gigante

Río Guarial

Santa Teresa

YOGA AND SURF RETREATS

Playa Santa Teresa

Carmen

LOS DELFINES GOLF AND COUNTRY CLUB

Paquera

Ferry

Malpaís

CATARATAS MONTEZUMA

Cóbano

Tambor

FERRY

PLAYA LOS SUECOS

PLAYA DE LOS ARTISTAS/ SUNTRAILS LODGE

Montezuma

Bahía Ballena

Refugio Nacional de Vida Silvestre Curú

Punta Coral

SEE "SANTA TERESA, CARMEN, AND MALPAÍS" MAP

Cabuya

Playa Las Manchas

Playa Cocalito

Playa Tambor

Playa Grande

TANGO MAR

Cabo Blanco

Isla Cabo Blanco

Reserva Natural Absoluta Cabo Blanco

ISLA TORTUGA

0   5 mi

0   5 km

☐ FORD (OFTEN IMPASSABLE IN WET SEASON)

© MOON.COM

northern Nicoya Peninsula, including Nosara, Sámara, Carrillo, Punta Islita, and Nicoya, the peninsula's transit hub; and the southern Nicoya Peninsula, including Tambor, Montezuma, Santa Teresa, Carmen, and Malpaís. Most visitors pick one sector to travel in. While it is possible to travel from one half to the other via Highway 21, you'll need a full day to do so.

Road 150, joining Nicoya and Sámara, is the main thoroughfare in the northern half of the peninsula. In the southern half, the principal route begins as Highway 21 just east of Nicoya. After passing the ferry terminal at Playa Naranjo, approximately 70 kilometers southeast of Nicoya, the route changes to an unnamed coastal road and curves south around the peninsula's coast. Due to several required river crossings (some of which are impassable during the low season), travel west of the route's turnoff to Santa Teresa, Carmen, and Malpaís is not recommended.

Nosara and Vicinity

In the remote northwest corner of the Nicoya Peninsula are Nosara, Pelada, and Guiones, a trio of tight-knit villages speckled with sublime surf spots and yoga studios. Less than ideal road conditions deter the growth of tourism, helping the community maintain its small-town, neighborly feel. But visitors still find their way here, including devoted wave runners in search of inspiring swells, soul searchers in pursuit of inner peace, and wildlife enthusiasts eager to see olive ridley turtles nesting north of Nosara in the Refugio Nacional de Vida Silvestre Ostional.

★ NOSARA

Spend a few days around Nosara and you'll learn what makes this down-to-earth coastal destination such a rewarding place to escape to. The area is home to steady surf, pale and silky sand, and a soothing yogic vibe.

The community's conservation and sustainability efforts, though, are what makes it stand apart from other beach towns. Everyone here works together to keep the area clean and safe so that everyone from residents to first-time visitors can enjoy Nosara's piece of the coast. The Nosara Civic Association (www.nosaracivicassociation.com) develops and maintains nature trails and constructs wildlife bridges. Nosara Recycles (www.nosararecycles.com) runs a weekly recyclables pickup and beach cleanups. Nightly quiet

hours, starting around 10pm, keep the place calm after dark. Choose this area if you want to relax in a quiet, well-kept, and stress-free destination.

Essentially three communities in one, the area referred to as Nosara comprises the Tico-inhabited inland village of Nosara (to the north), the low-key community of Pelada (in the middle), and the area's hopping tourist hub at Guiones (in the south). Guiones can be further divided into downtown Guiones, which provides the most direct route to the ocean, and North Guiones. Just north of Nosara village, the Río Nosara (Nosara River) flows east-west from the peninsula's inlands toward the ocean. The river marks the north end of the greater Nosara region.

Most foreigners choose either Guiones or Pelada as their home base. Both locations are dotted with restaurants and have bars that showcase the area's small live-music scene. Most tourist offices and shops center around Guiones, which is Nosara's commercial core and the gathering place of avid surfers who brave the break at Playa Guiones.

It's an eight-kilometer hike from Playa Guiones to the north end of Nosara. Choose an accommodation in the neighborhood you plan to spend the most time in to minimize travel while in the area. If you intend to hop between Nosara, Pelada, and Guiones

Nosara and Vicinity

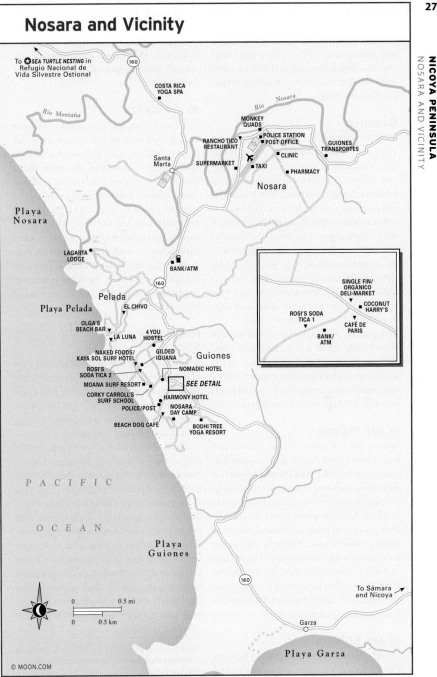

To ♻ *SEA TURTLE NESTING* in
Refugio Nacional de
Vida Silvestre Ostional

160

COSTA RICA
YOGA SPA

Río Montaña

Río *Nosara*

MONKEY
QUADS

RANCHO TICO
RESTAURANT

POLICE STATION
POST OFFICE

GUIONES
TRANSPORTES

Santa
Marta

SUPERMARKET

CLINIC

TAXI

PHARMACY

Nosara

Playa
Nosara

LAGARTA
LODGE

BANK/ATM

Pelada

160

EL CHIVO

Playa Pelada

OLGA'S
BEACH BAR

LA LUNA

4 YOU
HOSTEL

NAKED FOODS/
KAYA SOL SURF HOTEL

GILDED
IGUANA

Guiones

ROSI'S
SODA TICA 2

NOMADIC HOTEL

MOANA SURF RESORT

SEE DETAIL

CORKY CARROLL'S
SURF SCHOOL

HARMONY HOTEL

POLICE/POST

NOSARA
DAY CAMP

BEACH DOG CAFÉ

BODHI TREE
YOGA RESORT

SINGLE FIN/
ORGÁNICO
DELI-MARKET

ROSI'S SODA
TICA 1

COCONUT
HARRY'S

CAFÉ DE
PARIS

BANK/
ATM

PACIFIC

OCEAN

Playa
Guiones

0   0.5 mi

0   0.5 km

160

To Sámara
and Nicoya

Garza

Playa Garza

© MOON.COM

frequently, having a rental vehicle would be advantageous.

Road 160, the area's principal throughway, follows much of the Nicoya Peninsula's coastline from as far south as Carrillo to north of Ostional; it also connects Guiones, Pelada, and Nosara village.

Beaches
PLAYA GUIONES

Wide-open **Playa Guiones,** which fronts the community of Guiones, is Nosara's biggest attraction. Surfers, swimmers, stand-up paddlers, boogie boarders, beach walkers, and sunbathers occupy the area. This beach is full of swoon-worthy light sand but not much shade. My favorite thing about this beautiful beach is the endless trails of sand ripples hiding under the shallow, clear water. The calm scene is a contrast to the big waves that curl offshore and offer the region's best surf. This beach is also known for the aloof stray dogs that hang out here, hoping for scraps.

A path on the beach's north end leads to Playa Pelada, which is separated from Playa Guiones by a small, rocky headland. At the south end of Playa Guiones, Punta Guiones (Guiones Point) is a vegetation-covered headland that divides the beach from Playa Garza.

PLAYA PELADA

Nosara has a number of free, public, and well-marked trails. A path at the south end of small, tree-backed **Playa Pelada** connects it with Playa Guiones, making beach-hopping a breeze. Great for swimming, Playa Pelada is a local hot spot where Costa Rican children play in tide pools and adults kick soccer balls like Hacky Sacks. The light-sand beach is decorated with fishing boats, hides caves at its north end (accessible from the shore during low tide), and has a blowhole halfway down the beach that shoots water up like a geyser from a rocky outcrop.

PLAYA NOSARA

The black-sand **Playa Nosara** sits between Playa Pelada to the south and Playa Ostional

to the north. It's accessible from the south by wading across Nosara's river mouth—the confluence of Río Nosara and Río Montaña—at low tide. Most people forego visits to this volcanic beach in favor of the prettier shores farther south.

PLAYA GARZA

Less than a 15-minute drive south of Guiones (a 25-minute drive from Nosara) is one of my favorite beaches in all of Costa Rica: **Playa Garza.** Curving around the calm Bahía Garza, the beach has nearly white sand and fronts tropical waters that gleam in shades from turquoise to royal blue. Usually only fisherfolk frequent the spot, which offers shade under *almendro* (almond) trees, a few parking spaces, a small playground for children, and no other distractions. It's the perfect getaway spot, with the ocean practically empty and a beach you can lie on without being disturbed.

Recreation
YOGA

A variety of **yoga classes** (class times change monthly, 75-90 minutes, $15 pp) are run at the **Harmony Hotel** (just north of the police post in downtown Guiones, tel. 506/2682-4114, www.harmonynosara.com), conveniently located in downtown Guiones.

The beautiful **Bodhi Tree Yoga Resort** (150 m south of Road 160, 500 m southeast of the main road to Playa Guiones, tel. 506/2682-0256, www.bodhitreeyogaresort.com) provides public **yoga classes** (8:30am, 11am, 2:30pm, and 5pm daily, 75-90 minutes, $15 pp), but they specialize in yoga retreats, workshops, and teacher training sessions. If you're serious about yoga and you want more than a recreational class, Bodhi Tree's programs are the best in the area. The high-quality studios have pretty forest views. Supplement your yoga practice with the resort's on-site spa, gym, and juice bar.

1: the nearly white sand of Playa Garza 2: the beach at Refugio Nacional de Vida Silvestre Ostional, north of Nosara

If you're even more serious about your practice, you'll want to stay at a lodging that is all about yoga. North of Nosara is the **Costa Rica Yoga Spa** (Road 160, 6 km north of Guiones, tel. 506/2682-0192, www. costaricayogaspa.com, dorm $149 s, private $299 s, $448 d, all-inclusive). Here, at the remote mountaintop location, overnight guests can practice yoga in an open-air shala that overlooks the canopy of the Refugio Nacional de Vida Silvestre Ostional. A yoga retreat is in progress nearly every day of the year. Non-retreat visits are available in the form of all-inclusive yoga packages that include one yoga class and three organic vegetarian meals with each night's stay. Public yoga classes are offered when retreats are not in session, which is rare.

SURFING

Nosara is known for its consistent surf. The long beach break (with lefts and rights) that parallels much of **Playa Guiones** turns out impressive waves the entire year. Surfers of all skill levels are welcome in the lineups; some sections are ideal for beginners, and others challenge even experienced riders.

Novice surfers gravitate toward **Coconut Harry's** (Road 160, at the main road to Playa Guiones, tel. 506/2682-0574, www. coconutharrys.com, 8am-5pm daily). This iconic, trendy surf shop at Guiones's main intersection is stocked with beach gear and surf accessories. It carries the area's largest and most diverse inventory of **surfboard rentals** ($20-25 for 1 day; $120-150 for 1 week), and employs a fun group of instructors who teach daily **surf lessons** (1.5 hours), either group ($55 adults, $45 children 0-9, 2-3 students per instructor) or private ($75 adults, $65 children 0-9, 1 student per instructor). They also offer 5- and 10-lesson **surf packages** ($350-650 adults, $200-575 children 0-9), **water sport equipment rentals,** including stand-up paddleboards ($30 for 1 day; $150 for 1 week), boogie boards ($10 for 1 day; $50 for 1 week), and snorkeling equipment ($10 for 1 day; $50 for 1 week), and

beach rentals such as chairs, coolers, and umbrellas (each $5 for 1 day; $25 for 1 week). A satellite location rents water sport equipment near Playa Guiones. Lesson times are tide-dependent.

Most hotels have board rentals and surf lessons taught by in-house instructors or part-nered surf schools. Others, like the family-run **Corky Carroll's Surf School** (100 m southwest of the skate park between North Guiones and downtown Guiones, tel. 506/2682-0384, www.surfschool.net) and the luxurious **Moana Surf Resort** (200 m northeast of the beach at Playa Guiones in North Guiones, tel. 506/8989-2875, www.moanasurfresort.com), provide their own accommodations and operate multiday **surf packages** that combine lessons with room and board.

Entertainment and Events
NIGHTLIFE

You won't find a plethora of *discos* and clubs thumping late into the night around Nosara, but there are plenty of casual locales where you can let your hair down, grab a pint of beer or a glass of wine, and chat about the day's yoga class or surf. Since many residents and visitors rise early to surf or practice yoga, most nightlife venues in the area close at 10pm daily.

You can catch live music and open mic nights at the **Beach Dog Café** (175 m east of Playa Guiones, tel. 506/8337-5317, 8:30am-10pm Mon.-Sat. and 8:30am-3:30pm Sun., cash only), where the drink menu is full of creative cocktails, and at the Mexican bar **El Chivo** (on the main road to Playa Pelada, 500 m southwest of Road 160, tel. 506/2682-0887, www.elchivo.co, 11am-10pm Mon.-Sat.), which features nearly 30 different tequilas. **Olga's Beach Bar** (Playa Pelada, tel. 506/8711-0709, www.barolgasnosara. com, 11am-10pm daily) is your best bet if you want cheap brews and ocean views. Go on a Tuesday and you can get a bucket of six beers for 5,000 colones—less than US$10. This waterfront spot hosts friendly *fútbol* games on the sand and rounds of karaoke.

While the Kids are Away, the Parents Can Play

For parents, vacation planning can be a unique challenge. It can be difficult to put together an educational and entertaining trip for your child while still giving yourself the chance to escape to paradise. If you're struggling to balance both, register your kids for the awesome drop-in childcare program (8am Mon.-Fri., 5 hours, $70 per day children 4-14, $8 per additional hour 1pm-4pm) operated by the Nosara Day Camp (tel. 506/8606-8903, www.nosaradaycamp. com). Whether you want some alone time to practice yoga or to meditate, a few hours to surf the coast, or an opportunity to snooze on the sand, you can experience Costa Rica on your own terms, while your little ones explore the country through interactive field trips.

Lesson plans change regularly, but typical field trip activities include visiting waterfalls and caves, playing soccer, riding in oxcarts, spending time with local families, kayaking through mangroves, learning about the environment and sea turtle conservation, snorkeling in tide pools, and working alongside fisherfolk, farmers, and firefighters. Book for one day or an entire week. A snack, lunch, and transportation to planned outings (when required) are provided. Ask about the kid-friendly movie nights; they create an opportunity for you to slip away for a night out on the town. The camp's drop-off and pickup location is the Harbor Reef Hotel (400 m east of Playa Guiones) in Guiones, near the Beach Dog Café.

Traveling with tots under the age of four? Nosara Nannies (www.nosarananies.net), a division of Nosara Day Camp, is a reputable babysitting service utilized by many Nosara residents. Several of the nannies speak English and cater to both long-term visitors and travelers in town for only a few days.

Food

COSTA RICAN

The area's most authentic cuisine is served at the informal, patio-style Rosi's Soda Tica #1 (75 m southwest of Road 160 on the main road to Playa Guiones, tel. 506/2682-0728, 7am-3pm Mon.-Sat., $4.50-6) and Rosi's Soda Tica #2 (800 m southwest of Road 160 in North Guiones, tel. 506/2530-1363, 7am-3pm Mon.-Sat., $4.50-6). The small restaurants have only a few tables each, but they serve plentiful dishes made with quality meats, fresh fish, and tasty vegetables. Delicious *casados* (traditional dishes of rice and beans, accompanied by a variety of side dishes) draw in most regulars.

Awesome for groups, the large, open-air Rancho Tico Restaurant (150 m north and 300 m west of the airport, tel. 506/2682-0006, www.ranchoticonosara.wordpress.com, 11am-10pm Mon.-Sat., 3pm-10pm Sun., $6-17) has a menu packed with typical Costa Rican fare plus international favorites like pasta and pizza. Rustic wood tables, occasional live music, and local patrons fill the restaurant

and contribute to a laid-back atmosphere best described as *puro Tico*—purely Costa Rican.

INTERNATIONAL

To dine on the beach at sunset, grab one of the tables or benches spread out on the sand under the tall palms that tower over ★ La Luna (Playa Pelada, tel. 506/2682-0122, 7am-11pm daily, $9-21.50). The clean, classy, and nearly all-white restaurant serves a bit of everything, including spicy sausage pizza; Mediterranean beef, chicken, shrimp, or vegetable kebabs; and a kale, beet, and feta frittata. Lights strung across the place illuminate the beach after dark and create a warm environment perfect for a date night or low-key group socializing.

VEGETARIAN AND VEGAN

Plant-based cuisine is all the rage in Nosara. The organic, plant-based café Naked Foods (Kaya Sol Surf Hotel, tel. 506/8712-4463, 7am-3pm Mon.-Wed., 7am-3pm and 6pm-9pm Thurs.-Sun.) provides the greatest selection of meals, snacks, and beverages of this type. Its ever-changing menu features fresh, raw, and vegan creations, like mushroom and bean burgers, grilled jackfruit, and cold-pressed juices.

Fresh vegetarian poke bowls (served in 100 percent biodegradable dishes), salads, and vegan sushi rolls are whipped up by **Single Fin** (tel. 506/2682-1434, 10am-5pm Mon.-Sat., $5-12), inside the **Orgánico Deli-Market** (Road 160, at the main road to Playa Guiones, tel. 506/2682-1434, www.organico.webs.com, 7:30am-7pm daily). The market, too, has vegan and vegetarian food and drinks for sale, including sandwiches, burritos, fresh juices, and healthy smoothies; it also has the area's most diverse selection of wine.

Though it's not an entirely vegetarian establishment, ★ **Beach Dog Café** (175 m north of Playa Guiones, tel. 506/8337-5317, 8:30am-10pm Mon.-Sat., 8:30am-3:30pm Sun., $6-20, cash only) has mastered the meatless meal. Don't let the appearance of the unfussy, surf-inspired café and bar fool you; the mostly organic dishes on the upscale menu are executed to perfection and well worth paying a little extra for. Everything here deserves a taste, but the long list of healthy burger options is most impressive.

CAFÉS AND BAKERIES

At the principal corner in Guiones, **Café de Paris** (Road 160, at the main road to Playa Guiones, tel. 506/2682-1036, www.cafedeparis.net, 7am-5pm daily, $5-13) is perfect for popping in to pick up sweet treats or other snacks for a day trip to the beach. The deli-style bakery sells pastries, cookies, brownies, and breads baked fresh daily. Sandwiches and more substantial meals can be ordered at the café's sit-down restaurant or taken to go, if desired. Look for the tall, conical roof.

Accommodations

UNDER $50

Rooms around Nosara don't come cheap, but you can save a few bucks by staying at the **4 You Hostel** (200 m west of Road 160 in North Guiones, tel. 506/2682-1316, www.4youhostal.com, dorm $20 pp, private $34 s, $44 d). The industrial-style accommodation has squeaky-clean rooms, a modern and well-equipped kitchen, and tranquil outdoor lounge areas. Four private rooms sleep 1-4 people, and the one large dorm has 14 single beds—bye-bye, two-tier bunks! The owners provide warm and welcoming service. Ask them how they came to settle in Nosara; the account is quite the tale.

The price of a private room at the upscale, contemporary **Nomadic Hotel** (across from the skate park between North Guiones and downtown Guiones, tel. 506/2201-7342, www.nomadicnosara.com, dorm $49 pp, private $189 s/d) is out of reach for the average backpacker, but it hosts a handful of budget-minded travelers nightly in the eight-person shared room. If you're lucky enough to secure one of their teakwood dorm beds, you'll be able to enjoy the property's sophisticated but homey feel, luxe common area with a swing bench, and lagoon-like pool surrounded by paradisiacal tropical foliage.

$150-250

Open since 1988, Nosara's first establishment and hangout joint, the ★ **Gilded Iguana** (700 m southwest of Road 160 in North Guiones, tel. 506/2215-6950, www.thegildediguana.com, $249 s/d), initiated development in the area. The hotel, Nosara's most streamlined and sophisticated, has always been exclusive, and a 2018 renovation helped increase this vibe. Its one-of-a-kind, ultramodern design cleverly uses concrete paths and staircases to connect a series of two-story, whitewashed wood buildings. Underneath palm-thatched roofs are the hotel's 29 fresh, stylish, and superbly comfortable rooms, with surf-inspired decor, private outdoor bathrooms, and fine furnishings.

OVER $250

Deserving of the accolade "best panorama in Nosara," ★ **Lagarta Lodge** (at the south end of Playa Nosara, 1.5 km northwest of the 5-way intersection, tel. 506/2682-0035, www.lagartalodge.com, $320 s/d) perches above a 90-acre biological reserve; the property's restaurants, lounges, pools, rooms, and 360-degree *mirador* (lookout) boast marvelous river, beach, and ocean views. The boutique accommodation's 26 spacious junior suites spoil guests with private verandas, rainfall showerheads, and luxurious bedding. When you're not lounging in your quiet, comfortable room, you can make use of the hotel's spa, restaurant, bar, or wine cellar.

The ★ **Harmony Hotel** (just north of the police post in downtown Guiones, tel. 506/2682-4114, www.harmonynosara.com, room $390 s/d, bungalow $490 s/d) snagged one of the best locations in the area. It's a two-minute walk from Playa Guiones and a stone's throw from restaurants and shops. The hotel has 24 luxurious, crisp-white rooms and bungalows with striking wood beam-vaulted ceilings, king-size beds, air conditioning, outdoor showers, and private patios. Helping guests feel their best are the on-site health food restaurant, natural juice bar, spa, and yoga shala. Each overnight stay includes one complimentary yoga class.

Information and Services

Hospital La Anexión (Road 150, 300 m north of the justice courts, Nicoya, tel. 506/2685-5066, 24 hours daily) serves most of the Nicoya Peninsula. It's in Nicoya, a 1.5-hour drive northeast of Nosara.

Just below the north end of the airstrip are Nosara's **clinic, Ebais Nosara** (tel. 506/2682-0266, 24 hours daily), and **Farmacia Elimar** (tel. 506/2682-5149, 8am-7pm Mon.-Sat.), a **pharmacy.**

Nosara's **post office** (tel. 506/2682-0100, 8am-5pm Mon.-Fri.) and **police station** (tel. 506/2682-5126, 24 hours daily) are at the north end of the area's airstrip. A **tourist police office** (road to Playa Guiones, just south of the Harmony Hotel, tel. 506/2682-5332, 24 hours daily) in downtown Guiones has officers available to assist foreign tourists.

Banks with **ATMs,** including a branch of **Banco Popular** (tel. 506/2682-0011,

9am-4pm Mon.-Fri.) and an ATM belonging to **Banco de Costa Rica** (5am-midnight daily), are along Road 160 (between Guiones and Nosara) and on the road to Playa Guiones. Several **supermarkets** cluster around Playa Guiones and Nosara.

Fill up on fuel at the **gas station** on Road 160 between Nosara and Pelada, or on Road 150 just northeast of the turnoff to Nosara on your way into or out of town via Nicoya.

Transportation
CAR
Nosara is a 260-kilometer, 4.5-hour drive west from downtown **San José** via Highways 1 and 18 and Roads 150 and 160. From downtown **Liberia,** it's a 135-kilometer, three-hour drive south on Highway 21, Road 150, and Road 160 to Nosara. From **Sámara,** the 30-kilometer drive northwest on Road 160 to Nosara takes 45 minutes to an hour.

AIR
The local airport, **Aeropuerto Nosara** (NOB), is in the community of Nosara, roughly seven kilometers north of Playa Guiones. **SANSA Airlines** (tel. 506/2290-4100, www.flysansa.com) flies to Nosara daily from San José and Liberia. The flight time from San José is approximately 40 minutes.

BUS
Public **buses** travel daily to Nosara from **San José** (5:30am daily, 5.5 hours, $8.50) and **Nicoya** (multiple times 4:45am-5:30pm daily, 2 hours, $3.50).

To get to Nosara from **Sámara,** take the bus bound for Nicoya (multiple times 5:30am-6:45pm daily, 1-1.5 hours, $2.50) and get off partway, at the gas station (5 km north of Sámara). Ask the bus driver, "*¿Por favor, puede parar en la bomba?*" ("Please, can you stop at the gas station?"). You can then catch one of many buses that head to Nosara at the stop on the opposite side of the road, across from the gas station. To identify a bus bound for Nosara, look for signage in the bus's front window. Buses end their run in the village of

Nosara, on the north side of the *fútbol* field. If you need to get off at Guiones, ask the bus driver, *"¿Por favor, puede parar en Guiones?"* ("Please, can you stop in Guiones?"). The driver will drop you off in downtown Guiones on the corner of Road 160 and the unnamed road that leads to Playa Guiones.

PRIVATE TRANSFER SERVICE

Sámara Adventure Company (tel. 506/2656-0920, www.samaraadventure company.com), based in Sámara, provides **private transfer services** to Nosara from all over the country. Operating directly out of Nosara, the smaller **Guiones Transportes** (900 m east of the Nosara airstrip, tel. 506/8834-8904, www.guionestransports. com) can also deliver you to Nosara from multiple locations. Most vehicles accommodate up to eight people plus luggage. Prices average around $275 from San José, $150 from Liberia, and $70 from Sámara. Additional vehicles that fit 28 passengers can handle larger groups.

ORGANIZED TOUR

A few tour operators, including **Sámara Adventure Company** (tel. 506/2656-0920, www.samaraadventurecompany.com), offer **post-tour onward transportation** to Nosara. White-water rafting tours and safari float tours can be arranged to include a pickup from your hotel in Liberia, La Fortuna, or Monteverde, then a drop-off at your hotel in Nosara.

GETTING AROUND

The eight kilometers connecting Guiones, Pelada, and Nosara is best explored on wheels. If you don't have a rental vehicle, you can flag down one of the abundant **tuk-tuks** (a motorized rickshaw) in Nosara, or call for a ride with **Nosara Taxi Cab** (tel. 506/8973-7065, www.nosarataxicab.com, 24 hours daily). **Monkey Quads** (on the road to Playa Guiones, just south of the Harmony Hotel, tel. 506/2682-4067, www.monkeyquads.com) has **ATV rentals** ($55 for 1 day; $315 for 1 week)

and **golf cart rentals** ($65 for 1 day; $425 for 1 week).

REFUGIO NACIONAL DE VIDA SILVESTRE OSTIONAL

The elongated **Refugio Nacional de Vida Silvestre Ostional** (Ostional National Wildlife Refuge, tel. 506/2682-0400, 8am-4pm daily, beach access 5am-11pm daily, free) spans 15 kilometers of Pacific shoreline from just north of the community of Nosara all the way south to Punta Guiones. Surfers and swimmers fancy the refuge's nearly 20,000 acres of protected waters, but the star attractions are the groups of **olive ridley sea turtles** that come ashore to nest on the refuge's shores. A once-in-a-lifetime wildlife-viewing opportunity for most visitors, these events are the most dramatic showings of sea turtles in all of Costa Rica.

A small office of the Ministerio de Ambiente y Energía (Ministry of Environment and Energy, MINAE) in the community of Ostional marks the refuge's **official entrance.**

★ Sea Turtle Nesting

Unlike other sea turtle species spotted elsewhere in Costa Rica crawling ashore individually, the olive ridleys that frequent the refuge are notorious for nesting in groups. Swarms of pregnant female turtles gather in the ocean off Playa Ostional in the weeks prior to an *arribada* (literally, "arrival"). Together, they storm the beach over 2-6 days, stunning residents and visitors alike with a dramatic display of one of nature's wildest and most orchestrated events.

In 1995, a record-setting *arribada* saw a half million olive ridleys deposit their eggs in the sand at Playa Ostional. That's tough to top, but nesting periods from May to December routinely come close. It's not unusual for *arribadas* to see adult turtles in the hundreds of thousands, especially during the later months of August to December. Though olive ridley sea turtles nest at the refuge year-round, turtle sightings are much less common from January to April.

To plan for the event, brush up on your understanding of lunar cycles and tide charts. *Arribadas* are impossible to predict with certainty; most guides can't pinpoint dates more than a month in advance. However, olive ridleys tend to arrive at Playa Ostional during afternoon or evening high tides at least once every moon cycle, generally between the third quarter and the new moon. They nest between dusk and dawn, although smaller groups and stragglers come ashore throughout the day.

Arribadas are best witnessed after dark. Access to the refuge is restricted at night, so you'll need to join a guided **turtle nesting tour** ($10 adults, $5 children 0-5). Tours range in length from 45 minutes to four hours; only approved guides can lead them. During the tour, you'll wait on the beach while the guide searches for turtles. On nights during large *arribadas*, you may find yourself surrounded by the creatures. To avoid disrupting the nesting cycles, humans must stay one meter away from turtles that have laid eggs and are returning to the ocean. Tour guides provide special lights that can help you see the turtles in the dark. They also provide information about the turtles and their nesting behaviors throughout the experience. Tour groups are capped at a maximum of nine people per guide. Tour departure times are tide-dependent.

Tour guides can be hired through the **Asociación de Guías Locales de Ostional** (Ostional Local Guides Association, AGLO, tel. 506/2682-0428), though you'll need to ask specifically for an English-speaking tour guide. I highly recommend an alternate option: taking one of the tours offered by tour operators and agencies from nearby Nosara or Sámara, like **Sámara Adventure Company** (tel. 506/2656-0920, www.samaraadventurecompany.com) or **Eco Aventura Sámara** (tel. 506/2656-0606, www.ecoaventurasamara.com). Although taking these tours means paying more (prices start at $50 for adults, and $40 for children), round-trip transportation is included. This saves you a drive back to your home base in complete darkness. It also avoids the risk associated with leaving your vehicle parked by the beach at night while you trot off in search of turtles. Best of all, you avoid having to maneuver the bumpy stretch of Road 160 (complete with a river crossing) between the beach and its closest tourist destination, Nosara.

Getting There

Playa Ostional is a mere 10-15 kilometers northwest of Nosara, Pelada, and Guiones and 40 kilometers northwest of Sámara, but the unpaved stretch of Road 160 that leads to the site from the southeast is slow going. Vehicles must travel at a snail's pace to manage the loose rocks, and drivers will need to navigate a river crossing. Expect the route to take 30-40 minutes from Nosara, Pelada, or Guiones, and over an hour from Sámara. A 4x4 vehicle with high clearance is recommended. Significant rainfall can cause rivers to swell; before setting out, confirm with a local whether the road is passable.

If you plan to visit Playa Ostional from a beach town in Guanacaste, such as Tamarindo or Playas del Coco, Road 160 also provides access from the northwest. Traversing the road from this direction avoids the river crossing, but having a 4x4 vehicle is still a good idea. From Tamarindo, the route is about 60 kilometers, a 90-minute drive.

Sámara and Vicinity

One of the Nicoya Peninsula's most visited destinations is in its northern half. Sámara is a vibrant, geographically small, and easily accessible beach town. Much of Sámara's appeal—especially to families with young children—is its calm bay and swim-friendly waters. The town also serves as an ideal base for day trips to more remote communities scattered to the south along the coast.

South of Sámara, the secluded hamlets of **Carrillo** and **Punta Islita** are separated by the **Refugio de Vida Silvestre Camaronal.** These three areas allow off-the-beaten path explorers to explore beaches, surf spots, hotels, and attractions away from high-traffic areas.

SÁMARA

The coastal town of Sámara is the region's commercial and service hub, but it's no tourist trap. A handful of operators offer guided nature and adventure tours that showcase the area's hills and thrills, but equally recommended is downtime spent lounging on the long, inviting Playa Sámara.

The small and dense town has strong Italian and other European influences, conducts tourism in a professional but laid-back manner, and offers an eclectic vibe with its collection of beach bars, health stores, and art shops. In less than a half hour, you can walk around the entire core. Go ahead and do so in your bathing suit; you'll blend in just fine in this casual community.

Sámara is the easiest coastal destination on the Nicoya Peninsula to reach by car. The town is where **Road 150,** a paved, north-south route from Nicoya, joins **Road 160,** the area's pressed-dirt-and-gravel road from Nosara. In Sámara, Road 150 becomes the town's main drag, ending at Playa Sámara. The downtown core covers an area less than

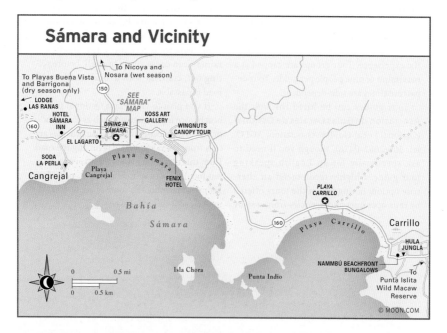

Sámara and Vicinity

To Nicoya and Nosara (wet season)

To Playas Buena Vista and Barrigona (dry season only) 150

LODGE LAS RANAS

HOTEL SÁMARA INN 160

SEE "SÁMARA" MAP

DINING IN SÁMARA

KOSS ART GALLERY

WINGNUTS CANOPY TOUR

EL LAGARTO

SODA LA PERLA

Cangrejal Playa Cangrejal

Playa Sámara

Playa Cangrejal

FENIX HOTEL

PLAYA CARRILLO

Bahía Sámara

160 Playa Carrillo Carrillo

HULA JUNGLA

NAMMBÚ BEACHFRONT BUNGALOWS

0   0.5 mi
0   0.5 km

Isla Chora

Punta Indio

To Punta Islita Wild Macaw Reserve

© MOON.COM

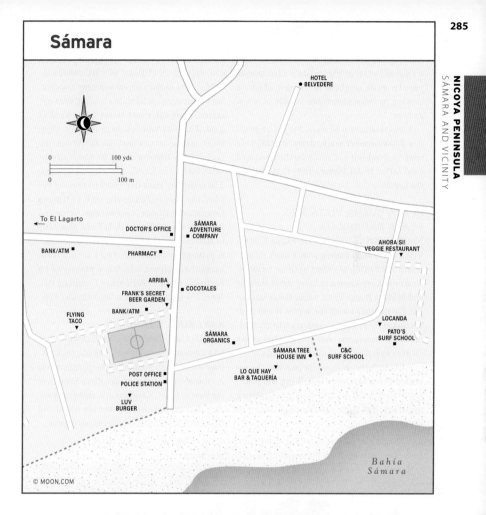

Sámara

HOTEL BELVEDERE

To El Lagarto →

DOCTOR'S OFFICE

SÁMARA ADVENTURE COMPANY

AHORA SI! VEGGIE RESTAURANT

BANK/ATM

PHARMACY

ARRIBA

COCOTALES

FRANK'S SECRET BEER GARDEN

FLYING TACO

BANK/ATM

LOCANDA

PATO'S SURF SCHOOL

SÁMARA ORGANICS

SÁMARA TREE HOUSE INN

C&C SURF SCHOOL

POST OFFICE

POLICE STATION

LO QUE HAY BAR & TAQUERÍA

LUV BURGER

Bahía Sámara

© MOON.COM

0 — 100 yds
0 — 100 m

---

one square kilometer and comprises a few unnamed side streets that branch off from Roads 150 and 160.

Beaches
PLAYA SÁMARA

The supple and slightly gray-tinged, light sand spread out across **Playa Sámara** is soothing to look at and comfortable to stretch out on. It's the kind of beach you can walk along barefoot, partly because the waves gliding along the shoreline keep the sand refreshingly cool but also because the forested headlands on

both sides of Bahía Sámara are worth admiring during a leisurely stroll.

Playing in the water here is largely stress-free due to small waves, a gradual slope, and a lack of riptides. This is Sámara's primary beach, and it fronts the entire town. Don't expect to find the place empty, but getting to hang out on a sliver of pretty Playa Sámara is reason enough to visit.

PLAYA CANGREJAL

On the west side of Bahía Sámara, **Playa Cangrejal** is separated from Playa Sámara by a small river mouth. This light-sand, wide beach backed by two rows of tropical palms remains off the tourist radar, even though it's equally as stunning and only a fraction as popular as its neighbor to the east. If you're looking to swim someplace outside of town, go here.

From downtown Sámara, Playa Cangrejal is a 1.5-kilometer walk, drive, or taxi ride west on Road 160 and south on the unnamed road (after Hotel Sámara Inn) that leads to the beach.

PLAYA BUENA VISTA AND PLAYA BARRIGONA

North of Playa Cangrejal are **Playa Buena Vista** and **Playa Barrigona.** I don't recommend swimming at either of these beaches. Crocodiles are known to hang out at the east end of Playa Buena Vista, where the estuary of Río Buena Vista meets the ocean. If you wish to relax at Playa Buena Vista, stick to the middle of the beach; the west end also has a tiny estuary that may also house crocodiles.

Although the snow-white beach at the secluded Playa Barrigona is striking and pleasant to stretch out on, the water hides a strong undertow that is easy to misjudge. It can be deadly.

Recreation

LOCAL GUIDES AND TOURS

Sámara Adventure Company (Road 150, just north of Road 160, tel. 506/2656-0920, www.samaraadventurecompany.com, 8am-6pm daily) is Sámara's leading tour operator. They offer just about every kind of guided activity you can do in the area, from local nature excursions like turtle nesting tours and mangrove tours, to ocean adventures including kayak and snorkel outings. The company runs day tours to regions beyond the Nicoya Peninsula, such as trips to Guanacaste's Parque Nacional Palo Verde and Parque Nacional Rincón de la Vieja, plus visits to attractions in La Fortuna and Monteverde. A prompt, professional, and friendly team backs the business, which is a partner of La Fortuna's Desafio Adventure Company (tel. 506/2479-0020, www.desafiocostarica.com).

KAYAKING, STAND-UP PADDLING, AND SNORKELING

Isla Chora (Chora Island), a small, rocky island with a blush-pink beach, is approximately 2.5 kilometers offshore from Playa Sámara at the base of town. Kayakers and stand-up paddleboarders can travel between the island and the mainland when tide conditions permit.

Rows of tropical palms back the secluded Playa Cangrejal in Sámara.

Sámara Adventure Company (Road 150 just north of Road 160, tel. 506/2656-0920, www.samaraadventurecompany.com, 8am-6pm daily) leads guided tours to the island. Their **Isla Chora Kayak and Snorkel Tour** (3 hours, $49 adults, $39 children 4-12, min. age 4) and **Isla Chora Stand-Up Paddle and Snorkel Tour** (3 hours, $49 adults, $39 children 4-12, min. age 4) both include all necessary equipment, round-trip transportation from Sámara hotels, a snack served on the island, and an opportunity to snorkel around a shallow reef. The times for these Isla Chora tours are tide-dependent. The operator's popular **Ocean Seafari Dolphin Sightseeing and Snorkel Tour** (8am daily, 4 hours, $55 adults, $40 children 4-12, children under 4 free) is an easy dolphin-watching expedition that docks near the island for snorkeling. During the trip, you can spot up to three different species of dolphins.

SURFING

Sámara's surf doesn't wow the pros or even intermediate-level surfers, but it's great for beginners who have never mounted a board. You'll get long and low waves, a sandy bottom, and hardly any rip current—ideal conditions for first-time surfers intimidated by rougher runs up and down the coast. If you're an avid surfer but you're stationed in Sámara, day trips to nearby breaks are in your future.

Any good surf instructor will tell you that it takes beginners more than one lesson to get the hang of how to surf. That's why I favor **Pato's Surf School** (on the beach at Playa Sámara, tel. 506/8373-2281, www.patossurfingsamara.com, 8am-6pm daily) and **C&C Surf School** (on the beach at Playa Sámara, tel. 506/8817-2203, www.cncsurfschool.com, 8am-8pm daily). Both schools ingeniously include a five-day surfboard rental with their classes, so you can have time to put theory into practice—at no extra cost.

Pato's Surf School runs two types of **surf lessons** (1.5 hours): group ($45 adults, $35 children 3-12, 2-4 students per instructor) and private ($55 pp, 1 student per instructor). They also include a five-day boogie board rental, in addition to the surfboard rental, in their rates. The team of instructors is particularly great with kids; this and the area's mild surf make Sámara the perfect place to introduce your young ones to the sport.

C&C Surf School runs three different types of **surf lessons** (1.5 hours): group ($45 pp, at least 3 students per instructor), semiprivate ($50 pp, 2 students per instructor), and private ($60 pp, 1 student per instructor). Their surprisingly affordable 8- and 15-day **surf camps** ($790-1,490 pp) include accommodations, some meals, surf lessons, surf video analyses, and board rentals.

All lesson times are tide-dependent. Surfboards can be rented ($4 for 1 hour; $15 for 1 day) at Pato's Surf School, C&C Surf School, and various other locations around town. If you plan to use the equipment for more than three days, a group surf lesson with a five-day board rental is the greatest value. Pato's Surf School has other **water sport equipment rentals,** including stand-up paddleboards ($12 per hour), kayaks ($10-12 per hour), boogie boards ($10 per day), and snorkeling equipment ($10 per day).

HORSEBACK RIDING

Horses are a common sight on Playa Sámara, and riding tours are widely available. My favorite are small-group horseback riding tours that explore relatively untouched beach areas north of town. The unoccupied sand makes for wide-open walks, and beautiful oceanside scenery and undeveloped land are on full display.

You cannot go wrong with any of the four horseback riding tours provided by **Horse Jungle** (just south of Road 160, 5 km northwest of Road 150, tel. 506/8650-1606, www.horsejungle.com). The outfitter welcomes children, focuses on the comfort levels of its riders, and takes good care of their horses. Their **Playa Buena Vista Horseback Riding Tour** (8:30am-3pm daily, 2.5 hours, $50 pp, min. age 4), **Playa Barrigona**

Horseback Riding Tour (8:30am-3pm daily, 3 hours, $60 pp, min. age 4), **Playa Buena Vista and Playa Barrigona Horseback Riding Tour** (8:30am-3pm daily, 4 hours, $80 pp, min. age 4), and **Full-Day Horse Ride** (8:30am-3pm daily, 8 hours, $130 pp, min. age 4) are equally worthy of your time and money. Each tour's course is slightly different; some pass through forest, visit the beach, or wade through rivers. If you're a devoted rider, consider committing to a three-, four-, or five-day horse trek ($295-555 pp) that combines daily horseback riding tours with extras like meals and a visit to a sunset *mirador*.

ZIP-LINING

While most Sámara travelers congregate at or near the beach, some opt to explore the area from above during the **Canopy Tour** (8am, 9am, noon, and 1pm daily, 2-3 hours, $65 adults, $50 children 3-12, min. age 3) created by the **Wingnuts Canopy Tour** (Road 160, 1.5 km east of Road 150, tel. 506/2656-0153, www.wingnutscanopy.com, 8am-4pm daily). Although it's exhilarating when you speed across each of the 10 zip-line cables, the trip overall has a down-to-earth feeling. Groups are small, and tour guides take time to make conversation. Partway through the treetop journey, juice and fruit are served picnic-style on one of the zip-line platforms. With a little luck, you'll spot monkeys or coatimundis during the experience, which traverses dry forest typical of the area and provides a beautiful view of the Pacific Ocean through the trees.

Entertainment and Events
NIGHTLIFE

Sámara isn't a party town, but there are a handful of low-key places that happily provide entertainment and drinks after dark. The longtime bar **Arriba** (Road 150, 50 m south of Road 160, tel. 506/8973-1618, noon-2am daily) in the center of town has darts and broadcasts live sports on televisions and projector screens. Down the road, **Frank's Secret Beer Garden** (on the corner of Road 150 and Calle Plaza, tel. 506/8710-4802, 7am-10:30pm daily) has poker, dominoes, billiards, and happy hours with discounted beer.

The **Flying Taco** (Calle Plaza, northwest corner of the *fútbol* field, tel. 506/2537-9566, 11am-2am daily) caters to an active crowd with live music and dance nights where people showcase their merengue, cumbia, and salsa moves.

Shopping

When I'm in Sámara, you'll likely find me perusing the shelves inside **Sámara Organics** (inside Natural Center on the main road that runs parallel to Playa Sámara, tel. 506/2656-3046, 8am-7pm daily). I love this small market, which doubles as a café. It has fresh fruit and vegetables, sandwiches, smoothies, superfoods, desserts, and the best banana bread I've ever tasted. The market also has souvenir-worthy gifts and artwork, hair and body products for pampering yourself, and essential oils.

Tons of shops selling typical souvenirs and beach supplies like sarongs, bathing suits, towels, and hats line the main drag. A unique find among them, **Cocotales** (Road 150, 100 m north of Playa Sámara, tel. 506/8807-7056, 8am-8pm daily) specializes in crafting products out of coconut, like jewelry and soap. You can buy bottles of 100 percent coconut oil and coconut-based massage oil too.

The **Koss Art Gallery** (on the beach at Playa Sámara, 650 m east of downtown Sámara, tel. 506/2656-0284, www.kossartgallery.com, 8am-5pm daily) sells upscale artwork. The eye-catching paintings are movement-filled and rich in primary colors. Canvasses crafted by Jaime Koss, Sámara's well-known artist and business owner, can also be ordered through the gallery's website and shipped internationally.

1: health food market Sámara Organics **2:** sunset at Playa Carrillo **3:** poolside at Hotel Leyenda in Carrillo **4:** the waterfront Lo Que Hay Bar & Taquería in Sámara

Food

★ BEACHSIDE RESTAURANTS

On a sun-kissed day in Sámara, a great way to relax and take in the tropical environment is by dining and drinking at a waterfront establishment. Stroll along Playa Sámara's three kilometers of beach and you'll find a line of restaurants with unspoiled ocean views. These are great places to watch or listen to waves crashing onto the shore, so grab a table on the sand and tickle your toes in its softness as you wait for your order to arrive. Go for lunch and you'll be entertained by watching beachgoers, horses trotting across the sand, and water sport adventurers arriving into and departing from the bay. Visit after dark and fall under the calming spell of soft lanterns or candlelight that dimly exposes the beach. You may even be serenaded by one of Sámara's traveling mariachi bands. On clear nights, the sky sparkles with stars.

The chill ★ **Lo Que Hay Bar & Taquería** (Playa Sámara, tel. 506/2656-0811, 7am-2am Mon.-Sat., 7am-midnight Sun., $5-19) has a great laid-back, beachy vibe, occasional live music, and a rotating list of food and drink specials. This self-described taqueria has seven delicious taco varieties, but the restaurant's diverse menu is equally impressive, with breakfast options, appetizers (try the melt-in-your-mouth grilled avocado), sandwiches and nachos, and even full entrées. The dress code here is bikinis and board shorts by day, but classier (albeit still casual) at night.

★ **Locanda** (Playa Sámara, tel. 506/2656-0036, www.locandasamarabeach.com, 7am-11pm daily, $9-18) provides one of the most romantic dining settings in the area. At this Italian restaurant, tables are spread out on the sand under palm-thatched huts lit with candelabras; the comfortable, oversize wood chairs have thick cushions. While the food quality doesn't match the fine-dining feel of the place, the pastas and desserts rarely disappoint. Beef, chicken, and fish plates, plus salads and sandwiches, round out the menu. Most appealing, though, is the ambience. Most evenings, a local guitar- and trumpet-equipped musical group serenades diners with tender Spanish and Latin American songs. (Expect to pay around $5-10 in cash if you request a serenade for your table.)

Jam-packed with healthy meal options is the 100 percent plant-based franchise ★ **Luv Burger** (Playa Sámara, tel. 506/2656-3348, www.luvburger.com, 8am-10pm Sun.-Fri., 8am-midnight Sat., $6-13). If the thought of a Power Fruit Bowl or Chocolate Superfood Banana-Based Ice Cream makes you happy, this venue's garbanzo-bean burger options (topped with coconut bacon, cashew cream cheese, or grilled pineapple) and Goddess Salad will get your mouth watering. Designed as a small, open-air patio with a few tables on the beach, this no-frills, vegan food station is a quiet spot where you can reset your mind while nourishing your body.

COSTA RICAN

My go-to diner for local cuisine is the tiny, roadside **Soda La Perla** (just west of Playa Cangrejal, tel. 506/2469-2275, 6:30am-5pm Mon.-Sat., $3.50-12.50). Just steps from Playa Cangrejal (a five-minute drive west of Sámara), this home-style restaurant serves authentic food in the least formal setting you can imagine. The floor is made of gravel, a surfboard serves as a table, and the kitchen is open (ideal if you like to watch your food being prepared), but the casual construction complements the tasty rice dishes and fish fillets.

INTERNATIONAL

For flavorful meals prepared *a la parrilla* (on the grill), look no further than the seafood, chicken, and steak joint **El Lagarto** (100 m south of Road 160, 200 m west of Road 150, tel. 506/2656-0750, www.ellagartobbq.com, 3pm-9:30pm Mon.-Thurs., 3pm-11pm Fri.-Sun., $10-33.50). The food quality is top-notch, thanks to the restaurant's preference for sourcing high-grade beef from the Northern Zone's plains and vegetables from the Central Valley. Seafood is caught just off the coast and served fresh. Come hungry and thirsty; portions are large, and the five-page drink menu provides plenty of refreshment options.

VEGETARIAN AND VEGAN

The colorful, mosaic-clad **Ahora Si! Veggie Restaurant** (just south of Road 160, 300 m east of Road 150, tel. 506/2656-0741, 8am-10pm daily, $6.50-11.50) is at the Casa Paraiso hotel on the east side of town. This small, hippieish restaurant is wonderfully welcoming. It promotes inclusivity and community with its unisex bathrooms and signage requesting that diners forgo their phones during their meal. The vegetarian Italian restaurant also caters to raw and vegan diners, winning over most with its homemade breads and pizzas as well as pastas including ravioli, gnocchi, fettucine, and lasagna.

Accommodations

$50-100

I'm partial to the 14-room, two-story ★ **Hotel Sámara Inn** (Road 160, 750 m west of Road 150, tel. 506/2656-0482, www. hotelsamarainn.com, $66 s, $80 d), which always delivers a quaint, cozy stay. I particularly love that the hotel is a 2-minute drive or 10-minute walk from Sámara's downtown core (it is far enough removed from town to be quiet) and roughly the same distance from nearby Playa Cangrejal. Rooms are well-equipped, with 1-3 comfortable beds, televisions, desks, air conditioning, modern bathrooms, and outdoor sitting areas that face the property's small pool.

Hotel Belvedere (100 m north of Road 160, 100 m east of Road 150, tel. 506/2656-0213, www.belvederesamara.net, $85 s/d), at the north end of downtown Sámara, offers 22 affordable rooms equipped with one double and one single bed for 1-3 people. Guest rooms are clean and have lots of shelving, air conditioning, and indoor and outdoor seating areas. The rooms and the friendly staff, well-kept grounds, on-site pool, and above-average complimentary breakfast make the Belvedere one of the area's best-value hotels.

$100-150

Perched on the hill that surrounds Sámara to the northwest, the charming ★ **Lodge Las Ranas** (just north of Road 160, 2 km northwest of Road 150, tel. 506/2656-0609, www. lodgelasranas.com, $110 s/d) feels a lot like a bed-and-breakfast, complete with warm hospitality and superb cleanliness. All 10 rooms are beautifully designed with rustic wood furnishings, tile floors, and canopy beds draped with soft white linens. Each one overlooks the varied landscape (howler monkeys are some of the inhabitants) around the peaceful lodge; you can also see the ocean from a distance. A restaurant, pool, and parking are available on-site.

The small, six-room **Fenix Hotel** (on the beach at Playa Sámara, 1.5 km east of downtown Sámara, tel. 506/2656-0158, www. fenixhotel.com, $120 s/d, cash only) on the eastern outskirts of Sámara wins big with its waterfront location. Set on the sand among a collection of shady palms and lounge chairs, the modest single-building property is popular among families, especially those with young children. All doors open to ocean views, and the water is steps away. Rooms, accommodating 1-4 people, are kept cool by screened windows and fans, not to mention the ocean's breeze.

$150-250

Uber cool describes the six freestanding apartments that form the **Sámara Tree House Inn** (on the beach at Playa Sámara, tel. 506/2656-0733, www.samaratreehouse. com, $160 s/d). The two-tier rustic apartments are unlike anything I've seen in Costa Rica: The enclosed top floor is the living space, and the open-air bottom floor (no more than a few posts that prop up the structure) hides hammocks, a grilling station, and an outdoor dining area. Facilities and amenities differ from one apartment to the next, but most have a queen bed, a living room, a kitchen, and a fan. Some offer air conditioning, and others reward occupants with ocean views.

Information and Services

Nicoya's **Hospital La Anexión** (Road 150, 300 m north of the justice courts, Nicoya, tel. 506/2685-5066, 24 hours daily) serves most of the Nicoya Peninsula. It's a 45-minute drive north of Sámara.

There is a **doctor's office,** signed as **Centro Médico Dr. Freddy Soto** (at the corner of Road 150 and Road 160, tel. 506/2656-0992, 8am-5pm Mon.-Fri., 8am-noon Sat.) in the heart of town. Across the street is a **pharmacy, Farmacia Sámara** (tel. 506/2215-6093, 8am-7pm Mon.-Sat., 8am-4pm Sun.).

A **post office** (tel. 506/2656-0368, 8am-5pm Mon.-Fri.) and **police station** (tel. 506/2656-0436, 24 hours daily) are south of the *fútbol* field at the end of the main road that leads to Playa Sámara (Road 150).

The **Banco de Costa Rica** (north side of the *fútbol* field, tel. 506/2211-1111, 9am-4pm Mon.-Fri.) has an **ATM** (5am-midnight daily). An additional bank and ATM can be found on Road 160.

The biggest supermarket is **Palí** (8am-8pm Mon.-Thurs., 8am-9pm Fri.-Sun.) on Road 160, just west of Road 150. Plenty of others line the road that runs parallel to Playa Sámara.

The closest **gas station** is on Road 150, five kilometers north of Sámara.

Transportation

CAR

Sámara is a 240-kilometer, four-hour drive west from downtown **San José** via Highways 1 and 18 and Road 150. From downtown **Liberia,** it's a 115-kilometer, two-hour drive south on Highway 21 and Road 150. To get to Sámara from **Nosara,** it's a 30-kilometer drive southeast on Road 160, which takes 45 minutes to an hour.

BUS

Public buses travel daily to Sámara from **San José** (noon and 5pm daily, 5 hours, $8) and **Nicoya** (multiple times 5:30am-8pm daily, 1-1.5 hours, $2.50).

To get to Sámara from **Nosara,** take the bus bound for Nicoya (multiple times 5am-3:30pm daily, 2-2.5 hours, $3.50) and get off partway (28 km east of Nosara), across the street from the gas station. When you get on, ask the bus driver, "*¿Por favor, puede parar en la bomba?*" ("Please, can you stop at the gas station?"). You can then catch one of many buses headed to Sámara at the stop in front of the gas station, on the opposite side of the road. To identify a bus bound for Sámara, look for signage in the bus's front window. Some buses pass through Sámara on the way to the village of Estrada. To ensure the bus will stop in Sámara, ask the bus driver, "*¿Por favor, puede parar en Sámara?*" ("Please, can you stop in Sámara?"). The driver will drop you off at the north end of Sámara, on the corner of Road 150 and Road 160.

PRIVATE TRANSFER SERVICE

Sámara Adventure Company (Road 150 just north of Road 160, tel. 506/2656-0920, www.samaraadventurecompany.com, 8am-6pm daily) surpasses their competition with a fleet of reliable vehicles (with free Wi-Fi on board) and a team of professional drivers. Their private transfer services can collect you in most popular tourist destinations around the country and bring you to their beloved hometown. Most vehicles accommodate up to eight people plus luggage. Prices average around $250 from San José, $130 from Liberia, and $70 from Nosara.

SHARED SHUTTLE SERVICE

Sámara Adventure Company (Road 150 just north of Road 160, tel. 506/2656-0920, www.samaraadventurecompany.com, 8am-6pm daily) offers shared shuttle services to Sámara, as does **Interbus** (tel. 506/4100-0888, www.interbusonline.com). Both companies provide service from San José, La Fortuna, and Monteverde. The Sámara Adventure Company covers additional routes from Liberia, Tamarindo, Montezuma, Santa Teresa, and Malpaís. One-way services cost $49-64 per person. Most shuttles fit eight people with luggage and offer drop-offs at Sámara hotels.

ORGANIZED TOUR

A few adventure and nature tours include **post-tour onward transportation** to Sámara. White-water rafting tours and safari float tours can be arranged to include a pickup from your hotel in Liberia, La Fortuna, or Monteverde, then a drop-off at your hotel in Sámara.

GETTING AROUND

Travel is casual in downtown Sámara. Foot traffic is the norm; even those who drive tend to leave their vehicles parked on side roads in favor of walking around town. If you're stationed on the outskirts, you can call **Elio Taxi** (tel. 506/8375-8303) to bring you to the core of the action, or else hire a taxi by the *fútbol* field (just north of Playa Sámara) to take you to wherever you need to go.

CARRILLO AND PUNTA ISLITA

Southeast of Sámara, the tiny hillside village of Carrillo hides one of Costa Rica's most beautiful beaches. Well worth visiting as a day trip from Sámara or Nosara, or perfect on its own if you want a low-key spot just outside of the bustle of a developed beach town, Carrillo and its magnificent half-moon beach should not be missed.

Those looking for an even more remote spot can head farther down the coast to the hamlet of Punta Islita, roughly 14 kilometers southeast of Carrillo. This tiny community, which houses a prominent resort, is spread out across dramatic hills. Largely undeveloped, Punta Islita is strikingly peaceful and a good choice if you want to spend time at a far-flung destination. Its mountainous gravel access road deters most peninsula travelers from visiting.

Immediately east of Carrillo is the Refugio de Vida Silvestre Camaronal, a quiet refuge where sea turtles come to nest and surfers come to ride advanced-level waves. The serpentine Río Ora (Ora River) weaves through the refuge and divides Carrillo from the refuge's main beach, Playa Camaronal. Travel

between the two areas is easy as far as the small, inland village of **Estrada** (4.5 km northeast of Carrillo), where a bridge crosses over the river. East of the bridge, the roads change to gravel and provide a bumpy course to the refuge and beyond.

The end of the northern half of the Nicoya Peninsula is considered to be some 20 kilometers southeast of Punta Islita. The roads along this stretch have earned the reputation for being some of Costa Rica's worst.

Punta Islita Wild Macaw Reserve

The Macaw Recovery Network, which runs the **Punta Islita Wild Macaw Reserve** (1 km north of Playa Islita, tel. 506/8505-3336, http://macawrecoverynetwork.org, 7:30am and 4pm daily by guided tour only, $20 adults, $10 children 4-14, children under 4 free), is actively involved in replenishing the world's population of scarlet macaws. This small but passionate organization, partially run by volunteers, is committed to increasing the birth and survival rates of the tropical bird species in Costa Rica. If you've ever wanted to see the rainbow-colored beauties up close, in groups, and outside the confines of a zoo, here's your chance. One-hour guided tours conducted at the informal breeding center and reintroduction station in Punta Islita begin with a slideshow and a brief talk but quickly shift focus to the birds themselves, as many can be seen flying freely around the center and visiting feeding stations. This is a unique, rewarding experience for anyone with an interest in spotting wildlife and will especially appeal to birders, photographers, and children. Advance reservations are required and can be made through the website.

Beaches

★ PLAYA CARRILLO

A short six-kilometer, 10-minute drive southeast of Sámara is the breathtaking **Playa Carrillo,** a crescent-shaped oasis well worth a visit and difficult to leave. It's a long beach full of soft, light sand glazed with water that's as clear and smooth as glass. Mounds of dry forest back the beach, as does a line of lime-green and yellow palms; hammocks hang from a few. Walk, swim, sunbathe, and don't miss the **sunset**. As the sun goes down over the western headland, the palm trees glow and the beach shines in a coral hue. Light reflects off the contours of clouds and waves, creating a stunning scene. The awe-inspiring setting is one of the reasons the spot is regarded as one of Costa Rica's best beaches.

You won't find restaurants or other facilities at Playa Carrillo, but you may spot the "Super Trailer" owned by **Hotel Leyenda** (Road 160, 2.5 km northeast of Playa Carrillo, tel. 506/2656-0381, www.hotelleyenda.com). The trailer provides a bathroom, a freshwater shower, chairs, and a food delivery service to beachgoers, all for free—but there's a catch. The complimentary services are available to hotel guests only.

Recreation

KAYAKING AND STAND-UP PADDLING

Just east of Carrillo, **Río Ora** runs from the inland part of the Nicoya Peninsula to the **Refugio de Vida Silvestre Camaronal,** where it empties into the Pacific Ocean. The quiet river setting amid mangrove and tropical forest ecosystems is perfect for a peaceful paddle. It is also the Sámara and Carrillo region's best site for bird-watching.

Guided river tours include the **Wildlife and Mangrove Kayak Tour** (3 hours, $49 adults, $39 children 4-12, min. age 4) and the **Stand-Up Paddle Mangrove Tour** (3 hours, $49 adults, $39 children 4-12, min. age 4). Both tours are provided by the **Sámara Adventure Company** (tel. 506/2656-0920, www.samaraadventurecompany.com). Tour times are tide-dependent.

Food and Accommodations

Up the hill from the community of Carrillo is the tiki-style **Hula Jungla** (500 m east of the beach at Playa Carrillo, tel. 506/2656-1118, 11am-10pm daily, $5.50-20.50). This tiny roadside restaurant serves pizzas, pastas, burgers, and plenty of cocktails—the kind of stuff you could probably go for after a lazy day at the beach. The seafood specials depend largely on what local fisherfolk reel in. Could be lobster, could be *pargo rojo* (red snapper). I go for the friendly service.

★ **Hotel Leyenda** (Road 160, 2.5 km northeast of Playa Carrillo, tel. 506/2656-0381, www.hotelleyenda.com, $126 s/d) is my preferred hotel in the Carrillo area for an endless list of reasons. I particularly love the immaculately manicured grounds that emit the subtle fragrance of ylang-ylang flowers; the welcoming staff; and the large, clean, comfortable, and well-furnished rooms (22 in total, equipped with 1 or 2 queen beds). This quiet place also has a restaurant and two pools on-site; discreet security cameras around the grounds maximize guests' safety. Stay here and you'll get access to the hotel's bathroom- and shower-equipped Super Trailer (which also dispenses complimentary beach chairs) on Playa Carrillo.

The 63-room resort complex known as the **Nammbú Beachfront Bungalows** (200 m east of Playa Carrillo, tel. 506/4002-1414, www.nammbu.com, $169 s/d) is Carrillo's most modern accommodation. Despite the resort's name, rooms are not on the beach—you must walk down a small hill to get to the water. Clean and minimalist white rooms with dark-wood floors and tiled bathrooms with glass-wall showers show off the hotel's chic design. The complex's best features include large sliding-glass room doors that open to balconies and terraces with ocean views, a wraparound infinity pool, and a yoga deck.

Journey uphill on the rough road to the Marriott-owned ★ **Hotel Punta Islita** (250 m north of the beach at Playa Islita, tel. 506/2656-3500, www.hotelpuntaislita.com, room $340 s/d, suite $600 s/d), one of the country's most remote resorts, where privacy reigns supreme. Set among rolling hills that tumble toward the ocean are 56 comfortable, well-furnished rooms and suites warmly decorated in Spanish and indigenous styles. Each has a terrace with a hammock, perfect for enjoying the property's unrivaled mountain or ocean views. Sprawling over 300 acres, the hotel has tennis courts, a golf course, a canopy tour, nature trails, two restaurants, a spa, a gym, and a waterfront club on the property's main beach, Playa Islita. Want a splash of Costa Rican culture? Sign up for an authentic activity hosted by the hotel, such as an art class, a cooking class, or a *mejenga* (an informal pickup soccer match).

Information and Services

Tiny Carrillo and Punta Islita offer very few services. There are a handful of **supermarkets** on Road 160 in Carrillo and another in Punta Islita.

The closest **gas station** is on Road 150, five kilometers north of Sámara.

Transportation

Both Carrillo and Punta Islita are best accessed by car. Carrillo is a 245-kilometer, 4.5-hour drive west from downtown **San José** via Highways 1 and 18 and Roads 150 and 160. From downtown **Liberia,** it's a 120-kilometer, two-hour drive south on Highway 21, Road 150, and Road 160. Carrillo is just five kilometers (an approximate 10-minute drive) southeast of **Sámara** on Road 160. Punta Islita is an additional 14 kilometers (an approximate 25-minute drive) southeast of Carrillo on Road 160. To reach Punta Islita, continue through Carrillo and watch for a turn southeast toward the Refugio de Vida Silvestre Camaronal; it will lead you along the coast to the hamlet.

Carrillo and Punta Islita are on the outskirts of Sámara. If you do not intend to drive yourself directly to either destination, your best bet is to obtain separate onward transportation once you've reached Sámara. Most transportation companies that service Sámara offer drop-offs at Carrillo-area and Punta Islita-area accommodations for an extra cost.

Carrillo can also be reached from Sámara by hopping on the **bus** that commutes between Nicoya and Estrada (multiple times 5am-8pm Mon.-Sat., 6am-8pm Sun., $2.50), a small, inland village between Carrillo and Punta Islita. (Buses bound for Carrillo pass through Sámara approximately 45 minutes after departing from Nicoya.) To get to Carrillo, catch the bus at the north end of Sámara, on the corner of Road 150 and Road 160. The ride is about 10 minutes. To identify a bus bound for Carrillo, look for signage in the front window. To ensure the bus stops in Carrillo, ask the bus driver, *"¿Por favor, puede parar en Carrillo?"* ("Please, can you stop in Carrillo?"). The driver will drop you off on Road 160 in the center of town, by the cemetery. To visit the beach, ask, *"¿Por favor, puede parar en Playa Carrillo?"* ("Please, can you stop at Playa Carrillo?").

Aeropuerto Punta Islita (PBP) is a small, privately owned airstrip 4.5 kilometers east of Punta Islita. It accepts chartered domestic flights.

East of Estrada—as far south as the hamlet of Manzanillo, eight kilometers shy of Santa Teresa—the Nicoya Peninsula earns its reputation for having some of the **worst roads** in the country. Paved highways turn to gravel, dirt, and dust roads that climb and drop steeply over headlands and hills. River crossings, sometimes impassable, are common. The majority of travelers avoid this stretch.

REFUGIO DE VIDA SILVESTRE CAMARONAL

It's no secret that massive groups of sea turtles nest on the Nicoya Peninsula within the Refugio Nacional de Vida Silvestre Ostional, but plenty of others climb ashore at beaches farther down the coast, most notably at Playa Camaronal. This shale-colored and driftwood-washed beach in the **Refugio de Vida Silvestre Camaronal** (Camaronal Wildlife Refuge, 100 m north of Playa Camaronal, tel. 506/2659-8190, 8am-4pm daily, beach access 6am-6pm daily, free) is where a variety of sea turtle species, including olive ridleys, leatherbacks, and hawksbills, lay their eggs.

A **ranger station** with a small museum

marks the refuge's entrance. The refuge's staff oversees a few informal hatcheries set up on the beach, which are used to protect incubating eggs from predators and poachers.

Sea Turtle Nesting

Although turtles nest at **Playa Camaronal** year-round, you're most likely to spot them between June and December. You can try your luck during the day by driving to the beach and strolling along the sand, but as with most turtle *arribadas* (arrivals), you're likely to catch more action after dark. The refuge is closed to the public from sunset to sunrise, so you'll need a guide if you wish to go at night.

I recommend the courteous **Sámara Adventure Company** (tel. 506/2656-0920, www.samaraadventurecompany.com). Their **Turtle Nesting Night Tour** (7pm daily, 4 hours, $45 adults, $35 children 4-12) includes round-trip transportation between the refuge and hotels in the Sámara and Carrillo areas, so you needn't worry about driving after dark.

You won't witness hordes of nesting sea turtles at Playa Camaronal like you might see at Playa Ostional farther up the coast, but you will find a less-frequented beach that hosts fewer tour groups. Choose this beach if you wish to avoid crowds and want to try your luck at spotting a variety of sea turtle types, including the hawksbill and the olive ridley. On a tour, your guide will search for turtles in the dark, then lead the group closer once a turtle has been spotted.

Surfing

With barely 500 acres of protected land to its name but an immense 40,000 acres of protected waters, the refuge is largely a marine reserve. It's also home to an advanced-level beach break that will let you ride left or right and at any time of day, regardless of the tide. The exact opposite of the calm waters off Playa Sámara and Playa Carrillo that swimmers love to wade in, **Playa Camaronal** has gnarly waves that expert surfers dream of playing in. Paddle out primed for the strong rip currents and undertow. The hazards are some of the most dangerous in the area. Plan on renting a surfboard in Sámara.

Getting There

The refuge is separated from Sámara and Carrillo to the west by Río Ora. The safest and most reliable way to get there is to take Road 160 from Carrillo to the northeast, then turn onto the road (marked with a sign for the refuge) that turns southeast toward the coast. The route crosses the river by bridge near the town of Estrada and leads to Playa Camaronal. From Carrillo, it's an eight-kilometer, 15-minute drive to the beach.

Nicoya Peninsula Inlands

The steep-rising vegetation that backs most of the region's smooth, outspread beaches hints that mountainous hills fill the Nicoya Peninsula's inlands. But you'd never know from standing at the ocean's edge that nearly the entire peninsula is enveloped in rugged terrain. Untouched forest blankets most of the region's interior, where there's little trace of tourism. Only a few modestly developed rural areas inhabited by farmers hide among the sector's slopes, which are laced with free-flowing rivers and trickling streams.

Few roads connect the peninsula's opposite sides. The area's principal course begins as Highway 21, travels east until Playa Naranjo, and then turns south and becomes an unnamed coastal road. It outlines much of the region's perimeter, providing access to most of the sought-after beach towns. Much of the route is paved, although sections of pressed gravel make for a slightly bumpy and sometimes dusty drive.

NICOYA

The mini metropolis of Nicoya is the commercial center of the inlands. Set in the northern half of the peninsula, the city provides services to much of the region and is a gateway to coastal destinations.

Apart from the small Iglesia San Blas (San Blas Church, corner of Calle 1 and Avenida Justo Flores), with its colonial architecture, Nicoya is void of notable attractions. Fill up on gas, find a bathroom, or grab snacks in town as you make your way to other destinations.

Information and Services

Services in the inland region of the Nicoya Peninsula cluster around Nicoya, including Hospital La Anexión (Road 150, 300 m north of the justice courts, Nicoya, tel. 506/2685-5066, 24 hours daily), the region's hospital.

The city also has a post office (corner of Avenida 2 and Calle Central, tel. 506/2686-6402, 8am-5pm Mon.-Fri., 8am-noon Sat.) and a police station (Road 150, upon entrance into Nicoya from the south, tel. 506/2685-5559, 24 hours daily).

A few pharmacies, most of which are open 8am-6pm daily, and supermarkets line Road 150 in the downtown core. There are several banks and ATMs in town. The easiest to access is the large Banco Nacional (tel. 506/2212-2000, 8:30am-3:30pm Mon.-Fri., ATM 5am-11pm daily) on the corner of Road 150 and Avenida 3.

There's a gas station on Road 150 (at Avenida 9) in downtown Nicoya. There's another station on Highway 21, just north of the exit for Nicoya.

Transportation

Nicoya is a 200-kilometer, 3.5-hour drive west from downtown San José via Highways 1, 18, and 21. From downtown Liberia, it's an 80-kilometer, 1.5-hour drive south on Highway 21.

Road 150, the main drag, makes a beeline through downtown Nicoya and continues south toward the coast, ending at Sámara.

The regional bus station is on the corner of Road 150 and Avenida 4, 250 meters north of the police station. Public buses travel daily to Nicoya from San José (multiple times 5am-5pm daily, 5 hours, $7), Liberia (multiple times 4:30am-8pm daily, 2 hours, $2.50), Sámara (multiple times 5:30am-6:45pm daily, 1-1.5 hours, $2.50), and Nosara (multiple times 5am-3:30pm daily, 2-2.5 hours, $3.50).

PARQUE NACIONAL BARRA HONDA

Southeast of Nicoya, Highway 21 meets Highway 18, which leads the way to the 5,675-acre Parque Nacional Barra Honda (Barra Honda National Park, 9 km northwest of Hwy. 18, 1.5 km north of Hwy. 21, tel. 506/2659-1551, 8am-4pm daily, $12 adults, $5 children 0-12). The national park is a 300-meter-tall elongated mound, mostly covered with forest. The landform has a raised, flat top that resembles a mesa, and steep sides that form an escarpment of exposed rock. The park houses a network of more than 40 underground caverns that drop into the mound like volcano craters. The park's deepest cave, Santa Ana, dives nearly 250 meters underground. Less than half of the attraction's multimillion-year-old caverns have been fully explored. Explorations have turned up carvings, artifacts, skeletal remains, and countless unanswered questions.

On the west side of the park at the base of the mound, a ranger station marks the official entrance. A few hiking trails explore the landform's top, where you can tour the caves with a guide. Due to the instability of most of the caves, only two, La Cuevita and Terciopelo, are accessible to the public.

Birds, deer, monkeys, coatimundis, agoutis, and anteaters inhabit the park, but it's not the varied wildlife that draws people here—it's the caverns.

Hiking

The park's public hiking trails begin at the top of the mound, just beyond a small forest clearing used as a parking lot. A rough, uphill road known as **Sendero Matapalo** (Matapalo Trail) connects the ranger station to the clearing. You must have a 4x4 vehicle to attempt the trip—the two-kilometer road follows a rugged, steep, narrow path through the forest. In-shape hikers can complete the journey without a car, but it's no easy task.

From the forest clearing, **Sendero Los Laureles** (Los Laureles Trail, 1.5 km one-way, 30 minutes, easy-moderate) departs to the right. **Sendero La Ceiba** (La Ceiba Trail, 1.5 km one-way, 30 minutes, easy-moderate) departs to the left. Each of these trails forms one half of the circular **Sendero Las Cavernas** (Las Cavernas Trail), which loops around the park through rare tropical dry forest. A tour guide is neither required nor needed to hike either trail. You'll pass turnoffs to La Cuevita and Terciopelo, the park's two publicly accessible caves, as you loop around the trail.

On the east side of the park, where Sendero Los Laureles connects with Sendero La Ceiba, an **unnamed trail** (250 m one-way, 10 minutes, moderate) climbs uphill to a *mirador* at the edge of an escarpment. Here, at the park's highest public access point, you have a jaw-dropping view of the Nicoya Peninsula's interior, including a valley filled with farms, pastures, and treetops; rows of mountains fading into the distance; and a vivid display of greens and blues. The sight is the most breathtaking and far-reaching panorama I've come across in the region.

★ Spelunking the Terciopelo Cave

One of the most unique journeys you can make in Costa Rica is the 63-meter descent into the park's **Terciopelo cave.** Not for the faint of heart or anyone who suffers from

claustrophobia, the heart-pounding journey requires you to join a guided tour, strap on a helmet and a harness, and climb down a metal ladder into a pit of darkness—or so the cave appears from its craggy entrance. During the tour, you'll walk around the cave's interior, visiting its various rooms before returning to the ladder and exiting the way you came. Only from the inside can you fully appreciate the limestone beauty of the cave, full of stalactites and stalagmites. Some formations are sharp as a tack. Others are curved, smooth, and look like hardened billows of smoke.

Cave tours (8am-1pm daily, 2 hours, $19 pp, min. age 12) include a descent into Terciopelo and exploration of its interior. Tour guides trained in cave exploration are provided when you sign up for the experience at the park's ranger station.

You can also join a Terciopelo tour through nearby operators and agencies, like **Eco Aventura Sámara** (tel. 506/2656-0606, www.ecoaventurasamara.com, $110 pp), which also goes by the name **Carrillo Adventures.** Transportation to and from the park is included in most rates. Expect your guide to accompany you around the hiking trails; a park guide will lead the cave descent portion of the tour.

Children must be at least 12 to enter Terciopelo. For younger children, there are guided cave tours that explore the less challenging La Cuevita (8am-1pm daily, 1.5 hours, $19 adults, $8 children, min. age 4). La Cuevita mirrors Terciopelo in its look and feel, but as a smaller cave, it takes a shorter time to explore, and it doesn't require as deep a descent. The narrow opening to this cave prevents entry by many adults. (Note that children are accompanied by a guide on this tour, not their parents—but parents can stick close by, at the opening to the cave.)

Getting There

The park is best accessed by car. If you plan to drive yourself to the park, coordinate your visit with a stop on the Nicoya Peninsula. Lodging options in the area are slim, so it's

1: Iglesia San Blas in Nicoya 2: Terciopelo Cave in Parque Nacional Barra Honda 3: view of the inland area of the Nicoya Peninsula

best to avoid staying overnight near the park. Visit early enough in the day to have time to tour the park and arrive at your next destination before sundown.

From Nicoya, it's a 15-kilometer, 15-minute drive east on Highway 21 and north on Highway 18 to reach the marked turnoff west to the park. From the turnoff, it's a nine-kilometer (15-minute) drive on flat, unnamed, country roads to the ranger station. The route zigzags through plains, passes the tiny communities of Barra Honda and Santa Ana, and requires a few turns (each is well-marked for the park).

Montezuma and Vicinity

The southern half of the Nicoya Peninsula has beach towns galore, many of them favored for their soft sand and swimmable, bright-blue waters. Throughout the area, you'll find yogis, surfers, and beachgoers who think of this distant area of Costa Rica as their happy place.

The southeast side of the peninsula curves around the Golfo de Nicoya in the north and juts into the Pacific Ocean to the south. The most frequented destination in the vicinity is Montezuma, a coastal village heavy in hippiedom that sits roughly 13 kilometers northeast of the peninsula's southernmost tip. You'll find a handful of hotels north of Montezuma in the community of Tambor; also nearby is the uninhabited, paradisiacal Isla Tortuga, a few kilometers offshore.

Nature trails cut through the Refugio Nacional de Vida Silvestre Curú and the Reserva Natural Absoluta Cabo Blanco, satisfying active visitors who seek nature exploration to supplement their beach time.

MONTEZUMA

The small coastal village of Montezuma is the destination of choice for the unconventional traveler. It's where bohemian locals, expats, and visitors converge to form a carefree community rich in the arts. On a visit here, you'll likely come across fire dancers, jugglers, aerial silk and trapeze artists, musicians, kirtan (a type of religious performance art) performers, and other surprising talents. Also here are equally free-spirited business owners, not all of whom care for tourism—or tourists.

Economy lodging and informal dining options are the standard, especially in the heart of Montezuma. They're also why Montezuma ranks highly among cash-strapped backpackers. Tucked away in the hills on the outskirts of the village are newer options that are changing the norm. To the delight of many, Montezuma is modernizing slowly but steadily to best compete with burgeoning beach towns elsewhere in the country. To the dismay of others, it's losing its allure as an unfiltered hippie hot spot.

Montezuma's tiny core comprises two unnamed roads. One runs parallel to Playa Montezuma, and the other runs perpendicular to the beach for no more than 100 meters until it connects with Road 624, the village's principal access road.

Sights

TOP EXPERIENCE

★ CATARATAS MONTEZUMA

The triad of cascades that form the **Cataratas Montezuma** (Montezuma Waterfalls, lower waterfall entrance: Road 624, 50 m north of the road to Delicias, 24 hours daily, free; upper waterfall entrance: at Suntrails, on the road to Delicias, 1.5 km northwest of Road 624, 8:30am-4pm daily, $4 pp) is not only a fine display of Mother Nature's remarkable craftsmanship but also home to Montezuma's most beloved swimming holes. Each waterfall has its own freshwater pool set among natural landscape with nothing made by humans in sight.

There's truly nowhere else you need to be in Montezuma than in one of the pools, soaking up your surroundings and patting yourself on the back for selecting Costa Rica as your travel destination. Technically, the three waterfalls are one giant cascade. Each is part of the Río Montezuma, which tumbles over three rockfaces one after the other. The top two waterfalls are known as the upper falls. Slightly downriver and closest to the village of Montezuma is the lower fall.

There are a few ways to access the Cataratas Montezuma and their respective swimming holes. The cheapest way is to follow the free entrance trail (1 km one-way, 20 minutes, moderate). It begins just beyond the bridge at the south end of town, roughly a 15-minute walk from Montezuma center. There's a parking lot at the trailhead. The trail leads to the lower waterfall, the most visited of the bunch. It has the largest swimming hole and is the tallest—some people say 24 meters, others say 30 meters. If you're on a budget or you're only interested in seeing the most impressive cascade, stop here, swim if you wish, then head back the way you came.

If you want to swing or jump into pools, or swim where fewer people are, opt to visit the upper falls. (If you're itching for adrenaline, you can give the rope swing at the uppermost fall a go.) One way to reach these two cascades is to take the unnamed trail (1 km one-way, 45 minutes, difficult) on the north side of the lower waterfall. This trail is free to access. The rough route will take you on a steep uphill trek through the forest and alongside rocks; ropes are provided to aid in the journey. Don't attempt to tackle this challenging terrain in flip-flops. To exit from the upper falls, carefully retrace your steps to the lower waterfall and return to Montezuma.

A third and much easier way to access Cataratas Montezuma is through the property of Suntrails Lodge (on the road to Delicias, 1.5 km northwest of Road 624, 8:30am-4pm daily, $4 pp), the providers of Montezuma's zip-line canopy tour. To enter, you need to pay a fee. Suntrails provides an unnamed trail that trades uphill hikes for hanging bridge crossings and descents to the waterfalls, saving more challenging ascents for your exit. The first section (1.5 km one-way, 20 minutes, easy-moderate) begins just beyond the Suntrails office and leads to the upper falls. The second section (500 m one-way, 10 minutes, easy-moderate) travels onward to the lower waterfall. The well-maintained Suntrails paths are the safest to trek and the better choice if you're traveling with children. The Suntrails office, which has a parking lot, is an approximate five-minute drive up the hill from downtown Montezuma.

If you're an American football fan, you may recognize the upper falls as the site of NFL quarterback Tom Brady's daring 12-meter cliff jump. Captured on video, it received millions of views on YouTube. The site is also where several less fortunate daredevils have lost their lives. If you plan to visit the area, please be cautious. Rocks can be slippery, flash floods are a possibility, and cliff jumps can be deadly.

Beaches
PLAYA MONTEZUMA

The light-sand Playa Montezuma is Montezuma's main beach. It's often awash with free-spirited beachgoers who gather at the spot to practice their arts, relax, drink a few brews, or have a bonfire. Socialize on the beach if you wish, but sunbathe and swim elsewhere. There's a lineup of better beaches both north and south of town.

PLAYA COLORADA, PLAYA GRANDE, AND PLAYA COCALITO

Northeast of Montezuma is a string of bare beaches that invite you to walk for miles. A quick, 200-meter coastal trail that begins at the Ylang Ylang Beach Resort at Playa Montezuma, a 15-minute walk from the center of town, leads to the pretty cove known as Playa Colorada. Here, you can spot rocks in coral, turquoise, amber, and purple hues.

Also accessible to the public beyond the Ylang Ylang resort, a moderate, one-kilometer, 20-minute forest trail cuts inland

around Playa Colorada and leads to the long **Playa Grande,** a decent place for swimming.

One kilometer up the coast from the northeast end of Playa Grande is the deserted **Playa Cocalito,** immediately south of Tambor. At the east end of this beach, you can watch the small Catarata El Chorro (El Chorro Waterfall), also known as Cocalito Falls, pour off a rockface into the ocean. It's a seven-kilometer, two-hour walk from the center of Montezuma to the waterfall at Playa Cocalito. Most sections of the walk offer no shade, so don't go without a hat, sunscreen, and water. Any of these three remote beaches, which are not accessible by car, is a good alternative to Playa Montezuma.

PLAYA LAS MANCHAS

My vote for the best beach in the area goes to **Playa Las Manchas,** 1.5 kilometers south of downtown Montezuma on Road 624. Many expats in the area also favor it, so you may not get the beach all to yourself although it remains off the tourist radar. This local hangout spot, less than a half-hour walk south of Montezuma, has white sand, turquoise water, and enough fish to warrant breaking out your snorkel gear. It also has a strong rip current at times, so remain mindful when you swim.

Recreation

LOCAL GUIDES AND TOURS

If you're in the market for tours around Montezuma or you need transportation to or from town, turn to longtime local outfitter **Zuma Tours** (50 m southeast of Road 624 on the main road in Montezuma, tel. 506/2642-0024, www.zumatours.net, 7am-9pm daily). This company has it all—a large staff of competent and professional individuals, reliable vehicles, fair prices, firsthand knowledge of the area, and a positive reputation that speaks for itself. They also provide nearly every service imaginable, from day trips to nearby

Isla Tortuga (from $65) to water taxi services (from $45) between the Nicoya Peninsula and the central Pacific coast to local ATV rentals (from $150 for 2 days). They rarely disappoint.

YOGA

A great way to take in Montezuma's laid-back vibe is to join one of the many **yoga classes** (8:30am and 6pm daily, 90 minutes, $14 pp) operated by **Montezuma Yoga** (Road 624, 250 m north of the road to Delicias, tel. 506/8704-1632, http://montezumayoga. com, 8:30am-7:30pm daily). Drop-ins are permitted.

Montezuma's best yoga resort, and arguably one of Costa Rica's top yoga resorts, is the **Anamaya Body, Mind, and Spirit Resort** (on the road to Delicias, 900 m west of Road 624, tel. 506/2642-1289, www.anamayaresort. com). The resort is known for their one-week **yoga retreats** ($795-1,995 pp) and 200-hour **yoga teacher training programs** ($3,438-5,155 pp), both of which include accommodations and all meals. Sway in a hammock, swim in a tranquil infinity pool, reward yourself with spa services, dine on gourmet organic cuisine, and surround yourself with nature; then breathe in fresh air and exhale any remaining stress. The resort encourages you to do it all and more, including practicing yoga in an open-air shala with a panoramic view of the Pacific Ocean. Retreats run back-to-back throughout the year. There is typically one teacher training program starting each month.

ZIP-LINING

The nine-cable **Canopy Tour** (9am, 1pm, and 3pm daily, 2.5 hours, $45 adults, $40 children 5-12, min. age 5) created by **Suntrails** (on the road to Delicias, 1.5 km northwest of Road 624, tel. 506/2642-0808, www.suntrails. com, 8:30am-5:30pm daily) is a basic zip-line tour with a twist: It includes a visit to the Cataratas Montezuma. During the fittingly nicknamed Montezuma Waterfall Canopy Tour, you'll have an opportunity to admire the two upper waterfalls between the sixth

1: a catamaran preparing for departure to Isla Tortuga **2:** lower fall of the Cataratas Montezuma **3:** view of the Nicoya Peninsula **4:** hanging bridge leading to Suntrails Lodge

and seventh zip-line cables. Wear your bathing suit under your clothes if you wish to plunge into the swimming hole at the bottom of either cascade. If you're coming from Santa Teresa, Carmen, or Malpaís, Zuma Tours (tel. 506/2642-0024, www.zumatours.net) can provide round-trip transportation ($20 pp) between the canopy tour site and Santa Teresa, Carmen, or Malpaís hotels.

Entertainment and Events

NIGHTLIFE

Chico's Bar (on the main road that runs parallel to Playa Montezuma, tel. 506/2642-0578, 11am-2am daily) is the main gathering place in town, but for no good reason other than there are few other places to go. During the day, the beachfront bar is a decent place to grab a drink. After dark, it is loud, attracts a mixed crowd, and has DJs and dancing.

The small but trendy Café Orgánico (on the main road that runs parallel to Playa Montezuma, tel. 506/2642-1322, 8:30am-9:30pm Wed.-Mon.) has live music and open mic nights.

Food and Accommodations

For high-quality food, Montezuma's standout restaurant is the beachfront ★ Playa de los Artistas (Road 624, 250 m north of the road to Delicias, tel. 506/2642-0920, 4:30pm-9:30pm Mon.-Fri., noon-9:30pm Sat., $7.50-19, cash only). The chef creates a new, handwritten short menu daily, so part of the fun of dining here is the element of surprise. Regardless of what is served (usually fish dishes), meals regularly receive rave reviews for their exquisite preparation, presentation, and taste. Grab a table on the beach before dark so you can fully appreciate the ocean view.

You cannot beat the atmosphere of the Clandestina Restaurant (on the road to Delicias, 700 m west of Road 624, tel. 506/8315-8003, noon-9pm Tues.-Sat., $8-11), which is warm, artistic, and even slightly sophisticated—although you're welcome to visit in your beach clothes. The small eatery has tacos, empanadas, sandwiches, and

more, plus an ever-changing specials board. Artisan beer and craft sodas are created by the on-site Butterfly Brewing Company (tel. 506/2642-1317). Try the Earthquake IPA and ask to hear the backstory of how the microbrewery was born.

The ★ Suntrails Lodge (on the road to Delicias, 750 m west of Road 624, tel. 506/2642-0808, www.suntrailslodge.com, $135 s/d, built in 2017, is my favorite Montezuma hotel. Perched atop the hill that descends into town, the property offers astounding ocean and forest views. Rooms have comfortable king or queen beds, shiny tile floors, air conditioning, flat-screen televisions, and a wall of glass with sliding doors. I've seen aracaris in the trees, heard monkeys howl, and even spotted a whale breaching offshore from the room's private balcony. As a guest, you'll have free access to the hotel's hanging bridge and a private trail that connects to the Cataratas Montezuma.

On the beach is the prestigious Ylang Ylang Beach Resort (Playa Montezuma, 1 km northeast of downtown Montezuma, tel. 506/2642-0636, www.ylangylangbeachresort.com, tent cabin $180 s/d, room $220 s/d, bungalow $295), an approximate 15-minute-walk up the coast from downtown Montezuma. This honeymooner hideout, which also hosts wedding ceremonies, has a spa, a pool, a yoga deck, and a restaurant serving organic gourmet cuisine; breakfast and dinner are included in the resort's nightly rates. Room choices (some sleep 1-2 people; others can accommodate up to 4) are screened tent cabins tucked away in the forest, standard rooms by the beach, and individual bungalows with floor-to-ceiling glass doors and private terraces.

One of the least expensive accommodations in town is Sano Banano (35 m southeast of Road 624 on the main road in Montezuma, tel. 506/2642-0638, www.elsanobanano.com, $70 s/d), although some say it's overpriced. The economy hotel has 12 simple rooms with 1-4 beds for 1-5 people, colorful tapestries, hand-painted walls, and air conditioning, but its greatest asset is its location. In Montezuma center, the hotel is steps away from restaurants, the beach, and the water taxi port. Guests are permitted to use the pool and hammocks at the Ylang Ylang Beach Resort, a sister hotel to Sano Banano.

Information and Services

There are few services in Montezuma proper. You'll need to go to nearby **Cóbano,** five kilometers northwest on Road 624, for most services.

Nicoya's **Hospital La Anexión** (Road 150, 300 m north of the justice courts, Nicoya, tel. 506/2685-5066, 24 hours daily) serves most of the Nicoya Peninsula. It's a 2.5- to 3-hour drive northwest of Montezuma.

In Cóbano, you'll find the **clinic Ebais Cóbano** (Road 624, 250 m west of the coastal road, Cóbano, tel. 506/2642-0208, 24 hours daily) and **Farmacia Montecristo** (Road 624, 75 m west of the coastal road, Cóbano, tel. 506/2642-1119, 7am-7pm Mon.-Fri., 7am-6pm Sat.).

There's an **ATM** (5am-midnight daily) in the heart of Montezuma, but it's rather unreliable. The closest **bank** is the **Banco Nacional** (corner of the coastal road and Road 624, Cóbano, tel. 506/2212-2000, 7:30am-2pm Mon.-Fri.) in Cóbano. Most businesses, with the exception of some small shops, accept credit cards.

Cóbano also has a **post office** (Road 624, 50 m east of the coastal road, Cóbano, tel. 506/2783-3500, 8am-5pm Mon.-Fri.) and a **police station** (on the coastal road, 350 m north of Road 624, Cóbano, tel. 506/2642-0770, 24 hours daily).

Fuel up at Cóbano's **gas station** (on the coastal road, 1 km northeast of Road 624); Montezuma doesn't have a *bomba* (gas station) of its own.

Transportation

Most routes at the southern end of the Nicoya Peninsula lead to Cóbano. From there, a quick five-kilometer (approximate 10-minute) journey down the hillside on **Road 624** ends in Montezuma.

CAR

Montezuma is a 140-kilometer, four-hour journey west from downtown **San José** that consists of a 100-kilometer, two-hour drive to Puntarenas, a one-hour ferry crossing to Paquera, and a 40-kilometer, one-hour drive to Montezuma. This combination of ground and water transportation is a prime opportunity to take in the views of the gulf. Montezuma can also be reached from downtown San José via a tiring 310-kilometer, 5.5-hour drive around the gulf via Highways 1, 18, 21, and the unnamed coastal road.

From downtown **Liberia,** it's a 210-kilometer, four-hour drive southeast on Highway 21 and the unnamed coastal road to Montezuma.

From **Santa Teresa** and **Malpaís,** a pressed-gravel road known locally as "the road to Delicias" cuts east-west across the peninsula and connects with Montezuma, passing the farming community of Delicias along the way. This 15-kilometer drive takes 40 minutes.

BUS

Public **buses** travel daily to Montezuma from **San José** (6am and 2pm daily, 5.5 hours, $13 includes ferry ticket). This route includes a timed transfer in Cóbano, where you'll get off the bus you boarded in San José and immediately board a bus bound for Montezuma.

To get to Montezuma from **Santa Teresa** and **Malpaís,** take the bus from Carmen (between Santa Teresa and Malpaís) to Cóbano (multiple times 3am-8pm daily, 45 minutes, $1.50-2) and catch one of many buses from there to Montezuma (multiple times 5:30am-7:30pm daily, 30 minutes, $1). When you board in Carmen, ask the bus driver, *"¿Por favor, puede parar en Cóbano?"* ("Please, can you stop in Cóbano?"). Buses stop in front of Banco Nacional, on the corner of Road 624 and the unnamed coastal road that runs through Cóbano. To identify a bus bound for Montezuma, look for signage in the front window. In Montezuma, buses end their run on

Road 624 by the waterfront, one block south of the village center.

PRIVATE TRANSFER SERVICE

Private transfer services can be hired through **Montezuma Expeditions** (10 m southeast of Road 624 on the main road in Montezuma, tel. 506/2441-3394, www. montezumaexpeditions.com, 8am-8pm daily). Prices average $275 from San José and $315 from Liberia. Vehicles vary in size; most accommodate up to eight people plus luggage.

SHARED SHUTTLE SERVICE

Operating shared shuttle services to Montezuma is local favorite **Zuma Tours** (50 m southeast of Road 624 on the main road in Montezuma, tel. 506/2642-0024, www. zumatours.net, 7am-9pm daily). Services departing from San José, Jacó, Manuel Antonio, Dominical, Uvita, and Sierpe consist of ground transportation and either a ferry or water taxi ride. Services departing from Liberia, La Fortuna, Monteverde, Tamarindo, Tambor, and Sámara are ground transfer services only. One-way services cost $40-140 per person. Most shuttles fit eight people with luggage and offer drop-offs at Montezuma hotels.

WATER TAXI

To get to Montezuma from the central Pacific coast, take one of the water taxis that commute daily between Playa Herradura and Montezuma. **Zuma Tours** (tel. 506/2642-0024, www.zumatours.net) operates a **taxi boat service** ($40 pp) that takes approximately 75-90 minutes.

GETTING AROUND

Walking around town is easy and only takes a few minutes. The **Ylang Ylang Beach Resort** (Playa Montezuma, 1 km northeast of downtown Montezuma, tel. 506/2642-0636, www.ylangylangbeachresort.com) has **bikes for rent** ($18 for 1 day) if you wish to speed up the process.

Accommodations and other businesses dot the hills that surround the village; several are on roads with a steep incline or decline. If you are driving, a 4x4 vehicle is not required but is recommended. Taxis, although scarce in Montezuma, can help you get up or down the area's hills if you prefer not to hike. Cóbano-based **taxi driver Gilberto Rodríguez** (tel. 506/8826-9055), who services the Montezuma area, is well-known and provides reliable service.

RESERVA NATURAL ABSOLUTA CABO BLANCO

Declared the country's first protected land area in 1963, the **Reserva Natural Absoluta Cabo Blanco** (Cabo Blanco Absolute Nature Reserve, Road 624, 9 km south of Montezuma, tel. 506/2642-0093, 8am-4pm Wed.-Sun., $12 adults, $5 children 2-12) has led the way for nature conservation in Costa Rica. Comprising roughly 3,400 acres of land and 4,200 acres of water, the reserve encompasses the entire southern tip of the Nicoya Peninsula and a wide perimeter of ocean.

Come to the reserve to walk its forested trails. After you've hiked up a sweat, spend some time relaxing on the beach near Cabo Blanco, the cape for which the reserve is named; this is the southernmost part of the peninsula. Two kilometers due south of the cape and visible from the beach is the rocky Isla Capitán (Capitán Island), sometimes called Isla Cabo Blanco (Cabo Blanco Island). Anteaters, armadillos, deer, monkeys, pacas, and the odd jungle cat inhabit the forest. Frigatebirds, brown boobies, pelicans, and other seabirds congregate at the cape, making it the region's best bird-watching locale. A seemingly endless list of marine life fills the reserve's protected waters and the expansive ocean beyond.

The reserve has two official entrances, but only the easternmost entrance, closest to Montezuma, is open to the public. A **biological station** equipped with bathrooms marks the public entrance.

Hiking

You can explore the reserve's three trails on your own, but tour operators around the peninsula will gladly sell you the services of a guide. Based in Santa Teresa, **Tropical Tours Shuttles** (on the main road parallel to Playa Santa Teresa, 50 m northwest of the intersection at Carmen, Santa Teresa, tel. 506/2640-1900, www.tropicaltourshuttles.com) runs a popular **Cabo Blanco Absolute Nature Reserve Tour** (7am daily, 5 hours, $75 pp) that includes round-trip transportation from Montezuma, Santa Teresa, Carmen, or Malpaís, a naturalist tour guide, snacks, and the reserve's entrance fee.

The **Sendero Arboretum** (Arboretum Trail, 1-km loop, 20-30 minutes, easy) is a quick loop that offers a peek at the reserve's rare tree collection, which flourishes within a contradictory mix of tropical dry forest and moist forest ecosystems.

The **Sendero Danés** (Danés Trail, 2-km loop, 45 minutes, moderate) and the challenging **Sendero Sueco** (Sueco Trail, 4 km one-way, 2 hours, difficult) are the park's most trekked trails. The Sendero Danés will lead you through secondary forest. The Sendero Sueco, an offshoot of the Sendero Danés, will have you trudging uphill and downhill through thick brush and humid air, and possibly muddy patches too, with the goal of reaching **Playa Cabo Blanco,** the reserve's principal beach. Although stones largely cover the light-sand coastline, visits to the spot are hardly disappointing. Simply being at this remote beach surrounded by dramatic hills, and viewing a limitless and thought-provoking sky and ocean, is rewarding enough.

Getting There

The reserve, in the southernmost corner of the Nicoya Peninsula, is best accessed by car from Montezuma. Follow Road 624 south out of Montezuma for 8.5 kilometers until it ends at the reserve's entrance. You'll pass through the hamlet of Cabuya along the way.

TAMBOR

About 20 kilometers north of Montezuma, an assortment of midrange and high-end hotels and homes arc around Bahía Ballena (Ballena Bay) and form the small community of Tambor. The town is spread out across flat, easy-to-navigate land on both sides of the Río Panica (Panica River), which drains into the bay. Largely geared toward international retirees (who both live and vacation here), Tambor is often overlooked. Here you'll find a quiet place with a noticeably mature vibe.

The largely undeveloped area has few services, making it feel remote despite the fact that the region's main thoroughfare, the unnamed coastal road, runs right through it.

Beaches

The compacted gray sand that fills **Playa Tambor** is rather drab, but the tall hills that back Bahía Ballena help beautify the scene. This beach is void of crowds and is almost always quiet. Swimming is pleasant in the ocean's calm waters, where local fisherfolk reel in and toss catches ashore at the south end of the beach.

Recreation

GOLF

Greens fees for the nine-hole **Los Delfines Golf Course** (7am-1pm daily, pro shop 7am-4pm daily, greens fees $100 pp 12 years and older), at the **Los Delfines Golf & Country Club** (on the coastal road, 1 km north of Aeropuerto Tambor, tel. 506/2683-0294, www.specialgolfdelfines.com), include two rounds of play to create an 18-hole, par-72 course. Guests of the nearby **Barceló Tambor** (on the coastal road, 650 m south of Aeropuerto Tambor, tel. 506/2683-0303, www.barcelo.com) receive a complimentary round of golf with each overnight stay at the resort.

Want to brush up on your swing? The resort **Tango Mar** (1.5 km south of the coastal road, 7 km south of Aeropuerto Tambor, tel. 506/2683-0001, www.tangomar.com) has an inexpensive, small, nine-hole, par-32 **golf** course (7am-4pm daily, $20 pp) that you're welcome to play on.

Food and Accommodations

Dining options in the Tambor area are limited, so plan to eat at your hotel's on-site restaurant. The hotels listed in this section each provide at least one restaurant that is open to the public.

The collection of 12 individual two-story suites that form the **Tambor Tropical Beach Resort** (on the beach at Playa Tambor, tel. 506/2683-0011, www.tambortropical.com, $215 s/d) is visually impressive. Built from a variety of Costa Rican woods, each open-concept, 93-square-meter, two-person suite feels like a rustic cabin and shines in multi-colored hardwoods. Upper floors have balconies that face the property's pool or the beach. Lower floors have wraparound patios adorned with privacy hedges, ornamental plants, and tropical palms. Each structure is conveniently close to the waterfront.

The 45 fresh, clean, and classy rooms at **Tango Mar** (1.5 km south of the coastal road, 7 km south of Aeropuerto Tambor, tel. 506/2683-0001, www.tangomar.com, $240 s/d) pop with beachy coral, aquamarine, and seafoam-green colors. One or two king or queen beds, wood furniture, and a television are inside each one. The resort has a romantic but casual restaurant, a beachside grill, a poolside wet bar, and a spa. The public, unnamed, brown-sand beach that fronts the property is the most attractive section of sand in the area.

The **Barceló Tambor** (on the coastal road, 650 m south of Aeropuerto Tambor, tel. 506/2683-0303, www.barcelo.com, $458 s/d, all-inclusive) was one of Costa Rica's first all-inclusive resorts. The whopping 402-room complex is a popular choice among Ticos who enjoy the beachfront property's three restaurants, three bars, tennis court, and pools. Rooms for 1-4 people have rainbow-colored textiles, stone floors, and king- or single-size beds. Expect much of the on-site entertainment to be provided in Spanish. Compared to

other all-inclusive accommodations elsewhere in Costa Rica, the Barceló is overpriced.

Information and Services

Tambor doesn't provide many services. Nicoya's **Hospital La Anexión** (Road 150, 300 m north of the justice courts, Nicoya, tel. 506/2685-5066, 24 hours daily) serves most of the Nicoya Peninsula. It's a 2- to 2.5-hour drive northwest of Tambor.

In the nearby town of Cóbano (a 15-minute drive south of Tambor), there's a **clinic, Ebais Cóbano** (Road 624, 250 m west of the coastal road, Cóbano, tel. 506/2642-0208, 24 hours daily), and a **pharmacy, Farmacia Montecristo** (Road 624, 75 m west of the coastal road, Cóbano, tel. 506/2642-1119, 7am-7pm Mon.-Fri., 7am-6pm Sat.).

Cóbano also has a **Banco Nacional** (corner of the coastal road and Road 624, Cóbano, tel. 506/2212-2000, 7:30am-2pm Mon.-Fri.), a **post office** (Road 624, 50 m east of the coastal road, Cóbano, tel. 506/2783-3500, 8am-5pm Mon.-Fri.), and a **police station** (on the coastal road, 350 m north of Road 624, Cóbano, tel. 506/2642-0770, 24 hours daily).

There's a **gas station** in Paquera (on Road 621), north of Tambor, and another in Cóbano (on the coastal road, 1 km northeast of Road 624).

Transportation

Tambor is a 120-kilometer, 3.5-hour journey west from downtown **San José** that consists of a 100-kilometer, two-hour drive to Puntarenas, a one-hour ferry crossing to Paquera, and a 20-kilometer, 30-minute drive to Tambor. This trip offers a chance to take in views of the gulf. Tambor can also be reached from downtown San José via a tiring 290-kilometer, five-hour drive around the gulf via Highways 1, 18, 21, and the unnamed coastal road.

From downtown **Liberia,** it's a 190-kilometer, 3.5-hour drive southeast to Tambor via Highway 21 and an unnamed coastal road.

The local domestic airport, **Aeropuerto Tambor** (TMU), is four kilometers north of Tambor. **SANSA Airlines** (tel. 506/2290-4100, www.flysansa.com) flies to Tambor daily from San José and Liberia.

To reach Tambor by **bus** from **Paquera**, where the ferry from Puntarenas docks, hop on a bus bound for Cóbano (multiple times 6:15am-6:15pm daily, 1.5 hours, $3.50). To get to Tambor from **San José**, take a bus bound for Cóbano (6am and 2pm daily, 5 hours, $13 includes ferry ticket), which can stop in Tambor on the way. To identify a bus bound for Tambor, look for signage in the front window. Ask the bus driver, "*¿Por favor, puede parar en Tambor?*" ("Please, can you stop in Tambor?"). Buses stop at the entrance to the Barceló Tambor resort.

REFUGIO NACIONAL DE VIDA SILVESTRE CURÚ

Off-the-beaten-path travelers, rejoice! Less touristy than most of the country's nature reserves is the small **Refugio Nacional de Vida Silvestre Curú** (Curú National Wildlife Refuge, on the coastal road, 15 km north of Tambor, tel. 506/2641-0100, www.curuwildliferefuge.com, 7am-4pm daily, $12). At this 200-acre reserve, you can wander along nature trails without a guide, observe various ecosystems, and relax on a beach with few other people in sight. Reminiscent of an earlier, undeveloped Costa Rica, Curú has forest and wildlife, not bells and whistles. It's not the cleanest attraction to tour, nor are trails and bridges in the ramshackle refuge in perfect condition, but its rustic feel is part of the draw. A small booth marks the entrance off the highway. Shack-like structures inside the refuge house a **visitors center.**

Turismo Curú (on the beach at Playa Curú, tel. 506/2641-0014, www.turismocuru.com, 7am-9pm daily) is the refuge's only tour operator. In addition to providing hiking guides, the small outfitter also rents kayaks and runs guided kayak, horseback riding, sportfishing, and scuba diving tours.

Beaches

PLAYA CÚRU

You can drive directly to **Playa Cúru,** the main beach in the refuge, from the entrance; the beach is 2.5 kilometers east of the entrance. The tour outfitter Turismo Curú operates from this beach, where a line of boats rests on the sand, ready to transport travelers to Isla Tortuga. You may find some hikers swimming at this gray-sand beach, but few other people. This stretch of the coast is only accessible to those who pay the refuge entrance fee.

The view from this beach is particularly pretty. Protected land backs the beach, and hilly headlands curve around the beach to the north and south; an island sits two kilometers offshore. The scenery makes this place feel private.

PLAYA QUESERA

The refuge's most beautiful beach, **Playa Quesera** has nearly white sand, a row of palm trees, and few visitors. You can swim in the calm, blue-green water. To reach Playa Quesera, take the challenging Sendero Quesera north from Playa Cúru and follow the trail until it ends at the beach.

Hiking

A network of over a dozen trails ranging from easy to challenging threads the refuge. Seven trails are open to the public. You can spot monkeys, coatimundis, raccoons, deer, peccaries, kinkajous, snakes, iguanas, and crocodiles throughout the refuge, but especially along the **Sendero Ceiba** (Ceiba Trail, 2 km one-way, 45 minutes, easy-moderate) and the **Sendero Finca de los Monos** (Finca de los Monos Trail, 2.5 km one-way, 1 hour, easy-moderate), both of which closely parallel and cross over Río Curú.

The **Sendero Quesera** (Quesera Trail, 5 km one-way, 2-2.5 hours, difficult) is the refuge's most challenging trail. It requires you to climb up and over the dense, forest-filled headland at the north end of the refuge, but your reward is a visit to beautiful Playa Quesera.

If you want a hiking guide, you can hire the services of one through **Turismo Curú** (on the beach at Playa Curú, tel. 506/2641-0014, www.turismocuru.com, 7am-9pm daily) for $15 per person.

Getting There

The refuge is best accessed by car. From Montezuma, it's a 35-kilometer, one-hour drive northeast on Road 624 and the un-named coastal road. The small entrance to the reserve is on the east side of the road; it resembles a parking booth. Turismo Curú is located within the refuge, so travelers planning to participate in one of the outfitter's tours must pay the refuge entrance fee separately, on the way into the refuge. Account for the added cost when budgeting for your trip.

★ ISLA TORTUGA

If you envision paradise as an island with lush vegetation and snow-white sand surrounded by gentle, turquoise-tinged waters, you're dreaming of **Isla Tortuga** (Tortuga Island). The uninhabited island lies a mere three kilometers off the coast of the Nicoya Peninsula, just east of the Refugio Nacional de Vida Silvestre Curú, yet it remains largely undeveloped. The smell of barbecued food, the warm touch of sunshine, and the sight of palm trees swaying in the breeze here are enough to make you giddy with glee.

The island, whose official name is Isla Tolinga (though you'll just hear it referred to as Isla Tortuga), is one of the Nicoya Peninsula's most popular destinations. Visits here are all-inclusive day trips that include boat transportation to and from the island, meals, and optional activities like snorkeling, banana boat rides, and kayaking. Overnight stays are not permitted. Most excursions are full-day adventures that depart in the early morning and return in the late afternoon.

Tours

Calypso Cruises (Avenida 3, 100 m east of Calle 7, Puntarenas, tel. 506/2256-2727, www.calypsocruises.com) has been operating classy excursions to the island since 1975. Their standout **Tour to Tortuga Island** (8:30am daily, 9 hours, $145 adults, $90 children 4-12) is far more than a boat trip—it's a comprehensive experience. First comes breakfast, served at a private dock in Puntarenas. After a 90-minute scenic cruise across the Golfo de Nicoya, you'll spend at least five hours on Isla Tortuga, where you can enjoy a complimentary **snorkeling excursion** and **banana boat ride,** along with plenty of free time at the beach. Included with the tour are unlimited nonalcoholic drinks (alcoholic drinks are available for purchase), a four-course gourmet lunch served under shade on the sand, and free downloadable photographs of the day's events. Calypso doesn't skimp on extras, like hiring local musicians to play marimba music and providing free beach chairs, hammocks, a volleyball net, a slack line, and private bathrooms. They even take different routes to and from the island to showcase unique views during each trip. Expect superior service from the outfitter, from their friendly staff to the use of a high-quality yacht, the *Manta Raya*, that delivers tour participants to the island in style. Calypso can provide ground transportation to their dock in Puntarenas from destinations including San José, Jacó, Manuel Antonio, and Monteverde.

To reach the island from Tambor, Montezuma, Santa Teresa, or Malpaís, go with **Zuma Tours** (50 m southeast of Road 624 on the main road in Montezuma, tel. 506/2642-0024, www.zumatours.net, 7am-9pm daily). The Montezuma-based operator, which generally services a young crowd, supplies boat transportation, snorkel gear, lunch, nonalcoholic drinks, and two cans of beer with their **Tortuga Island Snorkeling Tour** (9am daily, 7 hours, from Montezuma: $65 adults, $45 children 4-10; from Santa Teresa or Malpaís: $79 adults, $59 children 4-10).

The island's stunning beauty attracts hordes of travelers, but the destination is deserted in the early morning. Most tours start to arrive between 10am and 10:30am. **Turismo Curú** (on the beach at Playa Curú, tel. 506/2641-0014, www.turismocuru.com, 7am-9pm daily), a tour operator based out of Refugio Nacional de Vida Silvestre Curú, can get you there an hour earlier. You'll have the place to yourself for a short while. You'll need your own vehicle to drive to the outfitter's establishment on the beach inside the refuge, but once there, it's a quick 10-minute ride in a small boat over to the island. The no-frills operator's half-day **Tortuga Island Tour** (9am daily, 3.5 hours, $40 pp plus $12 pp wildlife refuge entrance fee) includes boat transportation, snorkel gear, and lunch.

Getting There

The island is typically accessed by boat. Excursions run year-round with departures from (and returns to) the Refugio Nacional de Vida Silvestre Curú, Tambor, Montezuma, Santa Teresa, Malpaís, Puntarenas, San José, Jacó, Manuel Antonio, and Monteverde.

Experienced kayakers can paddle to the island from the Refugio Nacional de Vida Silvestre Curú. Turismo Curú rents kayaks ($10 per hour).

Santa Teresa, Carmen, and Malpaís

The southwest side of the Nicoya Peninsula's tip is a long stretch of flat coastline comprising several beaches separated by rocky outcroppings, coves, and headlands. Spread out along the coast are three laid-back beachfront communities: Santa Teresa, Carmen, and Malpaís (sometimes styled as Mal País). Thanks to the monster waves that develop offshore here, surfing is one of the area's main attractions. Yoga is another principal draw. Travelers from around the world come to this remote part of the country for surf and yoga retreats. This is a place where it's easy to feel calm and relaxed.

There is little distinction between the adjoining communities of Santa Teresa and Carmen. Santa Teresa sits north of Carmen, but it's anyone's guess where one ends and the other begins. Together, they serve as the area's commercial hub, with the majority of the area's hotels, restaurants, offices, services, and shops. The two communities also front the area's best surf breaks, so either makes a good home base if you wish to catch some waves. Most places where you can practice yoga are centered in Santa Teresa.

Smaller and less-visited Malpaís, a dispersed settlement dotted with development, is five kilometers south of Camen. Stay in Malpaís only if you wish to isolate yourself from the area's low-key action.

The unnamed principal access road leads to Santa Teresa, Carmen, and Malpaís from the northeast at Cóbano. It enters the area just shy of the ocean at Carmen. It intersects with the main drag, an unnamed, north-south road that parallels the coast. The intersection, called *el cruce* (the crossing), is a common point of reference. Turn right at the intersection (head north) and you'll travel through the area's concentrated center, which blends with Santa Teresa. Make a left turn (head south) and you'll drive along a forlorn-feeling road through the spread-out community of Malpaís. Often discussed interchangeably, Santa Teresa, Carmen, and Malpaís share the various services provided within their six-kilometer span of coastline.

Beaches
PLAYA CARMEN

At the end of the main road that leads into town, **Playa Carmen** is close to several restaurants, shops, and services. It's the centermost beach in the area and a popular choice with visitors, but it's large enough that there's always enough space to stretch out on. The striking, light-colored sand pleases sunbathers, and the consistent beach break (with a long right and short left) speaks to surfers. Lifeguards are stationed at this beach.

Santa Teresa, Carmen, and Malpaís

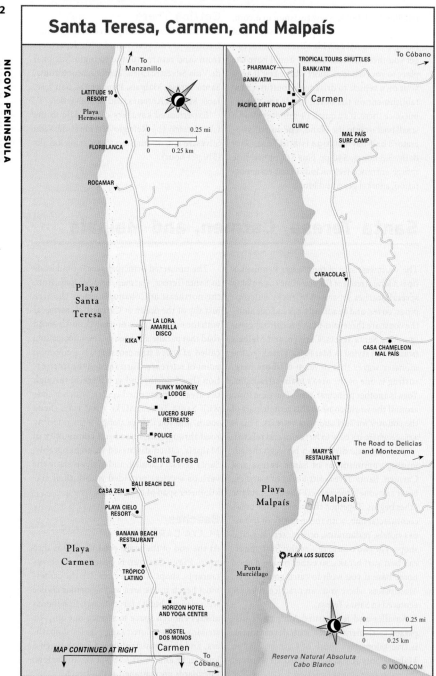

To Manzanillo

LATITUDE 10 RESORT

Playa Hermosa

FLORBLANCA

0   0.25 mi

0   0.25 km

ROCAMAR

Playa Santa Teresa

LA LORA AMARILLA DISCO

KIKA

FUNKY MONKEY LODGE

LUCERO SURF RETREATS

POLICE

Santa Teresa

BALI BEACH DELI

CASA ZEN

PLAYA CIELO RESORT

BANANA BEACH RESTAURANT

Playa Carmen

TRÓPICO LATINO

HORIZON HOTEL AND YOGA CENTER

HOSTEL DOS MONOS

Carmen

MAP CONTINUED AT RIGHT

To Cóbano

To Cóbano

PHARMACY

TROPICAL TOURS SHUTTLES

BANK/ATM

BANK/ATM

PACIFIC DIRT ROAD

Carmen

CLINIC

MAL PAÍS SURF CAMP

CARACOLAS

CASA CHAMELEON MAL PAÍS

The Road to Delicias and Montezuma

MARY'S RESTAURANT

Playa Malpaís

Malpaís

PLAYA LOS SUECOS

Punta Murciélago

0   0.25 mi

0   0.25 km

Reserva Natural Absoluta Cabo Blanco

© MOON.COM

PLAYA SANTA TERESA

The area's best-known beach, **Playa Santa Teresa** is beautiful: It has 2.5 kilometers of shimmery, cream-colored sand with hardly any debris and a verdant green backdrop. It's also an advanced surf site. There's plenty to impress the pros, from predictable beach breaks to first-rate point breaks. If you're a nonsurfer, you can watch the action from anywhere along the beach, especially at the waterfront restaurant and bar **Rocamar** (on the main road parallel to Playa Santa Teresa, 4 km northwest of the intersection at Carmen, tel. 506/2640-0250, noon-10pm Mon.-Sat., noon-7pm Sun. Nov.-July), which has a direct view of the area's best surf spot: **Suck Rock.** Lifeguards are stationed at this beach.

PLAYA MALPAÍS

The jagged coastline at Malpaís has rocky outcroppings and sandy stretches. Near the beached fishing boats at the *pescadería* (fish market) is **Playa Malpaís.** Locals hang out at this beach, which has beautiful turquoise water you can swim in. It also has sand strewn with stones and a shore roughened by several rock formations. While a much more pristine and secluded swimming spot awaits 400 meters down the coast at Playa Los Suecos, this beach is a decent option if you're centered in Malpaís and would prefer not to isolate yourself from most other beachgoers.

★ PLAYA LOS SUECOS

The primary reason to venture south from Carmen and Santa Teresa toward Malpaís is to experience the cove at **Playa Los Suecos.** Surrounded on three sides by lush vegetation and tall rock formations, the place is private, quiet, and the epitome of paradise. The beach has nearly white sand with finely crushed shells; the water is aquamarine—almost teal in places; and the shore deepens gradually. At high tide, the spot is great for snorkeling; marine life from the nearby Reserva Natural Absoluta Cabo Blanco comes to visit. Low tide exposes rocky areas and creates lovely little pools perfect for soaking in as if they were your own personal bath.

Low tide is also when **Punta Murciélago** (Bat Point) becomes the main attraction. You can't miss the charcoal-colored escarpment at the north end of the beach. Less obvious are the hundreds of bats that occupy the giant rock's crevice. To see the creatures, or at least to hear their communal squeaks, you'll need to wade through water and climb over large rocks. These rocks are uneven and slippery, and they also hide mollusks and tiny crabs. Watch out for waves that crash into the spot and can throw you off-balance. Strap-on shoes are a must. Only attempt the walk at low tide: If you get caught on the point as the tide rises and swallows your path, it's a rough, dangerous swim back to the shore. As you approach the bats, be sure to remain quiet. Don't disturb the colony by going too far into the rock's opening.

To find Playa Los Suecos, take the road to Malpaís as far south as it leads—roughly four kilometers from the intersection at Carmen, an approximate 15-minute drive. Just after the blocked gate that leads to the Reserva Natural Absoluta Cabo Blanco (a staff-only entrance), a clearing in the forest has room for a handful of vehicles to park. A short trail, sometimes with a small stream running through it, leads from the lot to the beach. As with any secluded beach, don't go alone.

Recreation

★ SURF AND YOGA RETREATS

The calmness that wafts throughout Santa Teresa, Carmen, and Malpaís makes the area an ideal and peaceful place to surf and practice yoga. It isn't too developed, and so lacks distracting sights and sounds, and it's remote enough to avoid big crowds. Both residents and visitors share an interest in the same recreational activities, lending an inclusive vibe to the area. Retreats here don't just teach surf skills and provide yoga classes; they also welcome you into a community that some call Costa Rica's surf and yogic soul.

To better yourself through focused and

cathartic surfing, I recommend the weekly **Lucero Surf Retreats** (east of the main road parallel to Playa Santa Teresa, 2 km northwest of the intersection at Carmen, tel. 506/8427-6587, www.costarica-surfvacations.com). Conducted in the heart of Santa Teresa, the social **surf retreats** ($1,675 pp) consist of six lessons, complete with in-depth surf theory and photo souvenirs, and unlimited surfboard rentals throughout the week. The retreat also includes accommodations, a healthy breakfast and lunch each day, a fun day trip via ATV to the Cataratas Montezuma, and a farewell dinner at the end of the retreat. A team of friendly, detail-oriented, and encouraging instructors works hard to make sure you enjoy the entire experience. Come ready to learn how to surf, have fun, and meet new friends.

For a remote retreat, look 20 minutes northwest of Santa Teresa and Malpaís to **Shaka Costa Rica** (main road parallel to Playa Santa Teresa, 6.5 km northwest of the intersection at Carmen, tel. 506/2640-1118, www.shakacostarica.com). The six- or eight-day **surf retreats** ($1,625-1,925 pp, min. age 15) here take place in a tranquil setting and include daily surf lessons, surfboard use, accommodations, a snack, brunch, and dinner

each day, plus complimentary yoga classes and snorkeling gear. A handful of Shaka's surf camps are designed for youths who use wheelchairs.

Diverse **yoga retreats** led by a revolving list of guest instructors are hosted by the **Pranamar Oceanfront Villas and Yoga Retreat** (on the main road that runs parallel to Playa Santa Teresa, 6 km northwest of the intersection at Carmen, tel. 506/2640-0852, http://pranamarvillas.com). Choose Pranamar if you wish to combine your yoga getaway with high-quality accommodations set among a beautiful tropical setting just steps from the beach. Retreats vary in duration and inclusions, but they typically last 1-2 weeks and, in addition to yoga classes, can include room and board, meditation, dharma talks, and beach walks. Prices vary by retreat.

If your time in Santa Teresa and Malpaís is limited or your budget is tight, consider the five-day **yoga retreats** ($590 pp) offered through the **Horizon Hotel and Yoga Center** (east of the main road parallel to Playa Santa Teresa, 500 m northwest of the intersection at Carmen, tel. 506/2640-0524, www.horizon-yogahotel.com). Along with accommodations, you'll get a yoga class, breakfast, and a power smoothie daily. The hotel is

Yoga and surfing are the Nicoya Peninsula's top activities.

smack-dab in the middle of the area's action, so you can easily combine this retreat with strolls around town and beach time.

Love yoga and surfing? The **Funky Monkey Lodge** (east of the main road parallel to Playa Santa Teresa, 2 km northwest of the intersection at Carmen, tel. 506/2640-0272, www.funkymonkeylodge.com) combines both pleasures during their **surf and yoga retreats** ($500-820 pp). Choose either a 6-, 8-, or 10-day camp to get accommodations, surf lessons, yoga classes, surfboard rentals, and breakfast and dinner daily. If you're into aerial silks, sign up for a **surf and aerial silk retreat** ($500-820 pp).

If retreats aren't your thing, just grab a board and hit the waves or attend a public yoga class. **Mal País Surf Camp** (main road parallel to Playa Santa Teresa, 500 m south of the intersection at Carmen, tel. 506/2640-0031, www.malpaissurfcamp.com) has competitive rates for **surfboard rentals** ($15 for 1 day; $75 for 1 week).

Casa Zen (south of the main road parallel to Playa Santa Teresa, 1.5 km northwest of the intersection at Carmen, tel. 506/2640-0523, www.zencostarica.com) has drop-in **yoga classes** (9:30am and 6:30pm daily, 90 minutes, $9 pp).

ZIP-LINING

The panoramic views of the ocean and the Reserva Natural Absoluta Cabo Blanco are the best reason to take the eight-cable **Canopy Tour** (9am, 11am, and 3pm daily, 1.5-2 hours, $50 pp, min. age 3) run by **Canopy del Pacífico** (700 m east of the fish market at Playa Malpaís, tel. 506/2640-0360, www.canopymalpais.com, 8am-5pm daily). If you're the gutsy type, you'll also love the forward-facing **superman cable** and the option to try zip-lining upside down. The tour's **surf line** is a zip-line cable you ride while standing on a dual-cable-controlled surfboard. It's unlike anything I've seen elsewhere in Costa Rica. Fun and attentive tour guides make this zipline tour full of zany adventures a blast to complete.

Entertainment and Events

NIGHTLIFE

On a Sunday, there's nowhere else you should be in Santa Teresa than soaking up the last of the day's rays at the family-friendly **Sunday Funday beach party** (3pm-8pm Sun. Nov.-July, weather permitting) hosted by **Rocamar** (main road parallel to Playa Santa Teresa, 4 km northwest of the intersection at Carmen, tel. 506/2640-0250). During the event, locals, expats, and travelers come together at the casual waterfront bar to catch an epic sunset and enjoy a bonfire on the sand. Variety acts demonstrate hula hooping, aerobatics, and poi (fire dancing). There's also live music and a tree swing. Don't expect a booze fest, although drinks are poured; the event is a laid-back gathering by the shore.

Thursdays are thumping at the chill beach bar **Kika** (main road parallel to Playa Santa Teresa, 2.5 km northwest of the intersection at Carmen, tel. 506/2640-0408, 6pm-10pm daily) when the house band puts on a live music show (10pm-midnight Thurs.). When they call it a night, you can walk up the street to **La Lora Amarilla Disco** (main road parallel to Playa Santa Teresa, 2.5 km northwest of the intersection at Carmen, tel. 506/2640-0132, noon-2am daily), Santa Teresa's classic dance spot. Thursday nights are reggae nights; other evenings have DJs and karaoke.

Food

COSTA RICAN

For typical Costa Rican food, including towers of ceviche and *patacones* (smashed and fried green plantains), try **Caracolas** (main road parallel to Playa Santa Teresa, 1.5 km south of the intersection at Carmen, tel. 506/2640-0189, 11:30am-8:30pm daily, $8.50-17). This relaxed spot in Malpaís has tables on the beach, brews in the fridge, and a book exchange.

INTERNATIONAL

Santa Teresa has several cafés, bakeries, and other small eateries. My favorite, the ★ **Bali Beach Deli** (main road parallel to Playa Santa

Teresa, 1.5 km northwest of the intersection at Carmen, tel. 506/2640-0797, 7:30am-3:30pm Mon.-Sat., $6-8.50), knows how to stack a sandwich, blend a smoothie, and artfully present bowls full of superfoods. This fun and colorful diner has seats out front—perfect for people-watching on the main drag—and knickknacks to smile at inside, like old school lunchboxes and Lego toys. It's wonderfully quirky.

★ **Mary's Restaurant** (main road parallel to Playa Santa Teresa, 3 km south of the intersection at Carmen, tel. 506/2640-0153, www.maryscostarica.com, 5pm-10pm Thurs.-Tues., $8.50-15.50) isn't just a place to eat; it's a piece of Malpaís history. What started in 1996 as a pizzeria and a spot to get some fried fish is now one of the area's best restaurants. It's still as unassuming as ever, with its booth seating, tin roof, and pool tables. Pie slices and the day's best catches continue to be served, along with other tasty choices like meat dishes, tacos, nachos, and salads, each featuring foods grown or raised on the restaurant's organic farm.

There's nothing better than cold ice cream on a hot, humid beach day. You'll need to ask around to hunt it down, but the traveling pop-up ice cream shop **Curly's** (tel. 506/8719-0618) rewards the effort in the coolest way possible. Their unique creations, called Ice Cream Rolls, are made from a liquid ice cream mix that's poured over an ice-cold block, mixed with toppings, flattened like a crepe, rolled like paper, and served in a cup. Flavors include coconut, coffee, brownie, and a variety of fruits.

VEGETARIAN AND VEGAN

Social crowds gravitate toward the **Banana Beach Restaurant** (south of the main road parallel to Playa Santa Teresa, 1 km northwest of the intersection at Carmen, tel.

506/2640-1117, 7am-1am daily, $9.50-16, cash only), given its beach-club feel. You can kick around a soccer ball, play a match of volleyball, and twist in aerial silks, or simply lounge in a hammock while waiting for your food. Order what you wish from hunger-hitting appetizers to succulent burgers and nontraditional mains like vegetarian moussaka. Everything goes at this beachfront Santa Teresa hangout spot with a great communal vibe and an even better ocean view.

Accommodations
UNDER $50

My favorite economy lodging in the area is ★ **Hostel Dos Monos** (main road parallel to Playa Santa Teresa, 200 m northwest of the intersection at Carmen, tel. 506/2640-1199, www.hosteldosmonos.com, dorm $27 s, private $37.50 s/d). This hostel has a laid-back surfer's vibe, the cleanest shared rooms in town, and a great location in the heart of Carmen within walking distance of restaurants and shops. There are two dorms (6-7 people each), six private rooms (1-2 people), air conditioning in all rooms, and a complimentary breakfast. It's the area's best-value hostel.

$100-150

A high-value, midrange accommodation in Santa Teresa is **Trópico Latino** (main road parallel to Playa Santa Teresa, 750 m northwest of the intersection at Carmen, tel. 506/2640-0062, www.hoteltropicolatino.com, room $150 s/d, bungalow $265 s/d). Scattered between the main road and the beach are rooms and bungalows that feature tiled bathrooms and floors, clean white walls, wood beams, natural stonework, and bohemian wall hangings. Some hide among tropical foliage, and others are on the beach. Air conditioning, hot water, mini-fridges, and coffee makers come standard with each.

OVER $250

The four individual beachfront villas at the **Playa Cielo Resort** (south of the main road

---

1: Punta Murciélago at Playa Los Suecos, south of Malpaís **2:** an ATV, a common way to explore the Nicoya Peninsula **3:** Bali Beach Deli, on the main drag in Santa Teresa parallel to Playa Santa Teresa, 1 km northwest of the intersection at Carmen, tel. 506/2640-1105, www.playacielo.com, $330 s/d) are relaxing pockets of paradise. Each villa has one king bed with a comfortable orthopedic mattress (plus a pullout couch for two additional guests), a fully equipped kitchen, a private bathroom with an outdoor shower, and a patio with sofas, tables, chairs, and a hammock. Paved, garden-fringed paths connect the villas to the beach, passing the property's saltwater pool along the way.

Visits to the ethereal ★ **Latitude 10 Resort** (main road parallel to Playa Santa Teresa, 4.5 km south of the intersection at Carmen, tel. 506/4001-0667, www.latitude10resort.com, $350 s/d) are rooted in the elements. The five open-air casitas (which forgo glass windows for roll-up shades) and private outdoor showers welcome warm breezes. Water from rainfall showerheads, accompanied by the sound of crashing ocean waves, provides the beachfront property's organic soundtrack. At night, the grounds are lit by candles and torches. A good 10-minute drive up the coast from Santa Teresa's action, the soothing spot, complete with a restaurant and pool, is a rewarding, at-one-with-nature kind of place.

If you're aiming for indulgence, your target should be the adults-only **Casa Chameleon Mal País** (main road parallel to Playa Santa Teresa, 2.5 km northwest of the intersection at Carmen, tel. 506/2103-1212, www.casachameleonhotels.com, $495 s/d). Blissful is the best way to describe stays at this cosmopolitan resort with 10 intimate and romantic villas, each with a king-size canopy bed, a palatial bathroom with modern facilities, and a personal plunge pool with an ocean view. Expect truly top-notch, personalized service from all staff, who go out of their way to make you feel welcome and help you enjoy your stay.

★ **Florblanca** (main road parallel to Playa Santa Teresa, 4.5 km northwest of the intersection at Carmen, tel. 506/2640-0232, www.florblanca.com, $600 s/d) is one of my favorite luxury accommodations in the entire country. It's where urban sophistication and rural naturalness meet, forming idyllic spaces where comfort comes first. Any one of the 10 villas equipped with bedrooms, bathrooms, and open-air living spaces will woo you with plush bedding, soaking tubs, cozy seating options, and tons of natural light. Each villa is also rich in exotic wood, bamboo, stone, and tile textures. The rest of the property will impress you with its two-tier pool, Pilates studio, and renowned health-conscious restaurant Nectar.

Information and Services

Nicoya's **Hospital La Anexión** (Road 150, 300 m north of the justice courts, Nicoya, tel. 506/2685-5066, 24 hours daily) serves most of the Nicoya Peninsula. It's about a 140-kilometer, three-hour drive northwest of Santa Teresa and Malpaís.

Santa Teresa has a **tourist police office** (northeast side of the *fútbol* field, tel. 506/2640-0856, 24 hours daily) with officers available to assist foreign tourists.

At the main intersection in Carmen, you'll find two **banks** with **ATMs,** one of which is **Banco de Costa Rica** (tel. 506/2640-1019, 9am-4pm Mon.-Fri., ATM 5am-midnight daily). Next door to the bank is a **clinic, Lifeguard Costa Rica** (tel. 506/2220-0911, 8am-5pm daily). Across the street is **Farmacia Amiga** (tel. 506/2640-0830, 8am-8pm Mon.-Sat.).

Head to Cóbano, a town about 10 kilometers north of Santa Teresa, to find the area's official **police station** (on the coastal road, 350 m north of Road 624, Cóbano, tel. 506/2642-0770, 24 hours daily), as well as the closest **post office** (Road 624, 50 m east of the coastal road, Cóbano, tel. 506/2783-3500, 8am-5pm Mon.-Fri.).

The area's only **gas station** is two kilometers northeast of Carmen.

Transportation

CAR

Carmen is a 145-kilometer, 4.5-hour journey west from downtown **San José** that consists of a 100-kilometer, two-hour drive to Puntarenas, a one-hour ferry crossing to Paquera, and a 45-kilometer, 75-minute drive to Carmen. If you'd prefer to skip the ferry crossing, Carmen, Santa Teresa, and Malpaís can also be reached from downtown San José via a tiring 315-kilometer, 5.5- to 6-hour drive around the gulf via Highways 1, 18, 21, and the unnamed coastal road.

Carmen is a 215-kilometer, 4.5-hour drive southeast from downtown **Liberia** via Highway 21 and the unnamed coastal road. From **Montezuma,** a pressed-gravel road known locally as "the road to Delicias" cuts east-west across the peninsula and connects with Carmen, passing the farming community of Delicias along the way. This 15-kilometer drive takes 40 minutes.

BUS

Public **buses** travel daily to Carmen and Santa Teresa from **San José** (2pm daily, 6 hours, $13 includes ferry ticket). There's also a 6am bus from San José each day that will get you to Carmen and Santa Teresa, but it requires transferring buses in Cóbano.

To get to Carmen or Santa Teresa from **Montezuma,** take the bus to Cóbano (multiple times 6:20am-8pm daily, 30 minutes, $1) and catch one of many buses from there to Carmen or Santa Teresa. To identify a bus bound for Carmen and Santa Teresa, look for signage in the front window.

If you're transferring buses in Cóbano, board your new bus and ask the driver, *"¿Por favor, puede parar en Carmen?"* ("Please, can you stop in Carmen?") or *"¿Por favor, puede parar en Santa Teresa?"* ("Please, can you stop in Santa Teresa?"). Buses can stop at the main intersection in Carmen or 2.5 kilometers up the coast (in front of the small commercial center signed as Plaza Kahuna) where they end their run in Santa Teresa.

PRIVATE TRANSFER SERVICE

Private transfer services can be hired through **Tropical Tours Shuttles** (main road parallel to Playa Santa Teresa, 50 m northwest of the intersection at Carmen, tel. 506/2640-1900, www.tropicaltoursshuttles.com, 8am-9pm daily). Prices average around $315 from San José and $275 from Liberia. Vehicles vary in size; most accommodate up to eight people plus luggage.

SHARED SHUTTLE SERVICE

Both Tropical Tours Shuttles and the Montezuma-based **Zuma Tours** (tel. 506/2642-0024, www.zumatours.net) provide shared shuttle services to the Santa Teresa and Malpaís area from most popular tourist destinations. Services departing from San José, Jacó, Manuel Antonio, Dominical, Uvita, and Sierpe consist of ground transportation and either a ferry ride or water taxi ride. Services departing from Liberia, La Fortuna, Monteverde, Tamarindo, Tambor, Nosara, Sámara, and a variety of Guanacaste beach towns are ground transfer services only. One-way services cost $50-150 per person. Most shuttles fit eight people with luggage and offer drop-offs at Santa Teresa, Carmen, and Malpaís hotels.

WATER TAXI

To get from the central Pacific coast to Santa Teresa or Malpaís, take one of the water taxis that commute daily between Playa Herradura and Montezuma. **Zuma Tours** (tel. 506/2642-0024, www.zumatours.net) operates a **taxi boat service** ($50 pp) that takes approximately 75-90 minutes for the water crossing, with an additional hour for ground transportation to Santa Teresa, Carmen, or Malpaís.

GETTING AROUND

Santa Teresa (in the north), Carmen (in the center), and Malpaís (in the south) are connected by the area's coastal road. The three-kilometer run from Carmen to Santa Teresa (also the main drag) is a wide-open, walkable stretch that showcases much of the area's development. From Carmen to Malpaís, the road is a rather desolate three-kilometer span with only a handful of hotels and restaurants along it. Stick to the area north of Carmen if you wish to walk around aimlessly, and only stray south of Carmen if you have a predetermined endpoint in mind.

If you need a taxi, Cóbano-based **taxi driver Gilberto Rodríguez** (tel. 506/8826-9055), who services the Santa Teresa, Carmen, and Malpaís areas, is well-known and provides reliable service.

If you really want to blend in with the crowd, rent an **ATV** to get around. ATVs are the most common method of transportation within the beach community, and tons of places in Santa Teresa and Carmen have them. The outfitter **Pacific Dirt Road** (road to Playa Carmen, 75 m southwest of the intersection at Carmen, tel. 506/8875-8452, www.quadtourscostarica.com, 8am-6pm daily) includes helmets, safe driving instruction, and hotel delivery with their ATV rentals ($50 per day).

Central Pacific

If you dream of road-tripping in Costa Rica, hop in a rental car and head to the central Pacific coast. It has over 200 kilometers of coastline to follow, and getting from one destination to the next is a breeze. Half of the experience is the journey: Drive alongside steep, verdant hills, pass through rows of swaying tropical palms, spot the sparkle of the glassy ocean, and marvel at a rainbow-colored sky come sunset. You'll have your pick of landing places along the way, such as party towns like Jacó, mountainside communities and adventure centers like Manuel Antonio, and quiet beachside villages that include Dominical and Uvita. Best of all, you can drive from one end of the region to the other in less than four hours, saving plenty of precious time for taking in some of the country's most raved-about experiences.

Highlights

Look for ★ to find recommended sights, activities, dining, and lodging.

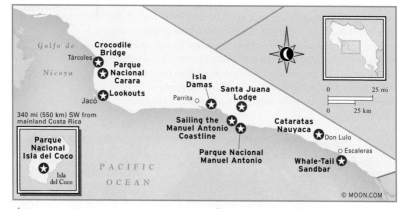

© MOON.COM

★ **Dive with hammerhead sharks** at uninhabited **Parque Nacional Isla del Coco** (page 331).

★ **Get a stunning view** of the coastline and the lush, green hills at **Jacó's lookouts** (page 335).

★ **Observe hundreds of crocodiles** under the **Crocodile Bridge in Tárcoles** (page 343).

★ **Search for macaws** and other tropical birds at the accessible **Parque Nacional Carara** (page 345).

★ **Take a boat tour** of the tranquil mangroves at Isla Damas (page 349).

★ **Fish for tilapia,** visit a traditional sugarcane mill powered by oxen, and enjoy a slower pace at the **Santa Juana Lodge** (page 354).

★ **Sail the Manuel Antonio coastline** for an unforgettable view of lush hills and sandy beaches (page 354).

★ **Lounge on the beach,** hang out with monkeys, and spot sloths and other wildlife at **Parque Nacional Manuel Antonio** (page 364).

★ **Swim** in pools at the idyllic falls of the **Cataratas Nauyaca** (page 367).

★ **Take a surreal walk** along the uniquely shaped **whale-tail sandbar** at **Parque Nacional Marino Ballena** (page 375).

The blanket of lush rainforest that envelops much of the central Pacific coast, butting up against the beach in areas, is bursting with wildlife, both land- and water-based. Take a national park or mangrove tour or go on an offshore excursion to a national marine park for rare up-close wildlife encounters. Waterfalls tumble down jungle-clad slopes where panoramic ocean and canopy views appear through cliffside clearings. Beaches line nearly the entire coast. Some showcase white-sand shores, a few remain unfrequented finds, and others are sought-after for their stupendous surf.

Ideal if you're looking for both nature and the beach, the central Pacific coast is Costa Rica's one-stop shop.

PLANNING YOUR TIME

If you plan to station yourself in **Manuel Antonio** or **Jacó,** the region's hubs, you'll want **three full days** at minimum, and ideally four or five, to experience the area's appeal. For in-demand Manuel Antonio, book accommodations **3-6 months in advance** if you will be in the country between the end of December and April—and even earlier, if your visit coincides with Christmas, New Year's, or Easter. Transportation and activity arrangements can be made a few weeks prior to your trip, as can accommodation arrangements if you plan to travel between May and mid-December.

Quieter coastal areas, including Herradura, Dominical, Uvita, and Ojochal, offer less to see and do, but that's part of their draw. You only need **one or two days** in each area to cover the must-see sights. Give yourself as much extra time as you wish to enjoy the beach.

Nature and wildlife-spotting activities in this region range from quick 10-minute stops at the **Crocodile Bridge** in Tárcoles to weeklong diving excursions at **Parque Nacional Isla del Coco.** Dedicate a half day to each of the region's highlights, which are all about wildlife-watching and enjoying the water. Search **Parque Nacional Carara** for tropical birds, play with monkeys in the mangroves at **Isla Damas,** and spy on sloths at **Parque Nacional Manuel Antonio.** Sail the **Manuel Antonio coastline,** play in the pool of the **Cataratas Nauyaca,** and take a relaxed adventure tour at the **Santa Juana Lodge.** Self-guided visits to **Jacó's lookouts** and the whale-tail sandbar at **Parque Nacional Marino Ballena** can take as little or as much time as you want or need.

Regardless of where you head to along the coast, familiarize yourself with the region's **tide schedule.** Some tours and attractions can only be experienced at high or low tide. If tide-dependent activities interest you, create a flexible itinerary that allows for activities with start times beyond your control.

Weather and Transportation

The central Pacific coast is such a striking emerald green and is home to rainforest in part because it receives a consistent dose of rain and sun. Showers ranging from drizzles to downpours are not uncommon throughout the year, but most of the region's annual precipitation falls between June and November. September through November is the wettest time to visit.

Most of the central Pacific coast's beaches average 80°F, rivaling some of the country's hottest areas. Temperatures drop as elevation rises inland. Prior to travel, prepare yourself for the two climates—pack plenty of sunscreen and a waterproof rain jacket or poncho.

Getting around the area is easy. There's not much mountainous terrain unless you break away from the highway to explore inland areas, and turnoffs to the region's numerous beach towns, villages, and communities are well marked. Drives to the most popular areas do not require a 4x4 vehicle. It's a good idea to have one if you plan to travel into the

CENTRAL PACIFIC

Previous: a two-toed sloth in the tree canopy; view of Costa Ballena at Uvita; an ox similar to the ones at Santa Juana Lodge.

Central Pacific

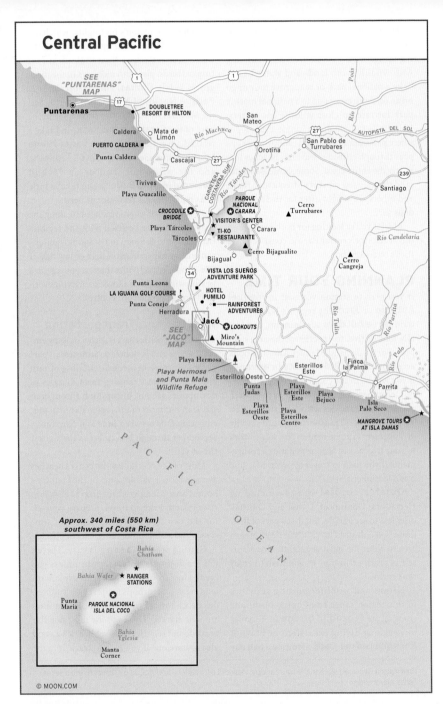

SEE "PUNTARENAS" MAP

Puntarenas

1

1

17

DOUBLETREE RESORT BY HILTON

San Mateo

Caldera

Mata de Limón

Río Machuca

27

San Pablo de Turrubares

AUTOPISTA DEL SOL

Río Poás

PUERTO CALDERA ■

Orotina

Punta Caldera

Cascajal

27

239

Tivives

CARRETERA COSTANERA SUR

Santiago

Playa Guacalilo

Río Tárcoles

PARQUE NACIONAL CARARA ✪

CROCODILE BRIDGE ✪

VISITOR'S CENTER ★

Cerro Turrubares ▲

Playa Tárcoles

TI-KO RESTAURANTE ▼

Carara

Río Candelaria

Tárcoles

Cerro Bijagualito ▲

Bijagual

Cerro Cangreja ▲

VISTA LOS SUEÑOS ADVENTURE PARK

34

Punta Leona

HOTEL PUMILIO ■

LA IGUANA GOLF COURSE ⛳

Punta Conejo

■ — **RAINFOREST ADVENTURES**

Río Tulín

Herradura

Jacó ✪

✪ **LOOKOUTS**

SEE "JACÓ" MAP

Río Palo

Miro's Mountain ▲

Río Parrita

Playa Hermosa ▲

Esterillos Este

Finca la Palma

Playa Hermosa and Punta Mala Wildlife Refuge

Esterillos Oeste

Parrita

Punta Judas

Playa Esterillos Este

Playa Bejuco

Playa Esterillos Oeste

Isla Palo Seco

Playa Esterillos Centro

MANGROVE TOURS AT ISLA DAMAS ✪ ★

P A C I F I C

O C E A N

Approx. 340 miles (550 km) southwest of Costa Rica

Bahía Chatham

Bahía Wafer ★ **RANGER STATIONS**

Punta María

✪

PARQUE NACIONAL ISLA DEL COCO

Bahía Yglesia

Manta Corner

© MOON.COM

Volcán Irazú ▲

SAN JOSÉ ✈ ㉗

② Cartago

Alto Cedral ▲

San Marcos
Cañon

PAN AMERICAN HIGHWAY

Cerro Caraigres ▲

0   10 mi
0   10 km

Fila de Bustamente

Cerro San Jeronimo ▲

Fila Chonta

Cerro Camorra ▲

Cerro Vueltas ▲

Cordillera de Talamanca

Parque Nacional Chirripó

Cerro Cuerici ▲

MIDWORLD COSTA RICA ■

SANTA JUANA LODGE ⊕

Río Naranjo

Cerro de la Muerte ▲

Cerro Urán ▲

RURAL MOUNTAIN ADVENTURE TOUR ★

Río Cañas

Río Damas

KIDS SAVING THE RAINFOREST ■

VILLA VANILLA ★

Fila San Bosco

Río Savegre

Cerro Lira ▲

Río Chirripó del Pacífico

Fila Zapotales

Río Ramón

Quepos

Londres

Manuel Antonio ⊕

PARQUE NACIONAL MANUEL ANTONIO ⊕

Silencio

San Isidro de El General

SAILING THE MANUEL ANTONIO COASTLINE ⊕

Savegre
Playa Savegre

㉞ Portalón

Matapalo

KALON SURF RESORT ■

CATARATAS NAUYACA ★

Cerro San Juan ▲

②

Playa Matapalo

SEE "MANUEL ANTONIO AND QUEPOS" MAP

Platanillo

㉔③

PACIFIC JOURNEYS ■

Barú

Playa Barú

DON LULO ★

CATARATA DIAMANTE/ CASA DE PIEDRA ●

Dominical

Escaleras

Cerro Uvita ▲

Río General

SEE "DOMINICAL AND VICINITY" MAP

Punta Dominical

WHALE-TAIL SANDBAR ⊕

Playa Hermosa

Uvita

Quebrada Grande

Río Pejibaye

SEE "UVITA" MAP

Playa Ballena

Piñuela

Fila Costeña

Costa Ballena

Parque Nacional Marino Ballena ▲

BEACH CAVE AT PLAYA VENTANAS ★

Tortuga Abajo

Ojochal

KUA KUA RESTAURANT ▼

㉞

Coronado

mountains or toward remote beaches, where you'll encounter some dirt roads.

ORIENTATION

The central Pacific coast spans nearly the entire southern coastline between the Nicoya Peninsula (to the northwest) and the Osa Peninsula (to the southeast). Passing through most of the region and paralleling the coast much of the way is the **Carretera Costanera Sur** (Southern Coastal Highway), also known as the **Pacífica Fernández Oreamuno** or Highway 34. It offers one of the country's easiest and most scenic drives.

The hamlet of El Roble, 95 kilometers due west of San José, is a major connecting point for cross-region travel. It is marked by the busy intersection of Highway 17 (east-west) and Highway 23 (north-south). To the west, Highway 17 leads straight into the port city of Puntarenas. To the east, it merges with Highway 1 on its way to the Central Valley and Highlands. To the north, Highway 23 ends at Highway 1 and carries on to Guanacaste. To the south, it becomes Highway 27, meets up with Highway 34, and extends the length of the entire central Pacific coast. If you plan to tour the coast directly from San José, you can bypass El Roble by taking Highway 27 west to Highway 34.

Puntarenas

Much of the region is contained within Puntarenas, Costa Rica's largest province. The province's capital city, also named Puntarenas, is set on a thin stretch of land that extends eight kilometers into the Pacific Ocean from the western edge of the mainland. No wider than 50 meters in some areas and just barely above sea level, the bustling port metropolis is perfect for sightseeing by car or on foot. The city's biggest attractions are its vibrant celebrations, tasty seafood and other local fare, and endless views of the Golfo de Nicoya.

Visit on a weekend and the place bustles with locals who escape to the city's beach from the concrete jungle of San José. Throughout the week, typically during cruise season from October to March, foreign visitors fill the area

picturesque Puntarenas, as seen from the Golfo de Nicoya

when ships are parked at Puerto Puntarenas (Puntarenas Port). Additional ships dock 20 kilometers down the coast at Puerto Caldera (Caldera Port). Ferries commute between Puntarenas and the Nicoya Peninsula, drawing in additional travelers.

A fearless few travelers depart from the city on liveaboard boats that sail the open ocean toward Parque Nacional Isla del Coco, a magnificent protected land area.

SIGHTS

As you drive along the peninsula to the city's small center, you'll be treated to views of crashing waves to the south and a calm estuary to the north. There's more to gaze at once you arrive, including the leaf-shaped **Anfiteatro Cultural La Concha Acústica** (La Concha Acústica Cultural Amphitheater, Avenida 4 at Calle 3), the mosaic-walled **Catedral de Puntarenas** (Puntarenas Cathedral, Calle 7 between Avenida 1 and Avenida Central), and the 17-meter lighthouse **Punta de Puntarenas** (Point of Puntarenas), also called El Faro, at the city's westernmost point.

Go to Puntarenas to explore the city, not to enjoy the beach. The brown-sand Playa Puntarenas is one of the least attractive sections of the Central Pacific coast. The rough, murky waters are swimmable if you absolutely must jump in.

Paseo de los Turistas

If you only do one thing while in Puntarenas, take a stroll along the **Paseo de los Turistas** (Tourist Walkway). The two-kilometer paved pedestrian path runs parallel to the beach on the south side of the city, offering the most pleasant way to discover the city. The palm-lined promenade passes by open-air restaurants where you can dine on fresh seafood, and pop-up souvenir stands sell handcrafted goods by local artisans. Watch a cruise ship enter or exit the dock, then follow the path to visit the peninsula's rocky tip and lighthouse.

Parque Marino del Pacífico

Showcasing many of the marine species found in the waters around Puntarenas, the **Parque Marino del Pacífico** (Marine Park of the Pacific, Avenida 4, 500 m east of the cruise dock, tel. 506/2661-5272, 9am-4:30pm Tues.-Sun., $10 adults, $5 children age 4-11) is not a park in the traditional sense of the word. Built within a historic building that was the city's railroad station, the park is a museum that houses aquariums and wildlife enclosures of various sizes. It also functions as a marine and wildlife rescue center. The park is home to more than 40 species of fish, plus crocodiles, caimans, turtles, sharks, rays, and pelicans. My favorite inhabitants are the delicate seahorses and the starfish.

With a spare hour in Puntarenas, you can easily walk around the park on your own. Alternately, you can sign up for a talk with an interactive **guided tour** (9am-3pm Tues.-Sun., 1.5 hours, $16 adults, $11 children 4-11). The informative 30-minute educational presentation on marine biology and conservation covers a variety of topics, including coral reefs, climate change, ocean pollution, marine species classifications, and more.

ENTERTAINMENT AND EVENTS
Nightlife

Capitán Moreno's (Paseo de los Turistas, 700 m west of the cruise dock, tel. 506/2661-6888, 11am-10pm Sun.-Thurs., 11am-2am Fri.-Sat.), the area's best beach bar, is packed with locals on Friday and Saturday nights when DJs spin reggaeton. The nautical-themed spot is also a small concert venue and brings in live bands from time to time; see their Facebook page for specific events.

Festivals and Events

The **Fiesta de la Virgen del Mar** (Virgin of the Sea Festival) is Puntarenas's most celebrated event. Weeks of religious ceremonies and sporting events around the city precede the grand festivity, which occurs annually on

Puntarenas

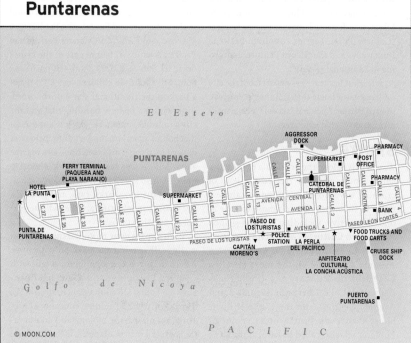

© MOON.COM

or around July 16, typically on a weekend. Music and dance enliven the city on the chosen date, as locals turn out in crowds to pay homage to their patron saint. It's especially entertaining to watch the boats decorated with flags, colorful banners, and fresh tropical flowers as they parade around the Golfo de Nicoya.

Mid-February is equally festive, as the city hosts the **Carnavales Puntarenas** (Puntarenas Carnivals), also known as the **Festival Perla del Pacífico.** Over 10-14 days, typically preceding the start of Lent, you can catch parades, concerts, and other live events, most of which take place along the Paseo de los Turistas.

FOOD

The city's local delicacies define Puntarenas. Porteños (Puntarenas residents) love *vigorones* and *churchills*. A *vigorón* is a tangy mix of cabbage, yuca, *chicharrones* (fried pork rinds),

and pico de gallo cradled in a leaf, sold in a plastic bag, and eaten with a fork. A *churchill* is a traditional Costa Rican *copo* (snow cone-inspired dessert topped with syrup and condensed milk) with fruit salad added in. Buy them from one of umpteen ★ **food trucks and food carts** parked along the beach and the Paseo de los Turistas. Fish and seafood dishes are the most sought-after entrées. Options sold by many restaurants in town include fillets of *corvina* (a fish similar to sea bass), *sopa de mariscos* (seafood soup), and *arroz con camarones* (rice with shrimp).

You can mingle with locals enjoying karaoke, pinball, and inexpensive drinks at **La Perla del Pacífico** (Paseo de los Turistas, near Calle 7, tel. 506/2661-1140, 10am-midnight Mon.-Tues. and Thurs., 8am-midnight Fri.-Sun., $4.50-14.50). At this understated beachside restaurant, you can dine on fresh ceviche, kick back with a fruit *batido* (smoothie), and watch cruise ships

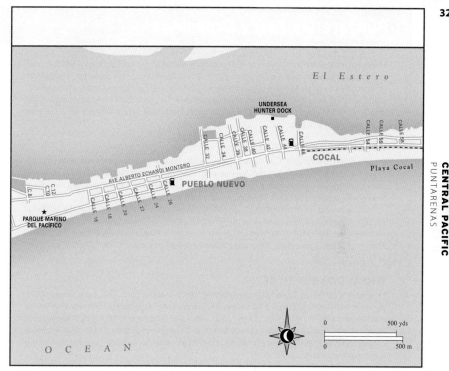

come and go from the dock. The vibe around the place is lively and carefree, which perfectly sums up life in Puntarenas.

ACCOMMODATIONS

Most visitors don't spend a night in the city, but if your itinerary requires it, stay at the small **Hotel La Punta** (Calle 35, 50 m south of Avenida 3, tel. 506/2661-0696, www. hotellapunta.net, $70 s/d). It's across the street from the ferry dock—ideal for catching an early morning ferry service out of town—and has clean, air-conditioned rooms, a pool, secure parking, and friendly staff.

The preferred resort of many Ticos, the 315-room **DoubleTree Resort by Hilton** (off Hwy. 23, 10 km east of Puntarenas, tel. 506/2663-0808, www. doubletreecentralpacific.com, $266 s/d all-inclusive) is on the outskirts of Puntarenas. Less touristy than the country's other all-inclusive resorts, the property is dominated by

locals, and much of the on-site entertainment is provided in Spanish. There are four restaurants, 10 bars, five pool areas, tennis courts, a game room, and a spa. Rooms come with one king or two double beds, all with comfy plush-top mattresses.

INFORMATION AND SERVICES

Hospital Monseñor Víctor Manuel Sanabria Martínez (Road 202, 350 m south of Hwy. 17, tel. 506/2630-8000, 24 hours daily) is the city's hospital. **Pharmacies** are found north of Avenida Central between Calle 4 and Calle 1. Most open at 8am and close anywhere between 5pm and 10pm daily.

Puntarenas also has a **post office** (Avenida 3 between Calle 1 and Calle Central, tel. 506/2661-2156, 8am-5pm Mon.-Fri., 8am-2pm Sat.), a **police station** (Avenida 4 just east of Calle 9, tel. 506/2661-3009, 24 hours daily), and several **supermarkets.**

Puntarenas Ferry Crossings

Ferries cross the Golfo de Nicoya several times daily between the city of Puntarenas and the small port towns of Playa Naranjo and Paquera on the Nicoya Peninsula. These passenger and vehicle services allow travelers to move efficiently between the central Pacific coast and the Nicoya Peninsula, but they also provide a relaxing way to experience the coast. You'll see pretty, jungle-filled islands along the way as you glide through the gulf's crystalline waters—there's even a chance you'll spot a whale or two.

WHICH FERRY DO I TAKE?

If you're going to Sámara, Carrillo, or Nosara (the northern section of the Nicoya Peninsula), board the ferry to Playa Naranjo. Service is provided by Coonatramar (tel. 506/2661-1069, www.coonatramar.com). Puntarenas departures are at 6:30am, 10am, 2:30pm, and 7pm daily. Playa Naranjo departures are at 8am, 12:30pm, 4:30pm, and 8:30pm daily.

If you're bound for Montezuma, Tambor, Malpaís, or Santa Teresa (the southern section of the Nicoya Peninsula), take the ferry to Paquera. Service is provided by Naviera Tambor (tel. 506/2661-2084, www.navieratambor.com). Puntarenas departures are at 5am, 9am, 11am, 2pm, 5pm, and 8:30pm daily. Paquera departures are at 5:30am, 9am, 11am, 2pm, 5pm, and 8pm daily.

WHERE DO I BUY TICKETS?

Ferry tickets can be purchased at *boleterías* (ticket offices) at ferry ports. The cost is roughly $1.75 per adult and $1 per child (ages 3-12) between Puntarenas and Playa Naranjo. Between Puntarenas and Paquera, tickets are about $1.50 per adult and $1 per child. Payment must be made in Costa Rican colones or small denominations of American dollars ($1 or $5 bills). Tickets for the service between Puntarenas and Paquera can be reserved and paid for in advance online by visiting www.quickpaycr.com.

There are many banks in the city, but the most convenient is Banco Popular, across from the bus station on Calle 2. It has an ATM (10:45am-6:30pm Mon.-Fri., 9:45am-1pm Sat.).

There are three gas stations on the east side of Puntarenas on Highway 17/Avenida Central.

TRANSPORTATION

Puntarenas is a 100-kilometer, two-hour drive west from downtown San José via Highway 1. From downtown Liberia, it's a 130-kilometer, two-hour drive southeast on Highway 1, and west on Highway 23 and Highway 17.

Highway 17 links up with Highway 1 to provide direct access to Puntarenas. The road becomes Avenida Central in the city's core.

The regional bus station is on Avenida 4 on the south side of the city, just east of the cruise dock. Public buses travel daily to Puntarenas from San José (multiple times 5:30am-7pm daily, 3 hours, $4.50-5), Liberia (multiple times 5am-5pm daily, 3 hours, $5-5.50), Jacó (multiple times 6am-7pm daily, 1.5 hours, $2.50), and Quepos (multiple times 4:30am-6pm daily, 3 hours, $4.50).

Desafio Adventure Company (tel. 506/2479-0020, www.desafiocostarica.com) offers private transfer services to Puntarenas with free onboard Wi-Fi. Prices average around $125 from San José, $250 from La Fortuna, and $150 from Monteverde.

Several ferries, including the *Tambor III*, depart from Puntarenas to destinations on the Nicoya Peninsula.

WHEN SHOULD I GET THERE?

Give yourself ample time to get to the ferry port. Arrive at least 30 minutes in advance of your departure time; come even earlier if you're traveling between December and April or if you plan to drive a vehicle on board.

CAN I BRING MY RENTAL CAR?

Rental vehicles can be driven onto the ferry at the cost of $16-25 per vehicle (between Puntarenas and Playa Naranjo) or $20-30 per vehicle (between Puntarenas and Paquera), depending on their size. You'll drive your own car aboard, but the vehicle must be clear of other occupants. You cannot access the car's contents during the cruise, so be sure to grab items you may want during the trip before leaving the vehicle. Remember to lock the doors.

Vehicles vary in size, but most accommodate up to eight people plus luggage. Some vehicles can fit up to 28 passengers.

Grayline Costa Rica (tel. 506/2220-2126, www.graylinecostarica.com) offers daily **shared shuttle services** to Puntarenas from San José, Dominical, La Fortuna, Playas del Coco, Brasilito, and Playa Flamingo. One-way services cost $42-89 per person. Most shuttles fit eight people with luggage and offer drop-offs at Puntarenas hotels.

★ PARQUE NACIONAL ISLA DEL COCO

Parque Nacional Isla del Coco (Isla del Coco National Park, tel. 506/2206-5701, www.isladelcoco.go.cr, $70 per diver per day, $50 per non-diver per day), more commonly known as Cocos Island National Park or simply **Cocos Island,** is Costa Rica's most illustrious destination. The park boundaries encase the 5,930-acre volcanic island, a Natural World Heritage Site and a breathtaking masterpiece with jagged mountains, virgin forests, soft cascades, trickling streams, and flowering plants. Uninhabited by humans except for a rotating crew of roughly 30 rangers who oversee park access and research, the tropical island is void of significant development and remains perfectly serene. If you're on a hunt to find Costa Rica's rarest jewel, Isla del Coco is the magnificent treasure you're looking for.

Visits to the park are not for the faint of

heart—or stomach. The remote territory lies nearly 550 kilometers off the coast of Puntarenas; reaching it requires a 32- to 36-hour boat journey across the Pacific Ocean. The island's extraordinary experiences include exploration of untouched land and scarcely chartered waters. Overnight stays on the island are not permitted, and there are no restaurants. Fully equipped liveaboard vessels provide room and board, with most expeditions lasting 8-12 days.

Visiting Isla del Coco is one of the most expensive experiences you can have in Costa Rica. Beyond the excursion's base cost, keep additional funds handy for dive equipment rentals, dive insurance, the park entrance fee, optional course instruction aboard the boat, fuel surcharges, and possible emergency evacuation fees. Most supplementary charges need to be paid in cash.

Excursions to Isla del Coco run year-round. High season (November to April) has slightly calmer ocean conditions and warmer water, but the low season tends to feature more shark sightings and an increased chance of seeing whales.

Scuba Diving

The park is a world-renowned scuba site. The best way to experience it is by diving into its iridescent green, turquoise, and royal blue waters. The ocean is replete with fish, rays, whales, and a variety of sharks, including the easily identifiable scalloped **hammerhead sharks** that feed, breed, and frequent underwater cleaning stations around Isla del Coco.

Park excursions depart from Puntarenas. Having performed their first run to the island in 1988, the most experienced outfitter is **Aggressor** (docks on the north side of Puntarenas at Calle 7, tel. 506/2289-2261, www.aggressor.com, $5,099-6,499 pp), offering 8- and 10-day expeditions on two yachts, the *Okeanos Aggressor I* (10 rooms, 22 passengers) and *Okeanos Aggressor II* (11 rooms, 22 passengers).

The **Undersea Hunter** (dock on the north side of Puntarenas at Calle 44, tel. 506/2228-6613, www.underseahunter.com, $5,645-6,745 pp) runs 10- and 12-day expeditions via two yachts, the *Argo* (9 rooms, 18 passengers) and the *Sea Hunter* (10 rooms, 20 passengers). Unique to the Undersea Hunter is the submarine-like *DeepSee* submersible ($1,450-1,850 pp, 3-person capacity including pilot). In the glass-enclosed pod of this motorized vessel, you can venture up to 300 meters below the surface. Provided as an add-on experience to Undersea Hunter's regular park excursions, the sub dive offers extreme (and dry) underwater exploration, as well as up-close and intense interaction with marine life.

Hiking

Exploration of the park's land is highly regulated. Should you wish to step onto the island, you'll need to check in at one of two **ranger stations** located at **Bahía Chatham** and **Bahía Wafer.** Hiking opportunities are limited.

The **Sendero Chatham-Wafer** (Chatham-Wafer Trail, 2.5 km one-way, 1 hour, moderate) connects Bahía Chatham and Bahía Wafer via rolling, forested terrain. From Bahía Wafer, a second trail, **Sendero Río Genio** (Río Genio Trail, 2 km one-way, 1 hour, moderate), leads to the **Catarata Genio,** where you can swim in a small pool at the base of the cascade.

The only mammals on the island are deer, goats, pigs, cats, and rats. You may come across lizards, birds, and insects too, but not much else, unless you're lucky enough to stumble upon what remains of pirate loot once stashed around the island. Hike for the thrill of exploring an area of Costa Rica that approximately 3,000 people get to visit each year, not for the wildlife.

Getting There

The park is accessible only by boat. Guided excursions run year-round out of Puntarenas. Each yacht makes approximately 2-3 trips to the island per month.

Help the Hammerheads

As spectacular as Isla del Coco is above water, equally spellbinding are scenes of the scalloped hammerhead sharks that swarm below the water's surface. The pelagic species is regularly spotted at several of the island's dive sites, but what makes them such a treat to see—apart from their uniquely shaped heads—is that schools can tally more than 100 sharks.

The immense gatherings are some of the largest hammerhead shark assemblies (and rarest shark sightings) in the world. But what has contributed to the island becoming a must-visit destination for avid underwater explorers has also fueled the brutal, gruesome act of shark finning: cutting off the fins of living sharks, who later die as a result of being unable to swim. Together with shark fishing, shark finning is responsible for the world's declining shark population and for making the hammerheads that congregate in Costa Rica an endangered species. The illegal fin market, propelled by the international use of shark fins in foods and medications, skirts the law in Costa Rica. There is a glimmer of hope that things are changing: The country brought its first-ever criminal charges denouncing the activity in 2017. But the battle is far from won.

Working to replenish the depleted shark population, the Costa Rican nonprofit organization **Misión Tiburón** (http://misiontiburon.org) is behind the creation of the country's first shark sanctuary and a 170,000-acre marine management area in the Golfo Dulce. The no-take zone helps protect hammerheads and other shark varieties from human (and marine) predators in the area, most notably around the critical nursery habitat in the wetlands of the Río Coto south of Golfito.

Though Costa Rica is known for its eco-awareness and environmental sustainability, shark preservation hasn't been a focus up to this point. Beyond Misión Tiburón, several other Costa Rican organizations, including the **Centro Rescate de Especies Marinas Amenazadas** (Endangered Marine Species Rescue Center, www.cremacr.org) and the **Programa Restauración de Tiburones y Tortugas Marinas** (Shark and Sea Turtle Restoration Program, www.pretoma.org), are doing what they can to raise awareness and incite change. To support the work being done to help save the hammerheads and other marine life from extinction, reach out to these organizations. You can volunteer your time, sign online petitions, evoke discussion through social media, or adopt a shark. Every little bit helps!

Jacó and Vicinity

One of the coastal regions closest to San José is the northern stretch of the central Pacific coast. Between the Pacific Ocean to the west and heavily forested hills to the east are various small, unobtrusive communities. Tárcoles, Herradura, and Playa Hermosa are all free of noise and congestion, offering seclusion instead of in-your-face tourism. Standing apart from this quiet crowd is Jacó, the vicinity's hub and one of the country's most boisterous, entertaining, and provocative beach towns. This area is also home to one of Costa Rica's most accessible national parks, the birding hot spot Parque Nacional Carara.

JACÓ AND PLAYA HERMOSA

Despite being rough around the edges, gritty Jacó is one of Costa Rica's liveliest beach towns. Myriad restaurants, bars, shops, tourism offices, and accommodations sandwiched next to one another line **Avenida Pastor Díaz,** the two-kilometer main drag that runs parallel to the beach. Notably absent from the strip is Costa Rican culture; American and Canadian influences dominate the town's eclectic food scene, unrestrained nightlife, and international festivals and events. At this happening destination, also known for

Jacó

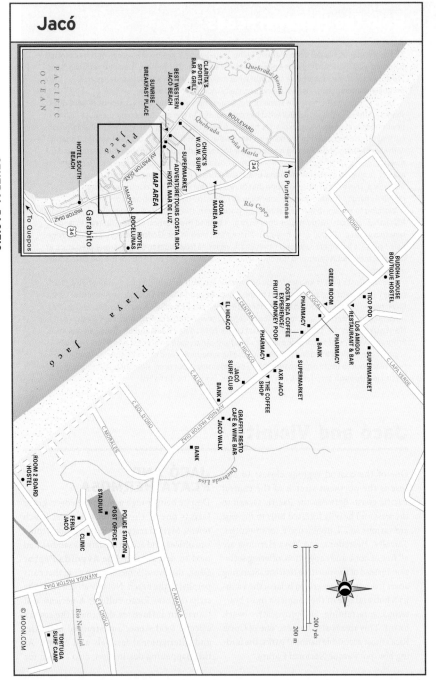

PACIFIC OCEAN

CLARITA'S SPORTS BAR & GRILL
BEST WESTERN JACÓ BEACH
SUNRISE BREAKFAST PLACE
HOTEL SOUTH BEACH
Garabito
Playa Jacó
Quebrada Bonita
BOULEVARD
Quebrada Doña María
CHUCK'S W.O.W. SURF
SUPERMARKET
ADVENTURE TOURS COSTA RICA
HOTEL MAR DE LUZ
AV PASTOR DÍAZ
AMAPOLA
PASTOR DÍAZ
HOTEL DOCELUNAS
SODA MAREA BAJA
Río Copey
To Puntarenas
34
To Quepos
34
MAP AREA

Playa Jacó

BUDDHA HOUSE BOUTIQUE HOSTEL
TICO POD
SUPERMARKET
GREEN ROOM
LOS AMIGOS RESTAURANT & BAR
PHARMACY
PHARMACY
COSTA RICA COFFEE EXPERIENCE
FRUITY MONKEY POOP
EL HICACO
PHARMACY
BANK
SUPERMARKET
AXR JACÓ
THE COFFEE SHOP
JACÓ SURF CLUB
BANK
GRAFFITI RESTO
CAFE & WINE BAR
JACÓ WALK
BANK
C OLLIO
C CENTRAL
C LOCAL
C CHICACO
CALICE
C SOL D ORO
AVENIDA PASTOR DÍAZ
C LAPA VERDE
Quebrada Lisa
C MORALES
ROOM 2 BOARD HOSTEL
STADIUM
FERIA JACÓ
POST OFFICE
POLICE STATION
CLINIC
AVENIDA PASTOR DÍAZ
C EL CHOLO
C AMAPOLA
Río Naranjal
TORTUGA SURF CAMP

0   200 yds
0   200 m

© MOON.COM

spectacular sunsets and decent surf, you'll find spirited and artistic townspeople, and social travelers looking to party. If you would prefer a low-key beach town, or if you plan to travel with children, Jacó may not be the best place for you.

Jacó sits just off Highway 34. The road known as the **Boulevard** provides access to Jacó from the north, and **Avenida Amapole** has access from the south. Both roads turn into Avenida Pastor Díaz in the downtown core.

From the south end of Jacó, **Playa Hermosa** is a five-kilometer trip down Highway 34. Not to be confused with the Playa Hermosa in Guanacaste (35 kilometers west of Liberia), this beach community harbors a small but mighty surf society. Avid surfers gather at the few accommodations in Playa Hermosa, where the very best are crowned surf champions. If you're not a surfer, there is little reason to visit.

Safety Concerns

Crime, mainly theft, is a problem in Jacó. Keep personal items close by or in your hotel's safe. Lock your vehicle's doors and never leave belongings in your car.

Remain extra vigilant in Jacó after dark. This is when theft and robberies increase, and the sale and consumption of drugs is obvious. At bars and clubs, keep a watchful eye on your beverages at all times. Stick to bars on or just off the main drag. If you wish to barhop, use a reliable form of transportation to get around town. Travel in groups if possible.

Prostitution, which is legal in Costa Rica, is big business in Jacó. It's common for people to receive solicitations at nightlife venues. It's okay to politely decline any offers that come your way and continue enjoying your night out on the town.

Sights

★ JACÓ LOOKOUTS

Life in Jacó centers around the beach, which can be seen from the many establishments that line the sand. The most stunning vistas showcase the coastline together with the

area's lush, green surroundings. In stark contrast to Jacó's flat and noisy commercial center, *miradores* (lookouts) on the outskirts of town capture the beach community from afar and portray its softer side, revealing the peacefulness of the mountainous landscape that surrounds the animated town.

Hidden in the hills at the south end of Jacó are the remnants of a restaurant and hotel abandoned partway through construction. The spot, known as **Miro's Mountain,** provides the most spectacular bird's-eye view of the area. From what would have been the structure's balcony, you can see the Pacific Ocean, the headland that separates Jacó from Playa Herradura, the small Isla Herradura off the coast, and, of course, the town's bountiful beachfront development. Take a moment to admire the ruins themselves; graffiti artists have tagged the place and their artwork merits appreciation. Free access to the lookout point is via a rough, steep road that is best hiked or biked: I don't recommend making the drive in a 4x4 vehicle as locals do. Find the road across the street from the gas station on Highway 34. A small parking lot marks the entrance.

Approximately one kilometer southwest of the road that leads to Miro's Mountain, you can see a similar picturesque scene along Highway 34 behind the brightly colored **JACÓ sign.** The lookout point is barely above sea level, but it still has a striking view of the ocean and the jagged skyline with Jacó in the forefront.

For a jaw-dropping view of the treetops that blanket Jacó's inlands, reserve a ride on the **aerial tram** (7:30am, 9:30am, 12:30pm, and 2pm daily, 1 hour, $65 adults, $32 children 3-12) operated by **Rainforest Adventures** (3.5 km northeast of Hwy. 34 between the two turnoffs to Jacó, tel. 506/8702-4566, www. rainforestadventure.com, 7:30am-4pm daily). This tour operator runs its own mini theme park, located north of the other two lookouts and tucked away in the hills that tower over Jacó from the east. The tram provides the best view of the area's forest, which sometimes feels close enough to touch through the open-air gondola. Along with the tram, the park also has a zip line, a hanging bridge, a waterfall, and gardens.

Beaches
PLAYA JACÓ

Great for sunbathing and surfing but less desirable for swimming, **Playa Jacó** spans the entire length of Jacó, from a small estuary at the north end of the beach to the town's southern end. A wide sweep of brown sand, often disturbed by the tracks of ATVs and other vehicles, separates the water from the row of businesses that fronts the beach. Finding space to park yourself is not difficult, even when the place gets busy. As tempting as the water is on steaming hot days, enter at your own risk. Rip currents and a strong undertow are known hazards.

In 2019, Playa Jacó became Costa Rica's first fully accessible beach. A flat, 63-meter, wheelchair-accessible boardwalk runs above the sand and perpendicular to the coast, nearly to the water. Built with recycled plastic, the boardwalk is a model of inclusive tourism and environmental sustainability.

PLAYA HERMOSA

Playa Hermosa is the namesake beach of the Playa Hermosa community. It runs from the small headland that separates the beach from Playa Jacó on the north to a small estuary that drains into the ocean at the south end of the beach. Despite its name, which translates to Beautiful Beach, this debris-washed stretch of the coast is full of dark, coarse volcanic sand that is neither appealing to the eye nor comfortable to lounge on. More importantly, it's home to some of the country's best swells and tubes. Amped-up surfers dig the area, but if you're not a betty or a brah, it's best to avoid this beach. Dangerous ocean conditions have led to drownings; leisurely swimming is a bad idea.

Recreation
SURFING

Some of Costa Rica's biggest waves barrel offshore at **Playa Hermosa**. The consistent swell is fantastic for experienced surfers, but the curls are generally too intense for newbies. Less challenging waves roll into **Playa Jacó,** where most of the area's surf schools have set up shop. A handful of surf schools in town have solid reputations; the two that I

view of Jacó and surroundings, as seen from the Miro's Mountain lookout

most recommend are Jacó Surf Club and the Tortuga Surf Camp.

To surf with former Costa Rican national surf team member Mauricio Umaña, book a lesson through Mauricio's company, the **Jacó Surf Club** (Avenida Pastor Díaz, 25 m southeast of Calle Hicaco, tel. 506/8810-5893, www.jacosurfclub.com, 7am-5:30pm daily). Choose from two different types of **surf lessons** (morning and afternoon daily, 2 hours): standard ($65 pp, 3 students per instructor) or private ($80 pp, 1 student per instructor). Each lesson includes a surfboard and rash guard rental for a full 24 hours. Umaña is the primary instructor, but other instructors may sub for him when he's unavailable.

If you want a comprehensive surf experience that includes multiple lessons, overnight accommodations, workshops, and video and photo reviews, the professional staff at **Tortuga Surf Camp** (Calle Santana at Hotel Perico Azul, tel. 506/2463-3348, www.tortugasurfcamp.com, 8am-8pm daily) excel at creating customizable **surf camps.** Prices vary according to camp length and inclusions. Four-day/three-night packages, the minimum during the high season, begin at $345 per person.

Nearly every surf school and surf shop around town has **equipment rentals. Chuck's W.O.W. Surf** (Avenida Pastor Díaz, 75 m southeast of Calle Ancha, tel. 506/2643-3844, www.wowsurf.com, 8am-8pm Mon.-Sat., 8am-6pm Sun.) has one of the better selections of surfboards ($15-20 per day). They also have stand-up paddleboards ($40 per day) and boogie boards ($10 per day).

ATV TOURS

Lots of companies offer ATV tours around Jacó. My favorite is **Adventure Tours Costa Rica** (Avenida Pastor Díaz at Calle Crotos, tel. 506/2643-5720, www.adventuretourscostarica.com, 8am-5pm daily). The group runs four different **ATV tours** (8am-6pm daily, 2-7 hours, $75-189 pp, min. age 16), each one tailor-made to suit diverse riding levels, interests, timelines, and budgets. Some excursions travel through the jungle and visit lookout points with beautiful views. Others roll through small towns and visit a waterfall.

Entertainment and Events

NIGHTLIFE

Jacó's nightlife is the town's most obvious appeal. The main drag is a bustling boulevard full of bars and *discos* (clubs) that stay open late. Some cater to millennial foreigners in search of casual spaces to socialize. Others offer velvet-rope experiences. Most venues don't charge a cover to enter, except on nights with special events, acts, or DJs.

No matter what kind of party vibe you're looking for, you'll find it in Jacó. The town hosts wild pool parties and themed events, has both swanky clubs and dive bars, is speckled with casinos, and even has a funky Polynesian-style bar that doubles as an art gallery. It also has a collection of casual but social bars that are great for kicking back with friends.

Barhopping around Jacó is easy, although walking anywhere in town after dark (especially along the beach) may put you at risk for robbery or theft. Stick to transportation provided by official red taxis and always travel in a group. Regardless of where you go, always keep a watchful eye on your drink.

Two decent choices are the fiery **Los Amigos Restaurant & Bar** (Avenida Pastor Díaz at Calle Lapa Verde, tel. 506/2643-2961, www.losamigosjaco.com, 11:30am-11pm Sun.-Thurs., 11:30am-midnight Fri.-Sat.), which has fridges full of craft beer and serves American pub grub; and **Clarita's Sports Bar & Grill** (Playa Jacó, near Calle Jardín, tel. 506/2643-3327, 8am-10pm Sun.-Thurs., 8am-11pm Fri., 8am-midnight Sat.), with live music and karaoke nights that reward singers with free tequila shots. Sports games play on multiple big screens in the background at both.

My favorite spot for hanging out after dark is the homey, hippieish **Green Room** (Calle Cocal, just south of Avenida Pastor Díaz, tel. 506/2643-4425, 9am-midnight daily).

Operating as a café by day, the low-key restaurant transforms at night into a relaxing bar that has live music every day of the week.

If you wish to start the party early—as in 11am early—you can sign up for the **Rainforest Adventure Booze Cruise** (4-7 hours, $99 pp, min. age 18) through **Adventure Tours Costa Rica** (Avenida Pastor Díaz at Calle Crotos, tel. 506/2643-5720, www.adventuretourscostarica.com, 8am-5pm daily). The trip traipses through the jungle in a 4x4 safari vehicle to remote villages, where you can down a few cold ones at local bars. A designated driver, a case of beer, and a shot of coconut-flavored moonshine (plus water and a meal) are included. Only in Jacó will you find an experience that combines cultural immersion with inebriation.

FESTIVALS AND EVENTS

Jacó hosts the large, annual, live-music festivals **Jungle Jam** (www.junglejam.com) and **Bamboo Bass** (www.bamboobassfestival.com). Jungle Jam is typically held in January, February, or March and brings in reggae, rock, and jam-band artists from all around the globe. Bamboo Bass is a spectacle of strobe lights, aerial arts, and poi that celebrates bass music, culture, and art. It's usually held in February. Both multiday events are outdoor gatherings.

You can catch other, smaller festivals around town throughout the year, including the **Festival de Arte** (Art Festival), usually in March each year, and the **Beer Fest,** which typically occurs twice annually, in February or March and in August or September.

Playa Hermosa lends its infamous surf break to surf tournaments year-round. Some are informal weekly battles. Others are as significant as the **National Surfing Championship,** typically held in July. The **Federación de Surf de Costa Rica** (http://fedesurfcr.com) oversees most competitions and posts event schedules on its website and Facebook page; look for listings for the Circuito Nacional. If you're in the area around 4pm on a Friday, head to the beachfront restaurant and bar at the **Backyard Hotel** (between Hwy. 34 and the beach in Playa Hermosa, tel. 506/2643-7011, www.backyardhotel.com) to watch local surfers go head-to-head as part of a weekly competition put on by the hotel.

Shopping

Countless shops blend in with the colorful restaurants and bars on the main street in Jacó. The open-air plaza **Jacó Walk** (Avenida Pastor Díaz at Calle Alice, tel. 506/2643-4757, www.jacowalk.com, hours vary by store) contains a collection of stores that are good for browsing.

On the main drag, **Tico Pod** (Avenida Pastor Díaz between Calle Cocal and Calle Central, tel. 506/2643-2068, 9am-9pm daily) is a small souvenir shop that resembles an art gallery. It sells the works of local artists, some of whom painted the giant murals you'll see around town. It features paintings, ceramics, glass creations, leather products, and indigenous masks.

The **Costa Rica Coffee Experience** (Avenida Pastor Díaz between Calle Cocal and Calle Central, tel. 506/2643-6197, 8am-9pm Mon.-Fri., 8am-10pm Sat.-Sun.), which also goes by the name **Fruity Monkey Poop,** is a fun shop to browse around. You can buy bags of Costa Rican coffee (both whole beans and ground) in a variety of roasts and flavors—some is even organic. The shop also sells an assortment of unique souvenirs you won't find at most other stores in Jacó, like handmade soaps and jewelry, local spices, and books written by locals, plus tasty treats like roasted cashews and licorice.

Jacó's decades-old farmers market, **Feria Jacó** (south side of the *fútbol* field, 7am-noon Fri.), sells fruit, vegetables, and handmade products. It's a great place to try rambutan, a fruit that most Ticos call *mamón chino*. The fruit is hairy on the outside and has a sweet and slimy center that looks and tastes like a peeled grape. Don't eat the pit!

Food

COSTA RICAN

Whenever hunger strikes, you can find flavorful eats at the 24-hour **Soda Marea Baja** (Hwy. 34, 1 km south of the Boulevard, tel. 506/2643-3530, 24 hours daily, $4-7). Perfect if your budget is tight or if you need something to eat on your way into or out of town, this small diner has one of the region's best buffet bars. It's always full of Costa Rican foods; try generous helpings of typical preparations like arroz con pollo (rice with chicken), *gallo pinto* (a traditional rice and bean blend), *patacones* (smashed and fried green plantains), and more. You'll pay significantly less here than you'll pay for the same amount of food in downtown Jacó.

INTERNATIONAL

What I love most about ★ **Graffiti Resto Café & Wine Bar** (Jacó Walk, Avenida Pastor Díaz at Calle Alice, tel. 506/2643-1708, 5pm-10pm Sun.-Thurs., 5pm-11pm Fri.-Sat., $10-19) is the dichotomy created by the restaurant's sophisticated menu and down-to-earth decor. Well-crafted dishes like the beloved coffee- and cacao-crusted beef tenderloin are served in a laid-back, funky space decorated with graffiti art and skateboards. You can dine on the exquisite Cajun yellowfin tuna steak while listening to electronic dance music and watching artists paint as a form of dinner entertainment. Operating in its own artistic world, this café is one of a kind.

Serving the area's best seafood since 1978, **El Hicaco** (at the end of Calle Hicaco, tel. 506/2643-3226, www.elhicaco.com, 11am-10pm daily, $11.50-33) fronts the beach and has a large outdoor patio, making it the perfect spot for a sunset dining experience. It's loved for its lobster dishes, but you can also order fish fillets, shrimp, and non-seafood selections like beef, pastas, and burritos. Although the popular establishment isn't as authentic as it used to be, it remains a quality seafood joint worth checking out.

The **Sunrise Breakfast Place** (Avenida Pastor Díaz at Calle Lido, tel. 506/2643-3361, www.sunrisebreakfastjaco.com, 6:30am-12:30pm daily, $5-9), appropriately nicknamed The Pink Place, has unmistakable bubble-gum-pink decor. Don't be fooled by the diner's name; in addition to the 15 breakfast options (try the Surfer's Burrito, loaded with eggs, bacon or ham, peppers, onions, and tomatoes), it also serves pizza, hamburgers, and hot dogs. Pop in if you need fast food before, after, or during your morning visit to the beach.

It's hard to miss the gourmet burger joint **Ridiculous Burgers** (Avenida Pastor Díaz at Calle Hicaco, tel. 506/2643-1010, www.ridiculousburgers.com, 11:30am-11pm Sun.-Wed., 11:30am-2am Thurs.-Sat., $9-21) on Jacó's principal street. This boisterous and touristy fast-food restaurant will catch your attention with its oversize signs that advertise more than 30 types of burgers. Try one stacked with onion rings or Doritos, one with a heart-shaped shrimp patty tossed in shredded coconut, or the Jacó Burger, which has beans, plantain, and Lizano sauce. Most patties are made from meats or fish, but quinoa burgers are also an option, as are low-carb, bun-less burgers. There's also a mini burger for kids.

VEGETARIAN AND VEGAN

Your best bet for vegetarian and vegan food in Jacó is the ★ **Green Room** (Calle Cocal just south of Avenida Pastor Díaz, tel. 506/2643-4425, 9am-midnight daily, $8-22). While this hippie café does serve meat and dairy products, it offers a fair number of vegetarian and vegan dishes too, including homemade vegan mushroom ravioli, a vegan quesadilla, vegan cacao-berry pie, and a handful of vegetarian options. The partly open-air space has a few tables on a front patio decorated with plants; several more tables are scattered around a cozy interior that mimics a big tent with its billowy, material-covered roof. At night, the laid-back place is a dimly lit bar with live music.

CAFÉS AND BAKERIES

A cute little breakfast and lunch spot worth stopping at is ★ **The Coffee Shop** (Avenida Pastor Díaz, 25 m south of Calle Central, tel. 506/8814-0893, 7am-2pm daily, $5.50-8.50). This tiny, informal café has a few tables inside and a handful more out front, but it's easy to pop in and pick up some delicious baked goods to go while you're strolling along Jacó's main drag. Quick snacks include pastries, bagels, and the shop's signature cinnamon rolls. If you find yourself with more time, dine in and try an omelet, a sandwich, or a bowl of fresh fruit. Coffees, teas, juices, and smoothies are also served.

Accommodations

UNDER $50

My favorite economy lodging in Jacó is the peaceful, clean **Buddha House Boutique Hostel** (Avenida Pastor Díaz, across from Calle Bohío, tel. 506/2643-3615, www.hostelbuddhahouse.com, dorm $20, private $40 s/d). This place isn't your standard hostel: It's a colorful, quiet, and Zen-inspired sanctuary. Buddha House is also conveniently located on the town's principal road, within walking distance of most establishments and the beach. Extras like linens, towels, and lockers are provided free of charge.

The futuristic-looking beachfront **Room 2 Board Hostel** (Playa Jacó, 350 m southwest of the post office, tel. 506/2643-4949, www.room2board.com, dorm $28, private $84 s/d) is refreshingly modern. Its dorms feature dark wood furniture, and the shared bathrooms have sloped sinks with high-end faucets. The hostel's large pool, waterslide, and outdoor movie screen contribute to the property's lively energy. Yoga classes ($10) and surf lessons (from $40) are available on-site.

1: *vigorón* and a *churchill*, both specialties of Puntarenas **2:** crocodiles under their namesake bridge near Tárcoles **3:** trail at Parque Nacional Carara **4:** a pair of scarlet macaws in an *almendro* (almond) tree

$100-150

If you're in the market for a standard hotel that provides clean rooms, a quiet environment, friendly staff, and an all-around pleasant stay, you cannot go wrong with **Hotel Mar de Luz** (Calle Crotos, 100 m northeast of Avenida Pastor Díaz, tel. 506/2643-3000, www.mardeluz.com, $115 s/d). The two-story hotel in the center of town—just 200 meters from the beach—has three pools, a Jacuzzi, and a cozy, inviting reading den. The colorful rooms are beautifully textured (some have cement-and-stone walls) and come equipped with a microwave, coffee maker, and refrigerator.

I like ★ **Hotel South Beach** (Avenida Pastor Díaz, 600 m south of the post office, tel. 506/2643-3419, www.hotelsouthbeachjaco.com, $125 s/d), located by the waterfront in a less chaotic area of town. The hotel's entrance is a bit drab, but the property redeems itself inside. Palm trees and banana plants sway peacefully by the pool and heighten the hotel's tropical feel. Middle- and top-floor rooms in the three-story, 38-room accommodation provide ocean and mountain views. Rooms have private terraces or balconies, air-conditioning, a television, and a safe. The on-site restaurant and bar borders the beach.

$150-250

The **Best Western Jacó Beach** (Playa Jacó, across from the bus station, tel. 506/2643-1000, www.bestwesternjacobeach.com, $166 s/d, all-inclusive) is one of Costa Rica's best-priced all-inclusive resorts. The beachfront complex is at the north end of Jacó and has two bars, one restaurant, sports courts, a game zone, and a pool. The hotel's 125 rooms are identical; none is jaw-dropping, but they are clean and bright, offering little to complain about. Choose this all-inclusive resort if you're looking for value, not luxury.

Separated from downtown Jacó by Highway 34 is **Hotel Docelunas** (500 m east of Hwy. 34 at the gas station, tel. 506/2643-2211, www.docelunas.com, $170 s/d). The accommodation is one of the few in the area that forgo beach access for proximity to nature. Twenty spacious, suite-style rooms fill the two-story hotel, which is set among five acres of jungle adorned with well-manicured gardens. Couples and honeymooners fancy the spot because of the romantic, intimate atmosphere. Crowded Jacó, a mere 10-minute drive down the road, feels light-years away from this modest mountain retreat.

Information and Services

Jacó sits roughly halfway between two hospitals—**Hospital Monseñor Víctor Manuel Sanabria Martínez** (Road 202, 350 m south of Hwy. 17, tel. 506/2630-8000, 24 hours daily) in Puntarenas, a 65-kilometer, one-hour drive up the coast from Jacó, and **Hospital Maximiliano Terán Valls** (Hwy. 34, 650 m northwest of the Quepos airport, tel. 506/2774-9500, 24 hours daily) in Quepos, a 70-kilometer, one-hour drive down the coast from Jacó. At the south end of Jacó is the town's **clinic, Ebais Jacó** (south side of the *fútbol* field, tel. 506/2643-1767, 24 hours daily).

Also at the south end of Jacó are a **post office** (east side of the *fútbol* field, tel. 506/2643-2175, 9am-2pm Mon.-Fri., 10am-2pm Sat.-Sun.) and a **police station** (east side of the *fútbol* field, tel. 506/2643-1213, 24 hours daily). A second police station (200 m north of Soda Marea Baja, tel. 506/2643-3011, 24 hours daily) is on Highway 34 between the two turnoffs to Jacó.

Jacó's jam-packed main drag has several **banks, supermarkets,** and **pharmacies.** Most pharmacies are open 9am-9pm daily. **Banco Nacional,** near the center of the strip, has two **ATMs** (5am-11pm daily).

Two **gas stations** serve Jacó. Both are on Highway 34, at either end of town. The northernmost gas station is on the west side of the highway, 350 meters north of the turnoff to Jacó via the road known as the Boulevard. The southernmost gas station is also on the west side of the highway, 1.5 kilometers south of the turnoff to Jacó via Avenida Amapola.

Transportation

CAR

Jacó is 100 kilometers southwest of downtown **San José** via Highway 27 and Highway 34, a nearly two-hour drive. From downtown **Liberia,** Jacó is a 185-kilometer drive southeast on Highway 1, Highway 27, and Highway 34; the trip takes just under three hours.

Highway 34 provides two entrances into town. If you arrive from the north, take the entrance to the west, at the road known as the Boulevard (350 m south of the gas station). If you arrive from the south, take the entrance to the west, at Avenida Amapola (1.5 km north of the gas station).

BUS

You can reach Jacó by **bus** from **San José** (multiple times 7am-7pm daily, 2 hours, $4-4.50), **Puntarenas** (multiple times 4:30am-5:30pm daily, 1.5 hours, $2-2.50), and **Quepos** (multiple times 4:30am-6pm daily, 1.5 hours, $2.50). The **regional bus station** is at the north end of Jacó's main drag, across from the Best Western Jacó Beach.

PRIVATE TRANSFER SERVICE

Desafio Adventure Company (tel. 506/2479-0020, www.desafiocostarica.com) offers private transfer services to Jacó with free Wi-Fi on board their vehicles. Prices average around $200 from San José and $250 from La Fortuna. Vehicles vary in size, but most accommodate up to eight people plus luggage. Some vehicles can fit up to 28 passengers.

SHARED SHUTTLE SERVICE

Interbus (tel. 506/4100-0888, www.interbusonline.com) has daily shared shuttle services to Jacó from San José, Manuel Antonio, La Fortuna, and Monteverde. **Grayline Costa Rica** (tel. 506/2220-2126, www.graylinecostarica.com) travels to Jacó from San José, Puntarenas, Dominical, Uvita, La Fortuna, Monteverde, Tamarindo, Brasilito, Playa Flamingo, Playas del Coco, Papagayo, and Rincón de la Vieja. One-way services cost $39-93 per person. Most shuttles fit eight people with luggage and offer drop-offs at Jacó hotels.

ORGANIZED TOUR
The tour operator **Desafio Adventure Company** (tel. 506/2479-0020, www.desafiocostarica.com) offers **post-tour onward transportation** to Jacó. White-water rafting tours, boat tours, and walks through Parque Nacional Carara can be arranged to include a pickup from your hotel in La Fortuna, Monteverde, or San José, then a drop-off at your hotel in Jacó.

WATER TAXI
To get to Jacó from the Nicoya Peninsula, take one of the water taxis that commute daily between Montezuma and Playa Herradura and include complimentary ground transportation to Jacó. **Zuma Tours** (tel. 506/2642-0024, www.zumatours.net) operates a **taxi boat service** ($40 pp) that takes approximately 75-90 minutes, depending on ocean conditions.

GETTING AROUND
Jacó's downtown core, a walkable area, has flat, paved roads lined with parking spaces. If you'd prefer not to walk, **AXR Jacó** (Avenida Pastor Díaz, 25 m southeast of Calle Central, tel. 506/2643-3130, www.axrjaco.com, 7:30am-6pm daily) has every kind of transportation rental you can imagine, from beach cruisers ($6 for 4 hours) and mountain bikes ($11 for 4 hours) to scooters ($28 for 4 hours) and ATVs (from $88 for 2 hours).

TÁRCOLES
Shortly after Highway 34 cuts over to the coast from the north, it flies by the quaint oceanside village of Tárcoles. A few foreigners venture into this community to take boat tours on the Río Tárcoles. Most visitors, however, are drawn to attractions on the village's outskirts, namely Parque Nacional Carara and the Crocodile Bridge.

A few accommodations and restaurants serve travelers who wish to spend a night in the area. Most people experience Tárcoles-area attractions via a day trip from Jacó or while on their way to other destinations in the region, such as Manuel Antonio.

★ Crocodile Bridge
One locale you can visit in Costa Rica that delivers wildlife on demand is the lower section of **Río Tárcoles** (Tárcoles River). Hundreds of **American crocodiles** lurk in the river's cloudy waters and sun their scaly bodies on the riverbanks. The bulky creatures are striking to look at, especially getting to see so many together in the wild.

A fast, easy, and cost-free way to spot the crocodiles at a distance is from the highway that crosses over the river, informally known as the **Crocodile Bridge** (Hwy. 34, 6 km north of the community of Tárcoles). You'll find small parking areas at both the north and south ends of the overpass. The north end has a few restaurants that cater to the busloads of foreigners that frequent the bridge, but you're more likely to come across a street vendor selling *pipa fría* (cold coconut water served in a coconut) at the south end. The crocodiles can be seen from anywhere along the stretch when you look over the bridge's west side. Just hold on to the guardrail tightly; cars and big rigs fly past the spot and could knock you off-balance. Regardless of where you park, lock your vehicle to best prevent theft. If you plan to use a shared shuttle or private transfer service to travel between destinations, most drivers will stop briefly at the bridge if you ask in advance.

Guided **boat tours** provide interactive, informative, and up-close crocodile-viewing experiences. Government organizations, tourism businesses, and area residents, however, debate whether the excursions cause more harm than good. Some sources suggest that the excursions cause the crocs to leave their known turf and turn up elsewhere along the coast, increasing the likelihood of an attack on an unsuspecting human. Others believe that the (illegal) practice of feeding the crocodiles during tours increases aggression in the animals. Most Tárcoles boat tour operators respect the law, but a few flaunt it. My recommendation is to ask any boat tour operator whether you'll witness a crocodile feeding during the tour; take your business elsewhere (or skip the crocodile safari experience altogether) if they respond in the affirmative.

If you wish to see the crocodiles by boat, stick to the tour operator **Costa Rica Birding Journeys** (tel. 506/8417-9015, www.costaricabirdingjourneys.org). Their **Mangrove Birding Journey** (7am, 10am, and 2:30pm daily, 2.5 hours, $85 adults, $55 children 6-12, children under 6 free) is a combined crocodile-viewing and bird-watching boat tour on Río Tárcoles. The bigger of their two boats has a capacity of 45 people and is equipped to carry travelers in wheelchairs. The team members behind this business are active in the Tárcoles community; they help keep the river clean through garbage pickups and other conservation efforts. Best of all, they adore the local wildlife—and they never feed the crocodiles.

LOCAL GUIDES AND TOURS

Tárcoles has two of the best nature tour guides along the central Pacific coast.

Víctor Mora Cháves is one of the nicest guys you'll meet in Costa Rica, and he's as knowledgeable about local flora and fauna as he is kind. His business, **Vic-Tours** (tel. 506/8723-3008, www.victourscostarica.com), runs nature expeditions—mainly hikes and boat tours—that explore Tárcoles-area parks, rivers, and mangroves. His passion and appreciation for the country is infectious. Tours start at $45 per person.

One of the country's best bird-watching guides and photographers is Randall Ortega Chavez of **Costa Rica Birding Journeys** (tel. 506/8417-9015, www.costaricabirdingjourneys.org). Not only is Randall well trained in bird spotting and species recognition, but he also taught photography and has a comprehensive portfolio that showcases his spectacular skills. He offers smartly designed journeys that provide bird-watching experiences of the highest caliber,

and his photography journeys will help you capture once-in-a-lifetime shots. He also guides boat tours to see the crocodiles on Río Tárcoles. Tour prices begin at $50 per adult and $20 per child (ages 6-12) for groups of four people.

Food and Accommodations

If you visit Tárcoles as part of an organized tour to see the crocodiles, your visit will likely include a meal at **Restaurante Nambí** (Hwy. 34, just north of the Crocodile Bridge, tel. 506/2449-5152, www.haciendanosavar. com, 7am-5pm daily, $6-16). The big open-air establishment, which has supports made of natural teakwood trunks, welcomes large groups and usually operates as a buffet restaurant. Hearty and home-cooked Costa Rican grub is served, including rice, beans, chicken, fish, vegetables, and salad. The friendly staff deliver pleasant service.

The small ★ **Ti-Ko Restaurante** (Road 320, 2.5 km northeast of Hwy. 34, tel. 506/4702-1000, www.tikorestaurante.com, 7am-7pm daily, $8-50) is absent of crowds and only a short detour off the main highway. The restaurant hides among the hills south of Parque Nacional Carara and has an unrivaled view of the area that overlooks the national park, Río Tárcoles, and the Pacific Ocean. Surf and turf options dominate the restaurant's menu, and the food is flavorful and fresh. Little-known to most foreigners, this local hangout spot is one of my favorite finds.

My preferred lodging in the area is the **Cerro Lodge** (3 km southwest of Hwy. 34, 3.5 km north of the Tárcoles bridge, tel. 506/2427-9918, www.hotelcerrolodge.com, $78 s/d). Sixteen standard rooms and bungalows provide basic accommodations with beds, end tables, and private bathrooms. Beware, though: Some rooms have semi-outdoor baths. The property at large is a wonderful birders' retreat. You can easily spot a variety of tropical birds while walking around the tree-lined grounds, taking a dip in the pool, or dining at the lodge's open-air restaurant. Best of all, the hotel is one of the quietest I've come across.

Information and Services

The closest hospital is **Hospital Monseñor Víctor Manuel Sanabria Martínez** (Road 202, 350 m south of Hwy. 17, Puntarenas, tel. 506/2630-8000, 24 hours daily) in Puntarenas, a 45-kilometer drive northwest of Tárcoles. The village's **clinic** is **Ebais Tárcoles Quebrada Ganado** (Calle 1, across from the school, tel. 506/2637-0466, 6am-5pm Mon.-Fri.).

Tárcoles has a few small **supermarkets** (most are on Calle Principal just off Hwy. 34) and a **police station** (Calle Principal, 50 m south of the central church, tel. 506/2637-0492, 24 hours daily).

The closest **gas station** is 15 kilometers south of Tárcoles on Highway 34 near Herradura.

Transportation

Tárcoles is an 80-kilometer, 1.5-hour drive southwest of downtown **San José** via Highway 27 and Highway 34. From downtown **Liberia,** it's a 165-kilometer, 2.5-hour drive southeast via Highway 1, Highway 27, and Highway 34. To get to Tárcoles from **Jacó,** it's a 20-kilometer, 15-minute drive north on Highway 34. Highway 34 zips right past the village.

To reach Tárcoles by **bus,** you can take one of a few *colectivo* (shared bus) routes.

- From **San José:** signed for **Jacó,** multiple times 6am-7:30pm daily, one hour and 45 minutes, $4-4.5

- From **Puntarenas:** signed for **Jacó,** multiple times 4:30am-5:30pm daily, one hour and 15 minutes, $1.50-2; signed for **Quepos,** multiple times 4:30am-5:30pm daily, one hour and 15 minutes, $1.50-2

- From **Jacó:** signed for **San José,** multiple times 5am-5pm daily, 15 minutes, $4-4.50; signed for **Puntarenas,** multiple times 6am-7pm daily, 15 minutes, $1

- From **Quepos:** signed for **Puntarenas,** multiple times 4:30am-6pm daily, one hour and 45 minutes, $3

Regardless of which route you take, ask the bus driver, *"¿Por favor, puede parar en Tárcoles?"* ("Please, can you stop in Tárcoles?"). The driver will drop you off alongside Highway 34 at the entrance to the village.

TOP EXPERIENCE

★ PARQUE NACIONAL CARARA

Parque Nacional Carara (Carara National Park, Hwy. 34, 2.5 km south of the Crocodile Bridge, tel. 506/2637-1083, www.sinac.go.cr, 8am-4pm daily, last entry 3pm, $10 adults, $5 children 6-12) is one of the best bird-watching locales in the country. Located between dry forest and humid climates, the protected land area not only provides refuge to more than 400 bird species (roughly half of all of Costa Rica's bird species), but it also offers an opportunity to see birds that aren't usually spotted in the same place.

The 13,000-acre park is also one of the most accessible national parks in the country, making it a top destination for visitors of all ages and mobility levels. It's easy to get to, one of its trails is accessible by wheelchair, and numerous informational placards make even unguided visits educational ones. Recorded audio narrations and Braille supplement the park's signage.

A **visitors center** marks the park's main entrance.

Hiking

Three of the park's trails are accessible beyond the visitors center. A fourth trail is located two kilometers up the road, just south of the Crocodile Bridge; stop at the visitors center first to pay the entrance fee. The trails here are easy to explore on your own; no advance reservations are needed. Most Tárcoles and Jacó tour operators run guided tours to the park daily.

The first trail beyond the visitors center is the **Sendero Acceso Universal** (Universal Access Trail, 1.2-km loop, 30 minutes-1 hour, easy). This paved, flat, and wheelchair-friendly trail provides ample resting stations, water fountains, and a bathroom halfway along the route. Leisurely walkers should give themselves an hour to complete the walk; however, speedier hikers can cover the trail in much less time. There is plenty to see as you meander through the forest, including leafcutter ants, iguanas, a giant ceiba tree, and the endemic cafecillo shrub.

The Sendero Quebrada Bonita (Quebrada Bonita Trail, 1.5-km loop, 30-45 minutes, easy-moderate) juts off from the Sendero Acceso Universal. In turn, the Sendero Las Aráceas (Las Aráceas Trail, 1.2-km loop, 30 minutes, easy-moderate) connects to the Sendero Quebrada Bonita. Each of these trails is its own loop and travels over flat land through an area of the forest where small bridges cross gentle streams. If you choose to explore Sendero Las Aráceas, backtrack through the Sendero Quebrada Bonita and the Sendero Acceso Universal when you wish to leave. (Note that the marked exit signs lead to a point where the park meets the highway. If you follow them, you'll need to walk alongside the high-traffic road to get back to the visitors center and your vehicle.)

Birders in particular love strolling through Sendero Laguna Meándrica (Laguna Meándrica Trail, 2 km one-way, 45 minutes, easy-moderate), the park trail that originates north of the visitors center. The out-and-back path darts into the protected land area and ends just beyond the large Laguna Meándrica (Meándrica Lagoon). Part of the trail crosses open areas, where there is little cover from the sun. Visit during the early morning when the sun is not directly overhead. You can explore the park's other trails, which are mainly shaded, at midday.

Bird-Watching

Birding tour guides proclaim that this park is one of the best—if not the best—bird-watching sites in Costa Rica.

There's an array of birds along the park's Sendero Laguna Meándrica (Laguna Meándrica Trail), including trogons, bellbirds, woodcreepers, hawks, owls, and a list of others. If you're lucky, you'll be dazzled by the smooth moves of a male red-capped manakin—nicknamed the Michael Jackson bird—as it moonwalks along tree branches as part of a mating ritual. Sightings of colorful scarlet macaws are most sought after. Hundreds inhabit the area, and several can often be seen flying overhead around the park; sightings are usually at dawn and dusk, but are possible throughout the day. All bird sightings vary significantly depending on the time of day and the time of year. Costa Rica Birding Journeys (tel. 506/8417-9015, www.costaricabirdingjourneys.org) and Vic-Tours (tel. 506/8723-3008, www.victourscostarica.com) are experts at pinpointing when you're most likely to see precise species. Both outfitters coordinate custom park tours that can help you spot the elusive birds you're eager to see. Prices typically begin around $45 per person.

Getting There

The park is to the immediate east of Tárcoles and is best accessed by car. It's a four-kilometer, five-minute drive from Tárcoles to the main entrance of the park. From Jacó, the park is a 25-kilometer, 20-minute drive north on Highway 34.

The well-marked turnoff to the entrance is along Highway 34, 2.5 kilometers south of the Crocodile Bridge. There's a large parking lot at the main entrance; a second, smaller lot is at the trailhead for Sendero Laguna Meándrica.

HERRADURA

Just north of Jacó is Herradura, a small community comprising a plaza, a few restaurants, and a 1,100-acre hotel and condominium complex. The development meets the ocean at Playa Herradura, which hugs the boat-filled Bahía Herradura up to the 200-slip Marina Los Sueños.

While Herradura's namesake beach draws in a few day visitors from Jacó who wish to relax on a quiet, bare stretch of the coast, most people who visit this destination are guests of the popular Los Sueños Marriott Ocean & Golf Resort. A handful of remote accommodations on the outskirts of Herradura cater to visitors who wish to stay outside of Jacó while remaining close to its bountiful offerings.

Beaches

Playa Herradura is a pebbly, brown-sand beach, backed by a row of palms, that spans much of the horseshoe-shaped Bahía Herradura. Locals and day-trippers congregate at the predominantly development-free southern end of the beach. Although Playa Herradura is a public beach, the northern section of sand is chiefly used by guests of Los Sueños Marriott Ocean & Golf Resort. This is a great beach for swimming if you wish to avoid Jacó's crowds and Playa Hermosa's big waves.

Recreation

SPORTFISHING

Inshore and offshore excursions from Herradura take advantage of first-rate sportfishing along the central Pacific coast. Year-round catches include yellowfin tuna (consistent Jan.-Dec.), marlin (best Oct.-Dec.), roosterfish (July-Sept.), sailfish (best Oct.-Mar.), mahi-mahi (best Oct.-Mar.), wahoo (best Jan.-Sept.), and snapper (best July-Dec.). The marina's own **Costa Rica Dreams** (Marina Los Sueños, tel. 506/2637-8516, www.costaricadreams.com, 6am-7pm daily) runs daily fishing charters with their fleet of five boats that fit 1-20 passengers. Prices vary by season, boat, excursion type, and number of anglers.

GOLFING

La Iguana Golf Course (tee times 6:30am-4pm daily, pro shop 6am-5pm daily, greens fees $180 adults, $85 children 0-18) at **Los Sueños Marriott Ocean & Golf Resort** (2 km southwest of Hwy. 34 at Herradura, tel. 506/2630-9000, www.marriott.com, $324 s/d) is a quintessential resort course, but its location will exceed your expectations. The

18-hole, par-72 course weaves through a lush, wildlife-rich rainforest north of Herradura. The course has well-kept gardens and tree-filled mountain views; it stuns at the end with a view of the bay. Bird, iguana, and monkey sightings are common.

ZIP-LINING

Zip-lining thrills are just up the mountain from Herradura at the **Vista Los Sueños Adventure Park** (1.5 km northeast of Hwy. 34 at the turnoff to Herradura, tel. 506/2637-6020, www.canopyvistalossuenos.com, 7am-6pm daily). The 10-cable **canopy tour** (8am, 9am, 10am, 11am, 1pm, and 3pm daily, 2 hours, $65 pp, min. age 5) offers gulf and bay views as it whizzes around the treetops. Those who dare are welcome to try upside-down, no-handed zip-lining. You can experience the optional **Tarzan swing** offered halfway through the tour for an additional $20 per person.

Food and Accommodations

The family-run **El Pelícano Restaurante** (across from Playa Herradura, tel. 506/2637-8910, www.elpelicanorestaurante.com, $10-60) has been around since the early 1980s. It's a great place to relax, especially around lunchtime when you can watch pearly-white yachts sail about the bay. The beach-front, open-air establishment prepares meat, chicken, vegetarian, fish, and seafood dishes; you can also have the restaurant cook what you catch.

If you love all things lavish, you'll melt over **Zephyr's Palace** (2 km southwest of Hwy. 34, 15 km south of the Tárcoles bridge, tel. 506/2630-3000, www.hotelvillacaletas.com, $238 s/d). The seven-suite mansion sits atop the mountain north of Herradura and is the epitome of grandeur in Costa Rica. Decorated with exquisite furnishings, each of its rooms represents a different part of the world or period of history. Guests are permitted to access the facilities of nearby sister property **Villas Caletas** (2 km southwest of Hwy. 34, 15 km south of the Tárcoles bridge, tel.

506/2630-3000, www.hotelvillacaletas.com, $238 s/d), a 43-room neoclassical-style luxury hotel that has three restaurants, an infinity pool, an amphitheater lookout, and a spa.

Adjacent to Herradura's golf course and marina is **Los Sueños Marriott Ocean & Golf Resort** (2 km southwest of Hwy. 34 at Herradura, tel. 506/2630-9000, www. marriott.com, $324 s/d). This resort caters to a mature crowd and trades romance for business-centric services and facilities. The four-story, 200-room property feels like a large Italian villa with its arches and pillars, natural stonework, and terra-cotta coloring. Rooms come with one king or two double beds and feature garden or ocean views.

When I'm in the area, I stay at the family-run ★ **Hotel Pumilio** (1 km east of Hwy. 34, 2 km south of the turnoff to Herradura, tel. 506/2643-5678, www.hotelpumilio.com, $223-288 s/d). Each of the property's 10 airy, spacious suites features a rainforest shower-head, fully equipped kitchen, and beautiful outdoor dining area. This hotel excels at the extras. I love the in-room flowers, abundance of throw pillows, industrial-style artwork, and complimentary snack basket. Equally appreciated are the kind hospitality and customer service.

Information and Services

The closest hospital is the **Hospital Monseñor Víctor Manuel Sanabria Martínez** (Road 202, 350 m south of Hwy. 17, Puntarenas, tel. 506/2630-8000, 24 hours daily) in Puntarenas, a 55-kilometer drive northwest of Herradura.

Most services in Herradura are in **Centro Comercial Plaza Herradura** (Hwy. 34), a large, modern strip mall. It has a location of **Banco Nacional** (tel. 506/2212-2000, 1pm-7pm Mon.-Sat.) with an **ATM** (5am-11pm daily); a location of the **Fischel** pharmacy (tel. 506/2637-8454, 9am-9pm daily); and an **Auto Mercado supermarket.**

There is a **gas station** on Highway 34 just south of the turnoff for Herradura.

Transportation

Herradura is a 95-kilometer drive southwest from downtown **San José** via Highway 27 and Highway 34 that takes about one hour and 40 minutes. From downtown **Liberia,** Herradura is 180 kilometers southeast on Highway 1, Highway 27, and Highway 34; the trip takes about two hours and 40 minutes. The turnoff to the village is off Highway 34, a seven-kilometer, five-minute drive north of **Jacó.**

To reach Herradura by **bus,** you can take one of a few *colectivo* (shared bus) routes.

- From **San José:** signed for **Jacó,** multiple times 6am-7:30pm daily, 2 hours, $4-4.5

- From **Puntarenas:** signed for **Jacó,** multiple times 4:30am-5:30pm daily, 1.5 hours, $1.50-2; signed for **Quepos,** multiple times 4:30am-5:30pm daily, 1.5 hours, $1.50-2

- From **Jacó:** signed for **San José,** multiple times 5am-5pm daily, 5 minutes, $4-4.50; signed for **Puntarenas,** multiple times 6am-7pm, 5 minutes, $1

- From **Quepos:** signed for **Puntarenas,** multiple times 4:30am-6pm daily, 1.5 hours, $3

Regardless of which route you take, ask the bus driver, *"¿Por favor, puede parar en Herradura?"* ("Please, can you stop in Herradura?"). The driver will drop you off alongside Highway 34 near the Centro Comercial Plaza Herradura.

Desafío Adventure Company (tel. 506/2479-0020, www.desafiocostarica. com) offers **private transfer services** to Herradura with free Wi-Fi on board their vehicles. Prices average around $200 from San José. Vehicles vary in size, but most accommodate up to eight people plus luggage. Some vehicles can fit up to 28 passengers.

Manuel Antonio and Quepos

Midway along the central Pacific coast is one of the country's must-visit beach destinations: the sprawling, mountainous community of Manuel Antonio, known for cliffside properties, ocean views, beach access, varied cuisines, and an energetic vibe. It's also close to the national park of the same name. This accessible park, Manuel Antonio's primary draw and one of Costa Rica's most visited attractions, impresses with soft and beautiful beaches, several hiking trails, diverse ecosystems, and abundant wildlife.

Acting as a gateway to Manuel Antonio, the flat, banana-port-turned-fishing-town of Quepos sits north of both the park and the community. Several shops, restaurants, and accommodations are scattered about the town.

Both Manuel Antonio and Quepos offer an endless number of day tours, mainly water-based activities and nature expeditions that showcase the area's wildlife and marine life. Others head up mountains north of the area and focus on authentic activities steeped in Costa Rican culture, like farm and plantation tours. Activity centers and tour operator offices can be found in Quepos and Manuel Antonio. All service guests of either area.

Orientation

Quepos is a bustling, concentrated town jam-packed with shops, restaurants, and other businesses that cater primarily to locals. It sits alongside the Pacific Ocean, just south of Highway 34. In Quepos center, the downtown corridor falls within **Avenida 5** to the north and **Avenida 2** to the south. Both are one-way streets; traffic on Avenida 5 flows west, and traffic on Avenida 2 flows east. Just southwest of town, the 195-slip **Marina Pez Vela** has some of the most tourist-friendly services, restaurants, and tour operator offices in Quepos.

From the southeast corner of Quepos, **Road 618** provides an easy but curvy 15-minute drive up and down the mountainside, ending at beach level. Lacking clear borders and an obvious center, Manuel Antonio sprawls across the entire stretch of Road 618 and down small side streets. Most accommodations, restaurants, and shops sit along this stretch. A handful of others cluster near **Playa Espadilla Norte,** Manuel Antonio's principal beach, at the southern terminus of Road 618, and on the side road that leads east to the national park.

Separating Playa Espadilla Norte in the south from Quepos in the north is **Punta Quepos** (Quepos Point), a small, forest-covered, hilly peninsula that extends into the ocean. A few of Manuel Antonio's upscale resorts dot the peninsula.

SIGHTS
Quepos

TOP EXPERIENCE

★ MANGROVE TOURS AT ISLA DAMAS

A mere seven kilometers northwest of Quepos is **Isla Damas** (Damas Island), a tranquil mangrove ecosystem. This area, technically an estuary, lends itself to quiet, slow, up-close exploration of nature—and it is truly replete with wildlife. You're bound to run into a capuchin monkey (or an entire troop) at the spot, which is full of birds, iguanas, lizards, caimans, and my favorite local inhabitants: tiger crabs.

You can learn about the important role tiger crabs and other creatures play in the ecosystem's life cycle during a **narrated tour** of the mangroves. Mangrove experts **Manuel Antonio Expeditions** (also known as Águila Tours, tel. 506/8365-1057, www.juanbrenes. blogspot.com) runs a fantastic guided **boat tour** (4 hours, $65 pp) as well as a guided

Quepos and Manuel Antonio

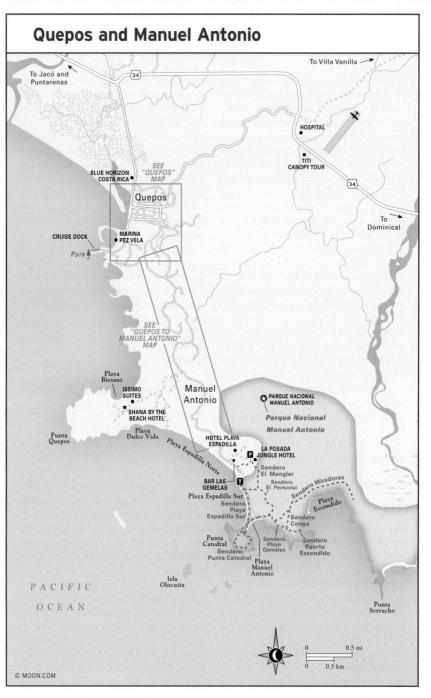

To Villa Vanilla

To Jacó and
Puntarenas

34

HOSPITAL

BLUE HORIZON
COSTA RICA

SEE
"QUEPOS"
MAP

TITI
CANOPY TOUR

34

Quepos

To
Dominical

CRUISE DOCK

MARINA
PEZ VELA

Park

SEE
"QUEPOS TO
MANUEL ANTONIO"
MAP

Playa
Biesanz

ISSIMO
SUITES

Manuel
Antonio

PARQUE NACIONAL
MANUEL ANTONIO

SHANA BY THE
BEACH HOTEL

Parque Nacional
Manuel Antonio

Punta
Quepos

Playa
Dulce Vida

HOTEL PLAYA
ESPADILLA

LA POSADA
JUNGLE HOTEL

Playa Espadilla Norte

Sendero
El Manglar

Sendero Miradores

BAR LAS
GEMELAS

Sendero
El Perezoso

Playa
Escondido

Playa Espadilla Sur

Sendero
Playa
Espadilla Sur

Sendero
Congo

Punta
Catedral

Sendero
Punta Catedral

Sendero
Playa
Gemelas

Playa
Manuel
Antonio

Sendero
Puerto
Escondido

PACIFIC

Isla
Olocuita

Punta
Serrucho

OCEAN

0   0.5 mi

0   0.5 km

Quepos

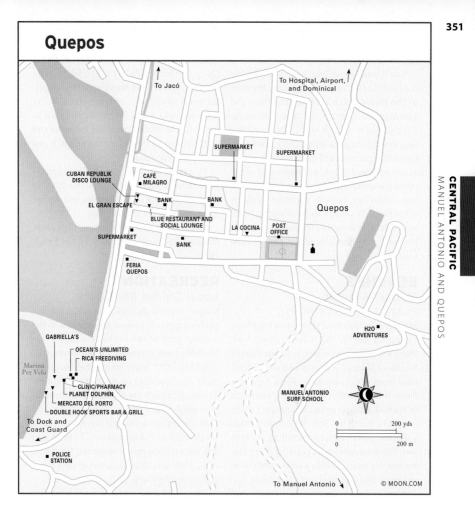

kayak tour (4 hours, $65 pp) through the swampy Isla Damas and its web of intertwined tree roots. Regardless of whether you're cruising through the ecosystem in a pontoon boat (with protection from the sun or rain) or floating through it in a kayak, you'll have an enjoyable and informative experience. Knowledgeable guides share tons of fascinating facts about mangroves and how their survival is vital to the protection of our oceans. The activity is a must if you're interested in ecology or unique ecosystems. The boat tour in particular is a favorite among less active travelers and families with young children. Tour times are tide dependent, and round-trip transportation from Manuel Antonio and Quepos hotels is included.

VILLA VANILLA

The spice plantation **Villa Vanilla** (14.5 km northeast of Quepos, Villa Nueva, tel. 506/2779-1155, www.rainforestspices.com, 9am-3:30pm Mon.-Fri., 9am-noon Sat.) is hidden in the mountainous landscape that towers over Quepos from the northeast. This 125-acre property has a sensational 27-acre farm dedicated to the production of high-quality vanilla and cinnamon, as well as other products including cacao and essential oils.

You'll learn about spice processing during the biodynamic farm's eye-opening **Flavors of the World Spice Tasting Tour** (9am and 1pm Mon.-Fri., 9am Sat., 2.5 hours, $50 adults, $25 children 6-12, cash only), a light walking tour around the plantation. The guided educational experience will overload your senses as you see, smell, touch, and taste many of the crops grown on-site. If you wish to take some home with you, you can purchase products at the property's small **Spice Shoppe.** Don't miss this farm if you're a foodie; the rich gastronomic experience is unlike any other in Costa Rica.

BEACHES
Manuel Antonio
PLAYA ESPADILLA NORTE

Manuel Antonio's most visited beach is **Playa Espadilla Norte.** Not to be confused with Playa Espadilla Sur, which is inside Parque Nacional Manuel Antonio and only accessible from within the park, Playa Espadilla Norte is the principal beach that spans much of Manuel Antonio up to the boundary of the park. The beach has soft, light-brown sand; a shallow shore perfect for strolling along in your flip-flops; and small, crashing waves that are fun to play in. There's a strong undertow, so keep a close eye on young swimmers.

Most visitors congregate at the south end of the beach, where there are restaurants, souvenir shops, and the occasional food cart. Park yourself farther north to avoid crowds or to watch local surfers maneuver the break that fronts the nearby **Playa Playitas,** which is accessible by crossing over the rocks that separate it from Playa Espadilla Norte. You can rent umbrellas and chairs from vendors on the beach ($15 per day for 1 umbrella and 2 chairs); however, lush vegetation backs the sand and provides plenty of shade for free.

PLAYA BIESANZ

Manuel Antonio's best-kept secret is out. Tucked away on the north side of Punta Quepos (Quepos Point) is the white-sand cove known as **Playa Biesanz.** When empty, the small spot is your own private oasis, but it doesn't take much for the small beach to feel full. The busiest times are from the end of December to the beginning of April and weekends year-round.

This is a great spot for snorkeling right off the beach, as schools of tropical fish frolic in the bay's warm waters. Vendors rent equipment on the beach ($10 per day).

The beach is accessed via a short but steep, forested trail near the Shana by the Beach Hotel.

RECREATION
Local Guides and Tours

Manuel Antonio abounds with naturalist tour guides, especially around the entrance to the national park. My go-to choice is the trio behind **Manuel Antonio Expeditions** (tel. 506/8365-1057, www.juanbrenes.blogspot.com), also operating under the name **Águila Tours.** Although the organization is small, tour guides Juan Brenes, Edgar Avila, and Paul Gonsalves know plenty about Costa Rica's wildlife and ecosystems. They're also fun, entertaining people to spend a few hours with. They specialize in national park tours and mangrove tours.

Tons of Manuel Antonio outfitters offer water-based activities and tours. Stick with **H2O Adventures** (Road 618, 300 m southeast of the central church, Quepos, tel. 506/2777-4092, www.h2ocr.com, 7am-8pm daily) or **Amigos del Río** (ADR, Road 618, 4.5 km north of the national park, Manuel Antonio, tel. 506/2777-0082, www.amigosdelrio.net, 6:30am-9pm daily). These two companies have both been operating since the 1990s and are detail oriented, safety conscious, and

---

1: sunshades and beach chairs on Playa Espadilla Norte in Manuel Antonio **2:** mangroves at Isla Damas

passionate. **White-water rafting tours** ($70-105 pp) and **ocean kayaking tours** ($70 pp) are provided by both outfitters. H2O Adventures, a division of the San José-based Ríos Tropicales, includes **jungle tubing** ($64 pp) in its list of water activities. Amigos del Río offers a fantastic **10-in-1 combo tour** ($139 pp) that fuses canyoneering, zip-lining, and other land-based adventures.

★ Santa Juana Lodge

The **Santa Juana Lodge** (road to Tarrazú, 26 km northeast of Quepos, tel. 506/8337-7337, www.santajuanalodge.com) is the perfect temporary escape from the region's many water sports and adrenaline-inducing adventures. Providing one of the region's top cultural experiences, this lodge welcomes you to learn about the lives and work of Costa Rican *campesinos* (farmers). Although the lodge has accommodations ($218 s/d, all-inclusive), the property caters to visitors who make day trips to the peaceful mountaintop from the Manuel Antonio vicinity.

The best way to explore the lodge is via their signature **Rural Mountain Adventure Tour** (7am daily, 6 hours, $125 adults, $79 children 6-11, min. age 6). Showcasing the country's hidden beauty and rural heritage, this guided tour is a wonderful compilation of authentic Costa Rican experiences. During the outing, you'll fish in a tilapia pond, watch oxen power a traditional sugarcane mill, explore nature during a three-kilometer hike through the private Cloudmaker Nature Reserve (accessible to lodge guests and day visitors only), swim under a natural waterfall, and enjoy a homemade, typical Costa Rican lunch.

The property's position above the clouds provides a spectacular view of steep hills and the Pacific Ocean from afar. As part of the lodge's reforestation program, the tour features tree planting, so you can help ensure the surrounding scenery remains vibrant for generations to come. Tours include round-trip transportation from Quepos or Manuel Antonio, but you're welcome to drive to the lodge on your own. The tour is also available to overnight guests at the standard rate.

To get to the lodge on your own from Quepos, a 4x4-vehicle is recommended for the rugged, uphill, hour-long drive.

★ Sailing the Manuel Antonio Coastline

Take to the ocean on a sailboat or catamaran to capture a stunning view of Manuel Antonio. From the water, you'll see luxury resorts adorning lush hills and sandy stretches speckled with beachgoers spanning the coast. Most boat tours sail as far south as Parque Nacional Manuel Antonio, where you can catch a glimpse of **Punta Catedral** (Cathedral Point), a wide, tall, tree-filled landform edged by a sharp, rocky escarpment that slices into the ocean. The pristine scene is particularly beautiful from the water, where waves crash into rough rock faces, and seabirds soar between the point's treetops and nearby islets.

My preferred sailing operator is the prompt and professional **Planet Dolphin** (at Marina Pez Vela, Quepos, tel. 506/2777-1647, www.planetdolphin.com, 7am-9pm daily). Their **sailing, snorkeling, and dolphin-watching tour** (9am and 2pm daily, 3.5 hours, $70-80 adults, $60-70 children 7-9) is one of the most enjoyable experiences I have had in Manuel Antonio. More a relaxing jaunt on the water than a booze cruise (although an open bar is included), the tour provides a leisurely sail along the coast, an opportunity to snorkel and swim at Playa Biesanz, and plenty of chances to see dolphins swimming alongside the boat. If you're lucky, you can spot sea turtles, rays, and whales in the waters too. Although the surrounding scenery is the tour highlight, a close second is the buffet of fish brochettes, pasta salad, and other delights prepared by the crew and served aboard the boat. Planet Dolphin's tour fleet includes two boats that hold 110 passengers and 150 passengers each.

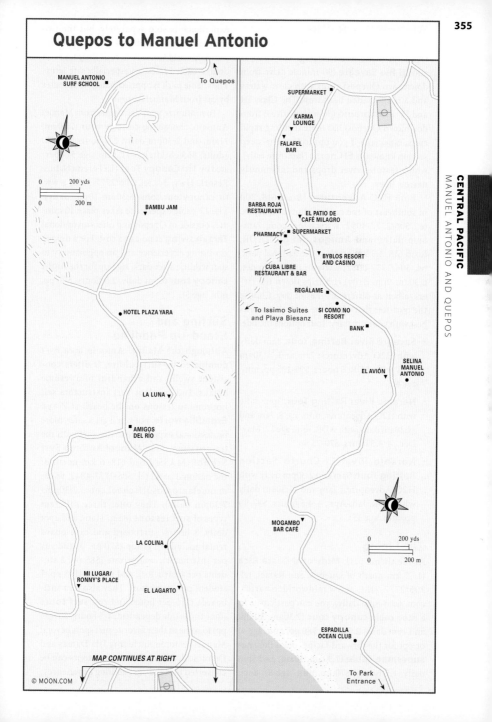

Quepos to Manuel Antonio

MANUEL ANTONIO
SURF SCHOOL

To Quepos

SUPERMARKET

KARMA
LOUNGE

FALAFEL
BAR

0   200 yds

0   200 m

BAMBU JAM

BARBA ROJA
RESTAURANT

EL PATIO DE
CAFÉ MILAGRO

PHARMACY   SUPERMARKET

BYBLOS RESORT
AND CASINO

CUBA LIBRE
RESTAURANT & BAR

REGÁLAME

HOTEL PLAZA YARA

To Issimo Suites
and Playa Biesanz

SI COMO NO
RESORT

BANK

SELINA
MANUEL
ANTONIO

EL AVIÓN

LA LUNA

AMIGOS
DEL RÍO

MOGAMBO
BAR CAFÉ

0   200 yds

0   200 m

LA COLINA

MI LUGAR/
RONNY'S PLACE

EL LAGARTO

ESPADILLA
OCEAN CLUB

MAP CONTINUES AT RIGHT

To Park
Entrance

© MOON.COM

White-Water Rafting

The Manuel Antonio area offers two prime rivers for white-water rafting. The Class II and III **Río Savegre** (90-minute drive from downtown Quepos) stuns with clear waters and a jungle-laden backdrop. The Class III and IV **Río Naranjo** (30-minute drive from downtown Quepos) has more thrilling rapid runs, especially if you opt to tour the steep section known as **El Chorro** (Jan.-Apr. only), which features river drops and infamously narrow lines.

Both **H2O Adventures** (Road 618, 300 m southeast of the central church, Quepos, tel. 506/2777-4092, www.h2ocr.com, 7am-8pm daily) and **Amigos del Río** (ADR, Road 618, 4.5 km north of the national park, tel. 506/2777-0082, www.amigosdelrio.net, 6:30am-9pm daily) run trips down the rivers, albeit at different times of day. Choose the outfitter that offers the time that works best with your itinerary. Tour options include:

- **Savegre River Rafting Tour:** 8am daily with H2O Adventures; 7am and 11:30am daily with ADR; 6 hours, $95-105 pp, min. age 6
- **Naranjo River Rafting Tour:** 1pm daily with H2O Adventures, min. age 8; 7am and 11:30am daily with ADR, min. age 12; May-Dec., 4-4.5 hours, $70-75 pp
- **Naranjo River El Chorro Section Rafting Tour:** 8am and 2:30pm daily with H2O Adventures; 7am and 11:30am daily with ADR, Jan.-Apr., 4-4.5 hours, $87-90 pp, min. age 15

Zip-Lining

At the theme park **Midworld Costa Rica** (15.5 km north of Quepos, San Rafael, tel. 506/2777-7181, www.midworldcostarica. com, 6am-8pm daily), you can participate in a nine-cable **canopy tour** (7:30am, 10am, and 1pm daily, 2.5 hours, $80 pp, min. age 4) or opt for the forward-facing, one-kilometer **superman cable** (7:30am, 10am, and 1pm daily, 1.5 hours, $70 pp, min. age 8). Each experience is sold separately, but the two activities can be combined for $125 per person. Midworld Costa Rica runs their tours on double-cabled lines, an especially safe setup. The theme park is approximately 45 minutes by car from Manuel Antonio.

To minimize your drive time from Manuel Antonio, choose the **canopy tour** (7:30am, 11am, and 2:30pm daily, 2.5 hours, $75-80 adults, $65 children 5-11, min. age 5) operated by **Tití Canopy Tour** (La Foresta Nature Resort, Hwy. 34, tel. 506/2777-3130, www. titicanopytour.com, 6:30am-10pm daily). The 12-cable experience takes place 10 minutes outside of Quepos and offers an optional **Tarzan swing** at no extra cost. For a unique zip-lining experience and an opportunity to spot wildlife after dark, sign up for the **night canopy tour** (6pm daily, 2.5 hours, $90 pp, min. age 5).

Surfing and Stand-Up Paddling

Although the Manuel Antonio area isn't dominated by surf culture, it offers consistent swells and a handful of awesome breaks. Independent surf instructors sell impromptu lessons on the beach at **Playa Espadilla Norte,** but you'll get a safer, more professional experience if you surf with the trained gang at the **Manuel Antonio Surf School** (MASS, Road 618, 6 km north of the national park, tel. 506/2777-4842, www. manuelantoniosurfschool.com, 7:30am-7:30pm daily). They offer three different types of **surf lessons** (8am, 11am, and 2pm daily, 3 hours, surfboard and rash guard rental included): group ($70 pp, 3 students per instructor), semiprivate ($85 pp, 2 students per instructor), and private ($95 pp, 1 student per instructor). They also rent surfboards ($15 per hour) and run **surf tours** (tour times tide dependent, 4-5 hours, $89-95 pp) to some of their favorite surf spots beyond Manuel Antonio, including Isla Damas and Dominical. All surf lessons and tours can be converted to stand-up paddling experiences.

Scuba Diving and Free Diving

The best dive operator in the area is **Ocean's Unlimited** (Marina Pez Vela, Quepos, tel. 506/2519-9544, www.scubadivingcostarica.com, 7am-5pm daily). They specialize in **local day dives** (7:30am and 12:30pm daily, 4.5 hours, $109 pp for 2 tanks) to one of nearly 20 dive sites just south of Quepos, and also run occasional **night dives** (5:30pm daily, 2.5 hours, $75 pp for 2 tanks) for advanced divers. Equipment rental is included with both options. They also offer a plethora of scuba certification courses including the Discover Scuba Diving course, the minimum accreditation you need to dive in Costa Rica.

If you have a specific interest in free diving (aka breath-hold diving), **Rica Freediving** (Marina Pez Vela, Quepos, tel. 506/8522-6783, www.ricafreedivers.com) teaches the sport to beginners with a basic free-diving course ($95 pp) and educates avid divers through a PADI-certified free-diving course ($295 pp).

Canyoneering

One of the wildest adventures you can have around Manuel Antonio is the adrenaline-pumping **10-in-1 Adventure Tour** (7am, 8am, and 9pm daily, 7 hours, $139 pp, min. age 6) offered by **Amigos del Río** (Road 618, 4.5 km north of the national park, tel. 506/2777-0082, www.amigosdelrio.net, 6:30am-9pm daily). The experience is a mash-up of waterfall and canyon rappels, zip lines, a Tarzan swing, a via ferrata walk (a route with ladders and cables) along a canyon's edge, a caving ladder, and a free fall into a river pool, plus a crazy 4x4 ride over rough terrain to get to the mountain clearing where the adventure begins. The entire ordeal is a thrilling hodgepodge of stunts and challenges.

NIGHTLIFE

Both Quepos and Manuel Antonio have lively nightlife, but the bar scene in Quepos is clustered together and a bit louder. In contrast, nightlife venues in Manuel Antonio are spread out around the community. Both Quepos and Manuel Antonio host a vibrant gay bar scene that is typically straight-friendly.

Quepos

The fishing-themed **Double Hook Sports Bar & Grill** (Marina Pez Vela, tel. 506/2519-9366, www.doublehooksportsbar.com, 11am-11pm daily) reels in anglers, both locals and foreigners, with cold beer and televised games, as well as other patrons who wish to enjoy the bar's view of the marina.

The underwater-themed **Blue Restaurant and Social Lounge** (Centro Comercial La Garzam, 2nd floor, Avenida 1, tel. 506/8433-6240, 11am-1am Mon.-Sat., 11am-midnight Sun.) is swanky but without attitude. It's a great place to hang out with friends alongside locals doing the same.

The **Cuban Republik Disco Lounge** (Avenida 3, near Calle 4, tel. 506/2777-7438, 8pm-4am Tues.-Sun., $4 cover charge Fri.-Sat.) is a hazy, neon-lit club that pumps out dance hits well into the morning. Visit after 11pm when the place begins to build its regular late-night crowd.

Manuel Antonio

There are plenty of places in Manuel Antonio to grab drinks after dark, and happy hours are everywhere you look. **Bambu Jam** (Road 618, 5.5 km north of the entrance to the national park, tel. 506/2777-3369, 6am-10pm daily) is wonderfully laid-back. It regularly has live music and is a great place to try Latin dancing.

The **Cuba Libre Restaurant & Bar** (Plaza Vista Manuel Antonio, 2nd floor, tel. 506/4700-9778, www.cubalibrerestaurantbar.wordpress.com, 11am-10pm daily) is an upscale, open-air establishment where you can sip your choice of wine, whiskey, cocktails, or beer while overlooking the Pacific Ocean.

Several restaurants and bars at the **Byblos Resort and Casino** (Road 618, 3 km northwest of the entrance to the national park, tel. 506/2777-0411, www.bybloshotelcostarica.com, 11am-10pm daily) encourage you to drink, dance, gamble, and play pool.

At the beachfront hole-in-the-wall **Bar Las Gemelas** (Road 618, across from Playa Espadilla Norte, tel. 506/2777-5238, 9am-1am daily), you can pass the evening while listening to waves roll in.

The hippest gay bars in the area are the **Karma Lounge** (Road 618, 3.5 km northwest of the entrance to the national park, tel. 506/2777-7230, 8pm-2:30am Tues.-Sun.), which has DJs, dancing, and an outdoor patio, and the **MoGamBo Bar Café** (Road 618, 2 km northwest of the entrance to the national park, tel. 506/7090-0883, 4pm-midnight Sun.-Mon. and Wed., 4pm-1am Thurs.-Sat.), which offers karaoke, cocktail parties, and a great ocean view.

SHOPPING
Quepos

On Friday nights and Saturday mornings, vendors peddle fruits, vegetables, meats, and cheeses by the waterfront at the outdoor **Feria Quepos** (Quepos Farmers Market, Calle 4 near Avenida 2, 5pm-11pm Fri., 6am-noon Sat.). Clothes and souvenirs are for sale too. Local residents turn out in droves to shop the market as part of their weekly routine. If it's hot when you visit, cool off with a refreshing *pipa fría*; the coconut-water drink is widely sold.

If you wish to buy coffee as a souvenir, do so at **Café Milagro** (Road 235 near Avenida 3, tel. 506/2777-1707, www.cafemilagro.com, 9am-5pm Mon.-Sat.). The small roastery produces its own coffee line, including light roasts, dark roasts, organic beans, espressos, and more. In addition to being a shop, this spot is a functioning café, so you can try their products before you purchase in bulk. You'll find other locally made items at the shop, such as sauces, chocolate bars, and beauty products.

1: Manuel Antonio's most recognizable restaurant, El Avión **2:** view from the Si Como No Resort in Manuel Antonio **3:** a refreshing and delicious *pipa fría* (cold coconut water) **4:** Punta Catedral, as seen during a coastal sailing tour

Manuel Antonio

The beachfront in Manuel Antonio hosts several souvenir shops and tables where artisans display their crafts. For higher-end products, visit **Regálame** (beside the Si Como No Resort, tel. 506/2777-0777, 7am-10pm daily). The large store carries most typical Costa Rican souvenirs, including T-shirts, wood products, and jewelry, but it also has a comprehensive collection of art pieces for sale, mainly paintings. There's ample parking out front.

FOOD
Quepos
COSTA RICAN

A good place in Quepos to get a *casado* (traditional dish of rice and beans accompanied by a variety of side dishes) is **La Cocina** (Avenida Central, 100 m west of the post office, tel. 506/2774-0036, www.lacocinaquepos.com, 6am-10pm daily, $4.50-12.50). The small diner is more modern than a typical *soda* (traditional Costa Rican family restaurant). Its low prices, large portions, and friendly service make it worth a stop.

INTERNATIONAL

One of my favorite restaurants in downtown Quepos is the family-friendly ★ **El Gran Escape** (corner of Avenida 1 and Calle 4, tel. 506/2777-7850, www.elgranescapequepos.com, 11am-11pm daily, $7-25.50). Its vibe is both social and laid-back. The establishment's varied menu, with chicken wings, nachos, tacos, burgers, steaks, sandwiches, and soups, satisfies foreigners. Larger than most restaurants in town, the spot is a great choice for groups.

Quepos's finest food selection is at the upscale **Gabriella's** (Marina Pez Vela, tel. 506/2519-9300, www.gabriellassteakhouse.com, 4pm-10pm daily, $20-70). A few of the restaurant's many mouthwatering (and pricey) dishes include grilled mahi-mahi topped with avocado and amaretto, lobster stuffed with shrimp, and a seafood platter doused in passion fruit with roasted almonds.

Save room for banana flambé or one of the other tempting desserts.

Fish and seafood dishes dominate most of this fishing town's menus, but you can find fabulous Italian food at **Mercato del Porto** (Marina Pez Vela, tel. 506/2519-9091, www. mercatodelporto.com, 7am-10pm daily, $7-26). The waterfront restaurant offers a front-row seat at the marina, allowing you to gaze at yachts while chowing down on pizzas, pastas, or antipasti. Go in the early morning and you can have Italian eggs, breakfast pizza, or one of several typical Costa Rican breakfast plates.

Manuel Antonio

COSTA RICAN

The Manuel Antonio area is blessed with several fabulous ocean views, but it's hard to top the one that fronts **Mi Lugar** (off Road 618, 750 m south of Amigos del Río, tel. 506/2777-5120, www.ronnysplace.com, noon-10pm daily, $5.50-22). Nicknamed and known by most as **Ronny's Place,** the restaurant has a few international dishes such as pastas, hamburgers, and burritos, but I like its Costa Rican preparations. Try one of four different types of ceviche or delicious black bean soup. The restaurant also has yummy fish, shrimp, and chicken brochettes.

INTERNATIONAL

Regarded by many as Manuel Antonio's must-see restaurant, **El Avión** (Road 618, 2.5 km northwest of the entrance to the national park, tel. 506/2777-3378, www.elavion.net, noon-11pm daily, $10-25) is built in and around a C-123 Fairchild cargo plane set among the mountains. The two-story dining establishment offers panoramic ocean and forest views that are spectacular at sunset. The menu lists salad, sandwich, seafood, beef, pasta, and rice selections, but the novelty of the restaurant's setting is what's most appealing. A small pub occupies the plane's fuselage. Grab a cocktail and take a photo in the cockpit!

★ **El Lagarto** (Road 618, 4 km northwest of the entrance to the national park, tel. 506/2777-6932, www.ellagartobbq.com, 3pm-11pm daily, $10-33.50) is the go-to spot for food prepared *a la parrilla* (on the grill). The restaurant offers barbecued chicken, vegetables, fish, lobster, shrimp, and octopus, plus loads of beef cuts. To produce meals of the highest caliber, El Lagarto sources ingredients from around the country, bringing in high-grade beef from the Northern Zone's plains, seafood caught off the coast of the Nicoya Peninsula, and vegetables grown in the Central Valley. The restaurant's open design allows you to watch chefs prepare your meal on wood-burning grills.

You would never know that the **Barba Roja Restaurante** (Road 618, 3 km northwest of the entrance to the national park, tel. 506/2777-0331, www.barbarojarestaurante. com, noon-10pm daily, $7-32) is one of Manuel Antonio's oldest restaurants just by looking at it. Established in 1975, the pirate-themed restaurant—named for the red-bearded pirate Jeireddín Barbarroja—is a fresh, fun hang-out spot that often has live music and sports broadcasts on big-screen TVs. It is also one of the few places in Manuel Antonio where you can get sushi and slow-cooked ribs, but it has plenty of other delicious delights, including six kinds of steak, six types of tacos, and a full breakfast menu. The ocean view at this place is *arrr*-guably the best around.

VEGETARIAN AND VEGAN

One of Manuel Antonio's best cafés is also a fantastic choice for diners who don't eat meat or dairy products. Not only does ★ **El Patio de Café Milagro** (Road 618, 3 km northwest of the entrance to the national park, tel. 506/2777-2272, 7am-10pm daily, $10-26) provide a warm and cozy ambience, but 18 of its menu items cater to vegetarians, and 10 are suitable for vegans. Several accommodate gluten-free diets too. My favorite thing to order for dinner is La Feria, which features quinoa and grilled vegetables purchased fresh from the market. Go for lunch and you can try the mango and chayote salad, with nuts and greens tossed with a passion fruit vinaigrette.

For a quick bite, head to the **Falafel Bar** (Road 618, 3.5 km northwest of the entrance to the national park, tel. 506/2777-4135, 11am-9pm daily, $6-11.50). You can order falafels on their own or as part of a pita sandwich with hummus. The place also has healthy fusion smoothies that come in unique flavor combinations, including pineapple and mint, banana and date, melon and honey, and blackberry and ginger. The food is best enjoyed while lounging on one of the comfy benches on the small establishment's shaded front patio.

★ **La Luna** (Gaia Hotel and Reserve, off Road 618, tel. 506/2777-9797, www.gaiahr. com, 6am-10pm daily, $10-35), a fine-dining restaurant, boasts a special menu for vegan and vegetarian customers separate from the restaurant's main menu. Ask for it if it isn't automatically given to you by waitstaff. Appetizers (including mango tartare with avocado, and grilled vegetables with chia and mustard dressing), various entrées, and dessert are offered by the mountaintop establishment. My favorite dish here is made of pasta, broccoli, almonds, and coconut milk.

ACCOMMODATIONS

Manuel Antonio has both mountain hotels and accommodations near the beach. While proximity to a beach is a must for many travelers, most of Manuel Antonio's best hotels are away from the water, perched cliffside on quiet, private, and luxurious properties. They require you to drive or take a bus, taxi, or hotel shuttle service to the beach, but the travel time is 10 minutes or less. Most visitors agree that the trip is worth making to have a peaceful mountaintop retreat to return to at the end of the day.

There's little reason to base yourself in Quepos. Most of its accommodation options are economical hostels and hotels. Instead, if you're on a budget, choose an inexpensive accommodation in Manuel Antonio so you don't miss out on the community's unique energy.

Manuel Antonio
UNDER $50
The happening hostel in town is **Selina Manuel Antonio** (Road 618, 2.5 km northwest of the entrance to the national park, tel. 506/2101-8823, www.selina.com, dorm $20, private $90 s/d). It attracts young travelers with its lantern-lit pool areas (complete with pool inflatables), a tiki-style bar, a pool table, and a yoga deck. Dorms with bunk beds sleep 4-12 people and are equipped with lights, shelves, and lockers for individual guest use. Most of the 38 private rooms accommodate two guests.

$50-100
An affordable accommodation in Manuel Antonio that offers good value is **La Colina** (Road 618, 4 km northwest of the entrance to the national park, tel. 506/6101-6007, www. lacolina.com, $80 s/d). This three-story hotel has 13 rooms with one or two queen beds, air-conditioning, a safe, and a private bath. Some rooms face the jungle, and others have an ocean view. Guests have access to two pools and the hotel's restaurant, which offers a complimentary breakfast. Though it feels outdated, this hotel remains one of the few solid options in Manuel Antonio that isn't overpriced.

$100-150
If you favor proximity to the national park, **La Posada Jungle Hotel** (off Road 618, 50 m northwest of the entrance to the national park, tel. 506/2777-1446, www.laposadajungle.com, $140 s/d) is right beside the protected land area. The two-story hotel has 12 beachy, brightly decorated rooms that add to the property's upbeat aura. The pool, common area, and restaurant are small but provide enough space for socializing. Reserve your stay a few months in advance; the property tends to sell out.

$150-250
One of the quietest places I've come across in Manuel Antonio is **Hotel Plaza Yara** (Road 618, 5 km northwest of the entrance to

the national park, tel. 506/2777-4846, www. hotelplazayara.com, $160 s/d). Fifteen oversize suites with kitchenettes and bamboo furniture fill the two-story structure. Located on the main road that connects Quepos to Manuel Antonio, the hotel hides a tropical forest out back. There are gathering areas in each suite, which, depending on the space, might be a balcony or might be an interior space set by large window. The hotel's pool and the lovely alfresco breakfast area border the peaceful jungle and provide scenic areas for relaxing.

Each time I stay at ★ **Hotel Playa Espadilla** (off Road 618, 400 m northwest of the entrance to the national park, tel. 506/2777-0903, www.espadilla.com, $220 s/d), I awake to the calls of howler monkeys in the nearby national park. Location is key at this hotel, which has 16 rooms in two buildings connected by a set of staircases. The spacious rooms are decorated in warm colors and feature cathedral ceilings with dark wood beams; second-floor rooms have balconies. On-site you'll find a restaurant with a bar, pools, and a tennis court.

OVER $250

My favorite upscale resort in the region is the family-friendly and rainforest-inspired ★ **Si Como No Resort** (Road 618, 2.5 km northwest of the entrance to the national park, tel. 506/2777-0777, www.sicomono.com, $275 s/d). The luxury here is understated. You'll notice it in the resort's multitiered design, beautifully landscaped property, colorful stained-glass decor, substantial buffet breakfast, friendly service, and sustainable practices. Each of the 58 spacious, comfortable rooms is perched on the Manuel Antonio mountainside and offers a private balcony where you can enjoy jungle or ocean views. There are no televisions around to distract you, and the resort's pools, bars, restaurants, and spa will spoil you. Resort guests can also access a nearby butterfly atrium for free.

Issimo Suites (off Road 618, 4 km northwest of the entrance to the national park, tel. 506/2777-4410, www.issimosuites.com, $311 s/d) is my recommendation for couples and honeymooners. The hotel just oozes romance. Each suite is outfitted with a king bed, flowers, walls of windows that feature jungle and ocean views, a Jacuzzi, and a bathroom with a bidet. Soothing live music at the hotel's restaurant (which also provides room service) and aromatherapy massages performed with essential oils at the on-site spa add to the intimate experience that Issimo aims to provide.

The four villas at the **Espadilla Ocean Club** (Road 618, 1 km northwest of the entrance to the national park, tel. 506/2777-6810, www.espadillaoceanclub.com, $495 s/d) are my preferred vacation rentals. Each one sleeps five people and has two floors, two bathrooms, a private pool, and an outdoor shower. The contemporary buildings are light and airy, outfitted with stainless steel appliances, and designed to showcase minimalist, "floating" elements including beds, seating areas, and staircases. Tucked away in the vegetation that separates Manuel Antonio's main road from Playa Espadilla Norte, the villas are within walking distance of the ocean.

INFORMATION AND SERVICES

On the outskirts of Quepos is **Hospital Maximiliano Terán Valls** (Hwy. 34, 650 m northwest of the Quepos airport, tel. 506/2774-9500, 24 hours daily), the hospital that serves much of the central Pacific coast.

In town, Marina Pez Vela has a **police station** (Quepos, tel. 506/2777-7140, 24 hours daily) and a **clinic,** called **Hospital Metropolitano** (tel. 506/2519-9733, 9am-7pm Mon.-Fri., 8am-1pm Sat.), with a **pharmacy.**

The downtown core has several **banks** and **supermarkets.** The **post office** (tel. 506/2643-2175, Quepos, 8am-4:30pm Mon.-Fri., 8am-noon Sat.) is on the north side of the *fútbol* field.

In Manuel Antonio, there are **supermarkets, pharmacies,** and **banks.** You'll find them along Road 618. You can have your clothes washed at **Lavandería Lucimaria** (Road 618 beside Amigos del Río, Manuel Antonio, tel. 506/8492-2233, 8am-9pm daily). However, many hotels in the vicinity offer laundry services to guests.

There is a **gas station** (1 km north of the airport) just east of Quepos where Highway 34, Road 235, and Road 616 meet. There's also a gas station to the north of town, on Highway 34, 2.5 kilometers before the turn-off to Quepos at Road 235.

TRANSPORTATION
Getting There
AIR
The **Aeropuerto Quepos** (XQP) is five kilometers (a 10-minute drive) northeast of downtown Quepos. **SANSA Airlines** (tel. 506/2290-4100, www.flysansa.com) offers direct flights to Quepos from San José daily. The flight time from San José is approximately 30 minutes.

Taxis operated by the **Manuel Antonio Taxi Service** (tel. 506/2777-3080, 24 hours daily) can be called to the airport to take you wherever you need to go. Expect to pay $20-25 for a ride to most hotels around Manuel Antonio.

CAR
To get to Quepos and Manuel Antonio from **San José,** it's a 170-kilometer drive west on Highway 27, then south on Highway 34; the trip takes nearly three hours. From **Liberia,** it's a 255-kilometer drive south on Highway 1, Highway 27, and Highway 34 that takes a little less than four hours. From **La Fortuna,** it's a 245-kilometer drive south on Road 702, Highway 1, Highway 27, and Highway 34 that takes almost five hours. From **Monteverde,** it's a 190-kilometer, 3.5-hour drive southeast on Road 606, Highway 1, Highway 27, and Highway 34.

Highway 34, the main road that leads to Quepos from the northwest and the southeast, is a paved highway that poses few obstacles, apart from occasional potholes, people walking along the side of the highway, and possible wildlife crossings. The turnoff to Quepos is at Road 235. Departing from the southeast corner of Quepos, Road 618 connects the town to Manuel Antonio and the national park. It's equally easy to drive, although it is curvy in some places.

BUS
The **regional bus station** is in the heart of Quepos on Avenida Central between Calle Central and Calle 2. Public **buses** travel to Quepos daily. You can catch one from **San José** (multiple times 6am-7:30pm daily, 3.5 hours, $8-8.5), **Puntarenas** (multiple times 4:30am-5:30pm daily, 3 hours, $4.50), **Dominical** (multiple times 6:30am-7:30pm daily, 1.5-2 hours, $3), and **Uvita** (5:30am, 11:30am, 1pm, and 4pm daily, 2 hours, $3-3.50).

PRIVATE TRANSFER SERVICE
Desafío Adventure Company (tel. 506/2479-0020, www.desafiocostarica.com) offers private transfer services to Quepos and Manuel Antonio with free Wi-Fi on board their vehicles. Prices average around $200-250 from San José, $250-300 from La Fortuna, and $200 from Monteverde. Vehicles vary in size, but most accommodate up to eight people plus luggage. Some vehicles can fit up to 28 passengers.

SHARED SHUTTLE SERVICE
Interbus (tel. 506/4100-0888, www.interbusonline.com) offers daily shared shuttle services to Quepos and Manuel Antonio from San José, Jacó, La Fortuna, and Monteverde. **Grayline Costa Rica** (tel. 506/2220-2126, www.graylinecostarica.com) travels to Quepos and Manuel Antonio from San José, Puntarenas, Dominical, Uvita, La Fortuna, Monteverde, Tamarindo, Brasilito, Playa Flamingo, Playas del Coco, Papagayo, and Rincón de la Vieja. One-way services cost $39-93 per person. Most shuttles fit eight

people with luggage and offer drop-offs at Quepos and Manuel Antonio hotels.

ORGANIZED TOUR

A few adventure and nature tours by **Desafio Adventure Company** (tel. 506/2479-0020, www.desafiocostarica.com) include **post-tour onward transportation** to Quepos from a variety of destinations. Tours can be arranged to include a pickup from your hotel in La Fortuna, Monteverde, or San José, then a drop-off at your hotel in Manuel Antonio.

Getting Around

The paved Road 618 that winds through Manuel Antonio has inclines, declines, curves, and barely any sidewalks. The safest way to travel this stretch is in a vehicle. Walking, biking, or relying on scooters or golf carts is not recommended.

CAR AND TAXI

Driving around Quepos and Manuel Antonio does not require a 4x4 vehicle. Quepos has a few one-way streets; traffic flows west on **Avenida 5** at the north end of town and traffic flows east on **Avenida 2** at the south end of town. **Road 618,** known as Avenida 2 in Quepos, is a two-way street. It goes through Manuel Antonio and ends at a roundabout in front of the beach.

BUS

Public **buses** (multiple times 5:45am-10pm daily, 25 minutes, $1) travel from Quepos to Playa Espadilla Norte and the national park (and vice versa), passing through Manuel Antonio along the way.

SHARED SHUTTLE SERVICE

Blue Horizon Costa Rica (Road 235, 1 km north of Marina Pez Vela, tel. 506/2277-9292, www.bluehorizoncostarica.com) operates a **beach concierge service** ($12 pp, cash only) that provides on-demand transportation to and from area hotels and the beach. Included in the service cost is the rental of a beach tent and chairs.

★ PARQUE NACIONAL MANUEL ANTONIO

One of Costa Rica's most beloved and busiest attractions, **Parque Nacional Manuel Antonio** (Manuel Antonio National Park, 500 m northeast of Road 618 at Playa Espadilla Norte, tel. 506/2777-5185, www.sinac.go.cr, 7am-4pm Tues.-Sun., last entry 3pm, $16 adults, free for seniors and children 11 and under) is also one of its smallest national parks, occupying less than 5,000 acres of land and an additional 60,000 acres of ocean. The park's nearly 500,000 visitors each year come for beautiful crescent beaches, where monkeys are known to fraternize with people on the sand. Despite its relatively small size, the park is jam-packed with trails, beaches, and lookout points. Well-designed and -maintained trails lead through forested areas, and sightings of sloths (both two-toed and three-toed varieties) are nearly guaranteed. If your ideal day in Costa Rica combines beach relaxation, light nature exploration, and wildlife encounters, you can tick all three off your travel list with just a few hours in this park.

Purchase tickets through the bank cooperative **Coopealianza,** which has an office (7am-3pm daily) on the unnamed road that connects Playa Espadilla Norte to the park, as well as another office in Quepos (Avenida 5 at Calle 3, 8am-5pm Mon.-Fri., 8am-noon Sat.). An iron gate 50 meters southeast of Manuel Antonio's Coopealianza office marks the **entrance** to the park. Just beyond the gate is the park's **ranger station.** Your park ticket is good for one entry; come-and-go access is not permitted.

Food is not available for purchase in the park. Additionally, in an effort to reduce trash and protect wildlife, most foods with wrappers aren't permitted inside the park. Cans, glass containers, aluminum foil, alcoholic beverages, foods that contain nuts or seeds, and prepackaged snacks (such as granola bars and chips) are not allowed on park property. You can, however, bring in peeled fruit and vegetables, unwrapped crackers and cookies, and sandwiches in either paper bags or reusable plastic containers (but you must pack all leftovers, bags, and containers back out when you leave, of course). Reusable bottles containing non-alcoholic beverages are also permitted. Expect your bags and backpacks to be searched upon entry.

An overwhelming number of tour guides congregate near the entrance, but the best guides are secured in advance. I've always had a blast touring the park with—and learning a lot from—the tour guides behind **Manuel Antonio Expeditions** (also known as Águila Tours, tel. 506/8365-1057, www.juanbrenes. blogspot.com). Their **Manuel Antonio National Park Tour** (8:30am and 1pm daily, 3 hours, $51 adults, $35 children 0-11) is a wildlife-spotting expedition. Guides come ready with spotting scopes, trained eyes, and years of experience that help them catch what others miss. The guided tour experience includes the park entrance fee and round-trip transportation from Manuel Antonio and Quepos hotels. If you have a rental car and buy your own park ticket, one of the company's guides can be hired for $25 per person. If you're drawn to the park for its beaches, you won't need a tour guide; simply buy your ticket and go.

Beaches

Upon entering the park, many visitors head straight for **Playa Manuel Antonio** to spend anywhere from 20 minutes to eight hours stretched out on one of the country's most idyllic stretches of supple white sand. Long visits are made easy by nearby bathrooms, showers, picnic tables, and a water station. You'll revel in calm waves, a shallow shoreline, and turquoise waters. Get there by taking the **Sendero El Manglar** (El Manglar Trail) and keeping straight toward **Sendero El Perezoso** (El Perezoso Trail) when the trail forks.

If Playa Manuel Antonio is too crowded for you to relax at comfortably, retreat to one of the park's other, equally stunning beaches, including the tiny cove at **Playa Gemelas** to the east of Playa Manuel Antonio, or the long **Playa Espadilla Sur** to the west.

Nearly enclosed by forest, Playa Gemelas is two small beaches split by a rocky outcrop; it's one of the quietest, most private beaches in the park. **Sendero Playa Gemelas** (Playa Gemelas Trail) leads right to it.

Playa Espadilla Sur is a wide, long beach regularly frequented by park visitors who find Playa Manuel Antonio too busy. From the south end of Playa Manuel Antonio, **Sendero**

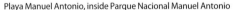

Playa Manuel Antonio, inside Parque Nacional Manuel Antonio

Wildlife Bridges

As you travel through Manuel Antonio, you'll notice several cables overhead. These ropes aren't mini zip lines; they're monkey bridges! Thanks to the 130-plus lines, monkeys and other wildlife can avoid run-ins with cars and electrocution caused by crossing high-voltage wires. The area's population of endangered mono tití monkeys (also called squirrel monkeys) has more than doubled since the initial placement of the monkey bridges.

The simple design is one of many projects crafted by **Kids Saving the Rainforest** (www. kidssavingtherainforest.org), an American charity formed in 1999 by two motivated young girls. Today, the organization has grown to include a wildlife rescue center and a wildlife sanctuary, both in the Manuel Antonio vicinity. The organization is also actively involved in area reforestation and community awareness.

If you're interested in learning more about the rainforest, its wildlife, and what you can do to help, the website for Kids Saving the Rainforest provides a wealth of information. In Costa Rica, you can get involved by touring or volunteering at the group's wildlife facilities, or by donating items that you have brought from home (see the Wish List section on the website for ideas). If, after returning home, you're still thinking about the cute animals that the center is working to protect, you can continue to support the cause by adopting an animal, fundraising for the cause, or sponsoring the maintenance of a monkey bridge.

Remember: Never feed any wildlife you encounter, as this can cause harm to the animals in myriad ways.

Playa Espadilla Sur (Playa Espadilla Sur Trail) provides access to Playa Espadilla Sur.

Hiking

The park's most popular trails are the **Sendero El Manglar** (El Manglar Trail, 785 m one-way, 15 minutes, easy), which is a raised boardwalk bordered on both sides by mangrove ecosystems, and the narrow forest path **Sendero El Perezoso** (El Perezoso Trail, 650 m one-way, 15 minutes, easy), which provides access to Playa Manuel Antonio. Sendero El Manglar's wheelchair-accessible boardwalk provides a peek at the area's woody mangroves. It also includes informational placards in Braille. Sendero El Perezoso is aptly named (*perezoso* means "lazy"), as its namesake sloths sleep in the trees that line the trail, while frogs, lizards, and iguanas scurry below with the sound of your footsteps.

From Playa Manuel Antonio, **Sendero Playa Espadilla Sur** (Playa Espadilla Sur Trail, 650 m one-way, 15 minutes, easy) leads west to Playa Espadilla Sur, then runs north along the beach and connects with Sendero El Manglar.

To really get to know the park and uncover its less obvious beauty, explore one of its other trails. The **Sendero Punta Catedral** (Punta Catedral Trail, 1.4-km loop, 1 hour, moderate-difficult) begins just south of Playa Manuel Antonio. This dense forest hike offers decent bird-watching and ocean and island views.

Sendero Playa Gemelas (Playa Gemelas Trail, 550 m one-way, 10 minutes, easy-moderate), **Sendero Puerto Escondido** (Puerto Escondido Trail, 450 m one-way, 10 minutes, easy-moderate), **Sendero Congo** (Congo Trail, 300 m one-way, 10 minutes, easy-moderate), and **Sendero Miradores** (Miradores Trail, 1.3 km one-way, 1 hour, moderate-difficult) connect with one another and are best completed as a set. They lead through the least visited areas of the park where you're most likely to run into one of the park's 107 animal varieties. (Keep an eye open for endangered squirrel monkeys, referred to by locals as mono tití monkeys; Manuel Antonio is one of only a few places in the country where you can spot the breed.) Lookout points that frame lush, textured headlands juxtaposed with soft stretches of sandy coast are abundant, but be prepared to climb lengthy staircases to reach them.

Getting There

The park is within walking distance of Playa Espadilla Norte and most beachfront hotels. Many high-end Manuel Antonio hotels include a complimentary shuttle to the park entrance.

To drive to the park from Quepos or the mountainous section of Manuel Antonio, take Road 618 south to beach level and turn left at the Marlin Restaurant. Follow the short side road until it ends just before the park's entrance. Parking lots are scattered all around; expect to pay roughly $10 for the day.

Costa Ballena

South of Quepos and Manuel Antonio, Highway 34 angles toward the coast and passes through dense plantations of lofty African palms, whose fruit produces oil for use in cosmetics, soaps, and other household products. The highway narrowly meets the water at the lackadaisical and popular surf town of Dominical, continues down the coast to the village of Uvita—home to Parque Nacional Marino Ballena—and then bypasses Ojochal, a small collection of upscale establishments.

Together, the trio of destinations forms the Costa Ballena (Ballena Coast), spanning roughly 35 kilometers of coastline. This burgeoning section of the central Pacific coast threw its hat into the tourism ring in 2010 after improved highway conditions eased access to the area. Leisurely drives through the region are particularly scenic, thanks to rainforest-covered mountains in the northern sections and up-close ocean views in the southern parts. Detours off the highway lead to empty beaches, forest-wrapped waterfalls, mountainside homesteads, and hotels with panoramic views. Though hopping between destinations along the Costa Ballena is easy, most visitors base themselves in one area, typically Dominical or Uvita, and make day trips to area attractions.

DOMINICAL

Dominical is a small, noncommercial surf town and the most popular of the three destinations along the Costa Ballena. From the moment you turn off the highway onto the main dirt road, you'll feel like you've entered a local community, not a tourist trap— except for the row of vendors who display souvenirs on tables near the waterfront. Development in the area is evident but subtle; the only high-rises around are the tall palms that back the beach, which mirrors the town's easygoing vibe. Backpackers and young travelers station themselves here to soak up the sun, socialize, and laze around like sloths.

The well-defined, triangle-shaped town sits immediately east of Río Barú, south of Highway 34, and north of Playa Dominical, the town's namesake beach. It's home to several expats who have applied English names to a few of the town's roads. **Main Street,** which connects with Highway 34, serves as the town's main drag and parallels the beach.

Sights

TOP EXPERIENCE

★ CATARATAS NAUYACA

North of Dominical, the two-tier, 65-meter **Cataratas Nauyaca** (Nauyaca Waterfalls, Road 243, 10 km north of Dominical, tel. 506/2787-0541, www. nauyacawaterfallscostarica.com, 7am-5pm Mon.-Sat., 8am-4pm Sun., last entry 2:30pm) are some of Costa Rica's most stunning cascades. Tucked among dense rainforest and scenic rolling hills, the two remote waterfalls are especially beautiful

Dominical and Vicinity

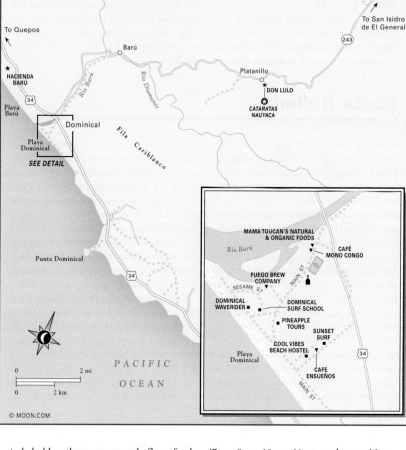

To Quepos

★ HACIENDA BARÚ

Barú

Río Barú

34

Playa Barú

Dominical

Playa Dominical

SEE DETAIL

Fila Cariblanco

Río Diamante

Platanillo

☆ DON LULO

◉ CATARATAS NAUYACA

To San Isidro de El General

243

Punta Dominical

34

PACIFIC

OCEAN

0   2 mi
0   2 km

© MOON.COM

MAMA TOUCAN'S NATURAL & ORGANIC FOODS

Río Barú

CAFÉ MONO CONGO

FUEGO BREW COMPANY

SESAME ST

MAIN ST

DOMINICAL WAVERIDER

DOMINICAL SURF SCHOOL

PINEAPPLE TOURS

SUNSET SURF

COOL VIBES BEACH HOSTEL

Playa Dominical

CAFE ENSUEÑOS

MAIN ST

34

to behold as the upper cascade flows freely into the lower. The taller **upper waterfall** is flanked on both sides by craggy canyon walls. Giant boulders at its base add to the dramatic scene. Water flows from here to the **lower waterfall,** where it tumbles into a natural pool that's great for swimming. At this cascade's base, you'll find a quiet, peaceful space, fresh water, bright-green flora, and few distractions.

The falls are on the private property of Don Lulo, who grants **hiking access** (trail access fee $8), runs **4x4 transportation** to the falls

(7am, 9am, 10am, 11am, and noon Mon.-Sat., $28 pp), and offers guided **waterfall tours** (8am Mon.-Sat., 5.5 hours, $70 pp) and **horseback tours** (8am Mon.-Sat., 5.5 hours, $70 pp, min. age 3).

The guided tours include breakfast, lunch, the trail access fee, and transportation to the falls. There's also plenty of time for swimming once you reach the falls. Your guide will show you how and where to safely climb and jump off the rocks into the cascade's refreshing pool.

If you choose to hike, be prepared for a long

walk. If you don't have a 4x4 vehicle, you'll be hiking six kilometers out to the falls and another six back. If you do have a 4x4, it's just four kilometers each way. The challenging trail is steep and rolling. Be sure to bring sturdy footwear; the dusty route gets muddy and slippery when it rains.

For those who don't want the full tour experience but also don't want to walk a long way, there is another choice. Referred to on Don Lulo's website as the Economic 4x4 Tour, this option is a transportation service rather than a tour. At the appointed time, you'll hop in the back of a 4x4 vehicle that will drive you to the falls. Note: Vehicle seats are limited, and preference is given to guided tour participants.

To get to Don Lulo's property from Dominical, take Road 243 northeast for about 10 kilometers. You'll find a small office, well signed for the waterfalls, on the east side of the highway.

HACIENDA BARÚ

Separated from Dominical by Rio Barú is the combined theme park and wildlife refuge **Hacienda Barú** (Hwy. 34, 3.5 km northwest of Dominical, tel. 506/2787-0003, www.haciendabaru.com, 6am-6pm daily). The 830-acre multifunctional property is a kaleidoscope of ecosystems. It contains primary forest, secondary forest, swamps, mangroves, riverbanks, and more than 2.5 kilometers of shoreline. Activities available here include hiking, bird-watching, an obstacle course, and zip-lining. Self-guided exploration of the property is possible with a **day pass** ($12 pp). If you wish to stay overnight, there's also a small lodge with six rooms and six cottages on-site.

You can explore a section of hilly terrain via the guided **Rainforest Experience** (7:30am Mon.-Sat., 3-4 hours, $44 pp) or take a light stroll along easy trails during the guided **Mangrove Walk** (6am and 3pm Mon.-Sat., 2-3 hours, $39 pp). Scale the seven-meter bird-watching tower—best visited before 7am or after 3pm—to increase your odds of spotting some of the 330 bird species seen in the area.

The on-site **Monkey Challenge** (8am, 11am, and 2pm daily, 15-30 minutes, $19 pp, min. age 10) is an obstacle course that combines tree climbing, rope-bridge crossings, and a free fall. The **Flight of the Toucan Canopy Tour** (8am, 11am, and 2pm daily, 2-3 hours, $49 pp, min. age 3) is ideal for timid or first-time zip-liners. I describe the tour as mild, not wild.

bottom tier of the Cataratas Nauyaca

To get here from Dominical, take Highway 34 north for 3.5 kilometers.

Beaches

Dominical's principal beach is **Playa Dominical.** From Rio Barú in the north, the beach fronts the entire town for one kilometer, then continues south for another kilometer along undeveloped coastline. Most of the beach's visitors come to surf, so they don't mind that the dark-gray sand is often awash with debris and not ideal for sunbathing. And, of course, where there's great surf, swimming conditions are usually dangerous. Watch yourself in the water here, as riptides reign supreme. The beach is one of the few in the country that have lifeguards, so help is close by if you get into trouble.

Recreation

SURFING

Despite its diminutive size, Dominical is rife with surf schools. You cannot go wrong with most; each has rave-worthy instructors, teaching techniques, and customer service. Nearly all provide surf lessons, but some provide unique offerings.

Sunset Surf (MAVI Surf Hotel, tel. 506/8917-3143, www.sunsetsurfdominical. com, 9am-5pm daily) has 7-, 10-, and 14-day **surf packages** ($1,575-2,819 pp), including an itinerary tailored toward families.

The **Dominical Surf School** (Sesame St., tel. 506/8853-4860, www.dominicalsurfschool. com, 8am-5pm daily) has an eight-day **women's surf camp** ($1,165 pp).

Dominical Waverider (Playa Dominical, 200 m northwest of Main St., tel. 506/8311-8950, www.dominicalwaverider.com, 8am-5pm daily) offers **advanced one-day surf tours** ($60-200 pp) to areas outside of Dominical.

Hidden in the mountains north of town, the **Kalon Surf Resort** (3 km north of Hwy. 34 at Hatillo, tel. 506/8708-3766, www. kalonsurf.com) couples surf lessons with luxury for an eight-day, **all-inclusive surf resort experience** ($2,740-3,210 pp).

Food

Start the day off right with one of nearly 20 sweet and savory breakfast options—many vegetarian and vegan—at ★ **Café Mono Congo** (Main St., 100 m west of Hwy. 34, tel. 506/8485-5523, www.cafemonocongo.com, 7am-5pm daily, $3-9.50). Wash it down with a cup of the café's signature Monkey Punch coffee, or my preferred smoothie, the Banana-Espresso Wake Up, a blend of coffee, banana, and cacao. Built on the southern bank of Rio Barú, the café has a river view that is almost as delightful as the staff is friendly.

For lunch, head to **Cafe Ensueños** (75 m north of the main street in Dominical, tel. 506/2787-0282, www.ensuenosdominical. com, 6:30am-8pm daily, $3.50-8) for flavorful, inexpensive Costa Rican food. This spot serves eight different *casados* plus soups, salads, pastas, and hamburgers.

Dinner and drinks are great at the two-story ★ **Fuego Brew Company** (Sesame St., tel. 506/8992-9559, www.fuegobrew.com, 11:30am-10:30pm daily, $8.50-26). Draped in bohemian decor, the upscale restaurant and bar stays true to Dominical's vibe while bringing a touch of class. The place serves more appetizers than entrées, likely so you'll have room to down glasses of their six kinds of craft beer. The brewery is on the bottom floor; the restaurant and bar are on the top.

To cure the munchies morning, noon, or night, check out **Mama Toucan's Natural & Organic Foods** (Main St., 100 m west of Hwy. 34, tel. 506/8433-4235, www. mamatoucans.com, 9am-8pm daily, $1-6). The shop is regularly stocked with fresh fruit, baked goods, chocolate bars, and ice cream. It also has a salad bar.

Accommodations

One of the most extraordinary overnight experiences you can have in Costa Rica is ★ **cave camping at the Catarata Diamante** (Diamante Waterfall), immediately east of Dominical. The group behind the tour operator **Pacific Journeys** (2.5 km south of Road 243, Tinamaste, tel.

506/2266-1717, www.pacificjourneyscr.com, 8am-5pm Mon.-Fri.) operates the two-day guided **Diamante Journey** (8:30am daily, $159 adults, $79.50 children 0-6), which features a hike to the 183-meter waterfall's highest point and an overnight stay in an open-air rock crevice—nicknamed Casa de Piedra, the Rock House—at the side of the cascade. Also included are exploration of an organic garden and three healthy vegetarian meals. Nature doesn't get any closer; you'll fall asleep to the sound of the water's soothing thunder while tucked away in a natural stone cave under a starry sky. For your convenience and comfort, the cave (which sleeps up to 25 people) is equipped with toilets, showers, and raised platform beds. Sleeping bags, pads, liners, and pillows are provided. You can even add rappelling down the waterfall ($70 pp) to your once-in-a-lifetime stay.

If you're strapped for cash, spend your nights at the **Cool Vibes Beach Hostel** (75 m north of the main street in Dominical, tel. 506/8353-6428, www.hosteldominical.com, dorm $14 pp, private $40 s/d). Living up to its name, the accommodation is a typical surf hostel complete with complimentary surfboard racks. It makes up for the bare-bones rooms with above-par facilities, including a cozy and comfy lounge area and a large communal kitchen. Best of all, the place is steps from the beach.

Information and Services

In Quepos, **Hospital Maximiliano Terán Valls** (Hwy. 34, 650 m northwest of the Quepos airport, tel. 506/2774-9500, 24 hours daily) serves most of the central Pacific coast's communities. It's a 40-kilometer drive northwest of Dominical.

Banco de Costa Rica (Centro Comercial Plaza Pacifica, Hwy. 34, tel. 506/2442-7700, 9am-4pm Mon.-Fri.) has an **ATM** (5am-midnight daily). It's on Highway 34, just east of the turnoff to Dominical. On Dominical's main road are a few **supermarkets** and a **police station** (tel. 506/2787-0406, 24 hours daily).

The closest **gas station** is three kilometers northwest of Dominical on Highway 34.

Transportation

There are two ways to get to Dominical from downtown **San José.** The easiest and fastest trip parallels the coast on Highway 34 and enters Dominical from the northwest. This **coastal route** is a 210-kilometer drive via Highway 27 and Highway 34 that takes a little over three hours. The alternate trip departs east from San José via Highway 2, climbing steeply over mountains and cutting through clouds at Cerro de la Muerte (Hill of Death). It then descends through the city of San Isidro de El General and enters Dominical via Road 243 from the northeast. This **mountain route** is a 170-kilometer, 3.5-hour drive—though it takes longer when cloud cover slows traffic.

From downtown **Liberia,** Dominical is a 295-kilometer drive via Highway 1, Highway 27, and Highway 34 that takes just over four hours. From **Uvita,** it's an 18-kilometer, 15-minute drive northwest on Highway 34. From **Quepos,** Dominical is a 40-kilometer, 30-minute drive southeast on Highway 34.

To reach Dominical by **bus,** catch one from **San José** (6am and 3pm daily, 5 hours, $8), **Quepos** (multiple times 5:30am-5:30pm daily, 1 hour, $3), or **Uvita** (5:30am-7pm daily, 20 minutes, $2-2.50). Buses end their run in Dominical next to the office for the Instituto Costarricense de Electricidad (ICE), the government-run electrical company.

Desafio Adventure Company (tel. 506/2479-0020, www.desafiocostarica. com) offers **private transfer services** to Dominical with free Wi-Fi on board their vehicles. Prices average around $250 from San José, $125 from Quepos and Manuel Antonio, $300 from La Fortuna, and $275 from Monteverde. Vehicles vary in size, but most accommodate up to eight people plus luggage. Some vehicles can fit up to 28 passengers.

Grayline Costa Rica (tel. 506/2220-2126, www.graylinecostarica.com) offers daily

Uvita

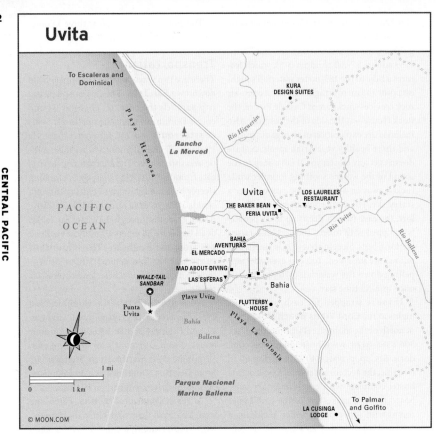

To Escaleras and Dominical

KURA DESIGN SUITES

Río Higuerón

Playa Hermosa

Rancho La Merced

PACIFIC OCEAN

Uvita

LOS LAURELES RESTAURANT

THE BAKER BEAN
FERIA UVITA

Río Uvita

Río Ballena

BAHIA AVENTURAS
EL MERCADO

MAD ABOUT DIVING

WHALE-TAIL SANDBAR
LAS ESFERAS

Bahía

Playa Uvita

FLUTTERBY HOUSE

Punta Uvita

Bahía

Playa La Colonia

Ballena

Parque Nacional Marino Ballena

To Palmar and Golfito

LA CUSINGA LODGE

0   1 mi
0   1 km

© MOON.COM

shared shuttle services to Dominical from San José, Puntarenas, Manuel Antonio, Jacó, La Fortuna, Monteverde, Tamarindo, Brasilito, Playa Flamingo, Playas del Coco, Papagayo, and Rincón de la Vieja. One-way services range $39-89 per person. Most shuttles fit eight people with luggage and offer drop-offs at Dominical hotels.

UVITA

Located 16 kilometers southeast of Dominical and in the middle of the Costa Ballena is the blossoming village of Uvita. Uvita is home to a small, tight-knit, and vibrant community comprised of locals and expats that gives off a warm and welcoming vibe. It is marked by plazas, restaurants, and hotels around Highway 34. The protected beaches and waters contained within Parque Nacional Marino Ballena draw in most visitors.

Bordering Uvita to the south is a neighborhood known as **Bahía** (sometimes called **Bahía Ballena**). You'll find most of Uvita's tour outfitters here, as well as the area's most inexpensive digs and diners. The national park, which sits on the south side of Bahía, is roughly 2 kilometers southwest of Uvita.

Recreation
SNORKELING AND DIVING
The area's most trusted dive operator is **Mad About Diving** (125 m north of the national park entrance, Bahía, tel. 506/2743-8019, www.madaboutdivingcr.com, 7am-2pm Mon.-Fri.). They offer a half-day **scuba diving tour** (7am daily, 3.5-4 hours, $100 per person for

2 tanks, $30 less per person for snorkeling) that explores the underwater world of Parque Nacional Marino Ballena. They also run full-day diving and snorkeling excursions to the Osa Peninsula's Reserva Biológica Isla del Caño ($170 per person for 2 tanks, $120 per person for snorkeling). Equipment rental is included with the cost of both tours.

Festivals and Events

September is a great time of year to visit, as Bahía hosts the annual **Festival de Ballenas y Delfines** (Whale and Dolphin Festival, www.festivaldeballenasydelfines.com). During this multi-day festival, which runs over two consecutive weekends, local tour companies and independent boat captains provide whale- and dolphin-watching boat tours. Each of these **Festival Tours** (7am, 9am, 11am, and 1pm, 2 hours, $35 per person, $25 children 3-9, free for children 2 and under) is planned so that whale and dolphin sightings are nearly guaranteed.

Uvita's famed **Envision Festival** (www.envisionfestival.com) aims to awaken higher levels of consciousness within its attendees. The energetic three-day camping event is a concoction of beats, body painting, yoga, health promotion, dance, meditation, and community collaboration. **Rancho La Merced** (Hwy. 34, 3 km northwest of Uvita, tel. 506/2743-8032, www.rancholamerced.com) hosts the festivities each year, which typically take place in February.

Shopping

Every Saturday, rain or shine, locals and expats meet at the covered **Feria Uvita** (Uvita Farmer's Market, 75 m south of Hwy. 34, opposite the main road in Uvita, 8am-noon Sat.) to sell all kinds of things, ranging from spices to souvenirs. The baked goods in particular are scrumptious! Many of the same products can be purchased on Wednesdays at the village's other farmer's market, **El Mercado** (The Market, between the *fútbol* field and the central park, Bahía, 8am-5pm Wed.), where you can shop while listening to live music.

Food

You can grab pub grub like quesadillas, wraps, nachos, tacos, wings, chilli fries, and more at the casual and homey ★ **Los Laureles Restaurant** (400 m northeast of Hwy. 34, Uvita, tel. 506/2743-8008, 11:30am-8:30pm Mon.-Sat., $7-13). This small, open-air restaurant has a few tables scattered under a wood roof with fans, and is surrounded by natural flora. It's clean and well-kept, and run by a hospitable and appreciative family who provides great customer service.

If you're passing through Uvita, pull over at **The Baker Bean** (Hwy. 34, 150 m southeast of the gas station, Uvita, tel. 506/2743-8990, www.thebakerbean.com, 5:30am-9pm Mon.-Fri., 5:30am-10pm Sat.-Sun., $1-6). This little café packs an amazing punch when it comes to food quality and cost. Quick to-go items include bagels, croissants, and empanadas. With more time, order a pizza or pasta.

Las Esferas (100 m north of the national park entrance, Bahía, tel. 506/2743-8135, 7am-9pm daily, $4.50-11) isn't much to write home about, but the tropical-themed roadside establishment is a convenient place to grab food or drinks while on your way to or from the beach or national park. The colorful spot serves refreshing fruit smoothies, sandwiches, hamburgers, and lots of seafood.

Accommodations

Dorm rooms at the **Flutterby House** (400 m north of Playa Uvita, Bahía, tel. 506/8341-1730, www.flutterbyhouse.com, dorm $15 pp, private $40 s/d) have handmade bunk beds made of natural wood. The hostel also has games, hammocks, a yoga deck, a bouldering wall, a book exchange, and a ping-pong table, but quiet hours (after 10pm) allow the area's natural soundtrack to be heard. Flutterby is eco-friendly: Notice the lack of air conditioning, their use of solar lights, and the upcycled surfboards that serve as furniture.

Most impressive about ★ **Vista Ballena** (1.5 km north of Hwy. 34, 2 km north of Uvita, tel. 506/2743-8150, www.vistaballenahotel.com, $129 s/d) is its panoramic view. From high up in the quiet and remote hills north of Uvita, this hotel overlooks the Pacific Ocean, the national park, and the famed whale-tail sandbar from each of its 20 rooms. The hotel is three separate buildings spread out vertically on a hillside. The top building provides a reception, restaurant, and lounge area complete with a two-tier infinity pool. In the bottom two buildings are fresh and modern rooms (for 1-4 people) with rich, dark-wood furniture, air conditioning, television, and a balcony with an outdoor sitting area perfect for taking in the view.

With some down time in Uvita, you can easily pass a day in a rocking chair on the open-air deck at ★ **La Cusinga Lodge** (450 m west of Hwy. 34, 4.5 km south of Uvita, tel. 506/2743-8271, www.lacusingalodge.com, $182 s/d), gazing at the forest and the sea. The tranquil ecolodge encourages relaxation at its yoga pavilion, restaurant, and lounge area, and invites exploration of nature through on-site trails. Ten simple, rustic, all-wood cabins aim to bring the outdoors in and unite with the jungle, not overpower it.

The eight minimalist, posh, and sexy **Kura Design Suites** (Calle La Colonia, 2 km east of Hwy. 34, tel. 506/8521-3407, www. kuracostarica.com, $790 s/d) will seduce you the moment you set foot on the exclusive resort's grounds. Glass walls, open-floor layouts, espresso machines, and rainfall showerheads are standout features. Resort facilities include a spa, a saltwater infinity pool, a restaurant, and two comfortable lounges.

Information and Services

The closest hospital is **Hospital de Osa Tomás Casas Casajús** (Hwy. 34, just west of Ciudad Cortés, tel. 506/2786-8148, 24 hours daily) in Ciudad Cortés, a 30-kilometer drive southeast of Uvita.

A few **pharmacies,** including **Farmacia Ibarra** (tel. 506/2743-8460, 8am-7pm Mon.-Sat., 8am-1pm Sun.), **banks,** and **supermarkets** huddle around the entrance to Uvita on Highway 34 near Río Uvita.

Additional supermarkets can be found in Bahía.

Just north of the highway is a **police station** (75 m north of Calle La Faralla, tel. 506/2743-8538, 24 hours daily) and the community's **clinic, Ebais Uvita** (tel. 506/2743-8170, 7am-4pm Mon.-Thurs., 7am-3pm Fri.).

There is a **gas station** on Highway 34, northwest of Río Uvita and the turnoff to the beach.

Transportation

There are two ways to get to Uvita from downtown **San José.** Via the **coastal route** (Highway 27 to Highway 34), Uvita is a 230-kilometer, 3.5-hour drive. Via the **mountain route** (Highway 2 to Road 243 to Highway 34), it's a 190-kilometer drive that takes just under four hours.

From downtown **Liberia,** it's a 315-kilometer, 4.5-hour drive southeast via Highway 1, Highway 27, and Highway 34. From **Quepos,** the 60-kilometer drive to Uvita south on Highway 34 takes roughly 45 minutes. From **Dominical,** it's an 18-kilometer, 15-minute drive down the coast on Highway 34. From **Ojochal,** it's a 16-kilometer, 15-minute drive north on Highway 34.

To reach Uvita by **bus,** hop on one from **San José** (6am and 3pm daily, 5.5 hours, $9.50), **Quepos** (multiple times 8:30am-5:30pm daily, 1.5-2 hours, $3), or **Dominical** (multiple times 4:45am-5:30pm daily, 20 minutes, $1.50). Buses end their run alongside Highway 34, 100 meters east of the turn-off to the community of Uvita.

Grayline Costa Rica (tel. 506/2220-2126, www.graylinecostarica.com) offers daily **shared shuttle services** to Uvita from San José, Puntarenas, Manuel Antonio, Jacó, La Fortuna, Monteverde, Tamarindo, Brasilito, Playa Flamingo, Playas del Coco, Papagayo, and Rincón de la Vieja. One-way services cost $43-95 per person. Most shuttles fit eight people with luggage and offer drop-offs at Uvita and Bahía hotels.

PARQUE NACIONAL MARINO BALLENA

The beach-filled **Parque Nacional Marino Ballena** (Ballena National Marine Park, 1.5 km southwest of Hwy. 34, Bahía, tel. 506/8946-7134, www.sinac.go.cr, 7am-4pm daily, $6 pp) is home to countless marine animals and plants, including dolphins, sea turtles, octopuses, crabs, sharks, sponges, and mollusks. Coral reef and mangrove ecosystems are protected by the park, which spans 15 kilometers of coastline from Uvita south to Punta Piñuela (Piñuela Point) on the outskirts of Ojochal. At this known mating site for humpback whales (*ballena* means "whale"), it is not uncommon to see pods of the giant mammals breaching offshore, especially from December to March, when whales migrate from the north, or from July to October, when whales migrate from the south. At the park's beaches, you can sunbathe, swim, and take a stroll along the whale-tail sandbar. You can also explore the park's protected waters during snorkeling excursions, kayaking trips, and whale- and dolphin-watching boat tours.

Four **ranger stations** scattered along Highway 34 provide access to the park's coastal areas. Most visitors come through the **Bahía entrance ranger station,** in the southwest corner of Bahía at the end of the main street that leads through the community from Highway 34. The Bahía entrance is the closest to the park's most visited beach, Playa Uvita, and the whale-tail sandbar.

You don't need a tour guide to enjoy the beaches in this park. Pack plenty of sunscreen; the unshaded beaches are piping hot. Hold on to your ticket; you can use it to enter any of the ranger stations over the course of the day.

★ Whale-Tail Sandbar

Playa Uvita is home to an intriguing natural feature: a sandbar in the shape of a whale's tail. Also referred to by Ticos as **Paso de Moisés** (Moses's Step), the **whale-tail sandbar** extends one kilometer into the Pacific Ocean, with its stretch of sand running perpendicular to the shore. Stroll out to the end for a surreal experience. When you've gone as far as you can, turn around and take in the view: You're almost completely surrounded by water. You'll see layer upon layer of mountains that gleam in multiple shades of green, plus waves that roll in to your left and to your right. For the best experience, visit the beach at low tide; the sandbar disappears into the ocean at other times of day.

Beaches

The park's principal beach is Playa Uvita. Several other stretches of sand are contained within the park's boundaries, including **Playa Arco** (2 km southeast of Playa Uvita), **Playa Ballena** (4 km southeast of Playa Uvita), and **Playa Piñuela** (7 km southeast of Playa Uvita). These three beaches are rarely visited.

PLAYA UVITA

Home to the whale-tail sandbar, **Playa Uvita** is the most visited beach in the park. It fronts the entirety of Bahía but is separated from the neighborhood by a thin strip of forested parkland that runs parallel to the beach. Particularly picturesque are Playa Uvita's smooth, beige-colored sand, sometimes decorated with shells and sand dollars, and the dense mix of tall and short palms that back the beach. This wide, sun-soaked, and bare beach is four kilometers from its easternmost end to its westernmost tip, which forms the end of the whale tail sandbar. Locals refer to the eastern half of the beach as **Playa Colonia.**

Access to Playa Uvita is via the park's main entrance at Bahía. A short two-minute walk on an unnamed, 50-meter trail departs from the entrance and leads through forest. Where the trail ends at the sand is the beach's midpoint, which also represents the divide between Playa Uvita and Playa Colonia.

Snorkeling, Kayaking, and Whale- and Dolphin-Watching

The park's waters are rich with marine life. Local tour outfitter **Bahía Aventuras** (beside

the school, Bahía, tel. 506/2743-8362, www. bahiaaventuras.com, 6:30am-8:30pm daily) runs water-based adventures in the park out of the Uvita area. They dominate tourism in the region with their friendly guides, knowledge of the Costa Ballena, and stellar service. Their **snorkeling tour** (2.5 hours, $75 adults, $35 children 3-10, min. age 3) provides an opportunity to spot several species of fish, including colorful parrotfish, funny-looking pufferfish, and even big fish varieties like marlin. During the tour outfitter's **kayaking tour** (3 hours, $78 adults, $38 children 6-10, min. age 6), you may see bottlenose dolphins, spinner dolphins, and spotted dolphins playing in the waves. Most sought after is the **whale- and dolphin-watching boat tour** (8:30am and 1:30pm daily, 3.5 hours, $78-90 adults, $30-50 children 3-10, min. age 3), offering an opportunity to spot a breaching humpback whale or, less likely, an orca. All three experiences include the park entrance fee. The times for the snorkeling and kayaking tours are tide dependent.

Getting There

The principal entrance to the park is in Bahía, at the end of the main street that leads through the community from Highway 34. Parking is available at the entrance.

OJOCHAL

The southernmost destination on the Costa Ballena is the quiet community of Ojochal. A tight-knit mix of locals and expats inhabits the area, which is spread out in the mountains just north of Highway 34. Many first-time visitors are surprised by Ojochal's greatest contribution to the central Pacific coast: topnotch international cuisine. A cluster of small but polished and revered restaurants puts this remote destination, nicknamed the culinary capital of Costa Rica, on the map.

1: the infinity pool at Vista Ballena, near Uvita
2: fruit harvested from African palm trees **3:** view from the whale-tail sandbar in Parque Nacional Marino Ballena **4:** beach cave at Playa Ventanas in Ojochal

Sights

BEACH CAVE AT PLAYA VENTANAS

The coolest thing to see in Ojochal is the **natural beach cave** at the pretty, light-gray **Playa Ventanas.** If you visit at low tide, you'll find a narrow passageway that cuts through the craggy rock face, separating the ocean from the beach. The cave's two entrances (or "windows") are large enough to walk through, but remain mindful of the tide. Water levels rise quickly and eventually engulf the tunnel with raging waves. The sight is neat to see from the outside, especially when the cave acts like a blowhole and spits out a powerful mist. Do not get caught in the middle at high tide.

Additional caves that decorate the vicinity with textured arches are accessible to kayakers. **Dominical's Pineapple Tours** (beside the police station, Dominical, tel. 506/8873-3283, www.pineapplekayaktours. com, 9am-5pm daily) runs the seasonal **Ventanas Cave Ocean Kayak Tour** (tour times tide dependent, Dec.-Aug., 4 hours, $75 pp, min. age 15) that paddles through the offshore caves, ocean conditions permitting. This tour is for experienced kayakers only.

Food

The food in Ojochal is a delight—both in quality and variety. Advance reservations are recommended for all restaurants in Ojochal. There are too many great choices to name them all, but at the top of the list is **Exotica** (main street in Ojochal, 1 km northeast of Hwy. 34, tel. 506/2786-5050, 5pm-10pm Mon.-Sat., $10-35). Softly lit with candles and lanterns, the intimate spot is perfect for a date night. Beef, chicken, and fish orders surpass the ordinary and feature flavors and cooking styles from countries around the world. Even the cocktails are a step up from most. Don't leave without indulging in the restaurant's sweet and slightly spicy chocolate cake, the Devil's Fork.

Tons of people gush over **Citrus** (2 km

north of Hwy. 34, tel. 506/2786-5175, 7am-10pm Mon.-Sat., 7am-11pm Sun., $18-28), which competes with Exotica for high-quality dishes that span a variety of international cuisines. Though diverse, Citrus's menu is French-inspired. This place offers a fine-dining experience in a sophisticated space with a laid-back, family-friendly vibe. The unique and eclectic decor includes funky pendant lights, tree-trunk tabletops, and modern chairs scattered throughout the dining rooms and outdoor courtyard.

Opened in 2018, the ★ **Kua Kua Restaurant** (Three Sixty Boutique Hotel, tel. 506/2100-9206, www.hotelthreesixty.com, 7am-9:30pm daily $15-21) is my preference when I visit Ojochal. The small menu offers a few fresh breakfast and lunch options, five exquisite dinner entrées, several tasty tapas, and delectable desserts. The superior-quality food is matched by an excellent view. Visit during the day or just before sunset so you can take in the sight of an endless ocean and a lush rainforest canopy while dining on the open-air patio perched on the side of a mountain.

Accommodations

If you're headed to Ojochal, treat yourself to a low-key yet luxurious stay at **El Castillo** (Calle Perezoso, 350 m southeast of Hwy. 34, tel. 506/2786-5543, www.elcastillocr.com, $245 s/d). The whitewashed, Spanish colonial-style building has nine elegant rooms with windows and doors that open up to ocean views or terraces near gardens. Stays at El Castillo, whose name in English means The Castle, feel like home. I particularly like the turret, which doubles as a reading nook. Other features include an infinity pool and guest deck that overlook the property's mountainside as it slopes toward the Pacific.

Information and Services

The closest hospital is the **Hospital de Osa Tomás Casas Casajús** (Hwy. 34, just west of Ciudad Cortés, tel. 506/2786-8148, 24 hours daily) in Ciudad Cortés, a 17-kilometer, 15-minute drive southeast of Ojochal.

Just east of Highway 34 at the turnoff to Ojochal are a **supermarket** and the community's **police station** (Calle Soluna, tel. 506/2786-5275, 24 hours daily).

The closest **gas station** is 15 km northwest of Ojochal on Highway 34 near Uvita.

Transportation

There are two ways to get to Ojochal from downtown **San José**. Via the **coastal route** (Highway 27 to Highway 34), Ojochal is a 245-kilometer drive that takes just under four hours. Via the **mountain route** (Highway 2 to Road 243 to Highway 34), it's a 205-kilometer drive to Ojochal that takes a little over four hours.

From downtown **Liberia,** Ojochal is a 330-kilometer drive southeast via Highway 1, Highway 27, and Highway 34; the trip takes a little less than five hours. From **Uvita,** Ojochal is a 16-kilometer, 15-minute drive southeast on Highway 34.

To reach Ojochal by **bus,** hop on one that commutes between Dominical and Ciudad Neily. From **Dominical** (multiple times 4:45am-4pm daily, $2-2.50), it's a 45-minute ride southeast to Ojochal. Be sure to ask the bus driver, *"¿Por favor, puede parar en Ojochal?"* ("Please, can you stop in Ojochal?"). The driver will drop you off alongside Highway 34 at the entrance to the community.

Osa Peninsula and the Southern Pacific

Costa Rica is known for its splendid biodiver- sity, and no region provides such a concentrated dose as the Osa Peninsula and the southern Pacific coast. Way down in the southern part of the country, among pristine primary and secondary forest, silent mountains, and unfrequented coastline, is a rugged wilderness. Sometimes referred to as the crown jewel of Costa Rica, the region is hardly flashy and polished. It's a rough, trying place that demands long travel days, strenuous hikes, and a tolerance for wet, steamy weather, but those brave and headstrong enough to visit will reap incomparable rewards. Wildlife and marine life, including many of the country's rarest species, are all around: along the tucked-away trails that lead through protected land areas, around the trees that

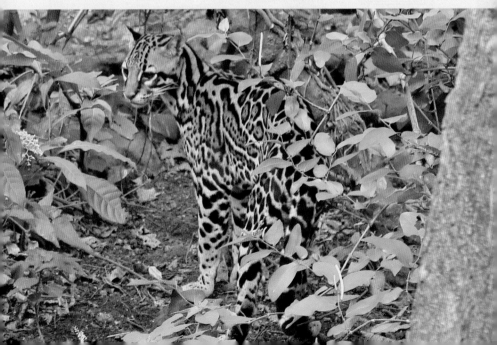

Highlights

Look for ★ to find recommended sights, activities, dining, and lodging.

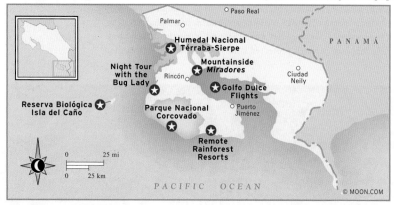

★ **Take a boat ride** through the **Humedal Nacional Térraba-Sierpe** to see varied wildlife and ecosystems (page 386).

★ **Search for creepy crawlers** after dark in Bahía Drake during the **Night Tour** with the **Bug Lady** (page 390).

★ **Snorkel or dive** at the **Reserva Biológica Isla del Caño** (page 394).

★ **Hike** and **spot wildlife** at the biodiverse **Parque Nacional Corcovado** (page 395).

★ **Take in picture-perfect views** from mountainside *miradores* on the way to **Puerto Jiménez** (page 398).

★ **Fly** into and out of the **Golfo Dulce** for spectacular views (page 402).

★ **Relax** at a **remote rainforest resort** (page 404).

tower over restaurant tables, and in the waters of the ocean. A kaleidoscope of ecosystems decorates the landscape and invites up-close exploration.

Lagging in modernization compared with other areas of the country, this region provides off-the-grid getaways—but don't expect a luxury experience. Many accommodations have outdoor showers (and sometimes full outdoor bathrooms), screened windows or walls, and limited electricity. Bare-bones lodging options cater to back-road backpackers. Several small-scale, all-inclusive ecolodges host big spenders. Most of these overlook the Pacific Ocean from Bahía Drake or are spread out around the picturesque Golfo Dulce, which divides the peninsula from the mainland and calms the wild, forest-filled region with still, blue-green waters.

PLANNING YOUR TIME

Travel to and throughout the Osa Peninsula and the southern Pacific coast takes time. A full day of exploration often requires two additional travel days—one to get to the region and another to backtrack out of it. A good length of time to budget for visiting this region is **five days,** which allows for three days of touring. Fortunately, many of the modes of travel to and from the region are themselves highlights, such as **flying into and out of the Golfo Dulce,** stopping at mountainside *miradores* (lookouts) if you're driving, and boating through the **Humedal Nacional Térraba-Sierpe.**

Whether and how you wish to explore the **Parque Nacional Corcovado** will largely influence the amount of time you'll need in the region. Day trips are possible, as are multiday expeditions. Most other attractions require no longer than a day to complete (including excursions to the **Reserva Biológica Isla del Caño**), if not only a few hours (like the **Night Tour with the Bug Lady**). If your purpose for trekking all the way down to the southernmost corner of Costa Rica is to escape to a **remote rainforest resort,** you'll have your pick of properties and you can stay as long as you wish.

Weather and Transportation

December to April is considered the dry season and May to November the wet season. Annual rainfall amounts are high, so it's more accurate to describe these periods as the sunny-with-sporadic-rain season and the soaked season. Temperatures average 75-79°F. Humid, densely forested areas can feel like saunas.

Long drives, even longer bus rides, and combined ground and boat or air travel make the region tricky to get around. If you stick to the main roads (Hwy. 34, Hwy. 2, Hwy. 14, Road 223, and Road 245 as far south as Puerto Jiménez), you won't need a 4x4 vehicle. With so much rain in the region, dirt roads quickly become slippery messes and may become impassable due to flooding and swollen river crossings. Even bus transportation isn't guaranteed in some areas. Boats and planes provide additional means of getting to, from, and throughout the region.

ORIENTATION

The Osa Peninsula and the southern Pacific coast occupy the southwestern corner of Costa Rica. The area is accessed from the central Pacific coast via the **Carretera Costanera Sur** (Southern Coastal Highway), also known as the **Pacífica Fernández Oreamuno** or simply Highway 34. Highway 34 ends in the town of Palmar, where it intersects with the **Carretera Interamericana** (Inter-American Highway), also known as the **Pan-American Highway** or Highway 2. Highway 2 continues southeast to the east side of the Golfo Dulce and the border at Panama. **Road 245** splits from the highway at Chacarita and travels to the west side

Osa Peninsula and the Southern Pacific

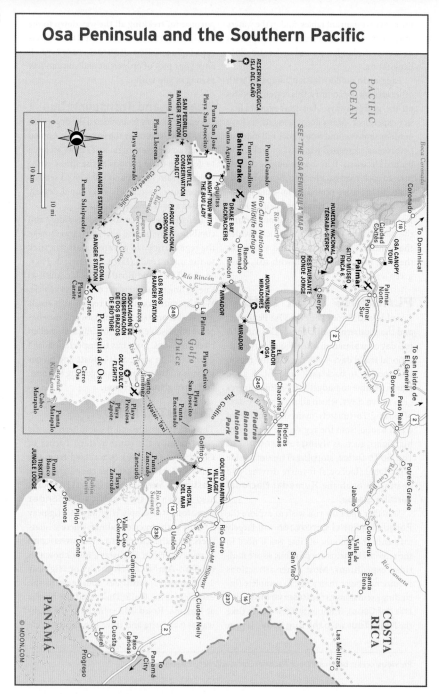

© MOON.COM

of the gulf and the southern half of the Osa Peninsula. **Road 223,** which originates from Palmar and runs south, provides access to the village of Sierpe, which acts as a gateway to Bahía Drake and the northern half of the peninsula.

Bahía Drake and Vicinity

It's possible to get a sense of the Osa Peninsula without traveling all that far south by visiting the rainforest-backed region named after its largest body of water, Bahía Drake (Drake Bay), exploring underwater at the Reserva Biológica Isla del Caño, and trekking through Parque Nacional Corcovado.

The towns of Palmar and Sierpe, near palm plantations, archaeological sites, and protected wetlands, provide access to this remote coastal destination.

PALMAR

Palmar is a crossroads community at the junction of Highway 2 and Highway 34. It provides little in the way of tourism. Split at its core by the east-west run of **Río Térraba,** Palmar is sometimes referred to as **Palmar Norte** (the section north of the river, where the highways intersect) and **Palmar Sur** (the section south of the river, which leads to the town of Sierpe along Road 223).

Just to the northwest of Palmar is Ciudad Cortés, home to the region's medical and governmental services.

Recreation
ZIP-LINING
Seemingly out of place, since there is hardly a trace of tourism within a 20-kilometer radius, is the zip-line outfitter **Osa Canopy Tour** (Hwy. 34, 8 km west of Palmar, tel. 506/2788-7555, www.osacanopytour.com, 8am-5pm daily). The nine-cable **canopy tour** (8am and 1pm daily, 3 hours, $65 pp, min. age 4) is jam-packed with fun surprises, including two rappelling stations where you'll free fall between vertical platforms, two wobbly wood-plank suspension bridges, and an exhilarating Tarzan swing that thrusts you into open air high above the treetops. The swing will wow you with an expansive view of the region's hills. Sign up for the tour if you want an adrenaline boost while passing through the area.

Food and Accommodations
The large, tile-floored, red-roofed, and open-air **Rancho Mi Tata** (Hwy. 34, 800 m northwest of the intersection of Hwy. 34 and Hwy. 2, Palmar, tel. 506/2786-6647, 6am-midnight daily, $3-10) is an informal restaurant with a ceiling propped up by tree limbs. I like it because you can mix and match your preferred mains and sides, each of which is priced individually. Order arroz con pollo (rice with chicken, $4) with *puré de papas* (mashed potatoes, $2), *ensalada verde* (green salad, $1), *plátanos maduros* (fried plantains, $1), and *queso blanco* (white cheese, $1), and you've got yourself a delectable plate of typical Costa Rican eats for less than $10.

There's little reason to stay in Palmar overnight, but if you must, check in at the **Brunka Lodge** (Calle 149, between Avenida 9 and Avenida 11, Palmar Norte, tel. 506/2786-7489, $35 s, $40 d). Each of the lodge's 25 cabins has a private bathroom and a plainly decorated bedroom with a television and one or two double beds. Around the property are two pools, two Jacuzzis, and tropical plants that spiff up the place. The best feature is the cute, colorful, comfortable restaurant, which also operates as an *heladería* (ice cream shop).

Information and Services
Palmar has **banks** with **ATMs** including **Banco Nacional** (just east of the intersection of Hwy. 34 and Hwy. 2, tel. 506/2211-1111, 9am-4pm Mon.-Sat., ATM 5am-midnight

The Osa Peninsula

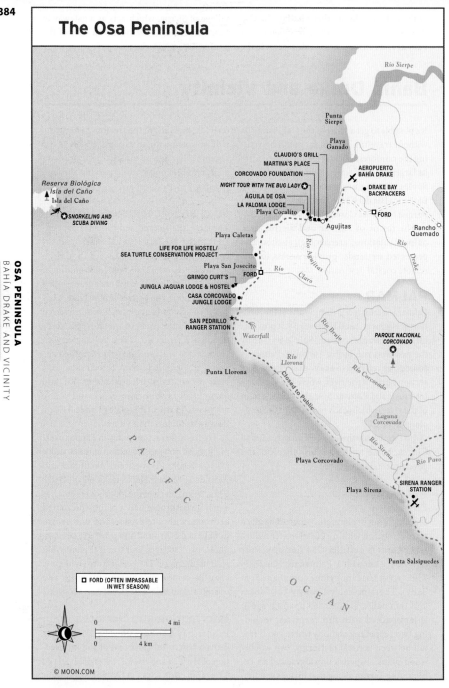

Río Sierpe

Punta Sierpe

Playa Ganado

CLAUDIO'S GRILL
MARTINA'S PLACE
CORCOVADO FOUNDATION
NIGHT TOUR WITH THE BUG LADY

AEROPUERTO BAHÍA DRAKE

DRAKE BAY BACKPACKERS

ÁGUILA DE OSA
LA PALOMA LODGE
Playa Cocalito

FORD

Agujitas

Rancho Quemado

Reserva Biológica
Isla del Caño
Isla del Caño

SNORKELING AND SCUBA DIVING

Playa Caletas

Río Agujitas

Río Drake

LIFE FOR LIFE HOSTEL/
SEA TURTLE CONSERVATION PROJECT

Playa San Josecito
GRINGO CURT'S
JUNGLA JAGUAR LODGE & HOSTEL
CASA CORCOVADO
JUNGLE LODGE

FORD
Río
Río Claro

SAN PEDRILLO
RANGER STATION

Waterfall

Río Brujo

PARQUE NACIONAL CORCOVADO

Río Llorona

Río Corcovado

Punta Llorona

Closed to Public

Laguna Corcovado

Río Sirena

Playa Corcovado

Río Pavo

SIRENA RANGER STATION

Playa Sirena

Punta Salsipuedes

P A C I F I C

O C E A N

FORD (OFTEN IMPASSABLE IN WET SEASON)

0   4 mi

0   4 km

© MOON.COM

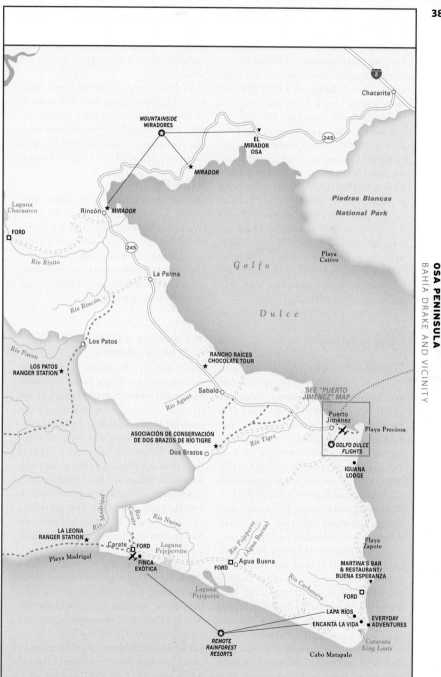

OSA PENINSULA
BAHÍA DRAKE AND VICINITY

daily), **supermarkets, pharmacies** including **FarmaSur** (Calle 143, just south of Avenida 11, tel. 506/2786-6686, 8am-8pm Mon.-Sat., 8am-noon Sun.), a **police station** (south side of the central park, tel. 506/2786-6320, 24 hours daily), and a **post office** (1 block north of Hwy. 2, 200 m east of Hwy. 34, tel. 506/2786-6291, 8am-5pm Mon.-Fri.).

Ciudad Cortés has a hospital, **Hospital de Osa Tomás Casas Casajús** (just south of Hwy. 34 upon entrance into Ciudad Cortés, tel. 506/2786-8148, 24 hours daily) and a **police station** (Calle Tagual, 50 m south of Avenida 21, tel. 506/2788-7567, 24 hours daily). It also has a **pharmacy, Farmacia Ibarra** (Calle 1, 450 m south of the gas station, tel. 506/2788-7087, 7:30am-7:30pm Mon.-Sat.), a branch of **Banco Nacional** (Calle 2, between Avenida 2 and Avenida 4, tel. 506/2788-8136, 8:30am-5pm Mon.-Fri.), and many **supermarkets.**

There are **gas stations** in both Ciudad Cortés (on Calle 1) and Palmar (at the corner of Hwy. 34 and Hwy. 2).

Transportation

Palmar is 270 kilometers (an approximate four-hour drive) southeast from downtown **San José** via the **coastal route** (Hwy. 27 to Hwy. 34). It's 230 kilometers (an approximate 4.5-hour drive) southeast from downtown San José via the **mountain route** (Hwy. 2, Road 243, and Hwy. 34). From downtown **Liberia,** Palmar is 355 kilometers (an approximate five-hour drive) southeast via Highway 1, Highway 27, and Highway 34. Ciudad Cortés is nine kilometers (less than a 10-minute drive) northwest of Palmar on Highway 34.

The **Aeropuerto de Palmar Sur** (Palmar Sur Airport, PMZ) is on the west side of Highway 2, one kilometer south of Highway 34. **SANSA Airlines** (tel. 506/2290-4100, www.flysansa.com) offers daily direct flights to Palmar from San José. The flight time from San José is approximately 40 minutes.

Public **buses** travel daily to Palmar from **San José** (multiple times 5am-5pm daily, 5.5-6 hours, $11), **Dominical** (4:45am, 8am, 11am, 12:30pm, and 4pm daily, 1.5-2 hours, $3.50), **Sierpe** (multiple times 4:30am-5pm daily, 30-45 minutes, $1), and **Ciudad Neily** (multiple times 4:45am-5pm daily, 1.5-2 hours, $1.50).

Additional public **buses** travel daily to Ciudad Cortés from **San Isidro de El General** (9am and 4pm daily, 3 hours, $3-3.50). From **Ciudad Cortés** (multiple times 5am-7pm Mon.-Fri. and 7am-5pm Sat.-Sun., 20 minutes, $1), buses travel daily to Palmar.

SIERPE

The tiny riverside village of Sierpe is the peninsula's gateway to Bahía Drake. It's quiet, save for the lively and entertaining boatmen who gather around the south-facing docks and tout all kinds of sales, from area tours to boat rides to *pipa fría* (cold coconut water). Sierpe is a pleasant place you'll pass through on your way to big adventure.

Sights
★ HUMEDAL NACIONAL TÉRRABA-SIERPE

Where the Osa Peninsula departs from the mainland are Costa Rica's **Humedal Nacional Térraba-Sierpe** (Térraba-Sierpe National Wetlands, www.sinac.go.cr). The protected 66,000-acre site is a mix of woodlands, marshy swamps, and rivers, most notably **Río Sierpe,** which flows south of Sierpe and connects wetlands on the east and west sides of the village, and **Río Térraba,** which cuts through Palmar and feeds the wetlands from the north. Here, birds, fish, crocodiles, and other reptiles, including nonvenomous boa constrictors, reside among remote estuaries and lagoons.

Organized tours visit the wetlands from Sierpe, Bahía Drake, and Uvita. Tour operators running similar slow-paced boat rides through the wetlands are **La Perla del Sur** (tel. 506/2788-1082, www.laperladelsur.cr), whose **River and Mangrove Tour** (3 hours, $50 adults, $30 children 5-10, children under 5 free) runs from Sierpe and Bahía Drake, and **Bahía Aventuras** (tel. 506/2743-8362, www.

bahiaaventuras.com), whose **Mangrove & Wildlife Tour** (3.5 hours, $85 adults, $40 children 0-10) departs from Uvita. Both guided excursions provide a rare opportunity to quietly explore the wetlands' innermost channels in search of resident wildlife and marine life. Tour guides narrate the trip and point out the different types of ecosystems you'll see along the way and their significance. Advance reservations are required by both tour operators. Tour start times vary according to the tide.

If you're merely passing through Sierpe on your way to Bahía Drake and you don't have time to tour the wetlands formally, you can see them at a distance during the one-hour **boat transfer** that commutes between Bahía Drake and Sierpe. The first half hour of the boat ride motors around Río Sierpe and passes by several of the wetlands' ecosystems. Tall, thin trees, sticklike mangrove root systems, wild brush, occasional ferns and palms, and minute leafy islets will fill your gaze as you travel downriver. Take mental pictures; the boat ride makes it tricky to capture still photographs. Boats depart for Bahía Drake twice daily (11:30am and 3:30pm) from the main dock in Sierpe, at the south end of the village in front of Restaurante Donde Jorge (south of Road 223). **La Perla del Sur** (tel. 506/2788-1082, www.laperladelsur.cr) runs the boat transfer service. It costs roughly $15-30 per person depending on where you're headed in Bahía Drake. Advance reservations are not required.

SITIO MUSEO FINCA 6

If you have an interest in pre-Columbian history, particularly indigenous cultures, don't miss **Sitio Museo Finca 6** (400 m northeast of Road 223, 6 km north of Sierpe, tel. 506/2100-6000, 8am-4pm Tues.-Sun., last entry 3pm, $6 adults, $4 children 0-11). The Finca 6 project is a small modern museum and an outdoor collection of archaeological artifacts that pays homage to Costa Rica's pre-Columbian Diquís culture. The group's mysterious, centuries-old stone spheres dot the region; to date, 300 have been discovered. I recommend visiting the museum first; the cultural theory presented there will help you understand and better appreciate the sights in the field, including grassy areas adorned with mounds (on which housing once stood) and authentic Diquís spheres. You can tour the museum and wander around the grounds during a self-guided visit. The grounds, on a deserted banana plantation, are flat and easy to explore within an hour. Take a moment to examine the stones at close range. No one can say with certainty how the sculptures were constructed, but they come within millimeters of being perfect spheres.

Food and Accommodations

I've never left disappointed from ★ **Restaurante Donde Jorge** (south of Road 223, tel. 506/2788-1082, 6am-9pm daily, $4-10). The flavorful but not too oily *arroz con vegetales* (rice with vegetables) is my go-to dish. Other large helpings that sell for a reasonable price include fish plates and fast food like hamburgers and sandwiches. Enjoy your pick at the open-air restaurant as you watch local captains ready their boats by the riverbank.

An early morning boat departure may require a night's stay in Sierpe. The two-story, motel-style **Hotel Sierpe River** (formerly Hotel Oleaje Sereno, south of Road 223, tel. 506/2788-1111, www.oleajeserenohotel. com, $36 s, $55 d) has 10 economy-priced, economy-quality rooms that face the street and hotel parking lot; overnight parking is free. Each room is equipped with air-conditioning, and first-floor rooms have barred windows. Guests have a complimentary breakfast at Restaurante Donde Jorge.

Restaurante Donde Jorge and Hotel Sierpe River share a riverfront location and an owner. The same owner also runs the tour and transportation service provider **La Perla del Sur** (tel. 506/2788-1082, www.laperladelsur.cr, 6am-9pm daily). To keep things simple, you can eat, stay overnight, and arrange area tours or boat transportation all in the same place.

Information and Services

Sierpe has a **police station** (on the riverfront, tel. 506/2788-1439, 24 hours daily); a small **clinic** called **Ebais Sierpe** (Road 223 upon entrance into Sierpe, tel. 506/2788-1189, 7am-4pm Mon.-Thurs., 7am-3pm Fri.); and a couple of **supermarkets.** The closest **bank** and **ATM** are in Palmar. There is no gas station in the area, so be sure to fuel up in Palmar before turning onto Road 223.

Transportation

Via the **coastal route** (Hwy. 27, Hwy. 34, and Road 223), Sierpe is a 285-kilometer drive southeast from downtown **San José** that takes a little over four hours. Via the **mountain route** (Hwy. 2, Road 243, Hwy. 34, and Road 223), it's a 245-kilometer drive southeast from downtown San José that takes nearly five hours.

From downtown **Liberia,** Sierpe is a 370-kilometer drive southeast via Highway 1, Highway 34, and Road 223 that takes a little over five hours. To reach Sierpe from **Palmar,** take Road 223 south; it zigzags for 15 kilometers (a 15-minute drive) and ends in the village near the waterfront.

To get to Sierpe from **Bahía Drake,** catch one of the **public boats** that depart from Playa Colorada twice daily (7:15am and 2:30pm). Area accommodations can arrange boat pickups at or near their property if needed. Expect to pay around $15-20 per person for transport from the main beach in Bahía Drake and upward of $30 per person for transport from the far-flung Casa Corcovado Jungle Lodge.

Public **buses** travel daily to Sierpe from San José (8:30am daily, 6 hours, $10.50) and **Palmar** (multiple times 5:30am-6pm daily, 30-45 minutes, $1).

Grayline Costa Rica (tel. 506/2220-2126, www.graylinecostarica.com) provides **shared shuttle services** to Sierpe from San José and Manuel Antonio. One-way services cost $48-98 per person. Most shuttles fit eight people with luggage and offer drop-offs near the dock, as well as at Sierpe hotels.

BAHÍA DRAKE

Bahía Drake, in the northwest corner of the Osa Peninsula, is the most touristy area in the region, but you won't feel like you've stationed yourself in an overly popular place when you visit. Development, in the form of low-key establishments and rustic all-inclusive ecolodges, is spread out along 25 kilometers of coastline between Río Sierpe (to the north) and the northwestern boundary of Parque Nacional Corcovado (to the south). Unless you travel by boat along the coast in search of buildings that peek through the forest, you'll assume they don't exist, which is exactly why many travelers adore this area. It offers seclusion and sublime privacy as well as popular guided excursions.

Locals reside around the sparse, coastal village of **Agujitas.** It's close to the center of the Bahía Drake region and the south end of the namesake bay. The village sits atop a hill just south of **Playa Colorada,** the area's principal beach, where boats transport visitors in and out of the area. A steep road connects the beach to the village and provides access to a handful of informal restaurants and accommodations.

Many travelers favor the waterfront accommodations southwest of the village along the coast. Stays at most of these spots are sold as all-inclusive two- or three-night packages that include a private room and three daily meals (dining options outside of Agujitas are scarce). In some cases, local tours and round-trip boat transportation from Sierpe—or combined ground and boat transportation from other locations, such as Palmar or San José—are included.

Recreation

HIKING

A 14-kilometer, **unnamed trail** referred to by locals as the **Sendero Costero** (Coastal Trail) connects the village of Agujitas to the

1: stone spheres at Sitio Museo Finca 6
2: the Humedal Nacional Térraba-Sierpe

San Pedrillo ranger station in the Parque Nacional Corcovado. A great way to spend a free day in Bahía Drake is to explore the first seven kilometers of this trail. It begins near Agujitas and offers a moderate, 2.5-hour, forested hike alongside the Pacific Ocean to **Playa San Josecito.** The trailhead, marked by a rickety wood suspension bridge, is at the west end of Playa Colorada, an approximate 20-minute walk from Agujitas center.

Roughly 1.5 kilometers beyond the trailhead, past the Río Agujitas and La Paloma Lodge, is the most accessible swimming beach in Bahía Drake, **Playa Cocalito.** Playa Cocalito has crystalline (albeit sometimes wave-filled) waters that are great for wading. The narrow beach is also quiet and just barely escapes Bahía Drake's lush forest, where monkeys can sometimes be seen playing in the trees that tower over the sand.

Hike an additional four kilometers south on the trail to get to a small café, souvenir store, and water sport rental shop run by local turtle conservationist Ricardo (nicknamed Clavito). Continue south on the trail for 1.5 kilometers and you'll arrive at **Playa San Josecito,** the coastline's prettiest beach. This remote beach with a *Castaway* feel is backed by a tall hill, has several bright-green palms spread out across light, gray-tinged sand, and features rocky islets near the shore. The calm waters between the islets and the sand are great for snorkeling. It can get busy midday, as the beach is a great spot to enjoy a picnic lunch.

Though it's possible to continue hiking south on the Sendero Costero (it's an additional seven-kilometer, four-hour hike to the San Pedrillo ranger station), most hikers turn around at Playa San Josecito to return to Agujitas.

★ THE NIGHT TOUR WITH THE BUG LADY

The **night tour** (tel. 506/8701-7356, www.thenighttour.com, 7:30pm daily, 2.5-3 hours, $40 pp) run by biologist Tracie Stice, also known as the **Bug Lady,** and photographer and naturalist guide Gianfranco Gómez is the best of its kind in the region. The duo leads a leisurely hike through the dark night of Bahía Drake's biodiverse forest, on a search for rare and photogenic insects, frogs, spiders, snakes, bats, and nocturnal animals. Stice and Gómez relate facts and stories that they've collected over decades of exploration and offer witty commentary, elevating the tour experience.

Advance reservations are required. Contact Stice and Gómez directly to avoid accidentally booking a different night tour through an area operator or hotel. This tour should be avoided if you're scared of the dark or if you cringe at the thought of creepy crawlers. Headlamps are provided. If you stay at an accommodation in Agujitas, the tour meeting place is the hotel Jinetes de Osa (at the west end of Playa Colorada). Pickups at hotels near Jinetes de Osa can also be arranged. Have Stice and Gómez confirm your meeting place and time when you book your tour.

Food

There aren't many restaurants in Agujitas. The best food here is served at **Claudio's Grill** (600 m southeast of the beach at Playa Colorada, tel. 506/6004-9910, 5am-10am and 2pm-9pm daily, $10-25), which cooks whole fish and meat cuts before your eyes on an outdoor barbecue. The rustic, open-air house-turned-restaurant has only a few tables, but doesn't disappoint with decent-size portions and staff with big smiles. Some preparations come neatly wrapped in banana leaves.

For years, the three-dish diner **Gringo Curt's** (Jungla Jaguar Lodge & Hostel, 1 km north of the San Pedrillo ranger station, tel. 506/8747-8929, www.gringocurt.com, 1pm-9pm daily, $8-12) was Agujitas's best restaurant. In 2018, it moved to a new location near the boundary of Parque Nacional Corcovado, and the unassuming restaurant is still a hit, especially for its spear-caught fresh

1: tree frog **2:** boats bound for the Reserva Biológica Isla del Caño **3:** coral snake in Parque Nacional Corcovado **4:** the rustic Águila de Osa lodge in Bahía Drake

fish. Choose from vegetarian pasta, a seafood wrap, or the specialty plate, which features the catch of the day. Come ready to ask your Bahía Drake questions; Curt, the expat owner, is a wealth of information.

Accommodations

One of the few accommodations in Bahía Drake that allows rooms to be booked without purchase of a package is the **Jungla Jaguar Lodge & Hostel** (1 km north of the San Pedrillo ranger station, tel. 506/8959-4067, www.jungladeljaguar.com, dorm $15 pp, private $50 s/d). The laid-back, solar-powered accommodation trades hot water, air-conditioning, and Wi-Fi for seclusion and an off-the-grid experience. Private rooms are simply outfitted and have one or two single or double beds. Dorms (one of which is open-air) come with mosquito nets. Low-key social spaces include the guest kitchen, yoga deck, restaurant, and bar.

The 13-room **Águila de Osa** (500 m northwest of the beach at Playa Colorada, tel. 506/8840-2929, www.aguiladeosa.com, 2-night package $811 s, $1,030 d, all-inclusive, 2-night minimum) is tucked away from the ocean by the mouth of Río Agujitas and feels like a sequestered jungle oasis. Rooms in the rustic lodge feature balconies and are constructed with fine Costa Rican woods; the furniture is made of wood too. Screened windows welcome comfortable tropical breezes. Daily meals at the hotel's open-air restaurant above the quiet river are included with the packages, as is the use of kayaks.

The 11 clifftop rooms and bungalow-style ranchos that form ★ **La Paloma Lodge** (500 m northwest of the beach at Playa Colorada, tel. 506/2239-0954, www.lapalomalodge. com, 3-night package $1,120 s, $2,240 d, all-inclusive, 3-night minimum) are utterly relaxing and exquisitely furnished. Each offers a touch of luxury with orthopedic beds, air-conditioning, in-room seating areas, gleaming hardwood floors, and wall-to-wall windows that take in the area's lush surroundings and ocean views. The hotel's superb service is second to none in the area. Guided tours of Parque Nacional Corcovado and the Reserva Biológica Isla del Caño are included in the package rates.

Adjacent to Parque Nacional Corcovado, the ★ **Casa Corcovado Jungle Lodge** (just north of the San Pedrillo ranger station, tel. 506/2256-3181, www.casacorcovado. com, 2-night package $792 s, $1,584 d, all-inclusive, 2-night minimum) is Bahía Drake's most upscale and environmentally sustainable accommodation. It's also the farthest hotel from Agujitas. Staying here means having a room with a romantic canopy bed and roofless outdoor shower. Guests have access to a 170-acre property with tropical gardens and nature trails as well as two swimming pools, a restaurant, a bar, a spectacular sunset viewpoint, and a waterfront boathouse. The lodge is perched atop a hill that overlooks the ocean. A steep road separates it from the beach. To get here, you'll take a tractor provided by the hotel.

If you must stay in Agujitas proper, your best option is **Martina's Place** (200 m southeast of Playa Colorada, tel. 506/8720-0801, www.puravidadrakebay.com, dorm $14 pp, private $40 s/d). It's the cleanest spot you'll come across in the village, and it has everything you need if you're a budget traveler. Rooms have tile floors, mosquito nets, oscillating fans, and wood beds; dorms have bunk beds. A communal kitchen and a restaurant are on-site.

Information and Services

Agujitas has a **police station** (just south of Playa Colorada, tel. 506/2775-0300, 24 hours daily), a **clinic** named **Ebais Bahía Drake** (just south of Playa Colorada, tel. 506/2775-1975, 7am-4pm Mon.-Thurs., 7am-3pm Fri.); a mini **pharmacy** called **Macrobiótica Hidalgo** (on the main road in Agujitas, tel. 506/2775-0909, 8am-7pm Mon.-Sat.); and a few **supermarkets.** There are no banks or ATMs in Bahía Drake, so bring as much cash to the area as you plan to spend, plus a little extra in case of unforeseen expenses.

Hostels with Heart

Hostelers around Bahía Drake are doing their part to ensure the Osa Peninsula remains rich in wildlife. You can support the cause by staying at either the nonprofit **Drake Bay Backpackers** (1.5 km southeast of Aeropuerto Bahía Drake, tel. 506/2775-0726, www.drakebaybackpackers.com, dorm $15 pp, private $50 s/d) or the **Life for Life Hostel** (8 km southwest of Agujitas, tel. 506/8581-7429, www.hostelindrake.com, $35 pp, all-inclusive). Proceeds from overnight stays at Drake Bay Backpackers fund local environmental and educational programs run by the esteemed **Corcovado Foundation** (www.corcovadofoundation.org), a group instrumental in the reduction of hunting and logging within area habitats. The cost of room and board at Life for Life Hostel buys protection for marine species through the **Life for Life Sea Turtle Conservation Project.** Both hostels and organizations welcome nightly guests and long-term volunteers.

Transportation

Bahía Drake is one of the few destinations in Costa Rica where access by car or bus is not recommended. A dirt road that requires a 4x4 vehicle connects Agujitas to the Golfo Dulce through the hamlet of Rancho Quemado, but it is often impassable due to the region's heavy rains. The route's condition is why Agujitas is predominantly vacant of vehicles and why boat transportation is the most popular method of travel to and from Bahía Drake.

BOAT

Most visitors to Bahía Drake arrive via a one-hour **boat ride** from Sierpe. The roughly 40-kilometer journey, which begins calmly along Río Sierpe and gradually increases in speed to battle the raging ocean at the river's mouth, can be fun or frightful, depending on the traveler. Climb aboard if you're up for an exhilarating ride. Skip the experience if you have a fear of small boats or the open ocean. Boats should be equipped with life jackets—don't board one that isn't.

Public **boats** offer drop-offs at hotels around Bahía Drake and at Playa Colorada; choose the latter if you're headed to Agujitas. Boats depart twice daily (11:30am and 3:30pm) from the main dock in Sierpe, at the south end of the village in front of Restaurante Donde Jorge (south of Road 223). The restaurant is owned by local tour operator **La Perla del Sur** (tel. 506/2788-1082, www.laperladelsur.cr, 6am-9pm daily), one of few Sierpe-based companies to offer boat service to Bahía Drake. La Perla is my preference for providers because of their skillful captains and coordinated, on-time service.

Expect to pay around $15-20 per person for transport to Playa Colorada and upward of $30 per person for destinations as far away as the Casa Corcovado Jungle Lodge. Advance reservations are not required. Wet landings, which require you to climb off the boat a short distance from the shore and wade through water toward the beach, are common. Wear shorts or quick-dry pants and secure footwear in preparation for this. If you drive yourself to Sierpe, you can leave your vehicle in the parking lot at La Perla del Sur for $6 per night. Be sure to lock the doors and remove any valuables.

Many of the area accommodations will handle boat travel arrangements and costs. Some accommodations use private docks, boats, and captains. Be sure to confirm the departure location, time, and the boat captain's contact information with your chosen hotel. Regardless of whether you travel via public or private boat, verify whether there's a luggage weight limit. Some vessels permit only 25 pounds of luggage per passenger.

AIR

The quickest way to get to Bahía Drake is to fly. The **Aeropuerto Bahía Drake** (Bahía Drake Airport, DRK) is six kilometers north of Agujitas. **SANSA Airlines** (tel. 506/2290-4100, www.flysansa.com) offers direct flights to Bahía Drake from San José daily. The flight time from San José is approximately 40 minutes.

BUS

If you need to reach Bahía Drake by **bus,** one departs from the village of **La Palma** (11am and 4pm Mon.-Sat., 2.5 hours, $2) on the eastern side of the peninsula, but the service is tricky to plan for because it only runs when road conditions permit. Be aware that if you're traveling by bus and staying at an accommodation outside of Agujitas, you'll likely need to hitch a boat ride from Playa Colorada to your hotel upon arrival in the area.

GETTING AROUND

Rough terrain in the area makes cycling around Bahía Drake a chore. Walking is the primary mode of getting around the village. Boat transportation, best arranged through your chosen accommodation, is the most common form of transport between Agujitas and areas of interest around the bay.

RESERVA BIOLÓGICA ISLA DEL CAÑO

About 24 kilometers off the coast of Bahía Drake is the tiny 800-acre, rainforest-filled island known as the **Reserva Biológica Isla del Caño** (Caño Island Biological Reserve, tel. 506/8946-7134, www.sinac.go.cr, 7am-3pm daily, $15 adults, $5 children 2-12). Abundant marine life congregates in the nearly 15,000 acres of protected waters that surround the reserve and its palm-fringed beaches. Once a pre-Columbian burial ground, the uninhabited island remains largely undeveloped, except for a small ranger station on its northwest side that welcomes visitors on organized day tours. The region's best snorkeling and scuba diving experiences take place at the reserve. Humpback whales frequent the area from December to March and July to October. There's a good chance you'll see one playing in the waves while you're boating to and from the island.

★ Snorkeling and Diving

Shallow inlets and offshore reefs are great spots for snorkeling, and year-round visibility in the area makes it easy to spot sharks, rays, eels, octopuses, sea turtles, and dolphins during open-water dives. Snorkeling and scuba diving tours to the reserve are most commonly operated out of Bahía Drake, Sierpe, and Uvita. From Bahía Drake, tour opportunities are seemingly endless, offered by hotels and tour outfitters alike. Expect to pay $80-85 per person for a snorkel tour or $125-135 per person for a two-tank dive. Both experiences typically last seven hours and begin around 7am-7:30am.

La Perla del Sur (just south of Road 223, Sierpe, tel. 506/2788-1082, www.laperladelsur.cr, 6am-9pm daily) runs **snorkeling and diving tours** (8am daily, 8.5 hours, $170 pp for 2 tanks, $90 pp for snorkeling) out of Sierpe. From Uvita, **Bahía Aventuras** (beside the school, Bahía, tel. 506/2743-8362, www.bahiaaventuras.com, 6:30am-8:30pm daily) operates a **snorkeling tour** (7:30am daily, 7 hours, $145 adults, $90 children 6-10, min. age 6), and **Mad About Diving** (125 m north of the national park entrance, Bahía, tel. 506/2743-8019, www.madaboutdivingcr.com, 7am-2pm Mon.-Fri.) provides a full-day **scuba diving excursion** (7am daily, 6.5-7 hours, $175 pp for 2 tanks, $130 pp for snorkeling).

The reserve has several dive sites. You can swim through an arch at **El Arco;** encounter whitetip sharks at the **Cueva del Tiburón, Paraíso,** and **El Barco** (the site of a washed-away shipwreck); and spot colorful coral at the **Coral Gardens.** Discuss the various options with your chosen tour provider when you book.

Getting There

The reserve is accessible by boat only. Guided snorkeling and scuba diving excursions depart from (and return to) Bahía Drake, Sierpe, and Uvita.

★ PARQUE NACIONAL CORCOVADO

Extraordinary biodiversity, vast primary forest, dense vegetation, and trails that go deep into remote wilderness make **Parque Nacional Corcovado** (Corcovado National Park, tel. 506/2735-5036, www.sinac.go.cr, 7am-4pm daily, $15 adults, $5 children 2-12) a bucket list experience for any big-hike adventurer or avid nature lover. Covering over 100,000 acres, the protected land and marine area occupies much of the Osa Peninsula's inland region, as well as a 40-kilometer stretch of its western coastline, and is the primary attraction in Costa Rica's south end. It's a jungle gym of ecosystems; visits here often lead to surprise encounters with some of the rarest wildlife species you can see in the country—and the world. Sea turtles nest on the shores of the park's perimeter. Bull sharks and crocodiles invade the area's rivers and swamps. Nearly 400 species of birds fill the forest's canopy. More than 70 varieties of reptiles, 45 types of amphibians, and a whopping 8,000 species of insects traverse the park. Tapirs, monkeys, peccaries, anteaters, agoutis, everelusive jungle cats, and other mammals roam freely. The raw, uncaged Corcovado welcomes you into a host of natural habitats.

The park has six sectors. The most visited are the **San Pedrillo Sector** (on the northwest side of the park near Bahía Drake), the **La Leona Sector** (on the southwest side of the park near Carate), and the **Sirena Sector** (on the west side of the park between the San Pedrillo and La Leona ranger stations). The **Los Patos Sector** (on the northeast side of the park near La Palma) and the **El Tigre Sector** (on the east side of the park near Puerto Jiménez) are less frequented. The **Los Planes Sector** (on the north side of the park near Bahía Drake) is closed to the public indefinitely.

Self-guided exploration is not permitted. The region's certified tour operators and agencies, many of which are based in Bahía Drake and Puerto Jiménez, run **guided day tours** and **overnight expeditions** through several areas in the park. Tour guides can also be reserved through area accommodations or the **Asociación de Conservación Osa** (Osa Conservation Association, on the west side of the airstrip in Puerto Jiménez, tel. 506/2735-5036, www.osaconservation.org). Visits to the El Tigre Sector are handled separately and best arranged through the nonprofit **Asociación de Conservación de Dos Brazos de Río Tigre** (Dos Brazos de Río Tigre Conservation Association, in the village of Dos Brazos, tel. 506/8323-8695, www.dosbrazosderiotigre.com).

Planning Your Time

It can be tough to choose a Corcovado experience. With **one day** to tour the park, visit either the San Pedrillo Sector or the Sirena Sector from Bahía Drake on a **boat tour.** Not only is the experience relatively affordable and easy to arrange through most hotels, but you'll also be able to set foot in the park (sign the guest book at the ranger station to record your presence), snap memorable photos, likely lay your eyes on some wildlife you've never seen, and be back in Bahía Drake reminiscing about the day long before sundown. If you're unable to spend a night in Bahía Drake, travel to Sierpe and catch a **full-day park tour;** tours typically depart at 8am and return to Sierpe at 4:30pm.

With **2-3 days** to spend in the area and ample energy, book a multiday Corcovado package that departs from Puerto Jiménez, enters the park via the Los Patos Sector, provides a downhill hike to the Sirena Sector, follows the coastal route through the La Leona Sector, and returns to Puerto Jiménez to complete the loop. You're bound to see abundant wildlife during the deep-woods circuit, not to mention a variety of the park's elevations, throughout the epic journey. Overnight stays take place at the Sirena ranger station, located halfway along the multiday route, in the thick of the park's wilderness. The well-known and respected operator **Surcos Tours** (on the west side of the airstrip in Puerto Jiménez, just south of the Asociación de Conservación Osa, tel. 506/2735-5355, www.surcostours. com, 8am-5pm Mon.-Sat.) offers my preferred multiday itinerary (2-day package $240 pp, 3-day package $415 pp) and plenty more that suit a variety of interests, timelines, departure locations, and budgets.

Hiking

An intertwined system of nature trails weaves throughout the park and connects several ranger stations. Dress and pack for high humidity, scorching sun, and torrential rain. Closed-toe shoes or boots, socks, insect repellent, canteens, sunscreen, a hat, a poncho or jacket, a small towel, a flashlight, and a basic first aid kit are must-haves. Hiking at night is not permitted in any sector of the park.

SAN PEDRILLO SECTOR

The San Pedrillo Sector operates as its own individual corner of the park. Five trails totaling 12.5 kilometers are accessible beyond a ranger station and offer treks of moderate difficulty alongside Río Pargo, through primary and secondary forest, and to a series of **small waterfalls.** Most people who tour this sector do so via organized day trips that depart from and return to Bahía Drake. **Day tours** typically start between 6am and 7am, last eight hours, and cost $80-90 per person.

SIRENA SECTOR

The Sirena Sector is the heart of the park, and its ranger station is the home base of most overnight visitors. Twenty kilometers of trails are spread out over eight routes around the station. Most trails, especially the **Sendero Río Pavo** (Río Pavo Trail), which sets off in the direction of the park's largest lagoon, offer prime wildlife-spotting opportunities. Guided **day tours** (expect to pay $90-125 from Bahía Drake) and guided **multiday excursions** (roughly $335 pp for a 2-day package from Bahía Drake or $240 pp for a 2-day package from Puerto Jiménez) visit the sector daily.

LA LEONA AND LOS PATOS SECTORS

The La Leona and Los Patos sectors are most often toured by hikers on their way to (or coming from) the Sirena Sector. Connecting to the ranger station at Sirena are a 16.5-kilometer **beach trail** that begins at the La Leona ranger station, and a 20-kilometer **forest trail** that departs beyond the Los Patos ranger station. The path through La Leona traces much of the coast and is a sweaty endeavor on sunny days, but occasional tree-shaded passage provides temporary relief. In contrast, the narrow, downhill trail (or uphill, if hiked from Sirena) that departs from Los Patos connects the area's highlands to the lowlands of the Corcovado basin. Both trails require river crossings, sometimes waist-deep. The Los Patos Sector also offers a second trail, a challenging three-kilometer hike that rewards brave trekkers with a waterfall, but it is unfrequented.

EL TIGRE SECTOR

A wildly difficult seven-kilometer trail that departs from the village of Dos Brazos enters El Tigre, the park's newest sector; the sector opened in 2015. Run partly on private property and partly within the park, the full-day hike will stun you early on with a nearly 400-meter rise in elevation. On your right upon entrance into Dos Brazos is the tourism office that oversees park access.

Food and Accommodations

Overnight stays ($30 pp) inside the park are permitted for 1-4 nights at the ★ **Sirena ranger station.** The open-air, solar-powered, dormitory-style accommodation has enough beds to sleep 70 tired souls, and it supplies linens, mosquito nets, potable water, and lockers (rented for $4). Meals ($20-$25 adults, children 3-12 pay half-price) are surprisingly gourmet versions of typical Costa Rican dishes. Vegetarian and gluten-free choices can be provided with advance notice. Outside food of any kind is not permitted at the station.

Meals and overnight stays at the Sirena ranger station require advance reservation. Most tour operators, agencies, and hotels that sell multiday guided park excursions include the cost of room and board in their tour rates and handle reservation arrangements on behalf of travelers. Direct booking is not sanctioned by the Costa Rican government, so you'll need one of these businesses to book your stay for you.

Getting There

Corcovado isn't a national park you can drive to leisurely. To reach most ranger stations, you'll need time, energy (some entrances are hike-in only), and a flexible itinerary that allows you to work around park permit availability and transportation schedules. Fortunately, outfitter-led day trips are the norm, and tour operators, agencies, and hotels handle most logistics, such as transportation arrangements, overnight stays, advance payment of the park entrance fee, and arrangement of a tour guide. You can get to the park from just about any destination in the region by booking a day tour or multiday package through a certified provider.

To get to the San Pedrillo ranger station, take one of the boats that depart from Bahía Drake and the dock in Sierpe.

To get to the La Leona ranger station, road access is permitted as far as Carate following a rugged two-hour drive (weather, vehicle, potholes, and river crossings permitting) from Puerto Jiménez. From Carate, also reachable via a charter flight into the community's airstrip, it's a 3.5-kilometer walk along the beach to the ranger station. Without a vehicle, you can hitch a ride on a flatbed truck that commutes between Puerto Jiménez and Carate daily (6am and 1:30pm). The slow ride, which makes stops along the way and is dubbed the *colectivo,* departs from the corner with the hardware store (100 m west of Road 245, just south of the bus station) and costs $10 per person. If you plan to stay in Matapalo, the truck passes through that area approximately one hour post-departure from Puerto Jiménez. The La Leona ranger station can also be accessed on foot via a 16.5-kilometer trail that departs from the Sirena ranger station.

Set in the park's interior, the Sirena ranger station is only accessible by boat (mainly from Bahía Drake, Puerto Jiménez, or the dock in Sierpe), by charter flight (the station has a small airstrip), or on foot (via trails from the La Leona and Los Patos sectors).

You'll need a reliable 4x4 vehicle, a wild sense of adventure, and luck that brings good weather to reach the Los Patos ranger station. The road to the station, which cuts south from the village of La Palma, is virtually impassable much of the year when rain swells the road's numerous river crossings. The only other way in is to hike the 15-kilometer road. The Los Patos ranger station can also be accessed on foot via a 20-kilometer trail that departs from the Sirena ranger station.

Refreshingly easy to reach, albeit over a dusty dirt road, is the El Tigre ranger station. By car, take Road 245 west out of Puerto Jiménez for four kilometers and turn left at the sign for the park. The trailhead is in the village of Dos Brazos, approximately eight kilometers beyond the turnoff; the way is well marked. If you're traveling from the north, the cutoff to Dos Brazos is 20 kilometers after La Palma. Dos Brazos can also be reached by bus during the week from Puerto Jiménez (11am and 4pm Mon.-Fri., 45 minutes, $2.50).

Golfo Dulce

A soothing contrast to the region's montane terrain is the tropical—and turquoise, in places—Golfo Dulce, with palm-lined beaches in some areas and piers packed with water taxis and fishing boats in others. On the gulf's west side, part of the Osa Peninsula, are Puerto Jiménez and Matapalo; on its east are Golfito and Pavones, part of the mainland. The region isn't yet overrun with tourists, but improved road conditions and the development of new attractions suggest it's only a matter of time before the southern part of the peninsula catches up with the north. For now, the area is still considered remote. Inviting villages provide authentic experiences, wildlife and marine life make spontaneous appearances, and tourism is kept to a minimum.

THE ROAD TO PUERTO JIMÉNEZ

Approximately 30 kilometers southeast of Palmar, Highway 2 meets **Road 245** at the community of **Chacarita.** While Highway 2 continues southeast to Ciudad Neily, Road 245 begins the 75-kilometer journey west and then south around the gulf to Puerto Jiménez. The paved but primarily mountainous route is a pleasure to drive as you sail past walls of feathery, lime-green ferns, horses carrying loads of palm fruit harvested from area plantations, and several spectacular *miradores.* Noticeably absent from the stretch are small towns, traffic, and commercial development. Most days, you'll have the curving, peaceful open road to yourself as you travel through one of Costa Rica's most primitive areas.

Sights

★ **MOUNTAINSIDE *MIRADORES***

Three of my favorite lookout spots in the region fall along Road 245 between Chacarita and Puerto Jiménez. With a rental vehicle, you can pull over to the side of the road and take in the scenic sights at each.

Nearly 20 kilometers southwest of Chacarita along Road 245, you can catch a beautiful view of the valley at the north end of the peninsula from the restaurant **El Mirador Osa** (Road 245, 20 km west of Chacarita). A distant Río Sierpe snakes through the scene. Sixteen kilometers west down the road, an opening in the forest (facing south) exposes a breathtaking view of the Golfo Dulce edged by five layers of rainforest-filled mountains. Park cautiously here; the lookout is located around a curve. The colorful scene is striking and includes the soothing blue hue of motionless water and vibrant greens patterned across verdant vegetation. Smooth white stones and terra-cotta-colored soil frame the bottom of the picture from the viewpoint.

Approximately 5.5 kilometers after the second viewpoint (after Road 245 descends down the mountainside), there's another clearing, which faces east. Here, at water level, you can appreciate the tranquility and beauty of the gulf up close. If you're lucky, you may also see whales breaching offshore, as pregnant and new mothers migrate to the spot to give birth and to nurse their young in its warm waters.

DOS BRAZOS

The community of **Dos Brazos** (12 kilometers west of Puerto Jiménez) was once the *X* on Costa Rica's treasure map during a gold rush in the 1970s. Today, the village of 295 residents runs on ecotourism thanks to the **Asociación de Conservación de Dos Brazos de Río Tigre** (Dos Brazos de Río Tigre Conservation Association, in the village of Dos Brazos, tel. 506/8691-4545, www.corcovadoeltigre. com, 7am-6pm daily), offering a handful of **nature tours** including botany tours, night tours, horseback riding tours, bird-watching

1: the scenic route between Chacarita and Puerto Jiménez **2:** the waterfront town of Golfito **3:** Rancho Raíces **4:** view of the Golfo Dulce from a mountainside *mirador* (lookout)

tours, visits to swimming holes, and cultural cooking classes. If you have time to spare in the area, there's no end to the experiences you can have in this tight-knit but welcoming community.

Dos Brazos's most unique offering, its **gold mining tour** (9am-2pm daily, 3 hours, $30 adults, $22.50 children 12 and under), provides an opportunity to mine for gold by hand in Río Tigre. As you'll learn during the interactive experience, panning is as much an artistic process as it is a profession. Older workers who reside in the village—you're bound to come across a few wading in the river—have spent years perfecting the efficient process. Younger generations lead the guided activity with the hope that you'll leave the area wealthy in new knowledge. On the tour, you'll hike through the forest to the river.

RANCHO RAÍCES CHOCOLATE TOUR

Entertaining from start to end is the **Chocolate Tour** (9am, noon, 2pm, and 3pm daily, 2.5 hours, $40 pp 7 years and older) conducted at **Rancho Raíces** (Road 245, 14 km west of downtown Puerto Jiménez, tel. 506/8603-0464). What begins as a medicinal plant tour conducted on a 50-acre family farm ends as an interactive and (spoiler alert!) delicious demonstration of the various stages of cacao processing. The best thing about the tour is Tico operator German Quirós Vivas, who leads passionate and informative walks around the property with his trusty machete in hand, ready to cut down fresh fruit for your enjoyment along the way. Fascinating and filling, this family-friendly foodie tour is one of the area's best learning opportunities.

Food and Accommodations

Serving typical Costa Rican cuisine, **El Mirador Osa** (Road 245, 20 km west of Chacarita, tel. 506/8823-6861, 6:30am-9pm daily, $4.50-19) is the best of a small selection of dining and lodging establishments between Chacarita and Puerto Jiménez. The quiet, open-air restaurant has a few rattan tables and chairs that overlook a beautiful valley. Below the restaurant, a path leads to a pool and a handful of quaint **bungalows** ($25 s, $45 d) with front porch areas perfect for bird-watching. In the middle of a non-touristy area, the restaurant and hotel are surprisingly customer-oriented.

Information and Services

Few services are offered between Chacarita and Puerto Jiménez, apart from a couple of small **supermarkets,** most of which are in the community of La Palma, approximately halfway between the two towns. There's a **gas station** on the corner of Highway 2 and Road 245.

Transportation

Chacarita is 300 kilometers (an approximate 4.5-hour drive) southeast from downtown **San José** via the **coastal route** (Hwy. 27, Hwy. 34, and Hwy. 2). It's 260 kilometers (an approximate five-hour drive) southeast from downtown San José via the **mountain route,** which begins on Highway 2, continues to Highway 34 (via Road 243), and returns to Highway 2.

Chacarita is 385 kilometers (an approximate six-hour drive) southeast from **Liberia** via Highway 1, Highway 34, and Highway 2.

PUERTO JIMÉNEZ

Puerto Jiménez is the only community of considerable size in the southern half of the Osa Peninsula. It's not large, but it's a bustling Tico town on the Golfo Dulce that's blessed with distant mountain views. Tourism here is understated. Except for a handful of hotels and outfitters, who mainly sell guided expeditions through Parque Nacional Corcovado, Puerto Jiménez is a quintessential Costa Rican fishing town.

Beaches
PLAYA PRECIOSA

Though the beach's official name is **Playa Platanares,** anyone who has spent more than a few days in Puerto Jiménez calls it

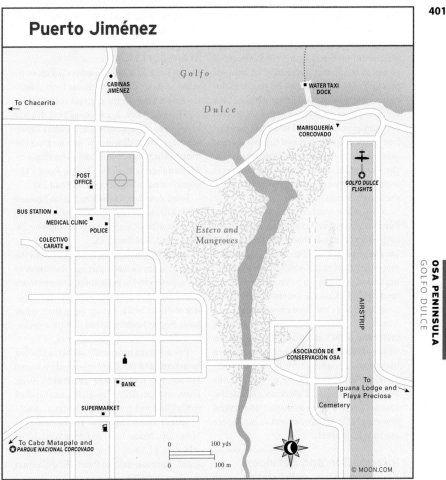

Puerto Jiménez

CABINAS JIMÉNEZ

To Chacarita

Golfo

Dulce

WATER TAXI DOCK

MARISQUERÍA CORCOVADO

POST OFFICE

GOLFO DULCE FLIGHTS

BUS STATION

MEDICAL CLINIC

POLICE

COLECTIVO CARATE

Estero and Mangroves

AIRSTRIP

BANK

ASOCIACIÓN DE CONSERVACIÓN OSA

To Iguana Lodge and Playa Preciosa

Cemetery

SUPERMARKET

To Cabo Matapalo and PARQUE NACIONAL CORCOVADO

0   100 yds

0   100 m

© MOON.COM

Playa Preciosa. The long, largely deserted stretch of coast east of town is the area's only swimming beach, but the water is consistently rough and suitable only for advanced swimmers. Often awash with driftwood, the brown-sand beach fronts a coastline of warm teal-hued water and crashing waves. Even storms are beautiful when they roll in here. Look and listen for scarlet macaws while sunbathing; they regularly fly overhead.

Food and Accommodations

On the waterfront, where you can practically see the day's catches being tossed on the mainland before they hit your plate, is my favorite eatery, the ★ **Marisquería Corcovado** (Oceandrive Blvd., 100 m east of the pier, tel. 506/2735-5659, 5am-11pm daily, $6.50-16). Everything fish-based is first-rate, including seafood pastas, seafood salads, sushi, and ceviches. Grab a table by the water's edge or a stool around the big tree that grows through the center of the restaurant, and down a bottle of Corcovado-brand beer.

The best budget lodging in town is ★ **Cabinas Jiménez** (100 m north of the *fútbol* field, tel. 506/2735-5090, www. cabinasjimenez.com, $45-105 s, $60-120 d), set right on the gulf. The hotel's 20 awesome air-conditioned and mini-fridge-equipped rooms make a great home base for area exploration. Most rooms sleep 1-5 people in single, double, or bunk beds. Many rooms have outdoor patios with views of the water; others face the pool. Extras, like secure parking, free kayak and bike use, and baggage storage (ideal if you're planning an overnight trip to the Parque Nacional Corcovado and don't want to drag your luggage with you), add to the accommodation's value.

A 20-minute drive from town down a bumpy, mangrove-lined road is the Bali-inspired and art-covered **Iguana Lodge** (on the road to Playa Preciosa, 4 km southeast of the airport, tel. 506/8829-5865, www. iguanalodge.com, club rooms $166 s/d, casitas $203 s/d). Upscale accommodation options include a three-story beach house and screened-in casitas with outdoor showers. I prefer the hotel's second-floor club rooms, which are clean and fresh and have modern bathrooms, bamboo-built beds, and comfortable mattresses. These rooms face the beach; the sunrises are glorious. Yoga decks, a tennis court, a ceramics studio, and several towering *ceiba barrigona* trees occupy space around the property.

Information and Services

Puerto Jiménez has a **police station** (south side of the *fútbol* field, tel. 506/2735-5114, 24 hours daily); a **clinic** called **Ebais Puerto Jiménez** (just west of the police station, tel. 506/2735-5029, 24 hours daily); a **pharmacy** called **Farmacia Hidalgo** (Road 245, 400 m south of the *fútbol* field, tel. 506/2735-5507, 8am-8pm Mon.-Sat.); **banks** with **ATMs,** including **Banco de Costa Rica** (Road 245, 375 m south of the *fútbol* field, tel. 506/2211-1111, 9am-4pm Mon.-Fri., ATM 5am-midnight daily); a **post office** (just east of the police station, tel. 506/2735-5045, 8am-5pm Mon.-Fri.); and several **supermarkets.** There's a **gas station** on Road 245, 500 meters south of the *fútbol* field.

Transportation

Puerto Jiménez is 375 kilometers (an approximate 5.5-hour drive) southeast from downtown **San José** via the **coastal route** (Hwy. 27, Hwy. 34, Hwy. 2, and Road 245). It's 335 kilometers (an approximate six-hour drive) southeast from downtown San José via the **mountain route,** which begins on Highway 2, continues to Highway 34 (via Road 243), then returns to Highway 2 and Road 245.

From downtown **Liberia,** Puerto Jiménez is 460 kilometers (an approximate seven-hour drive) southeast via Highway 1, Highway 34, Highway 2, and Road 245.

Road 245 enters Puerto Jiménez from the west, cuts north-south through the center of town, passes by the gas station, and continues down the coast to Matapalo before it eventually ends at Carate. Drives along the road as far as Puerto Jiménez do not require a 4x4 vehicle, but onward travel south does.

Public **buses** travel daily to Puerto Jiménez from **San José** (8am and noon daily, 8 hours, $12.50), **San Isidro de El General** (6:30am, 11am, and 3pm daily, 5 hours, $8), and **Ciudad Neily** (7am and 2pm daily, 3-3.5 hours, $4).

Water taxis (multiple times 7am-5pm Mon.-Sat., 10am, 1pm, and 3pm Sun., 30-90 minutes, $3.50-5), which vary in size and speed, commute daily to Puerto Jiménez from the dock in Golfito.

★ GOLFO DULCE FLIGHTS

If you want to fly somewhere in Costa Rica, fly to the Golfo Dulce, ideally to Puerto Jiménez. Not only does the quick 45-minute flight avoid five or more hours of driving or an eight-hour bus ride from San José, but the trip is also wonderfully scenic. Once your plane climbs steeply out of the Central Valley, you'll soar above the mountaintops past the country's highest peak and catch a bird's-eye view of cities, plantations, and national parks and other protected reserves. The best view, however, is saved for last, when you fly over the calm, blue, crystalline gulf. You'll descend over the water, just above fishing boats occupying the pier in Puerto Jiménez, before landing on the narrow airstrip in town. Although it's bumpy and not for the faint of heart, the aerial tour offers a look at the region's varied landscape like no other.

The **Aeropuerto Puerto Jiménez** (Puerto Jiménez Airport, PJM) is on the east side of town, a mere 500 meters from the main drag, Road 245. **SANSA Airlines** (tel. 506/2290-4100, www.flysansa.com) offers direct flights to Puerto Jiménez daily from San José. The flight time from San José is approximately 45 minutes.

MATAPALO AND CARATE

The hamlet of Matapalo occupies the southern tip of the Osa Peninsula, or more specifically, the craggy escarpment **Cabo Matapalo** (Cape Matapalo), which towers over the area. Access to the hamlet is via the rough, steep, downhill road known as the road to Playa Matapalo. The route begins off Road 245, travels a few kilometers south, and ends at the area's namesake beach, **Playa Matapalo.**

West of Matapalo, the tiny community of Carate serves as a small gateway to Parque Nacional Corcovado. Some of the country's most remote and elite rainforest resorts are in this area.

Wildlife here is known to stray from the forest and can make an appearance when you least expect it. Regardless of where you choose to stay, keep your eyes peeled for all four types of monkeys that reside in Costa Rica (capuchin, howler, spider, and squirrel), tropical birds, and other delightful surprises. If you hear caws, croaks, or squawks, you're probably in the presence of macaws, toucans, or linguistic *loras* (parrots), the last of which mimic the sounds of others in their company.

Recreation

Roughly 750 meters inland and upward from Playa Matapalo, the **Catarata King Louis** (King Louis Waterfall) tumbles down a rock face in the middle of pristine rainforest. The tall, beautiful 30-meter cascade, which can be reduced to a trickle during dry periods, usually has a small pool at its base where you can take a dip. Neither easy to get to (climbing over rocks and up a riverbed is part of the journey!) nor bursting with bathers, the majestic waterfall is one of my favorites to visit. Look for the trailhead on the west side of the road to Playa Matapalo, approximately 250 meters before the road ends at the beach. From the trailhead, it's about a 15-minute hike to the waterfall.

Up for a daring and fun experience? **Everyday Adventures** (on the road to Playa Matapalo, 2 km south of Road 245, tel. 506/8353-8619, www.psychotours.com, Dec.-July) offers a heart-pumping **waterfall rappelling tour** (8am daily, 3 hours, $95 pp, min. age 10). It will have you canyoning close enough to Catarata King Louis that your sweat will be washed away by the spray. A rappel down a smaller, 14-meter waterfall is also included in the tour experience. The tour operator's **combo tour** (8am daily, 5-6 hours, $130 pp, min. age 10) adds an opportunity to climb an 18-meter *higuerón* tree (strangler fig, or ficus) and free fall back to the forest floor. Have members in your travel group who aren't up for rappelling or tree climbing? They can participate in the **waterfall hiking** tour as an observer for $45 per person.

Food

Dining options in the Matapalo and Carate area are limited. Plan to eat at your hotel's on-site restaurant.

The pirate-themed **Martina's Bar & Restaurant** (Road 245, 1 km north of the road to Playa Matapalo, tel. 506/8720-0801, 11am-11:30pm daily, $4-15, cash only), which also goes by the name **Buena Esperanza,** is the local diner and watering hole, catering to anyone and everyone looking to hang out outside the bounds of a hotel. The chalkboard-written menu changes daily but sticks to pub grub. On Fridays after 4pm, the place hosts a small farmers market. Evenings bring loud music.

Accommodations
★ REMOTE RAINFOREST RESORTS

Accommodations around the southern tip of the Osa Peninsula form one of the country's best collections of remote rainforest resorts. There are many great options worth considering, including my favorites and more. Most invite you to relax in a luxurious but ecofriendly space, dine on meals prepared with locally sourced ingredients, hide out among curious wildlife, and truly immerse yourself in nature.

One of the best eco-resorts in the country is Matapalo's ★ **Lapa Ríos** (Road 245, just south of the road to Playa Matapalo, tel. 506/4040-0418, www.laparios.com, $670 s, $1,100 d, all-inclusive). Spread out across a hilltop, the secluded property has 17 spacious, open-concept bungalows with screened windows, wooden outdoor showers, and private decks with sitting areas and hammocks that face the water. Great for families, each sleeps up to five people. The lodge's culinary offerings (three daily meals are included in the cost of your stay) are rave-worthy: Food selections are gourmet, and vegan, vegetarian, gluten-free, and allergy-aware meal requests are addressed. The main restaurant's 360-degree canopy lookout tower, theme nights, and romantic poolside dinners keep dining experiences fresh and fun.

An awesome spot for groups is **Encanta La Vida** (on the road to Playa Matapalo, 750 m south of Road 245, tel. 506/8376-3209, www.encantalavida.com, $150-175 s, $300-350 d, all-inclusive). The eclectic place has a two-suite *casona* (house), a three-story, treehouse-like "pole house," two-story deluxe cabins, and an indigenous-style rancho. Most quarters are crafted out of hardwoods, have canopy beds, and feature indoor rooms or outdoor decks and patios that make great gathering areas. Three daily meals are included in the price. You can pass time between meals in the

on-site yoga shala or head to nearby Playa Pan Dulce to surf the area's best waves.

In Carate, **Finca Exótica** (Road 245, at the east end of the airstrip, tel. 506/4070-0054, www.fincaexotica.com, tent $90 s, $160 d; cabin $180 s, $300 d, all-inclusive) has five rustic, open-air cabins adorned with mosquito nets, beautiful textiles, and tropical plants. Bare-bones outdoor showers will test and hopefully increase your level of comfort with nature. Also available are a few raised, fully closable tiki tents that have beds for two occupants; bathrooms are shared. Contributing to the accommodation's quiet but social vibe is the large communal dining table. Mingling with other guests is encouraged during the three daily farm-to-table meals.

Information and Services
Except for a small *pulpería* (corner store) in Carate, both Matapalo and Carate rely heavily on services in Puerto Jiménez. Two hospitals serve much of the Osa Peninsula. **Hospital de Golfito Manuel Mora Valverde** (Hwy. 14, 1 km southeast of the airport, tel. 506/2775-7800, 24 hours daily) in Golfito and **Hospital de Osa Tomás Casas Casajús** (just south of Hwy. 34 upon entrance into Ciudad Cortés, tel. 506/2786-8148, 24 hours daily) in Ciudad Cortés are each roughly the same drive time from Matapalo (2.5 hours) and Carate (4 hours).

Transportation
Via the **coastal route** (Hwy. 27, Hwy. 34, Hwy. 2, and Road 245), Matapalo is a 395-kilometer drive southeast from downtown **San José** that takes a little over six hours. Via the **mountain route,** which begins on Highway 2, continues to Highway 34 (via Road 243), then returns to Highway 2 and Road 245, it's a 355-kilometer drive southeast from downtown San José that takes nearly seven hours.

1: the affordable Cabinas Jiménez in Puerto Jiménez **2:** La Playa restaurant at the Golfito Marina Village

From downtown **Liberia,** Matapalo is a 480-kilometer drive southeast via Highway 1, Highway 34, Highway 2, and Road 245 that takes just under eight hours.

From **Puerto Jiménez,** Matapalo is a 20-kilometer, 45-minute drive south on Road 245. Carate is another 25 kilometers (an approximate 1.5-hour drive) west of Matapalo on Road 245.

Be forewarned: The rough stretch of road from downtown Puerto Jiménez to Carate requires a 4x4 vehicle and includes river crossings. Your last chance to fill up on gas is in Puerto Jiménez center.

Visitors without a rental vehicle can catch a ride on the flatbed truck serving as the local *colectivo* that commutes between Puerto Jiménez and Carate daily (6am and 1:30pm, $10, $4 to Matapalo). It departs Puerto Jiménez from the corner with the hardware store (100 m west of Road 245, just south of the bus station) and stops in Matapalo roughly one hour post-departure. The full ride to Carate takes 2.5 hours.

GOLFITO

On the mainland side of the gulf, the waterfront town of Golfito is no more than a six-kilometer paved promenade (Hwy. 14) with steep-rising hills on one side and the low-lying Golfo Dulce on the other. It's eye-catching to say the least, a scene seemingly straight out of the Caribbean, with its colorful wood buildings and tall tropical palms. The area's largest, newest commercial development is the fancy 50-slip **Golfito Marina Village** that you'll pass roughly two-thirds of the way through town. The shopping center known as the **Depósito Libre Comercial de Golfito** (Golfito Duty-Free Warehouse, at the roundabout at the end of Hwy. 14) attracts Ticos from all over the country with low-cost household items. You'll know you're getting close to Golfito when you turn off Highway 2 at the village of **Río Claro** and are inundated with billboard advertisements for electronics, kitchen appliances, tires, and tools.

Beaches

PLAYA ZANCUDO

The pier-lined coast that stretches the length of Golfito offers little opportunity for swimming and sunbathing. South of Golfito is **Playa Zancudo**—the area's sandiest spot and a decent destination for a day trip. The route connecting Golfito with the beach is often underestimated; it's a long road trip to get here. The journey cuts inland to the east from Golfito via Highway 14 and travels south on Road 238 over the Río Coto before you turn west toward the coast and arrive at Zancudo. An hour is needed for the one-way trek. Alternately, Zancudo can be reached from Golfito by boat (noon daily, 30 minutes, $5). Boats depart from *el muellecito* (Avenida 10 off Hwy. 14), a small dock in the center of Golfito.

The quiet beachside community of Zancudo is spread out along a narrow land spit. Playa Zancudo edges the community's west side, while marshy wetlands encroach upon the area from the east. You can swim in the gulf off the light-gray-sand beach but be careful where you wade. The delta at the community's north end is a critical nursery habitat for hammerhead sharks.

Food and Accommodations

★ **La Playa** (at the Golfito Marina Village, tel. 506/2775-3100, www.laplayacr.com, noon-9:30pm daily, $9-35) is my favorite restaurant in Golfito. Its massive menu lists nearly everything from fish-and-chips, wood-oven pizza, meats, pastas, and Costa Rican entrées to salads, burgers, and wraps. It caters to yacht travelers and sportfishing aficionados, so don't expect bargain prices. But if you want high-quality food in a comfortable, casual setting that overlooks the beautiful gulf, La Playa offers it.

The Tica owners of ★ **Hostal Del Mar** (1 km south of Mar y Luna, tel. 506/4700-0510, www.hostaldelmargolfito.com, $20 s, $40 d) are sisters doin' it for themselves. A fantastic deal, this waterfront house provides breakfast and a clean private bedroom (bathrooms are shared) for less than the cost of shared accommodations elsewhere in the country. The vibe around the place is chill. Self-service laundry, a communal kitchen, and good Wi-Fi are pluses. The showstopper is the hotel's magnificent gulf view. Second- and third-place wins are the homey atmosphere and warm hospitality.

To treat yourself, stay at the **Playa Nicuesa Rainforest Lodge** (15 km from Golfito as the crow flies, tel. 506/2258-8250, www.nicuesalodge.com, $370 s, $590 d, all-inclusive, 2-night minimum). The remote accommodation, separated from Golfito by a protected reserve, is only accessible by boat (transport is provided by the hotel) and has a real *Swiss Family Robinson* feel. Private and quiet, it features five rustic cabins (plus two rentable jungle houses) with wraparound windows and terraces that show off the property's lush surroundings. Nature trails, paddleboards, kayaks, and yoga decks encourage exercise and wellness at the isolated lodge.

Information and Services

Golfito houses the **Hospital de Golfito Manuel Mora Valverde** (Hwy. 14, 1 km southeast of the airport, tel. 506/2775-7800, 24 hours daily); **pharmacies,** including **Farmacia San Ezequiel** (corner of Hwy. 14 and Avenida 50, tel. 506/2775-1632, 8:30am-8pm Mon.-Sat., 8:30am-noon Sun.); a **police station** (west side of the roundabout at the Depósito Libre Comercial de Golfito, tel. 506/2775-1022, 24 hours daily); a **post office** (Avenida 2, 50 m northeast of Hwy. 14, tel. 506/2775-1911, 8am-5pm Mon.-Fri.); **banks** with **ATMs,** including **Banco Nacional** (Hwy. 14 at Avenida 54, tel. 506/2775-1101, 8:30am-4pm Mon.-Fri., ATM 5am-11pm); and **supermarkets.**

Transportation

Via the **coastal route** (Hwy. 27, Hwy. 34, Hwy. 2, and Hwy. 14), Golfito is a 345-kilometer drive southeast from downtown **San José** that takes a little over five hours. Via the **mountain route,** which begins on Highway 2, continues to Highway 34 (via Road 243), then returns to Highway 2 and Highway 14, it's a 305-kilometer drive southeast from downtown San José that takes just under six hours.

From downtown **Liberia,** Golfito is a 430-kilometer drive southeast via Highway 1, Highway 34, Highway 2, and Highway 14 that takes nearly seven hours.

Highway 2 is a paved route to Golfito as far south as the village of **Río Claro,** where the equally easy-to-drive Highway 14 departs to the south and leads into Golfito center. The road ends at a roundabout just shy of the airport.

Public **buses** travel daily to Golfito from **San José** (6:30am, 7am, and 3:30pm daily, 7 hours, $13), **Ciudad Neily** (multiple times 5:20am-7:30pm daily, 1-1.5 hours, $1.50), and **Pavones** (12:30pm and 4:30pm daily, 1.5-2 hours, $3.50).

The **Aeropuerto Golfito** (Golfito Airport, GLF) is at the northwest end of town, at the end of the main drag. **SANSA Airlines** (tel. 506/2290-4100, www.flysansa.com) offers direct flights to Golfito daily from San José. The flight time from San José is approximately 40-50 minutes.

Water taxis (multiple times 6am-4:20pm Mon.-Sat., 6am, 11:30pm, and 2pm Sun., 30-90 minutes, $3.50-5), which vary in size and speed, commute daily to Golfito from the pier in Puerto Jiménez.

PAVONES

A long dirt road leads south to the quiet mainland beachside community of Pavones, where at least two assumptions are commonly understood: If you're crazy enough to make the trip down to Costa Rica's southernmost area, you deserve to be rewarded, and the only reward that counts is epic surf. Favored among experienced riders, this small surf mecca is suitable for any laid-back, board-toting, cash-carrying traveler who wants to kick it under coconut trees.

Six kilometers south of Pavones is the community of **Punta Banco,** the farthest south

Light Up the Night

Come nightfall, witnessing the bioluminescence that sometimes occurs in the waters off Costa Rica's coasts is a truly spectacular experience. The Disneyesque scene, which illuminates pitch-black gulfs, bays, and lagoons with specks of glowing blue, green, or white light, is merely a chemical reaction caused by startled plankton, but it feels supernatural, or rather, eerily extraterrestrial. Catching the event isn't easy; it requires clear skies, a dark night (typically the evening of a new moon), and a hint of luck, but when the conditions are right and the ocean shines, it's a majestic sight you won't soon forget.

Bioluminescence can be seen in various areas of Costa Rica, most notably in Bahía Drake, the Golfo Dulce, and the Golfo de Nicoya (best seen northeast of Paquera). Faded ocean glow can be spotted at a distance from some waterfront hotels, but the phenomenon is best viewed from a beach at close range. (Solo visits to any beach after dark are not safe; hire a local tour guide for company.) Kayak tours, which stimulate the chemical reaction with in-water movement, offer complete immersion.

Puerto Jiménez-based tour operator **Aventuras Tropicales** (750 m east of the airport, Puerto Jiménez, tel. 506/2735-5195, www.aventurastropicales.com, $50 adults, $25 children) is a reputable company that runs the thrilling trip around the Golfo Dulce. If you don't plan to travel that far south, the folks at the **Bahía Rica Fishing and Kayak Lodge** (1.5 km northeast of the ferry terminal, Paquera, tel. 506/2641-0811, www.bahiarica.com, $35 pp) run a great bioluminescence kayak tour in the calm waters of Bahía Paquera, a small bay adjacent to the Golfo de Nicoya.

you can travel in Costa Rica in a vehicle. Venture beyond this point on foot and you could unknowingly cross into the territory of the Ngäbe indigenous people (also known as the Guaymí and sometimes referred to as the Ngöbe) or tumble into Panama.

Recreation
SURFING

Pavones doesn't just offer surf—it's notorious for it. One of few Costa Rican surf towns that isn't bursting with surf shops, schools, and camps, Pavones offers what nearly every experienced rider desires: a kilometer-long river-mouth wave break in front of an off-the-beaten-path beach community. Despite the hype, the area's notorious left break—either the first, second, or third longest in the world, depending on who's bragging—is inconsistent. But when the stars align (or rather, when the waves connect), the peeling water provides a legendary two-minute hollow run. Get ready to get shacked, especially during the region's wet season when big swell hits and everyone gets wild.

If you need a board, you can rent one for $20 per day through the **Sea Kings Surf Shop** (on the northeast side of the *fútbol* field, tel. 506/2776-2015, www.seakingssurfshop.com, 8am-5pm daily), which doubles as an art store. Boogie boards go for $10 per day. If you lose or break your own gear, the shop has a lineup of replacements.

Food and Accommodations

Hungry after a long day of surfing righteous waves? What you need is a plate of loaded Mexican tacos or burritos stacked and stuffed by **Tico Mex** (75 m northeast of the *fútbol* field, tel. 506/8650-2315, 8am-9pm daily, $6-9). Fresh vegetables, flavorful meat, and cheese (lots and lots of cheese) help the hearty meals go down easy. Vegetarian varieties are also offered. Located across the street from the water, the informal restaurant has picnic-table seating and is a solid option for grabbing a bite by the beach.

To find Little Italy in Pavones, visit **Restaurante La Bruschetta** (on the road to Punta Banco, 2.5 km south of Pavones, tel. 506/2776-2174, 10am-9pm daily, $12-21), a fabulous—and romantic, come nightfall—

open-air restaurant with attentive staff and even better food. Locals adore Italian favorites like pastas, pizzas, and antipasti. This spot is suitable for a date or a sophisticated social outing. Adding to the ambience are desserts and wines.

The coolest hangout in town, **Caza Olas** (150 m southeast of the *fútbol* field, tel. 506/2776-2271, www.cazaolas.com, dorm $14 pp, private $50 s/d) also happens to be an affordable hostel. If you're a surfer on a budget, I bet you'll like it here. It's within walking distance of the beach, the break, supermarkets, and restaurants, plus the place is always abuzz with stories from the day's best waves. The hostel is also clean, has a trendy kitchen, and offers mixed and female-only dorms.

Tucked away in secondary forest five kilometers south of Pavones is the ★ **Tiskita Jungle Lodge** (on the road to Punta Banco, 2.5 km south of Pavones, tel. 506/2296-8125, www.tiskita.com, $285 s/d, all-inclusive). Nine cabins that provide a total of 17 rooms have comfortable beds, screened windows, fans, outdoor sitting areas, and half-walled outdoor bathrooms. Views from each cabin overlook jungle and water where the Pacific Ocean and the Golfo Dulce collide. Facilities include a pool (visited more frequently by wildlife than guests), a restaurant (three daily meals are included in the rate), a game area, a yoga deck, and, my personal favorite, an organic tropical fruit orchard.

Information and Services

Pavones has a **police station** (on the southeast side of the *fútbol* field, tel. 506/2776-2087, 24 hours daily) and a couple of small **supermarkets.** Forty minutes northeast of Pavones is a **clinic** called **Ebais Comte** (in the hamlet of Comte, tel. 506/2776-8205, 7am-4pm Mon.-Thurs., 7am-3pm Fri.). There are no banks or ATMs in Pavones. The closest **ATM** (5am-midnight daily) is in the community of **Laurel,** an hour's drive east.

Transportation

Pavones is 380 kilometers (an approximate 6.5-hour drive) southeast from downtown **San José** via the **coastal route** (Hwy. 27, Hwy. 34, Hwy. 2, Hwy. 14, Road 238, and Road 611). It's 340 kilometers (an approximate seven-hour drive) southeast from downtown San José via the **mountain route** (Hwy. 2, Road 243, Hwy. 34, Hwy. 2, Hwy. 14, Road 238, and Road 611).

From downtown **Liberia,** Pavones is a 465-kilometer, eight-hour drive southeast via

A water taxi in Puerto Jiménez waits for passengers heading to Golfito.

OSA PENINSULA
GOLFO DULCE

Highway 1, Highway 34, Highway 2, Highway 14, Road 238, and Road 611. Off Highway 14, 10 kilometers south of the village of **Río Claro** (at the junction of Highway 2 and Highway 14), a turnoff onto Road 238 leads to Pavones over paved and dirt roads. From Road 238, turn west onto Road 611 in the hamlet of. Comte and follow the signs to Pavones. A 4x4 vehicle is recommended, especially during wet times of year when the route is slick with mud.

Public **buses** travel daily to Pavones from **Golfito** (10am and 3pm daily, 2 hours, $4).

Southern Pacific

Past Río Claro and the turnoff to Golfito, Highway 2 sails through the region, where the Costa Rican portion of the road ends at the village of Paso Canoas, just at the border with Panama. Virtually absent of tourism, this area of Costa Rica is typically visited only by foreigners headed to (or coming from) Panama.

CIUDAD NEILY

The most notable town in the region is Ciudad Neily (18 km northwest of Paso Canoas and 16 kilometers east of Río Claro). It offers little to warrant a visit, but if you need food following a border crossing or you could use a good night's sleep after crossing over the mountains from San Vito via Road 237, the town makes an adequate rest stop.

Food and Accommodations

The best place to lay your head is **Hotel Neily** (corner of Calle 2 and Avenida 15, tel. 506/2783-3031, www.hotelneily.com, $70 s/d). Dressed up with touches of colonial style, the two-story motel has 77 standard-quality rooms with single or double beds, air-conditioning, flat-screen televisions, and spiffy bathrooms. The property has a large pool with a couple of short waterslides and its own *fútbol* field. The first-floor restaurant (2pm-10pm Mon., 6am-10pm Tues.-Sun., $6-15) sells typical Costa Rican cuisine and fast food. The sports bar has billiards and beer.

Information and Services

Ciudad Neily is home to the **Hospital de Ciudad Neily** (Hwy. 2, 1.5 km southeast of Road 237, tel. 506/2785-9600, 24 hours daily), a **post office** (corner of Calle 9 and Avenida 11, tel. 506/2783-3500, 8am-5pm Mon.-Fri.), a **police station** (Calle 5 at Avenida 18, tel. 506/2783-3150, 24 hours daily), and a few **supermarkets.**

Pharmacies (most of which are open 8am-5pm daily), including **Farmacia Villa Neily** (tel. 506/2783-5678), and **banks** with **ATMs,** including **Banco Nacional** (tel. 506/2212-2000, 8:30am-4pm Mon.-Fri., ATM 5am-11pm daily), can be found on Road 237.

Transportation

Via the **coastal route** (Hwy. 27, Hwy. 34, and Hwy. 2), Ciudad Neily is a 340-kilometer drive southeast from downtown **San José** that takes just over five hours. Via the **mountain route,** which begins at Highway 2, continues to Highway 34 (via Road 243), then returns to Highway 2, it's a 300-kilometer drive southeast from downtown San José that takes a little over 5.5 hours.

From downtown **Liberia,** Ciudad Neily is a 425-kilometer drive southeast via Highway 1, Highway 34, and Highway 2 that takes a little over 6.5 hours.

The north-south **Road 237** (from San Vito) is the main drag and connects with the east-west Highway 2 in the south end of town.

Public **buses** travel daily to Ciudad Neily from **San José** (multiple times 5am-6:40pm daily, 8 hours, $13), **Golfito** (multiple times 5am-8pm daily, 1-1.5 hours, $1.50), and **Puerto Jiménez** (5:30am and 2pm daily, 3-3.5 hours, $4).

Caribbean Coast

The pace of life in the Caribe—the Caribbean—
is gentler than in the rest of the country. It moves to reggae rhythms
and calypso claps. Bright colors saturate the region, and the cuisine is
rich and flavorful, something to be savored. Warm breezes sway the
branches of the palm trees.

Ask a Costa Rican about the Caribbean region and you're bound
to hear the phrase *"Lo mejor de Limón es su gente"* ("The best of
Limón is its people"). Contained entirely within the Limón province, the Caribbean coast is Costa Rica's cultural melting pot, where
Afro-Costa Rican, indigenous, Chinese, and mestizo traditions and
languages come together. In this notably diverse region, there are

Highlights

Look for ★ to find recommended sights, activities, dining, and lodging.

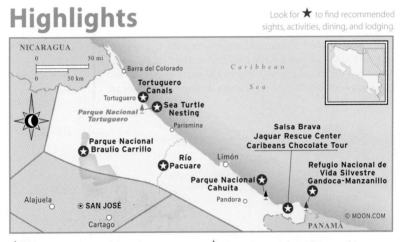

© MOON.COM

★ **Take a scenic drive** through steep forested slopes in the **Parque Nacional Braulio Carrillo** (page 417).

★ **Go white-water rafting** on the **Río Pacuare** (page 424).

★ **Watch monkeys** playing in the trees at **Parque Nacional Cahuita** (page 434).

★ **Surf the break** at **Salsa Brava** (page 437).

★ **Learn about wildlife** rescue and rehabilitation efforts at the **Jaguar Rescue Center** (page 444).

★ **Experience chocolate making,** from bean to bar, during the **Caribeans Chocolate Tour** (page 445).

★ **Hike** through varied ecosystems to beautiful beaches within the **Refugio Nacional de Vida Silvestre Gandoca-Manzanillo** (page 450).

★ **Float** through the **Tortuguero canals** (page 456).

★ **Watch sea turtles nesting** at **Parque Nacional Tortuguero** (page 456).

more Afro-Costa Rican and indigenous citizens than elsewhere in the country. Many Afro-Costa Ricans reside in waterfront communities along the coast. Most of the Caribbean's indigenous people inhabit the foothills of the Cordillera de Talamanca in the southern Caribbean's mountainous inland region. The Caribbean is also home to a number of Chinese descendants (the third-highest number in Costa Rica after San José and Heredia), many of whom live and own businesses in the city of Limón.

Culturally distinct from the rest of Costa Rica, the sultry Caribbean coast boasts an easygoing vibe and a no-frills approach to tourism. Most Limonenses (residents of Limón province) get by with little, and visitors are encouraged to do the same. Amenities that are standard in other areas of the country (like air-conditioning, reliable Wi-Fi, and private parking) are considered luxuries in the Caribbean. Economy accommodations and outdoorsy lodges equipped with fans, screened windows, and mosquito nets are the norm. This is also where hammocks are heaven, bikes outnumber cars, and dollars—when compared to spending on the Pacific coast—can stretch for miles.

The Caribbean's most obvious draws are the beautiful and rapid-filled Río Pacuare, and the laze-inviting beach town of Puerto Viejo de Talamanca. But the region is also home to a handful of ecological habitats where some of Costa Rica's rarest wildlife resides. Possible sightings of jaguars, manatees, sea turtles, and great green macaws delight visitors who flock to the Caribbean for its verdant forests and calm canals. Some sites here, primarily in Tortuguero and Puerto Viejo de Sarapiquí, are recognized around the world as key locales for marine life conservation and rainforest research.

PLANNING YOUR TIME

The northern Caribbean region's natural wonderlands provide fantastic bird-watching opportunities and immersion in a variety of ecosystems. Give yourself two days at the inland destination of Puerto Viejo de Sarapiquí or on the coast at Tortuguero. In Puerto Viejo de Sarapiquí, the overnight stay will provide you with time to experience the area's many rainforest trails during the day and night. In Tortuguero, you can tour the **Tortuguero canals** in the morning or afternoon. Then, if it's **turtle season** (March-October), catch an evening **turtle nesting tour** in the **Parque Nacional Tortuguero.**

If you plan to make the trip through the scenic **Parque Nacional Braulio Carrillo** toward Limón and onward to the southern Caribbean region, you'll need at least three full days in the southern Caribbean region to take in the highlights. The **Caribeans Chocolate Tour** and the **Jaguar Rescue Center** can be experienced in a few hours, but longer periods of time fly by while lounging on the beach at the **Parque Nacional Cahuita,** exploring the **Refugio Nacional de Vida Silvestre Gandoca-Manzanillo,** and surfing the break at **Salsa Brava.** How much time you should spend in the area depends largely on how much time you wish to spend lazing around. You can do that endlessly in the Caribbean, which is likely why so many foreigners arrive on vacation, sink into the slow-paced life, and never leave.

Don't forget to save a day for a white-water rafting trip down the remarkable **Río Pacuare.** The thrilling tour—regarded by many travelers as a top Costa Rica vacation experience—can either be combined with Tortuguero packages (experienced from towns in the southern Caribbean) or arranged as a travel connection between Caribbean destinations and other areas of the country. It's

Previous: sea turtle in Parque Nacional Tortuguero; Puerto Viejo de Talamanca; plates of flavorful Caribbean food.

Caribbean Coast

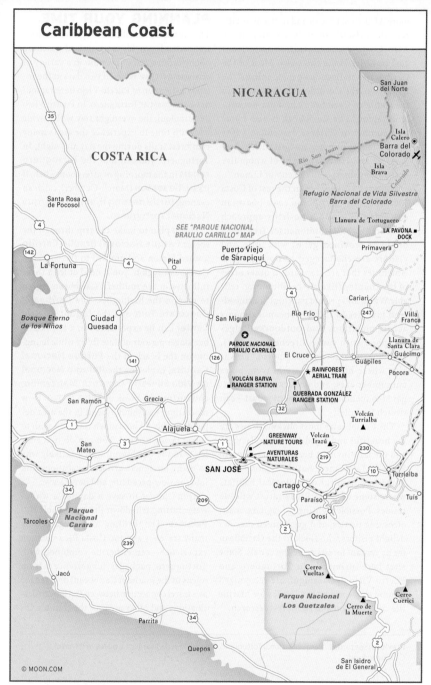

NICARAGUA

COSTA RICA

San Juan
del Norte

Isla
Calero

Barra del
Colorado

Isla
Brava

Rio San Juan

Santa Rosa
de Pocosol

Refugio Nacional de Vida Silvestre
Barra del Colorado

Llanura de Tortuguero

SEE "PARQUE NACIONAL
BRAULIO CARRILLO" MAP

LA PAVONA
DOCK

Puerto Viejo
de Sarapiquí

Primavera

La Fortuna

Pital

Bosque Eterno
de los Niños

Ciudad
Quesada

San Miguel

Río Frío

Cariari

Villa
Franca

Llanura de
Santa Clara

Guácimo

PARQUE NACIONAL
BRAULIO CARRILLO

El Cruce

Guápiles

Pocora

RAINFOREST
AERIAL TRAM

VOLCÁN BARVA
RANGER STATION

QUEBRADA GONZÁLEZ
RANGER STATION

Volcán
Turrialba

San Ramón

Grecia

Alajuela

Volcán
Irazú

GREENWAY
NATURE TOURS

San
Mateo

AVENTURAS
NATURALES

SAN JOSÉ

Turrialba

Cartago

Tuís

Paraíso

Tárcoles

Parque
Nacional
Carara

Orosí

Jacó

Cerro
Vueltas

Cerro
Cuéricí

Parque Nacional
Los Quetzales

Cerro de
la Muerte

Parrita

Quepos

San Isidro
de El General

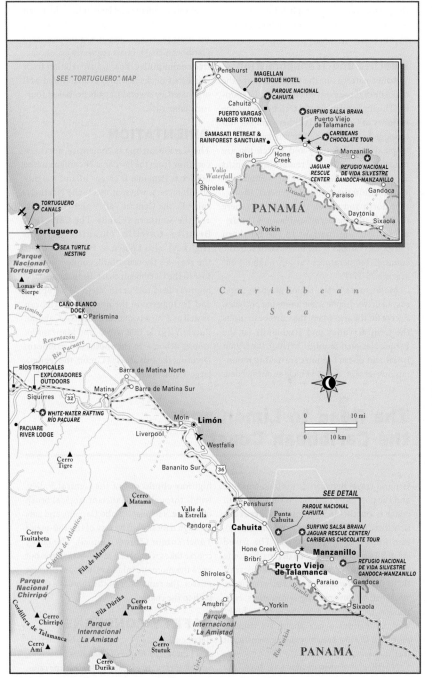

SEE "TORTUGUERO" MAP

Detail map (top right):

Penshurst

MAGELLAN BOUTIQUE HOTEL

PARQUE NACIONAL CAHUITA

Cahuita

SURFING SALSA BRAVA

PUERTO VARGAS RANGER STATION

Puerto Viejo de Talamanca

SAMASATI RETREAT & RAINFOREST SANCTUARY

CARIBEANS CHOCOLATE TOUR

Bribrí

Hone Creek

Manzanillo

Volio Waterfall

JAGUAR RESCUE CENTER

REFUGIO NACIONAL DE VIDA SILVESTRE GANDOCA-MANZANILLO

Shiroles

Gandoca

PANAMÁ

Paraíso

Daytonia

Sixaola

Yorkín

Main map:

TORTUGUERO CANALS

Tortuguero

SEA TURTLE NESTING

Parque Nacional Tortuguero

Lomas de Sierpe

Parismina

CAÑO BLANCO DOCK

Parismina

Reventazón

Río Pacuare

C a r i b b e a n

S e a

Barra de Matina Norte

RÍOS TROPICALES

EXPLORADORES OUTDOORS

Matina

Barra de Matina Sur

Siquirres

32

WHITE-WATER RAFTING RÍO PACUARE

Moín

Limón

PACUARE RIVER LODGE

Liverpool

Westfalia

Cerro Tigre

Bananito Sur

36

0   10 mi

0   10 km

Cerro Matama

Valle de la Estrella

SEE DETAIL

Pandora

Penshurst

PARQUE NACIONAL CAHUITA

Punta Cahuita

Cerro Tsuitabeta

Cahuita

SURFING SALSA BRAVA/ JAGUAR RESCUE CENTER/ CARIBEANS CHOCOLATE TOUR

Chirripó de Atlántico

Fila de Matama

Hone Creek

Bribrí

Manzanillo

Puerto Viejo de Talamanca

REFUGIO NACIONAL DE VIDA SILVESTRE GANDOCA-MANZANILLO

Parque Nacional Chirripó

Shiroles

Paraíso

Gandoca

Cerro Chirripó

Cordillera de Talamanca

Fila Dúrika

Cerro Punibeta

Coén

Amubri

Yorkín

Sixaola

Cerro Amí

Parque Internacional La Amistad

Parque Internacional La Amistad

Cerro Stutuk

Río Yorkín

PANAMÁ

Urén

Cerro Durika

the perfect way to accomplish interregional or cross-country travel while having the time of your life.

Weather and Transportation

Weather patterns in the Caribbean are the opposite of those everywhere else in the country. During September and October, when the majority of Costa Rica is either damp or waterlogged, much of the Caribbean basks in tropical sun. February and March too are notoriously sunny; the remaining months are splashed steadily with rain. Precipitation varies within the region. In general, the farther north you travel, the more rain there is. While the southern Caribbean is the driest section, destinations in the northern Caribbean rank as some of the wettest in the country. Temperatures vary throughout but average 75-77°F.

Major roads in the region are paved and easy to drive, despite some annoying potholes. Except for the area where the Caribbean meets the Central Valley and Highlands (at the Parque Nacional Braulio Carrillo), the region is flat and doesn't require traversing mountainous terrain. A 4x4 vehicle is not needed.

Highway accidents and landslides, which can cause road closures or driving delays, are the most pressing concern. On the northern Caribbean coast, boats regularly access car-free communities. Boat transportation from numerous docks is widely available and well organized by several Caribbean-based tourism companies.

ORIENTATION

The Caribbean spans the entire northern coastline from the border at Nicaragua to the border at Panama. It creeps inland roughly 60 kilometers, where it meets the Northern Inlands, the Central Valley and Highlands, and the Southern Inlands. The **Carretera Braulio Carrillo** (Braulio Carrillo Highway), also known as **Highway 32,** is the region's thoroughfare, connecting San José to the Caribbean coast. Branches off the highway lead to Puerto Viejo de Sarapiquí and Tortuguero in the northern Caribbean as well as a variety of beach towns—Cahuita, Puerto Viejo de Talamanca, and Manzanillo, among others—in the southern Caribbean. Dividing the two areas is Limón, the region's largest metropolis.

The Road to Limón and the Caribbean Coast

Ground travel between downtown San José and the port city of Limón on the Caribbean coast is on the 165-kilometer **Carretera Braulio Carrillo** (Braulio Carrillo Highway), also known as **Highway 32.** The paved stretch is relatively easy to drive (the route takes three hours); however, weekday traffic in the early morning and late afternoon, worsened by slow-moving semitrailers, contributes to congestion on the popular highway. Landslides occur about 2-3 times a month in the low season, causing significant traffic delays.

Northeast of downtown San José, the highway climbs out of the Central Valley, winds through the luxuriant tropical brush of Parque Nacional Braulio Carrillo, and cuts through a mountain by way of the 550-meter Túnel Zurquí (Zurquí Tunnel). The curvy course takes roughly 30 minutes to drive, but once the montane inland is in your rearview mirror, the remainder of the route is a direct path to the coast.

SAFETY CONCERNS

Between Parque Nacional Braulio Carrillo and Limón, the towns of Guapiles, Guacimo, and Siquirres are plagued by high crime rates.

This makes unguided stops risky, especially after dark. Tourism is practically nonexistent in this area. Stopping in these towns could put you at risk for robbery or assault.

In general, driving Highway 32, which bypasses the three towns, is safe. Exercise common sense and keep your wits about you. Fill up on gas, use the bathroom, and pack snacks before you leave so you can avoid making stops along the way.

A few restaurants at the side of the highway around Guapiles are connection points for Tortuguero excursions. Brief stops in the region for this purpose are typically safe, given that tour guides and a large group of travelers are often present.

If you must stop along the route, the best place to do so is at the intersection of **Highway 32** and **Highway 4.** A large bus station and the tourist-friendly **Restaurante Rancho Robertos** (tel. 506/2711-0050, www.restauranteranchorobertos.com, 6:30am-9pm Mon.-Fri., 6:30am-10pm Sat.-Sun., $8-35) mark the spot. Both the station and restaurant offer bathrooms, food, and drinks. There's also a **gas station** 350 meters southeast on Highway 32.

★ PARQUE NACIONAL BRAULIO CARRILLO

A backdrop that I never tire of seeing is the wall of steep, forested hills in the **Parque Nacional Braulio Carrillo** (Braulio Carrillo National Park, tel. 506/2206-5500, www.sinac. go.cr, 8am-3:30pm daily, last entry 2pm, $12 adults, $5 children 2-12). The awe-inspiring rainforest here feels like a scene straight out of *Jurassic Park.* In some places, lush mountains flank one side of Highway 32, which passes through the park; steep cliffs drop off the other. In other areas, the thoroughfare travels through thick forest rife with poor man's umbrella plants—recognizable by their long stems and broad, oversize leaves—and passes through a tunnel carved into the rocky mountainside. Travelers can best witness the sight in a vehicle, but several sharp curves that require drivers to remain alert

provide little opportunity to fully appreciate the view. Cloud cover, fast-moving vehicles, roadside cliffs, and narrow shoulders make stops along the highway dangerous. Still, the 25-kilometer, 30-minute drive through the park's virgin rainforest is a spectacular journey that shouldn't be missed.

The park has two sectors: the **Quebrada González Sector** (Hwy. 32, 45 km northeast of downtown San José, tel. 506/2206-5500) on the northeast side of the park, and the **Volcán Barva Sector** (30 km north of downtown San José, tel. 506/2266-1892) on the west side of the park. **Ranger stations** mark the entrance to each. Quebrada González is the most visited of the two, thanks to its easy trails and direct access from San José.

Hiking

Of the tens of thousands of visitors who pass through the mountainous park annually, only a small percentage tour it on foot. Covering more than 100,000 acres, the massive protected area is loaded with canyons, waterfalls, streams, and rivers, including the strikingly yellow and iron-rich **Río Sucio.** The two most-visited trails in the park are **Sendero Las Palmas** (1.5-km loop, 30-40 minutes, easy-moderate) and **Sendero El Ceibo** (1-km loop, 20 minutes, easy). Both trails are accessible beyond the main ranger station at Quebrada González.

Rainforest Aerial Tram

On Highway 32, three kilometers northeast of the Quebrada González ranger station, is the **Rainforest Aerial Tram** (7:30am, 10:30am, noon, and 2pm daily, 70 minutes, $65 adults, $33 children 0-12). Operated by tour outfitter **Rainforest Adventures** (tel. 506/2224-5961, www.rainforestadventure. com, 8:30am-4:30pm daily), this gondola ride takes place just outside of the park but provides a better look at the protected area from a distance. Beginning in a valley and climbing up through dense forest to the treetop canopy, the journey offers bird's-eye views of the rainforest from above and within. A tour guide

Parque Nacional Braulio Carrillo

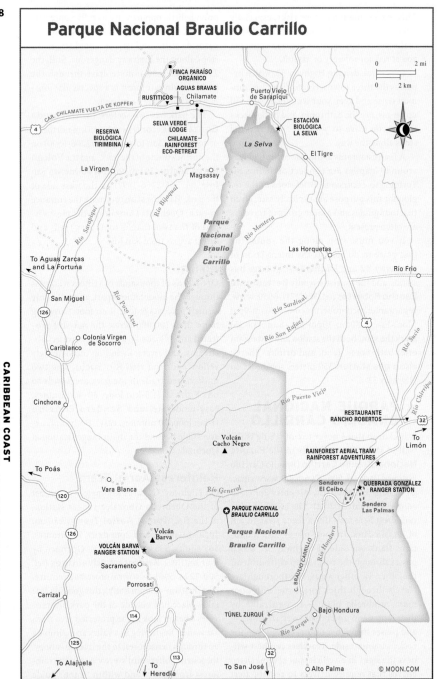

0   2 mi

0   2 km

FINCA PARAÍSO ORGÁNICO

AGUAS BRAVAS

RUSTITICOS   Chilamate

Puerto Viejo de Sarapiquí

CAR. CHILAMATE VUELTA DE KOPPER

4

ESTACIÓN BIOLÓGICA LA SELVA

RESERVA BIOLÓGICA TIRIMBINA ★

SELVA VERDE LODGE

CHILAMATE RAINFOREST ECO-RETREAT

La Selva

El Tigre

La Virgen

Magsasay

Río Bijagual

Parque

Nacional

Río Montera

Braulio

Las Horquetas

Carrillo

Río Frío

To Aguas Zarcas and La Fortuna

Río Sarapiquí

Río Poco Azul

San Miguel

126

Río Sardinal

Río San Rafael

4

Río Sucio

Colonia Virgen de Socorro

Cariblanco

Cinchona

Río Puerto Viejo

Río Chirripó

RESTAURANTE RANCHO ROBERTOS

32

To Limón

Volcán Cacho Negro ▲

RAINFOREST AERIAL TRAM/ RAINFOREST ADVENTURES ★

To Poás

Vara Blanca

Río General

Sendero El Ceibo

QUEBRADA GONZÁLEZ RANGER STATION ★

120

Sendero Las Palmas

🅟 PARQUE NACIONAL BRAULIO CARRILLO

126

Volcán Barva ▲

Parque Nacional

Braulio Carrillo

VOLCÁN BARVA RANGER STATION ★

Sacramento

C. BRAULIO CARRILLO

Río Hondura

Porrosati

Carrizal

114

TÚNEL ZURQUÍ

Bajo Hondura

125

Río Zurquí

To Alajuela

113

To Heredia

32

To San José

Alto Palma

© MOON.COM

Highway 32 Closures

Several times each year (most often during May to December), poor weather conditions close the section of Highway 32 within Parque Nacional Braulio Carrillo. Road closures can be confirmed by the Zurquí department of the Policía de Tránsito (Transit Police, tel. 506/ 2268-2157). Most officers do not speak English. Instead, check the status of the road as most locals do, by asking, *"¿Está abierta la ruta treinta y dos?"* ("Is Route 32 open?") This should return a quick *"Sí"* ("Yes") or *"No."*

ALTERNATE ROUTE TO THE CARIBBEAN

In the event of a road closure, you'll need to take one of the two alternate routes to the Caribbean. Both provide a mix of mountainous and flat terrain on paved highway.

- From downtown San José, take Highway 2 to Cartago, followed by Highway 10 through Turrialba to Siquirres, where the road ends at Highway 32. From downtown San José to Limón, the drive is 170 kilometers and takes about three hours and 45 minutes.

- From Aeropuerto Internacional Juan Santamaría in Alajuela, take Roads 712, 146, 120, and 126 to Highway 4. Follow Highway 4 through Puerto Viejo de Sarapiquí until the road ends at Highway 32. From Alajuela to Limón, the drive is 220 kilometers and takes roughly 4.5 hours. Although longer, this route avoids San José's chaotic downtown area.

---

narrates the experience with fun facts about the park.

Getting There

To reach the park from San José, take Highway 32 northeast for 43 kilometers, a one-hour drive. The signed entrance to the Quebrada González ranger station is on the southeast side of the highway. A tall wall of thick vegetation makes the turnoff easy to miss. Look for the road approximately two kilometers after crossing the bridge over Río Sucio. The ranger station is a mere 25 meters beyond the turn.

You can also reach the Quebrada González ranger station by public bus from San José (multiple times 5am-7pm daily, 1 hour, $2.50). When you board, tell the driver your destination; otherwise, the bus may not stop at the park. Say either the name of the park in Spanish or *"la entrada del parque nacional"* ("the entrance to the national park").

By taxi, a one-way trip from downtown San José costs approximately $40-50.

The ranger station at the Volcán Barva Sector is best accessed in a 4x4 vehicle. It is 4 kilometers north of the bus stop in the hamlet of Sacramento, 25 kilometers north of downtown San José.

PUERTO VIEJO DE SARAPIQUÍ

North of Parque Nacional Braulio Carrillo and sunken in the lush premontane forest that extends to the border at Nicaragua is the biodiverse community of Puerto Viejo de Sarapiquí. The area that encompasses Puerto Viejo de Sarapiquí, the hamlet of Chilamate (8 km west of Puerto Viejo de Sarapiquí), and the small village of La Virgen (16 km southwest of Puerto Viejo de Sarapiquí) is called Sarapiquí and is a respected hub of rainforest research. Many locals work on the banana and pineapple plantations that make use of the region's rich soil. Residents who don't work in the fields are part of the understated tourism industry that exists mostly in the form of a few rustic lodges, guided nature walks, farm tours, and trips down the Río Sarapiquí.

Puerto Viejo de Sarapiquí connects adventure tourism destinations in the northern inland area with getaways along the Caribbean coast. In 2017, completion of the Carretera Chilamate Vuelta de Kopper (Chilamate Vuelta Kopper Highway), an extension of Highway 4, improved travel significantly, easing the journey and shaving 60 kilometers (roughly 45 minutes) off the total drive time between La Fortuna and Puerto Viejo de Sarapiquí. This new highway avoids curvy roads and bypasses small towns that populate the old route, Road 140.

Sights
ESTACIÓN BIOLÓGICA LA SELVA

Though scientists and students from around the world account for most of the annual visitors to the **Estación Biológica La Selva** (Jungle Biological Station, off Hwy. 4, 3 km south of Puerto Viejo de Sarapiquí, tel. 506/2766-6565, by guided tour only), many of the forested trails that wind through the ecological research station's nearly 4,000-acre property are open to the public for touring. Flat paths (concrete in some places, wood in others) enable rainforest exploration for travelers of all abilities. If you have an interest in plants and trees, you'll marvel at La Selva's collection of over 2,000 varieties, including ferns, gingers, palms, threatened zamia neurophyllidias, and funny-looking monstera deliciosas, otherwise known as swiss cheese plants. Birds, snakes, frogs, howler monkeys, and peccaries make occasional appearances. The station is managed by the **Organization for Tropical Studies** (OTS, Universidad de Costa Rica, San José, tel. 506/2661-4717, www. tropicalstudies.org).

From the station, tour guides lead visitors on the gentle **Short Walk** (8am and 1:30pm daily, 3 hours, $35 adults, $28 children 5-12) through the station's trails. The narrated natural history tour details flora and fauna found in the area and provides information about on-site research projects. Opt to participate in the **Early Birding Tour** (5:45am daily, 2 hours, $50 adults, $33 children 5-12) and you'll head into the forest at the break of dawn alongside a tour guide, in search of new species to add to your bird list. You're sure to come across plenty, as La Selva is home to roughly half of the bird species documented in Costa Rica. If you're a night owl, sign up for the **Nocturnal Wildlife Walk** (7pm daily, 2 hours, $50 adults, $33 children 5-12), during which you'll encounter an assortment of amphibians, reptiles, mammals, and arthropods that contribute to the area's significant biodiversity. All guided experiences require advance reservations by telephone or through the OTS website; in addition, participants must wear completely enclosed footwear.

RESERVA BIOLÓGICA TIRIMBINA

The private wildlife refuge **Reserva Biológica Tirimbina** (Tirimbina Biological Reserve, Road 126, 14 km southwest of Puerto Viejo de Sarapiquí, tel. 506/4020-2900, www. tirimbina.org, 6:30am-5pm daily, last entry 4pm, $18 adults, $11 children 6-12) runs a multitude of **tours** ($29-31 adults, $19-20 children 6-12) on its 850 acres. The options include a guided bird-watching tour, a guided night tour, a guided natural history rainforest walk, and an educational cacao-processing tour. Proceeds finance on-site research and educational projects. You can also explore the reserve's nine kilometers of well-marked trails on your own if you'd rather hike and search for birds and other wildlife at your own pace. Along the way, you'll be treated to rainforest and river views, plus you cross the reserve's two hanging bridges, one of which sways 22 meters above the rapids of Río Sarapiquí.

Farm Tours

Sweet, juicy, and mouthwatering *piña* (pineapple) is ripe for the picking at **Finca Paraíso Orgánico** (4 km north of Hwy. 4, 10 km west of Puerto Viejo de Sarapiquí, tel. 506/2761-0706, www.organicparadisetour. com, 8am-5pm daily). You can learn just about everything there is to know about the tropical delicacy, from seeding and harvesting processes to its indigenous roots, during the farm's **Pineapple Tour** (8am, 10am, 1pm, and 3pm daily, 2 hours, $35 adults, $20 children 4-12). The experience takes you into the pineapple plantation for an up-close look at the world of organic pineapple farming and ends with a tasty treat of fresh pineapple slices and a delicious pineapple smoothie. The tour touches on the processing of yuca, lemon, guanabana, and pepper, too.

Recreation

WHITE-WATER RAFTING

In some areas around Puerto Viejo de Sarapiquí, the sound of ripping rapids disrupts the calmness of the quiet town. Roaring through **Río Sarapiquí** like a raging bull, the river has sections that boast impressive Class III and IV rapids ideal for white-water rafting. Longtime Sarapiquí-based outfitter **Aguas Bravas** (1.5 km west of Selva Verde Lodge, tel. 506/2761-1645, www.aguasbravascr.com, 8am-8pm daily) is one of the area's most experienced at running trips down the river. You can take the translation of the name, "angry waters," literally: The **Extreme Rafting Tour** (8:30am daily, 2.5 hours, $84 pp, min. age 12) is a 12-kilometer ride of mad fun. Although Aguas Bravas caters to travelers who stay in Sarapiquí, many rafters are shuttled in by outfitters that operate from La Fortuna and San José.

SAFARI FLOAT TOURS

Flat sections of **Río Sarapiquí** are ideal for leisurely safari float tours. The **Safari Float Tour** (9:30am daily, 2.5 hours, $84 pp, min. age 4) provided by **Aguas Bravas** (1.5 km west of the Selva Verde Lodge, tel. 506/2761-1645, www.aguasbravascr.com, 8am-8pm daily) is a river trip amid a pretty rainforest setting with plenty of opportunities to spot wildlife such as sloths, iguanas, and otters. The peaceful trip requires little to no effort and is great for kids.

Food and Accommodations

The best food and lodging options in this area are west of Puerto Viejo de Sarapiquí, around Chilamate. Most of these spots are on or close to Highway 4.

If you're hungry, your eyes will light up when you see the portion sizes that come out of the kitchen at **RustiTicos** (Hwy. 4, 8.5 km west of Puerto Viejo de Sarapiquí, tel. 506/8877-8928, 7am-8pm Mon.-Wed., 7am-10pm Fri., 9am-10pm Sat.-Sun., $5-8.50). The small restaurant serves *casados,* traditional dishes that marry servings of rice and beans on a plate, accompanied by a variety of side dishes, plus tons of other options such as seafood specialties, salads, hamburgers, nachos, soups, and a long list of breakfast plates. Good service and an unpretentious vibe add more reasons to dine at the spot.

If you plan to stay in Sarapiquí for a few days, plant yourself at the ★ **Selva Verde Lodge** (Hwy. 4, 6 km west of Puerto Viejo de Sarapiquí, tel. 506/2761-1800, www.selvaverde.com, $122 s, $141 d). Everything you might want is scattered around the tranquil grounds of the 500-acre private reserve, including two restaurants, a bar, and a pool. A nature trail ideal for bird-watching weaves throughout the leafy property, which aligns with the Costa Rican Bird Route (www.costaricanbirdroute.com), a biological corridor of rare great green macaws. The lodge has 40 cozy, comfortable white-walled rooms with striking wood floors, one or two beds, and forest or river views.

I'm partial to the family-run **Chilamate Rainforest Eco-Retreat** (just south of Hwy. 4, 5.5 km west of Puerto Viejo de Sarapiquí, tel. 506/2766-6949, www.chilamaterainforest.com, dorm $35 pp, private $90 s, $108 d), given the owners' commitment to the betterment of the Sarapiquí community through the development of local programs (one owner is a Sarapiquí native). Room options are 10 bunk bed-filled dorms with mosquito nets and shared bathrooms, and 6 private rooms for 1-3 people with a private bathroom and a shared patio. All overnight stays include breakfast and a half-hour guided walk around the hotel's rainforest reserve.

Information and Services

Puerto Viejo de Sarapiquí's **clinic** is **Clínica de Puerto Viejo** (Calle 1 at Avenida 3, tel. 506/2766-6734, 6am-6pm Mon.-Sat.). The closest **hospital** is the **Hospital de Guápiles** (Calle 1 and Avenida 7, 1.5 km north of Hwy. 32, Guápiles, tel. 506/2710-6801, 24 hours daily) in Guápiles, a 45-kilometer, 50-minute drive southeast of Puerto Viejo de Sarapiquí.

Puerto Viejo de Sarapiquí has a **post office** (north side of the soccer field at Calle Central, tel. 506/2766-9828, 8am-5pm Mon.-Fri.), **supermarkets,** and a **police station** (just south of Hwy. 4, 1.5 km south of Puerto Viejo de Sarapiquí, tel. 506/2766-6575, 24 hours daily).

Calle Central, which extends east from Highway 4 and runs north-south through town, has a few **pharmacies,** including **Farmacia Club** (50 m south of the soccer field, tel. 506/2766-6746, 8am-6pm daily), and **banks** with **ATMs,** including **Banco de Costa Rica** (150 m east of Hwy. 4, tel. 506/2211-1111, 9am-4pm daily, ATM 5am-midnight daily).

Transportation

Puerto Viejo de Sarapiquí is 85 kilometers (a drive of one hour and 45 minutes) north of downtown **San José** via Highways 32 and 4. It's 75 kilometers (a 75-minute drive) east of **La Fortuna** via Road 142 and Highway 4.

The **bus station** (southwest corner of the *fútbol* field), is on Calle Central in downtown Puerto Viejo de Sarapiquí. Public **buses** travel daily to Puerto Viejo de Sarapiquí via **San José** (multiple times 6:30am-6pm daily, 1.5 hours, $2-2.50) and **Ciudad Quesada** (multiple times 5am-7pm daily, 2.5 hours, $3).

Exploradores Outdoors (tel. 506/2222-6262, www.exploradoresoutdoors.com) offers Río Pacuare white-water rafting trips and Tortuguero expeditions with **post-tour onward transportation.** These tours can be arranged to include a pickup from your hotel in San José, Alajuela, La Fortuna, Puerto Viejo de Talamanca, or Cahuita, then a drop-off at your hotel in Puerto Viejo de Sarapiquí.

Río Pacuare

The stunning Río Pacuare is undoubtedly one of Costa Rica's most precious natural masterpieces. Set in the heart of virgin Costa Rican jungle, the 107-kilometer river is known for its lush mountainsides, rocky banks, tall waterfalls, and narrow canyons. Originating high in the Cordillera de Talamanca, south of the town of Turrialba, the river flows northeast down the mountains and empties into the Caribbean Sea, 35 kilometers northwest of Limón. Weaving through undeveloped land inhabited primarily by members of the Cabécar indigenous group, the remote Río Pacuare outshines Costa Rica's other rivers with dramatic and breathtaking scenery.

To experience the river yourself, sign up for a **guided white-water rafting tour.** Different from the rafting excursions on most other rivers, trips down Río Pacuare aren't just thrilling adventure tours. They're rare invitations to see, hear, and feel Costa Rica's wild jungle from within. Massive mountains tower above both banks of the river. Overgrown, verdant forests blanket the steep slopes. You'll float past rocky canyons and steer around giant, moss-covered boulders. The setting is grandiose and secluded. During calm floats between rapids, only the occasional birdsong, monkey howl, and whistle of wind can be heard. These river trips reward rafters with fresh air, clean water, and an invigorating connection to nature. Add the adrenaline rush of a white-water rafting expedition, and a journey down the enchanting Río Pacuare is a singular experience. Although guided kayaking tours down the river are also possible, these are for expert kayakers only.

Wildlife near Río Pacuare is abundant, but

1: the Río Sucio **2:** white-water rafting tour on Río Pacuare **3:** a tribute to Bob Marley **4:** pineapple plantation near Puerto Viejo de Sarapiquí

it can be difficult to spot. Look for iguanas and sloths in the trees that line the river. Herons, toucans, oropendolas, and other exotic birds make regular appearances. Swimming is permitted in the river's second canyon, where water flows quickly but calmly.

★ WHITE-WATER RAFTING ON RÍO PACUARE

Beyond its unrivaled landscape, Río Pacuare's claim to fame is its raging rapids. Rafting the river's renowned Class III and IV rapids requires physical effort but no previous rafting experience. One-day rafting tours are full-day excursions; depending on water levels, group size, and traffic to and from the river, the experience lasts 8-13 hours, 3-4 of which are spent paddling intermittently.

Planning Tips

Most river put-ins (rafting tour starting locations) take place off Highway 10 to the east, roughly halfway between Siquirres and the town of Turrialba, but many tour outfitters provide round-trip transportation. Exploradores Outdoors was one of the first companies in Costa Rica to combine adventure tours with free onward travel. Choose to raft Río Pacuare with this company and you can be picked up and dropped off at accommodations in any two of the following areas: San José, Alajuela, Puerto Viejo de Talamanca, Cahuita, Puerto Viejo de Sarapiquí, and La Fortuna.

The Class III and IV thrills are most aggressive from November to December when rainfall in the area is significant. Be aware that substantial overnight rain can cause the river to flood to dangerous levels by morning, resulting in possible last-minute rafting trip cancellations. If you prefer a tamer river trip, raft during February or March when rainfall is less significant and water levels are generally low.

Outfitters

Several Río Pacuare tour operators run boats down the river daily. The company I have rafted with more times than I can count is **Exploradores Outdoors** (tel. 506/2222-6262 or 506/2750-2020, www.exploradoresoutdoors.com), which operates daily **river tours** ($99 pp, min. age 12) from its modern, secure Exploration Center 2.5 kilometers east of Siquirres. The center has bathrooms, showers, oversize lockers, and a restaurant. I prefer this reputable rafting tour operator for its long-standing river operations and spotless safety record. Owners Miguel and Yency Cabrera Chan are a Costa Rican brother and sister team, as well as avid rafters and kayakers. Their tour guides are a professional, well-trained team whose lighthearted humor and playful camaraderie make trips down the river comfortable and fun. Exploradores Outdoors' tour includes a buffet breakfast before the river trip begins, as well as a buffet lunch served on the riverbank.

One of the country's most recognizable tour operators is the San José-based **Ríos Tropicales** (Calle 38, 200 m north of Highway 2, San José, tel. 506/2233-6455, www.riostropicales.com). They run daily Río Pacuare **rafting tours** (Dec.-May, mid-June-Nov., $129 pp, min. age 12) out of their operations center, 4.5 kilometers northwest of Siquirres. The rafting tour includes breakfast, lunch, and round-trip transportation from San José.

ACCOMMODATIONS

A few Río Pacuare tour operators offer two-day rafting tours with an overnight stay along the river's edge. Overnight rafting trips are typically all-inclusive one-night packages (longer stays are available upon request) that include a private room, meals, and two days of rafting. All river outfitters require advance reservations for overnight rafting trips as well as for one-day rafting tours.

If you choose to raft with **Exploradores Outdoors** (tel. 506/2222-6262 or

506/2750-2020, www.exploradoresoutdoors.com), you stay in the operator's own **Pacuare River Lodge** ($239 s, $478 d, all-inclusive 1-night package). Resembling a wilderness camp more than a lodge, it has 13 small, one-room (single or double occupancy) teakwood cabins with screen windows scattered about the property. Bathrooms are in the lodge's main building, a short walk from the cabins. Set atop a mountain, the camp overlooks the water from above and has an open-air bar and lounge area with top-notch rainforest and river views.

The **Ríos Tropicales Ecolodge** ($339 s, $650 d, all-inclusive 1-night package) is a full-fledged, 33-room riverside hotel. The 2,400-acre property has both private rooms (each one sleeps 1-3 people) with a private bathroom, and hostel-style dorms (each one sleeps 1-4 people) with bunk beds and a shared bathroom. If you stay for more than one night, you can fill time with on-site activities such as zip-lining, canyoning, and horseback riding. To stay here, take the rafting tour with

Ríos Tropicales (tel. 506/2233-6455, www.riostropicales.com).

The luxurious riverfront **Pacuare Lodge** (tel. 506/4033-0060, www.pacuarelodge.com, $1,448 s, $2,186 d, all-inclusive 2-night package, min. stay 2 nights) is one of Costa Rica's best resort-quality remote accommodations. Its 20 spacious bedroom suites have soaking tubs, canopy beds, high-quality linens and mattresses, outdoor showers, and private terraces. The architecturally stunning property's peaked roofs, beautiful stonework, and well-kept gardens are equally impressive, as is the lodge's restaurant, which serves spectacular gourmet cuisine in the middle of nowhere. Rafting tours that offer overnight stays at Pacuare Lodge are run by the lodge's affiliated outfitter, **Aventuras Naturales** (Avenida 5, 50 m east of Calle 33 and 300 m north of Hwy. 2, San José, tel. 506/2224-0505). The accommodation may also be accessed by helicopter or via a combined 4x4 vehicle, cable-crossing, and electric car ride provided by the hotel.

Limón

The tropical colors that surround the port city of Limón are a welcome contrast to the drab scenery along Highway 32 east of Parque Nacional Braulio Carrillo. The yellow gazebo in the city's central park, the lime-green *correos* (post office) building, the sky-blue Limón Municipality office, and the multi-colored checkerboard main street all provide warmth to the industrial metropolis and offer a glimpse of the vivacious Afro-Costa Rican style that dominates the coast. Look past yards full of stacked shipping containers, cruise ships docked at Puerto Limón (busiest during cruise season from October to March), and the city's rough edges, and you'll see a gateway to the southern Caribbean, home to a vibrant culture fundamentally different from what you'll find anywhere else in the country.

If you have two hours to spare, the best way to capture the essence of Limón is by taking the free narrated **walking tour** (tel. 506/8869-1653, www.explorelimon.com, 9am and 2pm daily, donations accepted) offered by local resident and city ambassador Sergio Bolaños. During the tour's easy 1.5-kilometer stroll, Bolaños succinctly details Limón's rich history, including its ties to the United Fruit Company and the role it played in the Banana Empire, as well as the city's modern-day services.

SAFETY CONCERNS

Numerous foreigners pass through Limón regularly without incident, but given the prevalence of crime in the city, some of it specifically targeted at tourists (theft, for example),

Limón

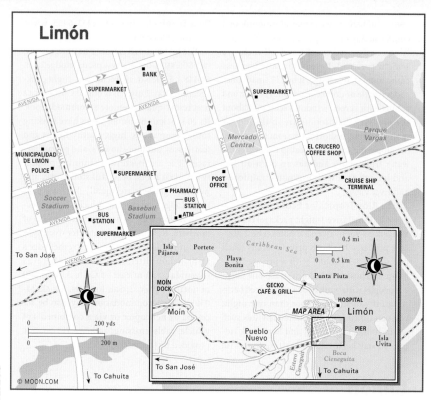

overnight stays are not recommended. Limit your exploration of the area to the city's downtown (bounded by Avenida 5, Calle 9, Highway 32, and the eastern coast) to avoid putting yourself at risk of theft or robbery.

FESTIVALS AND EVENTS

For 10-12 days in mid-October each year, corresponding with the nationwide celebration of Día de las Culturas (Culture Day), things get crazy in the Caribe. The **Carnaval del Caribe** (Caribbean Carnival) fills the streets of Limón with food stalls, calypso music, dance performances, and a joyous, infectious energy. Locals turn out in droves to catch the crowning of the carnival queen, to parade through the streets in extravagant and colorful costumes, and to watch spectacular fireworks displays. Originally designed to

celebrate the fourth voyage of Christopher Columbus and his arrival in 1502 at Isla Uvita (an island just east of Limón), today the event is one of the country's best demonstrations of multiculturalism in the Caribbean and the pride of Limonenses, the residents of Limón province.

FOOD

My favorite restaurant in Limón is the **Gecko Café & Grill** (Road 240, 1 km northwest of the hospital, tel. 506/2758-1558, 11:30am-10pm Mon.-Sat., 8am-9pm Sun., $4.50-19). This place gets casual waterfront dining right. The pub grub is tasty: Order the Caribeña, a hamburger stuffed with breaded shrimp in Caribbean sauce and sandwiched in one of the restaurant's homemade buns. The five-page menu has plenty of other options to choose from, including tasty breakfast fare on

Cruise Excursions from Limón

Almost two-thirds of the total number of passengers who arrive in Costa Rica by cruise ship each year dock at the port in Limón, and roughly 75 percent of that group participates in an excursion during their time in the Caribbean. A well-designed day tour can help you squeeze every drop out of the limited time you have to explore Costa Rica.

Most tours require light-to-moderate physical effort and cost $80-125 per person. To avoid paying an inflated price through your cruise ship's tour desk, book your day tour in advance through a local tour operator or agency. I like the shore excursion company Greenway Nature Tours (Montelimar de Guadalupe, San José, tel. 506/2297-0889, www.greenwaytours.com, 9am-6pm Mon.-Sat.). With years of experience tailoring tours to strict cruise schedules, the company will not only make sure you enjoy your day but also ensure that you return to the boat on time.

Here are some of the area's best cruise ship excursions:

· Exploring the Caribbean coast's vibrant Afro-Costa Rican culture during a city tour of Limón.

· White-water rafting Class II and III rapids on the Río Reventazón.

· Strolling along the beach during a rainforest walk through the Parque Nacional Cahuita.

· Boating through the quiet canals of Tortuguero in search of tropical birds and other wildlife.

Sundays, and the service is above par. Some evenings at the laid-back but social spot feature happy hours, live music, and open-air movie nights. This spot isn't in the safest area in the city, so it's a good idea to drive or take an official (red) taxi. Don't walk to or from the restaurant.

For a quick beverage or snack, head to El Crucero Coffee Shop (Hwy. 32 at Tomás Guardia, tel. 506/2758-7003, 7:30am-6pm Mon.-Sat.). The corner café is across the street from Parque Vargas (Vargas Park), near the water, and easily accessible to disembarking cruise ship passengers. It's a great spot if all you want is a coffee or an empanada.

INFORMATION AND SERVICES

Limón is the largest city in Costa Rica's Caribbean region. At the waterfront is Hospital Tony Facio Castro (Paseo Dr. Rubén Umaña Chavarría, 1 km north of the cruise dock, tel. 506/2758-2222, 24 hours daily). A few pharmacies are scattered throughout the downtown core, including Farmacia Caribeña (corner of Avenida 2 and Calle 6, tel. 506/2758-4121, 8am-8pm Mon.-Sat.), located three blocks east and one block

north of the intersection of Highway 32 and Highway 36.

Limón has a post office (corner of Avenida 2 and Road 240, tel. 506/2758-3471, 8am-5pm Mon.-Fri., 8am-noon Sat.), a police station (Avenida 3 between Calle 8 and Calle 9, tel. 506/2758-2435, 24 hours daily), and many supermarkets. There's a Banco Nacional (Plaza Puerto Limón, Avenida 5, tel. 506/2231-2220, 10am-5pm Mon.-Fri., 10am-3:30pm Sat.) as well as several other banks in the city. ATMs dot the downtown core; one that's easy to find is on Highway 32 at the bus station across from the cruise dock. It's open 5am-midnight daily.

The port town has more gas stations than you can count. If you're just passing through and need to fill up, you can do so at the intersection of Highway 32 and Highway 36.

TRANSPORTATION
Getting There

Most people visit Limón directly from San José, a 160-kilometer, three-hour drive east on Highway 32, or La Fortuna, a 215-kilometer, 3.5-hour drive southeast via Road 142 and Highways 4 and 32. Limón is a gateway to the southern Caribbean; many travelers revisit the city on their way out of the region. From **Cahuita,** it's a 45-kilometer, 45-minute drive northwest on Highway 36. From **Manzanillo,** it's a 75-kilometer, 1.5-hour drive west on Road 256 and northwest on Highway 36.

Both Highway 32 and Highway 36 are paved and easily manageable roads. Highway 36 can be riddled with potholes during rainy periods; drive slowly, especially at night, to avoid blowing out a tire.

The **Aeropuerto Internacional de Limón** (Limón International Airport, LIO) is 3.5 kilometers (a five-minute drive) south of downtown Limón. **SANSA Airlines** (tel. 506/2290-4100, www.flysansa.com) offers direct flights to Limón from San José daily. The flight time is approximately 40 minutes. From the airport, **Caribe Shuttle** (corner of Road 256 and Calle 213, Puerto Viejo de Talamanca, tel. 506/2750-0626, www.caribeshuttle.com) runs a handy **shared shuttle service** ($22 pp) to Puerto Viejo de Talamanca (departs Limón 7:50am, 12:40pm, and 3:50pm daily; departs Puerto Viejo de Talamanca 5:15am, 11am, and 2pm daily).

Limón's two regional **bus stations** are a block apart. Both are between Avenida 2 and Highway 32 (to the north and south) and Road 240 and Calle 8 (to the east and west). Public **buses** travel to Limón daily. You can catch one from **San José** (multiple times 5am-7pm daily, 3 hours, $5.50-6), **Cahuita** (multiple times 5:45am-8:15pm daily, 1-1.5 hours, $2-2.50), **Puerto Viejo de Talamanca** (multiple times 5:30am-8pm daily, 1-1.5 hours, $3-3.50), and **Manzanillo** (multiple times 5am-6pm daily, 1.5-2 hours, $4.50).

Getting Around

Downtown Limón is full of one-way streets. Except for Highway 32, both *calles* (streets), which run north-south, and *avenidas* (avenues), which run east-west, alternate the direction of traffic. Outside the downtown core, traffic moves in both directions. Official **taxis** line up by the city's westernmost bus station (Avenida 2 between Calle 7 and Calle 8).

Cahuita

The small, walkable beach town of Cahuita is a perfect example of the strong Jamaican influence that sweeps Costa Rica's southern Caribbean coast. Inhabitants proud of their Afro-Costa Rican roots cook up Caribbean fare, play calypso and reggae music, paint images of legendary figures on business walls, and live by the unifying mantra "one love." The town, sometimes referred to as a little Puerto Viejo de Talamanca, has a vibe every bit as laid-back and unapologetically slow as life elsewhere along the coast, but it escapes much of the region's tourism. (For more information on the area's Jamaican influence, see the sidebar *Roots, Reggae, and Rastas* on page 435.) The foremost attraction is the beach- and reef-filled, easy-to-trek Parque Nacional Cahuita at the east end of town.

If you're just here to visit the park, you'll need to set aside only a few hours. If you want to devote more time to relaxing on the beach, you could spend anywhere from a day to an entire week here.

BEACHES

Northwest of Cahuita center is **Playa Negra** (Negra Beach), not to be confused with the Playa Negra immediately west of Puerto Viejo de Talamanca. This is Cahuita's principal beach, an approximately one kilometer, five-minute drive from the center of the village. The dark-sand beach is surprisingly smooth and sinks gently into shallow waters. Big waves offshore churn up Cahuita's best surf. Gentler waves near the shoreline are decent for swimming, especially along the section of beach that fronts an establishment known as the Reggae Bar.

Cahuita

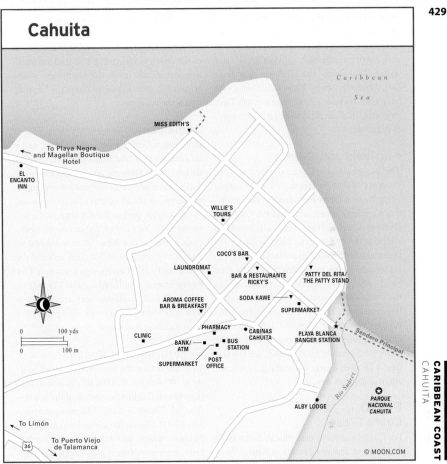

To Playa Negra and Magellan Boutique Hotel

EL ENCANTO INN

MISS EDITH'S

WILLIE'S TOURS

COCO'S BAR

LAUNDROMAT

BAR & RESTAURANTE RICKY'S

PATTY DEL RITA / THE PATTY STAND

AROMA COFFEE BAR & BREAKFAST

SODA KAWE

SUPERMARKET

PHARMACY

CABINAS CAHUITA

CLINIC

BANK / ATM

BUS STATION

PLAYA BLANCA RANGER STATION

SUPERMARKET

POST OFFICE

Sendero Principal

Río Suárez

ALBY LODGE

PARQUE NACIONAL CAHUITA

To Limón

To Puerto Viejo de Talamanca

Caribbean Sea

0   100 yds
0   100 m

© MOON.COM

The area's other main beach is Playa Blanca (Blanca Beach) in Parque Nacional Cahuita.

RECREATION
Local Guides and Tours

If you're based in Cahuita and unsure what to do in the Caribbean, reach out to the helpful folks at **Willie's Tours** (1 block northwest of Cahuita's main intersection, tel. 506/2755-1024, www.williestourscostarica. com, 8am-7pm daily). The staff are well versed on everything Cahuita and offer a ton of great local tours—most notably national park tours and indigenous community visits. Guides are enthusiastic about the activities and ready to please. Day tours cost $22-180 per person.

ENTERTAINMENT AND EVENTS
Nightlife

Barhopping around small-scale Cahuita is easy and mostly safe to accomplish on foot. After dark, stick to bars along the main street, particularly **Coco's Bar** (at Cahuita's main intersection, tel. 506/2755-0437, 10am-2:30am Mon.-Sat., 10am-midnight Sun.) and **Bar & Restaurante Ricky's** (at Cahuita's main intersection, tel. 506/2755-0305, 11am-10pm daily), both of which are in the middle of the village. As the sun goes down on the southern Caribbean, the music gets turned up at art-wrapped Coco's, where locals and foreigners dance well into the morning on a deck-board dance floor under the glimmer of a disco ball. Across the street, Ricky's competes with happy hours and is a great place to catch Ticos engaging in a much-loved pastime: rounds of dominoes.

Festivals and Events

The Panama-born, Cahuita-raised King of Calypso, Walter Ferguson, is acknowledged every year in mid-July during the multi-day **Festival Internacional de Calypso** (International Calypso Festival). Roadside concerts led by energetic calypso bands fill the streets with melodies perfect for dancing. I dare you not to twist your hips, clap your hands, and give in—at least momentarily—to the event's sweet sounds, synonymous with the coast. More than just great fun, the festival pays homage to calypso's Caribbean roots and celebrates Cahuita's contribution to the genre by way of its local legend. See the festival's Facebook page for more information about specific events.

FOOD
Costa Rican

For Caribbean food, many locals favor **Miss Edith's** (on the road to Playa Negra, 75 m northeast of the police station, tel. 506/2755-0248, 8am-10pm Mon.-Sat., 1pm-6pm Sun., $6-16). The restaurant is one of Cahuita's oldest. Dishes are a bit pricey (likely due to its popularity) but no doubt delicious. The *rondón,* a traditional fish and vegetable coconut-milk soup flavored with Caribbean spices, is to die for. Miss Edith and her family still run the place and provide friendly service.

My preferred eatery, thanks to its yummy food and fair prices, is ★ **Soda Kawe** (main street Cahuita, 100 m northwest of the park entrance to the Playa Blanca Sector, tel. 506/2755-0233, 5:30am-7pm daily, $4-8). Hearty breakfast options and fruit *batidos*

(smoothies) are great for starting off your day, but a plate of coconut rice and beans (with chicken, beef, pork, or vegetables) is my go-to lunch order. If you struggle to find an available picnic table inside the small, bare-bones restaurant, grab a stool and sit at the bar that fronts the property.

Jamaican

Jamaican influence thrives in Cahuita, so it's no surprise that traditional Jamaican patties do too. Often showing up on local menus as *patís,* the savory turnovers (stuffed with meat, pineapple, or plantain) make inexpensive and filling snacks, perfect for day trips to the national park. You can pick them up on weekends at **Patty del Rita** (50 m northeast of Soda Kawe, 10am-4pm Sat.-Sun. or until the patties sell out, $1 each), also known as **The Patty Stand.** On Tuesdays and Thursdays, a Patty Stand employee rides around town on a bike selling fresh treats. The patties are Cahuita's best street food.

Vegetarian and Vegan

You cannot beat the food selection and quality at ★ **Aroma Coffee Bar & Breakfast** (downtown Cahuita, just north of the bus station, tel. 506/8808-6445, 7:30am-6pm Mon.-Sat., $5-15). The vegetarian and vegan omelets, burgers, wraps, and rolls are each worth a taste. An array of meat dishes appeases visiting carnivores. The relaxing music, outdoor patio setting, and stack of board games are much-appreciated extras.

ACCOMMODATIONS
$50-100

Next to the national park, the **Alby Lodge** (150 m south of the park entrance to the Playa Blanca Sector, tel. 506/2755-0031, www.albylodge.com, $60 s/d, cash only) shares much of its vegetation, wildlife, and natural soundtrack, including early morning howler monkey calls. Four individual bungalows

1: view of Isla Uvita **2:** Soda Kawe in Cahuita **3:** coral reef **4:** Playa Blanca in Parque Nacional Cahuita

with palm-thatched roofs, covered porch areas with chairs and hammocks, private bathrooms, and beds draped with mosquito nets sleep 1-4 people. You're welcome to cook your own meals in the property's rancho, a shared kitchen space equipped with a barbecue; lovely gardens surround it. The lodge accepts payment in cash only.

Staying at **Cabinas Cahuita** (100 m east of the bus station, tel. 506/2755-1154, $45 s, $90 d) feels like you're on a homestay in a Caribbean *casa* (house). The small hotel's six rooms are close to one another and share access to a fully equipped kitchen and a comfortable common area (some rooms also share an entrance). Rooms provide one or two full beds, air-conditioning, and private baths. The gated entrance helps the place feel secure. Best of all is the property's location in the heart of town, steps away from nearly everything that Cahuita has to offer.

I like ★ **El Encanto Inn** (on the road to Playa Negra, 150 m east of La Union, tel. 506/2755-0113, www.elencantocahuita.com, $87 s, $98 d) because it offers decent value and a pleasurable stay. The two-story boutique hotel has 11 rooms amply furnished with beds, wardrobes, desks, end tables, safes, and fans. Two pools (one saltwater) and outdoor lounge areas are set among the property's attractive landscaping of palms and other tropical plants. Slump in a hammock or a chair on your room's terrace and enjoy the oasis-like feel of the fully enclosed hotel. Kind hosts add to the quality of the experience.

$100-150

The six simple but sophisticated guest suites at the ★ **Magellan Boutique Hotel** (Plaza Viquez, 50 m southwest of the road to Playa Negra, tel. 506/2755-0035, www.magellanboutiquehotel.com, $130 s/d) add a touch of class to a Cahuita stay. An aura of romance wafts throughout the hotel, where guests are treated to king-size beds with orthopedic mattresses, high-quality linens, flat-screen TVs, generously sized rooms, and French doors that open to views of the property's gardens. The rate includes a nourishing breakfast, complimentary beach mats, and access to the hotel's concierge service. Yogis should register for the hotel's yoga retreat package; classes take place in a tranquil open-air studio.

INFORMATION AND SERVICES

The town's **clinic, Ebais Cahuita** (tel. 506/2755-0383, 7am-4pm Mon. and Wed.-Fri.), is just west of Cahuita's mini-mall and bus station. **Hospital Tony Facio Castro** (Paseo Dr. Rubén Umaña Chavarría, 1 km north of the cruise dock, Limón, tel. 506/2758-2222, 24 hours daily), serving most of the Caribbean, is in Limón. It is a 45-kilometer, 45-minute drive northwest of Cahuita.

Cahuita has a handful of **supermarkets, laundromats,** and a **police station** (north end of town, road to Playa Negra, tel. 506/2755-0217, 24 hours daily). Just north of Highway 36 on the main road into town, the mini-mall and bus station have a **post office** (tel. 506/2755-0096, 9am-4pm Mon.-Fri.), a **pharmacy,** known as **Farmacia Cahuita** (tel. 506/2755-0505, 9:30am-5pm Mon.-Sat.), and Cahuita's only **bank, Banco de Costa Rica** (9am-4pm Mon.-Fri.), which has an **ATM** (5am-midnight daily).

TRANSPORTATION

From **San José,** Cahuita is a 200-kilometer drive east on Highway 32 and southeast on Highway 36, which takes around three hours and 45 minutes. From **La Fortuna,** the drive is 255 kilometers east on Road 142, Highway 4, and Highway 32, and southeast on Highway 36; it's a 4.5-hour journey. From **Limón,** Cahuita is a 45-kilometer, 45-minute drive southeast on Highway 36. From **Puerto Viejo de Talamanca,** it's just 15 kilometers, a 15-minute drive west on Road 256 and northwest on Highway 36.

The regional **bus station** in Cahuita is at the entrance to town, 500 meters east of Highway 36. You can reach Cahuita by **bus** from **San José** (multiple times 6am-6pm

The Bribri People

On the west side of Highway 36, 20 kilometers south of Cahuita and 13 kilometers southwest of Puerto Viejo de Talamanca, the small, inland village of Bribri serves as a gateway to several indigenous communities. The majority of the Caribbean's indigenous population, who are primarily members of the Bribri indigenous group, reside in reserves in the area that are spread out around the foothills of the Cordillera de Talamanca. The hardworking, remote group is largely self-sufficient. They survive by hunting for meat and fish, growing their own food (mainly corn, beans, bananas, plantains, and yuca), and trading cacao to chocolatiers for cash. Their earnings help the development of clinics, schools, and community centers, which in turn help sustain the communities themselves.

Many group members welcome the economic boost that tourism provides to indigenous reserves. Families in several communities— including Yorkin, Watsi, Shiroles, and Amubri, among others—take turns working with local outfitters to host tour groups and provide cultural presentations that demonstrate the group's way of life. Experiences vary; with some tours you can see how cacao is processed, visit a local waterfall, give archery a go, learn about medicinal plants, or participate in a purification ceremony performed by one of the group's doctors. Most visits include a home-cooked meal prepared with crops grown on the reserve. All visits provide an opportunity to interact with the Bribri people on their beloved land.

Indigenous community visits require traveling to remote areas of the Caribbean, sometimes via a combination of ground and canoe transportation. Book your experience through an operator familiar with the logistics and known to local groups. The Cahuita-based tour operator **Willie's Tours** (1 block northwest of the main intersection, Cahuita, tel. 506/2755-1024, www.williestourscostarica.com) is a reputable choice that runs a variety of day tours ($44-57 pp, 3-7 hours). The outfitter also operates multiday tours ($163-205 pp, 2-3 days) that permit overnight stays on a reserve. Another option is **Terraventuras** (Road 256 at Calle 213, Puerto Viejo de Talamanca, tel. 506/2750-0750, www.terraventuras.com), offering a day trip (8am daily, 8 hours, $85 adults, $42.50 children 4-11) to an indigenous reserve from Puerto Viejo de Talamanca.

daily, 4 hours, $8.50), **Limón** (multiple times 5:30am-8pm daily, 1-1.5 hours, $2-2.50), **Puerto Viejo de Talamanca** (multiple times 5:30am-8pm daily, 30 minutes, $1.50), and **Manzanillo** (multiple times 5:30am-6:30pm daily, 1 hour, $2-2.50).

To hire a private transfer service to Cahuita from anywhere in Costa Rica (as well as from destinations in Panama and Nicaragua), contact **Caribe Shuttle** (tel. 506/2750-0626, www.caribeshuttle.com). One-way prices average around $250 from San José, $450 from La Fortuna, and $500 from Monteverde for groups of 1-10 people.

In addition to private transportation, Caribe Shuttle provides **shared shuttle services** to Cahuita, as do **Interbus** (tel. 506/4100-0888, www.interbusonline.com) and **Grayline Costa Rica** (tel. 506/2220-2126, www.graylinecostarica.com). Together, the three companies cover routes to Cahuita from Limón, Puerto Viejo de Sarapiquí, San José, La Fortuna, and Liberia. Depending on the route chosen, one-way services range $22-64 per person. Caribe Shuttle is usually the least expensive by a few dollars per person. Most shuttles fit eight people with luggage and offer drop-offs at Cahuita hotels.

Exploradores Outdoors (tel. 506/2222-6262, www.exploradoresoutdoors.com) offers Río Pacuare white-water rafting trips and Tortuguero expeditions with **post-tour onward transportation.** These tours can be arranged to include a pickup from your hotel in San José, Alajuela, La Fortuna, Puerto Viejo de Sarapiquí, or Puerto Viejo de Talamanca, then a drop-off at your hotel in Cahuita.

Tiny Cahuita is easily explored on foot, but you may prefer to **rent a bike** if you plan to travel often between the town's center and

Playa Negra, a distance of 1.5 kilometers. Rent a bike from operators in downtown Cahuita; don't pay more than $10 per day.

★ PARQUE NACIONAL CAHUITA

Parque Nacional Cahuita (Cahuita National Park, tel. 506/2755-0302, www.sinac.go.cr, hours and admission vary by sector) is primarily a marine attraction that protects what remains of the region's damaged coral reef. The park's boundaries enclose a mere 2,700 acres of land but a whopping 57,550 acres of water. The site's tree-laden interior, home to raccoons, sloths, basilisks, birds, monkeys (look for howler monkeys near the entrance and capuchin monkeys farther into the forest), is overshadowed by the beautiful light-sand beaches that soften the outer edges of the park. Most visitors enter with a towel and sunscreen in hand, ready to laze the day away on **Playa Blanca** (Blanca Beach), one of the Caribbean coast's prettiest stretches of sand.

The park has two sectors: the **Playa Blanca Sector** (easternmost point of downtown Cahuita, 6am-5pm daily, donations accepted) and the **Puerto Vargas Sector** (east of Hwy. 36, 4.5 km southeast of downtown Cahuita, 8am-4pm daily, $5 pp). A **ranger station** marks the entrance to each. The Playa Blanca Sector is the most popular, the easiest to access from town, and technically free to enter; however, a $5 per person donation is respectful.

Playa Blanca

If you're bound for the beach, enter via the Playa Blanca Sector, stroll along the sand-swept trail until you find a section of coastline you'd like to station yourself at, and enjoy your stay. Beware of skittish ghost crabs that burrow in the beach; they're harmless, but the little critters camouflage themselves with the sand and can be startling when they dart out in front of you. Development along the beach is scarce. Bathrooms are provided at the sector's entrance.

Snorkeling

Reefs arc in the waters roughly 500 meters off **Punta Cahuita** (Cahuita Point), a 3.5-kilometer hike from the entrance of the Playa Blanca Sector and a 5-kilometer hike from the entrance of the Puerto Vargas Sector. Punta Cahuita is the park's peninsula and the site of Costa Rica's best coral reef. Snorkeling at the spot provides a peek at live coral and two shipwrecks, plus an opportunity to be surrounded by schools of tropical fish.

Nearly every tour company operating from Limón to Manzanillo runs **snorkeling tours** to the site. Snorkeling without a guide is not permitted, to help preserve the reef. Most tours couple snorkeling with a guided nature walk through the park. The **Snorkeling and Hiking in Cahuita National Park Tour** (8:30am daily, 5.5 hours, $40 per person) is a best seller of well-known Cahuita tour operator **Willie's Tours** (main street Cahuita, 300 m northwest of the park entrance to the Playa Blanca Sector, tel. 506/2755-1024, www.williestourscostarica.com, 8am-7pm daily).

Hiking

If you dread difficult hikes, you'll love touring this park. The flat **Sendero Principal** (Main Trail, 8.5 km one-way, 3 hours, moderate) parallels the coast much of the way and has ample opportunities to rest along the beach or take a refreshing dip in the Caribbean Sea. If you wish to tour the trail's entirety, you'll span the park's two sectors. The section of Sendero Principal that passes through the Puerto Vargas Sector is the least visited and densest, providing your best chance for spotting wildlife. Keep your eyes open for mustard-yellow snakes (venomous eyelash vipers) that inhabit the park.

Given the region's low elevation and the park's proximity to the water, floods are an unfortunate but common occurrence. Entrance staff can confirm whether any recent flooding has affected the trail.

Getting There

The park occupies the southeast end of

Roots, Reggae, and Rastas

In the late 1800s, thousands of Jamaicans came to Costa Rica and settled in Limón as railway workers. Much of Puerto Viejo's current population is composed of descendants of the Afro-Costa Rican group, as are the southern Caribbean communities of Limón, Cahuita, and Manzanillo.

Reggae music ties Afro-Costa Ricans to their Jamaican roots. You can't tour Puerto Viejo's center without hearing a Bob Marley tune or music from another reggae artist. You'll spot flags, towels, and souvenirs with the singer-songwriter's face on them. Reggae is like religion on the Caribbean coast, and for many who identify as Rastafarians ("Rastas" for short), that's exactly what it represents. Reggae lyrics often preach Rastafarianism (also known as "Rastafari"), a Jamaican religion established in the 1930s that gained momentum with the international success of Marley (1945-1981), a well-known ambassador of the faith. Puerto Viejo abounds with Rastas who practice the religion.

In Rastafari, ganja (marijuana) is considered a spiritual and healing substance. It's believed to cleanse the body and mind, bestow wisdom upon users, and, according to biblical references, award a closer connection to Jah (God). The smoking of ganja is ever-present and obvious in the Caribbean. While you're walking around Puerto Viejo, it's likely that you'll be offered a toke or two. Remember: The sale and purchase of marijuana is illegal in Costa Rica, regardless of its presence in the Caribbean. It's okay to politely decline any offers and continue on your way.

Cahuita. The Playa Blanca Sector entrance is within walking distance of nearly everything in the village. The Puerto Vargas Sector is best accessed by car. The turn-off to the entrance is off Highway 36, 4.5 kilometers southeast of downtown Cahuita.

Puerto Viejo de Talamanca

Southeast of Cahuita, Highway 36 leads the way to the popular Caribbean beach town of Puerto Viejo de Talamanca (not to be confused with the inland destination Puerto Viejo de Sarapiquí, 140 kilometers northwest of Limón), called Puerto Viejo for short. Puerto Viejo, the center of Afro-Costa Rican culture in Costa Rica, is where the Caribbean coast's Jamaican influence is most evident. It's also a laid-back beach town by day and a lively party town by night. This is a place that appears rather indifferent to tourism and lacks sightseeing attractions—and that's just how locals like it. The primary draw to this hub of the southern Caribbean isn't something you'll see; it's what you'll feel. Nourish yourself with flavorful Caribbean meals and let reggae music move your bones. Appreciate Afro-Costa Rican culture like a Rasta. Learn from the legend, Bob Marley (who is worshipped to no end in Puerto Viejo), and "don't worry... about a thing."

Puerto Viejo is a popular choice among free-spirited, easygoing travelers, but it isn't for everybody. The laid-back lifestyle doesn't deliver on a dime. Service in restaurants, shops, and hotels is typically less attentive and slower than what you'll get in beach towns along the Pacific coast. But that's part of Puerto Viejo's charm. The carefree attitude around town sets it apart from the rest of the country.

Road 256 is the town's main drag for roughly two kilometers, paralleling the Caribbean Sea much of the way before the road continues southeast along the coast toward the village of Manzanillo.

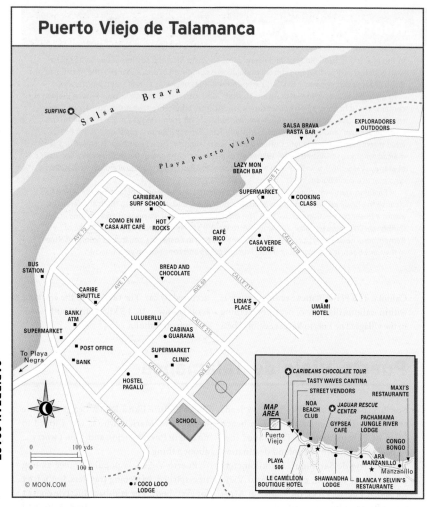

Puerto Viejo de Talamanca

BEACHES

The coastline that spans much of the town of Puerto Viejo is **Playa Puerto Viejo,** although it's not much to marvel at. The sand is often awash with debris, fishing boats occupy part of the water, and the waves can be rough. To enjoy picturesque beaches and more pleasant swims in the area, head east of town to any one of the beautiful beaches that line the Caribbean from Playa Cocles to Manzanillo.

Alternatively, you can travel 1.5 kilometers west of downtown Puerto Viejo to **Playa Negra** (not to be confused with the Playa Negra northwest of Cahuita), a long, dark-sand beach that you're likely to find empty. Apart from a sprinkling of accommodations and restaurants set back from the water, you won't find amenities directly on this beach. Visitors overlook the spot in favor of stretches of coastline with silkier sand that can be found northwest and southeast of the area. Still, if all you want is to take a dip in the sea with little distraction, hire a taxi, hop on a bike, or walk out to Playa Negra from Puerto Viejo and jump right in.

RECREATION
Local Guides and Tours

Exploradores Outdoors (Road 256, 150 m east of Lazy Mon Beach Bar, tel. 506/2750-2020, www.exploradoresoutdoors.com, 7:30am-9pm Mon.-Fri., 11am-9pm Sat.-Sun.) is one of Puerto Viejo's most reliable, safe, and professional tour operators. The company uses top-of-the-line equipment, employs a well-trained team of tour guides, and delivers experiences that are fun and cost-efficient. While they're best known for their white-water rafting excursions on Río Pacuare ($99 pp), their Caribbean operation offers trips to Tortuguero ($154-224 pp), snorkeling and hiking tours in Parque Nacional Cahuita ($55 pp), and kayak tours at Punta Uva ($55 pp), southeast of Puerto Viejo. The rafting tours and Tortuguero trips are city-to-city transportation-inclusive tours that provide onward transportation to San José, Alajuela, La Fortuna, or Puerto Viejo de Sarapiquí. Round-trip transportation to and from Puerto Viejo (or nearby Cahuita) can also be provided. Transportation fees are included in the cost of the tours.

★ Surfing at Salsa Brava

The Caribbean region isn't known for stupendous surf, but there are a handful of wicked waves. The best is **Salsa Brava,** a right-hand reef break that's a short paddle off the coast from Puerto Viejo. Best attempted by seasoned surfers, the powerful break (the name translates to "angry sauce") offers a full-speed, narrow, and gnarly ride. Besides common risks like riptides and undertows, the shallow break barrels over rocks and sharp coral reef. Surfers are spit out bloodied and bruised, yet the spot is one of the Caribbean coast's most crowded. Expect long lines and respect your fellow surfers by curbing your drop-ins; most are locals who have surfed the break for years and have earned priority. Novice participants should head 2.5 kilometers south to the beach

break at Playa Cocles, where less challenging surf awaits over a soft, sandy seabed.

Want to watch the pros from the shore? Seat yourself at a picnic table or in an Adirondack chair on the beach at the **Salsa Brava Rasta Bar** (Road 256 just east of Avenida 69, tel. 506/2750-0394, 10am-9pm Tues.-Sun.). The restaurant and bar offers a perfect view of the action.

Although local surfers offering up lessons are a dime a dozen in Puerto Viejo, the go-to guys are Hershel Lewis Gordon and his crew at the **Caribbean Surf School** (Calle 217, 50 m northwest of Road 256, tel. 506/8357-7703, www.crcaribbeansurf.com, 9am-6pm Sun.-Fri.). They stand out with their patience, professionalism, and passion for surfing. Choose from two different types of surf lessons (8am and 3pm daily, 2 hours): group ($55 pp, 2-3 students per instructor) or private ($60 pp, 1 student per instructor). Each lesson includes the use of a surfboard and rash guard. Also offered are lessons in **stand-up paddling** ($60 pp) at the same times.

Nonsurfers find it fun to play in Salsa Brava's residual waves as they roll into shore. Grab a **boogie board** from one of many rental shops in town or try **bodysurfing.** Local children give surfing with bikes a go, pedaling their two-wheelers into the sea.

Zip-Lining

If you have a need for speed while visiting the Caribbean, contact **Terraventuras** (Road 256 at Calle 213, tel. 506/2750-0750, www.terraventuras.com, 7am-7pm daily), one of Puerto Viejo's most reputable tour operators. Established in 1998, the company employs professional and informative tour guides. Their **Canopy Tour** (8am and 1pm daily, 4 hours, $58 adults, $29 children 4-11, min. age 4) was one of the first zip-line experiences I had in Costa Rica, and it still does not disappoint. Thirteen cables glide over indigenous plants and through primary forest in the foothills of the Cordillera de Talamanca (Talamanca mountain range). The best part of the tour is the exhilarating freefall from a tree platform in the middle of the jungle. For an extra fee ($12 pp), you can experience the forward-facing thrill of a **superman cable.**

White-Water Rafting

Puerto Viejo's own **Exploradores Outdoors** (Road 256, 150 m east of Lazy Mon Beach Bar, tel. 506/2750-2020, www.exploradoresoutdoors.com, 7:30am-9pm Mon.-Fri., 11am-9pm Sat.-Sun.) makes it easy for travelers to experience the country's most notorious Class III and IV river, the **Río Pacuare,** a two-hour drive from Puerto Viejo. The outfitter's full-day **Pacuare River Rafting Tour** (6:30am daily, 11 hours, $99 pp, min. age 12) is an exciting 30-kilometer jungle journey that passes through canyons and crosses 38 rapids.

Exploradores Outdoors also runs a less intense white-water experience on the Class II and III **Río Reventazón** (two-hour drive from Puerto Viejo). Their **Reventazón River Rafting Tour** (6:30am daily, 11 hours, $99 pp, min. age 6) is ideal for families with young children and cruise ship passengers. The trip is shorter than the one on the Pacuare—only 10 kilometers of river over nine rapids. Shorter trips can be arranged for cruise ship passengers with limited shore time.

ENTERTAINMENT AND EVENTS
Nightlife

Caribbean jam is alive and well in Puerto Viejo. There's no shortage of drinking holes and dance spots in town.

Note: Women may find themselves the object of unsolicited attention from men while in Puerto Viejo's bars and clubs. This behavior can include invitations to dance, offers to buy a drink, catcalling, or a man dancing too close to you in hopes that you'll turn to dance with him. The behavior tends to be forward rather than aggressive, and most men will back off when asked to do so. It's okay to say *"No, gracias,"* and return to what you were doing before you were approached. In the extremely rare case that a man's behavior is too aggressive, I recommend leaving and finding another bar to hang out at. Chances are, the man is a local, so the bar staff won't be especially helpful in managing the situation. Of course, if you ever fear for your safety, don't hesitate to call the police. Consider going with a group to experience Puerto Viejo's nightlife, as men are much less likely to approach women in groups.

Kick off your night at the **Lazy Mon Beach Bar** (Road 256 between Calle 219 and Avenida 69, tel. 506/2750-2116, www.thelazymon.com, noon-2:30am daily), where you can down drinks while playing billiards or table tennis. The large, open-air establishment is covered with vibrant murals and mosaics. It attracts a young, social crowd and is steps away from the water. Several tables are strewn about the sand, offering prime seats for sunset viewing. Some nights have live music, $1 shots, and Twister competitions.

Up the road from the Lazy Mon, the **Salsa Brava Rasta Bar** (Road 256 just east of Avenida 69, tel. 506/2750-0394, 10am-9pm Tues.-Sun.) has a killer view of the area's best surf break. This small place at the waterfront resembles an informal beach hut with a wraparound bar and several stools. On the beach, picnic tables and chairs provide additional seating. It oozes Afro-Costa Rican pride with red, yellow, and green walls, seats, and lights, not to mention countless signs that promote peace, love, and joy. Expect a chill vibe, smooth reggae beats that play on repeat, and happy hours on the beach.

Locals like the semi-outdoor **Hot Rocks** (Road 256 at Calle 217, tel. 506/8708-3183, 10am-2am daily). Though it serves all kinds of alcoholic beverages, it feels like a beer garden, thanks to its large, open-concept space filled with picnic tables. This place also has funky swing seating (for adults and children) and entertains crowds nightly with regularly scheduled events that feature live music,

1: art gallery and shop LuluBerlu **2:** souvenirs in Puerto Viejo de Talamanca **3:** the bright and airy Hostel Pagalu in Puerto Viejo de Talamanca

karaoke, free salsa dance lessons, and fire dancing shows. Some early evening events are family-friendly.

SHOPPING

Like most popular tourist hubs, Puerto Viejo is riddled with souvenir shops. Some are on the south/east side of the main street (Road 256) as it bends around town, but don't dismiss the less formal souvenir stands that line the north/west side of the road by the water. Some of the most unique items I've come across were spotted on tables set up by street vendors who rely on visitors' purchases to get by.

Browse the area's most eclectic gathering of nontraditional souvenirs at **LuluBerlu** (Avenida 69 between Calle 213 and Calle 215, tel. 506/2750-0394, 9am-9pm daily), a bohemian-style art gallery and shop that features the works of talented local artists. It is home to tons of paintings, jewelry, handbags, lanterns, and funky articles of clothing, including beachwear for men and women, and was the source of the cutest dress I've ever bought. A lot of its merchandise is handmade.

FOOD

For a once-in-a-lifetime opportunity to give Caribbean cooking a try under the helm of an Afro-Costa Rican matriarch, reserve a spot in chef Veronica Gordon's **cooking class** (tel. 506/8918-3238, www.veronicasplace.net, 10:30am and 5:30pm Sun.-Thurs., 2 hours, $40 pp, cap of 10 students per class). Veronica shares her love of Caribbean cuisine with these classes. Sign up for her lunch or dinner class to learn how to replicate traditional Caribbean meals like rice and beans or *rondón* in your own kitchen by cooking alongside the skilled, kindhearted chef. Then indulge and show off your newfound talent when you and Veronica sit down to enjoy the meal together. All of Veronica's healthy meals are vegetarian, but vegan meals are possible upon request. Advance reservations are required; a few days' notice is preferred. Make bookings by telephone or through Veronica's website.

Costa Rican

When in Puerto Viejo, I regularly dine at the authentic ★ **Lidia's Place** (corner of Avenida 67 and Calle 217, tel. 506/2750-0598, 1pm-9pm Tues.-Sat. and 11:30am-8pm Sun., $6-15). The simple *soda* (traditional Costa Rican family restaurant) may be unimpressive to the eyes, but it produces the most flavorful home-cooked meals in the region, most prepared by Lidia, the kind cook. Top dishes include chicken drenched in Caribbean sauce, coconut curry shrimp, *pargo rojo* (red snapper), and coconut rice and beans. Lidia's sons (and other relatives) demonstrate warm, genuine service that boosts the place from a delicious Caribbean diner to the best traditional-style restaurant in town.

Cafés and Bakeries

Your mouth will begin to water the moment you sift through the delectable menu options at the much-loved café ★ **Bread and Chocolate** (Calle 217 between Road 256 and Avenida 69, tel. 506/2750-0723, 6:30am-6:30pm Tues.-Sat. and 6:30am-2:30pm Sun., $5.50-9). The small, quiet, and rustic café is tucked away off the main street and has a slightly hippie vibe. Choose from pancakes, waffles, and French toast for breakfast; sandwiches, soups, and salads for lunch; cakes, pies, and tarts for dessert; plus loads of other fresh baked goods. Many items (including breads, butters, sauces, jams, and granolas) are prepared in-house. Other ingredients are sourced locally.

One block north of Bread and Chocolate, **Café Rico** (Avenida 69 just north of Calle 217, tel. 506/2750-0510, 7am-1pm Sat.-Wed., $3.50-7) competes for the early-riser breakfast crowd. You can treat yourself to crepes, fruit and granola, omelets, sandwiches, and huevos rancheros while trying your luck at spotting sloths in the trees that tower over the café's breezy veranda. Shelves and tables full of books make the trendy but cluttered eatery the town's best book exchange, so come ready to swap your used reading materials.

Vegetarian and Vegan

Vegan cakes, zucchini and eggplant burgers, avocado sandwiches, bruschetta, and a build-your-own salad are merely a few of the healthy options at the **Como En Mi Casa Art Café** (Road 256, just northwest of Playa Cocles, tel. 506/8674-2900, 7am-5pm Wed.-Mon., $4-10). Seats on the balcony of the tiny, second-floor hole-in-the-wall establishment provide a seaside view. Espressos, green smoothies, and fruit-based beverages fill the drink menu. Inside the colorful café, artwork and souvenirs adorn the walls and are available for purchase.

ACCOMMODATIONS

The best accommodations are located just south of Road 256 on the quiet back roads of Avenidas 67 and 69. Tucked away from the bustle of the main street, these spots remain within walking distance of restaurants, bars, shops, and other services.

Under $50

One of the quietest hostels in town, ★ **Hostel Pagalu** (Avenida 69 between Calle 211 and Calle 213, tel. 506/2750-1930, www.pagalu.com, dorm $12 pp, private $33 s/d) has a wonderfully relaxed vibe. The four dorms sleep four or six people each, and the six private rooms (three have shared baths) have a queen bed. Big lockers and hot water keep guests happy. The two-story building gets lots of light and is open concept and airy. In the main-floor common area opposite the shared kitchen, you can curl up with a book or socialize with others in a low-key setting.

I've spent many nights at the charming **Cabinas Guarana** (Avenida 69 between Calle 213 and Calle 215, tel. 506/2750-0244, www.hotelguarana.com, $36 s, $45 d), and I haven't yet tired of climbing the long ladder up to the property's hidden communal treehouse with a view of the town and the sea. The cozy space is wonderfully quiet, as is the rest of the hotel. Twelve cheery, colorful rooms decorated with handmade tapestries have beds for 1-4 people, private baths, and

secluded porch areas with hammocks. You're welcome to cook your own meals in the communal kitchen and enjoy them in the mosaic-plastered dining hall.

$50-100

The ★ **Casa Verde Lodge** (Avenida 69 between Calle 217 and Calle 219, tel. 506/2750-0015, www.casaverdelodge.com, $69 s/d) feels like its own little oasis in downtown Puerto Viejo. The small property packs a lot into its one-story structure, including 17 spacious and well-furnished rooms (each for 1-3 people), terraces with hammocks, and a decent-size pool. Pillow-top mattresses, safes, and mini-refrigerators are welcome in-room extras. Best of all, thick tropical vegetation completely encloses the hotel, creating a quiet, private place to rest where you'll forget you're in the middle of one of the most-visited destinations in the Caribbean.

Five individual bungalows line a paved, palm-fringed path that wends throughout the 4-acre property of the **Coco Loco Lodge** (at the southern end of Calle 211, tel. 506/2750-0281, www.cocolocolodge.com, $85 s/d). Visits are stress-free thanks to clean, spacious rooms (equipped with fans, safes, TVs, mosquito nets, coffee makers, and refrigerators), an outdoor misting garden (to help you stay cool on extra hot days), private parking, and overnight security. Expect to get a good night's sleep; the hotel is set back from the main street, away from the town's late-night bars.

$150-250

Luxury in downtown Puerto Viejo is practically nonexistent, but the 2018 addition of the adults-only ★ **Umāmi Hotel** (at the southern end of Calle 219, tel. 506/2750-3200, www.umamihotel.com, $209 s/d) is changing the scene. Twelve modern rooms with a comfortable king or queen bed, tile floors, high-end furniture, rainfall showerheads, air-conditioning, and designer finishes like indigenous-style wall art and sculptures create an aura of elegance in each room and encourage relaxation. The outstanding pool area has roofed cabanas with mattresses and lounge chairs with umbrellas. At night, the place sparkles in soft lighting and is ultraromantic. Breakfast is included in the rate.

The **Samasati Retreat & Rainforest Sanctuary** (in the community of Hone Creek, 8 km west of Puerto Viejo de Talamanca, tel. 506/2537-3418, www.samasati.com, $210 s, $235 d) is set atop the mountains that overlook Puerto Viejo and the Caribbean Sea from the west. This remote, rainforest-enclosed spot surpasses most in-town accommodations with its modern facilities, high-quality service, and resort-size grounds. The 250-acre property has an open-air restaurant, yoga shanti, Jacuzzi, meditation hall, and waterfall. Ten freestanding casitas (each sleeps 1-4 people) constructed with reclaimed wood are simply furnished, so as not to distract from the natural surroundings. Stay for a night or two, or register for one of Samasati's multiday yoga or wellness retreats.

INFORMATION AND SERVICES

The **Centro de Especialidades Médicas San Gabriel** (Calle 213, 100 m southeast of Road 256, tel. 506/2750-0079, 9am-9pm Mon.-Sat., 9am-6pm Sun.) is the town's **clinic.** It has a **pharmacy** on-site. Nearby Hone Creek has another clinic, **Clínica Hone Creek** (6 km west of Puerto Viejo de Talamanca, where Hwy. 36 meets Road 256, tel. 506/2756-8003, 24 hours daily). The **hospital** that serves most of the Caribbean is **Hospital Tony Facio Castro** (Paseo Dr. Rubén Umaña Chavarría, 1 km north of the cruise dock, Limón, tel. 506/2758-2222, 24 hours daily) in Limón. It is a 60-kilometer, one-hour drive northwest of Puerto Viejo.

The concentrated center of Puerto Viejo de Talamanca has a **post office** (Road 256 at Calle 211, tel. 506/2750-0404, 8am-5pm Mon.-Fri.), **laundromats,** and **supermarkets.** Two **banks** with **ATMs** are located near the corner of Road 256 and Calle 211; one is **Banco Nacional** (tel. 506/2212-1212, 9am-4pm Mon.-Fri., ATM 5am-midnight daily).

Surprisingly, the town does not have a **police station.** At Playa Cocles, 3.5 kilometers southeast of Puerto Viejo de Talamanca (just south of the Le Caméléon Boutique Hotel), a **tourist police office** (Road 256 at Playa Cocles, tel. 506/2750-0452, 10am-10pm daily) has officers available to assist foreign travelers. In the event of an emergency after hours, the closest official **police station** (Bribri, tel. 506/2751-0003, 24 hours daily) is 13 kilometers southwest of Puerto Viejo de Talamanca in the community of Bribri.

TRANSPORTATION
Getting There

Travelers arrive into Puerto Viejo de Talamanca, a popular coastal destination, from all over the country. From **San José,** Puerto Viejo is a 215-kilometer, four-hour drive east on Highway 32 southeast on Highway 36, and east on Road 256. From **La Fortuna,** the almost five-hour drive is 270 kilometers east on Road 142, Highway 4, and Highway 32, then southeast on Highway 36 and east on Road 256.

To get to Puerto Viejo from **Limón,** you'll travel southeast on Highway 36, following the Caribbean coast to the small community of Hone Creek (marked by a gas station along the highway). Highway 36 intersects with Road 256, which you'll follow east before reaching Puerto Viejo. This 60-kilometer drive takes one hour. From **Cahuita,** Puerto Viejo is just 15 kilometers southeast on Highway 36 and east on Road 256, a 15-minute drive.

The **regional bus station** in Puerto Viejo de Talamanca is by the water on Avenida 73 at Calle 213. You cannot miss it; the open-air station is one of Costa Rica's most colorful. You can reach Puerto Viejo de Talamanca by **bus** from **San José** (multiple times 6am-6pm daily, 4.5 hours, $10), **Limón** (multiple times 5:30am-8pm daily, 1.5 hours, $3-3.50), **Cahuita** (multiple times 5:30am-8pm daily, 30 minutes, $1.50), and **Manzanillo** (multiple times 5am-6pm daily, 30 minutes, $1.50). Make sure you board a bus to Puerto Viejo de Talamanca, not Puerto Viejo de Sarapiquí.

Must-Try Afro-Costa Rican Eats

Meat drenched in *salsa caribeña* (Caribbean sauce) and coconut-flavored rice and beans are staples of Caribbean cuisine.

The pristine beaches on Costa Rica's Pacific coast steal much of the country's spotlight, but where the Caribbean shines is in the kitchen. Caribbean cooking relies on freshly grated coconut milk, spices, and homemade sauces. You can taste the difference for yourself by trying any of the following dishes typically served on the Caribbean coast.

- **Coconut rice and beans:** Rice and beans is the Caribbean's take on the rest of the country's *gallo pinto* (a traditional rice and bean blend), although the grain and protein are sometimes served separately on the plate. The major difference between the two? The rice is cooked in coconut milk, so it's sweeter and a bit softer than regular rice. Much like *casado* (a traditional dish of rice and beans, accompanied by a variety of side dishes), coconut rice and beans is regularly enjoyed with meat and vegetables on the side.

- **Rondón:** Essentially fish soup, this slow-cooked stew also has vegetables, coconut milk, and curry powder. The result is a creamy, flavorful bowl of piping hot goodness.

- **Jerk marinades and *salsa caribeña*:** Caribbean food is rarely bland because it's often doused in delicious dressings. Jamaican-style jerk comes in a variety of flavors, but it's typically a smoky and spicy blend. My personal favorite, *salsa caribeña* (Caribbean sauce) is a slightly sweet brown sauce that looks like watered-down gravy. Both sauces are commonly rubbed on or poured over chicken, beef, and fish.

- **Patís:** The small, turnover-style snacks known as *patís* (also referred to as patties) are perfect if you're on the go. They're filled with either meat or fruit and can be baked or fried.

- **Pan bon:** Roadside stalls along Highway 32 sell *pan bon*. The dark, sweet bread is a local delicacy. Ingredients like coconut, cinnamon, and nutmeg are typical, but some varieties feature nuts and dried fruit.

- **Agua de sapo:** Ignore the off-putting translation (toad water): *Agua de sapo* is a delicious drink. The potent concoction of ginger, lime, and *tapa de dulce* (unrefined cane sugar) is part sweet and part sour. It will help clear your palate after a plateful of flavorful Caribbean food.

You may see Puerto Viejo de Talamanca referred to as Puerto Viejo de Limón or Puerto Viejo del Caribe at stations, on tickets and schedules, or on signs on the buses themselves.

The Puerto Viejo-based transportation service **Caribe Shuttle** (corner of Road 256 and Calle 213, tel. 506/2750-0626, www.caribeshuttle.com, 6am-9pm daily) is your best bet for **private transfer services** to the Caribbean region. They provide service to Puerto Viejo de Talamanca from all corners of Costa Rica, as well as from destinations in Panama and Nicaragua. They know the Caribbean inside and out and can provide you with helpful information while you're in transport. One-way prices average around $250 from San José, $450 from La Fortuna, and $500 from Monteverde for groups of 1-10 people.

Caribe Shuttle also provides **shared shuttle services** to Puerto Viejo de Talamanca, as do **Interbus** (tel. 506/4100-0888, www.interbusonline.com) and **Grayline Costa Rica** (tel. 506/2220-2126, www.graylinecostarica.com). Together, the three companies cover routes to Puerto Viejo de Talamanca from Limón, Puerto Viejo de Sarapiquí, San José, La Fortuna, and Liberia.

One-way services cost $22-64 per person. Caribe Shuttle is usually the least expensive by a few dollars. Most shuttles fit eight people with luggage and offer drop-offs at Puerto Viejo de Talamanca hotels.

Exploradores Outdoors (tel. 506/2222-6262, www.exploradoresoutdoors.com) offers Río Pacuare white-water rafting trips and Tortuguero expeditions with **post-tour onward transportation.** These tours can be arranged to include a pickup from your hotel in San José, Alajuela, La Fortuna, Puerto Viejo de Sarapiquí, or Cahuita, then a drop-off at your hotel in Puerto Viejo de Talamanca.

Getting Around

Downtown Puerto Viejo is small and best explored on foot or by bike. Rental vehicles are welcome, but there aren't a ton of great options for parking (especially overnight), unless you select an accommodation with a secure or private lot.

Bike rentals are everywhere you turn in town, so you'll never find yourself without means to get around. Prices vary, but you shouldn't pay more than $10 per day. Some hotels provide complimentary bikes for guest use.

Playa Cocles to Manzanillo

East of Puerto Viejo de Talamanca, splendid light-sand beaches stretch for 13 kilometers along the coast, from Playa Cocles and Playa Chiquita to Punta Uva and the village of Manzanillo. High-quality accommodations and restaurants, plus a handful of noteworthy attractions, line Road 256, which provides a direct path to each of the four areas. Where the road ends in Manzanillo, a forest trail begins, inviting visitors to explore the rainforest and wetlands of the Refugio Nacional de Vida Silvestre Gandoca-Manzanillo (Gandoca-Manzanillo National Wildlife Refuge).

SIGHTS
★ Jaguar Rescue Center

One of the area's most notable attractions, the **Jaguar Rescue Center** (Road 256, 4 km southeast of Puerto Viejo de Talamanca at Playa Cocles, tel. 506/2750-0710, www.jaguarrescue.foundation, 9am-4pm daily, by guided tour only) is located at the east end of Playa Cocles and the west end of Playa Chiquita. Named somewhat misleadingly, the site is commonly devoid of jaguars, although animal intake varies from day to day. Still, there are more than enough other kinds of wildlife here to feast your eyes on: The center usually has 130-200 temporary or permanent residents at any given time.

On average, the rescue center takes in 420-570 birds, reptiles, and mammals each year; slightly less than half are released back into the wild. Tour guides provide more information about the center's operations during the **Public Tour** (9:30am and 11:30am Mon.-Sat., 1.5 hours, $20 pp 10 years and older), a light walk around the property. During the experience, you'll have up-close but safe encounters with an ever-changing collection of species that usually includes monkeys, sloths, crocodiles, snakes, birds, and deer. Wildlife babies (many orphaned) are adorable, particularly the baby sloths. Though the center is a great place for kids, the stories behind each rescue—including electrocution, car accident, attack by other animals, and illegal trafficking—may upset some children.

While some wildlife-centered tours at other animal rehabilitation facilities focus on showing off their animals, this center prioritizes animal welfare. Visitors cannot pet, handle, or feed the animals. The center is not funded by the government; tour proceeds fuel the center and support its cause.

Ara Manzanillo

The Caribbean used to be replete with great green macaws, but the development of banana and pineapple plantations, the logging of *almendro* (almond) trees—the birds' primary source of food—and trafficking for the illegal pet market have chipped away at the population of this endangered species. Fortunately, conservation efforts are ongoing, and sightings of the birds (although still rare) are becoming more frequent.

One organization that's working to save the species is **Ara Manzanillo** (500 m southeast of Road 256, 2.5 km west of Manzanillo, tel. 506/8971-1436, www.aramanzanillo.org, 3pm-4pm daily, $20 pp 13 and older, by guided tour only). Within the tropical primary rainforest that surrounds Manzanillo, the organization operates a small reintroduction station where great green macaws

are released into the wild. You won't find a theme park, luxurious facilities, or hordes of visitors here, just a simple lookout point that provides an extraordinary opportunity to watch macaws flying freely around the treetops. At the **observation deck,** you'll sit with a tour guide (most of whom are volunteers) who will educate you on the birds' behaviors and habitats, as well as the work carried out by the organization to breed macaws and ready them for release. Other than the thrill of making the steep walk or drive from the main road up 100 meters above sea level to the entrance of the station (a 4x4 vehicle is recommended but not required), the hour spent chatting with the tour guide and admiring the macaws is a pleasant and relaxing experience. Advance reservations are required and can be made through Ara Manzanillo's website.

TOP EXPERIENCE

★ Caribeans Chocolate Tour

Some of Costa Rica's best chocolate comes from the Caribbean region. Taste it for yourself during the **Caribeans Chocolate Tour** (10am Mon., 10am and 2pm Tues. and Thurs.-Fri., 2pm Sat., 2.5-3 hours, $28 adults, $14 children 9-12), provided by café and bakeshop **Caribeans** (Road 256, just northwest of Playa Cocles, tel. 506/8341-2034, www.caribeanschocolate.com, 8:30am-6pm Mon.-Sat.). During the hands-on tour, you'll walk up the hill behind the shop to an operating cacao farm and chocolate factory, where a guide will explain how it's possible to get such smooth and rich dark chocolate from bumpy, bright-yellow cacao pods. What sets this experience apart from other chocolate tours around the country is Caribeans' focus on farming quality. You can literally taste differences across bars produced with cacao developed in different ways. The fact that fair wages are paid to local cacao farmers—and that an endless supply of organic chocolate samples are provided during the tour—are extra reasons to sign up; walk-ins are welcome. Don't forget

to purchase a drink or dessert from the café before you leave!

BEACHES

Few people know that much of the coastline east of Puerto Viejo to Manzanillo is part of the Refugio Nacional de Vida Silvestre Gandoca-Manzanillo. No official refuge entrances exist and no access fees apply along this stretch, so treat the beaches here as you would any other. Be sure to pack out whatever you bring in to help keep the refuge free of debris.

There is little development on the beaches themselves, but restaurants and the occasional street vendor are on Road 256, just south of the coast. No matter which beach you choose, food, drinks, and bathrooms are only a short walk away.

Playa Cocles

The area's best swimming and sunbathing beach, **Playa Cocles** is southeast of Puerto Viejo, within walking distance of town. You'll find a mix of swimmers and surfers here, with lifeguards keeping a watchful eye on both, plus plenty of surfboards available to rent. Choose this beach if you wish to remain close to town or socialize with other beachgoers. Even though it's a popular choice, the long, light-brown, sandy beach provides plenty of room to stretch out.

Playa Chiquita

East of Playa Cocles, **Playa Chiquita** is situated between the headlands of Punta Cocles and Punta Uva. This pristine cove, containing one of my favorite Caribbean beaches, boasts clear waters and sees few visitors. When you've had enough of the tropical sun or you tire of wading in the shallow waters, retreat to the line of leafy palms that backs the beach and provides cooling shade.

1: jaguar **2:** Andy's Caribbean BBQ, one of the street vendors on Road 256 **3:** chocolate bars for sale at the Caribeans café and bakeshop

Playa Punta Uva

The two crescent beaches that make up **Playa Punta Uva** are roughly 2.5 kilometers east of Playa Chiquita. The fine sand is lovely, but the coral reef offshore is even more beautiful. Swimming around the reef is permitted, provided you cause it no harm. A short **nature trail** climbs up and over the Punta Uva headland and connects the separate beach areas. Locals colloquially refer to the easternmost beach as **Playa Arrecife.**

Playa Grande

Fronting the village of Manzanillo (and aptly nicknamed **Playa Manzanillo**) is **Playa Grande.** On sunny days, the beach shimmers like gold, and the depths of the Caribbean Sea can be seen through turquoise waters. Don't expect to have the idyllic place to yourself, however, as it's the home beach of the area's residents. Stick to the east end of the beach if you wish to be close to the village and its handful of restaurants and supermarkets. Backed by a wall of dense vegetation, the west end of the beach is farther away from development. Swimming is best during September and October, when favorable weather calms the sea.

RECREATION

Local Guides and Tours

If you're headed to the Refugio Nacional de Vida Silvestre Gandoca-Manzanillo (Gandoca-Manzanillo National Wildlife Refuge), make sure **Florentino Grenald** (tel. 506/8515-4463 or 506/8841-2732) or **Abel Bustamante** (tel. 506/2759-9043) is leading the way. These independent, eagle-eyed tour guides know the area inside and out, and will show you all kinds of cool finds in the forest that you're likely to miss if you explore the area on your own. A guided tour through the refuge with Florentino ("Tino") costs $40 per person. Abel charges $35 per person for a refuge hike and $45 per person for a refuge tour with a bird-watching focus. Each tour runs about three hours.

Kayaking

A great way to get to know Punta Uva is to tour the area by kayak. Both river kayaking and coastal kayaking opportunities are available; combine the two and you'll be treated to scenes of rainforest and beach along the way. The guided **Punta Uva Sea Kayak and Rainforest Hike** (10am daily, 4.5 hours, $55 pp), coordinated by Puerto Viejo's **Exploradores Outdoors** (Road 256, 150 m east of Lazy Mon Beach Bar, Puerto Viejo, tel. 506/2750-2020, www.exploradoresoutdoors.com) fuses a number of Punta Uva highlights. It includes a paddle in the Caribbean Sea, where you can view coastal cliffs from the water; a paddle up the narrow, leaf-lined Río Punta Uva in search of iguanas, monkeys, birds, bats, and sloths; a hike to the area's best lookout; and transportation to and from Manzanillo-area hotels.

FOOD

Costa Rican

With a bit of luck, you can find ★ **street vendors on Road 256** selling Caribbean food. The fare is often the best around, even though some stalls look shabby. Near Manzanillo, **Andy's Caribbean BBQ** is no more than a bamboo hut that covers an old steel grill. It serves chicken, pineapple, and plantain straight off the grill. The red, yellow, and green food cart dubbed **Take It Easy** (typically parked around Playa Cocles) sells Caribbean chicken with a side of coconut rice and beans served on the leaf of an almond tree.

Since 1982, ★ **Blanca y Selvin's Restaurante** (Road 256, 7 km southeast of Puerto Viejo de Talamanca at Punta Uva, tel. 506/2750-0664, www.selvinpuntauva.com, noon-8pm Thurs.-Sun., $5.50-16) has been serving up some of the best local Caribbean fare, from bowls of *rondón* to plates of *patacones* (smashed and fried green plantains). For a roadside spot not far from the beach, the laid-back and open-air restaurant is

surprisingly clean; service is quick, and the entire operation feels organized.

If you stay in Manzanillo, you'll no doubt eat at least once at the beachfront **Maxi's Restaurante** (Road 256, 13 km southeast of Puerto Viejo de Talamanca at Manzanillo, tel. 506/2759-9073, 11:30am-10pm daily, $6-17), the village's main dining establishment. The large, two-story restaurant comes with a long family history, including a recipe for Caribbean-style lobster that has been passed down through generations. Eat here if all you want is a decent-size meal or a quick drink by the beach. Skip the spot if you're in search of gourmet food or stellar service.

Pub Grub

A great place to dine with friends is the social **Tasty Waves Cantina** (Road 256, 1.5 km southeast of Puerto Viejo de Talamanca at Playa Cocles, tel. 506/2750-0507, 10am-2am Tues., 10am-10pm Thurs.-Mon., $3.50-10.50, cash only). The roadside spot at the northwestern start of Playa Cocles appeases patrons who stumble in from the beach for $1 drinks and pub grub like fries, nachos, burgers, and burritos. The restaurant is famous for its tacos (sometimes available two for the price of one), served on handmade corn tortillas with beef, chicken, fish, shrimp, or vegetables. Trivia contests, karaoke, and movie showings reel in regulars and make for a good time. On Tuesdays, the restaurant stays open late, operating more like a bar. This spot is cash only.

Cafés

The eager-to-please chefs at the **GypSea Café** (Road 256, 6 km southeast of Puerto Viejo de Talamanca at Playa Chiquita, tel. 506/2750-2016, www.gypseacafe.com, 7am-9:30pm Tues.-Sun., $7-18) win over vegetarians with a great selection of healthy, plant-based meals as well as a promise to accommodate vegan and gluten-free dietary preferences. A handful of meat dishes are also served. Merely a bar with some stools stashed under a palm-thatched roof, the tiny café produces crafty creations you'd never expect, like the Chef's

Waffle—a vegetarian serving of avocado, spice, goat cheese, plantain, and egg on top of a waffle. New to the area in 2018, this surprising, funky, and minimalist-style café is quickly becoming a Playa Chiquita hot spot.

ACCOMMODATIONS
Under $50

If you're looking to socialize, head to the beachfront hostel ★ **Playa 506** (Road 256, 2.5 km southeast of Puerto Viejo de Talamanca at Playa Cocles, tel. 506/2750-3158, www.playa506.com, dorm $20 pp, private $70 s, $140 d). It has a fun energy and a laid-back vibe, and is a great place to grab a beer, play some beach volleyball, catch a movie, and meet new friends. The staff are helpful, the sea is steps away, and breakfast is included—what more could you want? Three mixed dorms sleep eight people each and have shared bathrooms. There are three private rooms; two of them share access to outdoor bathrooms.

$100-150

Two hundred meters shy of Playa Punta Uva is the riverside ★ **Pachamama Jungle River Lodge** (Road 256, 8 km southeast of Puerto Viejo de Talamanca at Punta Uva, tel. 506/8531-4845, www.pachamamacaribe. com, $110 s/d). A stay here is a lovely B&B-style experience, where the owners treat you like royalty in their jungle palace. Equipped with bedrooms, bathrooms, and kitchens, the five quaint, cozy villas are perfect for multi-day stays. Breakfast is delivered direct to your private terrace, where you'll start your day in the Caribbean's rainforest. Free use of snorkel gear, bicycles, and boogie boards is a thoughtful touch.

$150-250

The 14 bungalows scattered throughout the lush, jungle-like property of the **Shawandha Lodge** (Road 256, 6 km southeast of Puerto Viejo de Talamanca at Playa Chiquita, tel. 506/2750-0018, www.shawandha.com, $155 s/d) are within walking distance of Playa Chiquita. The lodge has a pool and a marvelous giant ceiba tree. Each bungalow features screened windows, 1-3 beds for up to four people, a seating area, wood furnishings, high ceilings, and large bathrooms. Many are starting to show some wear. Choose the hotel for its natural surroundings or proximity to the beach. Look elsewhere if you want polished finishes or a hotel with a fresher feel.

Congo Bongo (Road 256, 12 km southeast of Puerto Viejo de Talamanca at Manzanillo, tel. 506/2759-9016, www.congo-bongo.com, $185 s/d), a collection of eight vacation homes in the jungle west of Manzanillo, provides private access to Playa Grande. The homes vary in size and occupancy (1-7 people), but all feature an open-air, open-concept design that invites harmonious living within nature. Each has a fully equipped kitchen, private terrace, and lockable sleeping area. Laundry service is complimentary. For your peace of mind, security cameras aimed at each rental aid in keeping the airy accommodations safe.

The ultramodern, streamlined ★ **Le Caméléon Boutique Hotel** (Road 256, 4 km southeast of Puerto Viejo de Talamanca at Playa Cocles, tel. 506/2750-0501, www. lecameleonhotel.com, $250 s/d) trades Caribbean sway for grandiose swagger. Fans of avant-garde decor rave about the 23 upscale contemporary rooms, the property's tranquil ambience, and the hotel's nearby NOA Beach Club, where guests have access to a restaurant, bar, and hammock lounge on Playa Cocles. A contrast to the colorful buildings of the Caribbean, the nearly stark-white hotel may seem rather shocking, albeit squeaky clean. Only a few pops of color will catch your eye; these appear in extras like the pillows and wall art, which the hotel changes regularly, as if it were a chameleon.

INFORMATION AND SERVICES

Hospital Tony Facio Castro (Paseo Dr. Rubén Umaña Chavarría, 1 km north of the cruise dock, Limón, tel. 506/2758-2222, 24 hours daily) in Limón serves most of the Caribbean region. It is a 65-kilometer,

70-minute drive northwest of Playa Cocles and a 75-kilometer, 90-minute drive northwest of Manzanillo.

Several supermarkets can be found on Road 256 from Playa Cocles to Manzanillo. A tourist police office (Road 256 at Playa Cocles, just south of Le Caméléon Boutique Hotel, tel. 506/2750-0452, 10am-10pm daily) has officers available to assist foreign travelers. For after-hours emergencies, the closest official police station (Bribri, tel. 506/2751-0003, 24 hours daily) is 13 kilometers southwest of Puerto Viejo de Talamanca in the community of Bribri.

For additional services, visit Puerto Viejo de Talamanca.

TRANSPORTATION

The section of the southern Caribbean spanning Playa Cocles to Manzanillo is considered the eastern outskirts of Puerto Viejo de Talamanca. You'll drive through Puerto Viejo de Talamanca first. If you don't have your own vehicle, most accommodations in the area can pick you up in Puerto Viejo for an extra cost.

From Puerto Viejo, Playa Cocles is roughly three kilometers southeast on Road 256, a five-minute drive. Playa Chiquita is 6 kilometers (a 12-minute drive) and Punta Uva is 8.5 kilometers (a 15-minute drive) southeast of Puerto Viejo. Manzanillo is farthest from Puerto Viejo, at 13 kilometers (a 20-minute drive) southeast on Road 256.

Road 256 is paved and easy to walk, bike, or drive. If you plan to beach-hop, you'll appreciate having a rental car. Some hotels provide complimentary bikes for guest use. It's also possible to rent a bike in nearby Puerto Viejo for less than $10 per day.

Public buses travel to Manzanillo daily. You can catch one from San José (noon daily, 5-5.5 hours, $11), Limón (multiple times 5:30am-6:30pm daily, 1.5-2 hours, $4.50), Cahuita (multiple times 5:30am-6:30pm daily, 1 hour, $2-2.50), and Puerto Viejo de Talamanca (multiple times 5:30am-6:30pm daily, 30 minutes, $1.50). The bus that travels along Road 256 between Puerto Viejo de Talamanca and Manzanillo provides access to Playa Cocles, Playa Chiquita, and Punta Uva.

★ REFUGIO NACIONAL DE VIDA SILVESTRE GANDOCA-MANZANILLO

Much of the southern Caribbean coast south of Puerto Viejo is swathed in a mix of rainforest and wetlands that lies within the Refugio Nacional de Vida Silvestre Gandoca-Manzanillo (Gandoca-Manzanillo National Wildlife Refuge, tel. 506/2759-9100 or 506/2754-1103, www.sinac.go.cr, hours vary by sector, free). The refuge's 750-acre land reach contains some of the region's prettiest beaches, abundant and varied wildlife, much of the community of Punta Uva, and the entirety of the laid-back, predominantly Afro-Costa Rican community of Manzanillo.

Since 1985, government officials have been pushing for land conservation at the cost of losing several Manzanillo-area homes and businesses. Residents, many of whom are descendants of people who built the village in the 1800s, argue that the new rules were created without consideration for Manzanillo's townspeople. Today the debate is ongoing, and the refuge remains a gray area: It's acknowledged that the land is protected, but it is unclear how or if Manzanillo itself should be regulated.

The refuge consists of two sectors. The Manzanillo Sector (Road 256 as it enters Manzanillo, tel. 506/2759-9001, 8am-4pm daily) is the most visited. It's easily accessible from Manzanillo and offers a hiking trail that showcases both forest and beautiful beaches. The Gandoca Sector (8 km northeast of Hwy. 36 at Gandoca, tel. 506/2759-9100, 7am-5pm daily) provides access to Playa Gandoca, a small-scale turtle nesting beach that attracts a few researchers. Only a handful of travelers choose to visit this drab, dark-gray sand beach. Neither sector has public bathrooms.

Safety Concerns

Although the refuge is a well-known tourist attraction, its location at the southernmost end of the Caribbean coast limits the number of visitors it receives. You won't witness an endless flow of groups passing through, which increases opportunities for solitude—and vulnerability. Robberies have occurred within the area. If you wish to hike to Punta Mona, hire a tour guide who can help you navigate the trail, spot wildlife, and add an additional layer of security on your journey. Local guides **Florentino Grenald** (tel. 506/8841-2732) and **Abel Bustamante** (tel. 506/2759-9043) specialize in leading tours through the refuge.

Hiking

The refuge has an official entrance near the quiet community of Gandoca that's rarely accessed by the average traveler. Most people tour the refuge via Manzanillo by following the forest trail at the east end of Playa Grande that picks up after the village road ends. This trail is called the **Sendero Principal** (Main Trail, 5.5 km one-way, 2 hours, easy-moderate); it cuts through the refuge's rainforest and heads straight for **Punta Mona** (Mona Point), home to one of the Caribbean coast's most secluded beaches, with soft, nearly white sand. Near the start of the hike, you'll come across a wooden bridge that leads to **Punta Manzanillo** (Manzanillo Point), also known as **Miss May Point.** Traverse it for a postcard-worthy view of the Caribbean Sea at the opposite end.

Getting There

The refuge blankets much of the southeast end of the Caribbean coast. The Manzanillo Sector entrance is at the northeast corner of the village of Manzanillo. You can walk to the entrance if you're staying around town; otherwise, it is best accessed by car. Another option is to hop on one of the buses that commute between Limón and the village (multiple times 5:30am-6:30pm daily, 1.5-2 hours, $4.50). The bus picks up passengers as it passes through Cahuita, Puerto Viejo de Talamanca, Playa Cocles, Playa Chiquita, and Punta Uva. A sign for the refuge at the trailhead in the northeast corner of Manzanillo marks the sector's entrance.

The Gandoca Sector is best accessed by car. The turn-off to the entrance is off Highway 36, 4 kilometers shy of the hamlet of Sixaola and the country's border with Panama. A small outpost roughly 500 meters from the beach acts as the sector's entrance.

the Refugio Nacional de Vida Silvestre Gandoca-Manzanillo

Tortuguero

Most travelers who venture north of Limón are destined for Tortuguero, one of Costa Rica's most unique regions. Accessible only by small boat or plane, the area is a maze of natural and constructed waterways that snake through swamps, mangroves, and marshland among spits of land. An ideal destination for nature enthusiasts, the area's calm canals are peaceful, and the lush vegetation that towers over each canal is visually impressive. Enclosed within Parque Nacional Tortuguero (Tortuguero National Park), this area is a wildlife-packed destination. It's also a prime nesting site of four different species of sea turtles.

Locals reside in the colorful Tortuguero Village, a small concentration of homes and businesses on the isthmus that divides Laguna Tortuguero (Tortuguero Lagoon) from the Caribbean Sea. Although the village offers a handful of accommodations, most visitors stay at the waterfront hotels that are a short boat ride northwest of town. The majority of Tortuguero accommodations, as well as an endless list of tour operators and agencies around the country, offer all-inclusive one- to three-night packages that include a private room, meals, local tours (typically canal tours and a Tortuguero Village tour), and ground and boat transportation between Tortuguero and San José, among other cities. Also available are transportation-based packages that couple shared shuttle and boat transfer services to or from the destination; some operators also include a complimentary meal.

Safety Concerns

All-inclusive packages and **transportation packages** provide the safest experiences and the most reliable means of getting to and from Tortuguero. Unguided exploration of the area and self-arranged transportation in this remote region are not recommended due to tourist-targeted crimes like theft.

To ensure your personal safety, it's important to use a reputable hotel or tour outfitter to travel to and from Tortuguero. Traveling independently in this area can put you at risk. Instances of rental car break-ins, theft, and robbery along the roads and canals that connect with the dock at La Pavona have been known to occur. Tourists rarely use the local bus; those who do can be the target of theft while riding the bus or waiting for the next bus to arrive.

Three docks are used as gateways to Tortuguero: Caño Blanco, Moín, and La Pavona. **Caño Blanco** is generally the safest and is the preference of tour companies. I don't recommend that visitors use La Pavona, as it's unsafe due to instances of theft and robbery.

RECREATION
Local Guides and Tours

For help coordinating a Tortuguero visit, contact **Exploradores Outdoors** (tel. 506/2222-6262, www.exploradoresoutdoors.com). This trustworthy tour operator provides high-value Tortuguero packages ($154-224 pp) that depart from San José, Alajuela, La Fortuna, Puerto Viejo de Talamanca, Cahuita, and Puerto Viejo de Sarapiquí daily, with an option to continue on to a new location following your stay in the northern Caribbean region. If you're an adventure enthusiast, consider the operator's combined Tortuguero and white-water rafting tour package ($299-449 pp), which visits Río Pacuare.

Among the many businesses and independent tour guides that offer guided experiences in Tortuguero, my preference is **Costa Rica Roots Tours** (across from supermarket Las Tortugas in Tortuguero Village, tel. 506/2767-3107, www.costaricaroottours.com, 9:30am-6:30pm daily). You cannot go wrong with the

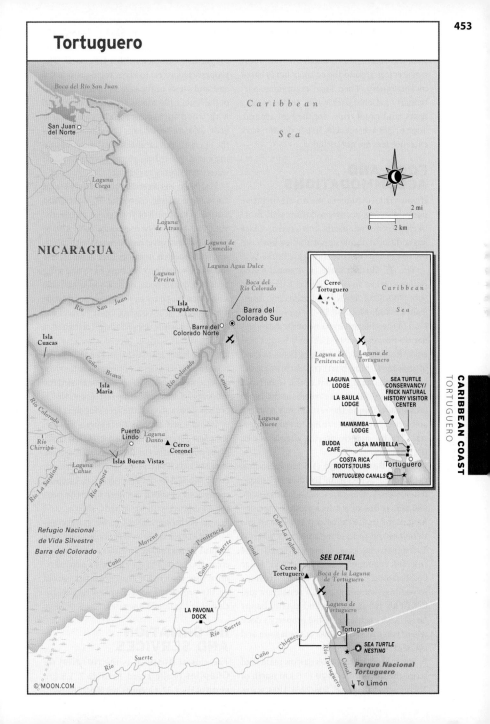

Tortuguero

Boca del Río San Juan

Caribbean

Sea

San Juan del Norte

Laguna Ciega

Laguna de Atras

Laguna de Enmedio

Laguna Agua Dulce

NICARAGUA

Laguna Pereira

Boca del Río Colorado

Isla Chupadero

Barra del Colorado Sur

Barra del Colorado Norte

Río San Juan

Isla Cuacas

Caño Bravo

Isla Maria

Río Colorado

Canal

Río Colorado

Río Chirripó

Puerto Lindo

Laguna Danto

Cerro Coronel

Islas Buena Vistas

Laguna Cahue

Río La Sardina

Río Zapote

Laguna Nueve

0   2 mi
0   2 km

Refugio Nacional de Vida Silvestre Barra del Colorado

Moreno

Río Penitencia

Caño

Suerte

Canal

Caño La Palma

SEE DETAIL

LA PAVONA DOCK

Río Suerte

Caño Chiquero

Cerro Tortuguero

Boca de la Laguna de Tortuguero

Laguna de Tortuguero

Tortuguero

SEA TURTLE NESTING

Parque Nacional Tortuguero

↓ To Limón

Caño

Río Suerte

Río Tortuguero

Detail inset

Cerro Tortuguero

Caribbean

Sea

Laguna de Penitencia

Laguna de Tortuguero

LAGUNA LODGE

SEA TURTLE CONSERVANCY/ FRICK NATURAL HISTORY VISITOR CENTER

LA BAULA LODGE

MAWAMBA LODGE

BUDDA CAFÉ

CASA MARBELLA

COSTA RICA ROOTS TOURS

Tortuguero

TORTUGUERO CANALS

© MOON.COM

collection of professional, knowledgeable, fun, and proficient tour guides who work with the organization, which provides tourism services around the country but is based in Tortuguero. Their local excursions, particularly national park walks, turtle-nesting tours, and canal trips, are the best around. Tour prices average $20-30 per person; park entrance fees are not included.

FOOD AND ACCOMMODATIONS

If you visit Tortuguero via an all-inclusive package, your accommodation will most likely provide your meals. Tortuguero Village has additional dining opportunities; however, the restaurants worth visiting are limited.

The ★ Budda Café (just south of the police station in Tortuguero Village, tel. 506/2709-8084, www.buddacafe.com, 1pm-8:30pm Wed.-Mon., $8.50-24) serves the best food in the village. Grab one of the café's signature pizzas, a pasta dish, or a burger and enjoy it while watching Panga boats (a kind of smaller fishing boat) travel through the lagoon and canal in front of the waterfront establishment. Patrons rave about the cocktails in addition to the restaurant's relaxing ambience. My favorite thing to order is dessert. Try the mouthwatering cheesecake or the brownies.

★ La Baula Lodge (1.5 km inland on the land spit across from Tortuguero Village, tel. 506/8951-8951, www.labaulalodge.com, $50 s/d) is one of a select group of accommodations in Tortuguero that allow rooms to be booked individually in cases where a Tortuguero package is not preferred. The colorful, economy-priced, motel-style lodge boasts fantastic value. It has 45 basic rooms, a refreshing swimming pool, a restaurant and bar (with swing seating and a daily happy hour), and a rest area by the property's dock where you can enjoy views of the lagoon and colorful sunsets.

Situated on Tortuguero's narrow main land strip, the Laguna Lodge (2.5 km north of Tortuguero Village, tel. 506/2253-1100, www.lagunatortuguero.com, $253 s, $446 d, all-inclusive) is surrounded by six acres of botanical gardens complete with a frog pond. The property has access to Playa Tortuguero to the east and views of the lagoon to the west. All of the hotel's 106 rooms are simply decorated with wood furnishings, have comfortable beds, and are kept clean. The showstopper is the open-air restaurant that extends out into the canal, providing guests with a tranquil waterfront dining experience.

Halfway between Laguna Lodge and Tortuguero Village, the quaint ★ Mawamba Lodge (1 km north of Tortuguero Village, tel. 506/2790-8181, www.mawamba.com, $297 s, $488 d, all-inclusive) has 56 rooms with cabin-inspired wooden interiors that demonstrate the lodge's rusticity. Rooms have one king bed, two queen beds, or one queen and one single bed. Each room features a porch with a hammock or a rocking chair perfect for lounging in while appreciating Tortuguero's quiet natural setting. Ideal for water sport fans, the hotel specializes in canal exploration and offers guests optional, gentle river experiences by kayak, by canoe, or aboard the property's Katonga floating restaurant, which cruises slowly around the area's lagoon.

If you must stay in Tortuguero Village, your best option is Casa Marbella (just north of the police station in Tortuguero Village, tel. 506/8833-0827, http://casamarbella.tripod.com, $40 s, $45 d). The B&B has 14 clean rooms (one of which can sleep up to five people) equipped with basic beds, shelves, and private bathrooms. Don't go for grand comfort but expect above-average hospitality. The helpful owners make an effort to ensure you enjoy your stay, and they know how to maximize your time in the area. Breakfast, served on the property's waterfront terrace, is included in the hotel's low rates.

INFORMATION AND SERVICES

The closest hospital is the Hospital de Guápiles (Calle 1 and Avenida 7, 1.5 km north of Hwy. 32, Guápiles, tel. 506/2710-6801,

24 hours daily) in Guápiles, a 75-minute boat ride followed by a 50-kilometer, 75-minute drive from Tortuguero.

Supermarkets, a police station (tel. 506/2767-1593, 24 hours daily), and the community's clinic, Ebais Barra Tortuguero (tel. 506/2767-0184, 8am-4pm Tues.-Wed.), form the small, walkable Tortuguero Village. There's an ATM (5am-midnight daily) in the north end of Tortuguero Village, east of the bird statues.

TRANSPORTATION

If you purchase an all-inclusive Tortuguero package, the outfitter or hotel you book with will handle all ground and boat transportation arrangements.

If you prefer to book your Tortuguero accommodations, meals, and tours individually, reserve a transportation package. Not only does this eliminate the stress of missed bus connections, driving through unsafe areas, leaving rental vehicles unattended overnight, buying boat tickets, and finding a safe boat operator, but it also makes your life easier. Simply reserve a seat on the all-in-one service: You'll get picked up at your hotel and transported directly to the dock, where you'll board a lifejacket-equipped boat with a professional captain and head out on the water with your luggage within arm's reach.

Several companies offer transportation packages in the form of combined shared shuttle and boat services. Exploradores Outdoors (offices in San José and Puerto Viejo de Talamanca, tel. 506/2222-6262, www.exploradoresoutdoors.com, 6am-9pm daily) offers pickups from San José, Alajuela, La Fortuna, Puerto Viejo de Sarapiquí, Cahuita, or Puerto Viejo de Talamanca. Their Tortuguero Shuttle Land & Water (6am daily, 5 hours, $55 pp), a convenient and high-value option, also includes a hearty breakfast buffet and provides a drop-off at your Tortuguero-area hotel. As an added bonus, they typically depart from the dock at Caño Blanco (approximately 135 kilometers and a 2.5-3-hour drive from downtown San José),

which is most often used by hotels and tour operators that run boats to Tortuguero on behalf of their customers.

Another dock at Moín, approximately 10 kilometers and a 15-minute drive west from downtown Limón, has boats to Tortuguero; however, you may find the 3.5-hour boat trip up the coast tough to take. Caribe Shuttle (on the corner of Road 256 and Calle 213, Puerto Viejo de Talamanca, tel. 506/2750-0626, www.caribeshuttle.com, 6am-9pm daily) combines ground transportation from destinations in the southern Caribbean region to the dock in Moín and boat transportation onward to Tortuguero if you wish to make the trip. Their Caribe Shuttle and Boat Service (8am daily, 5 hours, $75 pp) will drop you off at the dock in Tortuguero Village.

The quickest way to get to Tortuguero is to fly. The Aeropuerto Tortuguero (Tortuguero Airport, TTQ) is 4 kilometers (a quick boat trip) north of Tortuguero Village. SANSA Airlines (tel. 506/2290-4100, www.flysansa.com) offers direct flights to Tortuguero from San José daily. The flight time from San José is approximately 30 minutes.

PARQUE NACIONAL TORTUGUERO

The Parque Nacional Tortuguero (Tortuguero National Park, south end of Tortuguero Village, tel. 506/2709-8086, www.sinac.go.cr, 6am-6pm daily, $15 pp) is the foremost attraction of the northern Caribbean region and one of Costa Rica's most visited national parks. A truly remarkable diversity of species inhabits the protected land area, including more than 750 types of birds, mammals, reptiles, and amphibians, plus over 700 varieties of plants. Up-close bird-watching, crocodile and caiman sightings (or if you're lucky, endangered manatee sightings), and encounters with monkeys that drop in on boats are possible wildlife experiences. You may even spot the elusive jaguar that has been seen taking a dip in the park's rapid-free waters, hiding among the riverbank's brush, and roaming the southern end of the black-sand **Playa Tortuguero,** the area's principal beach. The beach spans 24 kilometers of Caribbean coastline but is unsuitable for swimming because of its rough, shark-ridden waters.

You can explore the park in a number of ways. The most popular option is to tour the *senderos acuáticos* (water trails) via a canal tour. A second, less popular option is to tour the park on foot by way of its nature trails. Since Playa Tortuguero is contained within park limits, walks along the beach and participation in turtle nesting tours are also considered park activities. Centers that monitor park access (especially by boat) surround the protected land space. The **ranger station** in Tortuguero Village marks the most visited entrance.

TOP EXPERIENCE

★ Tortuguero Canals

One of the most serene experiences you can have in Costa Rica is to take a boat, canoe, or kayak tour through the **canal system** entwined within Parque Nacional Tortuguero. This already remote destination begins to feel even more secluded as you float deep into the jungle and escape civilization. There are plenty of opportunities to spot wildlife along the way: Birders, keep an eye out for kingfishers, curassows, herons, hawks, jacanas, anhingas, cormorants, and toucans. The zone's ecological habitats are equally worthy of gawking. Simple shifts in scenery will catch your eye, such as how the water is chocolate brown in some areas and crystal clear in others, reflecting the waterway's verdant vegetation across canals that shine like glass.

For me, the highlight of the astonishingly quiet trip is listening to the chorus of the forest. It is sometimes enlivened by birdsongs, monkey howls, and the rustle of leaves as critters dart into hiding, and it is always peaceful. Few heavily visited tourist destinations in Costa Rica provide such a raw and unfiltered absorption of nature.

At their core, canal excursions are natural history tours. They should be led by a knowledgeable tour guide who can help you discover the park through its history, ecosystems, and inhabitants. Nearly every person with ties to tourism in Tortuguero sells the experience, however, qualified or not. To get the most out of your visit, choose a canal tour provided by **Costa Rica Roots Tours** (across from supermarket Las Tortugas in Tortuguero Village, tel. 506/2767-3107, www.costaricarootstours.com, 9:30am-6:30pm daily). The group's love for Tortuguero and knowledge of the park are tough to beat.

★ Sea Turtle Nesting

Sea turtles nest at several beaches in Costa Rica, but Tortuguero is fortunate to host the greatest variety, including leatherback turtles, loggerhead turtles, endangered green turtles, and critically endangered hawksbill turtles. To witness an *arribada*—when mother sea turtles crawl ashore, lay their eggs in the sand, and return to the sea—is to experience the joy of Tortuguero. There's a buzz of excitement in the air around the village during turtle season (March to October), when foreigners flood the area, eager to lay eyes on the town's main attraction, and the park is prepped to carry out its principal aim: protecting the reptiles and their delicate spawn.

Beach access during turtle season is highly regulated by the park. In order to experience an *arribada,* you'll need to reserve an authorized, guided **turtle nesting tour** (8pm-10pm or 10pm-midnight, tour time determined by the park each day, 2 hours, $30 pp). It's best to book your tour after you arrive in Tortuguero. Tour guides can be arranged through your accommodation or **Costa Rica Roots Tours** (across from supermarket Las Tortugas in Tortuguero Village, tel. 506/2767-3107, www.costaricarootstours.com, 9:30am-6:30pm daily).

During the tour, you'll visit the beach as

1: a Tortuguero canal **2:** the affordable La Baula Lodge in Tortuguero

part of a group (up to 10 people) and wait at a pavilion as a park ranger searches for turtles. Your tour guide will help pass the time by offering tons of information about sea turtle species, life and nesting cycles, and Tortuguero's conservation efforts. When a turtle is spotted, you'll be invited to get closer to the creature and witness its nesting behaviors with the help of a special light. Plan to wear dark clothing during the nighttime event; light colors are distracting and can disrupt the turtles' nesting cycles. Although seeing a turtle cannot be guaranteed, tours during September produce the most sightings.

Hiking

It is possible to explore the park by land, but doing so is less impressive than exploring the area's canals. A few trails weave throughout the park, the most notable being **Sendero El Gavilán** (El Gavilán Trail), a short two-kilometer loop that provides a walk through the area's humid, mosquito-ridden rainforest and a short visit to the beach. The trail is often impassable due to flooding, so be sure to verify open access through your hotel or the ranger station before setting out. When open, the trail could still be muddy, and rubber boots are a must, if not to help you maneuver the treacherous terrain, at least to help guard against rare but possible snake bites. Boots can be rented at the trail entrance.

A second trail, **Sendero Jaguar** (Jaguar Trail), parallels the beach. Short nature walks also take place here, but the trail is most often visited at night during turtle-viewing experiences.

Getting There

Technically, to reach Tortuguero is to reach the park, since the protected land space encompasses the area. You may travel within the park's limits, however, by boat or on foot. The park's most visited entrance (where the entrance fee is paid) is at the south end of Tortuguero Village and within walking distance of nearly everything else in the tiny town. You can hike to some hotels north of the village, but it's not safe to make the trip alone. If you plan to stay at a hotel separated from the village by water, you can hire a boat captain at the docks on the village's west side to take you wherever you need to go. Boat trips run $3-5 per person, depending on which accommodation you choose. Hotel staff can call a captain to their property if you need to head into town.

Southern Inlands

Costa Rica's least visited region is the inland area south of San José. This part of the country is dominated by undeveloped protected land that serves as habitats for the country's most elusive wildlife species and as the site of remote homes for indigenous groups. The mountainous region is stunning, contrasting high-altitude tundra and blunt ridges against rolling green hills that plummet into valleys. Covered in wild vegetation and etched with obscure trails, much of the region is accessible only to the adventurous.

Fit and fearless hikers come for the adrenaline-inducing ascents that lead through the rugged interior. Avid birders and naturalists are thrilled by frequent sightings of quetzals and the potent fragrance of beehive gingers. Thanks to its immense diversity of elevations and

Highlights

Look for ★ to find recommended sights, activities, dining, and lodging.

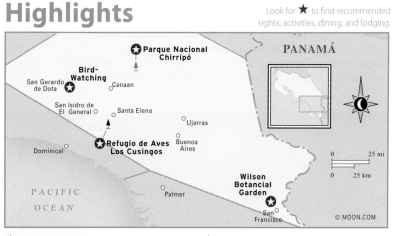

★ **Go bird-watching** around **San Gerardo de Dota** and try to spot an elusive quetzal (page 466).

★ **Take a guided tour** of the **Refugio de Aves Los Cusingos** to see many different types of birds (page 467).

★ **Summit** Costa Rica's highest peak in **Parque Nacional Chirripó** (page 472).

★ **Admire exotic and native plant species** at the **Wilson Botanical Garden** (page 477).

ecosystems, the southern inland area delivers complete immersion in nature within a quiet part of Costa Rica that still feels undiscovered.

The allure of the southern inland region is its detachment from overt tourism, commercialism, and, in some areas, civilization. Venturing out into the region's wilderness alone can be tempting. Apart from a few exceptions, though, the vast area is best experienced alongside a tour guide. This isn't a place you want to risk getting lost in.

PLANNING YOUR TIME

The amount of time you should spend in the region depends largely on whether you plan to climb **Cerro Chirripó.** If you do, you'll need two days to reach the summit and return to the trailhead. Give yourself three days if you want additional time to explore the park's interior. You also need to add an extra day before you begin the hike to travel to the area and register your arrival.

Other regional highlights, including birdwatching in **San Gerardo de Dota** or at the **Refugio de Aves Los Cusingos** and wandering through the **Wilson Botanical Garden,** can be experienced in a few hours. Plan at least one overnight stay in San Gerardo de Dota in order to take part in an early morning birding tour. Each activity or sight in this area can be worth adding to your itinerary as you pass through the region on your way to other areas, such as the central Pacific coast or the Osa Peninsula and the southern Pacific coast.

Weather and Transportation

Home to the highest elevation in the country, much of the region is downright cold, at least when compared with average temperatures elsewhere in the country. Temperatures range 60-70°F in the lowest areas and drop even more atop Cerro de la Muerte, around

San Gerardo de Dota, in San Gerardo de Rivas, and in other high-altitude destinations. Pack thick socks, pants, long-sleeve shirts, and sweaters. Additional gear, including warm jackets, hats, and gloves, may be required if you plan to engage in mountain ascents. Most accommodations ward off the overnight chill with electrical heaters, hot water bottles, sleeping bags, and layers of blankets. Although the wet season runs from May to December, fog in the region can make it feel damp year-round.

Road conditions vary throughout the region, from smooth highways to narrow, rocky back roads. If you're merely passing through (via Hwy. 2, Road 243, or Road 237), a 4x4 vehicle is not required. Most turns off the major roads and highways lead to remote areas that require either steep uphill drives or descents into valleys, some providing little opportunity to turn around once you've initiated the journey. In these areas, having a reliable 4x4 vehicle with high clearance and top-notch brakes is a must. Avoid driving after dark, amid bursts of rain, or during heavy cloud cover; the morning tends to be the clearest time.

ORIENTATION

The southern inland region occupies the middle stretch of southeastern Costa Rica. Geographically large, the region is comprised predominantly of protected land space. The paved but curvy Highway 2, the region's main thoroughfare, connects the Central Valley and Highlands to San Isidro de El General (the region's most populous city) over the mountaintop known as **Cerro de la Muerte** (Hill of Death). From San Isidro de El General, Highway 2 and Road 237 close in on Panama to the southeast, while Road 243 provides direct access to coastal towns like Dominical to the southwest.

Previous: Cerro Chirripó; butterfly; a stream northeast of San Gerardo de Rivas.

Southern Inlands

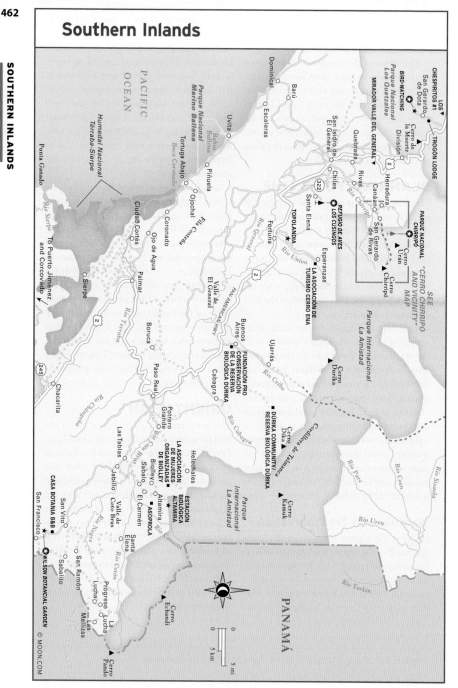

© MOON.COM

Driving Over the Hill of Death

Countless chats with other commuters have taught me there's no winning the debate over whether the winding drive over Cerro de la Muerte (Hill of Death) is best experienced or avoided. On one side are the many foreigners (who probably aren't accustomed to mountain driving) who argue that the steady 70-kilometer climb out of the city of Cartago and the 40-kilometer descent into the city of San Isidro de El General are intimidating challenges. On the other side are the many locals and experienced drivers (myself included) who feel the passage isn't as awful as first-time visitors are led to believe. In fact, the back roads that lead to remote areas all around the country give me greater stress than Cerro de la Muerte.

The section of Highway 2 between Cartago and San Isidro de El General weaves around mountainsides, edges steep cliffs in a few areas, and cuts through protected forest in many others. Traveled by Ticos daily, it is also a paved and popular road that passes through small communities and offers a few establishments where you can pull over, including restaurants and a gas station. On most mornings, when conditions are clear, the drive showcases rare highland ecosystems and breathtaking valley views. If you drive slowly, cautiously, and defensively around other drivers, especially trucks, the beautiful journey is usually an enjoyable one.

Weather conditions can significantly affect the drive; poor visibility makes it outright dangerous. Avoid the trip after dark or in the afternoon, when dense cloud cover shrouds the area. (The same advice applies to mountainous drives anywhere in the country.)

It might put your mind at ease to know that the mountain's terrifying name pertains to its frigid temperatures, not to deaths resulting from vehicular accidents—although accidents can and do happen. Still, if you'd rather not follow the route, you're in luck. The southern inland region can also be accessed from San José via the coastal route, Highway 34, which skirts the central Pacific coast. You'll spend an extra hour traveling to San Isidro de El General this way, but it's time well spent if you'd feel more comfortable skipping Cerro de la Muerte.

Cerro Chirripó and Vicinity

Southeast of San José and the Central Valley, Costa Rica's landscape changes dramatically, rising into mountains as it reaches the southern inland area. Along the way, you'll pass cloud-covered areas including Parque Nacional Los Quetzales and San Gerardo de Dota, both of which are chilly enough to make you wonder if you're still in Costa Rica. Following an elevation drop in San Isidro de El General, the road climbs again, this time northeast of the city in the direction of San Gerardo de Rivas. The tiny town is the jumping-off point for trips to Parque Nacional Chirripó, home to the country's highest peak.

PARQUE NACIONAL LOS QUETZALES

Midway over Cerro de la Muerte, Parque Nacional Los Quetzales (Los Quetzales National Park, Hwy. 2, halfway between Cartago and San Isidro de El General, tel. 506/2206-5020, 8am-4pm daily, free) is the favored stop of avid bird-watchers passing through the region, especially those in search of the park's namesake quetzals. Engulfed in cloud forest and rife with several of the country's eminent highland bird species, the alpine park is also known for its bountiful endemic flora and occasional tapir sightings. Quiet, soggy, foggy, and brisk (dress for temperatures of 40-55°F), the attraction feels less tropical than most of the country. Sometimes you'll

Cerro Chirripó and Vicinity

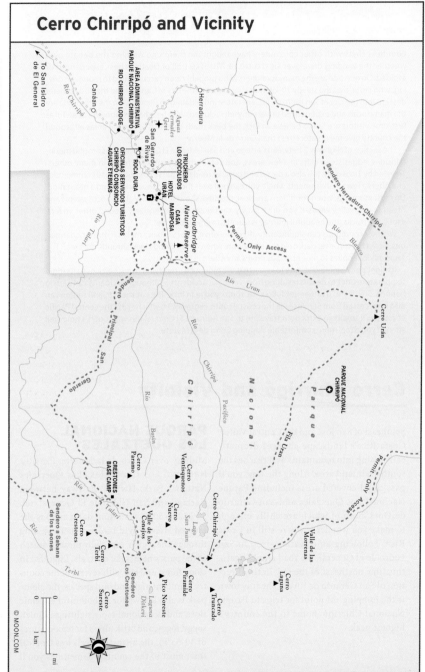

To San Isidro
de El General

Cañaán

Río Chirripó

ÁREA ADMINISTRATIVA
PARQUE NACIONAL CHIRRIPÓ
RÍO CHIRRIPÓ LODGE

Herradura

Aguas
Termales
Gevi

San Gerardo
de Rivas

OFICINAS SERVICIOS TURISTICOS
CHIRRIPÓ CONSORCIO
AGUAS ETERNAS

ROCA DURA

TRUCHERO
LOS COCOLISOS

HOTEL
URÁN

CASA
MARIPOSA

Cloudbridge
Nature Reserve

Permit Only Access

Río Blanco

Río Uran

Sendero Herradura-Chirripó

Cerro Urán

Río Talari

Sendero Principal San Gerardo

Río Chirripó Pacífico

Río Bosin

Río Uran

Chirripó

PARQUE NACIONAL
CHIRRIPÓ

Parque

Nacional

Fila Urán

Permit Only Access

CRESTONES
BASE CAMP

Cerro
Páramo

Cerro
Ventisqueros

Cerro
Nuevo

Lago
San Juan

Cerro Chirripó

Valle de las
Morrenas

Sendero a Sabana
de los Leones

Cerro
Crestones

Valle de los
Conejos

Cerro
Laguna

Río Talari

Cerro
Terbi

Sendero
Los Crestones

Cerro
Pirámide

Cerro
Truncado

Río Terbi

Cerro
Sureste

Pico Noreste

Cerro
Nuevo

Laguna
Ditkevi

0   1 km

0   1 mi

© MOON.COM

catch a glimpse of your own breath as you hike through the mountaintop's thin air. A walking stick can help ease the high-altitude journey.

There are 65 species of butterflies inhabiting the park in abundance, along with unique plants like *Psychotria elata*—also known as the hot lips plant—which has bracts that resemble the pout of voluptuous scarlet lips.

Visiting this park doesn't guarantee a quetzal sighting. The birds live in the park, but they're tricky to see. The likelihood of spotting one is much greater along trails in nearby San Gerardo de Dota. A few birding tours run through the park, but the better option is to take a guided bird-watching tour around San Gerardo de Dota.

The park is situated along the highway, so it's easy to tour it on your way to another destination. The park's entrance is just off the highway, marked by a **ranger station.**

Hiking

A network of eight trails threads throughout the park beyond the ranger station at the entrance. The majority are explored by researchers and students. If you're like most leisurely visitors, you'll choose to walk the out-and-back **Sendero Ojo de Agua** (Ojo de Agua Trail, 5 km round-trip, 2-2.5 hours,

moderate). The trail leads through secondary forest and is rarely busy, despite being the park's most popular trail.

Getting There

The park is on the south side of Highway 2, halfway between Cartago and San Isidro de El General. It is best accessed by car. You'll find the entrance (Hwy. 2, 58 km north of San Isidro de El General) and a large parking lot just off the highway, opposite the restaurant Los Chespiritos #1.

SAN GERARDO DE DOTA

A few kilometers southeast of Parque Nacional Los Quetzales, a side road departs from Highway 2 and descends deep into the Valle de Río Savegre (Savegre River Valley) toward a community of mountainside lodges collectively known as San Gerardo de Dota. The road plunges past hills thick in vegetation and drops toward the valley's namesake river, which flows swiftly but peacefully over a rocky bed. Moss-covered riverbanks, pretty orchards, and trout ponds dot the regularly misty, cool area. Occupying its own quiet crevice in one of the least visited regions of the country, San Gerardo de Dota remains off most travelers' radars, except those of devoted

view from the peak of Cerro Chirripó

birders who flock to the destination for its prime bird-watching.

Recreation

★ BIRD-WATCHING

Arguably, Costa Rica's most crowd-pleasing bird is the resplendent quetzal; it thrills patient gazers with its shimmery plumage, blue-green tail feathers, and crimson breast. To witness one in flight, especially a male with a flowing train in tow (some grow up to a meter long), is truly a spectacular sight. While the magnificent members of the trogon family aren't easy to spot around the country, they flourish here because of San Gerardo de Dota's high elevation and many *aguacatillo* trees.

Nearly every hotel in the valley offers guided birding excursions. I like the tours arranged by bird specialist Greivin Gonzalez, an administrator of the **Trogón Lodge** (Calle San Gerardo, 6.5 km south of Hwy. 2, tel. 506/2740-1051, www.trogonlodge.com). The hotel's **Quetzal Quest** (5:30am daily, 2 hours, $30 pp) is your best option if you've come to the area specifically to spot a quetzal, as the excursion aims to deliver you at least one sighting by visiting trees where the birds are most commonly spotted. Gonzalez suggests sightings are 90 percent guaranteed (on average, across the whole year). If you seek a variety of highland birds, the hotel's general **bird-watching tour** (9am and 2pm daily, 2 hours, $35 pp) explores riverbanks and nature trails in search of many of the area's 170 resident bird species. Both tours explore trails around the Trogón Lodge and provide a mild hiking experience.

Food and Accommodations

On Highway 2, a mere 3.5 kilometers northwest of the turnoff to San Gerardo de Dota, is ★ **Los Chespiritos #1** (Hwy. 2, 58 km north of San Isidro de El General, tel. 506/2571-2035, www.chespiritos.com, 5:30am-10pm daily, $5-12). I always stop at this informal cafeteria whenever I travel over Cerro de la Muerte, whether to pick a custom plate of Costa Rican foods from the buffet bar, to try

a sugary treat from the snack booth, or to simply enjoy a break from driving through the chilly mountaintop with a cup of hot coffee. The *chorreadas* (sweet corn pancakes) and empanadas are delish!

At the turnoff to San Gerardo de Dota, the cabin-style **El Jilguero** (corner of Hwy. 2 and Calle San Gerardo, 6am-7pm daily, $4-8, cash only) is an easy place to pull over if you wish to try the area's top dish: *trucha* (trout). It's practically a crime to visit the area and not dine on the local delicacy, and at $6 for a serving accompanied by rice and beans, you can't go wrong here. The restaurant also goes by the name **Soda San Gerardo** and opens early for breakfast.

Café Kahawa (Calle San Gerardo, 8 km south of Hwy. 2, tel. 506/2740-1081, www.kahawa.co, 8am-5:30pm daily, $8-10) brings gastronomic flair to modest San Gerardo de Dota with its unique approach to traditional trout dishes. Options include trout fillets served in coconut milk, trout-based pasta plates, and fried trout fingers with optional smoked trout dip. Set alongside the picturesque Río Savegre, the open-air restaurant radiates a very tranquil atmosphere in its rustic setting. It's a great place from which to admire the ecology of the region.

A handful of quiet lodges dot the valley. My favorite, the service-oriented ★ **Trogón Lodge** (Calle San Gerardo, 6.5 km south of Hwy. 2, tel. 506/2740-1051, www.trogonlodge. com, $124 s, $148 d), has 12 quaint, all-wood modules scattered around the hotel's property (some are up hills; come prepared to walk), with two separate rooms in each and a shared front porch. The cozy rooms sleep 1-4 people and are kept warm by an electrical heater and complimentary hot water bottles. Stay here if you wish to sequester yourself in nature—rooms have no television, Wi-Fi, or telephone service. Birdsongs at dawn function as alarm clocks. An eight-cable zip-line course through the treetops ($35 pp) provides on-site entertainment.

Off Highway 2, 10 kilometers northwest of the turnoff to San Gerardo de Dota, the remote **Las Vueltas Lodge** (2 km southwest of Hwy. 2, tel. 506/8391-1720, www. lasvueltaslodge.com, $45 s, $90 d) sits atop a mountain, overlooking the clouds. The owners built this simple, charming, two-story lodge from fallen wood. It houses 35 guests in private rooms and in dorms with bunk beds. Both the lodge and the on-site organic farm are run by a welcoming and attentive family who provide everything from home-cooked meals, cooking classes, and spiritual lessons to nature walks and garden tours around the 200-acre property.

Information and Services

Apart from its small collection of hotels and restaurants, San Gerardo de Dota is not a developed village. It offers next to no services, except for the small **supermarket** that you'll pass on Calle San Gerardo as you venture into the valley.

The closest **gas station** is on Highway 2, roughly 30 kilometers northwest of the turnoff to San Gerardo de Dota. From the south, your last opportunity to fill up on fuel will be in San Isidro de El General, about 50 kilometers southeast of the turnoff to San Gerardo de Dota.

Transportation

San Gerardo de Dota is 85 kilometers (an approximate two-hour drive) southeast from downtown **San José** via Highway 2 and Calle San Gerardo. It's 295 kilometers (an approximate 5.5-hour drive) southeast from downtown **Liberia** via Highway 1, Highway 27, Highway 2, and Calle San Gerardo, and 60 kilometers northwest of **San Isidro de El General** via Highway 2 and Calle San Gerardo, a drive of about 75 minutes. All routes to San Gerardo de Dota require at least partial travel over Cerro de la Muerte.

The turnoff to San Gerardo de Dota onto Calle San Gerardo from Highway 2 is 3.5 kilometers southeast of the roadside entrance to Parque Nacional Los Quetzales. From the turnoff, a 10-kilometer (approximate 30-minute) downhill drive leads into the

valley past local establishments. The drive is on a narrow, curvy road that borders cliffsides in places. Avoid driving the stretch after dark or when weather conditions make visibility poor.

SAN ISIDRO DE EL GENERAL

The compact and bustling agricultural city of San Isidro de El General, at the southern base of Cerro de la Muerte, serves as a gateway to the Central Pacific and destinations farther south. People also pass through the city on the way to Parque Nacional Chirripó and other attractions on the outskirts of town. Referred to by locals as **Pérez Zeledón** or simply Pérez, San Isidro de El General's modern-day claim to fame is the world-renowned *fútbol* goalkeeper Keylor Navas, who hails from the city. Many of the billboards in the area proudly feature the phenom.

As the hub of the southern inland region, San Isidro de El General is the best place to stock up on supplies. Restaurant prices are shockingly low. If you're merely passing through, plan to stop in the city and dine (rather informally) to save a few bucks.

Sights

★ REFUGIO DE AVES LOS CUSINGOS

Adding to the region's appeal to bird-watchers is the **Refugio de Aves Los Cusingos** (Los Cusingos Bird Refuge, Road 326, 3 km northeast of Road 322, tel. 506/2738-2070, 7am-4pm Mon.-Sat., 7am-1pm Sun., $17 adults, $6 children 0-12). This research-based attraction hides a half hour east of San Isidro de El General at the former house of the late Dr. Alexander Skutch. A highly respected botanist and ornithologist, the American naturalist produced several written works on avifauna in Costa Rica (and a handful on philosophy) between the 1950s and the late 1990s. Today, his property is a nearly 200-acre refuge protected by the Centro Científico Tropical (Tropical Science Center). You're welcome to wander the refuge's few short trails on your

own in search of the sights and sounds that captivated Dr. Skutch for decades; the bird species here include resident, migratory, and endemic varieties. I highly recommend taking a guided tour (7am-2pm Mon.-Sat., 7am-11am Sun., 2 hours, $32 adults, $21 children 0-12)—ideally in the early morning—to maximize spotting opportunities. Give yourself two hours at the attraction to tour the trail, peek inside the Casa Museo (the preserved home of Dr. Skutch), and marvel up close at the many social species that frequent the refuge's fruit feeders.

TOPOLANDIA

The Flintstones-feeling subterranean world of Topolandia (Road 327, 1 km northeast of Hwy. 2, tel. 506/2731-1322, www.topolandia. com, 8am-4pm daily, by guided tour only) is unlike anything I've ever experienced in Costa Rica. Sign up for a guided tour (8am-3pm daily, 1 hour, $20 pp) and explore the underground living quarters of the attraction's Tico owner, who began chipping away at his mountainside property with a pick and a shovel in 2004. He has since created a jaw-dropping, partly wheelchair-accessible, fully furnished (with tables, chairs, and beds) network of 12 walkable tunnels. The dwelling even has a bathroom and a meditation room! This creative passion project is a continual work in progress and is always expanding.

Food

There's really no reason to spend a night in San Isidro de El General. If you're merely passing through on your way to the Pacific coast (via San José), a handful of decent accommodations are provided in the beach town of Dominical, 35 kilometers southwest of the city. If you must stop beforehand, pull over at Mirador Valle del General before entering the city. If you're in the area to hike Cerro

Chirripó, book lodging in the gateway community of San Gerardo de Rivas.

As you descend into San Isidro de El General from the north, you'll come across ★ Mirador Valle del General (Hwy. 2, 15 km north of San Isidro de El General, tel. 506/2200-5465, www.valledelgeneral.com, 7am-7pm Mon.-Fri., 8am-7pm Sat.-Sun., $6.50-17). Perched on a mountain, this great little restaurant is blessed with an unobstructed view of the city below. It has typical Costa Rican food and a friendly Tico owner. Also on-site are eight basic rooms and bungalows (room $50 s/d, bungalow $80 s/d) with tile floors, wood-plank walls, one king or two double beds, and private bathrooms. Ask to hear the story behind the authentic oxcart stationed out front; it's a heartwarming tale of Costa Rican tradition passed down through generations.

In San Isidro de El General proper, across from the central park and great for people-watching, is the two-story La Reina del Valle (corner of Calle Central and Avenida Central, tel. 506/2771-4860, www.lareinadelvalle.com, 10am-midnight daily, $4-7). Since 1940, the restaurant and bar has been the city's go-to establishment for Costa Rican favorites like ceviche and patacones (smashed and fried green plantains). It's also the preferred evening hangout joint of many locals; beer and cocktails are cheap.

Healthy eaters, look no further than the Urban Farm Café (Calle Central, 200 m south of Avenida 10, tel. 506/2771-2442, 7am-7pm Mon.-Fri., 7am-4pm Sat., $3.50-6.50), which sells fresh, colorful, and wholesome salads, wraps, and quesadillas at its tiny storefront in a small commercial plaza. Organic, vegetarian, and vegan food and drinks fill the chalkboard menu, as does a list of creative smoothie blends featuring a host of tropical fruits.

Formerly a two-story home, Kafé de la Casa (Avenida 3, 20 m east of Calle 4, tel. 506/2770-4816, 7am-7pm Mon.-Wed., 7am-9pm Thurs.-Sat., 9am-5pm Sun., $4.50-10) has small dining tables in several rooms. It serves

---

1: Río Chirripó 2: green honeycreeper at the Refugio de Aves Los Cusingos 3: the snack booth at Los Chespiritos #1, near San Gerardo de Dota 4: the restaurant El Jiguero

great breakfasts as well as filling pasta dishes and meat and seafood plates. There are also separate vegetarian and children's menus. If you're in the mood for dessert, the restaurant prepares delicious *tres leches* (a sweet cake soaked with three kinds of milk) in vanilla and rare chocolate varieties.

Information and Services

San Isidro de El General has a hospital, **Hospital Fernando Escalante Pradilla** (1 block east of Calle Central, 800 m south of Hwy. 2, tel. 506/2785-0700, 24 hours daily), a **post office** (Calle 1, 300 m north of the hospital, tel. 506/2271-0346, 8am-5pm Mon.-Fri., 8am-noon Sat.), and a **police station** (750 m south of Hwy. 2, 3.5 km southeast of Road 243, tel. 506/2771-3608, 24 hours daily).

There are many **pharmacies, banks,** and **ATMs** in town, but the easiest to access are **Farmacia CVS** (tel. 506/2771-8545, 7am-6:30pm Mon.-Sat., 8am-2pm Sun.), a pharmacy on the south side of the central park; **Banco Nacional** (tel. 506/2212-2000, 8:30am-3:30pm Mon.-Fri.), a bank on the northeast corner of the central park; and the **ATM** (5am-midnight daily) at the gas station on Highway 2 (at Avenida 23) upon arrival into San Isidro de El General from the north.

A large **supermarket** is across the street from the gas station, and there are several others in town. **Gas stations** can be found on Highway 2 just north and south of the intersection with Road 243.

Transportation

San Isidro de El General is 135 kilometers (an approximate three-hour drive) southeast from downtown **San José** via Highway 2. It's a 325-kilometer drive southeast from downtown **Liberia** via Highway 1, Highway 27, Highway 34, and Road 243 that takes a little over five hours. The route from San José crosses over Cerro de la Muerte; the route from Liberia does not.

The main thoroughfare is Highway 2, which enters San Isidro de El General from the north and cuts through the city to the

southeast. At the north end of the mini metropolis, Road 243 splits from the highway and heads southwest to Dominical.

Public **buses** travel daily to San Isidro de El General from **San José** (multiple times 5am-6:30pm daily, 3 hours, $6), **Dominical** (6am, 9am, 12:30pm, and 4:30pm daily, 1-1.5 hours, $3), **Ciudad Cortés** (5am and 12:45pm daily, 3 hours, $3-3.50), **Puerto Jiménez** (5am, 9am, and 1pm daily, 5 hours, $8), **San Vito** (6:45am and 1:30pm daily, 3 hours, $6.50), and **San Gerardo de Rivas** (multiple times 5:15am-6:45pm Mon.-Sat. and 7am, 11:30am, and 4pm Sun., 1 hour, $2).

The **Aeropuerto Pérez Zeledón** (Pérez Zeledón Airport, IPZ) is 2.5 kilometers south of San Isidro de El General. **SANSA Airlines** (tel. 506/2290-4100, www.flysansa.com) offers direct flights to San Isidro de El General daily from San José. The flight time from San José is approximately 30 minutes.

SAN GERARDO DE RIVAS

Northeast of busy San Isidro de El General, speedy highways and traffic lights are traded for tranquility and narrow back roads that wind up mountainsides along the pristine Río Chirripó. At the hamlet of San Gerardo de Rivas, experienced hikers pause to collect information, last-minute purchases, and a good night's sleep—not to mention their nerves—before setting off on the daunting trek to Cerro Chirripó, Costa Rica's highest peak. An unspoken bond and tales of triumph unify the tiny town of 350 residents, where the summit-bound hikers arrive as thrill-seeking travelers and leave as highland heroes.

Sights
CLOUDBRIDGE NATURE RESERVE
To hike through cloud forest in an area few others frequent, head to the **Cloudbridge Nature Reserve** (2 km east of Road 242, 500 m northeast of the *fútbol* field, no phone, www.cloudbridge.org, 6am-6pm daily, $7 adults Sun. and holidays, donations accepted Mon.-Sat.). This remote private reserve abuts

Parque Nacional Chirripó and shares much of the flora and fauna encountered around the national park. Several trails of varying length and difficulty traverse the densely forested reserve's 700 acres. The easiest is a brief, 200-meter walk from the parking lot to the wild **Jardín de Memorial** (Memorial Garden). The most strenuous is the eight-kilometer **Sendero Montaña** (Montaña Trail), which curves around the property on a steep incline, slices through the clouds, and connects with the first four kilometers of the trail that leads to Cerro Chirripó before it enters the boundary of the national park. Other trails lead to the reserve's four waterfalls, including **Catarata Pacífica** (Pacífica Waterfall) and **Catarata Julia** (Julia Waterfall). Both of these waterfalls are close to the reserve's labyrinth-like **Jardín de Meditación** (Meditation Garden), a mere 20-minute hike from the entrance.

If you're in search of seclusion, you'll find it at Cloudbridge. At this off-the-beaten-path gem, it is unlikely you'll come across many—if any—other travelers during your visit. Don't attempt to visit without a reliable 4x4 vehicle. The route to the reserve, reached by turning right at the fork in the road just north of San Gerardo de Rivas, is an intimidating, steep, and bumpy uphill ride.

HOT SPRINGS

The three thermal-water pools (some of them covered for protection from sun and rain) at **Aguas Termales Gevi** (1 km northwest of Road 242, 500 m west of the *fútbol* field, tel. 506/2742-5210, 7am-5:30pm daily, visitor pass $8 pp 4 years and older) aren't much to write home about, but they're heavenly following completion of a strenuous hike. The hot springs work wonders on overworked muscles and ease wobbly, post-descent legs like a charm.

Food and Accommodations

Roca Dura (Road 242, across the street from the *fútbol* field, tel. 506/2742-5071, www.hotelrocadura.com, 8am-2am daily, $4.50-8.50) is your best option for dining and drinking in the heart of San Gerardo de Rivas. It serves protein-rich meals, including eggs and *gallo pinto* (a traditional rice and bean blend) for breakfast, and fish and meat plates (as well as hamburgers and veggie burgers) for lunch and dinner. Furniture built from giant tree trunks suits the area's mountain setting and the restaurant's easygoing, hiker-hangout vibe.

It's fun to try fishing for your food at ★ **Truchero Los Cocolisos** (Road 242, 700 m northeast of the *fútbol* field, tel. 506/2742-5054, 9am-4pm Fri.-Sun.). Less a restaurant and more a welcoming Costa Rican home, this spot just north of San Gerardo de Rivas invites you to catch your own fish from on-site trout ponds and then wait for a few minutes at a quaint riverside table while the friendly Tico homeowners prepare your catch on the spot. Dining in Costa Rica doesn't get much more authentic than this, nor does trout taste more delicious anywhere else, including at fancier establishments. The only menu item, the trout plate costs $7 and comes with a few sides and a drink.

Hotel Urán (1 km east of Road 242, 500 m northeast of the *fútbol* field, tel. 506/2742-5003, www.hoteluran.com, $40 s, $50 d), at the trailhead to Cerro Chirripó, counts 35 rooms with double beds and bunk beds; some share bathrooms. Catering to departing and returning hikers, the hotel provides much-appreciated services including hot showers, laundry service, and secure parking. Rental supplies (walking sticks, blankets, bags, and other items), packaged food to go, and the on-site mini-supermarket are handy extras. The hotel is near the Cloudbridge Nature Reserve.

Next to Hotel Urán, ★ **Casa Mariposa** (1 km east of Road 242, 500 m northeast of the *fútbol* field, tel. 506/2742-5037, www.casamariposachirripo.net, $56 s, $70 d) aims to make your stay as lovely and cozy as possible with good service and a woodsy accommodation perfect for snuggling up in. You'll be wowed by the hotel's construction: It is built into the mountainside and features impressive stonework; boulders serve as a wall in the Rock Room. Outdoors, you can wander along nature trails, visit an atrium and a *mirador* (lookout), or kick back in a hammock. Indoors, you can cook in the shared kitchen, socialize in the common area, or soak in a private hot bath ($5).

Above-average lodging is provided by the **Río Chirripó Lodge** (Road 242, 1 km southwest of the *fútbol* field, tel. 506/2742-5109, www.riochirripo.com, $159 s/d), which spoils guests with 10 spacious, clean, and comfortable rooms (for 1-4 people). Each has either a balcony or a deck that showcases the forest surrounding the lodge. Spoil yourself with soaks in the swimming pool and hot tub, or with meditation or yoga practice. You can also rest in the open-air, indigenous-style rancho, which functions as a communal lounge and a restaurant. The space is particularly inviting in the evening when the fireplace is lit and the mood is oh-so romantic.

Information and Services

Since 1974, the small **Abastecedor Las Nubes** (southeast corner of the *fútbol* field, tel. 506/2742-5045, 6:30am-8pm daily) has been the area's **supermarket.** It remains one of the few services in San Gerardo de Rivas and is your last chance to grab snacks and supplies before hiking to Cerro Chirripó.

Transportation

San Gerardo de Rivas is 155 kilometers (an approximate 3.5-hour drive) southeast from downtown **San José** via Highway 2 and Road 242. It's a 345-kilometer drive southeast from downtown **Liberia** via Highway 1, Highway 27, Highway 34, Road 243, and Road 242 that takes almost six hours. San Gerardo de Rivas is 20 kilometers (an approximate 30-minute drive) northeast from downtown **San Isidro de El General** via Road 242. The route from San José crosses over Cerro de la Muerte. The routes from Liberia and San Isidro de El General do not cross over Cerro de la Muerte.

Road 242, which departs from Highway 2

near the center of San Isidro de El General, follows a direct route northeast to San Gerardo de Rivas. Roughly halfway, in the town of Rivas, a right-hand turn is required to stay on the road; it is well marked. You won't need a 4x4 vehicle to reach San Gerardo de Rivas, but one is definitely required for continued travel northeast toward the Cerro Chirripó trailhead, area hotels, and the Cloudbridge Nature Reserve.

Public **buses** travel daily to San Gerardo de Rivas from **San Isidro de El General** (multiple times 5:45am-8pm Mon.-Sat. and 9:30am, 2pm, and 6pm Sun., 1 hour, $2).

★ PARQUE NACIONAL CHIRRIPÓ

Of the many mountains and volcanoes that give Costa Rica its rugged terrain, the most sought-after summit is **Cerro Chirripó** (Chirripó Hill), coveted for its reachable peak (3,820 meters above sea level). Hikes to this spot in **Parque Nacional Chirripó** (Chirripó National Park, tel. 506/2742-5084, 8am-4:30pm daily, $18 pp) provide the country's most extreme trekking experience. Rising more than **2,500 meters** in elevation, the route to the summit is a nearly **20-kilometer** uphill climb over the Cordillera de Talamanca (Talamanca mountain range) alongside rare paramo (high plains). To say the least, it's a wild and humbling adventure that will thrill your senses and reward you with a sense of accomplishment.

The primary sector is the **San Gerardo Sector,** on the west side of the park near San Gerardo de Rivas. Far less visited are the **San Jerónimo Sector** (on the south side of the park, due east of San Isidro de El General) and the **Herradura Sector** (on the west side of the park, north of the San Gerardo Sector).

Planning Your Trek

To some hikers, climbing Chirripó is a dream come true. To others, it's a logistical nightmare. Gone are the days when visits could be planned on the fly: Strict booking and payment requirements, which must be adhered to within tight timelines, are now enforced.

PERMITS AND RESERVATIONS

The first step of the Chirripó reservation process is to reserve a **park permit** ($18 pp per day) at www.sinac.go.cr, the website for Costa Rica's Sistema Nacional de Áreas de Conservación (National System of Conservation Areas, SINAC). Book as early as possible (up to **six months** in advance) because the 52 spaces available each day tend to sell out, especially on weekends, holidays, and between December and April when weather conditions are most favorable. At the end of the reservation process, you'll pay for your permit with a credit card.

After completing the process online, you'll receive a **permit confirmation number.** Email this number to info@chirripo.org, the address of the Oficinas Servicios Turísticos Chirripó Consorcio Aguas Eternas (Chirripó Eternal Waters Consortium Tourist Service Offices). This organization is the only outfit authorized to make base camp room and board arrangements. They'll provide you with a link to officially book your overnight stays and meals. The next step of the process requires that you pay (online, via credit card) for your accommodations and food within **48 hours** of the link being provided. If payment is not made within this tight timeline, your permit and reservation will be **canceled.** Same-day bookings, reservations made over the phone or in person, and cash payments are not accepted.

PORTERS

If you're wondering how best to manage the hike with your gear in tow, you're in luck: You don't have to. Several locals make a living as porters who transport luggage between San Gerardo de Rivas and the base camp either on their backs or by horse, weather permitting. The luggage-hauling service (one-way) costs $4.75 per kilogram. Porters can be hired at the **Oficinas Servicios Turísticos Chirripó Consorcio Aguas Eternas** (southwest corner of the *fútbol* field, San Gerardo de Rivas, tel. 506/2742-5097, www.chirripo.org, 8am-5pm Mon.-Sat., 9am-5pm Sun.). Bags are weighed, dropped off, and paid for at this same location. Return service down the mountain must be coordinated at the base camp no later than 3pm the day before your descent. Your bags will be weighed again at the base camp; you'll pay for them at the Oficinas Servicios Turísticos Chirripó Consorcio Aguas Eternas following your descent.

PACKING TIPS

Pack light to avoid carrying—or making porters carry—unnecessary weight up and down the mountain. Rent towels and extra items like blankets at the base camp to save space in your bag. Purchase your meals during the reservation process to avoid carrying large amounts of food. You can bring nonperishable items like granola and protein bars, but you must carry out your trash.

Temperatures on the mountain vary greatly, from nighttime lows of 15°F to daytime highs of 60°F. Pack comfortable hiking clothes, a good pair of hiking shoes, and a rain jacket or a poncho. Plan on layering your clothing. Be sure to bring a warm jacket, gloves, a hat, and a scarf in preparation for below-freezing temperatures at high elevations.

Other items to bring include two one-liter, durable water bottles (potable water is available at kilometer 7 and the base camp), a flashlight or a headlamp with spare batteries, sunglasses, sunscreen, insect repellent, toiletries, a small amount of money to pay for rentals at the base camp, and a first aid kit that contains treatments for cuts, blisters, burns, insect bites, muscle pain, allergic reactions, digestive upsets, and headaches. Be sure to bring any prescription medications you need. You may also want to bring a small alarm clock, earplugs, and water purification tablets in case of an emergency.

OTHER HIKING OPTIONS

The 2016 inauguration of a trail beyond the San Jerónimo Sector has led to increased interest in reaching Cerro Chirripó from areas other than San Gerardo de Rivas. While the route within the San Gerardo Sector remains the most frequented, adventurous travelers in search of an experience even more isolated from civilization can consider exploring the park from the tiny community of San Jerónimo. Hikes through that sector are organized through the San Jerónimo cooperative **La Asociación de Turismo Cerro Ena** (Cerro Etna Tourism Association, ATURENA, tel. 506/8374-3443, www. sanjeronimochirripo.com, 8am-4pm daily); a guide is hiked for these hikes.

Cerro Chirripó Trek
REGISTRATION

On the first day of your trek, you'll need to register your start at the **Área Administrativa Parque Nacional Chirripó** (Chirripó National Park Administrative Area, Road 242, 600 m southwest of the *fútbol* field, San Gerardo de Rivas, tel. 506/2742-5084, 8am-4:30pm daily) between 8am and 10am. Starting after 10am is not permitted, as this doesn't allow enough time to get to the base camp before nightfall. If you wish to set out earlier than 8am, you'll need to register one day in advance, between 8am and 4pm. Note that you don't need to make any changes to your reservation date if you want to depart before 8am; you only need to register the day before your reservation date.

Once you've registered, head up the street to the **Oficinas Servicios Turísticos Chirripó Consorcio Aguas Eternas** (southwest corner of the *fútbol* field, San Gerardo de Rivas, tel. 506/2742-5097, www.chirripo. org, 8am-5pm Mon.-Sat., 9am-5pm Sun.) to reconfirm your lodging and meal bookings.

The trailhead is approximately 1.5 kilometers northeast of San Gerardo de Rivas. From there, a 14.5-kilometer hike (roughly 4 kilometers to the park's boundary and another 10

kilometers within it) leads to the **Crestones base camp,** the only public lodging within the San Gerardo Sector.

ON THE TRAIL

Ready to go? The **Sendero Principal San Gerardo** (Principal San Gerardo Trail) is challenging from the start and will either spike your adrenaline in anticipation of what lies ahead or will leave you questioning what you've gotten yourself into. Forge forward and you'll find yourself counting down kilometers, each one well marked and named for the conditions, scenery, or wildlife associated with the area. Some stretches, like **El Jilguero** (Sooty Robin, km 3), travel through shaded, verdant cloud forest, and others, including **Los Quemados** (The Burned, km 11), explore open land cooked a few times over by incessant forest fires. **Llano Bonito** (Pretty Plain, km 7) offers a rest stop with **bathrooms** and **potable water,** and it's a good thing because the treacherous section that follows, **Cuesta de Agua** (Water Slope, km 8), is an uphill feat for the fittest that provides little opportunity to rest.

Going nonstop, the average fit hiker reaches the base camp **7-8 hours** after departing from the trailhead. Poor weather conditions, which can shift on a whim, can lengthen the journey by a few hours. Regular climbers can conquer the mountain in much less time.

BASE CAMP

Overnight stays ($33 pp) are permitted at the **Crestones base camp** for 1-2 nights from December to April and 1-3 nights between May and November. The solar-powered, dormitory-style accommodation sleeps 52 visitors plus 8 staff in bunk bed-equipped rooms. A sheet, a pillow, and either a sleeping bag or two blankets are provided to each guest at no additional cost. Extras of these items, as well as towels, are available for rent for $1.75-6.50 per night. Toilet paper and soap are stocked in the bathrooms; showers run ice-cold. Electricity-powered lighting is provided from nightfall (approximately 6pm) to 8pm. Camping and nighttime trail exploration is not permitted in the park.

Food options are selected and purchased during the reservation process. Meals range in price from $5.50 for a hot drink and snack to $10 for breakfast and $13 for lunch or dinner. Vegetarian options are available.

SUMMITING CERRO CHIRRIPÓ

There are many great firsts you can have in Costa Rica—your first adrenaline-inducing zip-line ride, your first encounter with a monkey in the cageless wild, your first sip of locally harvested coffee, and so many noteworthy others—but few top the feeling of summiting **Cerro Chirripó.** You can train for the climb, plan for mountain conditions, and pack for the trip, but it's difficult to prepare mentally for the experience. The hike is arduous—each kilometer a test of perseverance and a war with fatigue—not to mention a roller coaster of emotions that propels you forward with excitement and sickens you with self-doubt. But at the end is the moment of victory when you stand atop the mountain's peak, overcome with relief and joy. The 360-degree view you'll earn is sensational, filled with lakes and rock formations, valleys and peaks of distant volcanoes, the Caribbean Sea, and the Pacific Ocean. Equally rewarding is the sense of accomplishment. The invigorating mix of pleasure and pride can't be felt everywhere in Costa Rica, which is why ascents to Cerro Chirripó are such coveted experiences and make lifetime memories.

Cerro Chirripó awaits roughly five kilometers northeast of the base camp and squeezes another 1.5-2 hours of hiking out of weary travelers. Most hikers spend a night in the park in order to rise early the next morning and hike to the summit before sunrise—ideally under a clear sky full of stars. The descent to the trailhead takes about six hours.

EXTENDING THE TREK

Warranting an additional night's stay are a few side trails that depart from the camp and showcase hilltops with spectacular views. Southeast of the base camp, the **Sendero Los Crestones** (Los Crestones Trail, 3.4 km round-trip, 1 hour, moderate) is the most intriguing, as it leads past giant rock formations that look ablaze in shades of red and orange when the sun hits them. Should you choose to spend three days in the park, you can hike some of the side trails in the morning on your last day, but park policy requires that you begin your descent from base camp no later than noon.

Getting There

The trailhead for Sendero Principal San Gerardo is just beyond Hotel Urán, roughly 1.5 kilometers northeast of the center of San Gerardo de Rivas. Approximately 500 meters beyond the community's *fútbol* field is the turnoff for the steep, bumpy drive up to the hotel; a 4x4 vehicle is required.

Parque Internacional La Amistad and Vicinity

The giant Parque Internacional La Amistad covers much of the region, from east of San Isidro de El General to the border shared with Panama. It dwarfs the region with its majestic mountains, where tiny, quaint communities appear from a distance as striations on slopes. The far-flung but pleasant agricultural town of San Vito hides in the southeasternmost corner.

PARQUE INTERNACIONAL LA AMISTAD

Spanning Costa Rican and Panamanian territory, the 480,000-acre **Parque Internacional La Amistad** (La Amistad International Park, 20 km northeast of Road 237 at Las Tablas, tel. 506/2200-5355, 8am-4pm daily, $10 pp per day) is the largest protected land space in the country. The park occupies much of the southern inland area north and east of Highway 2 and connects with the Caribbean over the Cordillera de Talamanca (Talamanca mountain range). It serves as an important coast-to-coast corridor for resident wildlife, including 400 species of birds, more than 250 species of amphibians and reptiles, and all six varieties of jungle cats found in Costa Rica. The park is also full of diverse life zones and transition zones, and is home to several remote indigenous communities. Most visitors enter through the park's headquarters at **Estación Biológica Altamira** (20 km northeast of Road 237 at Las Tablas, tel. 506/2200-5355, 8am-4pm daily).

Hiking

Zealous, offbeat explorers love the rawness of this park. While difficult road conditions to and from its boundaries and scarce infrastructure within deter most visitors, a select few are seduced by the virgin forest and are drawn to the mysterious appeal of the park's rugged interior.

The **Sendero a los Gigantes del Bosque** (Trail to the Giants of the Forest, 3 km roundtrip, 1 hour, moderate) is good for a day trip and great for bird-watching, but if you choose the park over countless others in the country, I bet you long for a much greater challenge. The hike along the **Sendero al Valle del Silencio** (Trail to the Valley of Silence, 15 km one-way, 6-10 hours, moderate-difficult) provides a great one with scenes of lush vegetation, natural gardens, and a pretty lagoon. This hike is generally accomplished over two days—or three, if you wish to have an extra day to explore the park's interior. Overnight stays ($6 pp per night) are permitted at a small refuge equipped to sleep eight guests plus a tour guide. Reaching a height of 2,500 meters above sea level, the trail rivals those that provide multiday high-altitude climbs in Parque Nacional Chirripó.

Access to the Sendero al Valle del Silencio requires a tour guide. One can be hired through the park's official guide association, **AsoProLA** (2.5 km south of the Estación Biológica Altamira, 506/8621-5559, www.asoprola.com, 8am-6pm daily). Guided tours begin at $30 per person. You're welcome to tour the Sendero a los Gigantes del Bosque on your own, but I still recommend going with a guide trained in trail navigation and wildlife encounters, since the park is one of the most secluded in the country.

Getting There

The **Estación Biológica Altamira** is roughly 2.5 kilometers north of the community of Altamira, which is an 18-kilometer, 4x4-required, uphill drive northeast of Road 237. The marked turnoff is at the hamlet of Las Tablas.

Small Communities with Big Hearts

The 130-kilometer stretch between San Isidro de El General and San Vito offers little to stop for, but northeast of the highway, around the hamlet of Las Tablas, 30 kilometers northwest of San Vito, are tiny rural communities that long for your visit. A handful of community organizations have developed unique projects, services, and attractions that appeal to off-the-beaten-path explorers. Many survive off your purchases, and none is "touristy" in the common sense of the word. Visit these spots to support a good cause, meet some hardworking and friendly folk, and return with one-of-a-kind souvenirs—if not new and unparalleled memories.

Based in **Biolley, La Asociación de Mujeres Organizadas de Biolley** (Association of Organized Women of Biolley, ASOMOBI, www.asomobi-costarica.com) is an inspiring women's group of about 40 members that's all about empowering women to excel in the local workforce. Some women sell handmade jewelry and crafts. Others run guided tours around the area, mainly to the group's own coffee farm, which produces **Café Cerro Biolley.** To support the women (most of whom are working mothers), you can purchase bags of the coffee directly in Biolley or from shops around the country. Biolley is about 20 kilometers northeast of Road 237 in the community of Las Tablas.

La Asociación de Productores La Amistad (Association of La Amistad Producers, Aso-ProLA, www.asoprola.com), which is also responsible for running guided tours through Parque Internacional La Amistad, is dedicated to the growth and prosperity of the **Altamira** community in which it is based. It provides authentic, small-town experiences that are simple and sweet; you can check out a beloved ice cream shop, spend time with a family that crafts artisan chocolate, and tour a *trapiche* (sugarcane mill), among other activities. Altamira is just under 20 kilometers northeast of Road 237 in the community of Las Tablas.

The small community of **Dúrika** is a tight-knit group committed to sustainable and organic farming and the protection of sacred land. Thanks to the **Fundación Pro Conservación de la Reserva Biológica Dúrika** (Pro-Conservation Foundation of the Dúrika Biological Reserve, www.durika.org), or **Dúrika Foundation,** you can learn about locally produced dairy products, shop for crafts and baked goods, give a naturopathic treatment a go, or take guided tours of the community's biological reserve while learning about the foundation's efforts in forest conservation. Dúrika is 20 kilometers northeast of Highway 2 in the town of Buenos Aires.

SAN VITO

Among the foothills of the Cordillera de Talamanca adjacent to the border shared with Panama, plantations and cattle fields span much of Coto Brus, Costa Rica's easternmost district. San Vito, the district's capital, is a quiet agricultural town spread out across a mountain plateau. Founded by Italian settlers, the area still shows European influence, especially in the culinary offerings of Cotobruseños (Coto Brus residents).

Sights

★ WILSON BOTANICAL GARDEN

The best reason to travel to the eastern edge of the region is to immerse yourself in the impressive outdoor collection of plants, flowers, and trees that make up the **Wilson Botanical Garden** (Road 237, 6 km south of San Vito, tel. 506/2773-4004, 7am-5pm Mon.-Sat., 7am-1pm Sun., last entry 3pm Mon.-Sat. and 11am Sun., $10 pp 12 years and older). Located in the Estación Biológica Las Cruces (Las Cruces Biological Station), the 25-acre garden is an internationally recognized research and education center where botanists gather to see and study unique flora specimens. Overseen by Costa Rica's **Organization for Tropical Studies** (OTS, tel. 506/2661-4717, www.tropicalstudies.org), the garden is also open to the public and is a must-see for any devoted naturalist.

Some 5,000 botanical species make this garden a standout among others in the country. On display are roughly 3,000 exotic varieties and 2,000 native to Costa Rica; many are tagged for easy identification. Various exhibits from heliconias to bromeliads to *jengibres* (gingers) are scattered around the property and connected by trails—come prepared to walk. Most prized are the garden's 700 different species of palms from Costa Rica and all over the world. My favorite plants, which I always stop to gawk at as they tower overhead, are the giant bamboos. The well-marked, mapped garden is easy to explore at your own pace; give yourself a minimum of two hours.

Food and Accommodations

San Vito is, as a local might say, *todo italiano* (all Italian). If you're in the mood for a good pizza or a plate of pasta, you'll have no trouble finding one. **Ristorante La Casa Italiana** (Road 613, 6.5 km northeast of Road 237, tel. 506/2201-6690, 11:30am-10pm Wed.-Mon., $6.50-15) is my favorite, thanks to its mouthwatering lasagna, flavorful ravioli, and creamy fettucine. Built off the side of a house, the restaurant has only a few tables and offers a casual but intimate alfresco dining experience. I particularly love that the chef sticks to authentic Italian recipes.

There is little in San Vito to warrant spending a night, but if you must, the ★ **Casa Botania B&B** (Road 237, 3 km south of the hospital, tel. 506/2773-4217, www.casabotania.com, $88 s, $100 d) is the place to lay your head. It has five quaint, well-furnished rooms (most bungalows sleep 1-4 people) with spotless bathrooms and hot water, queen or king-size beds topped with orthopedic mattresses, and phenomenal valley views. Great for birders, Costa Rican co-owner Pepe is a bird-watching aficionado and runs spotting walks around the property's few nature trails.

Information and Services

On Road 612, the north-south passage through San Vito, you'll find a **police station** (400 m north of Road 237, tel. 506/2773-3225, 24 hours daily), a **post office** (500 m north of Road 237, tel. 506/2773-3130, 8am-5pm Mon.-Fri.), and **pharmacies,** including **Farmacia Coto Brus** (Road 612, 125 m north of Road 237, tel. 506/2773-3076, 7am-8pm Mon.-Sat.).

On Road 237, the principal access road, is **Hospital de San Vito** (750 m south of Road 612, tel. 506/2773-1100, 24 hours daily) and **banks** with **ATMs,** including **Banco de Costa Rica** (50 m south of Road 612, tel. 506/2211-1111, 9am-4pm Mon.-Fri., ATM 5am-midnight daily). A handful of **supermarkets** are scattered about town.

Transportation

San Vito is 265 kilometers (an approximate five-hour drive) southeast from downtown **San José** via Highway 2 and Road 237. It's 435 kilometers (an approximate 6.5-hour drive) from downtown **Liberia** via Highway 1, Highway 27, Highway 34, Highway 2, and Road 237. San Vito is 130 kilometers southeast of **San Isidro de El General** via Highway 2 and Road 237, a drive that takes roughly 2 hours and 15 minutes. The route from San José crosses over Cerro de la Muerte; the route from Liberia does not.

Road 237 is the principal access road. It begins 45 kilometers northwest of San Vito where Highway 2 veers southwest toward the Osa Peninsula. South of San Vito, Road 237 connects with Ciudad Neily. Traveling east-west through the south end of San Vito, Road 237 intersects with Road 612 (a north-west passage through the area) at the town's minuscule central park.

Public **buses** travel daily to San Vito from **San Isidro de El General** (5:30am, 9am, 11am, and 2pm daily, 3 hours, $6.50) and **Ciudad Neily** (multiple times 6am-5:30pm daily, 1.5 hours, $1.50).

Wildlife Guide

National parks, biological reserves, and wildlife refuges account for more than a quarter of Costa Rica's landmass. Dispersed throughout these areas are more than half a million species of mammals, birds, reptiles, amphibians, insects, and other living creatures, making it one of the most biologically diverse places on earth. Immerse yourself in the habitats of some of the world's most precious and distinctive species. Spotting wildlife is nearly guaranteed here—but you'll need to keep your eyes open, listen hard, and be in the right place at the right time.

Do you dream of laying eyes on an elusive wild cat? Watching an endangered species of sea turtle crawl ashore to lay its eggs? Observe multicolored birds take flight and spotting bright frogs among the foliage?

This guide is a selective list of the most interesting wildlife in the country, complete with recommendations for the best places to spot them. Use it to plan your adventures and you just might be rewarded with a life-changing wildlife encounter.

Land Mammals

SLOTHS

If there is one type of animal that draws wildlife-lovers to Costa Rica more than any other, it is the **sloth** (*perezoso*). Sloths live much of their life in the same area, making it easy for experienced tour guides to know exactly where to find them. If you're exploring Costa Rica's forests on your own, look for the cute creatures in **Cecropia trees,** identifiable by their white-washed bark and large fans of lime-green leaves.

Of Costa Rica's two sloth species, you're most likely to come across a **three-toed sloth** (especially around the Caribbean coast. The species has distinctive dark markings around the eyes like a racoon. Less commonly spotted are **two-toed sloths,** which have a more pronounced, pig-like nose. Rather confusingly, both species have three toes on each "foot." It's their "hands" that show the difference: Three-toed sloths have three "fingers" on each hand and the two-toed sloth has two.

WHERE TO SEE THEM? Fortunately, the sloths, which spend most of their time hanging upside down from treetop branches, can be seen all over the country, but especially within the Central Pacific's **Parque Nacional Manuel Antonio.**

MONKEYS

Three experiences are practically guaranteed in Costa Rica—you'll be served rice and beans, you'll encounter the slogan *pura vida,* and you'll see or hear a **monkey** (*mono*). Although spotting wildlife is unpredictable, monkeys are everywhere in the country. The **Osa Peninsula** and the **southern Pacific coast** are the only parts of Costa Rica where all four monkey species reside.

The most commonly spotted species is the social (and sometimes aggressive) **white-headed capuchin monkey,** colloquially referred to as white-faced monkeys.

WHERE TO SEE THEM? Capuchin monkeys frequent popular parks and beaches on a mission to steal travelers' food. Keep watch over your belongings—especially in **Parque Nacional Manuel Antonio** (on the central Pacific coast) and **Parque Nacional Cahuita** (on the Caribbean coast)—or they'll be gone before you know it.

Large, all-black **mantled howler monkeys,** referred to by many tour guides as congos, also abound in Costa Rica. You may not see them as often as you hear their startling, loud, low-toned roar, which can be heard up to nearly five kilometers away.

WHERE TO SEE THEM? Look and listen for troops of the territorial howler monkeys in the **treetop canopy**—they rarely frequent the forest floor. Countrywide, sightings are common during **forest hikes,** during **hanging bridge tours,** and on **safari float tours.**

Encounters with lanky and agile **Geoffroy's spider monkeys** are less frequent but not rare.

WHERE TO SEE THEM? Like most monkey species in Costa Rica, these spider monkeys can be seen in several natural areas around the country. However, I've had good luck spotting these brown-bodied creatures around **wetlands,** including the **Refugio Nacional de Vida Silvestre Mixto Caño**

Previous: resplendent quetzal.

1: mantled howler monkey **2:** two-toed sloth
3: puma

Negro (in the Northern Inlands) and **Parque Nacional Palo Verde** (in Guanacaste).

Most exotic-looking—and the smallest of the bunch—are **Central American squirrel monkeys,** also called mono tití monkeys, which have a cinnamon-colored body and a white- and dark-gray face.

WHERE TO SEE THEM? The adorable squirrel monkeys stick to the southern half of the country; they're best spotted in **Parque Nacional Manuel Antonio** (on the central Pacific coast) or **Parque Nacional Corcovado** (on the Osa Peninsula).

TAPIRS

The largest animal in Costa Rica's forests, the **Baird's tapir** (*danta*) is roughly two meters long and weighs anywhere between 325 and 775 pounds. The short-haired, gray tapir, sporting a wiggly nose not unlike a miniature elephant's trunk, helps regenerate Costa Rica's green zones through seed redistribution as they move about the land.

WHERE TO SEE THEM? Tapirs are difficult to see, although they course throughout several of the country's national parks, most notably **Parque Nacional Corcovado** (on the Osa Peninsula) and **Parque Nacional Los Quetzales** (in the southern inland region). Guided tours through the aptly named private reserve **Tapir Valley,** adjacent to **Parque Nacional Volcán Tenorio** in the Northern Inlands, produce occasional sightings. Look for the animals by riversides and shorelines; they love to take dips in the water.

WILD CATS

Costa Rica is home to six species of wild cats. The king of Costa Rica's jungle is the **jaguar,** which can grow to be 5 feet long, 2.5 feet tall, and weigh over 200 pounds. It's also the most elusive mammal. Many devoted naturalist tour guides spend much of their life hoping to see one in the wild and never do, but the few who have seen a jaguar tell marvelous tales of the beautiful creature's sleek look and cunning, predatory ways. Jaguars require

a forested territory large enough for them to roam and hunt.

One of the biggest wild cat species in the country, second only to the jaguar, is the **puma** (also known as a mountain lion, *león de montaña*). The big cat is easily recognizable by its short, smooth, and solid light-brown coat.

The most striking feline of the bunch is the **ocelot** (*ocelote* or *manigordo*), which is spotted like a jaguar but is roughly half its size and has notably large paws. Also spotted, and sometimes mistaken for small ocelots, are **margays** (*cauceles*) and **oncillas** (*tigrillos*). The margay weighs just under 10 pounds and has a long tail that can extend 1.5 feet beyond its body. The oncilla, sometimes referred to as the little spotted cat, weighs between 3.5 and 6.5 pounds, looks like a kitten, and is the smallest wild cat in Costa Rica's animal kingdom.

Weasel-like in appearance and slightly smaller than an ocelot is the **jaguarundi** (*león breñero*), which resembles a long and slender house cat. Jaguarundis can be greyish-brown, reddish-brown, or black in color.

WHERE TO SEE THEM? Sightings of jaguars most commonly occur in **Parque Nacional Corcovado** (on the Osa Peninsula), **Parque Nacional Tortuguero** (on the Caribbean coast), **Parque Nacional Santa Rosa** (on the northern Pacific coast) and **Parque Internacional La Amistad** (in the southern inland area). Recent years have seen the closure of public beaches in some protected land areas where jaguars have been spotted swiping turtle eggs and cracking the shells of sea turtles with their teeth. The other five species of wild cats inhabit many of the same remote, undeveloped spaces where jaguars hide, most notably **Parque Nacional Corcovado** and **Parque Internacional La Amistad** (in the southern inland region). They've also been spotted in the **Reserva Biológica Bosque Nuboso de Monteverde** (in Monteverde), among other protected land areas.

The majority of Costa Rica's wild cats are nocturnal. Your best chance of encountering one is during a **night tour,** though sightings are extremely rare. If you must see a wild cat during your time in Costa Rica, visit the **La Paz Waterfall Gardens** (in the Central Highlands), **Diamante Eco Adventure Park** (on the northern Pacific coast), or the **Proyecto Asis Wildlife Refuge Center** (near La Fortuna). Each attraction has wildlife exhibits that house rescued felines.

COATIMUNDIS, KINKAJOUS, AND OLINGOS

Relatively easy to see in Costa Rica are **coatimundis** ("coatis" for short, or *pizotes*), which resemble racoons but have a long, white nose and a slender tail. In less traveled areas, the animals are timid and will wander away when approached. In popular destinations, coatis turn out in droves, especially around **roadsides,** and are accustomed to getting attention from travelers.

WHERE TO SEE THEM? I've always had the best luck seeing groups of coatimundis around the **northern inland area,** especially near **Lago Arenal** at **Místico Arenal Hanging Bridges Park** and the **Arenal Observatory Lodge.**

Tougher to spot than coatis are other, less social members of the racoon (Procyonidae) family, including **kinkajous** (*martillas*) and **olingos** (*olingos*). Both are similar in appearance (though kinkajous are reddish-brown in color and olingos are greyish-brown); they have a thick, short coat, a long and flexible tail, and an elongated body like a ferret.

WHERE TO SEE THEM? Kinkajous and olingos reside in a variety of natural areas in most regions of Costa Rica, including cloud forest ecosystems such as the **Reserva Biológica Bosque Nuboso de Monteverde,** and lowland nature reserves, like the Nicoya Peninsula's **Refugio Nacional de Vida Silvestre Curú.**

BATS

Of the more than 200 species of mammals found in Costa Rica, approximately half are species of **bats** (*murciélagos*). Three of these are blood-sucking **vampire bats.** Vital for the survival of many plants and ecosystems is the process of chiropterophily, or plant pollination by bats.

WHERE TO SEE THEM? Primarily nocturnal, bats in Costa Rica are best admired in their natural habitats during **night tours.** However, a good tour guide can direct your eye to where they sleep during the day, especially during **cave tours** at **Cavernas Venado** (in the near San Rafael de Guatuso) or **Parque Nacional Barra Honda** (on the Nicoya Peninsula). Look for them tucked away in the curls of tree bark or under the protection of large leaves. You can hear bats chirping within the crevice of **Punta Murciélago** in Malpaís (on the Nicoya Peninsula). The country's best bat exhibit is the **Bat Jungle** in Monteverde. Species you may see or hear in exhibits and in the wild include **greater bulldog fishing bats, orange nectar bats, long-nosed bats,** and **white tent-making bats.**

PECCARIES

Essentially wild pigs, **peccaries** (*saínos*) roam about heavily in natural areas around the country. In search of food, they traipse through the forest, rustling leaves and branches. If the noise doesn't give them away, you can identify their recent presence by taking note of messy or muddy tracks, or by catching a whiff of their hog-like smell.

Two peccary species inhabit Costa Rica—**white-lipped peccaries,** which typically appear in groups and can be aggressive but are the most difficult to spot, and **collared peccaries,** which are generally smaller, nonaggressive, and encountered in forests on their own.

WHERE TO SEE THEM? Groups of white-lipped peccaries have been spotted in **Parque Nacional Corcovado** on the Osa Peninsula.

Though collared peccaries can be seen nearly everywhere in the country, sightings on trails within the **Estación Biológica La Selva** in the Caribbean region and **El Silencio Mirador y Senderos** near La Fortuna are common.

ANTEATERS

Crawling around Costa Rica's **lowlands** are two species of **anteaters** (*oso hormigueros*): the **collared anteater** and the **silky anteater.** A third species, the **giant anteater,** is critically endangered; it is unknown whether any still exist in the country. Easily recognizable by their long snout, anteaters (also known as tamanduas) are often seen rummaging around the ground in search of ant colonies or tearing open termite nests in trees.

WHERE TO SEE THEM? Occasional sightings of Costa Rica's two most common anteater species occur at the **Reserva Natural Absoluta Cabo Blanco** and **Parque Nacional Barra Honda,** both on the Nicoya Peninsula, as well as Guanacaste's **Parque Nacional Santa Rosa** produce.

AGOUTIS AND PACAS

As you trek through Costa Rica's national parks, you may spot a small rodent crossing the trail. If the critter's body resembles a large rat and is brown with a tinge of yellow, orange, or red, it is likely an **agouti** (*agutí,*

nicknamed a *guatusa*). You'll regularly come across them within natural areas as they eat fruits and seeds off the **forest floor.** They move quietly about the ground but can scurry when startled.

Small rodents encountered during **night tours** are most likely nocturnal **pacas** (*tepezcuintles*), which are slightly larger than agoutis. They are brown in color and usually have white markings on both sides of their body that resemble the spots on a deer or the stripe on a chipmunk.

WHERE TO SEE THEM? Agoutis and pacas can be seen all over the country, including within the **Reserva Natural Absoluta Cabo Blanco** on the Nicoya Peninsula and **Parque Nacional Carara** on the central Pacific coast.

DEER

Declared a national symbol of Costa Rica in 1995, the **white-tailed deer** (*venado*) is most commonly seen in **lowland areas,** mainly around **Parque Nacional Santa Rosa** (on the northern Pacific coast), as well as along the central Pacific and northern Caribbean coasts. More challenging to see is the **Central American red brocket deer,** which is slightly smaller, reddish-brown in color, and prefers mountain highland areas in remote sections of the central Pacific coastal region and the southern inland area.

Marine Life

SEA TURTLES

Costa Rica's beaches host five types of nesting **sea turtles** (*tortugas marinas*)—six if you count **Atlantic green sea turtles** and **Pacific green sea turtles** separately. Though sightings are never guaranteed, sea turtles are best witnessed during **turtle nesting tours,** which are highly regulated, guided excursions at popular nesting beaches

that typically run at **night.** With a lot of luck, you can spot sea turtles, mainly olive ridleys and leatherbacks (as well as the occasional hawksbill), swimming in the clear, open water of the Pacific Ocean while you participate in a snorkeling, scuba diving, stand-up paddling, or sailing excursion.

WHERE TO SEE THEM? The northern Pacific coast's **Playa Grande** (within **Parque Nacional Marino Las Baulas**) is known as one of the world's top nesting sites of giant

1: coatimundi **2:** margay **3:** agouti

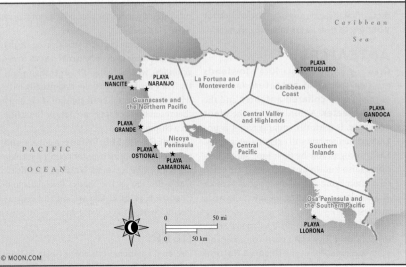

© MOON.COM

leatherback sea turtles (October-March). The **Refugio Nacional de Vida Silvestre Ostional** (on the Nicoya Peninsula) showcases mass gatherings of small **olive ridley sea turtles** (May-December). **Parque Nacional Tortuguero** (on the Caribbean coast) sees four turtle varieties, including leatherbacks, green turtles, **hawksbill sea turtles,** and **loggerhead sea turtles** (March-October), nest on its shores.

DOLPHINS AND WHALES

Costa Rica's **Pacific coast** is a known mating site for **humpback whales** (*ballenas*), which migrate to the region from the north (December-March) and the south (July-October). A few species of **dolphins** (*delfines*), including **bottlenose dolphins, spinner dolphins,** and **spotted dolphins,** can be seen playing in the Pacific Ocean year-round.

WHERE TO SEE THEM? Boat tours and sailing tours along the coast provide the best spotting opportunities, especially those that tour the waters of the **Reserva Biológica Isla del Caño** (24 kilometers off the coast

of the Osa Peninsula at Bahía Drake) and the **Parque Nacional Marino Ballena** (on the central Pacific coast).

SHARKS AND RAYS

Potential sightings of **sharks** (*tiburones*) and **rays** (*rayas*) draw in scores of scuba divers to Costa Rica each year. A reputable dive operator can help keep the encounters safe, especially run-ins with bull sharks, which have a reputation for being aggressive. Attacks on humans by any species of shark in Costa Rica are rare.

WHERE TO SEE THEM? Some extreme divers come to swim with schools of **scalloped hammerhead sharks** in the waters that surround the world-renowned **Parque Nacional Isla del Coco** (off the central Pacific coast). Closer to the mainland, dive trips to the Northern Pacific's **Islas Murciélago** (within **Parque Nacional Santa Rosa**) and **Islas Catalina** are known to produce exciting encounters with **bull sharks, whitetip sharks, giant manta rays,** and other ray varieties.

FISH

The waters of the **Pacific Ocean** and the **Caribbean Sea** are full of an extensive list of **fish** (*peces*). Tropical and colorful varieties, including species of **parrotfish, puffer fish,** and **butterfly fish,** can make appearances during snorkel and dive trips.

Sportfishing expeditions, which most commonly depart from the **Pacific coast,** reel in big fish like **marlins, sailfish, wahoos, snappers, roosterfish, dorado,** and **tuna.**

Birds

TOUCANS AND ARACARIS

If you're lucky, you'll get the chance to see a beautiful **toucan** (*tucán*) or **aracari** (a member of the toucan family, nicknamed a *pití*) in the wild. If not, plenty of **wildlife rescue centers** have resident varieties, including Alajuela's **Rescate Animal Zooave,** which houses the first toucan in Costa Rica to receive a prosthetic beak. Toucans are loved for their unique and sometimes colorful bill. You'll often hear the birds' boisterous, loud calls before you spot them high up in the canopy or soaring between trees.

WHERE TO SEE THEM? The **chestnut-mandibled toucan** makes a sweet, high-pitched sound; the bird is best seen in low elevations along the **Caribbean coast** and **central and southern Pacific coasts,** in the **northern inland area,** and on the **Osa Peninsula.** The **keel-billed toucan,** sometimes referred to as the rainbow-billed toucan, has a rougher and slightly lower-pitched caw. Toucans are commonly only spotted in the northern half of the country, including around **Guanacaste,** the **northern Pacific coast,** the **Nicoya Peninsula,** the **northern inland area,** and the **Caribbean region.**

Two similar-looking species of aracaris, the **fiery-billed aracari** (seen around the **central and southern Pacific coast** and the **Osa Peninsula**) and the **collared aracari** (seen around **Guanacaste,** the **northern Pacific coast,** the **Nicoya**

Peninsula, and the **Caribbean region**), can be found in Costa Rica and are best identified by their beak color. Fiery-billed aracaris have red on their beak. Keep watch for toucans and aracaris in the sky after rain showers; they tend to shy away from the sun and are most active when there is cloud cover.

MACAWS AND PARROTS

Talkative, lime-green **parrots** (*loras*) and loud-squawking **macaws** (*lapas*) are some of Costa Rica's most exotic birds. Parrots are found along both coasts, usually at low elevations. Macaws are monogamous and almost always seen in pairs.

WHERE TO SEE THEM? Look for red, yellow, and blue **scarlet macaws** along the Pacific coast, primarily on the **Nicoya Peninsula,** along the **central Pacific coast,** and on the **Osa Peninsula.** Seek out tough-to-find **great green macaws** around the **Tortuguero** and **Puerto Viejo de Sarapiquí** areas (both in the northern Caribbean region) or at the **Maquenque EcoLodge,** which is in a remote section of the Northern Inlands. You'll have the best chance of spotting either type in *almendro* trees; macaws enjoy their almonds. **Ara Manzanillo** (in the southern Caribbean region) and the **Punta Islita Wild Macaw Reserve** (on the Nicoya Peninsula) provide a chance to see wild macaws in abundance and learn about important breeding and re-introduction efforts.

QUETZALS AND OTHER TROGONS

Ten species of **trogons** (*trogones*) reside in Costa Rica, but the one every bird-watcher longs to see is the **resplendent quetzal.** Although female quetzals resemble most other trogons in appearance, males wow viewers with their unique colorful plumage and long tail feathers. Named after the Spanish verb *tragar* (to swallow), trogons are known for swallowing fruits whole and redistributing seeds around the forest upon regurgitation.

WHERE TO SEE THEM? While trogons can be seen all over Costa Rica, quetzals stick to **cloud forest ecosystems.** If you're lucky, you might spot one in the many nature reserves that blanket the **Monteverde vicinity.** Bird-watching expeditions around **San Gerardo de Dota** (in the southern inland area) produce the most frequent sightings. They're often seen feeding on small avocados in *aguacatillo* trees.

BIRDS OF PREY

Costa Rica has several varieties of birds of prey, including **hawks** (*gavilanes*), **vultures** (*zopilotes*), and **eagles** (*águilas*). The **harpy eagle,** one of the most sought-after birds in the country, is spotted so rarely that some people believe the species no longer resides here.

WHERE TO SEE THEM? If harpy eagles are still in the country, you'll likely only see it on the **Osa Peninsula** or in the **southern inland region.** A few types of **caracaras** (a kind of falcon) are a common sight throughout the country. Most are spotted mid-flight or perched on tall tree branches while they scope out their prey.

FLYCATCHERS

More than 70 species of flycatchers (nicknamed *pechos amarillos*) call Costa Rica home. Most have brown or olive-green backs and a yellow-tinged chest. You're bound to see

at least one **social flycatcher, boat-billed flycatcher,** or **great kiskadee** resting on cables and fences or visiting feeders at tourist attractions and accommodations **across the country.** The three species are nearly identical. Experienced birders search the Pacific side of the country high and low to view a **scissor-tailed flycatcher** or a rare **fork-tailed flycatcher,** both of which stand out from other family members with their long tails.

WHERE TO SEE THEM? Scissor-tailed flycatchers inhabit the **entire Pacific coast.** Fork-tailed flycatchers are mainly seen in the **southern Pacific region.**

HUMMINGBIRDS

The most delicate birds you'll come across are tiny **hummingbirds** (*colibríes*), which are always a treat to see zigzagging amid natural areas. More than 50 species whiz around Costa Rica. Endemic to Costa Rica and parts of Panama is the **fiery-throated hummingbird,** which has a beautiful, rainbow-colored throat.

WHERE TO SEE THEM? You can see many at once at **hummingbird gardens** scattered throughout the country, especially in **cloud forest ecosystems.** The attractions also permit up-close viewing, ideal if you wish to admire the birds' shimmery, jewel-tone bodies. It's rare to see a fiery-throated hummingbird; your best chance is while exploring attractions or staying at accommodations on the slopes of the **Cordillera Central** (in the Central Highlands) or the **Cordillera de Talamanca** (in the southern inland region).

MOTMOTS

Six species of motmots (nicknamed *pájaros bobos*) can be seen throughout Costa Rica. Except for one species (**Tody motmots**), all are easily identifiable by their long tail, which they sway back and forth like a pendulum when threatened.

WHERE TO SEE THEM? Tody motmots, which can be seen around the **foothills of**

1: northern jacana water bird **2:** keel-billed toucan **3:** scarlet macaws **4:** hummingbird

volcanoes in Guanacaste, are the smallest of Costa Rica's motmots and have a white breast, olive-green plumage, and a short tail. I've always had good luck getting close to motmots, so they're a good species to aim for if you're into bird photography. The black bands around the eyes and the blue, green, turquoise, and copper coloring add to the bird's striking appearance. Look for nests in holes along forest banks and walls.

CURASSOWS AND GUANS

Much like a wild turkey (*pavón*), a curassow or a guan is a medium-sized bird you might encounter wandering the forest floor in most areas of Costa Rica in search of food. They're able to fly, so you may also spot the birds in trees. Great curassows are regularly seen in pairs; the male is black and the female is brown. If you come across a set, approach them with caution because they scare easily and are quick to escape into the brush.

SONGBIRDS

Tons of songbirds fill Costa Rica's forests with sweet serenades. Small and colorful tanagers (*tangaras;* some species are nicknamed *viudas*) can be seen singing from the treetop canopy and hopping around the forest floor just about everywhere in the country. The clay-colored robin (*yigüirro*), also known as a clay-colored thrush, has been Costa Rica's national bird since 1977. It sings a nearly constant tune between March and June. Locals claim the birds *llaman la lluvia* (call the rain) since their song corresponds with the transition between the dry season and the wet season. Several warblers and orioles

add melodies to the natural symphony. These three types of songbirds can be seen and heard across the country.

One of the most distinct birdsongs you'll hear in Costa Rica, which plays on repeat throughout the northern inland area, the Caribbean region, and Guanacaste, is the combined squeak and gobble of the Montezuma oropendola. The blackbird species, which is dark-brown in color, has a yellow-tinged tail, and an orange-tipped beak, is a common sight around fruit feeders and in the wild. You may spot their funny-looking nests first, which hang from tree branches and appear as large, greyish-brown woven sacks, that can be up to six feet long.

WATERBIRDS

Costa Rica's countless wetlands, mangroves, rivers, lakes, lagoons, and beaches host flocks of waterbirds. Most species come looking for crabs, mollusks, fish, insects, and other foods in and around the water. Sandpipers (*andarríos*), gulls (*gaviotas*), herons and egrets (*garzas*), pelicans (*pelícanos*), cormorants (*cormoranes*), spoonbills (*espátulas*), anhingas (nicknamed *pato aguja*), kingfishers (*martín pescadores*), and storks (*cigüeñas*) are common varieties.

WHERE TO TO SEE THEM? Waterbirds can be found around the waterways of the Refugio Nacional de Vida Silvestre Mixto Caño Negro (in the Northern Inlands) and Parque Nacional Palo Verde (in Guanacaste). The canals in Parque Nacional Tortuguero (on the Caribbean coast) also produce sightings of water birds, including northern jacanas.

Reptiles and Amphibians

CROCODILES AND CAIMANS

American crocodiles (*cocodrilos*) are common sights on the banks of many of Costa Rica's **slow-moving rivers.** Remain alert when visiting natural lagoons or beaches next to river mouths, as crocodiles may lurk nearby. Never attempt to cross small rivers or estuaries unless you are certain crocodiles aren't in the area. Smaller and less aggressive are **spectacled caimans** (*caimanes*), seen in the Northern Inlands.

WHERE TO SEE THEM? Look for them as you travel through or participate in guided boat tours on **Río Tempisque** (in Guanacaste), **Río Peñas Blancas** (near La Fortuna), or **Río Tárcoles** (in the central Pacific coast). Passage through the **Humedal Nacional Térraba-Sierpe** (on the Osa Peninsula), the estuary within **Parque Nacional Marino Las Baulas** (on the northern Pacific coast), and the canals of **Parque Nacional Tortuguero** (on the Caribbean coast) provide additional opportunities for sightings. **Spectacled caimans** (*caimanes*) are seen in large quantities in **Río Frío** around the **Refugio Nacional de Vida Silvestre Mixto Caño Negro** (in the Northern Inlands).

FROGS

Costa Rica has more than 175 different types of amphibians, the majority of which are frogs (*ranas*). Several are entertaining to look at, like the **strawberry poison dart frog** (nicknamed the blue-jeans frog given the denim-colored legs that contrast with its bright-red body) or various species of **glass frogs,** whose transparent bodies put internal organs on full display. The nonpoisonous **red-eyed tree frog** is arguably the most sought-after, as its striking light-green body, blue legs, orange feet, and beady red eyes—all of which are used to trick predators into thinking it's poisonous—make it a unique sight. Most other frogs have earth-tone bodies that camouflage well with the environment. The majority of Costa Rica's frog species prefer moist environments to dry areas; look for poison dart frogs, glass frogs, tree frogs and more hopping

red-eyed tree frog

along wet or humid **nature trails,** sleeping **under leaves,** or depositing eggs in water-logged bromeliads, usually near small bodies of stagnant water in the **northern inland area,** the **Caribbean region,** the **central and southern Pacific coast,** and on the **Osa Peninsula.**

WHERE TO SEE THEM? After dark, when the temperature cools and nocturnal varieties awake, is the best time of day to see the largest number of frogs. Guided **night tours** through nature reserves and frog exhibits are available around the country. I particularly like La Fortuna's **Frog Watching Night Walk** at the **Arenal Oasis Eco Lodge & Wildlife Refuge.** Visits to **Frog's Paradise** in Bijagua (in the Northern Inlands) are also worthwhile.

GECKOS, IGUANAS, AND LIZARDS

The closest encounter you'll likely have with a lizard is in your hotel room, as tiny **house geckos** are common guests—wanted or not. Some geckos run across walls and ceilings, and others hide behind mirrors and hanging artwork. You'll hear them making clicking sounds every few minutes as they attempt to make a meal out of small flies, worms, and other insects. If you can't direct them out the door, don't fret. They're harmless.

Iguanas (*iguanas*) are also frequent finds in Costa Rica, especially along coastlines where there are plenty of sunny and sandy spots for females to bury their eggs. Black spiny-tailed iguanas and green iguanas can be seen basking in the sun on tree branches.

WHERE TO SEE THEM? For guaranteed iguana sightings, don't miss **Restaurante Las Iguanas** near La Fortuna, where hundreds of iguanas fill the trees beside the establishment.

Lizards (*lagartijas*), of which there are many varieties in Costa Rica, dash across **nature trails** and hurry up **tree trunks.**

Arguably the most remarkable species is the **common basilisk,** better known as a Jesus Christ lizard, which escapes land predators by scurrying across the surface of narrow bodies of water on its hind legs.

WHERE TO SEE THEM? Basilisks, along with most other lizards in the country, can be seen near **lowland rivers** and **streams** along the **Pacific coast.**

SNAKES

According to San José's Instituto Clodomiro Picado, the country's leading snake research center, which produces antivenom serums and exports the products around the world, Costa Rica has 140 species of **snakes** (*serpientes* or *culebras*), but only 23 are considered poisonous (22 species of land snakes and 1 species of sea snake). One of the most aggressive species is the pit viper known as the **fer-de-lance,** but the most poisonous is the **bushmaster.** Many snakes are brown in color and camouflage easily among natural settings; be mindful of where you walk and don't venture off flattened trails into **dense brush.** Other snake varieties are bright green or yellow.

It's worth noting that encountering a poisonous snake in Costa Rica is uncommon. In my many years of traveling throughout Costa Rica, I've only come across a handful in the wild, and most were encountered during non-routine activities like overnight deep-jungle expeditions. Although snakes can appear anywhere and at any time (carry a flashlight wherever you go at night), Costa Rica's most traveled trails rarely produce daytime snake sightings.

WHERE TO SEE THEM? Look for snakes in **trees** or curled up in **holes.** If you're fearful of snakes, visit forested areas with a knowledgeable and experienced tour guide, or examine them from behind glass walls at one of many **herpetariums** and other snake exhibits in the country.

1: baby green iguana **2:** golden silk orb weaver **3:** magnificent owl butterfly **4:** adult black spiny-tailed iguana

Insects and Arachnids

BUTTERFLIES AND MOTHS

More than 1,200 species of **butterflies** (*mariposas*) and roughly 8,000 species of **moths** (*polillas* or *mariposas nocturnas*) flutter **all around Costa Rica,** mainly in **natural areas** with plenty of **flowers.**

The most beloved butterfly in the country is the shimmery **blue morpho butterfly.** You're most likely to catch a glimpse of it up-close when it rests on plants or feeders to drink the juice of fermented fruit. With the blue side of its wings closed while it consumes the liquid, the butterfly displays a striking brown design with several circles meant to mimic eyes. The blue morpho is often misidentified as the **magnificent owl butterfly,** which displays similar brown markings on one side of its wings and an iridescent purple—not blue—hue on the other.

WHERE TO SEE THEM? To see them in abundance, visit one of the country's many **butterfly gardens,** which protect and breed several species within enclosed habitats.

ANTS

The tiny **leaf-cutter ants** (*hormigas*) you'll see marching across **nature trails** and up **tree trunks** in virtually every outdoor area in the country are wildly fascinating. If you plan to participate in a guided nature tour anywhere in the country, ask your tour guide about the ants' behavior. In short, the strong critters carry bits of leaves and other debris (sometimes 2-3 times their own weight) across forests to underground colonies, some of which consist of millions of ants. They later feed off the fungus of the decomposing materials. Colonies are overseen by queen ants, which run an impressively organized and smart operation. Watch out for the hardworking insects whenever you embark on forest treks to avoid stepping on their ingenious system.

SPIDERS AND SCORPIONS

Costa Rica has all kinds of **spiders** (*arañas*), from small varieties not unlike the ones you're used to shooing out of your home, to large **tarantulas** and plenty of weird-looking ones in between. A few are poisonous, including the *Phoneutria boliviensis* (one of the world's most feared spiders), but most are not. A common nonpoisonous variety you're bound to come across is the thin **golden silk orb weaver,** adored by some for its yellow-tinged web. If you're not up for running into one (literally), keep your head up as you walk through **forested areas** and approach exhibit enclosures; webs, often thin and easy to miss, are all around.

Dispelling several myths, findings from 2017 confirm that of Costa Rica's 14 species of **scorpions** (*escorpiones*), none is poisonous. Rarely seen in Costa Rica, the stinging arachnids shouldn't be feared; most hide behind **forest vegetation.**

Background

The Landscape

Costa Rica forms part of the Central American isthmus where the Caribbean and the Cocos (Pacific) tectonic plates converge. Millions of years of opposing pressure created the country's rugged, mountainous interior, which is strewn with active and dormant volcanoes. The landscape is a dramatic display of mountain peaks and plateaus made even more striking by deep valleys that emphasize the diverse terrain.

GEOGRAPHY AND GEOLOGY

North of the equator, Costa Rica stretches diagonally from the northwest, where it borders Nicaragua, to the southeast, where it borders Panama. Mountain ranges bisect the country in the same direction and nearly touch the Caribbean Sea and the Pacific Ocean in places.

Mountains and Volcanoes

Filling much of Costa Rica's interior are walls of mountains and volcanoes that provide stunning backdrops to many rural and city scenes. Four mountain ranges span the length of the country. Beginning in the northwest, they gradually increase in height and width as they stretch southeast.

Closest to Nicaragua and visible to the north from Costa Rica's Guanacaste region is the narrow **Cordillera de Guanacaste** (Guanacaste mountain range). The beastly **Volcán Rincón de la Vieja** (Rincón de la Vieja Volcano, 1,916 m above sea level), which has potent, smoking fumaroles, is contained within the range.

To the east, the **Cordillera de Tilarán** (Tilarán mountain range) wows mountain gazers with **Volcán Arenal** (Arenal Volcano, 1,670 m). The picture-perfect, cone-shaped volcano is one you'll want to capture on camera, even though it hasn't erupted since 2010. Tourism booms in La Fortuna, a town at the volcano's base, where spectacular volcano views and thermal water rich in volcanic minerals supplement many attractions.

In the middle of the country (north of the Central Valley), the **Cordillera Central** (Central mountain range) boasts **Volcán Poás** (Poás Volcano, 2,708 m), **Volcán Irazú** (Irazú Volcano, 3,432 m), and **Volcán Turrialba** (Turrialba Volcano, 3,340 m) in sequence. You're welcome to visit Volcán Poás and Volcán Irazú; you can peer into craters at

both. Access to Volcán Turrialba is prohibited indefinitely.

South of the Central Valley, the **Cordillera de Talamanca** (Talamanca mountain range) is Costa Rica's most expansive spread of mountains. It engulfs much of the southern half of the country and touches most of the border shared with Panama. Remote villages and virgin forest hide among the verdant range's hills and crevices, where opportunities for exploration are limited.

Protected land areas fan out over mountains and volcanoes, enclosing popular peaks and craters within their boundaries. Volcán Rincón de la Vieja, Volcán Arenal, Volcán Poás, Volcán Irazú, and Volcán Turrialba are all enclosed by national parks named after the resident volcano. **Cerro Chirripó** (Chirripó Hill, 3,820 m), Costa Rica's highest point, is within the **Parque Nacional Chirripó** (Chirripó National Park) and can be accessed via a challenging two- or three-day trek.

Valleys and Highlands

In the middle of the country, the Central Valley (also known as the Meseta Central) serves as an upland basin shared by agricultural fields and compact metropolises. San José, Costa Rica's capital city, marks the center of the depression. Roughly two million people, approximately 40 percent of the population, live in the valley or on its surrounding highlands.

Coastal Areas

Costa Rica borders both the Pacific Ocean and the Caribbean Sea. Two peninsulas along the **Pacific coast**, the **Nicoya Peninsula** (due west of San José) and the **Osa Peninsula** (in the far south), jut out into the ocean and curve southward. The peninsulas create the **Golfo de Nicoya** (Nicoya Gulf) and the **Golfo Dulce** (Dulce Gulf), respectively. Smaller peninsulas, including the Santa Elena Peninsula and the Papagayo Peninsula (both

---

Previous: a traditional dwelling of the Cabecar indigenous group.

in the northwest corner of the country) add to the jagged coastline. Mountains and hills back beaches in many places. Several stretches of the coast are divided by rocky headlands.

Separated from Costa Rica's interior by the Cordillera Central and the Cordillera de Talamanca, the **Caribbean coast** is a primarily flat region comprising pretty beaches (along the southern coast), lagoons and canals (along the northern coast), and rainforest (around Sarapiquí). The coastline is predominantly straight.

Earthquakes

Costa Rica's plate tectonics produce frequent earthquakes. Most are minor, unnoticed by residents and travelers, and acknowledged only by seismologists. Each year, a few earthquakes cause minor damage and are significant enough to feel near the epicenter. Disastrous earthquakes are extremely rare. Such events in recent history occurred in 2009 in the Poás vicinity and in 1991 in Limón.

ECOSYSTEMS

Costa Rica's 12 life zones—tropical dry forest, tropical moist forest, tropical wet forest, premontane moist forest, premontane wet forest, premontane rainforest, lower montane moist forest, lower montane wet forest, lower montane rainforest, montane wet forest, montane rainforest, and subalpine rain paramo—plus 12 additional transition zones make the country a hotbed of ecological habitats. Differentiated by several environmental factors (including temperature, humidity, and rainfall), each is its own precious gem in the country's treasure chest of natural jewels.

Tropical Rainforests

Costa Rica's thick and humid tropical rainforests are what you likely envision when you think of the jungle. In its interior, from the forest floor to the treetop canopy, the ecosystem is full of life. Dense with branches, vines, and giant tree roots, the rainforest is packed with insects, fungi, mosses, lichens, and decomposing fragments of the forest, not to mention bountiful wildlife. Trees that seem to stretch for miles toward the sky race one another for sunlight. The leafy canopy is always lush and green, and casts shade on nature trails below.

Tropical Dry Forests

Most endangered—due to significant deforestation during the development of pastureland—are Costa Rica's tropical dry forests,

Volcán Arenal

which span much of Guanacaste and the Northern Pacific, as well as parts of the Nicoya Peninsula. To the untrained eye, they appear like tropical rainforests (but sparser) during wet months, when the deciduous forest is lively and green. But drought-ridden months bring drastic change, as the trees drop their leaves and make for a bare and exposed ecosystem. If you visit during this period, you'd think the emerald-green lushness synonymous with Costa Rica is merely a ruse. Fortunately, several national parks, including **Parque Nacional Santa Rosa** and **Parque Nacional Barra Honda,** protect what remains of the precious ecosystem. Aiming to prevent irreparable damage caused by forest fires, the parks are equipped with *cisternas* (vehicles with water tanks) and have on-call teams of volunteer firefighters.

Cloud Forests

Thanks to the warm trade winds that roll in from the Caribbean Sea—rising alongside inland mountain ranges, cooling at high elevations, and eventually condensing—Costa Rica is blessed with several cloud forests. In these, a different world of biodiversity flourishes, and high-elevation bird and plant species are sights of interest. Compared with tropical rainforests and tropical dry forests, cloud forests are cooler, damper, denser, and often shrouded in fog. Experiencing one is as easy as traveling to a city, town, or area of Costa Rica that showcases the ecosystem. The two most well-known cloud forest destinations are **Monteverde** (in the northern inland area) and the vicinity of **Cerro de la Muerte** (in the southern inland region), but several others exist.

Mangroves

Fascinating to see are Costa Rica's waterlogged mangroves. Mazes of root systems, visible at low tide, make trees in the flooded forest look like they're walking on water. Tolerant of salt, mangroves exist in areas where freshwater rivers meet the ocean. **Red mangroves, black mangroves,** and **white mangroves** can be seen in Costa Rica. Each protects nearby land areas from harmful debris and shelters small but important marine life from large predators and other threats. Several areas along the Pacific coast and a few in the Caribbean region feature the ecosystem, which is best explored via guided boat or kayak tours.

Reefs

Climate change and warming ocean temperatures, which can lead to coral bleaching, have left Costa Rica's reefs in dire need of repair. Several reef restoration projects are underway to regenerate coral species with the hope of rebuilding reefs piece by piece. Protected marine zones in several national parks on both the Caribbean and Pacific coasts aim to safeguard reefs from human destruction by restricting access to guided snorkeling and diving tours.

If you're snorkeling or diving, kick your fins cautiously and never touch or remove coral or any other ocean fragments, including shells. With land exploration, the saying goes, "always take out what you carry in." When in the water, abide by the comparable rule, "take nothing out that you didn't bring in."

CLIMATE

Set within the tropics, Costa Rica is blessed with a warm and temperate climate year-round, although the country has an abundance of microclimates. Corresponding with the tourist high season (mid-December to the end of April), **summer,** also known as the **dry season,** provides, on average, longer periods of sunshine and shorter spurts of rain. Cloud cover and higher rainfall amounts are characteristic of **winter,** also known as the **green season** or the **wet season,** which lasts from May to mid-December and corresponds with the tourist low season.

On average throughout the year, lowland areas in the northwest region of the country—including much of Guanacaste, the Northern Pacific, the Nicoya Peninsula, and parts of the northern inland area—are the sunniest and the hottest, with temperatures averaging over

80°F. In part due to trade winds, rain is most common on the east side of the country, most notably in the northern Caribbean, on the Osa Peninsula, and in the Southern Pacific. Transition zones around the center of the country, including the Central Pacific, have a mixed bag of climate conditions. Destinations at high elevations, especially those within cloud forest ecosystems, are the coldest, dropping to 60°F, with near-freezing temperatures atop mountain peaks. They can also be foggy and windy, and produce a greater likelihood of rain.

If there's any truth to weather forecasts for Costa Rica, it's that they're often wrong. Because the country is a narrow land spit flanked by vast oceans, weather systems that roll in from the Pacific and the Caribbean wreak constant havoc on neatly arranged forecasts. Slight shifts in either (or both) systems can bring sudden change to several areas. The best way to plan for the weather in Costa Rica is to expect the unexpected.

On occasion, turbulent weather systems cause floods and landslides. During wet periods, always check with a local to be sure roadways are open before setting out. When mapping your trip, plan alternatives for each route in the event you encounter a road closure. Despite the blow that Tropical Storm Nate delivered to Costa Rica's natural areas and infrastructure in 2017, dangerous weather developments of this kind are infrequent.

ENVIRONMENTAL ISSUES

Costa Rica is a model of environmental conservation. Together with numerous private reserves and refuges, the country's complex national park system protects more than a quarter of the nation's total landmass, counting each of Costa Rica's 12 life zones within its borders.

Deforestation, Reforestation, and Protection

Once blanketed by thick, verdant vegetation, Costa Rica has been dealt a devastating blow thanks to deforestation. For centuries, and at an alarming rate in the latter half of the 20th century, Costa Rica's environment was nearly stripped bare due to the effects of logging, vast cattle farms, and the establishment of agricultural corporations. By the 1990s, before the tourism boom arrived, Costa Rica had already lost roughly four-fifths of its primary forest.

Soon after Costa Rica made its first appearance at the FIFA World Cup in 1990, foreigners flocked to the country to experience the exotic tropical paradise for themselves. As the tourism industry grew, businesses expanded and new establishments (including accommodations, tourist offices, attractions, and recreation centers) were erected around the country. Built before many modern-day policies came into effect, much of the development resulted in further loss of forested areas.

In response to Costa Rica's fast-changing landscape, the government developed several programs and regulations to help combat deforestation and spur reforestation. Many are managed by the **Sistema Nacional de Áreas de Conservación** (National System of Conservation Areas, SINAC, www.sinac.go.cr), which is governed by the **Ministerio de Ambiente y Energía** (Ministry of Environment and Energy, MINAE, www.minae.go.cr). SINAC is the leading organizational body responsible for the management of wildlife, forest resources, protected areas, watersheds, and water systems throughout the country. It also oversees Costa Rica's various conservation areas and its complex national park system.

Some argue that the well-intentioned SINAC falls short of its goals, because anti-conservation activities continue to operate in the shadows. But Costa Rica isn't a perfect nation. The country is actively working to right many wrongs, even though the feat will take generations. New initiatives that document the country's steady progress are always on the rise. Old ones are maintained and reviewed. The **Política Nacional de Saneamiento de Aguas Residuales** (National Wastewater Sanitation Policy) took aim at water pollution in

Low-Impact Travel Tips

Costa Rica has vowed to become the world's first carbon-neutral country by 2021. Here's how you can do your part to help the environment by traveling sustainably:

Choose environmentally friendly establishments. These can include accommodations, tour operators, agencies, and outfitters, transportation service providers, and restaurants. Most will indicate on their website if they have obtained a Certificate of Sustainable Tourism or if they employ sustainability practices.

Reduce, reuse, and recycle. The three pillars of environmentalism still apply when you travel. Reduce electricity by turning off lights and air conditioners in rooms. Reduce water use by taking quick showers. Reduce paper waste by relying on electronic confirmations. Reduce plastics by using refillable water bottles and asking for drinks without a straw. Reuse towels and bed linens (if possible) to cut back on laundry loads. Recycle whatever materials you can, whenever you can.

Respect nature and wildlife. Stick to posted trails and remain quiet in natural areas so you do not disrupt local inhabitants. Don't touch or scare wildlife, take flowers or shells, break tree branches, litter, or drive across the beach. Always watch where you're walking.

Tour an organic farm. Costa Rica has several fascinating farms that demonstrate organic agricultural practices. Some offer unique farm-to-table experiences where you can taste the difference that sustainable farming makes.

Walk or bike around town. Skip taxi rides in favor of greener ways to get around. If you require transportation, opt for public buses, shared shuttle services, or organized tour services, which transport multiple people at one time.

Choose tour experiences that don't damage the environment. Many attractions were built in ways that minimize harm to the environment. For example, some zip lines and tree-climbing excursions were constructed without causing damage to trees. Choose these kinds of activities whenever you can.

Travel consciously. Recognize the effect your actions have on your surroundings and remain conscious of their impact on today, tomorrow, and the future. It's easy to let go of concern while on vacation, but your stress-free trip shouldn't contribute added stress to your chosen destination. Awareness will help keep Costa Rica a paradisiacal place for us all to enjoy.

2016. The **Política Nacional de Humedales** (National Wetlands Policy), inaugurated in 2016, emphasized conservation efforts for Costa Rica's fluvial, estuarine, marine, lacustrine, and palustrine wetlands. The push to replace single-use plastics with biodegradable materials—countrywide by 2021—aims to spare oceans from receiving our trash. The **Programa Bandera Azul Ecológica** (Ecological Blue Flag Program), which began in 1996 and is updated every year, is a coastal community incentive that encourages beach cleanups along the Pacific and the Caribbean coasts.

Foreigners and expats contribute significantly to land and wildlife habitat protection. Many own private reserves purchased with the intent of restoring Costa Rica as close as possible to its original state. Others operate or volunteer with organizations that provide a diverse range of services from research studies and educational awareness to building structures that aid in wildlife proliferation and planting trees to replenish food sources. Most document their successes online to display their efforts and to instill hope. Together with equally earth-conscious Ticos, these groups are rebuilding the paradise lost.

Sustainable Tourism

Since 2000, Costa Rica's ecotourism stamp of approval has been the **Certificación para la Sostenibilidad Turística** (Certification of Sustainable Tourism, CST, www.turismo-sostenible.co.cr), handed out by the government-run **Instituto Costarricense de Turismo** (Costa Rican Institute of Tourism, ICT, www.ict.go.cr). The certification ranks tourism businesses according to their sustainability model. The program is wildly successful and a win for conservation. It also ignites competitive drive around the country, as businesses compete for top honors. You'll recognize the award, which appears as a circular leaf badge, on websites and in print marketing.

The program makes it easy to identify agencies, accommodations, attractions, and restaurants that are sustainable. A five-leaf ranking is the highest score. The majority of businesses receive a three- or four-leaf ranking. A full list of awardees is available on the certificate program's website.

Plants and Trees

PLANTS
Bromeliads

Bromeliads account for most of the spiky plants growing on trees, on the ground, and sometimes around rocks in Costa Rica. The majority are short and sharp to the touch but have beautiful pink, red, or orange flowers that soften the plant's appearance. Crevices formed where spikes depart from the plant's thick stem are where some frog species elect to deposit their eggs. The varietals that produce fruit attract birds. One of the most recognizable bromeliads in all of Costa Rica—and in the world—is the pineapple plant.

Coffee

Coffee production has long been (and remains) one of Costa Rica's most lucrative businesses. But you won't find tons of large coffee corporations here. Over 90 percent of the country's coffee plantations are small-scale, family-owned operations.

If you travel around Costa Rica, you'll see plantations of medium-sized **coffee plants** arranged in rows on sloped terrain. Monteverde in the northern inland area, several areas around the Central Valley and Highlands, and parts of the Southern Inlands have many. The plants are easily identifiable by their shiny, almost plastic-looking dark-green leaves and, when in season, small red fruits. Although Costa Rica's small size doesn't allow for the production of vast quantities of coffee, where the country differs from other coffee-growing nations is in the perfection of its bean. Faring well in international

tasting competitions, Costa Rica is a model country in high-quality arabica bean production, as well as in organic and sustainable coffee farming.

Heliconias

Quintessentially tropical in appearance, many kinds of **heliconias** fill gardens and forests with bursts of bright colors. Beautiful enough to be used in hotel decor and wedding arrangements, the flowers of heliconia plants (technically called bracts) are regularly exported from Costa Rica to nations around the world. Some heliconias are low-lying plants with spiky flowers that stand upright, much like a bird-of-paradise. Others are tall, towering plants that allow strands of flowers to hang freely through oversize leaves. Most attract several types of birds, namely hummingbirds.

Medicinal Plants

Several plants grown in Costa Rica can be used as analgesics, sedatives, anti-inflammatories, and antidepressants. Most *plantas medicinales* (medicinal plants) play important roles in indigenous cultures, but many are also used by nonindigenous Costa Ricans and expats who favor traditional approaches to medicine. A few of the more common remedies include **jackass bitters** (*gavilana*), *Lippia alba* (nicknamed *juanilama*), and **mint** (*menta*). Most are consumed as tea prepared with leaves from the plant. To learn more, visit the garden at the **Sacred Seeds Sanctuary** near La Fortuna, which has roughly 300 medicinal plants. Sprigs or leaves of dried plants can be purchased in many shops and markets around the country, including San José's **Mercado Central.**

Orchids

Costa Rica's national flower (chosen in 1939) is the bright-purple *Guarianthe skinneri* (*guaria morada,* also known as *Cattleya skinneri*), one of more than 1,500 species of orchids found in the country. Many hide among thick forest brush and are too small for the average traveler to notice, which is why you might not see as many in the wild as you hope to come across. To fully appreciate Costa Rica's abundance of orchids, visit an **orchid garden.** The **Monteverde Orchid Garden** (in the northern inland area) is an excellent choice, as Monteverde is thought to have the greatest diversity of orchids in the world. Another fantastic garden is the **Jardín Botánico Lankester** (in the Central Valley and Highlands), which displays several kinds of plants but counts roughly 1,000 orchid varieties in its collection.

TREES

Cacao

Medium-sized **cacao trees** fill cacao farms around Costa Rica. Sporting hard fruit pods bigger than the size of your hand, cacao is one of the most identifiable trees in the country. Pods can be green, red, or yellow, depending on the tree species and the pod's ripeness. Inside each pod are several deep-purple seeds covered in a white, fibrous, edible skin. The seeds, first fermented and then dried and broken into bits, are called nibs. Fatty content (known as cocoa butter) drawn out from ground nibs is the foundation of white chocolate. The nib remnants, following the extraction of cocoa butter, are pulverized to create cocoa powder. Regular chocolate, which can range from sweet milk chocolate to bitter dark chocolate, is typically comprised of ground nibs, cocoa butter, sugar, and milk. It's created by combining the ingredients, refining them (usually with rollers) until they're smooth, and heating and mixing the blend to achieve a desired flavor during a process known as "conching."

Ceiba

Centuries-old **ceiba trees,** some more than 60 meters tall, are showstoppers in several of Costa Rica's natural areas, including **Parque Nacional Volcán Arenal** (near La Fortuna) and **Parque Nacional Carara** (on the central Pacific coast). The property of the **Shawandha Lodge** (in the Caribbean region) has one of the country's largest. Look for the tree's noticeably branchless trunk and its giant buttresses, which appear to climb out of the forest floor as they stabilize the tall growth.

Cortez

Among scenes of brown and green, the bright-yellow flowers of the **cortez tree** are a shocking sight, most often spotted in Guanacaste. Look for the blooms if you plan to be in Costa Rica during the summer season. They make a prominent but brief appearance before dropping to the ground.

Guanacaste

Since 1959, the robust **guanacaste tree** has served as Costa Rica's national tree. Sometimes called the **elephant-ear tree** because of the shape of its seed pods, the large, umbrella-shaped tree is easy to spot in the Guanacaste region but can also be seen in other areas of the country. Its wood is used for furniture, and its little brown seeds (which sport a copper-colored ring) adorn jewelry pieces in souvenir shops. The sap is sometimes used for medicinal purposes.

Palm

Much of Costa Rica's Caribbean and Pacific coastline is backed by tall, tropical **palm trees** (*palmas*) that provide an endless supply of **coconuts** (*cocos*). Some palms are desired

1: palm tree 2: heliconias 3: ceiba tree 4: orchid

for the edible, white coconut meat contained within their fruit. The fruits of others, called **pipa,** are cracked open for their refreshing juice. **African palms** (*palmas africanas*) are harvested for their oil, which is used in cosmetics, soaps, and other household products. **Peach palms** (*pejibayes*) supply *palmito* (heart of palm), a staple vegetable in Costa Rican cuisine.

Strangler Fig
Costa Rica's many **strangler fig trees** (*higuerones*, of the ficus tree variety) are vastly interesting to see and learn about. These trees often begin their life on the trunk or within the canopy of another tree (depending on the location of seed germination), where roots sprout and grow toward the ground. Over years, the new tree expands and encloses or "strangles" the host tree, eventually stripping it of the elements and nutrients it needs to survive. Mid-process, the sight is a wild display of twisted roots wrapped around tree trunks. With early growths, you can witness the trees on their journey to the forest floor. Most of Costa Rica's **tree-climbing tours** (namely in Monteverde and on the Osa Peninsula) scale strangler figs because the tangled roots make decent footholds. Some hollow varieties allow tree climbing from within.

History

EARLY HISTORY
Although humans are believed to have resided in Central America as far back as 10,000 years ago, little is known about them. Artifacts and legends suggest that several **indigenous groups** roamed the area, but apart from findings within the **Monumento Nacional Guayabo** (Guayabo National Monument) in the Central Valley and Highlands, archaeological evidence of settlements is sparse. Unlike the history of Aztec and Mayan cultures in northwestern Central America and other indigenous civilizations in South America, much of Costa Rica's early history is undocumented.

SPANISH COLONIALISM
When Christopher Columbus first arrived on the Caribbean coast in 1502, he was met by gold-toting members of small indigenous communities established near modern-day Limón. Dazzled by the metal (and even more so by the tribe's quantity of it), Columbus returned to Europe with tales that ignited tremendous greed and ambition. Spanish explorers came to Costa Rica—literally, the "Rich Coast"—soon after in search of wealth. Colonization attempts by several Spanish conquistadores including Columbus's successor, Diego de Nicuesa, were thwarted by challenging terrain and territorial native peoples. In 1513, Vasco Núñez de Balboa managed to travel over the mountains of the Central American isthmus to discover the Pacific coast. By the 1520s, most invaders had either died or returned to Europe. For the most part, Costa Rica was left alone.

Roughly 40 years later, Spaniards returned to the territory to brutally claim it as their own. They waged a bloody war on the native peoples, who defended themselves with equally violent guerrilla tactics. Tuberculosis, smallpox, and ophthalmia, brought over by the Europeans, spread like wildfire, which resulted in a significant decline in the indigenous populations. Many native Costa Ricans who escaped the inadvertent germ warfare retreated to remote mountain areas.

In 1563, Spaniard Juan Vázquez de Coronado chose Cartago as the colony's capital city. Officially part of the **Spanish Empire,** cities in the Central Valley, known today as San José, Heredia, and Alajuela, were formed. The aristocratic colonists, with little agricultural experience and no indigenous labor force, struggled to cultivate the land and construct their settlement.

ERA OF INDEPENDENCE

Following Mexico's 11-year **War of Independence** with Spain, which won Mexico its independence in 1821, Central American nations fell under the **Mexican Empire**. Not wanting to be governed by Mexico, the Central American countries briefly formed their own coalition in 1823 before going their separate ways. Although full independence wasn't granted to Costa Rica until 1838, citizens celebrate the country's 1821 separation from Spain on September 15 each year.

The century that followed Costa Rica's acquisition of independence was a tumultuous but promising era. Several setbacks deferred progress, including attacks on San José by its neighboring cities during the 1835 **Guerra de la Liga** (War of the League), in which San José proved victorious, and the 1856 invasion (and eventual defeat) of American William Walker and his troops via Nicaragua.

There were plenty of successes as well, propelling Costa Rica to power and self-sufficiency. President Juan Mora Fernández, Costa Rica's first elected head of state (1824-1833), helped establish the country's judicial and education systems. President Braulio Carrillo Colina (1835-1842) developed public administration and fought for Costa Rica's autonomy from the rest of Central America, which earned him the nicknames the "liberator" and the "architect" of the state.

Coffee brought small-scale farmers and elite manufacturers together, and was considered the new gold of the nation by the mid-1800s. The coffee baron Juan Rafael Mora Porras was even president during this period (1849-1859). Liberal leader Tomás Guardia Gutiérrez (two-time president, 1870-1882) abolished capital punishment, invested in infrastructure, and guaranteed free primary education to all Costa Ricans.

The era also saw the construction of Costa Rica's national railroad, connecting the Central Valley to the Caribbean port in Limón. Until the railroad's completion, coffee was transported by oxcart from the Central Valley to the Pacific port in Puntarenas, then shipped by boat via a three-month journey around South America to Europe. Minor Keith, a nephew of American railroad builder Henry Meiggs, oversaw construction of the track and planted bananas throughout the process. As a side business, he exported the fruit, which received rave reviews. Together with the Boston Fruit Company, Keith co-founded the **United Fruit Company** (known today as **Chiquita Brands International**), which propelled the growth of Costa Rica's **Banana Empire**. By the early 1900s, bananas surpassed coffee as the nation's top export.

CIVIL WAR AND CONTEMPORARY TIMES

From the turn of the 20th century until the mid-1900s, Costa Rica endured a period of increased tensions. Changes in tax laws that required higher payments from the wealthy drew outrage from the upper class. The **Great Depression** and a simultaneous downturn in the coffee industry brought economic struggle and social unrest. Polarization across political parties divided the nation. Some residents, mainly the elite, were frustrated with the government under the rule of controversial president Rafael Ángel Calderón Guardia (1940-1944), who aimed to help the non-wealthy through the development of national healthcare and the public University of Costa Rica.

Election years in 1944 and 1948 produced presidential results stained with fraud. On March 10, 1948, activist José María Figueres Ferrer (nicknamed Don Pepe) led a revolution to overthrow the government alongside the **Ejército de Liberación Nacional** (National Liberation Army). The six-week civil war won Calderón Guardia's surrender and cost the lives of roughly 2,000 people, most of whom were civilians. That same year, Figueres Ferrer, who served as president on three separate occasions following the revolt, abolished the nation's army in an act of peace meant to stabilize turbulent times. One of

Costa Rica's most respected leaders, he went on to give women the right to vote and Afro-Costa Ricans the right to apply for citizenship.

Following the civil war, Costa Rica experienced a relatively uneventful 30-year run until economic crises set in during the 1980s. The first presidential term of economist Óscar Arias Sánchez (president 1986-1990 and 2006-2010) couldn't have come at a better time; he got to work on broadening the country's sources of income, especially with respect to tourism. A supporter of international amity, Arias Sánchez also helped alleviate stress on the country through the development of peace plans shared with other Central American nations; the progress earned him a Nobel Prize in 1987. The wheels he set in motion to make Costa Rica a carbon-neutral country by 2021 are still chugging away. If the goal is met, it will no doubt add further acclaim to the former president's legacy.

Today, issues surrounding social and economic inequality continue to weigh on the nation and take precedence in political platforms. Equality is becoming more evident in Costa Rica's highest office, which younger generations hope will trickle down to the rest of the republic. Laura Chinchilla Miranda was the country's first female president (2010-2014). Current leader Carlos Alvarado Quesada, who became Costa Rica's 48th president in 2018, is a politician, a novelist, a rock singer, and the youngest of Costa Rica's elected presidents. He was 38 at the time of his inauguration. His pick for vice president was the country's first female Afro-Costa Rican to hold the title.

Tensions remain high between Costa Rica and Nicaragua, largely due to long-running disputes over ownership of **Río San Juan** (San Juan River) despite resolutions being handed down (in Costa Rica's favor) from the United Nations' top court. Ongoing civil unrest in Nicaragua, which has led to an increase in illegal Nicaraguan immigrants in Costa Rica, has only worsened the conflict.

Government and Economy

GOVERNMENT

Costa Rica is a democratic republic with a stable, responsible government. Governance is divided among three branches: executive, legislative, and judicial. The executive branch is overseen by the president, who is responsible for choosing two vice presidents as well as various cabinet ministers, ambassadors, and provincial governors.

The legislative branch largely represents the people. Fifty-seven *diputados* (deputies) from various political parties fill seats within the **Asamblea Legislativa** (Legislative Assembly) and act as voices for residents of all seven provinces.

The judicial branch manages various courts, from local civil courts to Costa Rica's **Corte Suprema de Justicia** (Supreme Court of Justice) in downtown San José. It also operates the **Organismo de Investigación**

Judicial (Judicial Investigation Agency, OIJ, www.sitiooij.poder-judicial.go.cr), the country's top crime investigation unit. The OIJ has offices around the country but is headquartered in the capital.

Political Parties and Elections

In order to become president, candidates must be older than 30, and they must have been born in the country; candidates cannot have been employed with the government for at least two months prior to running for office. Once elected, a president is in power for a four-year term. While running for a second term is permitted, serving consecutive terms is not.

National elections are held every four years in Costa Rica and often require three voting rounds. During the first, citizens elect party leaders from proposed party candidates.

Following competitive campaigns, Ticos take to the polls on election day. The legal voting age in Costa Rica is 18 years.

The presidency is won with 40 percent of the vote, but since this is rarely received, a follow-up vote between the top two parties determines the winner. Costa Rica has many political parties (more than 10), but 4—the Partido Liberación Nacional (National Liberation Party) (PLN, green and white), the Partido Acción Ciudadana (Citizens' Action Party) (PAC, red and yellow), the Partido Unidad Social Cristiana (Social Christian Unity Party) (PUSC, red and blue), and the Partido Restauración Nacional (National Restoration Party) (PRN, blue and yellow)—regularly complete for the presidency and seats in the Asamblea Legislativa. Current leader Carlos Alvarado Quesada, who became Costa Rica's 48th president in 2018, belongs to the PAC; however, the PLN hold majority seats in the assembly.

On a municipal level, additional elections are held in many cities and towns to determine an *alcalde* (mayor) and *regidores* (aldermen).

ECONOMY

Costa Rica pulls its income from a variety of sources, most notably agricultural and technological product exports, and the country's booming tourism industry. In 2017, product and service exportation brought in a whopping US$11 billion, nearly 20 percent of the country's gross domestic product (US$57 billion) for the same year. Tourism is estimated to contribute an additional 17 percent to the total GDP.

Agriculture

The many agricultural fields and warehouses that can be seen all over Costa Rica are responsible for the country's 4,000 different types of product exports, most of which end up in North American, European, or Central American countries. Top products are bananas and pineapples (mainly grown in the Caribbean region) and coffee (much of which comes from the Central Valley and Highlands). Other exports include watermelons and cantaloupes (from Guanacaste); meat and dairy products (from the northern inland area); vegetables, flowers, and ornamental plants (from the Central Valley and Highlands); mangoes (from the central Pacific region); palm oil (from the central and southern Pacific regions, and the Osa Peninsula); and cacao (from the Caribbean region).

Medicine and Technology

Recent years have seen Costa Rica make a name for itself in the medical technology industry as a producer of high-quality medical devices. Supplying employment to more than 20,000 residents (more than half of whom are women), the growing field brings in millions of dollars annually and has helped Costa Rica forge important relationships with medical companies around the world.

The technology company Intel, which established itself in the country in the 1990s and helped fuel the economy through microchip processing, shocked employees when it abruptly closed its production plant in 2014. Although Intel's microchips are no longer manufactured in Costa Rica, the corporation continues to offer employment opportunities in software support. Textile factories, located mainly in and around the Central Valley, provide additional earnings and jobs.

Tourism

With just over three million international arrivals per annum as of 2018, Costa Rica owes much of its stable economy to tourism. Roughly 9 percent of working Costa Ricans are direct employees of the tourism industry, which spans a multitude of jobs from hotel, restaurant, and airport workers to tour guides and tourism office staff. Indirectly, tourism's reach is immeasurable, as everyone from the farmers who cultivate the foods travelers eat to the accountants who handle tourism tax payments are part of the industry. Accommodations and food represent more than 40 percent of the industry's earnings.

People and Culture

DEMOGRAPHY

In 2018, Costa Rica's population surpassed five million people. More than 70 percent live in urban centers, mainly in and around the Central Valley, with the remaining inhabitants spread out across rural areas. Foreign nationals account for roughly 8 percent of the country's total population. The average life expectancy is 80 years, 77.5 years for men and 82.5 years for women.

Life in Costa Rica is *pura vida*. Literally translated as "pure life," the phrase represents the low-stress, unrushed lifestyle practiced by most Ticos. You'll hear and see the slogan no matter where you travel in the country, and it's a constant reminder of the positive vibe that pulses throughout the nation.

In practice, *pura vida* appears in many forms. It is the strong familial bonds that unify many Ticos, including families that choose to live close to one another throughout their lives and spend time together on a regular, sometimes daily, basis. Elders, usually matriarchs, are looked up to as the head of the household.

Pura vida is also the social atmosphere that wafts about most towns. Friends gather in restaurants, bars, and parks to chat. Celebratory events, like birthdays and weddings, are often neighborhood affairs where everyone is welcome. Strangers, when they pass each other on the street, exchange smiles and salutations without hesitation. At its core, *pura vida* is Costa Rica's openness to interaction. Within the tourism industry, non-damaging immersion in nature and peaceful interaction with wildlife embody the *pura vida* way.

A typical workday in the life of a Tico varies. Many businesspeople, most of whom work in and around the Central Valley, lead fast-paced, high-pressure lives. The majority of Costa Ricans, however, carry out their work in an easygoing but professional manner in offices, institutions, and factories around the country. Those who have jobs requiring manual labor, most notably in the agriculture industry, are notoriously hardworking. My husband, who earned his strong work ethic from an early age picking coffee beans on the steep slopes of Costa Rican plantations, is one of many Ticos who can attest to the physical and mental struggle that often comes with making a living in the nation.

Family structures vary as well. Traditionally, women had several children, but families are slowly decreasing in size as more women opt to enter the workforce. Women who choose to extend their education at postsecondary institutions typically start their family later in life, which also contributes to the decline in family size. Many families are blended, as mothers and fathers bring together children from previous relationships to form new family units. Marriage is common, but many people prefer to live as common-law couples. Divorce is legal.

According to the national census in 2011, Costa Rica is largely a homogeneous nation where more than 90 percent of the population self-identifies as being White or of mixed ancestry (either Mestizo or Mulatto). Other individuals self-identify as being Indigenous (2.5 percent), Black or an Afro-Descendant (1 percent), or Chinese (0.2 percent). Remaining individuals (6 percent) either declare their ethnicity or race as Other or None, or don't report having an ethnicity or race at all.

Caribbean Descendants

One of the most heterogeneous regions in Costa Rica is the Caribbean, which is a mosaic of Afro-Costa Rican (also called Afro-Caribbean), indigenous, Chinese, and Mestizo cultures. Afro-Costa Ricans, many of whom are descendants of Jamaicans who traveled to the country in the late 1800s to help build

Pura Vida and the Tico Spirit

There's a pleasantness that permeates Costa Rica and makes the country a warm, inviting destination. Locals call it *pura vida,* referring to their famously laid-back lifestyle. Foreigners call it happiness. According to the **Happy Planet Index,** which considers life expectancy, well-being, equality, and a country's ecological footprint in its evaluation, Costa Rica is one of the happiest nations in the world. The country regularly ranks high on the index and claimed the top spot in 2009, 2012, and 2016. Perhaps the vibe can be attributed to peace, synonymous with Costa Rica ever since the country abolished its army in 1948. According to the **Global Peace Index** (2018), Costa Rica has a "high state of peace" and is the most peaceful nation across Central America and the Caribbean.

I like to call this force the "Tico spirit." I believe it has a lot to do with the mindset and behavior of many Costa Ricans who approach life in a straightforward way. They're not averse to working hard, but they know money and prestige aren't everything. Family, friends, exercise, and downtime are most important, and, if you believe Dan Buettner's work on Blue Zones (regions of the world where people live the longest; Costa Rica made the top five), each is crucial for longevity. Since Costa Rica's average life expectancy is higher than that of the United States, the locals must be doing something right.

The Tico spirit can also be enlivening and inspiring. I've seen it pull people together during thrilling sport competitions and devastating natural disasters. I've seen it encourage conservation and changes in outdated laws. I've seen it teach many people—locals and travelers alike—how to take notice of, appreciate, and learn from what gives them joy.

the national railroad, are largely responsible for the region's distinct feel. Due to segregation laws that prohibited Afro-Costa Ricans from residing outside of the Limón province until 1949, much of the Caribbean influence brought to the country stayed by the coast. Today, Afro-Costa Rican culture enlivens the country with catchy music, colorful dwellings, flavorful food, and expressions of peace and love. This culture is largely what draws travelers to the Caribbean. It's also a beloved part of Costa Rica's rich soul.

Asian and European Descendants

A small percentage of Costa Ricans are descendants from Asian and European nations, mainly China, Spain, and Italy. Like the ancestors of many Afro-Costa Ricans, the ancestors of some Asian-Costa Ricans and Italian-Costa Ricans were brought to the country to construct the railroad. Following the arrival of many Asian-Costa Ricans by boat via the Pacific, the port town of Puntarenas became a settling ground for the group. A noticeable community of Asian-Costa Ricans remains present in the city today, as well as in San José, which has its own **Barrio China** (Chinatown). European descendants are spread out around Costa Rica. The largest concentration of Italian-Costa Ricans can be found in the San Vito area of the Southern Inlands, where many settled in the mid-1900s to escape postwar socioeconomic crises in Europe. Italian influence is also felt in the beach town of Sámara on the Nicoya Peninsula.

Indigenous Groups

The 2.5 percent of Costa Ricans who self-identify as indigenous span eight ethnic groups. Typically residing in mountainous areas are the **Chorotega** (sometimes cited as the **Matambú,** on the Nicoya Peninsula), the **Maleku** (in the Northern Inlands), the **Huetar** (sometimes cited as the **Quitirrisí,** in the Central Valley and Highlands), the **Bribri** and the **Cabecar** (both in the Caribbean and the southern inland region), the **Boruca** and the **Térraba** (both in the southern inland region), and the **Guaymí** (sometimes referred to as the **Ngäbe** or the **Ngöbe,** on the southern Pacific coast). Great diversity exists across group members. Roughly 75 percent of all indigenous people in Costa Rica live in traditional communities on indigenous reserves and have limited interaction with non-indigenous Costa Ricans. The remaining 25 percent have assimilated into Costa Rican society at large. Some even work in the tourism industry to help non-indigenous Costa Ricans and foreigners better understand their beliefs and traditions through cultural presentations.

Much like the devastating effects of deforestation on Costa Rica's natural environment, the acquisition of indigenous land by non-indigenous individuals has contributed to Costa Rica's diminishing indigenous culture. Although the **Indigenous Law of 1977** aimed to curb land loss within indigenous reserves and to ensure that stolen land be returned to indigenous ownership, the groups today still only govern a fraction of the land they are due. Sadly, when indigenous groups speak out on issues that impact their communities, especially in opposition to encroaching development projects, their opinions are given only marginal attention.

RELIGION

Nearly three-quarters of Costa Rica's population self-identify as **Roman Catholic,** with roughly two-thirds of the group claiming to actively practice the religion. Most remaining Ticos are **Evangelists.** Small percentages represent **Jehovah's Witness** and other faiths or individuals who choose to follow no religion at all. Some people in the Caribbean practice **Rastafari,** also known as Rastafarianism, a Jamaican religion established in the 1930s.

Faith is well celebrated in Costa Rica. Religious holidays, including Navidad (Christmas) and Semana Santa (Holy Week), which corresponds with Easter, call for church visits, decorative displays that depict religious scenes, and parades during which crosses and statues of religious figures are carried through town centers. Other events, like the **Romería de la Virgen de los Ángeles** (Pilgrimage of the Virgin of the Angels) and the **Fiesta de la Virgen del Mar** (Virgin of the Sea Festival) pay homage to patron saints. Even the local language incorporates religion in many uses. Personal requests are often followed with *"si Dios quiere"* ("God willing"), and departures typically receive a blessing of *"que Dios lo acompañe"* ("may God accompany you").

LANGUAGE

Latin American Spanish is the primary language spoken in Costa Rica. *Tiquismos* (Costa Rican slang words and phrases) like *mae* (dude) and *tuanis* (good, used to imply coolness) add local flair. In the Caribbean, **Jamaican Patois** (also called **Patwah,** an English-based creole language) is used. Elsewhere in the country, primarily on protected land reserves, the use of Chibchan languages is maintained by members of some of Costa Rica's indigenous groups. In regions with tourism, English is spoken and understood, although to varying degrees.

THE ARTS

Costa Rica's contribution to the arts is somewhat understated, especially with respect to visual and performance arts; contributions in literature, cinema, and fashion are fewer still. Some of the most beloved artworks displayed in the country weren't crafted by Costa Ricans, and many that were drew little attention from international critics. Slowly gaining popularity are small but mighty community organizations committed to saving the arts. They're responsible for the few small-scale art festivals and large-scale street murals you may encounter along the coasts, especially in Jacó and Tamarindo.

If you're looking for Costa Rican art, several museums in San José showcase rotating exhibits, including the **Museo de Arte Costarricense** (Museum of Costa Rican Art) and the **Museo de Arte y Diseño Contemporáneo** (Museum of Art and

Costa Rican Traditions: Punto Guanacasteco and *Bombas*

A common sight at festivals, events, and holiday celebrations in Costa Rica, especially in Guanacaste, is the Punto Guanacasteco—an animated and synchronized folkloric dance that is a treat to see. Dancers circle around one another while men wave *pañuelos* (handkerchiefs) and women twist colorful, ruffled *enaguas largas* (long skirts). The display is enlivened by the tropical sounds of marimbas, guitars, and horns, joined by several enthusiastic *güipipías* (shouts) from delighted spectators.

Midway through the dance, the music and action halts, and one of the performers yells "*Bomba!*" The term refers to poetic, four-line rhyming statements used to show endearment to loved ones or imaginary figures. (Don't confuse this with the more literal translation of the word, which can mean "gas station" or "firework.") The expressions are usually good-humored and invite big laughs, but they can also be used to deliver zingers or insults in nontraditional settings. Men, women, and children perform the bits, delivering classic lines that have been passed down through generations. The country's best recitalists, however, are adept at improvisation and regularly invent new statements.

If you plan to visit Costa Rica in mid-September, you can catch the dance as part of festivities hosted around the country for **Día de la Independencia** (Independence Day). The dance can also be seen in Guanacaste—mainly in Liberia, Tamarindo, and Playas del Coco—during celebrations of the **Anexión de Guanacaste** (Annexation of Guanacaste) near the end of July. Another option is to see the spectacle at restaurants that couple traditional shows with dining, including **Mirador Ram Luna** and **Mirador Tiquicia** in the Central Valley and Highlands.

Contemporary Design). Studios, galleries, and art shops dot the nation; I particularly like the informal collection in the Monteverde vicinity. Indigenous communities almost always have local art available for purchase, and **Galería Namu** in downtown San José displays and sells pieces that represent a variety of groups. The Central Valley and Highlands town of Sarchí has several *fábricas de carretas* (oxcart factories) that reveal the artistry behind the craftsmanship and decoration of Costa Rica's vibrant oxcarts. Other towns and cities display sculptures or topiary art that may catch your eye. Accommodations, regardless of where you travel, almost always incorporate local art into their decor, whether it's tribal art or paintings of flora, fauna, and rural scenes.

Admired locally, music and dance are regular inclusions in traditional Costa Rican celebrations. Live music in a range of styles fills many bars and restaurants, and cultural dance presentations are provided at a few, including **Mirador Tiquicia** and **Ram Luna** in the Central Valley and Highlands.

Calypso and **reggae** music resound throughout the Caribbean. Numerous music festivals are hosted around the nation. Catchy mariachi-inspired **rancheros** (ranch music) and songs played on the **marimba,** Costa Rica's national instrument, are frequently heard. Common dances include **merengue, cumbia, salsa,** and the folkloric dance known as the **Punto Guanacasteco.**

Professional performing arts liven San José's large collection of small theaters, but the country's best (including theater shows and orchestral symphonies) are held at the capital's **Teatro Nacional de Costa Rica** (National Theater of Costa Rica).

Essentials

Transportation

GETTING THERE

Air

Most visitors to Costa Rica arrive by flying into one of the country's two primary international airports. Which to choose (beyond schedule availability and flight costs) depends largely on where you intend to travel in Costa Rica.

JUAN SANTAMARÍA INTERNATIONAL AIRPORT

The most popular of the two airports is the large and modern **Aeropuerto Internacional Juan Santamaría** (Juan Santamaría International Airport, SJO, tel. 506/2437-2400, http://sjoairport.com), located just outside of Alajuela city, an approximate 20-minute drive northwest of San José. Centrally located, the airport is the preferred starting point of most travelers, who find it easy to depart from the hub in a variety of directions. Choose this airport as a starting base if you plan to travel to the following regions: La Fortuna and Monteverde, the central and southern Pacific regions, the Osa Peninsula, the southern inland region, or the Caribbean region.

The airport has snack bars and full-service restaurants, complimentary Wi-Fi, currency exchange booths, and a SIM card vendor—everything you might want to access before hitting the road. Over 25 airlines travel between the airport and roughly 45 destinations worldwide. The airport's website provides a comprehensive list of airlines, including telephone numbers for each. It also displays up-to-date arrival and departure information.

DANIEL ODUBER QUIRÓS INTERNATIONAL AIRPORT

Just west of Liberia, in the northwest corner of the country, the **Aeropuerto Internacional Daniel Oduber Quirós** (Daniel Oduber Quirós International Airport, LIR, tel. 506/2666-9600, http://lircr.com) serves travelers destined for coastal areas in Guanacaste and the northern Nicoya Peninsula. (If you plan to travel to the southern Nicoya Peninsula, you can choose either LIR or SJO.) Renovated twice between 2012 and 2018, the airport is smaller and less chaotic than SJO, but it still offers useful amenities, including a few restaurants and shops. Most of these can only be accessed by departing passengers.

Some 17 airlines use the airport. Real-time flight arrivals and departures are found on the airport's website.

Boat

More than 200 cruise ships arrive at Costa Rica each year, from cruise lines including **Royal Caribbean, Carnival, Princess, Windstar, Disney, Celebrity, Regent, Marella,** and **Oceana.** Most visit the ports in Limón (on the Caribbean coast) or Puntarenas (on the Pacific coast), but others dock at ports in Caldera, Quepos, and Golfito (also on the Pacific coast).

Overland

Tica Bus (tel. 506/2296-9788, www.ticabus. com) offers routes into Costa Rica from both Nicaragua and Panama. Regardless of your origin point, you'll be limited to two bags, each weighing a maximum of 15 kilograms; additional baggage is permitted at an extra cost when space permits. Tickets must be reserved in advance via the Tica Bus website. The website also permits seat selection. One-way ticket purchases are permitted. Round-trip tickets are available for purchase but do not usually provide monetary savings. Tica Bus uses air-conditioned coach buses equipped with reclining seats, televisions, Wi-Fi, and a bathroom.

FROM NICARAGUA

Some travelers (mainly backpackers) cross into Costa Rica from the northwest via Nicaragua. The most common border crossing is in the Guanacaste town of **Peñas Blancas.** A far less common border crossing is offered farther east, in the La Fortuna and Monteverde region, at **Las Tablillas/ Los Chiles.**

Tica Bus operates daily buses to San José from Nicaragua's capital city of **Managua** (6am, 7am, and noon daily, 10 hours, $29). Buses depart from Tica Bus's main terminal

---

Previous: pretty pastures and volcano views along one of Costa Rica's highways.

Crossing Costa Rica's Borders

I have a love-hate relationship with Costa Rica's border crossings. It's great being able to explore the neighboring countries of Panama and Nicaragua. But long lines, piles of paperwork, and the ambiguity of border crossing requirements can be downright frustrating for travelers. There are some things you cannot control, like delays and grumpy customs officials, but you can help your travel experience be as stress-free as possible by arriving at a *frontera* (border) prepared.

You'll need to **pay an exit tax** ($8 pp) to leave Costa Rica, **complete paperwork** at a Costa Rican *oficina de migración* (migration office), physically **cross the border, complete additional paperwork** at the destination country's migration office, and possibly **pay an entrance fee** ($14 pp to enter Nicaragua; entrance to Panama is free). Some border regions require the exit tax to be paid at a booth steps away from the migration office. Don't be alarmed if representatives hand you paperwork to fill out as you approach a migration office line. This is to help expedite processing times, especially during busy periods.

Border towns are not safe tourist destinations. Most don't offer decent lodging or dining opportunities, so avoid staying overnight. If you're traveling by bus, depart in the morning so you arrive at the border as early as possible. The later you arrive, the more likely an unforeseen delay will lead to a missed connection, which could leave you stranded in an unsafe area.

MIGRATION OFFICE LOCATIONS

- **Southern Caribbean region:** Costa Rica's migration office at **Sixaola** (tel. 506/2754-2044, 7am-5pm daily) is 200 meters north of the border with Panama.

- **Southern Pacific region:** Costa Rica's migration office at **Paso Canoas** (tel. 506/2732-1534, 6am-10pm daily) is across from the bus station, 100 meters northwest of the border with Panama.

- **Guanacaste:** Costa Rica's migration office at **Peñas Blancas** (tel. 506/2677-0230, 6am-midnight daily) is by the bus station, 350 meters south of the border with Nicaragua.

in Managua and can offer pickups at six other destinations in the country. Drop-offs are provided at Tica Bus's main terminal in San José. Alternately, you can deboard at one of 18 stops along the way, including Liberia and the Aeropuerto Internacional Juan Santamaría in Alajuela.

FROM PANAMA

To reach Costa Rica from the southeast via Panama, border crossings take place in Sixaola (in the southern Caribbean region) and in Paso Canoas (in the southern Pacific region). Tica Bus operates daily buses to San José from Panamá City (11:55pm daily, 16 hour duration, $40), Panama's capital city. Buses depart from the main terminal in Panamá City and can pick up passengers from eight other destinations in the country.

Drop-offs are provided at Tica Bus's main terminal in San José. Alternately, you can get off at one of seven stops along the way, including several popular beach towns along the Central Pacific coast.

GETTING AROUND
Air

Several popular destinations in Costa Rica have domestic airports, and a few remote areas provide private landing strips. On the western edge of San José is the **Aeropuerto Internacional Tobías Bolaños** (Tobías Bolaños International Airport, SYQ). Though it's technically an international airport, it operates primarily as a domestic one. It used to be the country's most visited small-scale airport but has dwindled in popularity since losing the well-known local flight provider

- **Northern Inlands:** Costa Rica's migration office at **Las Tablillas/Los Chiles** (tel. 506/2299-8048, 7am-5pm daily) is immediately south of the border with Nicaragua.

BE PREPARED

- You can pay exit and entrance fees in **cash** and by **credit or debit card.** Some border offices accept one form of payment but not the other, so be ready to pay either way.

- You may be **pulled over** on the side of the highway as part of a routine police check within a few kilometers of any border town.

- You should be able to provide **proof of funds** (roughly US$500) and/or **proof of exit** from the country you plan to enter within 90 days. Proof of exit must be in the form of a confirmed bus ticket, flight, or cruise ship departure.

- You may have your **bags searched** after crossing into a new country.

- Have your **passport** and at least two hard copies of the identification page handy. Bring a **pen** to fill out paperwork.

- Keep all **paperwork and receipts** you are given. You may need to show them later, especially if you plan to reenter Costa Rica.

- Make sure your passport gets marked with **entrance and exit stamps** when you enter and depart countries.

- Exchange your **Costa Rican colones** into Panamanian balboas or Nicaraguan córdobas before arriving at a border (if desired). Another option is to exchange money through unofficial parties who loiter around border crossings, but make sure you know the going exchange rate to avoid a bad deal.

- Set your watch or clock **one hour ahead** of Costa Rica time if you're entering Panama.

Nature Air in 2018. **SANSA Airlines** currently serves as the best provider for in-country flights.

Domestic flights offer several advantages and disadvantages. They can be more or less expensive than other modes of transportation, but there's no question they save a ton of time, especially getting to and from the distant Osa Peninsula and southern Pacific region. Environmentally conscious travelers can (and should) be concerned about the carbon output of each flight; however, especially given that most planes seat only 12 people. SANSA Airlines claims their fleet is fuel efficient; their partnership with the **Fondo Nacional de Financiamiento Forestal** (National Fund for Forest Financing, FONAFIFO, www.fonafifo.go.cr)—which helps protect primary forest on the Osa

Peninsula—helps offset carbon dioxide emissions.

If money is no concern, private air travel in the form of charter flights can be arranged through providers like SANSA Airlines.

Bus

Costa Rican buses are known for being crowded and having windows that slide open just a crack; bumpy roads mean rides aren't always comfortable. However, Costa Rica's public bus system is a model transportation operation in Central America. There are plenty of routes, and buses are generally punctual.

Most passengers are Ticos, so ticket prices are refreshingly inexpensive, making buses a great option for travelers on a tight budget. Those in search of an authentic Costa Rican experience will love riding the bus, especially routes marked *colectivo* (collective), which make several stops in small towns along the way. If you're itching to get to your next destination, hop on a bus marked *directo* (direct), which should provide nonstop service or make only one or two quick stops along the way.

Travel around Costa Rica by bus sometimes requires connections, and these may call for a walk or taxi ride between bus stations. It pays to plan out your routes before you travel to avoid ending up at the wrong destination or spending more time and money than necessary getting to where you need to be. Check (and double-check) destination names carefully. Beware of similar names, like Puerto Viejo de Talamanca and Puerto Viejo de Sarapiquí; these two places are 200 kilometers apart!

If you plan to travel by bus, it's a good idea to prepare yourself for the unexpected. Every bus, operator, and route is different. In some cases, usually for longer routes, you'll be riding in a comfortable air-conditioned bus with your luggage tucked away in a storage compartment below the vehicle. In others, you'll be sandwiched between your neighbor and a humidity-drenched window with your belongings stacked on your lap. Sometimes you can arrive at a station, prepurchase a ticket with an assigned seat number, and board the bus when it's time to go. For another route, after purchasing a general ticket, you may need to join a line by the bus's front door and claim a seat on a first-come, first-served basis. If you can, arrive at bus stations at least an hour before departure so you have time to sort out logistics and wait in line if necessary.

Rental Car

Renting a vehicle in Costa Rica rewards you with complete freedom. As you drive around the country, you can stop to shop, dine, or take photos; follow detours whenever you desire; and get to know the open road. Most rental agencies have multiple offices scattered around popular tourist towns. Many (some

for a fee) allow vehicle pickups in one city and drop-offs in another, as well as convenient vehicle deliveries and returns at airports and accommodations. Nearly all agencies require renters to be at least 25 years of age and have a valid driver's license in their home country as well as a credit card.

You should rent a vehicle in Costa Rica only if you feel comfortable driving abroad, you are familiar with Costa Rica's driving laws, and you have access to a reliable GPS system (either rented through a vehicle agency or brought from home) for navigational support. In most areas of the country where Wi-Fi signal is decent, you can get away with using Google Maps on devices like cell phones, laptops, and tablets.

Vehicle types vary across agencies. Nearly all offer a few sedans, several 4x4 options that vary in size, and your choice of a manual or automatic transmission. Rental costs are determined by a variety of factors, including vehicle size, rental duration, rental pickup and drop-off locations, insurance preferences, and optional add-ons. Among these are a GPS system, cell phone, car seat, cooler, and a rooftop carrier known as a *canasta*. Each add-on is subject to availability and best requested at the time of reservation.

If you're unsure whether you need a 4x4 vehicle, rent one anyway. Road trips to beaches and attractions, as well as entrances to some accommodations, lead down rugged roads that are a far cry from paved highways. Routes in backroad areas can be steep, rocky, or overrun with flooded rivers. Some areas of the country are known for having roads that become impassable during the green (wet) season. Other times, a fallen tree might be enough to halt your journey.

For years, my go-to provider has been **Mapache Rent-A-Car** (offices in San José, Alajuela, Liberia, and La Fortuna de San Carlos, tel. 506/2586-6300, www.mapache. com, hours vary by office). I like that the rental agency offers transparent price quotes, which helps renters avoid surprise charges. I also appreciate that the organization has earned the

Car Rental Insurance

Driving around Costa Rica can be freeing, but car rental insurance is a tangled issue. Not only is there a ton of fine print to deal with, but surprise charges not disclosed at the time of reservation can be downright frustrating. Before you travel, and even before you reserve a car for your trip, be sure to review this information.

There are two types of car rental insurance in Costa Rica. As mandated by the Instituto Nacional de Seguros (National Insurance Institute) (INS), the first type, commonly cited as **SLI insurance** (also known as **TPL insurance**), must be acquired in Costa Rica. Typically purchased through the rental agency, this insurance provides coverage for damage caused to other drivers and their vehicle. The second type, which provides **limited coverage** for damage caused to you and your rental car (according to a set deductible), can be acquired from providers outside of Costa Rica, such as credit card companies in your home country. It's important to note that there's no universal term for either type of insurance, so you may see other names used.

Most rental agencies require renters to purchase both types of insurance. Many rental agencies will require you to supply proof that the second type of insurance was acquired elsewhere, usually in the form of a letter from the insurance provider).

Not all rental agencies include the cost of both insurance types in their quotes. Some agencies market the two insurance types together and automatically include the combined insurance cost in their quotes. If you're able to provide proof of partial insurance acquired elsewhere, the quote can then be reduced to reflect the cost of SLI insurance only.

Other rental agencies opt to include only SLI insurance in their quotes, which helps them appear less expensive than competitors. If you choose one of these companies and you haven't arranged partial insurance from home, you'll likely learn when you pick up your car that astronomical fees have been added to your bill to cover the second type of insurance. Almost always, this type of rental will end up costing more than one of the seemingly more expensive agencies. When comparing quotes, don't be swayed by low costs. If a price seems too good to be true, it likely is!

Additional insurance is available for purchase. Most rental agencies sell **extra insurance** that can broaden coverage for damage caused to you and your rental car, as well as lower the deductible amount (typically to $0). Although beneficial, extra insurance is optional.

Supplemental fees (some mandatory and others optional) can increase your rental price. Confirm with your chosen agency whether a license plate fee, additional driver fee, roadside assistance fee, smoke damage fee, cleaning fee, airport fee, pickup fee, drop-off/delivery fee, late return fee, refueling fee, green/environmental fee, and/or sales tax have been or will be applied to your quote. Some supplemental fees apply per day and others are one-time charges.

highest ranking of the **Certificación para la Sostenibilidad Turística** (Certification of Sustainable Tourism, CST). Through water recycling, material composting, and practically turning their head office in San José into a greenhouse, Mapache earned the distinction of being one of few sustainable vehicle rental agencies in the country.

GAS STATIONS

Most gas stations around the country do not offer self-service pumps or English-speaking attendants. When an employee approaches your window, say *"Lleno, por favor, regular,"* which translates to "Full, please, regular," assuming you want standard unleaded fuel. Payment is typically accepted in cash (colones or US dollars) or by credit card. In remote areas, gas stations are few and far between, and it helps to know where they are before getting on the road. Always keep your tank above the halfway mark, filling up wherever you can, so you're less likely to find yourself strapped for gas if you end up in an area without fuel.

TRAFFIC REGULATIONS

You must be at least 21 years of age and have a valid driver's license from your home country and passport to drive in Costa Rica. The *policía de tránsito* (transit police), who typically ride in navy blue pickup trucks, are responsible for traffic enforcement. You must abide by the speed limit (generally 80 kilometers per hour on highways and 60 kilometers per hour on other roads), wear a seat belt when driving, and be able to provide your license, passport, and vehicle documentation if asked.

Officers with radar guns hide along highway edges; locals typically alert one another of their presence with a quick flash of the high beams. Speed cameras, mainly around the Central Valley and Highlands, provide added vigilance. If you receive a ticket, you can pay the fine through your rental agency, which will handle the necessary paperwork. In the rental agreement fine print, some agencies require you to notify them immediately after you receive the ticket.

ACCIDENTS AND BREAKDOWNS

In the event of an accident, Costa Rican law dictates that you must not move your vehicle. It can be tempting to do so if you're holding up traffic (now you can appreciate why road accidents in Costa Rica cause such awful delays), but the scene of the accident will be treated much like the scene of a crime, and evidence cannot be tampered with.

First and foremost, call 911 if you or anyone else has been injured. Next, phone your vehicle rental agency (many will provide a 24-hour emergency line) as well as the traffic accident report line of the **Instituto Nacional de Seguros** (National Insurance Institute, INS, 1-800-800-8000). If you have a camera or cell phone, take photos of the scene and all vehicles involved for your own records; then wait for assistance to arrive.

Taxi

Taxis serve all major cities and popular tourist areas in Costa Rica. They're a good way to get around towns and cities but aren't the safest or the most economical mode of transportation between destinations. Most **official taxis** are red and display a yellow triangle with a black number on the door. **Official airport taxis** are the exception—they're orange. Most taxi drivers do not speak English, but simply saying the name of your destination is sufficient. You can also ask, *"¿Por favor, me puede llevar a…?"* ("Please, can you take me to…?"), filling in the name of your destination. Plan to pay the exact fare in colones to avoid losing money on a poor exchange rate. Many *taxistas* (taxi drivers) do not carry change. Unofficial taxi drivers, known as *piratas,* are everywhere, but unless you know and trust the driver (as locals often do), they're best avoided.

Organized Tour Transportation

For travelers looking to maximize their time and minimize the cost and hassle of arranging separate transportation services and tours, **city-to-city transportation-inclusive tours** are a helpful tool. This form of transportation, sometimes referred to as an **Adventure Connection** or **post-tour-onward transportation,** allows you to move between destinations while participating in an activity along the way. How it works: You'll get picked up in one city in the morning, participate in an adventure or nature tour (like white-water rafting) during the day, and get dropped off in a different city in the afternoon or evening. You choose the route and the tour, and the tour operator coordinates the rest. Lunch and sometimes breakfast are included.

Trailblazer tour operators that offer this service include **Exploradores Outdoors** (offices in San José and Puerto Viejo de Talamanca, tel. 506/2222-6262, www.exploradoresoutdoors.com) and **Desafío Adventure Company** (Calle 472 behind the central church, La Fortuna, tel. 506/2479-0020, www.desafiocostarica.com). The most common destinations selected as tour start or end locations are San José, La Fortuna, Monteverde, Tortuguero, Puerto Viejo de Sarapiquí, Manuel Antonio, Sámara, Puerto Viejo de Talamanca, Cahuita, and beaches along Guanacaste's northern Pacific coast.

Crossing Flooded Roads and Rivers

My favorite way to explore Costa Rica is by car. I love the flexibility and the opportunities to explore the extraordinary. But there's nothing worse than setting off on an exciting journey only to turn a corner and be confronted by a flooded road or a swollen river. You can't go over it, you can't go under it, and you can't go around it. Unless you turn back, you must go through it. Before you hold your breath and plunge in, make sure you know the following information.

- Having a **4x4 vehicle with high clearance** is a must, not only to best avoid flooding the engine but also to ensure that water doesn't enter through low side doors.

- Rental agencies **do not cover damage** to vehicles as a result of river crossings. Admitting that you crossed a river (even when no damage is caused) can jeopardize your insurance.

- A dirty river (marked by opaque, brown water) can be a sign that the water came from a mountain. Rainfall at higher elevations increases the likelihood of **flash floods** at lower elevations. These can engulf rivers (and vehicles) at any moment. Although still dangerous, clear and still water is the least risky to enter. Don't attempt to cross a river if it is moving swiftly; you could get swept away. If you misread river currents, flash floods can be deadly.

- Your best chance for success is to **shadow another driver,** ideally a local driver who knows the area well. Watch how other vehicles proceed and follow the same course. If no one else is around, look for entrance and exit tracks. Sometimes the best route proceeds through the water on an angle and doesn't follow a straight and obvious path.

- It's smart to **prepare for the worst.** Don't attempt to cross a river if you don't have access to a phone and a reliable signal to call for help in case of an emergency. In remote areas of the country where river crossings are most common, it can be hours (or longer) before you meet other people.

- Don't forget to assess the area for **dangerous wildlife.** I wouldn't want to stall a vehicle in the middle of a river with a crocodile on its bank, would you?

- Avoid crossing a river **after dark** when it's next to impossible to assess water depth, condition, and current, not to mention roadblocks and other hazards. Stranding yourself anywhere at nighttime is never safe.

If and when you're good to go (make sure your windows are down and your doors are unlocked), drive slowly but steadily through the water. Don't stop halfway in and don't gun the vehicle to create unnecessary and potentially engine-drowning waves. When you make it across, give yourself a pat on the back for journeying through the jungle like a pro—but don't make it a habit. Each crossing is different, and river conditions can change instantaneously. You can never fully predict what lies ahead.

Private Transfer Service

A great option for families, private transfer services can transport you and your travel companions between destinations in air-conditioned tourist vans typically built for 8-12 occupants. Modern services include complimentary onboard Wi-Fi. Included in the cost, which may be $75-400 each way, is the driver's service and your choice of pick-up time. Some service providers apply a surcharge for departures between 7pm and 7am. Brief stops along the way, typically up to one hour, are permitted. Longer stops require extra payment to cover the driver's time. If you're headed to a remote location, this service type may be the only possible means of transport.

Shared Shuttle Service

Shared shuttle services, which operate vehicles similar to those used by private transfer services, are a form of public transportation.

They're also one of the most popular ways to get around Costa Rica. Van seats are reserved on an individual basis and are priced per person per way; some service providers offer reduced rates to child travelers. Connecting the most popular tourist destinations around the country, the services run according to set schedules and typically offer one or two departure times daily per route. A scheduled bathroom stop is provided along the way.

Boat, Ferry, and Water Taxi

Alternatives to ground transportation are boat, ferry, and water taxi rides. Common crossings take place over the Golfo de Nicoya, the Golfo Dulce, and Lago Arenal. Most ferries are large and can carry vehicles on board. Boats and water taxis are significantly smaller; some resemble safari boats, and others look like speedboats). Each service runs according to set schedules and is priced per person per way.

Visas and Officialdom

Many countries, including the United States and Canada, detail entrance requirements to Costa Rica on their own government websites. However, the official source of Costa Rica entry regulations is **La Dirección General de Migración y Extranjería** (General Directorate of Migration and Immigration, www.migracion.go.cr). Up-to-date entry requirements are posted on the department's website.

DOCUMENTS AND REQUIREMENTS
Entry

Entry into Costa Rica requires presentation of a signed, legible, and unexpired **passport** with enough space to receive official stamps. Although you may not be asked to provide this documentation, legally you must come to Costa Rica prepared to provide **proof of intent to exit** before your entry stamp expires; most entry stamps are valid for 90 days. A prepurchased onward flight or bus ticket to another country qualifies as proof of your intent to depart Costa Rica, as does a cruise ship vacation confirmation if you plan to arrive and leave by boat. You must also be able to show that you have **access to at least $300** ($100 for each potential 30-day stay within the standard 90-day access period) to support you during your visit.

Your country of origin determines whether you need a **visa** to enter Costa Rica, as well as whether your passport must be valid for a minimum of one day, three months, or six months. More than 60 countries, including the United States and Canada, are awarded the one-day validity period and do not need a visa. Countries that must abide by the three-month validity period do not require a visa. Countries that must have a passport valid for six months also require a visa to enter Costa Rica. See the website of La Dirección General de Migración y Extranjería for lists of countries that form the various groups.

Minors traveling on their own to Costa Rica must have both a valid passport and **written authorization** to travel from their parents or legal guardians.

In addition to passport requirements, travelers from several African and South American countries must provide proof of **yellow fever vaccination** in order to enter Costa Rica. This requirement could also apply to other nationals who have recently traveled to the flagged countries. A list of the flagged countries can be obtained from the World Health Organization's website (www.who.int) or by calling La Dirección General de Migración y Extranjería (tel. 506/2299-8100). According to some foreign health organizations, vaccinations that protect against hepatitis A, hepatitis B, typhoid, and rabies are suggested but not mandatory. Make sure your routine vaccinations are up to date.

Departure

In order to leave Costa Rica by air, you must pay the **departure tax** ($29 pp). Most airlines incorporate the cost of the tax into the price of their flights. Double-check your airfare's fine print—the charge is usually noted in the price breakdown—to determine if the tax has already been paid. If not, you'll need to pay it at the airport's departure tax desk prior to approaching the airline counter. Some hotels and vehicle rental agencies can pay the tax for you in advance if you'd prefer to save the time and hassle the day you fly.

FOREIGN EMBASSIES

Most foreign embassies are in San José. The **U.S. Embassy** (just north of Road 104, 1.5 km northwest of the Parque Metropolitano La Sabana, tel. 506/2519-2000, www.cr.usembassy.gov, 8am-4:30pm Mon.-Fri.), the **Canadian Embassy** (just east of Road 177, on the south side of Parque Metropolitano La Sabana, tel. 506/2242-4400, www.canadainternational.gc.ca/costa_rica, 8am-4pm Mon.-Thurs., 7:30am-1pm Fri.), and the **British Embassy** (corner of Paseo Colón and Calle 38, tel. 506/2258-2025, www.gov.uk/world/organisations/british-embassy-in-costa-rica, 8am-4pm Mon.-Thurs., 8am-1pm Fri.) are all on the west side of the city.

Recreation

When you depart from one of Costa Rica's international airports, you may be approached by a representative of the **Instituto Costarricense de Turismo** (Costa Rican Institute of Tourism, ICT) and asked a few brief questions about the activities you engaged in during your visit. The polls, published on the ICT website in Spanish and English, primarily help tourism businesses understand which excursions garner the most attention. But the findings can also help you build your bucket list. The fact that 18 of the top 25 experiences cited in the poll (2013-2017) are recreational activities speaks volumes. Getting out and experiencing Costs Rica is a large part of what traveling here is all about.

The activities described in this guide are some of Costa Rica's most prominent. Consider participating in at least two or three— ideally as many as your itinerary, budget, and energy level permit—to understand for yourself why Costa Rica is considered an adventure destination. Most activities require advance reservations.

Your safety is never fully guaranteed. Accidents can and do happen, sometimes because of a negligent tour operator and other times due to unforeseen events. Select your preferred tour operators carefully; at minimum, stick to those that come recommended in this guide or by other trusted sources. Many won't allow people with health conditions, individuals who are recovering from an operation, or pregnant women to participate in their activities out of concern for participants' well-being.

ZIP-LINING

A favorite recreational activity of many travelers is zip-lining. After being secured in a harness and connected to a pulley with carabiners, you'll be thrust through the forest or skim the top of it while you glide (or "zip") across thick cables (most routes have 7 to 13 cables). While these tours are offered all around Costa Rica, most take place in lush, verdant areas where the scenery is most impressive. The best ones are in **La Fortuna** and **Monteverde.**

Nearly all zip-line tour operators enforce a minimum age requirement; typically, children must be at least 3-8 years old. A few also enforce maximum weight limits. Contact the operator for details, as limits depend on the particular zip line's materials and equipment.

Zip-lining activities are also called **canopy tours** in Costa Rica. This term can apply to any experience that takes place around the treetop canopy, including **hanging bridge tours.** As a rule, if an experience is advertised as a canopy tour, it's a zip-line tour.

Most commonly, zip-lining tours require participants to brake manually, with their hands, which requires you to wear a thick glove and place gentle pressure on the cable to slow yourself down. The process sounds more difficult than it is, but if you're concerned about it, go with a tour operator that uses a handlebar system. With this option, you grasp the handlebars and jostle them back and forth to reduce your speed. If you have a fear of heights, skip zip-lining altogether; the experience requires you to stand atop high platforms and soar above the forest floor. In most cases, once you begin the circuit, there's no turning back.

Although zip-line tours take place around the forest, they're hardly wildlife-spotting excursions. While you may get lucky and see birds, butterflies, insects, frogs, monkeys, and maybe even sloths along the way, it's best not to expect any sightings to avoid disappointment.

WHITE-WATER RAFTING

White-water rafting tours are one of the most exciting adventures you can have in Costa Rica. They're also loved for the scenery they showcase, especially the tall walls of jungle you'll raft through if you go out on **Río Pacuare.** The most popular rivers for rafting in the country flow through the Caribbean, the Central Pacific, and Guanacaste regions, but rafting tour operators are spread out around the country and offer tours with round-trip transportation to several rivers from most other regions. Most companies enforce a minimum age requirement that varies by river according to the class of the rapids. On average, tours on Class III and IV rivers (the most common for white-water rafting in

Costa Rica) require child participants to be at least 12 years old. Class II and III rivers, typically rafted only by families with young children, tend to allow kids as young as 6 years old to participate.

No previous experience is necessary for participation in white-water rafting tours; however, you should be in good physical condition, be able operate a paddle, feel comfortable around water, and have a thirst for thrills. Don't forget to smile as you maneuver each rapid. Most rafting tour outfitters employ photographers and sell photos at the end of the trip as souvenirs.

The chance of getting sunburned can be high, and the results severe, given the many hours spent on the water. Make sure you apply a waterproof variety of high-SPF sunscreen generously and frequently throughout the day. Most rafts have a waterproof barrel for storage, and many tour guides carry dry bags as well. Any medication you may need during the day can be stored in the raft. Tour outfitters provide also secure storage for other items that you won't need in the raft, such as a set of dry clothes to change into, a towel, and money.

HOT SPRINGS

Offering supreme relaxation are the country's several hot spring attractions, located primarily around the **La Fortuna** and **Rincón de la Vieja** areas. Hot spring visits, where you soak in rejuvenating thermal-water rivers and pools, are one of the best rewards you can give yourself, not to mention a great way to recover from physically demanding, adventure-filled days. Some attractions are small and informal, with a limited number of pools. Others occupy resort properties and are rich with beautiful views, waterfalls, and swim-up bars.

Visitor passes may be purchased for a block of time or a full day, depending on the property. Purchase passes well in advance if you plan to travel during the high season, as spaces will sell out. Most sites offer complimentary towels (with a deposit) and the option to rent a locker. Outside food and drinks are not permitted, but most attractions have at least one restaurant on-site. Some visitor passes include lunch or dinner in their rates.

SURFING, SNORKELING, AND SCUBA DIVING

Scheduling water sports during your trip depends greatly on ocean conditions. Always have your chosen water sport provider confirm the latest conditions to avoid snorkeling or diving when the water visibility is poor, or surfing when waves are lackluster.

The long Pacific coast provides breaks for surfers of all skill levels. Lessons are offered in abundance if you want them. Surf trips to popular breaks are available to advanced-level riders. Beware of riptides, rip currents, and undertows that make many coastal areas downright dangerous.

Scuba diving requires a valid certification through **PADI** (the Professional Association of Diving Instructors). If you don't obtain one before you travel, you can do so through most dive shops in beach communities, assuming you have two full days to commit to the course. If your dream is to dive at **Parque Nacional Isla del Coco**—the world-renowned dive spot 550 kilometers off Costa Rica's Central Pacific coast—you'll need to sign up months in advance for an 8- to-12-day ship excursion and have roughly $5,000-7,000 to shell out for the experience.

SEA TURTLE NESTING TOURS

Several varieties of sea turtles are known to nest on many of the beaches in Costa Rica. You'll have the best luck witnessing an *arribada* (arrival) by visiting **Parque Nacional Marino Las Baulas** between October and March, the **Refugio Nacional de Vida Silvestre Ostional** from May to December, the **Refugio de Vida Silvestre Camaronal** between June and December, or **Parque Nacional Tortuguero** from March to October. Visits to most sites during off-season periods produce few sightings. Gatherings within the Refugio Nacional de Vida Silvestre Ostional, especially between August and December, are particularly impressive because adult sea turtles storm the beach in massive groups.

Turtle nesting tours aren't for the impatient. They involve very little activity, apart from waiting on a beach for turtles to arrive. In many cases, the experience takes place in the late evening, and in almost all cases, it is guided by a government-approved tour guide. Dark clothing is required, and the use of lights (beyond a flashlight used by the guide) is not permitted.

HIKING

Nature trails in government-regulated or private land areas known as *parques nacionales* (national parks), *reservas biológicas* (biological reserves), or *refugios* (refuges) exist in all regions of Costa Rica. Self-guided exploration is permitted at most, typically without advance reservations, but it's still a good idea to visit these places with a guide. There is a lot to gain from having a guide at your side, the most obvious benefit being the guide's wealth of knowledge. Knowing where to walk to avoid stepping on a snake, which trees to look at to see birds and sloths, which insect species produce the sounds you hear, why certain root systems look the way they do, and countless other lessons are what turn ordinary walks into educational journeys and extraordinary wildlife-spotting opportunities. In some areas of the country—generally remote regions—guides are strongly recommended for the navigational support and extra security they provide.

Hiking conditions and experiences vary immensely due to Costa Rica's diverse terrain, elevation, weather, and ecosystems. Some hikes are quick walks along paved and sometimes wheelchair-accessible paths. Others are incredibly challenging multiday climbs through narrow clearings in the forest. You can feel the coolness of clouds on your cheeks in several areas; in others, you may need to wipe sweat from your brow due to the humidity. Familiarize yourself with trail lengths and levels of difficulty before setting out, to avoid hiking a route that is either too physically intense or not stimulating enough.

HANGING BRIDGES

There are plenty of ways to explore nature in Costa Rica; one of them is by touring a series of hanging bridges. Essentially a calm and quiet nature hike with uphill and downhill sections, this experience allows you to walk through the forest and cross a series of bridges along the way. The best place for these is in **La Fortuna** or **Monteverde.** Most hanging bridge attractions offer a combination of stationary bridges and suspension bridges, the latter typically being the highest and the longest. There's a rush that comes with standing in the middle of a suspension bridge, completely surrounded by the sights and sounds of the rainforest or the cloud forest. Amid the leafy treetop canopy, you'll have decent bird-watching and wildlife-spotting opportunities. Hanging bridge attractions can be explored with or without a tour guide.

Food

TYPICAL DISHES

Costa Ricans consume fruit, meat, rice, and beans multiple times daily in a variety of forms. Literally meaning "spotted rooster" in English, **gallo pinto** (a traditional rice and bean blend) is served each morning. In addition to *gallo pinto,* a typical Costa Rican **desayuno** (breakfast) includes fresh fruit, a tortilla with a slice of cheese, or made-to-order *huevos* (eggs). Eggs can be requested *fritos* (fried), *picados* or *revueltos* (both terms mean scrambled), *tiernos* (over easy), or sometimes *duros* (hard boiled). *Café* (coffee), *té* (tea), *agua* (water), and *jugo* (juice) are commonly served drinks.

Casado (a traditional dish that marries servings of rice and beans on a plate, accompanied by a variety of side dishes) is consumed at **almuerzo** (lunch) and/or **cena** (dinner). *Queso frito* (fried cheese) and *plátano frito* (fried plantain, also called *plátano maduro*) commonly accompany the meal, as does a mix of vegetables, typically including *palmito* (heart of palm). **Tres leches** (a sweet cake soaked with three kinds of milk and topped with whipped cream) and **flan de coco** (coconut flan) are delectable, must-try desserts.

Costa Rican food in general is flavorful but lightly seasoned. Spices are passed over for herbs, and the leafy, dark-green cilantro adds a flavorful zip to most dishes. Although some preparations are bland on their own, vinaigrettes, oils, and homemade salsas like *pico de gallo* (diced tomato, pepper, onion, and pineapple mixed with cilantro and lemon juice) enhance the flavors of most foods.

During holidays or special events, **tamales, chicharrones** (fried pork rinds), and **churros** appear on many Costa Rican tables. Sold from carts regularly stationed at beaches and in public parks are **ceviche** (raw seafood or fish marinated in citrus) and **copos** (snow cone-inspired desserts topped with syrup and condensed milk). On the Caribbean coast, Afro-Costa Rican specialties take center stage, including **rondón** (a fish and vegetable coconut-milk soup flavored with Caribbean spices), **patís** (savory turnovers often stuffed with meat, pineapple, or plantain), and **pan bon** (a dark sweet bread).

DIETARY RESTRICTIONS

Over the last decade, Costa Rican cooking has shifted toward worldwide culinary trends. Most chefs and waitstaff are conscious of gluten-free diets, as well as what vegetarians and vegans will and won't eat. Organic fruit, vegetable, and coffee plantations dot the country, making for fabulous farm-to-table meals at health-conscious restaurants and accommodations.

Being a **vegetarian** in Costa Rica isn't difficult. Some dishes, like *arroz con vegetales* (rice with vegetables), are naturally vegetarian, and others can be made so simply by asking for the serving without meat. Since Costa Rica's bean-based diet is packed with protein, you shouldn't need to supplement your meals. If you're a **pescatarian,** you'll find yourself surrounded by variety, as many menus include meat and fish plates equally. Not surprisingly, the best fish and seafood in the country are served along the coasts.

Vegans may struggle to find meal options at most run-of-the-mill restaurants. But every day it seems a new little café, diner, or high-end restaurant has popped up with the purpose of catering to vegans. Seek out these specialty eateries and you'll find a fantastic repertoire of creative, innovative, and delicious meals worth eating more than once.

If you avoid **gluten,** it is best to have restaurant waitstaff confirm which menu items contain it. Recipes vary across establishments, so treating meals on a case-by-case basis is the smartest approach. Gluten-free cooking is one of the more recent trends to hit Costa Rica, and not all restaurants have caught up with suitable menu options. A select few have opted to be 100 percent gluten-free.

DRINKS

On humid days, you can quench your thirst with nonalcoholic **batidos** (smoothies) made to order with fresh tropical fruits including *banano* (banana), *piña* (pineapple), *mora* (blackberry), mango, and papaya. The drinks can be made with milk or water. If you're up for something different, give the local delicacy *cas* (guava) a go, or try a glass of **agua de tamarindo** (juice produced from tamarind pulp). **Pipa fría** (cold coconut water) is typically consumed directly from the coconut and is sold all over Costa Rica, generally on beaches, in markets, and at roadside stands. Locally produced alcoholic drinks include **Imperial** and **Pilsen beer, Ron Centenario rum,** and **Cacique guaro** (sugarcane liquor).

By a landslide, **café** (coffee) wins as the most beloved drink in the nation. It's consumed morning, noon, and night. Some restaurants and attractions like coffee plantations and roasteries prepare the beverage traditionally and tableside in a *chorreador* (a wood device equipped with a cloth filter used to brew coffee).

RESTAURANTS
Sodas

Inexpensive *sodas* (traditional Costa Rican family restaurants) are much more than restaurants; they're authentic establishments, popular gathering places, and sources of the best Costa Rican cuisine. Often found in city centers or markets frequented by locals, these informal establishments, which are sometimes open-air structures filled with picnic tables, are bursting with unassuming character.

Menus feature Costa Rican staples, usually with a few pasta or sandwich options thrown in. Several offer small buffet bars— usually in the back, near the kitchen—where you can try an assortment of traditional foods. The best spots will top off your visit with a small, complimentary bowl of *arroz con leche* (rice pudding). With hundreds to *sodas* pick from all over Costa Rica (even small towns typically have more than one), you can dine at many throughout your trip if you're looking to save money, indulge in the local cuisine, and feel what it's like to live like a Tico.

Tourist-Geared

If you grow tired of eating at *sodas*, there's no shortage of tourism-oriented restaurants that will happily accept your business. Choices span all kinds of establishments from large steak houses to cozy pizzerias to tiny cafés. Cuisines from all over the world are represented, with a slant toward American, Argentinean, Italian, French, and Chinese influences. There are also many Costa Rican restaurants (more formal than *sodas*) that serve *comida típica* (typical food) with fancy presentations and above-average service. Some proudly showcase the nation's culture through employee uniforms that copy traditional dress; live music; and dance performances.

Fine Dining

Fine dining isn't the norm in Costa Rica, but several fantastic options exist. The Central Valley and Highlands offer the greatest concentration and cater to capital city business-people. Spread out around the country are some others, many of which are at resort-quality hotels but are open to the public. (Some restaurants at all-inclusive resorts serve hotel guests only.) Fine dining in Costa Rica translates to a nice restaurant with a warm or romantic ambience, top-notch service, and enjoyable food and drinks—and not much else. You can leave your black-tie attire at home, as there's little use for it here.

Accommodations

Costa Rica offers an immense selection of accommodation types. The types, however, are difficult to define, due to the fluid use of terminology across the industry. As you familiarize yourself with the options, keep in mind that similar hotels may describe themselves in completely different ways. Likewise, two accommodations that couldn't be more different from each other may label themselves as the same kind of establishment—for example, a resort. Use the categories here as a guide, but also recognize that many places don't fall neatly into one.

Lodging prices are determined by many factors, including reputation, location, size, style, room amenities, on-site facilities, travel season, and inclusions (such as meals). **Prices vary significantly within each category.** Hostels, the least expensive lodging option, offer beds in shared rooms as low as $10 per person, but I've seen private rooms in a hostel go for more than $150 a night. A room at a hotel might cost $50 per night in a rural area during the low season but $200 per night at a popular destination during the high season. Adding to the confusion, some resorts cost less than some rustic lodges. Don't make presumptions about cost or quality based on accommodation type.

When selecting your accommodation, **prioritize location.** Accommodations can be in downtown cores where noise may be an issue; on the outskirts of town and a taxi ride, walk, or drive to dining options; down a poorly maintained road; in sketchy areas you may prefer to avoid; or even in areas only accessible by small plane or boat. They may also fall outside of common tour excursion pickup zones, which means you'll end up paying surcharges to tour operators for pickups and drop-offs every time you wish to participate in a guided activity. Find accommodations with desirable locations first, according to your interests, needs, and comfort level, before narrowing down the choices according to secondary factors like price, style, and ambience.

Be aware that the sewage lines below some accommodations in the country don't process toilet paper well. Most places will ask that you deposit paper into waste bins.

HOSTELS

Hostels in Costa Rica are not unlike hostels elsewhere in the world. Each typically offers a few dormitories—capacity ranges from 4 to 16 people—and many provide women-only rooms. Most are outfitted with bunk beds, but a few offer single beds. Bathrooms are also shared, as are kitchens and common areas.

Although nearly all hostels cater to young travelers, the ambience in hostels varies significantly. Some have game rooms, television lounges, swimming pools, and a vibrant social atmosphere, while others have libraries or reading nooks and a calmer vibe. Almost all offer a handful of private rooms, usually for 1-4 people.

HOTELS

Hotels range from small and informal buildings to modern high-rises, some with 5 individually styled rooms and others with 100 nearly identical suites. Many resemble one- or two-story motels. Most others comprise multiple structures separated from one another by paved paths or nature trails. Sometimes these structures are called *cabinas* or *cabañas* (both mean cabins), **bungalows, villas,** or **casitas** (little houses). The five terms are used interchangeably.

BED-AND-BREAKFASTS

Many B&Bs in Costa Rica are no different than hotels. Several strive to provide guests with the quintessential homey, service-oriented experience that differentiates B&Bs from other accommodations elsewhere in the world, but others simply use the name. If you plan to stay at a B&B, research the accommodation thoroughly to determine the type of experience you'll have.

RANCHES AND LODGES

If you plan to stay at a ranch or lodge, expect accommodations that are rustic in design and decor. Although hotels built as *cabinas, cabañas,* bungalows, villas, and casitas often provide a similar look and feel, ranches and lodges are almost always bucolic. Sometimes they're set on farms and offer a slew of rural activities from horseback riding to cow milking. It's worth noting, however, that these kinds of experiences aren't limited to ranches and lodges; many hotels and resorts (as well as theme parks and small-scale attractions) operate similar activities.

RESORTS

Where Costa Rican accommodations really play it loose is with the term "resort." In most cases, the word refers to a high-quality accommodation, but I've come across several that are mid-range hotels at best. Always research resort options before you select one,

and don't rule out small properties; sometimes they're the most intimate and provide the best service.

Most resorts are not **all-inclusive,** meaning that three daily meals and beverages are not automatically included. However, several all-inclusive resorts do exist, especially in Guanacaste (which is home to many of the country's most exclusive accommodations) and in the Osa Peninsula and southern Pacific region (where remoteness and a lack of dining establishments require meals to be provided).

An **eco-resort,** an unregulated title some accommodations bestow upon themselves, is an accommodation that engages in environmentally friendly practices. Not necessarily high-quality accommodations, eco-resorts may be small, family-run hotels, woodsy lodges, or high-end contemporary resorts. Some eco-resorts have earned a **Certificación para la Sostenibilidad Turística** (Certification of Sustainable Tourism). The program is a good starting point for finding green businesses in Costa Rica, but don't dismiss an eco-resort (or any Costa Rican business) if it doesn't have the CST. There are plenty of sustainable properties worth your consideration that aren't part of the program.

VACATION HOME RENTALS

With the rise of companies like **Airbnb** (www.airbnb.com), **VRBO** (www.vrbo.com), **FlipKey** (www.flipkey.com), and **HomeAway** (www.homeaway.com), it has never been easier to find a house to crash at throughout your Costa Rica travels. But the option isn't always safe, especially if you plan to travel alone or to remote areas. If you like the idea of having a large space to spread out in and an opportunity to cook your own meals, you'll find many hotels offer both. **Apartotels,** hotels outfitted with apartment-style rooms, may be exactly what you're looking for.

HOMESTAYS

Homestays are typically coordinated in conjunction with volunteer stints. Some school and research groups use them as well. Arrangements are usually handled by program administrators. It is uncommon for foreigners to stay with Costa Rican families otherwise, unless a personal connection exists between the groups.

Conduct and Customs

Many Costa Ricans value humility; off-putting behavior typically receives a wry expression of *"¡Qué humilde!"* ("How humble!"). Costa Rican culture also prioritizes relationships with family and friends over money. This means that rude behavior, typically with respect to showing off money, isn't well received. Bartering for lower prices is viewed as tacky, as is waving around cash or acting entitled.

SALUTATIONS AND ETIQUETTE

The most common greeting in Costa Rica is *"Hola"* ("Hello"), followed by either *"Buenos días"* ("Good morning"), *"Buenas tardes"* ("Good afternoon"), *"Buenas noches"* ("Good evening"), or *"¿Cómo está?"* ("How are you?"). Shaking hands takes place in the workplace. Kissing on one cheek is common among family members and close friends. Use of either is rare within tourism settings.

Costa Ricans practice most of the same rules of etiquette that the majority of North Americans are accustomed to. Act politely, don't dress provocatively around religious centers and during homestays, and give up your seat on the bus if you see an elderly person or a parent with a child standing in the aisle.

PUNCTUALITY

Within the tourism industry (which is partially driven by expat business owners), operations from guided tours to transportation services run like clockwork on set schedules. Outside the realm of tourism, Costa Rica's laid-back *pura vida* attitude contributes to a general lack of urgency across personal and business affairs. **Tico time,** a phrase describing the slow pace at which things tend to progress, is a reality in Costa Rica. Be patient if service is slow.

HOLIDAYS, FESTIVALS, AND EVENTS

Costa Ricans rarely miss an opportunity to gather with family and friends. Holidays are always celebrated, and cultural events draw crowds of locals. *Fiestas cívicas* (civic festivals), which take place in towns throughout Costa Rica, usually during the summer, are an excuse to party, indulge in fair food, and catch live performances.

The country also hosts a ton of great festivals and events. A few to consider planning your trip around include the **Ocaso Underground Music Festival** (www. ocasofestival.com) in Tamarindo, **Jungle Jam** (www.junglejam.com) and **Bamboo Bass** (www.bamboobassfestival.com) in Jacó, and the **Envision Festival** (www. envisionfestival.com) in Uvita. Plenty of sporting events add to the list, including international *fútbol* games held at San José's **Estadio Nacional de Costa Rica** (National Stadium of Costa Rica). Schedules and sometimes locations change from year to year; see event websites for details.

Costa Rican Celebrations

- January 1: **Año Nuevo** (New Year's Day; nationwide)

- Mid-January: **Fiestas de Palmares** (Palmares Festivals; Palmares)

- February/March: **Mardi Gras** (Playa Flamingo); date corresponds with Lent

- March/April: **Semana Santa** (Holy Week; nationwide); date corresponds with Easter

- March 14: **Día de los Boyeros** (Day of the Oxcart Drivers; San Antonio de Escazú)

- Late March: **Feria de la Mascarada** (Masquerade Fair; Barva)

- April 11: **Día de Juan Santamaría** (Juan Santamaría Day; nationwide)

- May 1: **Día Internacional del Trabajo** (International Labor Day; nationwide)

- Mid-July: **Fiesta de la Virgen del Mar** (Virgin of the Sea Festival; Playas del Coco, Puntarenas, and a few other coastal towns) and **Festival Internacional de Calypso** (International Calypso Festival; Cahuita)

- July 25: **Anexión de Guanacaste** (Annexation of Guanacaste; nationwide but mainly Guanacaste)

- August 2: **Día de la Virgen de los Ángeles** (Virgin of the Angels Day; nationwide but mainly Cartago)

- August 15: **Día de la Madre** (Mother's Day; nationwide)

- September/October/November: **Feria de Pejibaye** (Peach Palm Fruit Fair; Turrialba)

- September: **Festival de Ballenas y Delfines** (Whale and Dolphin Festival; Uvita)

- September 15: **Día de la Independencia** (Independence Day; nationwide)

- October 12: **Día de las Culturas** (Culture Day; nationwide)

- Mid-October: **Carnaval del Caribe** (Caribbean Carnival; nationwide but mainly in Limón)

- Early December: **Iluminación del Museo de los Niños** (Lighting of the Children's Museum; San José)

- Mid-December: **Festival de la Luz** (Festival of Light, San José)

- December 25: **Navidad** (Christmas; nationwide)

Health and Safety

HEALTH

Potential health hazards are ubiquitous in Costa Rica, but most won't cause a problem if you pay attention and take normal precautions. Pack a basic first aid kit so you can treat minor cuts, scrapes, burns, stings, bites, and sprains. Cleanse and disinfect your hands often, especially after visiting areas where wildlife is present. If you fall ill or suffer a major injury (severe bleeding, bruising, vomiting, or having a high fever are clear indicators), seek medical attention immediately.

In most developed areas of the country where tourism is present (except for the Caribbean), tap water is considered safe to drink and is consumed by locals. Bottled water is preferred by most travelers and is widely available for purchase at grocery stores and restaurants.

Diseases and Common Ailments

Dengue, chikungunya, malaria, and the **Zika virus** are the most pressing health concerns for visitors. However, cases of each are rare. Travelers are more likely to encounter episodes of **traveler's diarrhea,** which can be treated with over-the-counter medications or by letting it run its course. Most of the time, the upset is caused by a sudden change of diet; eating or drinking lots of fresh tropical fruit can bring it on too. Don't let yourself get dehydrated; drink water regularly.

Bites, Stings, and Sun Exposure

There's no shortage of bugs, bees, spiders, scorpions, and snakes in the forests, and there's little you can do after you've been bitten or stung by one—apart from waiting out the itch or burn or seeking medical care. Travel proactively. Use **waterproof sunscreen** and a strong **insect repellent.** Some people swear by Avon's **Skin So Soft** line, which has a few bug guard options. Others prefer products with **DEET.** Regardless of which product you purchase, buy it in a spray bottle (not an aerosol) so it's suited for air travel.

Use **mosquito nets** whenever they're provided with accommodations. Shake out shoes, towels, and clothes, especially items that have been left outside, before putting them on or packing them away. Check under beds and tables and in baths and showers for surprise guests. Keep unscreened windows closed as often as you can. Limit time spent around swampy areas or walking around at night. Avoid being out in the sun for long periods of time to prevent sunstroke. If you have open wounds, keep them fully covered while you're active during the day to help prevent infection.

MEDICAL CARE

In the event of an emergency, call **911.** Ambulances can also be reached by phoning **128** or the central office of the **Cruz Roja** (Red Cross, tel. 506/2542-5000, www. cruzroja.or.cr), which has several stations around the country. Serious illnesses and injuries should be treated at the *emergencias* (emergencies) department of a **hospital.** The majority of hospitals in Costa Rica have one.

If you're far from a hospital, you can visit a **clinic.** Some are small, informal public clinics, and others are top-of-the-line private medical centers. Nearly every town has at least one clinic, typically an *ebais* overseen by the government-run **Caja Costarricense de Seguro Social** (Costa Rican Social Security Fund, CCSS or simply the Caja, www.ccss.sa.cr). The CCSS also oversees public hospitals. Several private hospitals dot the nation and are known for providing the highest level of medical care in Costa Rica.

For non-urgent concerns, some large hotels have on-call medical professionals on retainer. Most towns have at least one **pharmacy** (cities typically have many) stocked with run-of-the-mill items including medications for headaches, stomachaches, muscle soreness, itch relief, and countless other conditions. Pharmacies also carry a range of contraceptives. A surprising number of pharmacies in touristy areas have English-speaking staff.

SAFETY

When common sense is exercised, traveling throughout Costa Rica is generally safe. Travelers should be extra alert in San José and cities around the Central Valley. These areas account for roughly 70 percent of all victim-based crimes in Costa Rica); the Caribbean accounts for an additional 10 percent. Always keep your wits about you wherever you go.

In case of an emergency, it's easiest to call **911,** which will connect you to the police for assistance. If you're a victim of a crime, you can contact the **tourist police** (tel. 506/2286-1473), who typically have English-speaking staff, and/or the **Organismo de Investigación Judicial** (Judicial Investigation Agency, OIJ, tel. 506/2295-3000, www.sitiooij.poder-judicial. go.cr), Costa Rica's central crime investigation unit. For assistance with less pressing matters, you can ask for help from accommodation or restaurant staff, vehicle rental agencies, or tourism companies. Most Ticos are willing to lend a helping hand.

If you need to reach the fire department, dial **118,** or call the regular emergency dispatch via 911 and ask for the *bomberos* (firefighters).

Police

Costa Rica has two police forces that operate under different divisions of the government. Under the watch of the **Ministerio de Obras Públicas y Transportes** (Ministry of Public Works and Transportation, MOPT), the *policia de tránsito* (transit police) oversee transportation-related matters that pertain to permissions and licenses, driving laws, and parking infractions. They usually wear uniforms with white shirts and vests (typically with *Tránsito* on them) and drive navy-blue pickup trucks or motorcycles. You'll see them along the sides of roads and highways with their radars ready to catch speeders.

Under the umbrella of the **Ministerio de Seguridad Pública** (Ministry of Public Security, MSP), the *fuerza pública* (public force) maintains public safety in Costa Rica. Divisions of the group include border police, coast guards, and tourist police, the last of which have English-speaking officers to best assist travelers when problems arise. Officers of the *fuerza pública* usually wear navy-blue uniforms and vests (with *Policía* on them) and drive white pickup trucks, motorcycles, or sedans.

Police stations, open 24 hours daily, are scattered throughout the country. Most cities and large towns have one, but they're noticeably absent from several beachside communities.

Robbery and Theft

Countrywide, theft is a problem. Instances usually occur in the form of **pickpocketing** or theft of possessions left in or on unattended areas like beaches, parked vehicles, and bus storage compartments. To minimize risk, use hotel safes whenever provided, hide your camera equipment while sightseeing, and don't wear jewelry. Always keep your eyes on your luggage, especially at bus stations and airports, and keep your cash concealed; divide cash and hide it in various pockets across your body and belongings. Travel with a copy of your passport and important documents so you have backups in the event the originals are stolen. Better yet, email yourself electronic copies so there's always a copy to retrieve if needed.

Assault

Episodes of assault against travelers, especially violent assault, are rare, but they do happen. Some of the most unfortunate incidents are the result of opportunistic nighttime attacks. There are actions you can take to lower your risk of becoming a target. Being vigilant at night is a must. After dark, don't withdraw money at ATMs, drive (if possible), or hang out on the beach or in any city park.

There is safety in numbers; travel with others whenever possible and stick to areas where people are regularly present. If you are a solo traveler—and especially if you're traveling during the low season, when many towns become desolate—visit popular destinations. If you decide to go out at night alone, especially to drink, you're an easy target.

Water and Beach Safety

Dangerous riptides, rip currents, and undertows exist off the shores of many beaches along both coasts. Do yourself a favor and research how to get out of a riptide before you travel. Most beaches in Costa Rica are not staffed with lifeguards, but an increasing number have signposts that issue stern warnings. Abide by them! Costa Rica's open water

Travel Smartly and Safely

Maintaining awareness of your surroundings while you travel can save your life. Vacationing in Costa Rica is exciting, and it's easy to get caught up in the thrill. When you vow to leave your troubles behind on vacation, you may detach yourself from other realities too. Try to maintain a clear head, even while it's pumped full of adrenaline and clouded by the chaos of travel. At the very least, these suggestions should help you become a more conscious and prepared traveler.

Don't sacrifice safety for selfies. Accidents and sometimes deaths have occurred as a result of people taking selfies. Remember, your trip is just a trip! No Instagram-worthy photo of you in a risky place or position is worth your life.

Trust your instincts. Your gut knows when something is wrong. If you're unsure about an experience, such as the safety of a vehicle or an activity, the remoteness of a town, the qualifications of a tour guide, the preparation of a meal, or the condition of a back road route, don't take the chance.

Remain cautious when befriending strangers. Ticos are friendly and social people. Making a friend or two is common, and it isn't a bad idea so long as you keep your willingness to trust others in check. Exercise caution if strangers invites you out, whether to a bar, the beach, or their home, especially at night.

Be (and stay) organized. Balance relaxation with organization. You can be lazy on vacation; just don't forget to monitor your belongings and watch where you walk. When you let your guard down, someone (with sticky fingers and their eyes on your stuff) or something (like a fallen tree limb you could easily trip over) could make your travel experience miserable.

Plan the details too. Beyond the time you've put into choosing accommodations, securing transportation, and reserving tours, consider other details that will contribute to your travel experience. Estimate travel times between destinations so you can plan stops for snacks. Schedule ample sleep and rest each day to avoid physical exhaustion. Review restaurant menus online ahead of time.

claims far too many lives every year; it's one of the leading causes of accidental deaths in the nation. You may be a strong swimmer, but you're no match for the ocean.

Extreme caution should also be exercised around waterfalls and swimming holes, which are often surrounded by jagged rocks that make it easy to slip. Don't climb up the side of a waterfall, swim near the base of a powerful cascade, or jump from the top unless accompanied by a tour outfitter who has appropriately scouted out hazards and measured pool depth. Always keep young children and weak swimmers within arm's reach near oceans, lakes, rivers, streams, waterfalls, swimming holes, hot springs, and hotel pools.

As silly as it may sound, don't station yourself directly under the tall palms that back many of Costa Rica's beaches. Coconuts have been known to fall, and they can cause significant damage when dropped from great heights. Pick a shady spot elsewhere if you can. If you can't, lie under palm fronds as far away from the center of the tree as possible.

Getting Lost

Occasionally, hikers get lost in wooded areas because they either accidentally veered off course or chose to explore an area where access is not permitted. Most of Costa Rica's national parks, biological reserves, and wildlife refuges provide well-marked trails that are easy to follow. It's not difficult to stick to the paths, but it's always a good idea to take a photo of the attraction's map when you enter, or take a hard copy if one exists. Some attractions are notorious for having untended trails. In these cases, having a tour guide who knows the area well is a must.

Travel Tips

WHAT TO PACK

Packing for Costa Rica depends largely on which destinations you intend to visit and which activities you plan to participate in. If you plan to engage in water activities or visit the beach often, consider packing **quick-dry clothing,** more than one bathing suit, and non-terrycloth towels. (Large microfiber cloths are great because they're thin, light, and super absorbent.) Sunscreen is widely available in Costa Rica, but it's more expensive than what you'll likely pay for it at home. Although flip-flops are suitable for the sand, if you plan to do a lot of walking around beach communities, you may prefer a sandal with a more supportive sole.

If most of your time will be spent out in nature, you'll want at least one pair of long pants (ideally of a light material), a long-sleeved shirt, and a broken-in pair of hiking boots or trail runners. Several attractions won't permit you to enter if your shoes have an open toe or slits of any kind, as Keen footwear often does. Insect repellent can be purchased in Costa Rica, but it comes at a premium. A small cloth is handy to keep in your pocket to wipe drips of sweat from your eyes as you traverse humid forests.

If you're into bird-watching or wildlife-spotting, **camouflage clothing** is best. Most tour guides supply spotting scopes, but bring your own set of binoculars so you can spot birds even when you're not on a guided adventure. If you plan to explore nature at high elevations, pack for colder temperatures. Multiday excursions may require overnight supplies, such as a sleeping bag.

Pack a pair of pants for adventure tours like horseback riding and activities that use harnesses (like zip-lining and canyoneering); a pair of strap-on sandals or running shoes (most adventure tours cannot be done in flip-flops); and clips or bands for eyeglasses or sunglasses.

Recommended items for all travelers include a **waterproof rain jacket** or **poncho** (umbrellas are impractical as they're difficult to use in dense forests and during adventure tours); a waterproof case or bag big enough to carry your phone, identification, and money; a small alarm clock for early morning tour or transfer service starts; a flashlight (it's dark by 6pm in Costa Rica); and **anti-nausea medication** to help you manage Costa Rica's curving, mountainous roads. A **backpack** (with a waterproof rain cover) is best for packing all your gear, but if you only have a suitcase, make sure it's small and light enough to lift with ease. Some routes—like trails to hotel rooms or bumpy roads to bus stations—aren't flat enough to allow luggage to be dragged.

Remember to leave some space in your suitcase for bringing home souvenirs. Popular choices include bagged coffee, bottled rum or *guaro* (sugarcane liquor), artwork (especially indigenous pieces), and wood products.

MONEY

The local currency in Costa Rica is the colón (pronounced coh-lohn). The plural form is colones (pronounced coh-loh-nays). Bills are offered in denominations of 50,000 (purple), 20,000 (orange), 10,000 (green), 5,000 (yellow), 2,000 (blue), and 1,000 (red). *Mil* (one thousand) is written on each: A bill stamped 50 mil colones is worth 50,000 colones. Gold-colored coins come in denominations of 500, 100, 50, 25, 10, and 5. Common monetary terms and phrases are: *dinero* (money), *plata* (a slang term for money used to imply cash), and *en efectivo* (to pay in cash).

Prices in Costa Rica appear in U.S. dollars or colones. Costa Rica uses a period instead of a comma in depicting numbers of 1,000 or greater. For example, if items in a shop are priced in colones, the price might appear as 10.000. This figure is equivalent to 10,000 colones. To make things even more complicated for U.S. and Canadian visitors, the symbol for colón (₡) is similar to the symbol that the United States and Canada use for cent (¢).

In popular tourist destinations, U.S. dollars are accepted by most businesses including accommodations, tour operators, transportation service providers, restaurants, souvenir stores, grocery stores, pharmacies, and gas stations. The majority will not accept Canadian dollars, euros, or other currencies unless their owner has a connection to the foreign country. Businesses in non-touristy towns and remote areas prefer payment in colones. Most establishments won't accept bills greater than US$20, so be sure to bring money in low denominations.

If you don't want to pay in cash, credit card payments (with Visa, Mastercard, and in fewer cases, American Express and Discover) are accepted by most establishments. If you have two cards, bring both to Costa Rica, in case the *cajero automático* (ATM) eats one, you lose one, or one gets stolen. Your card provider may charge fees if you use a credit card in the country, including one fee for out-of-country purchases and another for foreign exchange when charges are processed in colones. If you plan to visit ATMs often throughout your trip—only taking out small increments of money every few days of travel—you'll get hit with hefty service fees. To avoid paying unnecessary fees, travel with as much cash as you'll spend throughout your trip. If doing so makes you nervous, rely on ATMs and credit cards, and consider the extra fees payment for your peace of mind.

Payment Requests

Although Costa Rica is a popular tourist destination, many businesses are behind the times with respect to payment options. Payment policies vary across companies. Some will ask you to sign a **credit card authorization form** in order to guarantee bookings. This gives them permission to charge your credit card in the event of a last-minute cancellation or if you're a no-show. Some companies don't use credit card processing machines and only accept payment in cash.

Nearly every business will accept payment via **international wire transfer** (note that there's a transfer fee associated with this method), but only a small fraction of businesses will collect payment via convenient online tools like **PayPal.** A handful, including many water sport outfitters and vehicle rental agencies, need a copy of your identification.

Tax

Sales tax is 13 percent in Costa Rica. Tourism businesses are legally entitled to charge sales tax on top of their service rates. Most tour operators and transportation service providers automatically factor sales tax into their published rates.

Policies at accommodations and restaurants vary. Look for the phrase *impuesto de ventas incluido* (sales tax included, IVI) on websites and menus for confirmation. Be aware that many restaurants also impose a 10 percent service fee separate from sales tax. Restaurants might include one charge but not the other, so keep your eyes open for both.

Currency Exchange

The currency exchange rate hovers around US$1 to 600 colones. Always know the going rate to avoid losing money when making purchases. It helps to have a small conversion chart in your back pocket while you shop: 2,000 colones is roughly $3.50, 5,000 colones is roughly $8.50, and so on. Some businesses insist on applying their own exchange rates if you want to pay in U.S. dollars, which, not surprisingly, lean in their favor.

Money can be exchanged at airport counters, banks, and some hotels. No matter where you go in the country, if you pay for an item in U.S. dollars, you'll likely receive change in colones. You'll collect the currency over the course of your trip, so there's no need to convert all your money before you travel.

Tipping

Tipping isn't common among locals. But

since many foreigners, mainly Americans and Canadians, are accustomed to awarding gratuities at home, tipping has made its way to Costa Rica and is now an expectation in the tourism industry. If the level of service you receive warrants a tip, don't hesitate to give one.

Tour guides earn the highest amount, ranging around $5-10 per person per guide for short excursions and $5-15 per person per guide for full-day adventures. In most cases, tips can be handed directly to your tour guide. Some attractions provide tip boxes, and pooled tips are then divided among the staff.

Some restaurants charge an automatic 10 percent gratuity. In general, *sodas* don't do so, but tourist-geared establishments do. Look to the menu or waitstaff for confirmation. For exceptional service, a tip of up to 20 percent (including the automatic gratuity) is appropriate.

It's also kind to give a few dollars to hotel porters and to leave the same amount on your night table (sometimes an envelope is provided) for hotel housekeeping staff. Taxi drivers aren't usually tipped, but you can round up the fare if you like. You can also give a few dollars to private transfer service and shared shuttle service drivers, as well as boat and water taxi captains, as a thank you for providing safe travel.

COMMUNICATIONS
Telephones and Cell Phones

Telephone numbers in Costa Rica have eight digits. Most landlines begin with 2, and most cell phone numbers begin with 8. Many landline numbers correspond with geographical regions. For example, most landlines around La Fortuna begin with 2479, landlines around Manuel Antonio begin with 2777, and so on. Newer number assignments, which aren't yet common in the country, can start with 3, 4, 5, 6, or 7. Costa Rica's country code is 506, which does not need to be dialed when making local calls.

It's smart to have access to a cell phone in Costa Rica for navigational and emergency purposes. Unless your phone provider offers a phenomenal deal on international calling and data usage, you'll want to purchase a service plan in Costa Rica to avoid astronomical long distance and roaming fees. There are several Costa Rican providers to choose from, but I've found **Kölbi** (www.kolbi.cr) to be the most reliable. They have a small desk near baggage claim at the Aeropuerto Internacional Juan Santamaría where you can buy service and a SIM card ($4-20, depending on the quantity of data). Your phone must be unlocked to work in Costa Rica. Hold on to the casing of the SIM card and the paperwork you receive; the documents contain codes and numbers you'll need to activate and reload the service. Although Kölbi works well in most areas of the country, signal strength weakens as you venture into remote areas; this is the case regardless of which provider you choose.

Without a cell phone, you can make calls from phone booths in towns; they're usually in public parks or near street corners. Calling cards can be purchased from telecommunication offices and supermarkets. Several hotels offer free local calls, and some offer free international calling too.

Internet Access

Wireless internet is readily available in Costa Rica. Most accommodations provide it for free, but service may be limited to common areas like lobbies.

SPANISH-LANGUAGE SCHOOLS

Several Spanish-language schools are spread out around the country. Not surprisingly, institutes by the beach are popular. I like the **Nosara Spanish Institute** (tel. 506/2682-1460, www.nosaraspanishinstitute.com) in Nosara and the **WAYRA Instituto de Español** (tel. 506/2653-0359, www.spanishwayra.co.cr) in Tamarindo, both of which offer combined language and surf programs. **La Escuela del Sol** (tel. 506/8884-8444, www.laescueladelsol.com) near Montezuma combines Spanish with yoga. For an intimate learning experience, go with the small-scale

Instituto Estelar Bilingüe (tel. 506/2665-6921, www.estelarcr.com), based out of Liberia. One of the country's largest language schools, the **Centro Panamericano de Idiomas** (CPI, tel. 506/2265-6306, www.cpi-edu.com) has campuses in Heredia, Monteverde, and Playa Flamingo.

OPPORTUNITIES FOR VOLUNTEERING
La Fortuna and Monteverde

Several of Costa Rica's wildlife rescue centers accept long-term volunteers, but the **Proyecto Asis Wildlife Refuge Center** (www.institutoasis.com) offers half- and full-day volunteer experiences. These short and inexpensive volunteer stints, which can easily be added to most trip itineraries, are a great way to see and learn about rescued Costa Rican wildlife while lending your time and effort to a noble cause. Volunteer duties change regularly but can include preparing toys, cleaning enclosures, and feeding animals. If you have more time to commit, arrange a local homestay through the center and volunteer for 2-4 weeks.

Nicoya Peninsula

In Punta Islita, the **Macaw Recovery Network** (www.macawrecoverynetwork.org), which operates a scarlet macaw breeding and reintroduction station, invites volunteers to aid in their efforts. If you're interested in avifauna, consider signing up for one of the station's volunteer stints or apprenticeship programs. Some volunteer opportunities and programs run according to set schedules and require a minimum time commitment (see the Macaw Recovery Network's website for details). Depending on which you choose, you may find yourself running guided tours, maintaining aviaries, preparing food, or monitoring resident birds.

Central Pacific

On the Pacific coast, hidden in the hills north of Manuel Antonio and Quepos, are a wildlife rescue center and wildlife sanctuary overseen

by the nonprofit organization **Kids Saving the Rainforest** (www.kidssavingtherainforest.org). Here, you can volunteer for as little as one day or as long as a month, working alongside staff members to care for sick or injured wildlife. Volunteer responsibilities vary, but usually include enclosure cleaning and food preparation. If you have at least three months to spend in Costa Rica and a university or college degree in the field of veterinary medicine, wildlife management, biology, or animal conservation, consider applying for one of the organization's internship positions for a chance to interact more closely with the animals.

Another way you can make a difference is to travel to Costa Rica with items on the organization's wish list and donate the items directly to the wildlife sanctuary. You can also sponsor an animal from afar. See the Kids Saving the Rainforest's website for their wish list and sponsorship details.

Osa Peninsula and the Southern Pacific

The nonprofit **Corcovado Foundation** (www.corcovadofoundation.org) is one of the Osa Peninsula's most active organizations. They operate and accept volunteers for several great projects that focus on sea turtle conservation, environmental education, and sustainable tourism. Most projects are centered around Bahía Drake, but some take place in different regions of Costa Rica. Volunteer duties vary by project, but range from monitoring and relocating sea turtle nests to teaching kids about the environment. The foundation also challenges youth around the world to lead fundraising campaigns for the organization from home.

The **Life for Life Sea Turtle Conservation Project** (www.hostelindrake.com) is all about supporting one man on a mission to do good. This project operates out of a small beachfront hostel in a remote area of Bahía Drake, approximately eight kilometers southwest of Agujitas. It's run by Ricardo, a local who has dedicated decades of his life to protecting sea turtle eggs. Volunteer to help

Ricardo and you can stay at his hostel, enjoy traditional home-cooked meals, and help relocate turtle eggs to safe areas. This is one of the least touristy volunteer experiences you can have in the country.

Caribbean Coast

Each year, some of the world's most endangered sea turtles storm the beach in Parque Nacional Tortuguero, much to the delight of tourists, ecologists, and volunteers. The sea turtle conservation organizations that operate in the northern Caribbean region are regarded as some of the best wildlife initiatives in the country, given the work being done to tag, monitor, and study marine species.

To help protect sea turtle species in this region, you can take your pick of volunteer opportunities along the Caribbean coast. In Tortuguero, you can learn about local efforts and sponsor a satellite-tracked sea turtle during a visit to the **H. Clay Frick Natural History Visitor Center** (north end of Tortuguero Village, tel. 506/2709-8091, 10am-noon and 2pm-5pm daily, $2 pp) or donate your time to the **Sea Turtle Conservancy** (www.conserveturtles.org). Volunteer opportunities offered by the conservancy provide a chance to work alongside a research team that tags, surveys, and measures sea turtles, identifies nests, counts eggs, and patrols beaches.

In Parismina, a community roughly 30 kilometers down the coast from Tortuguero, volunteer opportunities are offered by **Association Save the Turtles of Parismina** (ASTOP, www.parisminaturtles. org). Volunteer with ASTOP and you can help protect sea turtle eggs from poachers and predators by joining a team that monitors turtle hatcheries and operates nightly beach patrols.

If you want to support sea turtles from afar, the American organization **Save the Turtles** (www.costaricaturtles.com) is a reputable nonprofit that has its hand in a variety of Caribbean sea turtle projects. It will happily pass along any donation you wish to make through its website.

Also available in the Caribbean are opportunities to help Costa Rica's avifauna population. The Manzanillo-based organization **Ara Manzanillo** (www.aramanzanillo.org) welcomes volunteers to assist with the operation of their great green macaw breeding and reintroduction station. Volunteers help forage the forest for natural foods, maintain feeders, monitor nests, clean the field station, run guided tours, and release macaws into the wild.

ACCESS FOR TRAVELERS WITH DISABILITIES

Unfortunately, much of Costa Rica is inaccessible to travelers with disabilities. Pothole-ridden roads, broken sidewalks, and unpaved paths make it tough to get around, but doing so isn't impossible. Some taxis, buses (mainly in San José), shared shuttle services, and private transfer services can provide wheelchair-suitable transport if requested in advance. Most modern hotels provide at least one wheelchair-accessible room and wheelchair-accessible facilities; however, many hotel restaurants don't have wheelchair-friendly tables.

If you're in search of attractions that provide inclusive experiences, check out the **Jardín Botánico Lankester** in Cartago, **Parque Nacional Carara** near Jacó, the **Reserva Biológica Bosque Nuboso de Santa Elena** near Monteverde, **Parque Nacional Santa Rosa** on the northern Pacific coast, and **Parque Nacional Manuel Antonio** in Manuel Antonio, all of which offer wheelchair-accessible trail systems.

At **Parque Nacional Volcán Poás** (near Alajuela) and **Parque Nacional Volcán Irazú** (near Cartago), paved paths connect visitors centers to the parks' principal volcano craters. For wildlife exhibits, don't miss Alajuela's **Rescate Animal Zooave.** The rescue center has smooth trails but you'll need to be able to maneuver inclines and declines—or have a travel companion who can assist with these parts of the trails.

Philanthropy for Travelers

Ever since my husband and I developed a *fútbol* shoe donation project for underprivileged Costa Rican kids enamored with the sport, I've been a proponent of travel philanthropy. The idea is simple—that a vacation can also be an opportunity to help your intended destination. This is done by bringing items from home to donate during your travels.

The American nonprofit **Pack for a Purpose** (www. packforapurpose.org) offers a great way to get involved. Simply visit the organization's website to learn which Costa Rican companies (mainly hotels) are involved in the project and which common items, ranging from school supplies to lightly used clothing to health products (medication excluded), are on the current wish list. Purchase or collect the items from home, bring them to Costa Rica, and drop them off at a project-approved hotel. (Note: If you plan to donate items with a combined value of over US$500, you may need to pay an import tax to bring the items into the country.) Of the many accommodations I recommend in this guide, **Águila de Osa**

a child receiving *fútbol* shoes and gear

(in Bahía Drake), the **Arenal Kioro Suites & Spa** (in La Fortuna), **Casitas Tenorio** (in Bijagua), the **Chilamate Rainforest Eco-Retreat** (in Puerto Viejo de Sarapiquí), the **Pura Vida Hotel** (in Alajuela), the **RipJack Inn** (in Playa Grande), the **Selva Verde Lodge** (in Puerto Viejo de Sarapiquí), the **Si Como No Resort** (in Manuel Antonio), the **Springs Resort & Spa** (near La Fortuna), and the **Villa Blanca Cloud Forest Hotel** (near San Ramón) all participate in Pack for a Purpose.

To see the crocodiles in **Tárcoles** by boat, take a tour with **Costa Rica Birding Journeys** (tel. 506/8417-9015, www.costaricabirdingjourneys.org). The bigger of their two boats has a capacity of 45 people and is equipped to carry travelers in wheelchairs.

If your dream is to surf, Santa Teresa's **Shaka Costa Rica** (on the main road that runs parallel to Playa Santa Teresa, 6.5 km northwest of the intersection at Carmen, tel. 506/2640-1118, www.shakacostarica.com) runs youth surf camps for wheelchair-using adventurers in collaboration with the **Ocean Healing Group** (www.oceanhealinggroup.org).

Visually impaired travelers will encounter information written in Braille within Parque Nacional Carara and Parque Nacional Manuel Antonio. But even areas of Costa Rica without such placards make great travel destinations. Costa Rica has an invigorating natural

soundtrack, rich and earthy smells, and flavorful tastes. Make it a priority to sense Costa Rica—listen to a howler monkey's territorial call, smell the hint of smoke in the cloud forest, feel the breeze carried in with the waves, and taste the best cup of coffee you've ever had.

TRAVELING WITH CHILDREN

Costa Rica is a family vacation destination. It's also an adventure destination in a tropical jungle. Prepare your children for hot days, winding drives around mountains, and unexpected creepy crawlers. Insects and small geckos often find their way into accommodations. Pack snacks for long car rides. A few transportation services offer free onboard Wi-Fi to help pass the time, and if you plan to drive yourself around Costa Rica, bring or rent (through your chosen vehicle rental agency) a child car seat. Costa Rican law dictates that children under the age of 12 who are smaller than 1.45 meters (57 inches) must ride in one.

Several tour operators impose minimum age limits for activity participation. Some activities, primarily those that require use of a harness, have additional minimum height and weight limits. Verify each tour in advance to avoid disappointment on the day of your reserved excursions. It's also a good idea to confirm tour durations and any potential difficulties (like uphill treks) in advance to avoid surprises. Many tour operators, accommodations, and shared shuttle service providers offer discounted rates for child travelers. A few restaurants have children's meals.

WOMEN TRAVELING ALONE

Violent attacks on women travelers are rare, but when they do occur, they most often involve women traveling alone. Be vigilant about where and when you travel. In general, daytime visits to popular destinations and attractions are safe. Don't go out at night, especially to a bar, a park, or the beach. If possible, stay at known and secure hotels or hostels in town centers, not vacation homes or other accommodation types in the outskirts of an area. Travel during the high season when you're most likely to share accommodations, restaurants, and transportation vehicles with others. If you must travel during the low season, avoid remote areas of the country: These empty during down periods and will leave you feeling like you're on your own.

LGBTQ TRAVELERS

Costa Rica isn't as progressive in LGBTQ matters as the United States and Canada. But it's not an intolerant country by any means. Public displays of affection should be kept to a minimum, but this applies to couples of all orientations.

Marcha de la Diversidad, also known as **Pride Costa Rica,** is an annual event that draws LGBTQ community members and allies to the streets of downtown San José each June or July. It's marked with a lively, colorful, and musical parade.

Costa Rica is making strides toward inclusion and unity, allowing its citizens the option to alter their name and gender on identification documents. Court rulings are inching the country closer to legalizing same-sex marriage.

SENIOR TRAVELERS

Life in the tropics can be hot and humid. Carry plenty of water to ensure you stay hydrated. If you're active at home, you'll love being active in Costa Rica. If you're not, don't overdo it while here. Bring all the medication you'll need from home; you may find having a doctor's note and a medication list eases travel through the airport. Also bring any medical equipment you may need. Although Costa Rica has reliable hospitals, clinics, and pharmacies, they may not carry the items you need or be open or nearby when you need them. Cold temperatures at high elevations can be chilling, so travel with warm clothing if you're headed to the mountains.

If you're thinking of retiring to Costa Rica, Erin Van Rheenen's *Moon Living Abroad in Costa Rica* (www.moon.com) outlines everything you need to know to successfully relocate and join the country's large network of expats.

WEIGHTS AND MEASURES

Costa Rica utilizes the metric system. The country also uses the same 110- to 120-volt, 60-hertz electrical sockets found in the Unites States and Canada. Newer accommodations provide at least one three-prong connector per room, but sometimes only in the bathroom. Older properties may only have two-prong sockets.

TIME ZONE

Six hours earlier than Greenwich Mean Time, Costa Rica falls within the **Central Time Zone** shared with the United States and Canada. The country does not observe Daylight Saving Time.

BUSINESS HOURS

Business hours vary significantly by business type and region. Government offices typically operate 8am-5pm Monday-Friday, give or take an hour. Police stations and hospitals are open 24 hours daily. Businesses centered in touristy areas, where the flow of new buyers is constant, offer extended hours and are usually open on weekends. Some establishments are closed or open late on Sundays. Tourism operations, including adventure and nature tours, transportation services, and accommodations, operate every day of the year, including holidays.

TOURIST INFORMATION
Tourist Offices
The government-run **Instituto Costarricense de Turismo** (Costa Rican Institute of Tourism, ICT, Avenida Central, between Calle 1 and Calle 3, tel. 506/2222-1090, www.ict.go.cr, 8am-5pm Mon.-Fri.) and the private organization **Canatur** (National Chamber of Tourism, tel. 506/2234-6222, www.canatur.org, 8am-5pm Mon.-Fri.), both based in San José, are Costa Rica's leading tourism organizations. Innumerable travel agencies and tour operators extend tourism services to nearly every corner of the country. You don't need to look far to find people willing to answer your questions or sell you tours and activities.

Maps
Maps are handed out generously in Costa Rica. Most vehicle rental agencies, tourism offices, and even some hotels provide them free of charge. Through their website **Essential Costa Rica** (www.visitcostarica.com), the ICT offers several detailed, well-keyed maps that can be downloaded for free as PDFs. It's also worth knowing that Google Maps permits downloads for offline use. If you use the tool to map out your driving routes or to create itineraries while planning your trip, download copies to keep on file in case you lose access to the Internet.

Resources

Glossary

agua de tamarindo: juice produced from tamarind pulp

águila: nickname for Imperial beer; also means eagle

alcalde: mayor

algodones: cotton candy

almendro: almond

arrecife: reef

arribadas: literally "arrivals," referring to sea turtle nesting events

arroz cantonés: Cantonese rice

arroz con leche: rice pudding

arroz con pollo: rice with chicken

arroz con vegetales: rice with vegetables

artesanos: artisans

barrio: neighborhood

birra: slang word for beer

boca: appetizer; Costa Rica's take on Spanish tapas

bomba: poetic, four-line rhyming statement used to show endearment to loved ones or imaginary figures; can also mean gas station or firework

bomberos: firefighters

bosque: forest

boyero: oxcart driver

cabañas: cabins (similar to *cabinas*)

cabinas: cabins (similar to *cabañas*)

cajeta: sugary, chewy dessert bar

campesino: small-scale farmer

caña de azúcar: sugarcane

canastas: rooftop carriers

cantina: informal bar

Caribe: Caribbean

carreta: oxcart

cas: guava

casa: house

casado: traditional dish that marries servings of rice and beans on a plate, accompanied by a variety of side dishes

casitas: small houses

ceniza: ash

ceviche: raw seafood or fish marinated in citrus

chayote: squash

Chepe: nickname for San José

chicharrones: fried pork rinds

chifrijo: mixed bowl of rice, beans, and fried pork rinds, among other fixings

Chiliguaro: cocktail that blends *guaro* with mandarin lime, Tabasco, and salt

chorreadas: sweet-corn pancakes

chorreador: device for brewing coffee made of wood and equipped with a cloth filter

churchill: *copo* (similar to a snow cone) topped with fruit salad

churros: fried-dough pastry sticks rolled in sugar and cinnamon

cisternas: vehicles with water tanks

colectivo: collective, referring to shared transportation (most often a bus) that makes several stops

colón: Costa Rican currency; plural form is colones

comida típica: typical food

copo: snow cone-inspired dessert topped with syrup and condensed milk

costillas: nickname for turnover-style pastries, often filled with apple, pineapple, guava, or other fruits

diputados: deputies

directo: direct, referring to transportation that doesn't make stops

disco: nightclub

dulce de leche: caramel

ejecutivo: executive

empanada: fried or baked turnover pastry typically stuffed with meat, beans, or cheese

en efectivo: to pay in cash

enagua larga: long skirts, typically worn during the traditional Punto Guanacasteco dance

ensalada rusa: Russian salad; a beet, potato, egg, and mayonnaise mixture

ensalada verde: green salad, referring to a garden salad

fábricas de carretas: cart factories

fiestas cívicas: civic festivals

finca: farm

flan de coco: coconut flan

fogón: stove

fresas: strawberries

frontera: border or boundary

fuerza pública: Costa Rica's safety police

fútbol: soccer

gallo pinto: traditional rice and bean blend, typically served for breakfast

graderías: stands, referring to rodeo seating

guanábana: soursop

guapote: rainbow bass

guaro: sugarcane liquor

guía: tour guide

güipipías: authentic shouts

heladería: ice cream shop

horchata: sweet and creamy blend of ground rice, condensed milk, and cinnamon

huevos rancheros: eggs served in a tomato-based sauce

jengibre: ginger, referring to flavor and the plant

lazos de lujo: roping, referring to rodeo activity

leche condensada: condensed milk

legislativo: legislative

lomito: beef tenderloin

mae: dude

mamón chino: rambutan, a fruit with a sweet and slimy center that looks and tastes like a peeled grape

maracuyá: passion fruit

maría: taxi meter

mariposario: butterfly garden

máscaras: masks

mejengas: informal *fútbol* matches

mercados: markets

mirador: lookout

montas de toro: bullfights

mora: blackberry

oficina de migración: migration office

olla de carne: beef stew

palenques: communities

palmito: heart of palm

pan bon: dark sweet bread

pan dulce: sweet bread

pañuelo: handkerchief, typically worn during the traditional Punto Guanacasteco dance

para llevar: to go, referring to food or drink orders

páramo: high plains

pargo rojo: red snapper

parques nacionales: national parks

patacones: smashed and fried green plantains

patís: savory turnovers often stuffed with meat, pineapple, or plantain

payasos: clowns

pejibaye: peach palm fruit

peajes: tollbooths

pescadería: fish market

pico de gallo: salsa comprised of diced tomato, pepper, onion, and pineapple mixed with cilantro and lemon juice

piña: pineapple

pipa fría: cold coconut water, typically served in the coconut, with a straw

piratas: unofficial taxi drivers

plata: slang term for money, used to imply cash

plátano frito: fried plantain (similar to *plátanos maduros*)

plátanos maduros: fried plantains (similar to *plátano frito*)

playas: beaches

plaza de toros: bullring

policía de tránsito: transit police

pollo asado: roasted chicken

pulpería: corner store

pulpo: octopus

Punto Guanacasteco: an animated and synchronized folkloric dance

pura vida: Costa Rica's slogan; translates to "pure life"

puré de papas: mashed potatoes

puro Tico: purely Costa Rican

queso blanco: white cheese

queso frito: fried cheese

queso maduro: aged cheese

rancheros: ranch music

refugios: refuges

regidores: aldermen

reserva biológica: biological reserve

retahílas: rehearsals, referring to recitation of cultural poems

rompope: eggnog-like drink

rondón: traditional fish and vegetable coconut-milk soup flavored with Caribbean spices

rotunda: traffic roundabout

sabanero: slang term for cowboy, specific to Guanacaste

salsa caribeña: Caribbean sauce; a slightly sweet brown sauce that looks like watered-down gravy

senderos acuáticos: canals

siesta: nap

soda: traditional Costa Rican family restaurant

sopa negra: black bean soup

talabarterías: saddleries

tapa de dulce: unrefined cane sugar

temazcal: sweat lodge

Ticos: Costa Ricans

tiquismos: Costa Rican slang words and phrases

tope infantil: infant equestrian parade

tope: equestrian parade

tortillas rellenas: stuffed corn tortillas

trapiche: sugarcane mill

tres leches: sweet cake soaked with three kinds of milk

trucha: trout

tuanis: good; slang term to imply coolness

vainilla: vanilla

vaquero: cowboy

vigorones: tangy mix of cabbage, yuca, *chicharrones,* and *pico de gallo*

yuca frita: fried yuca; similar in taste and appearance to thick French fries

yuca: cassava

Spanish Phrasebook

Spanish commonly uses 30 letters—the familiar English 26, plus four straightforward additions: ch, ll, ñ, and rr, which are explained in "Consonants," below.

PRONUNCIATION

Once you learn them, Spanish pronunciation rules—in contrast to English—don't change. Spanish vowels generally sound softer than in English. (*Note:* The capitalized syllables below receive stronger accents.)

Vowels

a   like ah, as in "hah": *agua* AH-gooah (water), *pan* PAHN (bread), and *casa* CAH-sah (house)

e   like ay, as in "may:" *mesa* MAY-sah (table), *tela* TAY-lah (cloth), and *de* DAY (of, from)

i   like ee, as in "need": *diez* dee-AYZ (ten), *comida* ko-MEE-dah (meal), and *fin* FEEN (end)

o   like oh, as in "go": *peso* PAY-soh (weight), *ocho* OH-choh (eight), and *poco* POH-koh (a bit)

u   like oo, as in "cool": *uno* OO-noh (one), *cuarto* KOOAHR-toh (room), and *usted* oos-TAYD (you); when it follows a "q" the u is silent; when it follows an "h" or has an umlaut, it's pronounced like "w"

Consonants

b, d, f, k, l, m, n, p, q, s, t, v, w, x, y, z, ch   pronounced almost as in English; h occurs, but is silent—not pronounced at all

c   like k as in "keep": *cuarto* KOOAR-toh (room); when it precedes "e" or "i," pronounce **c** like s, as in "sit": *cerveza* sayr-VAY-sah (beer), *encima* ayn-SEE-mah (atop)

g like g as in "gift" when it precedes "a," "o," "u," or a consonant: *gato* GAH-toh (cat), *hago* AH-goh (I do, make); otherwise, pronounce **g** like h as in "hat": *giro* HEE-roh (money order), *gente* HAYN-tay (people)

j like h, as in "has": *jueves* HOOAY-vays (Thursday), *mejor* may-HOR (better)

ll like y, as in "yes": *toalla* toh-AH-yah (towel), *ellos* AY-yohs (they, them)

ñ like ny, as in "canyon": *año* AH-nyo (year), *señor* SAY-nyor (Mr., sir)

r is lightly trilled, with tongue at the roof of your mouth like a very light English d, as in "ready": *pero* PAY-doh (but), *tres* TDAYS (three), *cuatro* KOOAH-tdoh (four)

rr like a Spanish r, but with much more emphasis and trill. Let your tongue flap. Practice with *burro* (donkey), *carretera* (highway), and *Carrillo* (proper name), then really let go with *ferrocarril* (railroad)

Note: The single small but common exception to all of the above is the pronunciation of Spanish **y** when it's being used as the Spanish word for "and," as in *Ron y Kathy*. In such case, pronounce it like the English ee, as in "keep": Ron "ee" Kathy (Ron and Kathy).

Accent

The rule for accent, the relative stress given to syllables within a given word, is straightforward. If a word ends in a vowel, an "n," or an "s," accent the next-to-last syllable; if not, accent the last syllable.

Pronounce *gracias* GRAH-seeahs (thank you), *orden* OHR-dayn (order), and *carretera* kah-ray-TAY-rah (highway) with stress on the next-to-last syllable.

Otherwise, accent the last syllable: *venir* vay-NEER (to come), *ferrocarril* fay-roh-cah-REEL (railroad), and *edad* ay-DAHD (age).

Exceptions to the accent rule are always marked with an accent sign: (á, é, í, ó, or ú), such as *teléfono* tay-LAY-foh-noh (telephone), *jabón* hah-BON (soap), and *rápido* RAH-pee-doh (rapid).

BASIC AND COURTEOUS EXPRESSIONS

Most Spanish-speaking people consider formalities important. Whenever approaching anyone for information or some other reason, do not forget the appropriate salutation—good morning, good evening, etc. Standing alone, the greeting *hola* (hello) can sound brusque.

Hello. *Hola.*

Good morning. *Buenos días.*

Good afternoon. *Buenas tardes.*

Good evening. *Buenas noches.*

How are you? *¿Cómo está?*

Very well, thank you. *Muy bien, gracias.*

Okay; good. *Bien.*

Not okay; bad. *Mal* or *no bueno.*

So-so. *Más o menos.*

And you? *¿Y usted?*

Thank you. *Gracias.*

Thank you very much. *Muchísimas gracias.*

You're very kind. *Muy amable.*

You're welcome. *Con mucho gusto.*

Goodbye. *Adios* or *chao.*

See you later. *Hasta luego.*

please *por favor*

yes *sí*

no *no*

I don't know. *No sé.*

Just a moment, please. *Un momentico, por favor.*

Excuse me, please (when you're trying to get attention). *Disculpe* or *Con permiso.*

Excuse me (when you've made a boo-boo). *Lo siento.*

Pleased to meet you. *Mucho gusto.*

How do you say . . . in Spanish? *¿Cómo se dice . . . en español?*

What is your name? *¿Cómo se llama usted?*

Do you speak English? *¿Habla usted inglés?*

Is English spoken here? (Does anyone here speak English?) *¿Se habla inglés?*

I don't speak Spanish well. *No hablo bien el español.*

I don't understand. *No entiendo.*

My name is . . . *Me llamo . . .*
Would you like . . . *¿Quisiera usted . . .*
Let's go to . . . *Vamos a . . .*

TERMS OF ADDRESS

When in doubt, use the formal *usted* (you) as a form of address.

I *yo*
you (formal) *usted*
you (familiar) *tu*
he/him *él*
she/her *ella*
we/us *nosotros*
you (plural) *ustedes*
they/them *ellos* (all males or mixed gender); *ellas* (all females)
Mr., sir *señor*
Mrs., madam *señora*
miss, young lady *señorita*
family *familia*
wife *esposa*
husband *esposo*
friend *amigo* (male); *amiga* (female)
sweetheart *novio* (male); *novia* (female)
son; daughter *hijo; hija*
brother; sister *hermano; hermana*
father; mother *padre; madre*
grandfather; grandmother *abuelo; abuela*

TRANSPORTATION

Where is . . . ? *¿Dónde está . . . ?*
How far is it to . . . ? *¿A cuánto está . . . ?*
from . . . to . . . *de . . . a . . .*
How many blocks? *¿Cuántas cuadras?*
Where (Which) is the way to . . . ? *¿Dónde está el camino a . . . ?*
the bus station *la terminal de autobuses*
the bus stop *la parada de autobuses*
Where is this bus going? *¿Adónde va este autobús?*
the taxi stand *la parada de taxis*
the train station *la estación de ferrocarril*
the boat *el barco*
the launch *la lancha*
the dock *el muelle*
the airport *el aeropuerto*

I'd like a ticket to . . . *Quisiera un boleto a . . .*
first (second) class *primera (segunda) clase*
roundtrip *ida y vuelta*
reservation *reservación*
baggage *equipaje*
Stop here, please. *Pare aquí, por favor.*
the entrance *la entrada*
the exit *la salida*
ticket office *boletería*
(very) near; far *(muy) cerca; lejos*
to; toward *a*
by; through *por*
from *de*
the right *la derecha*
the left *la izquierda*
straight ahead *directo; adelante*
in front *en frente*
beside *al lado*
behind *atrás*
the corner *la esquina*
the stoplight *el semáforo*
a turn *una vuelta*
right here *aquí*
somewhere around here *por aquí*
right there *allí*
somewhere around there *por allá*
road *el camino*
street; avenue *calle; avenida*
block *la cuadra*
highway *carretera*
metro *meter*
kilometer *kilómetro*
bridge; toll *puente; cuota*
address *dirección*
north; south *norte; sur*
east; west *este; oeste*
one-way *una vía*
one-way up ahead *una vía adelante*

ACCOMMODATIONS

hotel *hotel*
Is there a room? *¿Hay una habitación?*
May I (may we) see it? *¿Puedo (podemos) verla?*
What is the rate? *¿Cuál es el precio?*
Is that your best rate? *¿Es su mejor precio?*

Is there something cheaper? *¿Hay algo más barato?*

a single room *una habitación sencilla*

a double room *una habitación doble*

a shared room *una habitación compartida*

double bed *cama matrimonial*

twin beds *camas gemelas*

with private bathroom *con baño privado*

with shared bathroom *con baño compartido*

hot water *agua caliente*

shower *ducha*

towels *toallas*

soap *jabón*

toilet paper *papel higiénico*

blanket *cobija*

sheets *sábanas*

air-conditioned *aire acondicionado*

fan *abanico; ventilador*

key *llave*

manager *gerente*

FOOD

I'm hungry *Tengo hambre.*

I'm thirsty. *Tengo sed.*

breakfast *desayuno*

lunch *almuerzo*

dinner *cena*

snack *bocadillo*

menu *carta; menú*

order *orden*

plate of the day *plato del día*

the check *la cuenta*

glass *vaso*

fork *tenedor*

knife *cuchillo*

spoon *cuchara*

napkin *servilleta*

soft drink *refresco*

coffee *café*

tea *té*

drinking water *agua pura; agua potable*

bottled carbonated water *agua mineral*

bottled uncarbonated water *agua sin gas*

beer *cerveza*

wine *vino*

milk *leche*

juice *jugo*

smoothie *batido*

cream *crema*

sugar *azúcar*

cheese *queso*

eggs *huevos*

bread *pan*

salad *ensalada*

fruit *fruta*

mango *mango*

watermelon *sandía*

papaya *papaya*

banana *banano*

plantain *plátano*

apple *manzana*

orange *naranja*

lime *limón*

fish *pescado*

shellfish *mariscos*

shrimp *camarones*

meat *carne*

without meat *sin carne*

chicken *pollo*

pork *cerdo*

beef; steak *res; bistec*

bacon; ham *tocino; jamón*

fried *frito*

hard-boiled *duros*

scrambled *picados* or *revueltos*

over-easy *tiernos*

roasted *asada*

grilled *a la parrilla*

barbecue; barbecued *barbacoa; al carbón*

SHOPPING

money *dinero*

money-exchange bureau *casa de cambio*

ATM *cajero automático*

I would like to exchange traveler's checks. *Quisiera cambiar cheques de viajero.*

What is the exchange rate? *¿Cuál es el tipo de cambio?*

Do you accept credit cards? *¿Aceptan tarjetas de crédito?*

How much does it cost? *¿Cuánto cuesta?*

expensive *caro*

cheap *barato*
more *más*
less *menos*
a little *un poco*
too much *demasiado*
sales tax included *impuesto de ventas
  incluido*

HEALTH

Help me please. *Ayúdeme por favor.*
I am ill. *Estoy enfermo.*
Call a doctor. *Llame un doctor.*
Take me to . . . *Lléveme a . . .*
hospital *hospital; clínica*
drugstore *farmacia*
pain *dolor*
fever *fiebre*
headache *dolor de cabeza*
stomach ache *dolor de estómago*
burn *quemadura*
cramp *calambre*
nausea *náusea*
vomiting *vomitar*
medicine *medicina*
antibiotic *antibiótico*
pill; tablet *pastilla*
aspirin *aspirina*
ointment; cream *pomada; crema*
bandage *venda*
cotton *algodón*
sanitary napkins use brand name, e.g.,
  Kotex
birth control pills *pastillas anticonceptivas*
contraceptive foam *espuma
  anticonceptiva*
condoms *preservativos; condones*
toothbrush *cepillo*
dental floss *hilo dental*
toothpaste *pasta dental*
dentist *dentista*
toothache *dolor de muelas*

POST OFFICE AND COMMUNICATIONS

long-distance telephone *teléfono larga
  distancia*
I would like to call . . . *Quisiera llamar a . . .*
collect *por cobrar*

person to person *persona a persona*
credit card *tarjeta de crédito*
post office *correos*
general delivery *lista de correo*
letter *carta*
stamp *estampilla, timbre*
postcard *tarjeta*
aerogram *aerograma*
air mail *correo aereo*
registered *registrado*
money order *giro*
package; box *paquete; caja*
string; tape *cuerda; cinta*

AT THE BORDER

border *frontera*
customs *aduana*
immigration *migración*
tourist card *tarjeta de turista*
inspection *inspección; revisión*
passport *pasaporte*
profession *profesión*
marital status *estado civil*
single *soltero*
married; divorced *casado; divorciado*
widowed *viudo*
insurance *seguros*
title *título*
driver's license *licencia de manejar* or
  licencia de conducir

AT THE GAS STATION

gas station *gasolinera* or *bomba*
gasoline *gasolina*
unleaded *sin plomo*
full, please *lleno, por favor*
tire *llanta*
tire repair shop *llantera*
air *aire*
water *agua*
oil (change) *aceite (cambio)*
grease *grasa*
My . . . doesn't work. *Mi . . . no funciona.*
battery *batería*
radiator *radiador*
alternator *alternador*
generator *generador*
tow truck *grúa*

repair shop *taller mecánico*
tune-up *afinación*
auto parts store *venta de repuestos*

VERBS

Verbs are the key to getting along in Spanish. They employ mostly predictable forms and come in three classes, which end in *ar, er,* and *ir,* respectively:

to buy *comprar*
I buy, you (he, she, it) buys *compro, compra*
we buy, you (they) buy *compramos, compran*
to eat *comer*
I eat, you (he, she, it) eats *como, come*
we eat, you (they) eat *comemos, comen*
to climb *subir*
I climb, you (he, she, it) climbs *subo, sube*
we climb, you (they) climb *subimos, suben*

Here are more (with irregularities indicated):

to do or make *hacer* (regular except for *hago,* I do or make)
to go *ir* (very irregular: *voy, va, vamos, van*)
to go (walk) *caminar*
to love *amar*
to work *trabajar*
to want *desear, querer*
to need *necesitar*
to read *leer*
to write *escribir*
to repair *reparar*
to stop *parar*
to get off (the bus) *bajar*
to arrive *llegar*
to stay (remain) *quedar*
to stay (lodge) *hospedar*
to leave *salir* (regular except for *salgo,* I leave)
to look at *mirar*
to look for *buscar*
to give *dar* (regular except for *doy,* I give)
to carry *llevar*
to have *tener* (irregular but important: *tengo, tiene, tenemos, tienen*)
to come *venir* (similarly irregular: *vengo, viene, venimos, vienen*)

Spanish has two forms of "to be":

to be *estar* (regular except for *estoy,* I am)
to be *ser* (very irregular: *soy, es, somos, son*)

Use *estar* when speaking of location or a temporary state of being: "I am at home." *"Estoy en casa."* "I'm sick." *"Estoy enfermo."* Use *ser* for a permanent state of being: "I am a doctor." *"Soy doctora."*

COLORS

red *rojo*
pink *rosado*
orange *naranja*
yellow *amarillo*
green *verde*
blue *azul*
purple *morado*
white *blanco*
brown *café*
black *negro*
rainbow *arco iris*

NUMBERS

zero *cero*
one *uno*
two *dos*
three *tres*
four *cuatro*
five *cinco*
six *seis*
seven *siete*
eight *ocho*
nine *nueve*
10 *diez*
11 *once*
12 *doce*
13 *trece*
14 *catorce*
15 *quince*
16 *dieciseis*
17 *diecisiete*
18 *dieciocho*
19 *diecinueve*
20 *veinte*
21 *veinte y uno* or *veintiuno*

30	treinta
40	cuarenta
50	cincuenta
60	sesenta
70	setenta
80	ochenta
90	noventa
100	ciento
101	ciento y uno or cientiuno
200	doscientos
500	quinientos
1,000	mil
10,000	diez mil
100,000	cien mil
1,000,000	millón
one half	medio
one third	un tercio
one fourth	un cuarto

TIME

What time is it? ¿Qué hora es?
It's one o'clock. Es la una.
It's three in the afternoon. Son las tres de la tarde.
It's 4 a.m. Son las cuatro de la mañana.
six-thirty seis y media
a quarter till eleven un cuarto para las once
a quarter past five las cinco y cuarto
an hour una hora

Monday lunes
Tuesday martes
Wednesday miércoles
Thursday jueves
Friday viernes
Saturday sábado
Sunday domingo
today hoy
tomorrow mañana
yesterday ayer
January enero
February febrero
March marzo
April abril
May mayo
June junio
July julio
August agosto
September septiembre
October octubre
November noviembre
December diciembre
a week una semana
a month un mes
after después
before antes

(Courtesy of Bruce Whipperman, author of Moon Pacific Mexico.*)*

Suggested Reading

HISTORY AND CULTURE

Hiltunen Biesanz, Mavis, Richard Biesanz, and Karen Zubris Biesanz. *The Ticos: Culture and Social Change in Costa Rica.* Boulder, CO: Lynne Rienner Publishers, 1998. This is the quintessential book on Costa Rican culture as shaped by its social institutions.

Leiva Coto, Asdrúbal. *Traditional Costa Rica Cookbook.* San José, Costa Rica: Ediciones Jadine, 2004. A no-frills cookbook with basic recipes for Costa Rican cuisine.

Van Rheenen, Erin. *Moon Living Abroad in Costa Rica.* Berkeley, CA: Avalon Travel, 2017. A practical and detailed guide to moving to Costa Rica, written by an American expat who successfully made the jump.

LITERATURE

Ewing, Jack. *Monkeys Are Made of Chocolate: Exotic and Unseen Costa Rica.* Masonville, CO: PixyJack Press, 2005. This book offers entertaining tales of interaction among people, plants, and animals in Costa Rica's rainforest.

Ras, Barbara, ed. *Costa Rica: A Traveler's Literary Companion*. San Francisco: Whereabouts Press, 1994. A compilation of 26 stories by Costa Rican writers that capture day-to-day life in Costa Rica.

NATURE AND FIELD GUIDES

Garrigues, Richard, and Robert Dean. *The Birds of Costa Rica: A Field Guide*. Ithaca, NY: Cornell University Press, 2007. A 387-page field guide to over 820 of Costa Rica's bird species, including a color illustration and map of regions with each one.

Leenders, Twan. *A Guide to Amphibians and Reptiles of Costa Rica*. Miami: Distribuidores Zona Tropical, S.A., 2001. A 305-page field guide to nearly all of Costa Rica's amphibian and reptile species, including in-depth descriptions and helpful tips for easy species identification.

Pucci Golcher, Sergio. *Costa Rica Aérea: Retratos de un País Inédito*. San José, Costa Rica: GSPG, 2014. A fantastic coffee-table book that features striking, colorful full-page photographs of Costa Rica as seen from above.

Pucci Golcher, Sergio. *Costa Rica from Above: Landscapes Over Time*. San José, Costa Rica: GSPG, 2018. The sequel to *Costa Rica Aérea: Retratos de un País Inédito*. Photographs in this edition predominantly feature volcanoes and beaches.

Zuchowski, Willow. *Tropical Plants of Costa Rica: A Guide to Native and Exotic Flora*. Ithaca, NY: Cornell University Press, 2007. A 529-page field guide to over 430 of Costa Rica's plant species. A scientific name, a detailed description of appearance and behavior, and a color photograph or pen drawing are included with each.

Suggested Films

A Bold Peace: Costa Rica's Path of Demilitarization. Directed by Matthew Eddy and Michael Dreiling, 2016. An English-language documentary that explores correlations between the abolition of Costa Rica's army and happiness.

Escape to Costa Rica. 2017. A trilogy of episodes ("Connected with the Earth," "The Jungle Story," and "The Call of the Earth") delves into Costa Rica's indigenous cultures, natural environments, and vast coastlines.

Maikol Yordan Traveling Lost. Directed by Miguel Gomez, 2014. This film (*Maikol Yordan de Viaje Perdido* in Spanish) is a shared favorite among locals. The comedy tells the story of a humble Tico who travels the world to save his family farm. The 2018 sequel, *Maikol Yordan 2: La Cura Lejana*, sees the same protagonist search for a cure to aid his ailing grandmother.

Internet Resources

Many Costa Rican websites are in Spanish. However, most are enabled to work with Google Translate, which can provide quick and free translation.

TOURISM INFORMATION

Costa Rica Travel Blog
http://costaricatravelblog.com
This site offers information, photographs, and personal travel stories, written by the author of this guide.

Essential Costa Rica
www.visitcostarica.com
This is the online presence of the Costa Rican Institute of Tourism. The website is a good starting point for first-time Costa Rica visitors.

Sistema de Información Cultural de Costa Rica (Sicultura)
http://si.cultura.cr
Sicultura is an online platform for discussion pertaining to Costa Rican culture. It provides cultural event listings and descriptions of traditional attractions and celebrations.

PARKS AND RECREATION

Sistema Nacional de Áreas de Conservación (SINAC)
www.sinac.go.cr
The National System of Conservation Areas is the go-to website for information regarding Costa Rica's various government-protected land areas, including several national parks, biological reserves, and wildlife refuges.

TRAVEL INFORMATION

La Dirección General de Migración y Extranjería
www.migracion.go.cr
The General Directorate of Migration and Immigration is the official source of Costa Rica's entry regulations. Check the website for up-to-date entrance requirements.

Aeropuerto Internacional Juan Santamaría
www.sjoairport.com
The official website of the Juan Santamaría International Airport provides everything you need to know about travel through Alajuela.

Aeropuerto Internacional Daniel Oduber Quirós
www.lircr.com
The official website of the Daniel Oduber Quirós International Airport provides helpful information about travel through Liberia.

CONSERVATIONS AND NONPROFIT ORGANIZATIONS

Corcovado Foundation
www.corcovadofoundation.org
Operating from the Osa Peninsula, this nonprofit organization conducts marvelous work in the fields of sea turtle conservation, sustainable tourism, environmental education, and community development.

Kids Saving the Rainforest
www.kidssavingtherainforest.org
Based in Manuel Antonio, Costa Rica, this American nonprofit organization has several rainforest conservation and wildlife protection projects on the go, with a focus on helping mono títi (squirrel) monkeys. Wildlife rescue center tours and volunteer opportunities are offered.

Macaw Recovery Network and Ara Manzanillo
www.macawrecoverynetwork.org;
www.aramanzanillo.org
These two Costa Rican nonprofit organizations are dedicated to the protection and

proliferation of avifauna, specifically scarlet and great green macaws. Breeding and reintroduction stations on the Nicoya Peninsula (operated by the Macaw Recovery Network) and in the Caribbean (run by Ara Manzanillo) welcome visitors.

Misión Tiburon
www.misiontiburon.org
This Costa Rican nonprofit organization aims to replenish the depleted shark population through the development of shark sanctuaries (no-take zones) and educational awareness.

Sea Turtle Conservancy
www.conserveturtles.org
Based in Tortuguero, Costa Rica, this longtime American nonprofit organization tags, monitors, and studies sea turtles. It also serves as a model for the many other sea turtle conservation initiatives that operate from Costa Rica's Caribbean coast.

Index

WXYZ

List of Maps

Photo Credits

Acknowledgments

To Ricky—my husband, travel companion, business partner, *heroe*, and best friend—thank you for your unconditional love. Without complaint, you contributed long workdays and sleepless nights to the development of this book, all because one of your dreams is to see me fulfill one of mine. I'm grateful for your passion for exploration, your knowledge of nature and wildlife, your photography skills, and the Tico heart and soul you gave to this book. Your never-ending encouragement helped bring the manuscript to fruition and reminds me every day that I'm the luckiest person in the world.

I'm indebted to my newfound professional family at Hachette Book Group and Avalon Travel, especially acquisitions editor Nikki Ioakimedes for her encouragement and guidance; senior editor Leah Gordon for her spot-on leads and eloquent writing style; graphics coordinator Lucie Ericksen for making this book such a visually appealing read; and map editor Kat Bennett for her attention to detail. Thank you for inviting me to contribute to the Moon series and for making me feel welcome from day one of our collaboration.

To my international family and friends, I appreciate your patience and understanding while work and travel commitments monopolized my time. Your unwavering support means more to me than you will ever know. To my mom, whose giddy excitement throughout the book-writing journey kept me smiling during stressful times, thank you for believing in me always, all ways, and for teaching me to dream big. To my dad, who, from afar, was at my side helping me write each page, thank you for instilling in me the drive to succeed and the determination to see things through.

To my Costa Rican family, your invaluable traditions and teachings grace the pages in this book and continue to enrich my life. Thank you for accepting me as a foreigner and loving me like a daughter, sister, and aunt. I am a proud Tica at heart and feel honored to write about your country.

Keeks, Gabriel, Clay, Marianita, Kar, Ángel, Moni, Ben, and Josie: There are purposes to life that only you can fulfill. Seek them then serve them to the best of your abilities and that will forever be enough. Thank you for filling my down time with infinite joy and bursts of laughter.

To Ricky's and my network of faithful Costa Rican friends and colleagues: Thank you for the facts, figures, stories, support, and jovial camaraderie. You contributed substantial detail to this book and made research fun and memorable.

To past and present Pura Vida! eh? Inc. clients and *Costa Rica Travel Blog* readers: Thank you for sharing your Costa Rica experiences with me. They informed my own travels and made this book a compilation of lessons learned.

To all Ticos who embody *pura vida* and cherish Costa Rica's precious land, water, and wildlife: Thank you for capturing the essence of what makes your country beautiful and unique. Your blissful spirit and ecofriendly mindset are the travel souvenirs I wish for every *Moon Costa Rica* reader.

MAP SYMBOLS

≡≡≡	Expressway	✪	Highlight	✈	Airport	⚲	Golf Course
≡≡≡	Primary Road	○	City/Town	✗	Airfield	🅿	Parking Area
≡≡≡	Secondary Road	◉	State Capital	▲	Mountain	🛕	Archaeological Site
┄┄┄	Unpaved Road	⊛	National Capital	✦	Unique Natural Feature	🍶	Church
------	Trail	★	Point of Interest	🏳	Waterfall	⛽	Gas Station
··········	Ferry	•	Accommodation	⛲	Waterfall	🐟	Dive Site
⤬⤬⤬	Railroad	▼	Restaurant/Bar	⛺	Park		Mangrove
≡≡≡	Pedestrian Walkway	■	Other Location	🚩	Trailhead		Reef
▥▥▥	Stairs	Λ	Campground	⚓	Lighthouse		Swamp

CONVERSION TABLES

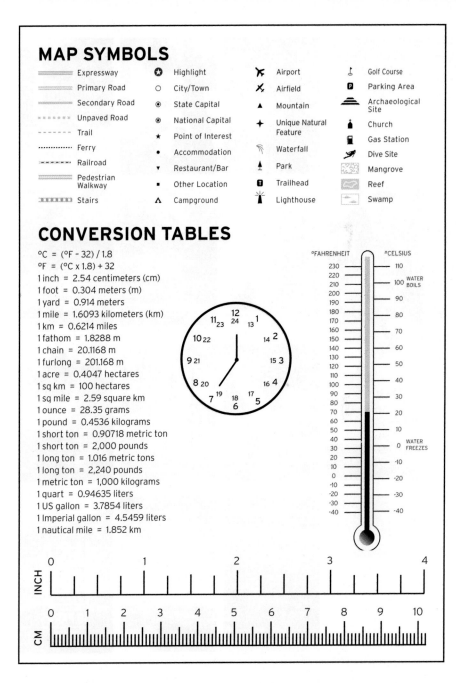

°C = (°F - 32) / 1.8
°F = (°C x 1.8) + 32
1 inch = 2.54 centimeters (cm)
1 foot = 0.304 meters (m)
1 yard = 0.914 meters
1 mile = 1.6093 kilometers (km)
1 km = 0.6214 miles
1 fathom = 1.8288 m
1 chain = 20.1168 m
1 furlong = 201.168 m
1 acre = 0.4047 hectares
1 sq km = 100 hectares
1 sq mile = 2.59 square km
1 ounce = 28.35 grams
1 pound = 0.4536 kilograms
1 short ton = 0.90718 metric ton
1 short ton = 2,000 pounds
1 long ton = 1.016 metric tons
1 long ton = 2,240 pounds
1 metric ton = 1,000 kilograms
1 quart = 0.94635 liters
1 US gallon = 3.7854 liters
1 Imperial gallon = 4.5459 liters
1 nautical mile = 1.852 km

Trips to
Remember

MOON

TRIP OF A LIFETIME

ANGKOR WAT

MOON

TRIP OF A LIFETIME

**GALÁPAGOS
ISLANDS**

MOON

ICELAND

JENNA GOTTLIEB

MOON

TRIP OF A LIFETIME

**MACHU
PICCHU**

MOON

MOROCCO

MOON

**NEW
ZEALAND**

JAMIE CHRISTIAN DESPLACES

MOON

NORWAY

MOON

TRIP OF A LIFETIME

PATAGONIA

WAYNE BERNHARDSON

MOON

**PRAGUE, VIENNA
& BUDAPEST**

MOON

**ROME,
FLORENCE
& VENICE**

ALEXEI J. COHEN

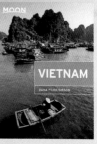

MOON

VIETNAM

DANA FILEK-GIBSON

Epic
Adventure

MOON

Drive & Hike

**APPALACHIAN
TRAIL**

THE BEST TRAIL TOWNS, DAY HIKES,
AND ROAD TRIPS IN BETWEEN

TIMOTHY MALCOLM

MOON

**CAMINO DE
SANTIAGO**

SACRED SITES,
HISTORIC VILLAGES,
LOCAL FOOD & WINE

BEEBE BAHRAMI

MOON

**USA
NATIONAL
PARKS**

THE COMPLETE GUIDE TO ALL
59 PARKS

BECKY LOMAX

Beachy Getaways

MOON.COM
@MOONGUIDES

GO BIG AND GO BEYOND!

These savvy city guides include strategies to help you see the top sights and find adventure beyond the tourist crowds.

OR TAKE THINGS ONE STEP AT A TIME

Packed with colorful photos, helpful lists of top experiences, and strategic tips for visiting America's National Parks, this top-selling travel guide is a practical keepsake.

Moon USA National Parks includes a pull-out souvenir map and a designated section to collect each park's stamp.

5 ³/₈" x 8 ³/₈" • 700pp • $24.99 US | $32.49 CAN

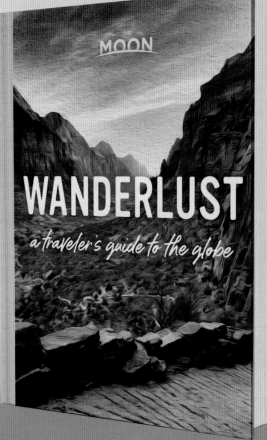

BUILD YOUR BUCKET LIST
WITH MOON WANDERLUST!

Find travel inspiration in this handsome coffee table book full of illustrations and photos of destinations all around the globe.

10" x 13" Hardcover • 368pp • $40 US | $50 CAN

MOON COSTA RICA

Avalon Travel
Hachette Book Group
1700 Fourth Street
Berkeley, CA 94710, USA
www.moon.com

Editor: Leah Gordon
Acquiring Editor: Nikki Ioakimedes
Series Manager: Kathryn Ettinger
Copy Editor: Linda Cabasin
Graphics and Production Coordinator:
 Lucie Ericksen
Cover Design: Faceout Studios, Charles Brock
Interior Design: Domini Dragoone
Moon Logo: Tim McGrath
Map Editor: Kat Bennett
Cartographers: Erin Greb, Brian Shotwell,
 Kat Bennett
Proofreader: Ann Seifert
Editorial Assistance: Anna Ho
Indexer: Rachel Kuhn

ISBN-13: 9781640490864

Printing History
1st Edition — November 2019
5 4 3 2 1

Front cover photo: Catarata del Toro © Kryssia
 Campos, Getty Images
Back cover photo: keel-billed toucan © Nikki Solano

Printed in China by RR Donnelley

Avalon Travel is a division of Hachette Book Group,
 Inc. Moon and the Moon logo are trademarks of
 Hachette Book Group, Inc. All other marks and
 logos depicted are the property of the original
 owners.